A football compendium

A Football Compendium

A Comprehensive Guide to the Literature of Association Football

Compiled by

Peter J Seddon

Introduction by the Rt Hon Roy Hattersley, M.P.
Edited by C McKinley and A E Cunningham

To a true Oxford United supporter –
Best Wishes –
Peter Seddon

THE BRITISH LIBRARY
1995

First published 1995 by

The British Library
National Bibliographic Service
Boston Spa
Wetherby
West Yorkshire LS23 7BQ

ISBN: 0-7123-1075-4

Typographic Design *by* Cynthia McKinley

Series Editor: A E Cunningham

Printed by Redwood Books, Trowbridge

Acknowledgements

The compiler and editors wish to thank all those who helped in the compilation and production of this bibliography and especially Linda Briggs; Malcolm Brodie; Robert Corbett; Phil Crossley; John Eastwood; Norman Gannaway; Ian Garland; Chris Harte; George Holland; Peadar Ivers; Brenda Jackson-Hill; Steve James; John Jarman; Clive Leatherdale; David McKinley; Rebecca Marshall; Richard Marshall; Murray Cards International of London; Rob Rowbotham; Ray Spiller; Aidan Taylor; and, John Weir.

During the course of compilation the following kindly took the time to check and add to draft entries for the clubs as shown: Gordon Allan (Wigan Athletic); Peter A. Bishop (Tranmere Rovers); Mike Blackstone (Exeter City); Kate Bouchard (West Ham United); Pam Bridgewater (Aston Villa); R. Briggs (Grimsby Town); S. Briggs (Bradford City); Mick Brown (Oxford United); A. T. Bullock (Stenhousemuir); John Byrne (St. Mirren); Tim Carder (Brighton & Hove Albion); I. R. Davies (Barnsley); G. Dickson (Berwick Rangers); M. D. Deavin (Woking); Steve Durham (Workington); Prof. D. H. Farmer (Swansea Town/City); H. Finch (Crewe Alexandra); C. F. Graham (Hibernian); J. Harrison (Bristol City); Jim Hendry (Falkirk); P. M. Hough (Lincoln City); Mike Jay (Bristol Rovers); Paul Joannou (Newcastle United); Derek Johnston (Everton); George C. Johnston (Brechin City); Dominic Keane (Celtic); Alec King (Sunderland); Richard Lindsay (Millwall); Paul Mace (Leicester City); Gordon Macey (Queen's Park Rangers); D. McGregor (Forfar Athletic); John Maddocks (Manchester City); Robin W Marwick (Albion Rovers); Ian Moat (Notts County); Mike Noye (Ipswich Town); Tom Ogilvie (Cowdenbeath); Richard Owen (Portsmouth); Alistair Paton (Dumbarton); L. W. Porteous (Heart of Midlothian); Andy Porter (Tottenham Hotspur); Robert W. Reid (Partick Thistle); Ian Rigby (Preston North End); A. D. Rowing (Scunthorpe United); J. C. Rutherford (Queen's Park); Rev. Nigel Sands (Crystal Palace); Lesley Scott (Hereford United); M. J. Spinks (Barnsley); J. S. Steedman (Clydebank); David Steele (Carlisle United); Steven Stride (Aston Villa); Scott Struthers (Hamilton Academical); John Swinburne (Motherwell); Ian J. Taggart (Aberdeen); Clare Tierney (Gateshead); Dennis Turner (Fulham); Andrew J. Warrington (Arbroath); James Watson (Hamilton Academical); E. S. J. White (Brentford); Geoffrey S. Wilde (Southport); Brian Williams (Sutton United); and, Phil Yelland (Barrow).

Thanks also to the following clubs which responded to our request for information: Airdrieonians; Aldershot; Alloa Athletic; Arsenal; Ayr United; Blackpool; Cambridge United; Cardiff City; East Fife; Heart of Midlothian; Hull City; Kilmarnock; Leicester City; Manchester United; Norwich City; Port Vale; Queen of the South; Queen's Park Rangers; Raith Rovers; Rochdale; Sheffield Wednesday; St. Johnstone; Stoke City; Torquay United; and, West Bromwich Albion.

Peter Seddon would particularly like to thank Mary Grix for her secretarial assistance, members of the 'B'-Stand Matchday Club for their interest and encouragement and, most of all, Kate Ibbitson for her understanding, tolerance and support.

Contents

Preface

ASSOCIATION FOOTBALL IS REGARDED BY MANY as the world's greatest game. In the British Isles it is part of the very fabric of life for millions of followers, whether as players or spectators or simply those taking a quiet but steady interest in the game. It is not surprising therefore that so many books have been published on all aspects of the game since the formation of the Football Association in 1863. What has been surprising has been that unlike cricket, which since 1977 has had E W Padwick's celebrated *A Bibliography of Cricket* to draw upon, football has had no single work of reference to bring together and focus attention on this wealth of material.

It is to redress this state of affairs that *A Football Compendium* has been compiled. The genesis of the work comes from a combination of my passion for football and my interest in book collecting. There was also a feeling that football had somehow been short-changed in the treatment accorded to its literature and I knew that others, particularly within the Association of Football Statisticians and the Association of Sports Historians, shared this sense of injustice. I had found myself studying Padwick's bibliography on a number of occasions, musing what a soccer equivalent might look like, and when Arthur Cunningham, Head of Publications at the British Library's National Bibliographic Service, approached me early in 1993 concerning a projected new series of subject bibliographies, the opportunity arose to fill this gap. I am most grateful to the British Library, and to Arthur Cunningham and Cynthia McKinley in particular, for having the foresight and enthusiasm to back this project and the fortitude to see it through. Their support has been an essential ingredient in seeing the work through to completion.

It is my hope that this bibliography will serve to raise the profile of football literature and make the titles listed within it more readily identifiable and thus available to a wider audience. I would like to think that librarians in particular will find this book useful in responding to enquiries and in the selection of stock most suited to the needs of their users.

Queries concerning football may arise for a number of reasons: the local historian looking to complete the definitive history of his town or region; a novelist looking for authentic background material; the enthusiast wishing to read up on his team and perhaps see the game in its wider context. This bibliography should be a useful first step for them all.

However, as well as addressing the needs of researchers and the librarians and others who assist them, my hope is that this bibliography will be of equal interest and value to those with a straightforward love of the game – the armchair soccerphile, the book collector as well as the season ticket holders. Most of my annotations have been written with these fans in mind. I have tried, as entertainingly as I can, to guide the reader through the mass of material which exists, to show what is important, to highlight the rare and significant, to enthuse and amuse.

From a purely personal point of view, perhaps the best thing about compiling *A Football Compendium* is that is has given me a perfect excuse to indulge my lifelong habit of diving into bookshops at every opportunity – without having to offer apologies to either family or friends. It has been a mammoth task albeit a hugely enjoyable one (for the most part!)

There is only one *real* game of football. It has been called 'the peoples' game', the 'world game', the 'greatest game', the 'beautiful game'. Whichever epithet one chooses they can all be illustrated in one way or another in the more than 5,000 entries in *A Football Compendium*.

PJS
June 1995

Introduction
by Roy Hattersley

ON THE SUNDAY BEFORE THE OPENING MATCH of the 1994 World Cup, Channel 4 Television devoted the whole evening to a celebration of 'the beautiful game'. The programme included recordings of the greatest matches and the worst fouls, a good deal of pretentious discussion about strategy and tactics, and an examination of crowd psychology. At the end of the broadcast, the voice of a small boy summed up the real importance of football in a single sentence. 'You get a ball and a few of your mates, and it's tea time before you know where you are'. Football is meant to make us glad. The rule applies to spectators and players alike.

As far as top players are concerned, these days it is also meant to make them rich. But although huge wages and enormous bonus payments have changed the status of the football professional, the men who earn more in a week than many of the fans take home in a year still find real pleasure in the game. It could not be otherwise. There is something intrinsically joyful about the principles on which football is based. Anyone who does not find real delight in kicking a ball is not likely to run his heart out every Saturday afternoon – at least, not to much effect.

Part of football's charm is its essential simplicity. The American game which goes by the same name is a version too complicated to be comprehensible. Rugby Union seems to change its rules for no better reason than to prove that it is a game designed to be played by public school boys and ancient universities. And Rugby League indulges in a similar rule-book just to prove that anything that the amateurs of the Union can do, the professionals of the north of England can do better. But football remains straightforward. Even the modern sophistications – no passing back to the goalkeeper and no tackles from behind – are intended to keep play flowing in constant rhythm. Football was born in the industrial cities of Britain. The men who stood on the terraces on Saturday afternoon paid their one-and-nines for an emotional rather than an intellectual experience.

It may be that, unconsciously, football spectators enjoy another experience of which they are not fully aware. Neville Cardus believed that cricket made aesthetes out of men who had never heard the word and would be frightened of it if they ever did. Perhaps the same can be said of football. J. B. Priestley writing seventy years ago about fictional Bruddersford, said that, for a few coppers on a Saturday afternoon, 't'United' provided both 'conflict and art', and that to describe a match as 'twenty two hirelings kicking a ball' was like describing a Stradivarius as wood and cat-gut and Hamlet as paper and ink. Despite Priestley's ennobling opinion, football has been notable for an absence of accompanying literature. Football novels, as the section in this bibliography sadly demonstrates, are few and often far from any claim to being classified as serious fiction. Good football poetry is equally scarce. And until recent times much of football reporting has been of 'the leather sphere flew from his cultivated instep with the speed of light and, leaving the glovesman rooted to the spot, buried itself in the back of the net' variety. There has been no Ring Lardner in Britain to write about football in the way that the greatest of all sports journalists wrote about American games – that is to say inherent romance combined with the brutal reality.

In *The Good Companions*, J. B. Priestley also wrote about the social importance of football. In Bruddersford, a man who had missed 't'United's' last home match 'must walk on tiptoe' when he got to work on Monday. Overstatement though that may be, there is no doubt that between the wars football dominated the lives of the northern industrial towns. Pre-war Bradford had a population of about 100,000, Huddersfield rather less. Yet crowds of 60,000 – almost entirely male – watched Huddersfield Town during their glory years of three consecutive First Division Championships. At Bradford – where there were two, less exalted teams – the average home-gate was still almost 30,000. Those are hard facts. Social scientists would confirm that the statistics demonstrate football's importance in the life of both working class pre-war Britain and the nation which faced a further ten years of austerity after the war was won. That judgement is based neither on nostalgia nor sentimentality. Though as so much of *A Football Compendium* demonstrates – nostalgia and sentimentality are abiding characteristics of the true football enthusiast.

Football supporters all believe in a golden age. Basically they are divided between those who think that the golden age is passed and those who know that it is yet to come. Only a handful – most of them children – believe that the golden age is here and now. Even those who believe that their team is 'playing better than ever before' and 'bound to win something next year' talk incessantly about old heroes and the exploits of teams which they have never seen or barely remember.

That is why the section of *A Football Compendium* which is boldly entitled 'Club Histories' and the following section, 'Personalities' are the two most substantial parts of the whole work. *The Glory Game*, by Hunter Davies is one of the genuinely literary and literate accounts of a football year. But it no doubt became a best seller because it described a season in the life of Tottenham, one of the great and most successful clubs in England. But the famous names of football are not the only teams to be immortalised in print. Enthusiasts can buy a 272-page *History of Walsall Football Club*. Welsh football fans can obtain a 416-page 'complete record' of Wrexham AFC between 1873 and 1992. Perhaps the most poignant entry of all is Northampton Town – the unhappily named 'Cobblers'. This struggling Third Division side – saved from disappearance from the league only because the team which was to take its place played on an unacceptable ground – offered its fans both a history of its club and a 'Who's who' of its players since 1920. But both books have a steady sale.

Biographies in particular have a special appeal to the long time football enthusiast. On receipt of the British Library's bibliography, I immediately turned, within the 'Personalities' chapter, to 'R' for Robinson. Jackie Robinson was my first football hero. He played for Sheffield Wednesday before, and in the first couple of years after, the war and became the youngest player to win an England cap. He was transferred to Sunderland in 1947 and, since my regular presence at Wednesday's Hillsborough ground did not begin until that year, I am not even sure that I ever saw him play. I certainly cannot remember watching him wear the blue and white striped shirt and I have no idea what he looked like. But he was my first hero. So I looked for his name amongst the Ramseys, the Revies, the Robsons (Bryans and Bobbys) and the Rushes. All real football fans would behave in exactly the same way.

The introduction to the section entitled 'Theory and Practice' correctly contains a disclaimer 'It is doubtful whether a single soul would attribute his success to the fact that he 'once read a book' which taught him all he knew'. Though, as the game grows more sophisticated, it is bound to generate an extended body of work which acts as a manual for players who wish to improve. Football success begins with natural ability and is then extended by hard work and application which is directed normally by verbal coaching. Even then, the advice has to be advanced with some care and discretion. Folklore has it that Jimmy Greaves complained about one manager who 'thought that, because I play for England, he can talk to me about peripheral vision and purposive running. Honestly, I cannot understand a word he is talking about'. The truth is that most coaching manuals are to be read for pleasure. A few enthusiastic school teachers may pore over them during the summer holidays and retired professionals may think it necessary to quote some titles and authors when they apply for FA Coaching Certificates. But most of the 'text books' will be read by little boys who dream of putting the theories into practice at Wembley.

The most quoted recent comment on football is Bill Shankly's judgement that the game is not 'a matter of life and death' but, 'much more important than that'. Since most supporters and players share that view it is hardly surprising that there is a notable dearth of football humour beyond the stages of working men's clubs where the jokes are almost always against the local team. In the years when both Birmingham City and Aston Villa were performing badly, I heard in a single night, three equally improbable stories. The City manager was said to possess visual aids which he held up before the team as he discussed tactics. When told that the foreign players could understand such English terms as 'shoot' and 'goal', he explained that the drawings were to help the local players who did not understand the meaning of the words. It was also revealed that Birmingham City were the only club in football history not to score during the entire reign of a Pope – who turned out to be John Paul I who lasted for only thirty-three days. Finally, there was a monologue about the city's most famous team and the manager who had just taken over the club that can rightly claim to have created the Football League, 'Now his hand is on the tiller, God help poor old Aston Villa'.

It is not surprising that jokes of this quality are not collected in anthologies to stand on the library shelves next to the works of S. J. Perelman, Dorothy Parker and Steven Leacock. They are however superior (as a form of humour) to the Colemanballs quotations which have found their way into no less than six volumes. Colemanballs are verbal errors made by football commentators in the heat of battle. The surprising thing about them is that they happen so rarely. At the final of the World Cup, Barry Davis talked more or less continually for two hours – only interrupted by half time, the pause between the ninety-minute whistle and extra time and the occasional comments by the experts who assisted him. What is more, he described – spontaneously and with no more preparation than his years of experience – continuous action. If he said anything that sounded foolish, I did not hear it. But that was only good luck. Commentators are bound to make mistakes. Most of their errors may raise a smile at the time, but are essentially unmemorable.

Inevitably, the chapter on 'Football & Society' contains a lengthy list of works on soccer hooliganism. They range from the quasi-academic to the biographical. Happily, when the bibliography is updated it seems unlikely that very much will be added to that section. Soccer violence has almost been extinguished – though not by the Government's conscious determination to 'change the culture' of the game. The real football fans – who never rioted on the terraces, or smashed the stands or ran amok across the pitches – simply reasserted their influence over the game. The fans have changed – and will change even more with all seater stadia and the provisions of facilities which the old grounds lacked. But the basic charm of the game will remain. Football was meant to make us glad. That will shine through everything that is written about it.

How To Use This Book

✱ Scope

A Football Compendium is a bibliography of all books and serials published in the United Kingdom or the Republic of Ireland about the game of association football in all its aspects. Additionally, in Chapter 1, there are a small number of books about the game before the formation of the Football Association in 1863. *A Football Compendium* covers publications issued up to March 1995 and includes titles whose publication was imminent after this date and for which advance information had been submitted by publishers to the British Library.

This bibliography does not cover periodicals, newspapers, boys' annuals, programmes, club yearbooks, testimonial brochures, unpublished research, dissertations, theses, promotional and souvenir items, although occasional instances of some of these categories are included to make or illustrate a specific point. Reprints are not included, but new editions *are* listed. In the case of serials such as *Yearbooks*, *Guides* and *Annuals*, the entry gives the year in which the title started publication and, if known, the year in which publication ceased.

In the main, the entries in this bibliography are derived from the holdings of the British Library, the national library of the United Kingdom. By law, all publishers in the United Kingdom (and, under Irish law, publishers in the Republic of Ireland) are required to deposit on publication and without waiting to be formally requested to do so, one copy of every title they issue. For a number of reasons, including ignorance of this obligation, the British Library does not in fact hold a copy of every book published in this country and various bibliographic and other sources have been used to ensure that *A Football Compendium* is as comprehensive as the compiler and editors could make it.

Although most of the entries in this bibliography have been derived from the catalogue of the British Library, many have not. In some instances (particularly in the Fanzine and Music chapters) the only information available to the compiler has been the title and perhaps the date of an item. In these cases, although the compiler is confidant that the item exists, it has not been possible to obtain further information. Further information on these items, and indeed on any omissions or mistakes in this bibliography, will be gratefully received by the editors and incorporated in the next edition.

✱ Arrangement

The chapter headings used reflect the categories to be found in the literature and it has thus been possible to list most items just once. Where the scope of a work cuts across the boundaries of the chapter headings, the book has been listed in the most relevant chapter. Index entries have been created under all other appropriate headings. In cases where it has been thought helpful to the user, books have been listed in more than one section.

The information contained in each entry is laid out in a standard format and contains certain standard pieces of information. Not all records will contain all pieces of information. Some books, for example, do not carry information on them saying where the book was published. In these instances the catalogue record will not contain this information.

Books are numbered sequentially within each chapter. A new sequence of numbers starts with each chapter. In this way, every book listed in the bibliography has been given a unique reference made up of the chapter letter and the number of the book within the chapter, e.g. A165, B178 etc. Entries within most sections are arranged chronologically by date of publication. When more than one book has been published in the same year, they are arranged alphabetically by title. A few chapters are arranged alphabetically by name, e.g. Chapter C, *Personalities*, where the entries are arranged by the *biographee*, Chapter I, *Football in Literature*, where the entries are listed alphabetically by *author*, and Chapter B, *Club Histories*, where entries are in *club* order.

Those records relating to items not held by the British Library have been laid out in a similar way and every effort has been made to include all the information necessary to uniquely identify the item in order to facilitate its purchase, or enable users to obtain it on loan from a public or other library.

A typical entry is set out below:

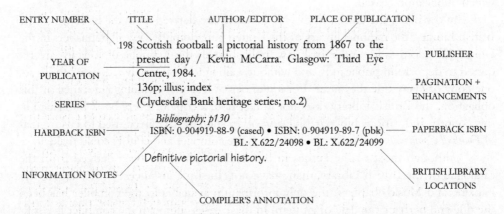

ENTRY NUMBER   TITLE   AUTHOR/EDITOR   PLACE OF PUBLICATION

198 Scottish football: a pictorial history from 1867 to the present day / Kevin McCarra. Glasgow: Third Eye Centre, 1984.
136p; illus; index
(Clydesdale Bank heritage series; no.2)
Bibliography: p130
ISBN: 0-904919-88-9 (cased) • ISBN: 0-904919-89-7 (pbk)
BL: X.622/24098 • BL: X.622/24099
Definitive pictorial history.

YEAR OF PUBLICATION — PUBLISHER — PAGINATION + ENHANCEMENTS — SERIES — HARDBACK ISBN — PAPERBACK ISBN — INFORMATION NOTES — BRITISH LIBRARY LOCATIONS — COMPILER'S ANNOTATION

(The index entries would refer to this book as item A5)

N.B. The location numbers for books held in the British Library refer to books which are not available for loan. They are only available for consultation in the Reading Rooms of the Library when it is not possible for a reader to consult them elsewhere. Various restrictions may also apply to particular items. Enquiries concerning access to the British Library should be made in writing to:

British Library
Reader Admission Office
Great Russell Street
London WC1 3DG

✳ *Abbreviations Used in the Entries*

BL	British Library
Cm/Cmd/Cmnd	Command paper
D	BL copy destroyed during WW2
ed.	edition
fps	frames per second
geneal.	genealogy
illus	illustrated
ISBN	International Standard Book Number
ISSN	International Standard Serial Number
mins	minutes
p	pages
pbk	paperback
pseud.	pseudonym
rev.	revised
SBN	Standard Book Number
t.p.	title page
vol.	volume

CHAPTER
A

History &
Development

FOR WELL OVER A HUNDRED YEARS association football has been able to capture the attention of publishers as a subject worthy of coverage. The result has been the publication of a vast number of titles dealing with the history and development of the game. From early works of particular appeal to the collector to more recent histories and reference works, this chapter lists all the books which the researcher or interested reader might wish to consult to learn about the origins, growth and development of a very simple game which has been so passionately embraced by a world-wide public.

Football had been played as a street game for many centuries before the formation of the Football Association in 1863, though it seems to have resembled more of an organised brawl than a game. This phase of the game is covered in the section Folk Football [A224-226]. Some general descriptions of the game played in pre-association days can be found in the section Football Before 1863 [A284-294]. It was the public schools and universities, however, which exerted the most influence in transforming an unstructured pastime into an organised game with its own set of distinct rules. Works covering this period, at A252-255, give a fascinating record of the differing varieties of 'football' played at Charterhouse, Eton, Harrow, Winchester and Westminster which were the direct forerunners of the association game.

The Victorian and Edwardian titles listed at A1-36 describe from a contemporary standpoint how the game evolved into a highly organised sport. Of particular interest, many of these works contain contributions from leading administrators of the day. These were the individuals to whom football as we know it owes its very existence. The style and quality of these early books very much reflects the social status of the game in that period. Lavishly produced and expensive, they were suited to grace the mahogany shelves of a gentleman's study or country house library, for football in the nineteenth and early twentieth century was indeed a gentleman's pursuit.

Notable examples from this period are *Football: Our Winter Game* [A4] by Charles Alcock and *Athletics and Football* [A7] by Montague Shearman published as part of the renowned 'Badminton Library' series. Shearman's work presents one of the very best contemporary accounts of the growth of the game up to the formation of the Association in 1863 and beyond. Pre-dating the formation of the Football League by just one year, it presents a particularly well rounded and apposite summation of the pre-league era.

Used in conjunction with *The Rise of the Leaguers* [A16] which covers the years 1863 to 1897, these two books alone convey the complete story of the game up to the turn of the century. Updated editions of Shearman's book and Nicholas 'Pa' Jackson's monumental *Association Football* [A18] are also well worthy of consultation. Indeed, hardly any of these nineteenth century works could fail to fascinate the serious football student. Whilst much of the information they contain can be found repeated in more recent publications there is a particular satisfaction in handling and consulting these early titles. Now scarce collectors' pieces these primary sources continue to evoke the atmosphere and spirit of the times and are handsome additions to any football library.

Nothing could epitomise this better than Gibson and Pickford's *Association Football & and the Men Who Made It* [A29], a classic four volume set which must be regarded as essential reading for all serious students and justifiably cherished by anyone fortunate enough to own these marvellous books. Not far behind in both quality and content is *The Book of Football* [A30] while for pure opulence *Cricket and Football* [A34], published by 'The Sportsman' cannot be bettered.

A distinct publishing trend becomes discernible in the inter-war years. Football had ceased to be a game favoured only by gentlemen and had become firmly established as a popular sport championed by the working class. The ordinary man in the street had neither the money nor the inclination to purchase quality books – very few items of any note were published in the inter-war years. There are nonetheless a number of classic works from the period which should not be overlooked. Notable examples are *Wickets and Goals* [A39] and *The Mighty Kick* [A43].

This dearth of significant material continued during the wartime years. But although little material was published, this is not to say that the period 1939-1945 is poorly documented. Jack Rollin's classic *Soccer at War* [A49] provides an extremely comprehensive account of one of the lesser known eras of soccer's rich history.

The post-war era [A50-163] includes a splendid range of works, with specialist studies covering every decade to the present and a number of general titles giving a full overview. Those by William Lowndes [A65], Geoffrey Green [A67], Morris Marples [A68], Brian Glanville [A71] and Percy Young [A73] stand out amongst those published before 1960 while James Walvin's *People's Game* [A114] and Wray Vamplew's *Pay Up and Play the Game* [A143] present a scholarly retrospective analysis of the growth of football in its early years with particular reference to economic and social influences.

Whilst most of the works cited thus far are general in terms of their geographical coverage, researchers requiring specific emphasis on Scotland, Wales or Ireland are adequately catered for. In terms of numbers there are fewer works to consult, but in terms of quality and comprehensiveness the content is excellent, particularly for Scotland. The same might be said regarding coverage of the non-league and amateur game – items A227-251 are a real credit to the publishers and authors whose efforts have ensured such a detailed coverage of the game in the lower echelons.

Finally, it should be noted that a number of specialist works have been written which chronicle the history and work of both the Football Association and the Football League – two key organisations in the administration of the game. In particular, Geoffrey Green's massive work *The History of the Football Association* [A261] and Simon Inglis' *League Football and the Men Who Made It* [A280], tell the story of both bodies and bring vividly to life the characters of those who have held office in them.

The entries in this chapter show that there can be no doubt that association football has generated a comprehensive and thoroughly worthwhile literature – a rich source of research material indeed and physical proof of the popularity and tradition of what must surely be regarded as the world's greatest game.

History & Development ~ Contents

The Victorian Era

1   Beeton's football / Frederick Wood. London: Frederick
Warne, 1865.
96p   BL: D

   *Scarce early commentary published just two years
   after the formation of the Football Association.*

2   Routledge's handbook of football. London: Routledge,
1867.
                          BL: Mic.A.12484(1) (microfilm copy)
   Another scarce early item worthy of consultation.

3   The goal: the chronicle of football. London: 1873-1874.
12 parts   BL: Hendon

4   Football: our winter game / Charles W. Alcock. London:
Field, 1874.
139p   BL: D

   *One of the first truly comprehensive accounts of the
   game during its years of growth following the formation of the Association in 1863. The author was an
   extremely influential figure – he played for the famous
   Wanderers side and served on the Association Committee in its early years prior to taking the helm as
   Secretary for 25 years until 1895. His part in developing the game through its junior and teenage years
   into 'adulthood' cannot be underestimated; it was
   also Alcock who suggested the FA Cup competition.
   Well worth consultation.*

5   Foot-ball: its history for five centuries / Sir Montague
Shearman and James Edmund Vincent. London: Field
and Tuer, 1885.
72p
(Historical sporting series)   BL: 7908.c.43

   *Scholarly study charting the ancient origins of foot-
   ball as played in centuries past, culminating in the
   formation of the Association and the formalisation
   of a previously rough-and-tumble pastime. Much of
   this material was repeated two years later in the
   Badminton Library publication by Shearman.*

6   The year's sport: a review of British sports and pastimes
for . . . 1885 / edited by A. E. T. Watson. London: 1886.
                                               BL: P.P.2489.zcb

7   Athletics and football / Montague Shearman; with a
contribution on paper-chasing by W. Rye; and an
introduction by Sir Richard Webster. London:
Longmans, Green, 1887.
xxvi, 446p; illus; index
(The Badminton Library)   BL: K.T.C.103.a.1/5
                                        BL: 7919.aaa.20

   *This is an essential work for all researchers of the
   game in its early years. Four detailed chapters cover
   the history and development of association football.*

The first chapter offers an extremely comprehensive
account of the ancient origins of football, whilst the
second chapter charts the progress of the various
codes of play in use by the public schools. This is followed by a twenty-nine page description of the
association game concentrating particularly on positional and tactical developments. The concluding
chapter gives a short overview of the place of football
in modern society. The book is illustrated by several
evocative engravings taken from action photographs
– 'the first occasion in which the newest development
of photography has been utilised for illustrating a
work upon athletic sports'. This work also serves well
for researchers studying folk football – the games at
Chester, Derby, Scone, Corfe Castle and Ashbourne
are all covered. It should be noted that individual
teams and players are not chronicled here as the
Football League was not formed until 1888. For a
history up to this date, this work is invaluable.*

   ☞   Subsequent ed. A19

8   Football: a popular handbook of the game / Dr. Irvine,
C. W. Alcock, and other . . . authorities; edited by
G. A. H. 1887.
(The boy's own bookshelf; vol. 2)

   Edited by George Andrew Hutchison   BL: D
   *Interesting early study with contributions from some
   of the leading names of the day.*

9   Camsell's game of football. 1889.
                          BL: Mic.A.9961(13) (microfilm copy)
   ☞   Subsequent ed. A10

10 Camsell's game of football : description and rules. New
ed. 1890.   BL: Mic.A.9961(14) (microfilm copy)
   ☞   Previous ed. A9

11 Football: the association game / Charles W. Alcock.
London: G. Bell, 1890.
80p
(All England series)   BL: 7908.df.23/2
   *Short study of the game and its rules, part of the
   well-known 'All England' series.*

   ☞   Subsequent ed. A31

12 Football / edited by Rev. Francis Marshall. Rev. and
enlarged ed. London: Cassell, 1894.
xvi, 560p; illus

   Previous ed. untraced   BL: 07905.i.6
   *Extremely comprehensive and essential work of refer-
   ence.*

   ☞   Subsequent ed. A37

13   A sporting pilgrimage: riding to hounds, golf, rowing,
     football, club and university athletics, studies in English
     sport, past and present / Caspar W. Whitney. London:
     Osgood, 1895.
     xii, 397p; illus   BL: 07905.i.30

     The author presents personal observations on the
     variety of sporting activities which might be wit-
     nessed on a journey through England – football is
     amongst them.

14   The encyclopædia of sport / edited by the Earl of
     Suffolk and Berkshire, Hedley Peek, and F. G. Aflalo.
     London: Lawrence & Bullen, 1897-1898.
     2 vols; illus   BL: 7904.dd.8

     Includes a section on football illustrated with photo-
     graphs.

     ☞ See also: A15; A22

15   Football / A. Budd, C. B. Fry, T. A. Cook and B. F.
     Robinson. London: Lawrence & Bullen, 1897.
     95p
     (Suffolk sporting series)

         Reprinted, with additions and alterations, from part 7 of the
         Encyclopædia of Sport   BL: 7912.df.13

     This is the relevant section from the previous entry,
     published here in its own right. The association game
     shares the volume with rugby and American football.
     C. B. Fry presents the soccer content which is largely
     an analysis of the skills and methodology to be em-
     ployed in varying positions. One wonders how Fry
     might fare as a coach today – 'It is sound policy to
     shoot whenever there is a good chance of scoring,
     and certainly in this case "bis dat qui cito dat". . . .
     Usually the outsides should be rather in front of the
     other forwards, but they should avoid loafing.'

     ☞ See also: A14

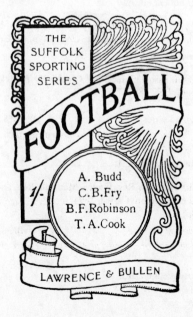

16   The rise of the Leaguers from 1863-1897 / Tityrus.
     London: Sporting Chronicle, 1897.
     159p; illus

         Pseudonym for J. A. H. Catton

     Catton's introduction states that 'the object of this
     little book is to tell in simple language, and with such
     detail as the official records obtainable and limited
     space will allow, the history of the most powerful
     clubs in the League today.' This is precisely what it
     does, offering valuable material to the club historian.
     The clubs covered are Aston Villa, Blackburn Rovers,
     Bolton Wanderers, Burnley, Bury, Derby County, Ever-
     ton, Liverpool, Nottingham Forest, Preston North
     End, Sheffield Wednesday, Sheffield United, Stoke,
     Sunderland, West Bromwich Albion and Wolverhamp-
     ton Wanderers. Each chapter includes line drawings
     of the clubs' leading personalities and there are some
     interesting advertisements at the front and rear.
     Certainly one of the gems of football literature. It has
     lately been published in facsimile by the Association
     of Football Statisticians.

17   Association football / John Goodall; edited by S. A. De
     Bear. Edinburgh: W. Blackwood & Sons, 1898.
     108p   BL: 07905.ee.15

     Part instructional, part historical coverage from one
     of the day's most prominent footballers. Goodall had
     been a member of the all-conquering Preston North
     End side in 1888-89 but was playing for Derby
     County when he penned this work. He was a pioneer of
     scientific football and the passing game and also
     played cricket for Derbyshire and Hertfordshire. Such
     was his exemplary character he was known universally
     as Johnny Allgood! Certainly a valuable contribution
     to football literature and notable as one of the earli-
     est examples of a work written by a leading player of
     the day.

18   Association football / Nicholas L. Jackson; with
     contributions by the Rev. W. W. Beveridge, A. H. Tod,
     'Old Forester', A. T. Hay, E. Tudor-Owen, and an 'Old
     Boy', Westminster. London: G. Newnes, 1899.
     xii, 412p; illus

         'Old Boy', Westminster is T. S. Oldham
                             BL: Mic.A.8124(2) (microfilm copy)

     Extremely worthwhile study fronted by 'Pa' Jackson, a
     leading administrative figure in Victorian and Ed-
     wardian soccer and well known as the founder of the
     Corinthians in 1882.

19   Football history / M. Shearman. New ed. London:
     Longmans, Green, 1899.
     xii, 379p; illus
     (The Badminton Library)

         Contents: The association game / W. J. Oakley and G. O.
         Smith; The rugby union game / F. Mitchell
                                                 BL: 7913.pp.1/20

     Football takes centre stage in this updated edition
     from this classic sporting series – in the 1887 work it
     had to share its place with athletics and paper chas-

ing. This in itself is an indicator of the growth in stature which the game had experienced in little over a decade. An essential work of reference.

☞   Previous ed. A7; subsequent ed. A27

20   Association football / Ernest Needham. London: Skeffington, 1900.
91p   BL: Mic.A.10965(5) (microfilm copy)
Ernest 'Nudger' Needham was a leading player of the day, a wing-half with Sheffield United and England. Interesting in itself but may offer particular material for historians of the 'Blades'.

21   The real football: a sketch of the development of the association game / James A. H. Catton. London: Sands, 1900.
215p   BL: Mic.A.6656(1) (microfilm copy)
Certain of the more substantial early works stand out as essential for any serious student of the game's history. This is one such work.

22   The young sportsman / edited by A. E. T. Watson. London: Lawrence & Bullen, 1900.
viii, 663p; illus
The greater part is reprinted from the Encyclopædia of Sport
BL: 07905.l.18

☞   See also: A14

The Early Twentieth Century

23   The sports of the world / edited by F. G. Aflalo. London: Cassell, 1902-1903.
viii, 416p   BL: 7915.i.6
Includes a short section on football.

24   English sport / edited by A. E. T. Watson. London: Macmillan, 1903.
viii, 361p; illus   BL: 7907.dd.30

25   Men famous in football and footballers' almanack / edited by E. C. Price. London: 1903-   BL: P.P.2489.wfe
Portraits of leading players of the day – this work has recently been published in facsimile by the Association of Football Statisticians.

26   Association football / J. L. Jones. London: C. Arthur Pearson, 1904.
112p   BL: Mic.A.8208(13) (microfilm copy)
The author was a Welsh International whose clubs included Rhyddlan, Sheffield United and Tottenham Hotspur.

27   Football: history / Sir Montague Shearman. New ed. London: Longmans, Green, 1904.
xii, 387p; illus; index
(The Badminton Library of sports and pastimes)

Contents: The association game / W. J. Oakley & G. O. Smith; The rugby union game / Frank Mitchell; other contributions by R. E. MacNaghten, M. C. Kemp, J. E. Vincent, Walter Camp, and A. Sutherland
BL: 2270.c.1

☞   Previous ed. A19

28   Weddell's unique record of league football, first and second divisions, 1888-1904 / Albert J. Weddell. Liverpool: The author, 1904.
67p   BL: D

ASSOCIATION
FOOTBALL &
THE MEN WHO MADE IT
BY ALFRED GIBSON & WILLIAM PICKFORD

IN FOUR VOLUMES
VOL. I

FULLY ILLUSTRATED

LONDON
THE CAXTON PUBLISHING COMPANY
CLUN HOUSE, SURREY STREET, W.C.

29   Association football & the men who made it / Alfred Gibson and William Pickford. London: Caxton, 1905-1906.
4 vols; illus; index   BL: 7913.g.18
If ever there was a case for a brief bibliographic citation failing to do full justice to its subject, then this is surely it. These four volumes, each extending to over two hundred pages, make up what is generally regarded as the most sought after set of books in

football literature. From the delightfully illustrated cover to the very last index entry, this is a journey through football history which should not be missed at any price. The subject matter is extremely wide – many of the leading players and teams are placed under the spotlight, as are the top-hatted administrators of the day. All researchers of the early years should procure a set, but be aware that copies in good condition seldom surface. The Association of Football Statisticians has sensibly produced a facsimile edition in recent years.

30 The book of football: a complete history and record of the association and rugby games with numerous illustrations and photographs. London: Amalgamated Press, 1906.
xii, 292p; illus   BL: 7912.k.14

This is one of the classics of football literature, originally published in twelve parts in 1905. It is particularly strong on club histories – each club is accorded 3-4 pages along with a team photograph. The clubs covered are Aston Villa, Arsenal, Newcastle, Sheffield United, Blackburn, Southampton, Bristol Rovers, Chelsea, Tottenham, Stoke, Burnley, Fulham, Bolton, Small Heath, Reading, Liverpool, West Bromwich Albion, Queens Park Rangers, Everton, Burton United, Queens Park, Plymouth, Sunderland, Blackpool, Portsmouth, Sheffield Wednesday, West Ham, Wolverhampton Wanderers, Luton, Middlesbrough, Corinthians, Notts County, Chesterfield, Nottingham Forest, Leeds City, Preston North End, Manchester United, Leicester Fosse, Bury, Barnsley, Watford, Brentford, Northampton, New Brompton, Derby County, and Manchester City. Other chapters cover Scottish and Irish football. There is also an unusual section entitled 'The ball and the boot – how they are made'. Yet further sections cover football in the army, public schools football, university football and the aptly titled 'Much abused referee'. Certainly a vital contribution to football history. A facsimile edition has been published by the Association of Football Statisticians.

31 Football: the association game / Charles W. Alcock. New ed. London: G. Bell, 1906.
103p
(All England series)
                                             BL: 7908.df.23/3
☞ Previous ed. A11

32 Football / B. O. Corbett, William McGregor, Ernest Needham, J. H. Gettins, L. Richmond Roose, Stanley S. Harris, W. Pickford, Andrew Aitken, J. Sharp, James W. Crabtree and C. W. Alcock. London: Greening, 1907.
128p
(Greening's useful handbook series)
                          BL: Mic.A.7125(7) (microfilm copy)

Well worthy of study for its contributions by leading figures of the day – particularly notable in the list of authors is William McGregor, a redoubtable Scotsman dubbed 'Father of the Football League' and elected its first chairman in 1888. There is no better way to learn about the game at this time than from observations by contemporary figures presented in volumes of this type.

☞ See also: H97

33 The book of football / Edward Humphrey Dalrymple Sewell. London: Dent, 1911.
xiv, 304p; illus   BL: 7911.c.14

Effectively the last substantial survey of the game prior to the outbreak of World War One.

34 Cricket and football / compiled and edited by 'The Sportsman' (Sporting Life). London: British Sports & Sportsmen, 1917.
xiii, 579p; illus
(British sports and sportsmen past & present; vol. 5)
                                             BL: L.R.255.b.1

The cricket and football volume of this fine series was in preparation during the First World War and was very nearly abandoned. In the event, it was published in 1917, largely out of loyalty to advanced subscribers. What a blessing that it did proceed, for it is surely the most lavish book listed in this bibliography – it is certainly the heaviest with its large gilt-edged pages bound between bevelled leather boards with fine marbled endpapers. The football content extends to just 70 or so pages, but it is well worth consulting. Two limited editions each of 1,000 copies were published: the de-luxe is in red leather whilst the popular is in green cloth. Collectors will need deep pockets whichever they choose.

35 Edwardians at play: sport, 1890-1914 / Brian Dobbs. London: Pelham, 1973.
186p; illus   ISBN: 0-7207-0642-4
                                             BL: X.629/5894

Excellent study of sporting developments during an important transitional era for football itself – includes much of relevance for the football historian.

The Inter-War Years

36 The rise and progress of modern football / Harras Moore. London: Bowman & Murdoch, 1922.
32p; illus   BL: Mic.A.10909(7) (microfilm copy)

37 Football . . . / edited by the late Rev. F. Marshall. New ed. edited and revised by L. R. Tosswill. London: Cassell, 1925.
xi, 408p   BL: 7904.f.25

   Extremely comprehensive and essential work of reference.

   ☞ Previous ed. A12

The author starred with Sunderland and Arsenal before contributing this work upon his retirement from the playing side of the game. Valued contribution from one whose experiences spanned both sides of the First World War; Buchan went on to become a highly respected football journalist.

42 The philosophy of sport / Peter MacBride. London: Heath Cranton, 1932.
ix, 190p   BL: 07912.h.47

   A refreshing approach to the subject of sport — might well yield footballing material of interest.

A War-time Match from Reg Carter's Sketchbook

38 A book about football / Hayte Mayfield. London: Epworth Press, 1926.
132p; illus   BL: 07912.f.63

39 Wickets and goals: stories of play / James A. H. Catton. London: Chapman & Hall, 1926.
ix, 303p; illus   BL: 07911.gg.23

   Football shares its place with cricket here but soccer students must in no way be deterred by this. This is one of the classics of the era.

40 Association football / J. Dimmock. London: C. Arthur Pearson, 1927.
124p; illus   BL: 07912.g.20

   In the 1919/20 season Tottenham Hotspur scored 102 goals with only 32 in reply, losing just 4 out of 42 games to run away with the Second Division Championship. James Dimmock was a member of that side.

41 Association football / Charles Murray Buchan. London: Hutchinson, 1928.
192p; illus   BL: Mic.A.9930(8) (microfilm copy)

43 The mighty kick: romance, history and humour of football / W. Capel Kirby and Frederick W. Carter; first words by Hugo Meisl; a last word by George Allison. London: Jarrolds, 1933.
288p; illus   BL: 7916.b.28

   Any collector of pre-war soccer books would do well to procure this volume — much of relevance including some good anecdotal material.

44 British sport and games / Bernard R. M. Darwin. London: Longmans, Green, 1940.
42p; illus
(British life and thought; no. 6)   BL: 10353.k.3/6

   ☞ Subsequent ed. A50

45 The psychology of the history and organisation of association football / R. W. Pickford. 1940.
2 vols

   I have not had sight or verification of this item though the title suggests interesting and original content.

The Second World War

46 POW football competition. Hereford: 1944-1945.
    2 issues   BL: 7918.a.7

    Amongst the variety of Services and Inter-Allied
    Forces games organised during the war period were
    also those for Prisoners of War. This is a scarce
    ephemeral item which outlines the rules of the compe-
    tition and lists the competing clubs.

    ☞ See also: A48

47 Victory was the goal: soccer's contribution in the war of
    1939-45. London: Football Association, 1945.
    48p; illus; pbk

    Soccer did indeed make a contribution to the war ef-
    fort, not least in terms of general morale. This scarce
    FA publication explains its role from a contemporary
    stance. Twenty-five photographs are included. In the
    foreword, the Earl of Athlone, President of the FA,
    wrote: 'This book is at once a record and a tribute – a
    record of the many ways in which football and the
    Football Association contributed to the war effort
    and a tribute to that great army of footballers
    whose valiant service in many fields helped so materi-
    ally to bring us victory and peace . . .'

48 St Dunstan's football competition: annual handbook.
    Hereford, 1948-

Continues the handbooks of the POW football competition
                                              BL: W.P.14065

    ☞ See also: A46

49 Soccer at war 1939-45 / Jack Rollin. London: Collins,
    1985.
    308p   ISBN: 0-00-218023-5
                                  BL: X.800/42211

    Rollin's work makes a very valuable contribution to
    historical football literature, covering an era when
    matters of far greater importance than soccer were
    being fought on the world stage. At home, many
    grounds suffered bomb damage, personnel were re-
    quired for war service and some stadiums were
    utilised for training exercises. Massive disruption to
    the normal football programme was inevitable, yet
    the business as usual British spirit ensured that
    some football did continue and undoubtedly this
    must have helped raise spirits; 75 professional play-
    ers lost their lives in the course of the war – many
    others picked up their careers again afterwards, not
    only older, but surely much wiser. Rollin's is the defini-
    tive and essential account for all researchers
    interested in this fascinating period.

The Post-War Years & General Histories

50 British sport and games / Bernard R. M. Darwin. Rev.
    ed. London: Longmans, Green, 1945.
    39p; illus
    (British life and thought; no. 6)   BL: 10353.k.3/6a

    ☞ Previous ed. A44

51 An intimate talk on soccer – the ace of games / Alec E.
    Whitcher; cartoons and sketches by Reg Carter.
    Brighton: Southern Publishing, 1945.
    145p; illus   BL: 7915.v.10

    When all the standard sources have been exhaustively
    researched it is to this engaging study that the
    football historian might profitably turn for something
    new. Whitcher had been an amateur player and sup-
    porter but here writes from his seat as a director of
    Brighton and Hove Albion. He covers all aspects of
    the game's history whilst also addressing the prob-
    lems of the time and musing on soccer's future. The
    style is often idiosyncratic and amusing, supported
    by appropriate cartoons and photographs. Well worth
    consulting and likely to yield something new, including
    particular observations on wartime soccer.

52 Soccer calling / Alec E. Whitcher; illustrated by Reg
    Carter; foreword by A. B. Campbell. 6th ed. Brighton:
    Southern Publishing, 1945.
    207p; illus

    Previous editions untraced   BL: X.629/3730

    Surprise is the element of Whitcher's style. Again
    there are informative snippets relating to wartime
    soccer.

    ☞ Subsequent ed. A54

53 Dynamo – and all that: the history of football from the
    dark ages to the Dynamos, BC to 1946 AD. London:
    Valiant, 1946.
    32p; pbk

                                           BL: 7918.bb.4

    Whilst in the process of establishing a mill outside
    Moscow in 1887, English mill owners, Clement and
    Harry Charnock, advertised in *The Times* for 'engi-
    neers, mechanics and clerks capable of playing
    football well'. Thus was founded Orekhovo Football
    Club, later to become Moscow Dynamo. The club es-

tablished an international reputation on their British tour in 1945, a tour which prompted this modest, yet fascinating, publication. Effectively a potted history of football from ancient time to the modern era by several authors.

> # DYNAMO
>
> ## —and all that
>
> The History of Football
> from the Dark Ages
> to the Dynamos
>
> B.C. to 1946 A.D.
>
> *Published by*
> VALIANT PUBLICATIONS LIMITED
> 153 FENCHURCH STREET
> LONDON, E.C.3

54 Soccer calling / Alec E. Whitcher; illustrated by Reg Carter. 7th ed. Brighton: Southern Publishing, 1946.
207p; illus

BL: 7918.b.24

☞ Previous ed. A52

55 The voice of soccer / Alec E. Whitcher; with a foreword by B. Howard-Baker; sketches by Reg Carter. Brighton: Southern Publishing, 1947.
232p; illus BL: 7919.cc.49

Like Whitcher's previous works, well worthy of consultation and likely to yield lesser known observations – includes references to Brighton, where Whitcher was a director.

56 Sportsman's club / Alec E. Whitcher; illustrated by Reg Carter. Brighton: Southern Publishing, 1948?
229p BL: 7920.aaa.28
The final book in the author's four volume series.

57 The story of soccer / various authors. Westcliffe-on-Sea: Michael Mason, 1948.
28p; pbk BL: 7917.c.42

58 Association football / Wilf Mannion. London: Nicholas Kaye, 1949.
119p BL: 7920.aaa.48
Mannion, whose playing career with Middlesbrough ran from 1936 to 1954 before a move to Hull City,

was an outspoken voice amongst the players of this era. At one point he spent months out of the game without wages when he refused to re-sign for Middlesbrough. His observations on football at this time present an informative account from the player's point of view.

59 The book of football for boys. London, 1949-
BL: P.P.6754.acn

60 English sports and pastimes / Christina Hole. London: B. T. Batsford, 1949.
viii, 182p; illus BL: 7920.c.24

Whilst football is only mentioned in Chapter 4, which it shares with hurling and cricket, this work makes interesting observations on the ancient origins of the game with particular reference to folk football at Atherstone, Chester-le Street and Haxey. There is just one football illustration, but it is one of the lesser known, entitled 'Street Football at Barnet – 1775'. Includes a comprehensive bibliography which may be of further interest to the serious student of folk football.

61 A popular history of association football / George J. S. King. London: Findon, 1949.
95p; illus BL: 7920.de.10

62 The story of the First Division / John E. Reynolds. London: Day & Mason, 1949.
22p; pbk BL: 7919.b.49

63 Soccer from the press box / Archibald William Ledbrooke and Edgar Turner. London: Nicholas Kaye, 1950.
224p; illus BL: 7921.aaa.7

This book is not just an insight into the art of football journalism – more than that, it is an extremely well-informed account of soccer between 1930 and 1950 presented from the perspective of an independent observer.

☞ Subsequent ed. A70

64 This football business / Joseph P. W. Mallalieu. London: Tribune Publications, 1951.
16p; pbk
(Tribune pamphlet) BL: W.P.12828/7

This curious short essay is delivered by one of the most academically learned observers of the game – a history degree and an MA from Trinity College, Oxford, followed by a Commonwealth Fellowship at the University of Chicago preceded his career as a journalist and then MP for Huddersfield in 1945. Huddersfield Town loom large in his affections. Worthwhile reading.

65 The story of football / William Lowndes. London: Thorsons, 1952.
127p; illus BL: 7920.aaa.75

Well researched, drawing from many early sources. Students having difficulty obtaining authentic nine-

teenth century works will find this modest book worth consulting for an historically accurate, scholarly yet light treatment of the subject.

66 The story of soccer / Patrick Pringle. London: Harrap, 1952.
    77p; illus   BL: W.P.A.112/2
    Aimed at the junior reader.

67 Soccer: the world game: a popular history / Geoffrey Green. London: Phoenix House, 1953.
    215p; illus   BL: 7921.ee.37
    This authoritative work covers the full spectrum in the following chapters: The beginnings; The game spreads; The coming of professionalism; The amateur game; The turn of the century; Soccer's world-wide popularity; League clubs and their traditions; Style and tactics; Great moments, great matches, great men; Global football; and, Stray ends. Eminently readable and nicely illustrated.

68 A history of football / Morris Marples. London: Secker & Warburg, 1954.
    xi, 276p; illus   BL: 7922.bb.3
    Largely concerned with the growth and development of football before the codifications of the mid-nineteenth century. This is a fine and scholarly work.

69 Soccer: a history of association football / Denzil Batchelor. London: Batsford, 1954.
    xii, 164p; illus
    (British sports: past & present)   BL: W.P.b.353/2
    A good general overview of the history of football from its earliest origins to the date of publication. Notable for its attractive dust jacket depicting a match in 1890 reproduced from a painting by W. H. Overend. This is an entertaining if not hugely detailed read from an accomplished journalist. Batchelor was sports editor of the *Picture Post* and raises a smile here with a most interesting piece of biographical blurb beneath his photograph on the dust jacket: 'Mr Batchelor is a member of most wine drinking clubs in existence, takes no exercise and wishes he lived in Somerset instead of Knightsbridge. He dislikes abstract painting, poetry which does not rhyme or scan, the very rich, gin and zoos!'

70 Soccer from the press box / Archibald William Ledbrooke and Edgar Turner. Entirely revised and re-set. London: Nicholas Kaye, 1955.
    208p; illus   BL: 7922.e.6
    Updated version of the journalist's view of soccer – Ledbrooke was regarded as one of the finest of his time, sports editor of the *Manchester Evening News* before the war, then of the *Daily Dispatch* before joining the *Daily Mirror* in 1955. This book is a fitting memory to his craft for Ledbrooke was three years later to be one of seven journalists who lost their lives in the Munich air crash.
    ☞ Previous ed. A63

71 Soccer nemesis / Brian Lester Glanville. London: Secker & Warburg, 1955.
    189p   BL: 7922.aa.78
    Relates the story of British football and the foreign challenge – the blurb states that the book 'traces the growth of that challenge from its almost comic beginnings early in the century, to the present day, when British football has far more to learn from other countries than it has to teach them'. Described as exciting and controversial, this work is authentically researched and regarded as a classic of football literature. It includes chapters on Vittorio Pozzo and Hugo Meisl, analysing their roles in the rise of football in Italy and Austria respectively.

72 The art of modern football / Frank Butler. London: Faber Popular Books, 1956.
    124p; illus   BL: W.P.388/16

73 Football through the ages / Percy Marshall Young; with illustrations by Reginald G. Haggar. London: Methuen, 1957.
    68p; pbk   BL: W.P.A.543/31
    One of football's best historical writers presents his own short study.

74 Sixty seasons of league football / Reginald Charles Churchill. Harmondsworth: Penguin, 1958.
    ix, 310p   BL: 12208.a.2/171
    One of the first publications to include all the final tables and full statistical records to this date.
    ☞ Subsequent ed. A79

75 Your book of soccer / H. T. L. L. Tottenham. London: Faber & Faber, 1958.
    54p; pbk   BL: 7923.n.20

76 Soccer round the globe / Brian Lester Glanville. London, New York: Abelard-Schuman, 1959.
    99p; illus   BL: 7925.b.44
    Short but wide-ranging study from one of soccer's best writers.

77 Association football / edited by A. H. Fabian and Geoffrey Green. London: Caxton, 1960.
    4 vols
    Various supplements were later issued to update this work
                                                  BL: 7925.c.19
    Over 400 pages in each volume ensures extremely comprehensive coverage of all facets of the game. The structure of the work is unashamedly modelled on *Association Football & The Men Who Made It*, a true gem from 1906. Stanley Rous, Secretary of the Football Association, described the 1960 version as a 'monumental effort'. It would be churlish to disagree with him – this set is a fine addition to any football library. In fact it might well be described as indispensable.

78   Sport international / edited by Charles Harvey. London:
     Sampson Low, Marston, 1960.
     415p; illus; index

        Football section compiled by Bernard Joy

                                                    BL: 7923.w.6

        ☞ Also listed at: E175

79   English league football / Reginald Charles Churchill.
     Rev. ed. London: Nicholas Kaye, 1961.
     303p   BL: X.449/819

        Invaluable reference book which includes historical
        material on all the league clubs up to the late 1950s.

        ☞ Previous ed. A74

80   Football / Barrington Julian Warren Hill. Oxford: Basil
     Blackwell, 1961.
     94p; illus

                                                    BL: X.449/555

81   Football today / John Norman Haynes. London: Arthur
     Barker, 1961.
     127p; illus   BL: X.441/193

        In the year of publication, Haynes became England's
        first £100 a week footballer. The Fulham inside-for-
        ward makes some telling observations.

        ☞ Also listed at: C253

82   Soccer now / Denzil Batchelor. London: Newman
     Neame Take Home Books, 1961.
     15p; illus; pbk   BL: X.449/583

83   A century of soccer . . . a centenary publication of the
     Football Association / Terence Delaney. London:
     Published officially for the Football Association by
     William Heinemann, 1963.
     166p; illus   BL: 7926.pp.5

        Informative general overview endorsed by the FA.

84   The Gillette book of cricket and football / edited by G.
     Ross. London: Frederick Muller by arrangement with the
     Gillette Safety Razor Co., 1963.
     207p   BL: 7926.f.24

        Modestly titled and easily overlooked volume, yet it
        includes some less common material: the transcript
        of an interview with Real Madrid star, Alfredo di Ste-
        fano; a section on refereeing by experienced official
        Jack Clough; the art of continental goalkeeping by the
        great Hungarian Gyula Grosics; as well as short sec-
        tions on specialist positions by Jack Kelsey, Jimmy
        Armfield, Billy Wright, Stanley Matthews and Jimmy
        McIlroy.

85   Association football / Frank Taylor. London: W. & G.
     Foyle, 1964.
     90p; illus   BL: W.P.2940/237

        ☞ Subsequent ed. A113

86   Football / Charles Molin. London: Hamish Hamilton,
     1966.
     32p; illus
     (Dormouse tales)   ISBN: 0-241-90761-6

        Aimed at the junior market.

87   The soccer syndrome: from the primeval forties / John
     Moynihan. London: Macgibbon & Kee, 1966.
     203p; illus   BL: X.449/2253

        This work has rightly come to be regarded as a clas-
        sic of football writing. It concentrates on the first
        twenty years of post-war British football through a
        study of the great games, teams and names of the
        era. The lower divisions are covered as well as the up-
        per end and even the author's own Sunday morning
        football adventures with the Chelsea Casuals are
        chronicled. Extremely well written account of an im-
        portant two decades for soccer.

88   Football / Norman Geddes; illustrated by Peter
     MacKarell. London: Methuen, 1968.
     20p; illus
     (Matter-of-fact books)   ISBN: 0-423-76380-6

        Another title for the juvenile market.

89   The football man: people and passions in soccer /
     Arthur Hopcraft. London: Collins, 1968.
     253p; illus   BL: X.449/3352

        This is a highly regarded book which offers a refresh-
        ingly different approach to many of the standard
        works on the game. The writing is perceptive and at
        times both humorous and poignant. One section cov-
        ers The Player, and refers particularly to George
        Best, Stanley Matthews, Derek Dooley, Duncan Ed-
        wards and Bobby Charlton. A similar section on The
        Manager covers Stan Cullis, Alan Brown, Stan
        Mortensen, Matt Busby and Alf Ramsey. A valuable
        research tool and a jolly good read to boot.

        ☞ Subsequent ed. A98

90   The game of soccer / Ted Smits. Englewood Cliffs,
     London: Prentice-Hall, 1968.
     v, 164p; illus; index   BL: X.441/1197

91   A history of British football / Percy Marshall Young.
     London: Stanley Paul, 1968.
     xiii, 224p; illus   BL: X.441/1060

        Much of the material here comes from well re-
        searched early sources. Young is one of the most
        highly respected historians of the game – contempo-
        rary reviewers have likened him to cricket writer
        Neville Cardus. There can surely be no finer recom-
        mendation.

        ☞ Subsequent ed. A105

92   The Park Drive book of football / edited by Gordon
     Banks. London: Wolfe, 1968.
     271p; illus   BL: X.449/3333

93 Soccer: a panorama / Brian Lester Glanville. London: Eyre & Spottiswoode, 1969.
254p; illus
SBN: 413-27520-5
BL: X.441/1233

Good general historical survey from one of football's most accomplished writers.

94 The A to Z of soccer / Michael Parkinson and Willis Hall; with drawings by Bob Monkhouse. London: Pelham, 1970.
174p; illus
SBN: 7207-0383-2
BL: X.629/2967

A well-known broadcaster here joins forces with a re-nowned writer to present their own survey of the game. Neither contributor hails from the football world but both have an obvious feeling for the game – especially when it's played on good old Yorkshire soil.

95 A century of great soccer drama / John Cottrell. London: Hart-Davis, 1970.
208p, illus
ISBN: 0-246-63997-0
BL: X.619/5004

A history of the game since 1870 told through the great events and memorable matches.

96 David Coleman's world of football / reporter Norman Harris; assisted by Chris Mills. London: Purnell, 1970-
(World of sport library)

Published annually
BL: X.622/820

General survey from one of the game's most noted television commentators – never was the scoreline 1-0 enunciated more emphatically than when Coleman was behind the microphone for BBC's *Match of the Day*.

97 The Puffin book of football / Brian Glanville; illustrated by Helen Fisher. Harmondsworth: Penguin, 1970.
122p; illus; pbk

A potted history of the game aimed specifically at the juvenile reader.

☞ Subsequent ed. A115

98 The football man: people and passions in soccer / Arthur Hopcraft. Rev. ed. Harmondsworth: Penguin, 1971.
215p
SBN: 14-003297-5
BL: X.619/5372

Revised edition of one of the classics of soccer litera-ture.

☞ Previous ed. A89

99 Bedside book of soccer / George L. Hough. London: Pelham, 1972.
149p; illus
ISBN 0-7207-0614-9
BL: X.629/4938

100 The football revolution: a study of the changing pattern of association football / George W. Keeton. Newton Abbot: David and Charles, 1972.
196p; illus
ISBN: 0-7153-5688-7
BL: X.629/4890

101 Great moments in sport: soccer / Geoffrey Green. London: Pelham, 1972.
208p; illus
ISBN: 0-7207-0590-8
BL: X.629/4803

Includes accounts of 33 games from the British, European and world scene.

102 The observer's book of association football / Albert Sewell. London: F. Warne, 1972.
192p; illus
(The observer's pocket series; 47)
SBN: 7232-1511-1
BL: W.P.12066/108

Almost certainly the smallest volume in this bibliog-raphy – this pocket-size history is one of the famous Observer series. There is no new material here, yet this is an evocative little book and the full colour illus-trations of club and international shirts, 108 in all, are a charming reminder of the quaintly simple de-signs prevalent in the 1960s – not a sponsor's name in sight and white 'Dennis Law pull down' cuffs in abundance.

☞ Subsequent ed. A110

103 Book of football / John Goodbody and Allen Wade. London: Macmillan, 1973.
112p; illus; pbk
(Topliners)
ISBN: 0-333-14372-8
BL: X.619/16696

Readily absorbed survey, ideal for the teenage mar-ket.

☞ Also listed at: G125

104 The football industry / Peter Douglas. London: Allen and Unwin, 1973.
175p
ISBN: 0-04-796041-8
BL: X.629/5744

Includes much on the early years of the game with chapters on administration, economics, the govern-ment of football, the Players' Union, and the media.

☞ Subsequent ed. A109

105 A history of British football / Percy Marshall Young. London: Arrow Books, 1973.
320p; illus
ISBN: 0-09-907490-7
BL: X.619/7598

Updated and enlarged edition of this first-class work.

☞ Previous ed. A91

106 All about football / Joseph Edmundson. London: W.H. Allen, 1974.
125p; illus; index

Answers included; Bibliography: p121-122

BL: X.619/15197

☞ Subsequent ed. A121

107 Football / compiled by Geoffrey Nicholson. London: Macdonald, 1974.
63p; illus   ISBN 0-356-04652-4
BL: X.622/1825

108 Football fever: John Moynihan's international survey of the players, the teams and their influences. London: Quartet Books, 1974.
160p; illus
ISBN: 0-7043-2042-8 (cased) ● ISBN: 0-7043-1092-9 (pbk)
BL: X.611/3879 ● BL: X.620/7490

109 The football industry / Peter Douglas. Rev. ed. London: Howard House, 1974.
175p   ISBN: 0-904257-00-2
BL: X.619/15001

☞ Previous ed. A104

110 The observer's book of association football / Albert Sewell. 2nd ed. London: F. Warne, 1974.
192p; illus
(The observer's pocket series; 47)   ISBN 0-7232-1536-7
BL: W.P.12066/126

☞ Previous ed. A102; subsequent ed. A118

111 Soccer / John Moynihan. London: Macmillan, 1974.
95p; illus
(Leisureguides)   SBN: 333-15755-9
BL: X.629/6809

112 Soccer in the fifties / Geoffrey Green. London: Allan, 1974.
288p; illus   ISBN: 0-7110-0566-4
BL: X.620/7787

The fifties is regarded by many as a golden age for football whilst others view this decade as something of a wilderness between the good old days and the swinging sixties. The fact is, the way one perceives a particular era of football depends largely upon one's date of birth – whatever perspective might be taken, there is no doubt that Geoffrey Green here presents a most authoritative overview of the period.

113 Football / Frank Taylor. 2nd ed. London: Foyle, 1975.
102p; illus; pbk   ISBN: 0-7071-0549-8
☞ Previous ed. A85

114 The people's game: a social history of British football / James Walvin. London: Allen Lane, 1975.
xi, 201p; illus
Bibliography: p187-193   ISBN: 0-7139-0768-1
BL: X.629/7112

Essential work of reference for those wishing to obtain a full perspective of the game's development, especially during its formative years. The bibliography is particularly comprehensive and contains references to non-British books as well as to magazines and journals not listed in this compendium.

☞ Subsequent ed. A160; Also listed at: H13

115 The Puffin book of football / Brian Glanville; illustrated by Helen Fisher. 1st ed. reprinted with revised postscript. Harmondsworth: Puffin Books, 1975.
131p; illus; pbk   ISBN 0-14-030462-2
BL: X.619/15219

☞ Previous ed. A97

116 Football in colour / Jim Bebbington. Poole: Blandford Press, 1976.
211p; illus   ISBN: 0-7137-0749-6
BL: X.629/10551

117 Great moments in football / Martin Tyler. London; Macdonald & Janes, 1976.
142p

118 The observer's book of association football / Albert Sewell. 3rd ed. London: Warne, 1976.
192p; illus   ISBN: 0-7232-1558-8
BL: WP.12066/149

☞ Previous ed. A110; subsequent ed. A125

119 The sportsman's world of soccer / edited by Martin Tyler. London: Marshall Cavendish, 1976.
152p; illus
(Golden hands books)
    'Some of this material has previously appeared in the partwork The Game' – title page verso
ISBN: 0-85685-120-5
BL: X.0975/4(93)

☞ Also listed at: E196

120 The story of football / Martin Tyler. London: Marshall Cavendish, 1976.
249p; illus, 1 map; index
    Bibliography: p245   ISBN: 0-85685-177-9
BL: X.622/6252

Very comprehensive survey.
☞ Subsequent ed. A126

121 All about football / Joseph Edmundson. Rev. ed. London: W. H. Allen, 1977.
157p; illus; index; pbk
    With answers; Bibliography: p153-154
ISBN: 0-491-00452-4
BL: X.629/11924

☞ Previous ed. A106

122 The big match: Brian Moore's world of soccer, 1976-77 / Brian Moore. London: Arthur Barker, 1977.
3-125p; illus   ISBN: 0-213-16663-1
BL: X.622/6175

As David Coleman was to the BBC so Brian Moore was to ITV as their leading football commentator.

123 The Dunlop footballer's companion / Ken Rice. Lavenham: Eastland Press, 1978.
viii, 120p; illus; index

   Bibliography: p115   ISBN: 0-903214-11-3
                                        BL: X.620/18079

124 The Marshall Cavendish football handbook. London: Marshall Cavendish, 1978-
illus

   In 63 weekly parts; folded wallchart as insert in issue 1
                                        BL: P.441/884

   The full 63 parts present a very comprehensive coverage of all elements of football on a truly worldwide basis. Charity shops are a good hunting ground for those in search of a full set – underneath the bottom shelf, in the plastic clothes basket next to the 45 rpm records.

125 The observer's book of soccer / Albert Sewell; revised by Alan Hughes. 4th ed. London: Warne, 1978.
192p; illus

   Spine title: Soccer   ISBN: 0-7232-1587-1
                                        BL: WP.12066/179

   ☞ Previous ed. A118; subsequent ed. A128

126 The story of football / Martin Tyler. Updated and revised ed. London: Marshall Cavendish, 1978.
265p; illus, 1 map; index

   Bibliography: p261   ISBN: 0-85685-525-1
                                        BL: X.622/6676

   ☞ Previous ed. A120

127 The Beaver book of football / Tom Tully; illustrated by Mike Jackson; cartoons by David Mostyn. London: Beaver Books, 1979.
126p; illus; pbk
                                        ISBN: 0-600-33699-9
                                        BL: X.619/22523

   ☞ Also listed at: G152

128 The observer's book of soccer / Albert Sewell. 5th ed. London: Warne, 1980.
191p; illus, coats of arms
                                        ISBN: 0-7232-1616-9
                                        BL: X.629/18966

   ☞ Previous ed. A125

129 Soccer / Derek Henderson; foreword by Joe Mercer. London: Hamlyn, 1980.
217p; illus; index

   Bibliography: p217   ISBN: 0-600-34653-6
                                        BL: X.622/9301

   Sections entitled: The global game; The giants; Disasters and tragedies; The game abroad; Soccer's blackest days; and, Great upsets. Well worth consulting.

130 Soccer / Jim Bebbington; colour photographs by Tony Duffy, All-Sport Limited. Hove: Wayland, 1980.
64p; illus; index
(InterSport)   ISBN: 0-85340-773-8
                                        BL: X.629/13350

131 As I see soccer ? / Lawrence Sutton. Newport: Starling, 1981.
122p; illus; pbk
                                        ISBN: 0-903434-44-X

132 The book of football / Norman Barrett. Maidenhead: Purnell, 1981.
157p; illus; index   ISBN: 0-361-05078-X
                                        BL: X.622/10988

   Sections on: The stars; The action; The teams; The goals; and, The results. Extensively illustrated.

133 The football industry: the early years of the professional game / John Hutchinson. Glasgow: R. Drew, 1982.
95p; illus; pbk   ISBN: 0-904002-81-0

134 Football / Keith Styles. Cambridge: Cambridge University Press, 1983.
31p; illus; pbk
(Sport masters)   ISBN: 0-521-27532-6
                                        BL: X.622/20571

135 Industry analysis: the English football industry / David Palmer. Dudley: D. Palmer, 1983.
71 leaves; illus; spiral   BL: X.622/21675

136 Soccer / Norman Barrett; illustrated by Paul Buckle. London: Granada, 1983.
63p; illus, plans; index   ISBN: 0-246-11980-2
                                        BL: X.990/21770

137 Soccer!: the road to crisis / Anton Rippon. Ashbourne: Moorland, 1983.
200p; illus; index   ISBN: 0-86190-019-7
                                        BL: YC.1986.a.669

   A history, a snapshot view of the present, and a concerned look at the future of the game as perceived by the author.

138 Football recollections. Basildon: Association of Football Statisticians, 1986-

   This was published from time to time by the AFS from 1986 – the accent was towards coverage of items from football's past, offering a wide-ranging spectrum of subjects.

139 The story of football / Phil Soar and Martin Tyler. Twickenham: Hamlyn, 1986.
264p; illus, 1 map; index   ISBN: 0-600-50245-7
                                        BL: YK.1987.b.670

140 Back page football: a century of newspaper coverage / Stephen F. Kelly. London: Macdonald/Queen Anne, 1988.
208p; illus   ISBN: 0-356-17110-8
                                        BL: YK.1989.b.3224

141 The footballer: the journal of soccer history and statistics. Cleethorpes: Sports Promotions (International), 1988-
illus

Six issues yearly   BL: ZK.9.b.1578

As a source of excellent period photographs and journalistic articles on a wide variety of footballing subjects, this magazine style publication is of great value. Researchers with a taste for pure nostalgia will find it in abundance here.

142 A major initiative in support of football. London: Football Trust, 1988.
24p; pbk   BL: YK.1989.b.3046

Founded in 1979, the Football Trust provides financial support for developing the game at all levels. As an adjunct to their publication of meaningful demographic and trend statistics relating to the game, this short booklet effectively presents their raison d'être at a most important time in the game's history, one hundred years on from the formation of the Football League.

143 Pay up and play the game: professional sport in Britain, 1875-1914 / Wray Vamplew. Cambridge: Cambridge University Press, 1988.
580p; index

Includes bibliography   ISBN: 0-521-35597-4
                                 BL: YK.1989.b.3364

An essential part of the football historian's library. A scholarly study of the Victorian and Edwardian eras with much emphasis on economic and social elements and particular coverage of the Scottish experience.

144 Head over heels: a celebration of British football / Jim Hossack; introduction by Don Revie. Edinburgh: Mainstream, 1989.
218p; illus
   ISBN: 1-85158-209-6 (cased) • ISBN: 1-85158-210-X (pbk)
                                 BL: YK.1990.b.5115

145 The secret life of football / Alex Fynn and Lynton Guest with Peter Law. London: Queen Anne Press, 1989.
288p; illus; pbk

Bibliography: p283-284   ISBN: 0-356-17494-8
                                 BL: YK.1990.a.1939

An examination of football's problems and the author's suggestions of a blueprint for the future. Their analysis is incisive and not always comfortable reading but this volume certainly addresses soccer's difficulties in great depth.

146 Soccer focus: reflections on a changing game / John Moynihan; foreword by David Miller. London: Simon & Schuster, 1989.
224p; illus
(Sports pages)

Bibliography: p223-224   ISBN: 0-671-69709-9
                                 BL: YK.1990.a.3355

Includes some of the more original and controversial observations from one of football's 'thinking' contributors.

147 Belles of the ball / David J. Williamson. Exeter: R&D Associates, 1991.
100p; illus; pbk   ISBN: 0-9517512-0-4
                                 BL: YK.1992.a.2064

This very informative and entertaining account traces the development of ladies' football from the early eighteenth century in the hills above Inverness through to its heydays in the 1920s. Essential reading for all historians of the ladies' game.

148 The blueprint for the future of football. London: Football Association, 1991.
119p

149 Football back in time / compiled by R. E. Day. Harefield: Dave Twydell, 1991.
46p; pbk   ISBN: 0-9513321-5-5
                                 BL: YK.1992.a.11695

150 The golden age of football / Peter Jeffs. Derby: Breedon Books, 1991.
255p; illus

'1946-1953' – Dust jacket; includes bibliographical references
                                 ISBN: 0-907969-91-7
                                 BL: YK.1993.b.11184

On Saturday 31 August 1946 the League restarted in earnest after its wartime break – that same day was the 217th day of the Nuremberg trials and 388,000 German prisoners of war still remained in Britain. For the people who had lived through six years of horror, soccer represented an escape and proved to be an irresistible pull. Attendance figures were astonishing and it is not surprising that many still look back on the period as the 'golden age'. The author, however, gives a very balanced account by studying both the virtues and the ills of the game during this period. Very entertaining and valuable study.

151 The golden age of the English Football League. Worthing: Worthing Typesetting, 1991.
8 vols   ISSN: 0964-5608

This title was published in eight parts, each concentrating on just one particular month in the football calendar. Part two, for example, chooses September 1958 and dissects the month's achievements in the context of the times, giving all the news and results. This snapshot in time treatment is novel and might usefully be consulted by those studying fifties football.

152 The sixties revisited / Jimmy Greaves with Norman Giller. Harpenden: Queen Anne, 1992.
256p; illus; pbk   ISBN: 1-85291-536-6
                                 BL: YK.1995.b.909

The swinging sixties was a time of change for the game. Jimmy Greaves is well qualified to comment on this decade in which Celtic and Manchester United secured the European Cup and England won the World Cup.

153 The Daily Telegraph football chronicle: a season-by-season account of the soccer stories that made the headlines from 1863 to the present day / Norman Barrett. London: Stanley Paul, 1993.
272p; illus; index
ISBN: 0-09-178228-7
BL: YK.1994.b.1797

A lightly presented and entertaining overview of the leading football stories year by year since the formation of the Football Association.

☞ Subsequent ed. A156

154 Great sporting moments: soccer, the last 25 years / Norman Barrett. Swindon?: W H Smith, 1993.

155 Code war: English football under the historical spotlight / Graham Williams. Harefield: Yore, 1994.
192p; illus
ISBN: 1-87442-765-8

Excellent retrospective study.

156 The Daily Telegraph football chronicle: a season-by-season account of the soccer stories that made the headlines from 1863 to the present day / Norman Barrett. Updated ed. London: Stanley Paul, 1994.
272p; illus; index
ISBN: 0-09-179061-1

Of the recently published volumes covering the general history and development of the game, this is well worth consultation.

☞ Previous ed. A153

157 Football: a history of the world game / Bill Murray. Aldershot: Scolar Press, 1994.
xvi, 297p; index
Includes bibliographies
ISBN: 1-85928-091-9
BL: YK.1994.b.8339

Comprehensive and highly scholarly account of the growth of the game, charting its spread throughout the world; an essential reference work.

158 Kicking and screaming: an oral history of football in England / Rogan Taylor and Andrew Ward. London: Robson, 1994.
224p; illus
ISBN: 0-86051-912-0

Rogan Taylor's speciality is the study of football from the fan's perspective; this volume offers some fascinating and original material.

159 The mavericks: English football when flair wore flairs / Rob Steen. Edinburgh: Mainstream, 1994.
192p; illus
ISBN: 1-85158-641-5

The jacket blurb gives a subtle foretaste of what's to come – 'Admiral sock tags, platform shoes and kipper

ties mingle with cod wars, Harrods bombings and three day weeks in a recreation of the early seventies, the era when football joined the vanguard of English youth culture.' This wry and evocative account of the period studies seven players to support its theme, each of them proud to be individuals amid an increasingly corporate environment. The stars of the show are Stan Bowles, Tony Currie, Charlie George, Alan Hudson, Rodney Marsh, Peter Osgood and Frank Worthington. An excellent study approached in a bold and highly individual manner.

160 The people's game: the history of football revisited / James Walvin. Rev. ed. Edinburgh: Mainstream, 1994.
224p; illus; index
Includes bibliography
ISBN: 1-85158-642-3

Essential update of Walvin's earlier work – extremely thorough and scholarly approach to the game's history and development with much emphasis on the discipline of social history. The dust jacket shows a selection of football paraphernalia.

☞ Previous ed. A114

161 The seventies revisited / Kevin Keegan. Harpenden: Queen Anne, 1994.
256p; illus
ISBN: 1-85291-549-8

162 Shot!: a photographic record of football in the seventies / compiled by Doug Cheeseman, Mike Alway and Andy Lyons; foreword by Eamonn McCabe. London: Witherby, 1994.
chiefly illus; pbk
Published in association with: When Saturday Comes
ISBN: 0-85493-237-2
BL: LB.31.b.9599

Eamonn McCabe was Sports Photographer of the Year in 1978, 1979, 1981 and 1984. This volume presents a selection of photographs chosen by him – not surprisingly this results in a fascinating portfolio which brings to life one of the most vivid decades in football history. Many of the pictures are presented for the first time. My personal favourite shows a grim-faced Don Revie leaving Molineux on 8 May 1972 after Leeds lost their last game of the season to Wolves – well worth enlarging to poster size! Close on its heels though, is the one of the Tottenham tea ladies looking distinctly 'Pythonesque' and totally oblivious to the on-field action. This is a fun book which preserves the frozen images we must all have seen but never truly looked at. One to savour.

163 The Sunday Times illustrated history of football / Chris Nawrat & Steve Hutchings. London: Hamlyn, 1994.
352p; illus
ISBN: 0-600-57918-2

Extremely thorough coverage including a very broad variety of photographs and other visual material.

Pictorial Histories

164   100 years of soccer in pictures: a centenary publication
of the Football Association, 1863-1963. London: William
Heinemann, 1963.
160p; chiefly illus   BL: 7926.bb.8

*Comprehensive pictorial summary of one hundred
years of the association game.*

165   The picture story of football / Frank Butler. London:
World Distributors, 1963.
157p; illus   BL: 07926.aa.2

166   A pictorial history of soccer / Dennis Signy. London:
Spring Books, 1968.
316p; illus   BL: X.441/1151

*This is the first truly comprehensive pictorial history
of the game – lightweight text accompanies some
striking images.*

☞   Subsequent ed. A167

167   A pictorial history of soccer / Dennis Signy. 2nd rev.
ed. Feltham: Hamlyn, 1970.
316p; illus, 1 plan

☞   Previous ed. A166; subsequent ed. A168

168   A pictorial history of soccer / Dennis Signy. New ed.
London: Hamlyn, 1971.
316p; illus   SBN: 600-36978-1
                                                       BL: X.622/1069

*Revised to include separate chapters on South
America, North America and world soccer.*

☞   Previous ed. A167

169   A source book of football / compiled by Jack Rollin.
London: Ward Lock, 1971.
160p; illus   ISBN: 0-7063-1176-0
                                                       BL: X.629/4260

☞   Subsequent ed. A170

170   Soccer: a picture survey / compiled by Jack Rollin. Fully
revised. London: Pan Books, 1973.
156p; illus   ISBN: 0-330-23669-5
                                                       BL: X.619/7559

☞   Previous ed. A169

171   Soccer: a pictorial history / by Roger Macdonald; with a
foreword by Bobby Moore. Glasgow: Collins, 1977.
192p; chiefly illus; index   ISBN: 0-00-434554-1
                                                       BL: X.620/17144

Scotland

172   Football sketches, or, The tale of the travellers / Milo.
1889.

Scarce early ephemeral item.

173   Heads and tales: being a biographical and pictorial
record of the clubs composing the Scottish Football
League: season 1890-91 / edited by 'Gush'. Glasgow,
1890-1891.   BL: P.P.1832.m(1)

*Neatly titled early item likely to yield material of in-
terest to historians of clubs playing in the Scottish
League at that time. The League was formed in 1890,
with just eleven members – Abercorn, Cambuslang,
Celtic, Cowlairs, Dumbarton, Heart of Midlothian,
Rangers, Renton, St Mirren, Third Lanark, and Vale of
Leven.*

174   Scottish football reminiscences and sketches / D. D.
Bone. Glasgow: Aird & Coghill?, 1890.

*The Scottish Football Association was formed in
1873, a short while after the English FA had organised the first of many Internationals between the two
countries – this work contains interesting reminiscences from the early days of the game.*

175   Sports and pastimes of Scotland, historically illustrated /
Robert Scott Fittis. Paisley: A. Gardner, 1891.
212p   BL: 7908.dd.12

*Includes some football references on the early years
of the game in Scotland.*

176   25 years football / 'Old International'. Archibald Steel,
1896.

*By this date the game was well established north of
the border – a Second Division had been added to the
League in 1893. This study covers the entire era during which the game began and became established.*

177   The Scottish junior portfolio of photographs and history
of the Scottish Junior Football Association / J. C.
Chalmers, G. Denny and W. Prentice. 1897.
120p

*Extremely scarce early item containing material of in-
terest to all students of the early years of the game
in Scotland.*

178   Scottish League football: history of the Scottish League / 'Bedouin'; with photographs of grounds and players. Glasgow: James Cameron, 1908.
56p; illus

      Author's real name is R. M. Connell
           BL: Mic.A.9947(13) (microfilm copy)

      Updated history covering the first eighteen years of the League.

179   The story of the Scottish League 1890-1930 / John McCartney. 1930.

      A Third Division had been created in 1923 only to be disbanded three years later and not revived again until 1946. This work covers the first forty years of the League.

180   Alan Breck's book of Scottish football / Alan Breck. Scottish Daily Express, 1937.

181   Scottish football through the years / George Graham. 1947.

182   The Highland League through the years. Dundee: Simmath, 1949.

      A scarce early ephemeral item giving a brief overview of the early history of the Highland League.

183   Through the years with the Scottish League. Dundee: Simmath, 1949.

184   The Scottish football book. London: Stanley Paul, 1955-

      Published annually   BL: P.P.2489.wlf

  ☞   Also listed at: J91

185   The Scots book of football. London: Wolfe, 1969.
207p; illus; pbk   ISBN: 0-7234-0141-1

186   Daily Record book of Scottish football / edited by Jack Adams. Glasgow: Collins, 1970-
illus

      Published annually

187   100 years of the Scottish Football Association / Rod McLeod. 1973.

      Centenary publication of the SFA – essential reference work for all historians of the Scottish game.

188   One hundred years of Scottish football / John Rafferty. London: Pan Books, 1973.
vi, 234p; illus   ISBN: 0-330-23654-7
                     BL: X.611/3521

      Researchers unable to seek out the scarce early works on the Scottish game will find much of the material drawn together here in a comprehensive coverage since the formation of the SFA in 1873.

189   Banned!: an investigation into the Scottish Football Association and a look at Scottish football / Alan Nixon and Charlie Tremayne. Glasgow: Strathclyde University Press, 1976.

190   We'll support you evermore: the impertinent saga of Scottish 'fitba' / edited by Ian Archer and Trevor Royle. London: Souvenir, 1976.
236p; illus; index

              ISBN: 0-285-62224-2
              BL: X.629/10729

      A view of Scottish football from 19 contributors.

191   When will we see your like again?: the changing face of Scottish football / edited by Mike Aitken. Edinburgh: Edinburgh University Press, 1977.
78p; illus
     ISBN: 0-904919-17-X (cased) • ISBN 0-904919-18-8 (pbk)
              BL: X.619/19102

192   The Scottish footballer / Bob Crampsey. Edinburgh: Blackwood, 1978.
7, 77p, illus; pbk

      Bibliography: p77   ISBN: 0-85158-128-5
              BL: X.619/18780

      This slim volume presents a celebrated essay on the special characteristics of the Scottish game and the players that represent it.

193   Mackinlay's A-Z of Scottish football / compiled and edited by Forrest Robertson. Loanhead: Macdonald, 1979.
100p; illus; pbk; index   BL: X.619/22420

Useful general reference book covering all elements of the game.

☞ Subsequent ed. A194

194 Mackinlay's A-Z of Scottish football / compiled and edited by Forrest Robertson. New ed. Loanhead: Macdonald Publishers, 1980.
118p; illus; pbk; index
ISBN: 0-904265-41-2
BL: X.629/18914

☞ Previous ed. A193

195 In a different league: Highland football / Rodwill Clyne. 1981.
Useful overview of the Highland League and its clubs.

196 The birth of football in the Burns country / John G. McIlvean. 1982.
Retrospective study of the very early days of Scottish football.

197 Scottish football: souvenir brochure. Glasgow: Third Eye Centre, 1983.
Exhibition catalogue

198 Scottish football: a pictorial history from 1867 to the present day / Kevin McCarra. Glasgow: Third Eye Centre, 1984.
136p; illus; index
(Clydesdale Bank heritage series; no.2)
Bibliography: p130
ISBN: 0-904919-88-9 (cased) • ISBN: 0-904919-89-7 (pbk)
BL: X.622/24098 • BL: X.622/24099

Definitive pictorial history.

199 The new Scottish football factbook / Forrest H. C. Robertson. Sports Data Services, 1985.
62p; pbk

200 Juniors' one hundred years: centenary history of Scottish junior football / David McGione. Edinburgh: Mainstream, 1986.
320p; illus; pbk
ISBN: 1-85158-056-5
Scottish junior football should not be confused with the juvenile game; its closest analogy would be to the English non-league scene. This is an extremely thorough history of great value to all historians of the lower echelons of the game in Scotland.

201 The Maryhill Charity FA: 100 years 1888-1988 / Albert Moffat and Charles McCulloch. 1988.

202 Scottish junior football: the early years / edited by Stewart Davidson. Renfrew: Scottish Non-League Review, 1990.
30p; pbk
Short study giving brief descriptions of the formation of several of the earliest local Scottish football associations, including club colours, early cup finals and anecdotal material.

203 Scottish university football: a review / George Campbell. 1990.
An unusual study of the game as played at university level.

204 The Central League: 1931-1991 / Duncan Hoskins and Stewart Davidson. Renfrew: Scottish Non-League Review, 1991.
51p; pbk
This includes statistical records for all the League's participants with a guide to the location of each club.

205 Hampden Babylon: sex & scandal in Scottish football / Stuart Cosgrove. Edinburgh: Canongate, 1991.
144p; illus; pbk
ISBN: 0-86241-296-X
BL: YK.1991.b.3771

Once in a while a refreshingly different football book comes along – this is one such volume. It might seem unfair to suggest that it is Scottish football alone which supplies the sort of steamy and seedy revelations found here – indeed, a similar volume could certainly be published based on the English fraternity. That being the case, though, it is equally certain that the Scottish version could run to many revised and updated editions! This is a glossy account centred around drink, with a hint of women and sectarianism thrown in for good measure, creating a heady mixture which has all too often been the downfall of Scottish football. Extremely entertaining.

206 The Scottish Football League: the first 100 years / Bob Crampsey. Glasgow: The League, 1991.
ix, 306p; illus; index; pbk
ISBN: 0-9516433-0-4
BL: YK.1992.b.1293
Essential work for all researchers into the Scottish game – a good starting point for any study.

207 The South Ayrshire Junior League 1920-1932 / Jim McAulay. 1991.

208 Drink, religion and Scottish football 1873-1900 / edited by John Weir. 1992.
72p; pbk

A most interestingly titled publication which not only charts the interrelationship between the three stated elements but also offers a more general overview of the game in Scotland at the time. This is a scholarly piece of research revealing very interesting insights. The presentation is by way of individual articles and essays, some written well over a hundred years ago, told in an entertaining and sometimes amusing fashion. The chapters are: The SFA's formation and early years; John K. McDowall and the SFA's financial crisis; Drink up and play the game; Junior football – what is it?; The clergy and early Scottish football; Morals status and the Scottish football player; and, The SFA's early homes. This book certainly presents some unusual and surprising material and is well worth consulting.

209 Highland hundred: centenary history of the Highland League / B. McAllister. The League, 1993.
206p

Definitive history of this important and romantically perceived Scottish League.

210 Scottish sport in the making of the nation: ninety minute patriots? / edited by Grant Jarvie and Graham Walker. Leicester: Leicester University Press, 1994.
viii, 200p   ISBN: 0-7185-1454-8
                                                   BL: YC.1994.b.5896

Scholarly approach with some interesting football references.

Wales

211 Association football in Wales 1870-1924 / G. G. Lerry. Wrexham: The author, 1924.

Scarce early publication covering the development of the game in Wales from its pre-Association days and throughout its formative years.

212 The Football Association of Wales: 75th anniversary, 1876-1951 / G. G. Lerry. Wrexham: Football Association of Wales, 1952.

Here the same author updates the story of Welsh football up to the 75th anniversary of the formation of its Association.

213 100 years of Welsh soccer / P. Corrigan. Cardiff: Welsh Brewers, 1976.

Complete centenary overview.

214 Gol! / Gwyn Jenkins. Talybont: Y Lolfa, 1980.
60p; illus   ISBN: 0-904864-93-6

215 Pêl-droed / Geraint H. Jenkins. Talybont: Y Lolfa, 1983.
96p; illus; pbk
(Dewch i chwarae; 1)   ISBN: 0-86243-055-0
                                                   BL: X.629/21537

216 Welsh annual 1939-46 / G. Andrews. London?: Datasport, 1984.

Contains material of interest to researchers of Welsh soccer during the war years.

217 Ciciwn ymlaen: Clwb y Cymric 25: cronicl y dathlu. Caerdydd: Clwb Cymric, 1994.
60p; illus; pbk

Ireland

218 Irish Football League 1890-95 / Malcolm Brodie. Belfast: Universities Press.
264p; illus; pbk

During the first five years of the League in Northern Ireland, Linfield were champions no less than four times, with Glentoran alone interrupting their progress in 1893. This is a detailed retrospective study of these early days of organised league football in Ireland and is essential reading for all serious historians.

219 Twenty years of Irish soccer / Thomas Walsh. Dublin?: Sports Publicity Services, 1941.

Although football was played in Southern Ireland since early times, it had always suffered from intense competition from rugby, Gaelic football and hurling. The first Southern club, Dublin Association, was formed in 1883, but it was not until 1921 that the Football Association of Ireland came into being. This important study covers the first years of organised football in the South.

220 History of Irish football / Malcolm Brodie. London: Stanley Paul, 1961.

A study of the Irish game from Malcolm Brodie, well established as the leading historian of soccer in Ireland.

221 History of Irish soccer / Malcolm Brodie. Glasgow: Arrell, 1963.
269p; illus

Updated version of the previous study.

222 100 years of Irish football / Malcolm Brodie. Belfast: Blackstaff Press, 1980.
ix, 187p; illus; pbk   ISBN: 0-85640-225-7
                            BL: X.622/8058

At a meeting in the Queen's Hotel, Belfast on 18 November 1880, the Irish Football Association came

into being to govern football in Northern Ireland. This is a definitive history and an essential work of reference. The Football Association of Ireland which governs the game in the South was not formed until 1921.

223 Six glorious years 1980-1986 / Ronnie Hanna. Coleraine?: Causeway Press, 1986.
246p; illus; pbk

Northern Ireland outshone England, Scotland and Wales in 1980 and again in 1984 to win the Home International Championship. In 1982 and 1986, they reached the World Cup finals, beating the hosts, Spain, in a memorable game in the first of these tournaments. This detailed study covers those 'six glorious years'.

Folk Football

224 The history of the County of Derby / Stephen Glover; edited by T. Noble. Derby: H. Mozley & Son, 1829.
2 vols   BL: 2367.b.8

Long before the formalisation of the game of football, street games resembling a general scramble had been played for many centuries. Some of these games had developed into annual events. The most celebrated of these, now no longer played, was at Derby. Glover's history gives a full account of the game – 'broken skins, broken heads, torn coats and lost hats are amongst the minor accidents of this fearful contest, and it frequently happens that persons fall owing to the intensity of the pressure, fainting and bleeding beneath the feet of the surrounding mob'. The full graphic account is well worth reading; the vivid picture of play is not entirely in keeping, however, with the rather quaint image which folk football tends to evoke.

225 Survivals of folk football, Great Britain / Frank N. Punchard. King's Norton: The Editor of School Hygiene and Physical Education, 1928.
12p; pbk   BL: D

Short study covering some of the survivals of folk football still prevalent in 1928.

226 The Ashbourne custom of Shrovetide football / G. J. Corbishley. Yeldersley: P. J. Wood, 1953.
20p; illus   BL: 7921.e.63

Whilst many of the folk football games around the country have fallen by the wayside over the years, the annual Shrovetide game at Ashbourne in Derbyshire still takes place today. This short study gives an informed account of the game although researchers into folk football would do well to supplement their reading matter with a visit to the game – only the robust would be advised to take full part as the action can still be on the rough side, but observed from a suitable fringe position with a little imagination, this is an event which transcends the centuries and is well worth taking in.

Non-League & Amateur

227 The Amateur Football Association annual. London: Amateur Football Association, 1908-   BL: P.P.2489.wff

This is the first annual of the Association following the approval of the formation of the Amateur Football Association in 1907 at a meeting held at the Holborn Restaurant in London. For many years amateur teams had competed side by side with paid professionals, but the legalisation of professionalism in 1885 prompted a split which was to grow wider as

the twentieth century progressed. Whilst the professional game receives the highest media profile, it is a fact that the majority of matches played week in week out on the minor fields and public parks throughout the land are played on an amateur basis despite the FA officially dropping the distinction in 1974.

228 The Hawser: the official organ of the Liverpool Shipping Football League, the London Shipping Football League, the London Shipping Athletic Association, the London Shipping Boxing Club. London: E. H. Jackson, 1929.
BL: P.P.1832.gan

A scarce item covering two of the more unusual amateur leagues – one based in the capital and the other on Merseyside.

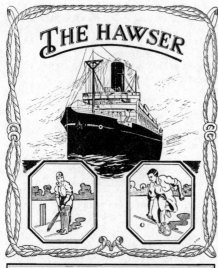

229 Amateur sport: amateur football annual, 1949-50. London: Amateur Sport, 1949.

Only one issue published   BL: P.P.2489.wkn

230 Norman Ackland's handbook of amateur football. London: Dennis Yates, 1950-
illus; pbk

Library has only one edition   BL: P.P.2489.wky

The author began writing about amateur soccer as 'Philistine' in the Westminster Gazette back in 1923 and is very well qualified to present this work.

231 The history of the Amateur Football Alliance / Walter Edward Greenland. Dovercourt: published for the Amateur Football Alliance by the Standard Printing and Publishing Co., 1966.
102p; illus   BL: X.449/1889

The Amateur Football Alliance was founded in 1907, the same year the Amateur Football Association was formed. It was originally styled the Amateur Football Defence Federation. Its role was to promote amateur football at a time when professionalism was increas-

ingly dominating the game.

☞ See also: A236

232 The Northern Premier League 1968-69: non-league soccer on the march / Paul Doherty. London: The People, 1968.
64p; pbk

The Northern Premier League was formed in 1968 from the amalgamation of the Cheshire County League, Lancashire Combination, Midland League, North Regional League, and the West Midlands Regional League. The sub-title of this volume might be explained by the fact that the establishment of the League gave non-league sides a potential route into the highest level of the game. Both Scarborough and Wigan Athletic were ultimately to gain election to the Football League following earlier successes in the Northern Premier. The League has subsequently been known as the Multipart League and the HFS Loans League after its sponsors.

233 Seventy five years of Southern League football / Lionel Francis. London: Pelham, 1969.
195p; illus   SBN: 7207-0262-3
BL: X.449/3879

In the modern pyramid structure this important League feeds into the Conference and thus into the Football League itself. It was formed in 1893 as a counterpart to the Football League and eventually its clubs were elected to form the Football League's Third Division. It has an important history, well told in this first definitive coverage.

234 The FA non-league football annual / edited by Tony Williams. London: Macdonald and Jane's, 1978-1980.

Continued as: Rothman's FA non-league football yearbook
ISSN: 0142-6257
BL: P.441/865

Detailed study covering the non-league scene – volumes of this type assisted greatly in winning recognition for football played and followed at this level. There is now a thriving interest amongst non-league aficionados and a continuing development in the study of the historical and statistical elements attached to clubs not playing in the Football League or the Premiership.

☞ Also listed at: J106

235 Non league football in Hertfordshire / Derek Fieldsend. 1981-

Published annually

Results, tables and profiles of all the teams in the county.

236 The history of the Amateur Football Alliance. Vol. 2: 1967-1982 / A. J. Suggate and W. P. Goss. 1982.
48p

This item should be studied in conjunction with W. E. Greenland's earlier history of the Alliance to 1966.

This second study updates the history to 1982. The Alliance continues to oversee many amateur competitions today.

☞ See also: A231

237 Non league: a history of league and cup football / Bob Barton. Newcastle upon Tyne: The author, 1983?
304p; illus; pbk   ISBN: 0-9508941-0-9
          BL: X.629/22345

When this book was published it won an award from the Association of Football Statisticians – as a pioneering effort in covering the non-league scene with such thoroughness, its acclaim was well deserved. Essential work for all non-league students.

☞ Also listed at: D66

238 Non league / Bob Barton. Newcastle upon Tyne: The author, 1986.
639p; illus; pbk   ISBN: 0-9508941-5-X
          BL: YC.1986.a.2514

All students of the non-league game must regard this extremely thorough work as an essential part of their history. Every major league from the past and present has been reviewed along with coverage of the cup competitions and much more of interest besides.

239 Manchester Amateur Sunday Football League: 40th anniversary brochure (1947-1987) / written and edited by Peter Moulds. Manchester: The League, 1987.
48p; illus; pbk   ISBN: 0-9512925-0-1
          BL: YK.1991.a.8034

Contains some history of interest to' historians of amateur football in and around Manchester.

240 Southern League football: the post-war years / Paul Harrison. Gravesend: The author, 1987.
62p; illus; pbk   ISBN: 0-9515001-2-0
          BL: YK.1988.b.4164

A thorough study of the Southern League from 1946 with substantial statistical information alongside history, photographs and newspaper reports. Founded in 1893 as a counterpart to the Football League which at that time comprised only northern clubs, this League is an important one. Consequently the Southern League initially contained some of the big London clubs and indeed Spurs won the 1901 FA Cup whilst still playing as a Southern League side. The clubs were gradually assimilated into the Football League and after the Second World War, the Southern League effectively served as the leading semi-professional league.

☞ Subsequent ed. A246

241 Midland Counties League 1889-1982: a historical look at semi-professional football leagues / David Webster. Sheffield: The author, 1988?.
71p; unbound   BL: YK.1990.b.5642

The Midland Counties League was long considered one of the leading minor leagues before it merged with the

Yorkshire League in 1982 to form the Northern Counties Eastern League. Barnsley, Chesterfield, Doncaster Rovers, Lincoln City, Rotherham, Peterborough United, Scunthorpe United, and Shrewsbury Town have all played in the Midland Counties League at one time – historians of those clubs may find material of interest here.

242 Northern goalfields: the centenary history of the Northern League / Brian Hunt. 1988.
458p

Very substantial official history comprising a detailed look at the clubs which have made their mark in a league which in itself is not noted for its wider achievements in the football world.

243 Non-league football. Windsor: Burlington, 1989-1991.
illus

Also entitled: Mail on Sunday's non-league football magazine
Published monthly   ISSN: 0958-6474
          BL: ZK.9.b.4192

244 Southern League football: the first fifty years / Paul Harrison. Gravesend: The author, 1989.
62p; illus; pbk   ISBN: 0-9515001-0-4
          BL: YK.1992.b.6743

Read in conjunction with the author's earlier work covering the League's post-war years, the researcher may gain a complete picture of almost one hundred years of the Southern League.

245 The Corinthian & Delphian Football Leagues / Mike Wilson. 1992.
75p

Includes a brief history of each of the leagues – every team and all the results. The Corinthian League began in 1945 but was disbanded in 1963. Its most successful sides were Hounslow Town, Maidenhead United, and Walton and Hersham. This is a well written account and record of particular interest to historians of the non-league game in the south.

246 Southern League football: the post war years/ Paul Harrison. Rev. ed. Gravesend: The author, 1992.
70p; illus; pbk   ISBN: 0-9515001-2-0

Updated version of an earlier work but containing largely new material.

☞ Previous ed. A240

247 A view from the terraces: one hundred years of the Western Football League, 1892-1992 / as recalled by Tom with the help of Sandie & Doug Webb. Chippenham: The authors, 1992.
iv, 351p; illus; pbk

Bibliography: p351   ISBN: 0-9520085-0-5

The treatment of the subject here is an innovative one. The history of the League is told through the eyes of Tom, who was born on the date of the League's first game – 24 September 1892. The

League itself started out as the Bristol and District Football League, yet it strangely included many London clubs amongst its members. All the League tables are presented and the various challenges facing the League and its administrators over the years are fully chronicled.

248 Non-league football pocket annual / edited by Bruce Smith. St Albans: Words on Sport, 1993-
pbk
BL: ZK.9.a.2279

☞ Also listed at: J129

249 The Athenian Football League 1912-1939 / Mike Wilson. 1994.
70p; pbk

An excellent study of this former amateur football league, founded in 1912, disbanded in 1984. Distinguished former members have included Barnet, Kingstonian, Southall, and Wimbledon. This thorough work includes a history of the League by Ray Spiller of the Association of Football Statisticians. This is an essential reference tool.

250 Every picture tells a story: the pictorial history of the Midland Counties Football League / David Kirkby. 1994.
200p

The Southern League Race of 1902/03

251 The official centenary history of the Southern League 1894-1994 / Leigh Edwards. Paper Plane, 1994.
336p   ISBN: 1-871872-08-1

Highly acclaimed definitive history of this important League — a valuable addition to non-league football literature.

University & Public Schools

252 Some remarks on the game of football as played at Winchester College / James Arthur Fort. Winchester: J. Wells, 1890.
15p; pbk   BL: 7923.d.4

The public school movement had a profound influence on the development of all manner of organised games. In the early part of the nineteenth century, football the street game became football the gentleman's game — this was a vital step towards the formation of the Football Association in 1863. Indeed, many of the founder figures of the association game came directly from the public school and university systems. The Winchester game discussed here is a distinct part of the lineage from which the modern game descended. As such, the serious soccer student should not neglect its study.

253 A complete record of scores, with bowling analyses, of all cricket matches, and full particulars of all football matches and rifle contests between Charterhouse and other public schools, from 1850 to 1890 / edited by B. Ellis. London: Wright, 1891.
103p   BL: D

Charterhouse, along with Eton, Harrow, Winchester, and Westminster, enjoyed its own peculiar brand of football. One factor, however, unites all these schools: they were bound by the all-important principle of kick-

SOME REMARKS

ON THE

GAME OF FOOTBALL

AS PLAYED AT

WINCHESTER COLLEGE.

WINCHESTER
J. WELLS BOOKSELLER TO THE COLLEGE.
—
1890.

ing the ball, which ranged them jointly against the collective force of Rugby and other followers of the handling game.

254 'Upon St Andrew's Day' 1841-1901: a list of football teams / compiled by R. A. A. L., i.e. R. A. Austen Leigh. Eton: Spottiswoode, 1902.

x, 62p   BL: 07906.de.29(1)

The Eton field game predominated at the school during this period; all serious students of the association game, however, will find that its origins and development may only be understood fully in conjunction with a thorough knowledge of the various school codes. There are distinct parallels, as one contemporary observer of the field game eloquently observes: 'I saw the perfect specimen of the art of dribbling – a long and tortuous run through a multitude of opponents, none of them touching or touched by him, the ball always at his foot, without a fluke or stumble, the perfection of easy mastery.'

255 Fifty years of sport at Oxford, Cambridge, and the great public schools / arranged by the Right Hon. Lord Desborough; edited by A. C. M. Croome. London: Walter Southwood, 1913-1922.

3 vols; illus

Vol. 1, 2: Oxford and Cambridge; Vol. 3: Eton, Harrow and Winchester / edited by Hon. R. H. Lyttleton, Arthur Page and Evan B. Noel

BL: L.R.37.a

These huge volumes are invaluable to any researcher of university and public school football. The various rules peculiar to each of the public schools are covered in detail along with passing comparative reference to the more familiar association version; it is quite evident that in the eyes of many an old boy, the association game came a very poor second to the school's own brand. For example, the Harrow correspondent states that 'The Old Harrovian Football

FIFTY YEARS OF SPORT

AT OXFORD, CAMBRIDGE

AND THE

GREAT PUBLIC SCHOOLS

ARRANGED BY

THE RIGHT HON. LORD DESBOROUGH OF TAPLOW, K.C.V.O.

EDITED BY

HON. R. H. LYTTELTON, ARTHUR PAGE AND EVAN B. NOEL

ETON, HARROW AND WINCHESTER

LONDON

WALTER SOUTHWOOD & CO., LIMITED

1922

Club ("soccer") has rarely been very active', whilst he extols the virtues of the real game – 'nothing can drive the dumps away, like Harrow footer on Harrow clay'. Despite the relative subservience of the association game as portrayed within these pages, each of these books offers observations of great value to any historian of the game. The photographic content is comprehensive.

The Football Associations

256 Annual of the Norfolk County Football Association / edited by W. E. Hansell. Norwich: Fletcher, 1888.

BL: 7908.a.78

Norfolk is not the first county to spring to mind when considering the history of soccer, yet this early publication serves to amply illustrate the countrywide appeal of the game and the part played by the lesser known outposts.

257 History of the Lancashire Football Association, 1878-1928 / compiled by C. E. Sutcliffe, President, and F. Hargreaves, Secretary. Blackburn: Toulmin, 1928.

280p; illus

Subsequently reprinted in facsimile: Harefield: Yore, 1992

BL: X.629/6431

There is no doubt that Lancashire has been a hotbed of soccer talent and interest for many years; this acclaimed early chronicle of its County Football Association includes histories of around twenty Lancashire clubs, full records of the Lancashire Cup, histories of the regional leagues and biographies of leading figures together with an abundance of team and portrait photographs. Such is the scarcity of many of the early works on football, that a trend for facsimile reprints has recently arisen. This could well represent a growing market – certainly the historic works deserve a wide and renewed readership beyond the confines of serious football book collectors. Both Dave Twydell's Yore Publications and the Association of Football Statisticians have recognised this market niche.

258 The Hampshire Football Association: golden jubilee book / compiled by W. Pickford. Bournemouth: Bournemouth Guardian, 1937.

286p; illus, 1 map   BL: 07908.e.40

A very detailed study and invaluable source for tracing early developments of the game in Hampshire — contains particular material of interest to historians of Portsmouth, Southampton and Aldershot. The author was one of the leading figures in administration and was elected President of the English Football Association in the same year this was published. Includes a pull-out county map and has attractive decorated boards.

259 A glance back at the Football Association Council, 1888-1938 / William Pickford. Bournemouth: Bournemouth Guardian, 1938?

75p   BL: X.449/2974

Pickford was a member of the FA Council throughout this period. His eyewitness account of developments from the very early days is invaluable.

260 Bulletin no. 1-9, 20 Sept. 1946-Dec. 1947. London: Football Association, 1946-1947.

Continued as: The Football Association bulletin no. 10-27. London: Football Association, 1948-1951;
Continued as: New series. vol. 1. no. 1-vol. 5. no. 10. (Aug. 1951-May/June 1956). London: Football Association, 1951-1956;
Continued as: FA news: official journal of the Football Association vol. 6. no. 1 (August 1956). London: Football Association, 1956-

BL: P.P.1832.maf

261 The history of the Football Association / Geoffrey Green; Harley V. Usill, general editor. London: Naldrett, 1953.

691p; illus   BL: 7919.ff.42

This massive scholarly work cannot be praised too highly. It gives an extremely comprehensive account of the conception and development of the Association, drawing on contemporary correspondence and minutes to present a living 'as it happened' portrayal. Yet it is not purely an historical study as it also analyses prevailing problems and the way forward for the future. Chapter 13, for example, covers Sunday football, the women's game, floodlighting and the Pools. This is certainly a most valuable work for all serious students of the game.

262 The Portsmouth Football Association / E. G. Whiteaway. Portsmouth: Portsmouth FA, 1965.

48p; pbk

Small ephemeral item which may yield material of interest to followers of the game in and around Portsmouth.

263 The centenary book of the Birmingham County Football Association, 1875-1975 / S. W. Clives. Birmingham: The Association, 1975.

164p; illus   ISBN: 0-9504713-0-5
                                        BL: X.622/5436

Includes much of interest to historians of clubs in the West Midlands.

264 100 years of county football / Robert Speake. Stafford: Staffordshire Football Association, 1977.

Although Staffordshire is one of the lower profile associations, the county has always enjoyed a keen football following — indeed Burton upon Trent at one time boasted no less than three League teams. All researchers of Staffordshire clubs will find something of value here.

265 Centenary history of the Gloucestershire Football Association / C. Timbrell. Gloucester: The Association, 1986.

68p; pbk

This short study, with a foreword by Sir Stanley Rous, presents a knowledgeable overview; Bristol Rovers and Bristol City historians in particular will find it an informative work.

266 From Clegg to Clegg House: the official centenary history of the Sheffield and Hallamshire County Football Association, 1886-1986 / Nicholas Fishwick. Sheffield: Sheffield & Hallamshire County Football Association, 1986.

101p; illus; pbk   BL: YK.1988.a.2482

The Sheffield area can rightly lay claim to having exerted a distinct influence on the shaping of the association game. The formation of the Sheffield Club in 1855 was prompted by the presence of certain Old Harrovians residing in the area. They very much favoured the kicking rather than the handling game and are said to have equipped the local youth with spotless white gloves and silver florins to clutch in their hands as an inducement to concentrate on kicking. Two years later the Hallam Club was formed, and the Sheffield based sides were to help spread the popularity of the association game at a vital time in its formative years. The officially named Sheffield and Hallamshire County Football Association did not come into existence until 1886, but it was born very much as a result of earlier activity in the county. This excellent study will yield material of interest to all followers of the Yorkshire clubs.

267 Centenary: a history of Hampshire Football Association 1887-1987 / Norman Gannaway. Hampshire County FA, 1987.

136p

Excellent narrative of the Association throughout its one hundred year life with some material relevant to even earlier times. Contains information of relevance to all followers of Hampshire soccer.

268 The first one hundred seasons: a centenary history of
Dorset County Football Association 1887-1987 /
Norman Gannaway. Dorset County FA, 1987.
131p

This informed study looks briefly at football in its very
earliest days before charting the history of the last
100 years of the game in Dorset. Much of interest to
followers of soccer in that delightful county.

269 100 years of schools football: a history of the
Nottingham Schools FA 1891-1991 / R. F. Chaplin.
1991.
40p; pbk

270 The official history of the Football Association / Bryon
Butler. London: Macdonald, 1991.
xii, 300p; illus; index   ISBN: 0-356-19145-1
                                      BL: YK.1992.b.6

In conjunction with Geoffrey Green's earlier classic,
this is the definitive and most up-to-date work covering the history of the FA.

271 The ball keeps rolling: one hundred years of the Isle of
Man Football Association / Eric Clague and Colin
Moore. 1993?
100p

This excellent study covers everything you might want
to know about Manx football from its early days in

the shadow of rugby to becoming a thriving participation and spectator game. An Isle of Man League
actually began in 1896 and this study covers all the
clubs which have played in it over the years — an essential work of reference indeed.

272 A coast of soccer memories 1894-1994: the centenary
book of the North Wales Coast Football Association /
edited and compiled by Gareth M. Davies. Holyhead:
The author for the North Wales Coast Football
Association, 1994.
368p; illus; pbk   ISBN: 0-9524950-0-7

A marvellous piece of detailed research with over 200
photographs and 40 articles from officials, players,
referees and journalists associated with the North
Wales Coast FA. The resourcefulness of the author in
compiling this definitive work is astonishing — an excellent example of what can be achieved when covering
the lesser known areas of soccer history.

273 The Guernsey Football Association: one hundred years
and onwards 1893-4 to 1993-4 / Graham Skuse. 1994.
124p

Includes histories of the clubs playing in Guernsey
and the competitions they have played in — a fascinating insight into the game on this small island,
where soccer is far removed from the glamour of the
Premiership, but no less keenly fought.

The Football League

274 The story of the Football League, 1888-1938 / compiled
by Charles E. Sutcliffe, J. A. Brierley, F. Howarth.
Preston: The Football League, 1938.
300p; illus   BL: Cup.1247.i.13

This classic of football literature is eagerly sought as
a collector's item. Celebrating the fiftieth year of the
League, it gives a detailed account of its foundation
and is particularly strong in highlighting the leading
personalities involved, with supporting photographs.
There are contributions by the elderly statesmen of
the game whose own lives paralleled football's development from the Victorian era right through to the
second World War. In this respect, the viewpoint is
both unique and extremely valuable. The photographic
content is first class too. A pleasure to read and an
essential work of reference.

275 The Football League jubilee book / compiled by Ivan
Sharpe. London: Stanley Paul, 1963.
xii, 304p; illus

*Includes an abridged version of: The Story of the Football
League / C. E. Sutcliffe and others*

BL: 07926.a.2

Updates the history of the League to its 75th year.
The compiler was truly qualified to present this work,
having experienced the game from the late nineteenth

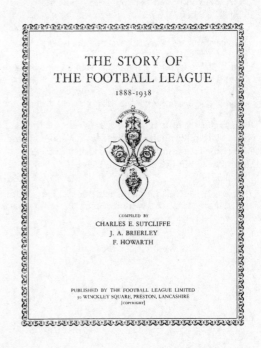

THE STORY OF
THE FOOTBALL LEAGUE
1888-1938

COMPILED BY
CHARLES E. SUTCLIFFE
J. A. BRIERLEY
F. HOWARTH

PUBLISHED BY THE FOOTBALL LEAGUE LIMITED
30 WINCKLEY SQUARE, PRESTON, LANCASHIRE
[COPYRIGHT]

century to the date of publication, hence this is very much an eyewitness account. Must be regarded as an essential volume for the serious student.

☞ See also: A274

276 Football League review: the official journal of the Football League. Leicester: The League, 1966-

BL: P.441/49

This glossy magazine-style publication was the official voice of the League; it was issued regularly and given away free with club programmes. The contents present a good evocation of the times and of the prevailing issues, yet strangely, probably because they were never club-specific, these items are regarded with some disdain by historians and collectors. Nevertheless, it is such lesser used sources that can throw up curious items and anecdotal material of interest. Any researcher of sixties soccer might find the Football League Review a worthwhile hunting ground.

277 We are the champions: a history of the Football League champions, 1888-1972 / Maurice Golesworthy. London: Pelham, 1972.
288p; illus   ISBN: 0-7207-0598-3
BL: X.629/4679

Much sought after by collectors. The League Championship is generally regarded as the greatest and most difficult prize to achieve in domestic soccer — this surprisingly scarce volume tells the story of all the winners from the first season to date.

278 The Football League 1888-1988: the official illustrated history / Bryon Butler. London: Macdonald, 1987.
352p; illus; index   ISBN: 0-356-15072-0
BL: YK.1987.b.6678

This centenary celebration work is an essential starting point for all students of the Football League and, indeed, for the game in general. Whilst the text is informative, the treatment is largely pictorial and this is the particular strength of this volume. It is best used in conjunction with the following two items.

279 The League: the official centenary souvenir / written and edited by Ken Reynolds and Bob Blair. London: Mirror Publications in association with the Daily Mirror and Mercantile Credit Football League Centenary, 1987.
48p; illus; pbk   BL: YK.1990.b.5657

Relatively lightweight treatment; useful, but unlikely to add anything to the contents of the previous and following items.

280 League football and the men who made it: the official centenary history of the Football League, 1888-1988 / Simon Inglis. London: Willow, 1988.
288p; illus   ISBN: 0-00-218242-4
BL: YK.1988.b.5382

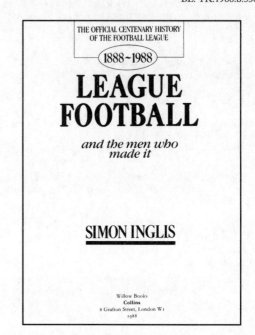

THE OFFICIAL CENTENARY HISTORY OF THE FOOTBALL LEAGUE

1888~1988

LEAGUE FOOTBALL

and the men who made it

SIMON INGLIS

Willow Books
Collins
8 Grafton Street, London W1
1988

The dustjacket states that 'never before has the history of the Football League been told in such depth'. It is impossible to dispute this. Inglis is a history graduate and his work here is indeed scholarly. Don't expect an array of quaint photographs – the presentation is almost entirely written. The detail is astonishing, covering the formation and development of the League and including many personal details of the leading men involved. Set against some of the more romantic treatments of the same subject, this book reminds us just how strong the human element must be in creating anything of value. Certain chapters will be of interest to those engaged in the study of particular elements of the game – the Pools, wartime soccer and the impact of television and sponsorship are all well charted. Certainly an essential work for the serious student but perhaps a little daunting for the casual observer.

The Professional Footballers' Association

281 The professional footballer. London: Football
Association, 1968.
47p; illus   BL: X.619/10211

282 For the good of the game: the official history of the
Professional Footballers' Association / John Harding.
London: Robson Books, 1991.
xii, 403p; illus; index

   Bibliography: p391-392   ISBN: 0-86051-770-5
                                     BL: YK.1993.b.9325

   The footballers' trade union was founded in 1907 to
   protect players' rights – this excellent and scholarly
   study covers the history and development of the Association, highlighting the experiences of key
   personalities and significant events which have af-
   fected the footballer's lot. As such, all researchers of
   the game throughout this century would be well advised to keep this volume at hand in interpreting all
   developments through the eyes of the men who play
   the game.

283 PFA footballers' world. Hampton: Newton Wells, 1993-
illus

   Six issues yearly   BL: ZK.9.b.6147

Football Before 1863

284 The boke named the governour / Sir Thomas Elyot.
Londini: T. Berthelet, 1531.
516p

   Includes manuscript notes   BL: G.735

   When the majority of nineteenth and twentieth century football historians discuss the very early origins
   of the game they often refer to a notable quotation
   by Sir Thomas Elyot. The serious researcher may wish
   to consult this at firsthand. Elyot certainly thought
   the game unfit for gentlemen owing to the violence
   with which it was played – 'Footballe, wherein is nothing but beastlie furie and exstreme violence, whereof
   procedeth hurte, and consequently rancour and mal-
   ice do remain with them that be wounded, wherefore
   it is to be put in perpetual silence.' Whilst Elyot had
   some foundation for his strictures, as the coroner's
   records of the day graphically show, all followers of
   the modern game must surely be thankful that his
   wish to banish the game forever came to nought. This
   would be an extremely slim bibliography if Elyot had
   had his way.

285 The anatomie of abuses: containing, a discoverie, or
briefe summarie of such notable vices and imperfections,
as nowe raigne in many . . . countreyes of the worlde: but
(especially) in . . . Ailgna [Anglia]: together with most
fearefull examples of Gods judgements . . . / made
dialogue-wise by P. Stubbes. London: R. Jones, 1583.
250p   BL: 697.a.34

   Long before the birth of football in its modern form,
   contemporary observers expressed forthright views
   on popular football as played in the streets and fields
   of our island. This entry is included here as it offers
   one such famous observation putting the game firmly
   in its place, condemning in a most forceful manner
   the 'football playing and other develishe pastimes on
   the Sabbath day'. Stubbes continues: 'For as concerning football playing I protest unto you that it
   may rather be called a friendlie kinde of fyghte than a
   play or recreation, a bloody and murthering practice
   than a felowly sport or pastime. For dooth not everyone lie in waight for his adversarie, seeking to
   overthrow him and picke him on his nose . . . and he

that can serve the most of this fashion he is counted the only fellow, and who but he.' Very tempting, perhaps, to say 'What's new?' The quote continues in even stronger vein. Extremely fascinating and well worthy of consultation for all students wishing to go back directly to early source material.

286 Glig-Gamena Angel Deod., or, The sports and pastimes of the people of England ... from the earliest period to the present time, illustrated by engravings selected from ancient paintings / Joseph Strutt. London: LP, 1801. 301p; illus

BL: 7915.k.9 • BL: G.2221 • BL: 143.e.7

Joseph Strutt, the most learned student of contemporary manners and customs, might justifiably claim to be one of the first football historians. Were he alive today he might be known as 'Statto Strutt'! He had a fascination for all the pastimes of the people and commented thus on the early rough and tumble known as football – 'When a match at football is made, two parties, each containing an equal number of competitors, take the field and stand between two goals placed at a distance of eighty or a hundred yards the one from the other. The ball, commonly made of a blown bladder and cased with leather is delivered into the midst of the ground and the object of each party is to drive it through the goal of their antagonists. When the exercise becomes exceedingly violent the players kick each other's shins without the least ceremony and some of them are overthrown at the hazard of their limbs.' He speaks little more of football – nonetheless a charmingly wry early observation.

287 A set of humerous *[sic]* and descriptive illustrations in twenty-one engravings ... of the sports and pastimes of the people of England: from paintings of the XVII and XVIII century ... / Stephenhoff and others in continuation of J. Strutt's. 1810?   BL: 7905.d.35

Includes an engraving entitled 'Foot ball'

288 Englishmen at rest and play: some phases of English leisure, 1558-1714 / Members of Wadham College; edited by R. Lennard. Oxford: Clarendon, 1931. vi, 248p

BL: 010360.bbb.37

Scholarly overview of the leisure pursuits prevalent amongst Englishmen from the sixteenth to the eighteenth centuries. Includes material of interest to researchers chronicling the origins and development of football.

289 Sport in England: a history of two thousand years of games and pastimes / Norman G. Wymer. London: Harrap, 1949. 271p; illus

BL: 7917.bbb.27

Includes references to both ancient and historic origins of the game of soccer.

290 Physical education in England since 1800 / Peter Chisholm MacIntosh. London: G. Bell, 1952. 259p

BL: 7921.e.54

Many football players enjoyed their first serious taste of organised football under the supervision of schoolteachers. This thorough work chronicles the development of all forms of physical education over a century and a half; some of the material has a direct bearing on the development of football as an organised sport.

291 Landmarks in the history of physical education / J. G. Dixon, P. C. MacIntosh, A. D. Munrow, R. F. Willetts; edited by P. C. MacIntosh. London: Routledge & Kegan Paul, 1957. ix, 218p; illus

BL: 7923.m.19

Effectively an updated version of the above item.

292 Sports and pastimes through the ages / Victor Peter Cannings Moss; illustrated by A. Hossack. London: Harrap, 1962. 222p

BL: X.441/42

293 Popular recreations in English society, 1700-1850 / Robert W. Malcolmson. Cambridge: Cambridge University Press, 1973. xii, 188p; illus

Bibliography: p174-184   ISBN: 0-521-20147-0
                                   BL: X.620/6817

This serves as an ideal companion volume to Englishmen at Rest and Play, extending the coverage of English leisure pursuits into the mid-nineteenth century, the very point at which organised football began to emerge as a force to be reckoned with, leading in turn to the formation of the Football Association in 1863. This work contains observations of relevance to the emergence of soccer.

294 Sports and games: history and origins / Brian Jewell. Tunbridge Wells: Midas Books, 1977. 148p; illus; index
(Heritage of the past)

Bibliography: p141-142   ISBN: 0-85936-075-X
                                   BL: X.622/5936

Chapter 3 of this work covers ball games. There is a short overview of the historical development of football – the treatment is light and would particularly suit school age children seeking easily assimilated material for project work.

Club

Histories

'IT'S ALL ABOUT THE CLUB'; a rather trite phrase much favoured by managers and administrators seeking to explain some particular action or other to a pressing media – yet therein lies a basic truth. Elsewhere in this bibliography I expand upon the importance of players and spectators in keeping football clubs alive. Without the club in the first place however, there would be no players, no fans, no ground, no memorable matches, – absolutely nothing at all. The moment of the club's formation is the spring from which all else flows. Little wonder then, that club histories are both numerous and extremely popular.

Those needing to study a specific club will find this a very easy chapter to use as the listings are arranged by club name. Where there is more than one club history, the entries are arranged chronologically by date of publication. If more than one book has been published in the same year, these are listed alphabetically by title. As a rule, the researcher would do well to consult the most recent works first. The older items are fascinating and most have a curiosity value all of their own but, typically, the later works will have extracted all relevant material from these sources. The serious club historian will no doubt wish to consult all available material. It is as well to leave no stone unturned – the earlier works may supply an obscure fact or enlightening quote which can add authority and depth to their research.

There is a pattern to the publication of club histories. Nineteenth century works are few in number and often ephemeral in nature – the clubs were then too young to warrant detailed historical treatment. Even Notts County, founded in 1862 and the oldest of the Football League clubs, did not see its history appear in print until 1927 and even then it only amounted to a scant sixteen pages. Blackburn Rovers had been lauded a little earlier. Such was their record of success around the turn of the century that they were honoured as early as 1906 with a sixty-two page history. Such examples, it must be stressed, are more the exception than the rule.

Often, it was a club's fiftieth anniversary celebrations that prompted the publication of its history and this led to a mini-boom in the 1920s when many truly substantial works began to appear. Those covering Everton, Sheffield Wednesday, Rangers, Hearts and Queen's Park are all excellent examples from the 1920s. The history of Queen's Park extends to a magnificent 446 pages to stake a valid claim as the best of the 'antiquarian' works. If only all the clubs had been so richly covered! What a treasure trove of material we would now have at our disposal.

The majority of clubs had to wait until the late 1940's before their stories were first told. Many appeared in Tom Morgan's *Let's Talk About* . . . series, published by Sentinel. But how disappointing these curious little booklets were; most included only eight pages about the club itself, the remainder being made up of general material and advertisements. The Scottish clubs were covered by similar booklets published by Simmath. The *Famous Football Clubs* series, published by Newservice throughout 1948, added much more flesh to the bare bones of the Sentinel booklets and are worth seeking out, whilst the slightly later Convoy *Football Club* series went a step further on a number of occasions. A notable example is Brian Glanville's 1952 volume on Arsenal. At 133 pages it can reasonably lay claim to being one of the first comprehensive histories published post-war and is now particularly collectable.

It wasn't until the 1970s and later though that the world of football publishing really found its feet. Much of this was due to an increasing number of clubs celebrating their centenaries. Authors and publishers alike were presented with an opportunity they were quick to seize. Organisations such as the Association of Football Statisticians, founded in 1978, served as a catalyst to the process by providing an invaluable forum for the promotion and encouragement of such material and nurturing a market place for it. Their contribution is a most significant one and many key publications have been written by their members.

Central to the entire future of club history publishing was the year 1984, when Derby-based Breedon Books celebrated the centenary of their home town club by the publication of *Derby County: The Complete Record*. As well as giving an historical account of the club's growth and activity over the years, it added a comprehensive season-by-season statistical summary of results, appearances and scorers; full career records of all the players; biographical details of one hundred 'greats', and much more besides. If ever there was a landmark publication in modern football publishing, this was surely it.

Breedon put out feelers for volunteer authors to cover other clubs, a winning formula was established, and the series has grown into a classic. Moreover, some of the ideas included in these volumes have been expanded upon to suggest entire books in their own right – memorable matches, who's who, A to Z – all of these whet the appetites of historically inclined club followers with the result that many authors, some with no previous experience, set about putting pen to paper with a vengeance. The rest, as they say, is history. The last decade has witnessed a boom in club-based works, seeing ever resourceful writers applying the basic principles of product segmentation in successive publications. Cynics might suggest that this is nothing more than the same material being recycled in different ways. There is of course a vein of truth in this, especially with regard to the larger clubs. It is more useful though to note that the search for something new has encouraged imagination and innovation amongst the football writing fraternity, resulting in a multi-angled coverage. Cartoon histories, picture postcards, pictorial records, quiz books, supporter reminiscences, ground histories – these are just some of the ways in which historians have chosen to write about their clubs. Although this phenomenon has been most marked amongst the first class English clubs, the same enthusiasm has extended to Scottish football and, to a lesser degree, Wales and Ireland.

As coverage of the leading clubs reaches near saturation point writers have inexorably turned their attention to clubs lower down the pecking order. This has been excellent news for followers of the non-league game as an ever increasing number of relatively minor clubs are now being chronicled.

To this phenomenon may be added the legendary work of Dave Twydell in studying the ex-league clubs and extinct non-league teams, and similar work in Scotland by Norman Nicol and Stewart Davidson. The result is a breadth of coverage which was simply unthinkable even ten years ago.

The message to all club followers is a simple one – keep reading and keep writing – this will guarantee a flow of new material and this can only be good for football. Certainly the game has come a long way since its conception in 1863, but football publishing has come even further. Readers who consult the entries in this chapter may judge for themselves but I suspect, indeed I *know*, that they will be well rewarded.

Club Histories ~ Contents

FA Premiership & Football League

Arsenal

1 Woolwich District football handbook, 1894-5.
Woolwich: Arsenal Football Club, 1894.
illus   BL: 1578/1424

Founded in 1886 as Dial Square, the club subsequently played as Royal Arsenal until 1891 when they turned professional. This early handbook echoes the name Woolwich Arsenal which the club took in that year.

2 History and fixtures. London: Arsenal Football Club, 1936-1939.

Continued as: The official handbook of Arsenal Football Club, Ltd
BL: P.P.8005.rz

☞ See also: B4

3 Let's talk about Arsenal: including football personalities and points of interest / Tom Morgan. London: Sentinel, 1946.
32p; illus; pbk
(Football handbooks. Series 1; no. 3)   BL: W.P.1144/3

Interesting but lightweight early study.

4 The official handbook of Arsenal Football Club, Ltd. London: Arsenal Football Club, 1947-1949.

Continued as: The official history and handbook of Arsenal Football Club Limited   BL: P.P.8005.rz

☞ See also: B2; B6

5 Gunflash. London: Arsenal Football Supporters' Club, 1950-   BL: P.P.1832.mae

Early example of a supporters' club magazine.

☞ Also listed at: L16

6 The official history and handbook of Arsenal Football Club Limited. London: Arsenal Football Club, 1950-
BL: P.P.8005.rz

☞ See also: B4

7 Arsenal Football Club / Brian Glanville. London: Convoy, 1952.
133p; illus; pbk
(Famous football clubs); (Football club series)
BL: 7923.f.14/3

One of a generally lightweight series, though this is rather fuller than most. It is effectively the first history of the club – surprising that one of our greatest footballing institutions had to wait until 1952 to be properly chronicled.

8 Forward, Arsenal!: a history of the Arsenal Football Club / Bernard Joy. London: Phoenix House, 1952.
xvi, 208p; illus   BL: 7921.bb.47

Whilst the previous item can be regarded as the first attempt at a history of the club, this work can justifiably be regarded as the first detailed history. It has become something of a collector's item for followers of 'The Gunners'.

9 Forward Arsenal! / Bernard Joy. London: Hamilton, 1957.
190p
(Panther books; no. 725)   BL: W.P.B.29/725

10 Tom Whittaker's Arsenal story / Tom Whittaker; edited by Roy Peskett. London: Sporting Handbooks, 1957.
351p; illus   BL: 7923.ff.35

Whittaker served the club from 1919 in a variety of roles. This work was published shortly after his death – it offers a rare eyewitness insight and is written in an entertaining and informal style.

☞ Also listed at: C502

11 Gunners on the target: a record of the Arsenal Football Club / Geoffrey Mowbray. London: Stanley Paul, 1961.
207p; illus   BL: X.449/516

Notable for 60 pages of player biographies – 92 in all.

12 Arsenal: Chapman to Mee / Ralph Leslie Finn. London: Hale, 1969.
176p; illus   ISBN: 0-7091-1068-5
BL: X.449/3997

Herbert Chapman managed the club from 1925 to 1934. Bertie Mee filled the same role from 1966 to 1976. This book covers the full fifty years.

13 The Arsenal football book / edited by R. Hayter.
London: Stanley Paul, 1969.
128p; illus
               ISBN: 0-09-097890-0
               BL: X.441/1243

Profuse illustrations are a feature of this annual which was to run for six issues.

14 Arsenal from the heart / Bob Wall. London: Souvenir, 1969.
192p; illus
               ISBN: 0-285-50261-1
               BL: X.449/4278

Reminiscences of one of Arsenal's truly long-serving administrative stalwarts – Wall was secretary from 1928.

☞ Also listed at: C495

15 The Arsenal football book no. 2 / edited by R. Hayter.
London: Stanley Paul, 1970.
128p; illus
               ISBN: 0-09-103310-1
               BL: X.441/1243

16 Arsenal, Arsenal!: Football League champions FA Cup winners 1971 / edited by Harry Langton. London: Arsenal FC, 1971.
160p

Official souvenir of the double.

17 The Arsenal football book no. 3 / edited by R. Hayter.
London: Stanley Paul, 1971.
128p; illus
               ISBN: 0-09-108280-3
               BL: X.441/1243

18 Inside the Gunners. 1971.
48p; pbk

Ephemeral item published during the club's double-winning year.

19 The Arsenal football book no. 4 / edited by R. Hayter.
London: Stanley Paul, 1972.
128p; illus
               ISBN: 0-09-112610-X
               BL: X.441/1243

20 The Arsenal story / Deryk Brown. London: Arthur Barker, 1972.
151p; illus
               ISBN: 0-213-16412-4
               BL: X.629/4789

Concentrates largely on the 1960s and the double year with the result that it is rather light on early history.

21 The battle of London: Arsenal versus Tottenham Hotspur / Rex Pardoe. London: Tom Stacey, 1972.
xix, 220p; illus
               ISBN: 0-85468-150-7
               BL: X.629/4130

An overall history of the rivalry between these two clubs from the 1880s through to the 1970s – it was fitting for Arsenal that they clinched the 1970/71 Championship at White Hart Lane, home of their arch enemy. This achievement provides the climax to this excellent work.

☞ Also listed at: B796

22 The Arsenal football book no. 5 / edited by R. Hayter.
London: Stanley Paul, 1973.
128p; illus
               ISBN: 0-09-117210-1
               BL: X.441/1243

23 The Arsenal football book no. 6 / edited by R. Hayter.
London: Stanley Paul, 1974.
129p; illus; pbk
               ISBN: 0-09-121000-3
               BL: X.441/1243

24 Arsenal FC official annual / edited by Harry Harris.
Ilford: Circle Publications, 1979-
illus

    Spine title: Arsenal annual
               BL: P.441/1030

25 The story of Arsenal / Anton Rippon. Ashbourne: Moorland Publishing, 1981.
95p; illus
               ISBN: 0-86190-023-5
               BL: X.622/11884

Rather light on narrative but good pictorial content.

26 Arsenal / John Robertson. Twickenham: Hamlyn, 1985.
123p; illus; index
               ISBN: 0-600-50178-7
               BL: YC.1986.b.815

Extensively illustrated; includes some rare early photographs.

27 Arsenal 1886-1986: the official centenary history of Arsenal Football Club / Phil Soar & Martin Tyler. Twickenham: Hamlyn, 1986.
256p; illus, 2 coats of arms; index
               ISBN: 0-600-35871-2
               BL: YK.1988.b.4064

Excellent detailed study giving every team line-up since 1919.

☞ Subsequent ed. B30

28 Arsenal / Bill Day; illustrated by Craig Warwick.
London: Purnell, 1988.
96p; illus; index
(Football clubs)
    ISBN: 0-361-08356-4 (cased) ● ISBN: 0-361-08357-2 (pbk)
               BL: YK.1989.a.827

29 Arsenal: a complete record 1886-1988 / Fred Ollier.
Derby: Breedon Books, 1988.
416p; illus
               ISBN: 0-907969-41-0
               BL: YK.1991.a.10597

Essential work of reference – extremely comprehensive. Later updated editions cover a greater span of years.

30 Arsenal: official history / Phil Soar & Martin Tyler.
London: Hamlyn, 1989.
272p; illus; index; pbk
               ISBN: 0-600-56784-2
               BL: YK.1990.b.3755

☞ Previous ed. B27; subsequent ed. B43

31 Wembley 1927: the Cardiff-Arsenal FA Cup Final 1927 / Derrick Jenkins and Ceri Stennett. Cardiff?: The authors?, 1989?
    45p; illus; pbk   BL: YK.1990.a.6154

    Probably of more interest to Cardiff followers – Arsenal were surprisingly beaten in this famous final.

    ☞ *Also listed at: B174*

32 Arsenal: a complete record 1886-1990 / Fred Ollier. Derby: Breedon Books, 1990.
    416p; illus   ISBN: 0-907969-77-1
                                                        BL: YK.1991.a.12995

    Updated complete record – essential work of reference.

33 Arsenal greats / Keith Fisher; foreword by George Graham. Edinburgh: Sportsprint, 1990.
    vii, 178p; illus; pbk   ISBN: 0-85976-314-5
                                                        BL: YC.1990.b.7066

    Largely a coverage of great post-war players and managers.

34 Arsenal: history and full record 1886-1988 / Scott Grant and Colin White. Lingfield?: Lingfield Press, 1990.
    552p

    Published as a limited edition of 3,000 copies. Extremely comprehensive coverage – it even includes full results for the reserve team.

35 Arsenal – the champion's year: the inside story of the Gunners' 1989-90 season / the Arsenal 1st team squad with Harry Miller. London: Partridge, 1990.
    159p; illus   ISBN: 1-85225-122-0
                                                        BL: YK.1991.b.1089

36 Arsenal: player by player / Ivan Ponting. Enfield: Guinness, 1991.
    176p   ISBN: 0-85112-997-8
                                                        BL: YK.1991.b.6607

    Covers Arsenal players since the war.

    ☞ *Subsequent ed. B41*

37 Green Gunners: Arsenal's Irish / Stephen McGarrigle. Edinburgh: Mainstream, 1991.
    160p; illus   ISBN: 1-85158-442-0
                                                        BL: YK.1993.b.6234

    An A-Z of Irish players who have played for the club – niche marketing at its more obvious.

38 Heroes and villains: the inside story of the 1990-91 season at Arsenal and Tottenham Hotspur / Alex Fynn and Lynton Guest. London: Penguin, 1991.
    373p; illus; pbk   ISBN: 0-14-014769-1
                                                        BL: YK.1991.a.9721

Arsenal were champions in this year, whilst Spurs won the FA Cup.

☞ *Also listed at: B809*

39 Arsenal: a complete record 1886-1992 / Fred Ollier. Derby: Breedon Books, 1992.
    432p; illus   ISBN: 1-873626-12-6
                                                        BL: YK.1993.a.9548

    Another full update.

40 Arsenal: a pictorial history / compiled by Neal Simpson, Kevin Alcock. Derby: Breedon Books, 1992.
    256p; illus   ISBN: 1-873626-26-6
                                                        BL: YK.1993.b.12603

    A most comprehensive presentation of photographic material of the club.

41 Arsenal: player by player / Ivan Ponting. 1993. Previous ed. B36

42 The end: 80 years of life on Arsenal's North Bank / Tom Watt; foreword by David O'Leary. Edinburgh: Mainstream, 1993.
    347p; illus

    Includes bibliographical references   ISBN: 1-85158-567-2
                                                        BL: YK.1994.b.4458

    Like many clubs, Arsenal were forced to convert a famous section of terracing into seating in order to comply with the Taylor Report. This is a superb work evoking many memories of supporters and personalities from all eras. The writer is one of Arsenal's many celebrity fans, best known for his role as Lofty in the TV soap Eastenders. Many supporters have boasted in moments of fantasy or inebriation of 'taking' the North Bank, but only Justice Taylor and the developers might stake their claim with any justification.

    ☞ *Also listed at: H131*

43 Arsenal: official history / Phil Soar & Martin Tyler. Rev. ed. London: Hamlyn, 1994.
    304p; illus, coats of arms; index
                                                        ISBN: 0-600-58342-2

    ☞ *Previous ed. B30*

44 Gunning for glory: the full story of Arsenal's victorious 93-4 season / compiled by David Emery. London: Simon & Schuster, 1994.
    159p; illus; pbk   ISBN: 0-671-71368-X

45 The Highbury encyclopedia: an A-Z of Arsenal FC / Stephen F. Kelly. Edinburgh: Mainstream, 1994.
    192p; pbk
                                                        ISBN: 1-85158-659-8

Aston Villa

46 Aston Villa Cup record 1880-1924. 1924.
Scarce early item.

47 Let's talk about Aston Villa: including football
personalities and points of interest / Tom Morgan.
London: Sentinel, 1946.
32p; illus; pbk
(Football handbooks. Series 1; no. 5)   BL: W.P.1144/5
Collectable but lacking in serious content.

48 The story of Aston Villa: a cartoon history / Norman
Edwards. Birmingham: Birmingham Evening Dispatch,
1947.
92p; illus
Scarce and unusual item.

49 Aston Villa / Fred Ward. London: Newservice, 1948.
32p; illus
(Famous football clubs)   BL: 7922.k.15/7
Rather lightweight coverage.

50 Aston Villa: the history of a great football club,
1874-1960 / Peter Morris. London: Naldrett, 1960.
xv, 308p; illus   BL: 7925.f.10
*Few clubs had been comprehensively covered in print
by this date – this is an excellent effort albeit
eclipsed by later studies.*

51 Aston Villa: the first 100 years 1874-1974 / Peter Morris.
Birmingham: Aston Villa Football Club, 1974.
96p
Good coverage of the early days.

52 Play up Villa!: the story of a unique FA Cup tie / Rob
Woolley with foreword by Johnny Dixon. Sutton
Coldfield: The author, 1977.
20p; pbk
(Midland tales; no. 1)   BL: X.619/18495

53 The Aston Villa story / Ian Johnson. London: Arthur
Barker, 1981.
x, 170p; illus   ISBN: 0-213-16794-8
                                         BL: X.622/10940

54 Ron Saunders' Aston Villa scrapbook. London: Pictorial
Presentations, 1981.
143p; illus
     ISBN: 0-285-62512-8 (cased) • ISBN: 0-285-62513-6 (pbk)
                                         BL: X.622/11531
*Manager Ron Saunders presents his personal im-
pressions in the year when Villa won the First Division
championship.*

55 The story of Aston Villa / Anton Rippon. Ashbourne:
Moorland, 1981.
96p; illus   ISBN: 0-903485-99-0
                                         BL: X.622/11077
Heavy concentration on illustrations.

56 The great years of Aston Villa 1886-1982 / David
Goodyear. Birmingham: The author, 1983.
200p; illus; pbk   ISBN: 0-9508826-0-7
*Very strong on statistics – full line-ups, results and
scorers for all league and cup matches.*

57 Aston Villa: a complete record 1874-1988 / David
Goodyear and Tony Matthews. Derby: Breedon Books,
1988.
448p; illus   ISBN: 0-907969-37-2
                                         BL: YK.1991.a.8659
Essential definitive text.

58 The Aston Villa quiz book / Derrick Spinks. Edinburgh:
Mainstream, 1989.
141p; illus; pbk   ISBN: 1-85158-282-7
                                         BL: YK.1991.a.3948

59 Aston Villa greats / Leon Hickman. Edinburgh:
Sportsprint, 1990.
vi, 197p; illus; pbk   ISBN: 0-85976-313-7
                                         BL: YK.1991.a.4079
*The author, chief sports writer with the Birmingham
Evening Mail, chooses ten players as his all time
greats: David Platt, Johnny Dixon, Dennis Mortimer,
Gerry Hitchens, Gordon Cowans, Andy Gray, Peter
Withe, Brian Little, Charlie Aitken and Stan Lynn.*

60 The Aston Villa who's who 1874-1989 / Tony
Matthews. Paper Plane, 1990.
144p   ISBN: 1-871872-01-4
Potted biographies of all first team players.

61 Aston Villa: a portrait in old picture postcards /
compiled by Derrick Spinks. Market Drayton: S. B.
Publications, 1991.
viii, 88p; chiefly illus; pbk
(A portrait in old picture postcards)
     Bibliography on inside cover   ISBN: 1-870708-88-1
                                         BL: YK.1992.a.4924

Part of a series which covers a number of clubs. A total of 88 postcards are presented including many fascinating early images. High on nostalgia content.

62 Aston Villa: a complete record 1874-1992 / David Goodyear & Tony Matthews. Derby: Breedon Books, 1992.
432p; illus

ISBN: 1-873626-17-7
BL: YK.1993.a.9582

Update of this key historical text.

63 Aston Villa on cigarette & trade cards / Derrick Spinks. Studley: Brewin Books, 1993.
93p; all illus; pbk

Spine title: Aston Villa

ISBN: 1-85858-030-7
BL: YK.1994.a.7052

One of very few such studies. This is a treatment which might admirably be applied to many other clubs – it would certainly make a good series. Delightful images – excellent source of illustrations.

64 Aston Villa review 1993 / edited by Denis Shaw. Birmingham: Sports Projects, 1993.
160p
(Match by match)

ISBN: 0-946866-09-0

65 The Aston Villa story / Anton Rippon. Derby: Breedon Books, 1993.
239p; illus

ISBN: 1-873626-49-5
BL: YK.1994.b.6574

A substantial reference work.

66 Aston Villa review 1994 / edited by Denis Shaw. Birmingham: Sports Projects, 1994.

Barnet

67 Barnet Football Club diamond jubilee 1888-1948 / edited by T. H. Cooper. 1948.
44p; pbk

Scarce item chronicling the club's earliest years in their amateur pre-league days; Barnet did not turn professional until 1965.

68 Barnet Football Club: a souvenir brochure to commemorate Barnet's historic rise into the Football League. London: Barnet Football Club, 1991.

The club are latecomers to the Football League – they gained entry in 1991, having triumphed in the Conference League.

69 The club that wouldn't die: Barnet FC from Barry Fry to disaster and back / Tony Thornton. London: Tiger, 1994.
207p; pbk

ISBN: 0-9523862-0-8

Despite crippling financial difficulties the club did survive – this is essential reading for all 'Bees' historians.

Barnsley

70 Barnsley FC 1887-1910.

This is an unverified item covering Barnsley's early history. They were formed in 1887 as Barnsley St Peters, but changed their name upon joining the League in 1898.

71 Let's talk about Barnsley Football Club: including football personalities and points of interest / Tom Morgan. London: Sentinel, 1948.
32p; illus; pbk
(Football handbooks. Series 3; no. 42)

Curious but distinctly lightweight early study.

72 Oakwell: the official history of Barnsley Football Club / Grenville Firth. Barnsley: The author, 1978.

☞ Subsequent ed. B73

73 Oakwell: the official history of Barnsley Football Club / Grenville Firth. Rev. ed. Wakefield: EP Publishing, 1979
10, 443p; illus; pbk

ISBN: 0-7158-0742-0
BL: X.629/13972

Substantial definitive history – essential work of reference.

☞ Previous ed. B72

74 The Reds: a pictorial history of Barnsley Football Club / Grenville Firth. Wakefield: EP Publishing, 1980.
96p; chiefly illus; pbk

ISBN: 0-7158-0755-2
BL: L.49/1800

Largely photographic in content.

75 Barnsley: a study in football 1953-59 / Andrew Ward & Ian Alister. Barton-under-Needwood: Crowberry, 1981.
139p; illus; index; pbk

ISBN: 0-9507568-0-6
BL: X.629/15861

In 1953 the club were relegated to Division Three but regained their Division Two status for the period 1955-1959. The apparently arbitrary choice of era for this study is not what it seems – this was the period during which the club was managed by Tim Ward, father of the co-author of this interesting work.

76 Oakwell heroes: a who's who of Barnsley footballers, 1945-86 / Graham Noble. Barnsley: Glenwood, 1986.
96p; illus   ISBN: 0-9511359-0-2
Comprehensive study of post-war players.

77 Oakwell Saints go marching on / Keith Lodge. Barnsley: Barnsley Football Club, 1987.
112p; illus

78 Oakwell centurions: a collection of biographies of Barnsley FC's leading players of modern times – almost all of whom have played 100 first team games / David Watson. Barnsley: Barnsley Libraries, 1990.
276p; illus   ISBN: 0-9516227-0-6
                         BL: YK.1992.b.8273
Very comprehensive study of leading players.

79 Barnsley: seasons 1983-84 to 1992-93 / season-by-season commentary by Keith Lodge; statistics and history by Mike Ross; editors, Michael Robinson, John Robinson & Philip Norminton. Cleethorpes: Soccer Book Publishing, 1993.
52p; illus; pbk
(The 10 seasons series)   ISBN: 0-947808-34-5
                         BL: YK.1995.a.1173

81 Let's talk about Birmingham City Football Club: including football personalities and points of interest / Tom Morgan. London: Sentinel, 1948.
32p; illus; pbk
(Football handbooks. Series 3; no. 44)
   Rather sketchy coverage of little value to the serious historian.

82 The history of Birmingham City since 1875 / Neil Edwards. Birmingham: Birmingham Evening Dispatch, 1956.

83 One hundred years history of Birmingham City Football Club 1875-1975: centenary souvenir. Birmingham: Birmingham City FC, 1975.
98p

84 Birmingham City: a complete record, 1875-1989 / Tony Matthews. Derby: Breedon Books, 1989.
416p; illus   ISBN: 0-907969-48-8
                      BL: YK.1992.a.9047
Essential definitive coverage.

85 Who's who of Birmingham City 1875-1991 / Tony Matthews and Roger Baker. Warley: Sports Leisure Concepts, 1991.
96p   ISBN: 1-873171-04-8
   Features 750 players and managers from all eras.

Birmingham City

Blackburn Rovers

80 Birmingham Football Club. 1906.
   The club was founded in 1875 and played under the name of Small Heath. They changed their name to Birmingham City in 1906, moving to their St Andrews ground in the same year. This extremely scarce handbook celebrates this double event.

86 Jimmy Forrest's career and a brief history of the Blackburn Rovers Club 1874-1893 / J. Baron. 1893.
   Extremely scarce item – Jimmy Forrest was the only player who appeared in all Blackburn's nineteenth century cup winning sides.

87 Blackburn Rovers: the Blackburn Weekly Telegraph's handy history of the famous 'Blue and Whites' from origin to 1906-7 / Baron Joseph of Blackburn. Blackburn: 1906.
ii, 62p   BL: D

Scarce early study charting the years 1875 to 1906.

88 History of Blackburn Rovers 1875-1925 / Charles Francis. Preston: Toulmin, 1925.
219p

This rare volume chronicles fifty years of the club – Blackburn are one of just a few teams covered so comprehensively at such an early date.

89 Let's talk about Blackburn Rovers Football Club: including football personalities and points of interest / Tom Morgan. London: Sentinel, 1946.
32p; illus; pbk
(Football handbooks. Series 1; no. 7)   BL: W.P.1144/7

Short on historical detail but an interesting collector's item.

90 Things about Blackburn Rovers / Harry Livesey Kay. Blackburn: J. Dickinson, 1949.
165p   BL: 7920.b.23

Uses an unusual question and answer format to convey facts and figures about the club and its personalities.

91 Blackburn Rovers Football Club: a century of soccer / Harry Berry. Blackburn: Blackburn FC, 1975.
188p

Good general historical survey.

92 Safe hands: 111 years of Blackburn Rovers goalkeeping / Harry Berry. Blackburn: Berry Books, 1987.
194p

First in a rather innovative series profiling players in particular positions during the entire history of the club.

93 Blackburn Rovers Football Club: a pictorial history 1875-1988 / Peter White. Runcorn: Archive Publications, 1988.
128p; illus; pbk   ISBN: 0-948946-25-3

Excellent content, though it would have benefited from the use of more early photographs.

94 Blazing bullets: Blackburn's memorable goals / Harry Berry. Blackburn: Berry Books, 1988.
150p

95 Strong backs: the history of the Blackburn full back / Harry Berry. Blackburn: Berry Books, 1988.
150p

96 Hard centres: the evolution of the Blackburn stopper / Harry Berry. Blackburn: Berry Books, 1989.
160p

Centre halves under the spotlight.

97 Blackburn Rovers: a complete record 1875-1990 / Mike Jackman. Derby: Breedon Books, 1990.
416p; illus   ISBN: 0-907969-63-1
                                           BL: YK.1992.a.10724

Best starting point for any historical study of the club.

98 Characters and caricatures / Harry Berry. Blackburn: Berry Books, 1991.
illus

180 cartoons portray players from all eras.

99 Blackburn Rovers: an A-Z / Dean Hayes. Preston: Palatine, 1993.
156p; illus; pbk
(Carnegie soccer A-Z; vol. 1)   ISBN: 1-874181-10-1

Interesting facts and anecdotes about players and events arranged alphabetically.

100 Blackburn Rovers: the official encyclopaedia / Mike Jackman. Derby: Breedon Books, 1994.
250p; illus   ISBN: 1-873626-70-3

Essential reference work.

Blackpool

101 The souvenir history of the Blackpool Football Club / W. Hartley-Bracewell. Manchester: Holt Publishing Service, 1931.
64p; pbk

Scarce item – half the book covers the club's history while the remainder is made up of photographs of contemporary players and officials.

102 Blackpool / Archie Quick. London: Newservice, 1948.
35p; illus
(Famous football clubs)   BL: 7922.k.15/9

Brief history – rather lightweight.

103 Let's talk about Blackpool Football Club: including football personalities and points of interest / Tom Morgan. London: Sentinel, 1948.
32p; illus; pbk
(Football handbooks. Series 3; no. 46)

Lightweight content only.

104 Blackpool Football Club players' handbook 1956-57. Nottingham?: Clearpoint, 1957.
24p; pbk

By the players for the players

105 Blackpool football: the official club history / Robin Daniels. London: Hale, 1972.
364p; illus   ISBN: 0-7091-3501-7
                                           BL: X.620/6117

Includes a foreword by famous cricket writer Sir Neville Cardus.

106 Seasiders – the first 100 years: a history of Blackpool FC 1887-1987 / H. Ellis Tomlinson. Blackpool: Blackpool Football Club, 1987.
88p; illus

Weighted towards more recent times.

107 Blackpool: a complete record 1887-1992 / Roy Calley. Derby: Breedon Books, 1992.
416p; illus

ISBN: 1-873626-07-X
BL: YK.1994.a.15521

Essential starting point for all serious research.

Bolton Wanderers

108 History of Turton Football Club / W. T. Dixon. 1909.

Turton Football Club came into existence in 1871 – whilst not the direct forerunner to Bolton Wanderers, the club had a marked influence on the development of soccer in this area. One of the club's captains, J. J. Bentley, was to become an important administrative figure for Bolton Wanderers and the Football Association.

109 Bolton Wanderers FC, 1872-1925 / Bolton Wanderers Football Club. Bolton: Blackshaw, 1925.
64p

BL: D

Scarce item covering the team's early history.

110 Let's talk about Bolton Wanderers Football Club: including football personalities and points of interest / Tom Morgan. London: Sentinel, 1946.
32p; illus; pbk
(Football handbooks. Series 1; no. 8)   BL: W.P.1144/8

Contains little in the way of historical detail.

111 All about Bolton Wanderers: club, personalities, matches, facts, figures, fancies. James Bland, 1950.
48p

112 Bolton Wanderers / Percy Marshall Young. London: Stanley Paul, 1961.
192p; illus

BL: 7926.w.6

The first major history of the club, here presented by one of football's most respected writers.

113 Bolton Wanderers: a complete record, 1877-1989 / Simon Marland. Derby: Breedon Books, 1989.
416p; illus

Updated paperback editions subsequently published to cover 1989-90, 1990-91, 1991-92 and 1992-93

ISBN: 0-907969-51-8
BL: YK.1992.a.10136

Serious researchers should consult this volume first.

114 Bolton Wanderers A-Z / Dean Hayes. Preston: Palatine, 1994.
192p; illus; pbk
(Carnegie soccer A-Z; vol. 3)

ISBN: 1-874181-13-6

AFC Bournemouth

115 The official souvenir of the Boscombe Football Club. Bournemouth: Boscombe Football Club, 1913.

Extremely scarce item; gives a brief résumé of the club's foundation in 1899 following the demise of the Boscombe St John's Institute team, itself formed in 1890.

116 Bournemouth and Boscombe Athletic FC golden jubilee. Bournemouth: Bournemouth and Boscombe Athletic Football Club, 1949.
40p; illus

Includes photographs of the team squad.

117 Up the cherries: the complete story of Bournemouth and Boscombe FC 1899-1959 / Tony Pullein. Bournemouth: Bournemouth and Boscombe FC, 1959.

Quite a scarce item – certainly the definitive work when published and unusual for a relatively small club to be seriously chronicled at a time when club histories were thin on the ground.

118   AFC Bournemouth official club history and championship souvenir / Leigh Edwards and John Treleven. Bournemouth: Bournemouth FC, 1987.
76p; pbk

Published to celebrate the club's first ever promotion to the Second Division, this doubles as a good historical account with appreciable coverage of their early history.

Bradford City

119   The remarkable history of the Bradford City AFC: pioneers of English league football in West Yorkshire / W. H. Sawyer. Bradford: Bradford City Supporters Club, 1927.
44p; pbk

Subsequently published: Wetherby: City Gent, 1986

The club was founded in 1903 and played in Division One from 1908 to 1922, then Division Two from 1922 to 1927. They won the FA Cup in 1911. This rare item covers all this as well as their early history.

120   Let's talk about Bradford City Football Club: including football personalities and points of interest / Tom Morgan. London: Sentinel, 1948.
32p; illus; pbk
(Football handbooks. Series 3; no. 47)

Early ephemeral study, light on serious content.

121   The jubilee story: Bradford City AFC 1903-1953 / W. H. Sawyer. Bradford: Bradford City Shareholders & Supporters Association, 1953.
76p; pbk

This updated version of the 1927 edition extends the Bradford City story to 1953. Proceeds from sales went towards the fund for the Midland Road stand.

122   Memorable matches: Bradford City AFC / Denis Blyth. Milnthorpe: Byways, 1981?
64p; illus; pbk

Includes an 8p supplement   BL: X.629/20684
From Gainsborough Trinity in 1903 to Liverpool in 1980.

123   Bradford City: a complete record 1903-1988 / Terry Frost. Derby: Breedon Books, 1988.
416p; illus   ISBN: 0-907969-38-0
          BL: YK.1992.a.8143

Definitive coverage – an essential work.

124   A game that would pay: a business history of professional football in Bradford / A. J. Arnold. London: Duckworth, 1988.
xi, 217p; illus; index

Bibliography: p209-212   ISBN: 0-7156-2506-3
          BL: YC.1988.b.6581

This is an unusual study of universal interest. Using Bradford football as an example, this study focuses on the place of football clubs in society, how they are run and the effect on the local economy. Much of the material relates to the early days of the game.

☞   Also listed at: B922

125   Of boars and bantams: pictorial history and club record of Bradford City AFC / D. R. Gillam, John Dewhirst, Tim Clapham and Keith Mellor. Bradford?: Temple Printing, 1988.
216p   ISBN: 1-870010-06-X

Two pages are devoted to each season.

126   How City won t' cup: the story of Bradford City's 1911 cup campaign told by the newspapers of the day / written and compiled by Mick Dickinson. Wetherby: City Gent, 1990?
65p; illus; pbk   BL: YK.1991.b.8967

Story of City's 1911 cup victory seen through the newspapers of the day – this unusual retrospective work charts their 1-0 victory over Newcastle to become the first winners of the present trophy.

Brentford

127   Let's talk about Brentford Football Club: including football personalities and points of interest / Tom Morgan. London: Sentinel, 1947.
32p; illus; pbk
(Football handbooks. Series 2; no. 30)

Extremely limited in content – curious, but not for the serious student.

128   The Brentford story 1888-1979 / Graham Haynes and Geoff Buckingham. Brentford: Brentford Football Club, 1979.
60p

Rather lightweight, includes many adverts.

129 Brentford match facts & figures 1920-1981 / Graham Haynes and Eric White. 1981.
72p

> Every result, appearance, scorer and attendance for the period – extremely thorough but purely statistical.

130 Brentford FC: three visits to Wembley / Graham Haynes and Dave Twydell. Brentford?: The authors, 1985.
48p; pbk

> The eye-catching title is a little mischievous – three glorious FA Cup Final victories perhaps? The reality is less grand but no less interesting. The first visit took place on 22 November 1930 for an away match against Clapton Orient whilst Orient's ground was being altered; the second was 30 May 1942 for the London War Cup Final, which Brentford won 2-0 against Portsmouth; the final glory was 1 June 1985 when 'The Bees' finished runners up to Wigan in the Freight Rover Trophy. Cynics might suggest 'clutching at straws' as a good subtitle, but this is nonetheless an interesting idea and includes some lesser known material.

131 100 years of Brentford / Eric White and others. Brentford: Brentford Football Club, 1989.
400p; illus; pbk

ISBN: 0-9515262-0-0
BL: YK.1993.b.1348

> Excellent definitive work and key historical text covering all aspects of the club's history.

132 Albion: an illustrated history of Brighton & Hove Albion FC / John Vinicombe. Norwich: George Nobbs, 1978.
112p

> An informed first account from the leading sports journalist with the Brighton Evening Argus. Brighton's Southern League days are covered as well as their time in the Football League from 1920, as founder members of the Third Division.

Brighton & Hove Albion

133 Up, up and away: Brighton & Hove Albion's rise to the 1st Division / John Vinicombe. Norwich: George Nobbs, 1980.
100p

Narrow coverage concentrating entirely on the 1978/79 season when 'The Seagulls' first achieved promotion to the First Division.

134 Super Seagulls: an account of Albion's first season in the top flight / John Vinicombe. Norwich: George Nobbs, 1981.
84p

> Story of their first season in Division One – a natural follow-up to the previous entry.

135 Seagulls!: the story of Brighton & Hove Albion FC / Tim Carder & Roger Harris. Hove: Goldstone, 1993.
328p; illus; index

ISBN: 0-9521337-0-9
BL: YK.1993.b.14334

> Essential reading – comprehensive coverage.

136 Brighton and Hove Albion: a portrait in old picture postcards / compiled by David Tilehurst. Seaford: S. B. Publications, 1994.
96p; chiefly illus; pbk
(A portrait in old picture postcards)

ISBN: 1-85770-070-8

Bristol City

137 Let's talk about Bristol City Football Club: including football personalities and points of interest / Tom Morgan. London: Sentinel, 1948.
32p; illus; pbk
(Football handbooks. Series 3; no. 48)

> Limited serious content.

138 Bristol City: 75 years in the League / Bruce Parry. Bristol?: The author?, 1976.
48p; pbk

> Relatively recent but scarce brochure-style publication.

139 Bristol City: the complete history of the club / Peter Godsiff. Norwich: Wensum, 1979.
112p; illus   ISBN: 0-903619-31-8

This is the first serious effort at historical coverage and includes the foundation of the club in 1894 as Bristol South End – their present name was adopted three years later upon turning professional.

140 Bristol City: a complete record 1894-1987 / David M. Woods with Andrew Crabtree. Derby: Breedon Books, 1987.
368p; illus   ISBN: 0-907969-27-5
BL: YK.1991.a.12332

Ideal volume to use as a starting text for any research project.

141 City greats / Ivan Ponting. Bristol: Evening Post, 1992.

142 Bristol Babe: centenary history of Bristol FC, 1894-1994 / David M. Woods. Harefield: Yore, 1994.
320p; illus   ISBN: 1-874427-95-X

Comprehensive coverage – essential historic text.

Bristol Rovers

143 Let's talk about Bristol Rovers Football Club: including football personalities and points of interest / Tom Morgan. London: Sentinel, 1947.
32p; illus; pbk
(Football handbooks. Series 2; no. 32)
Simple, ephemeral, study lacking detail.

144 Bristol Rovers: a book of cartoons / 'Pak'. Bristol: 1950.
28p; illus; pbk
Scarce and unusual item chronicling the 1949 and 1950 seasons through cartoons.

145 Inspection of Bristol Rovers Football Club Limited: report / A. Frank Ward. London: HMSO, 1951.
vii, 81p; pbk   BL: B.S.41/140(47)

I have not had sight of this or the following item but one assumes the club was suspected of some sort of misdemeanour – serious Rovers historians will undoubtedly wish to consult these official publications.

146 Companies Act, 1948 investigation under Section 172 of Bristol Rovers Football Club Limited: report / E. H. C. Wethered. London: HMSO, 1952.
viii, 44p; pbk   BL: B.S.41/140

147 Bristol Rovers: match by match summary 1946-47 to 1961-62. Bristol: Bristol Rovers FC, 1962.

148 Bristol Rovers: a complete record 1883-1987 / Mike Jay. Derby: Breedon Books, 1987.
352p; illus   ISBN: 0-907969-26-7

This is the key historical text for the research student.

149 Champions and cup finalists 1990 / Mike Jay. Bristol: Bristol Rovers Supporters Club, 1990.
36p; illus; pbk

Covers the club's Third Division Championship triumph and their Leyland Daf Cup Final appearance.

150 Joy of the Rovers! / Jack Steggles. Edinburgh: Mainstream, 1990.
143p; illus   ISBN: 1-85158-347-5
BL: YK.1994.b.6140

151 'The Pirates' at Wembley 1990 / Mike Jay. Bristol: Bristol Rovers Football Club, 1990.
48p; illus; pbk

Covers the club's Leyland Daf Cup Final appearance which ended in defeat by Tranmere Rovers.

152 Pirates in profile: Bristol Rovers players who's who 1920-1994 / Mike Jay and Stephen Byrne. Bristol: Potten, Bayer & Murray, 1995.
320p; illus   ISBN: 0-9524835-0-5

This is the best study of players and personalities.

Burnley

153 The story of our epic double bid. Burnley: Burnley Football Club, 1947.
36p; pbk

Burnley actually finished as runners-up to Manchester City in Division Two whilst also losing out in the Cup Final to Charlton.

154 Let's talk about Burnley Football Club: including football personalities and points of interest / Tom Morgan. London: Sentinel, 1948.
32p; illus; pbk
(Football handbooks. Series 3; no. 50)
Curious item of little value to serious researchers.

155 75th anniversary handbook, 1889-1964 / Burnley
Football Club. London: Pyramid Press, 1965.
44p; illus
BL: X.441/302

156 'Up the Clarets': the story of Burnley Football Club /
David Wiseman. London: Hale, 1973.
207p; illus
ISBN: 0-7091-4310-9
BL: X.629/5827

Studies the club's history on a season-by-season basis.

157 Vintage claret: a pictorial history of Burnley Football
Club / David Wiseman. Nelson: Hendon Publishing,
1975.
50p; illus
ISBN: 0-902907-69-7
BL: X.619/8490

Largely team photographs and portrayals of players
on cigarette cards.

158 Burnley Football and Athletic Co. Ltd: centenary
handbook 1881-2 to 1981-82 / compiled by Robert
Bradshaw. Burnley: Burnley Football Club, 1982.
200p; illus

Well illustrated with rather a lot of advertisements.

159 Burnley Football Club: a pictorial history of 'The Clarets'
/ Tony Durkin. Runcorn: Archive, 1988.
128p; illus; pbk
ISBN: 0-948946-33-4

One of a series covering a number of clubs – rather
disappointing in terms of the balance between eras
as the early years receive little coverage.

160 Burnley: a complete record 1882-1991 / Edward Lee &
Ray Simpson. Derby: Breedon Books, 1991.
416p; illus
ISBN: 0-907969-90-9
BL: YK.1993.a.8936

An ideal volume on which to base all serious research
projects or for quick general reference.

161 The best ground in the Fourth Division: a history of
Burnley Football Club (1960-1988) / Andrew Procter.
London: Janus, 1992.
ix, 94p; illus; pbk
ISBN: 1-85756-010-8
BL: YK.1992.a.4920

Covers the period 1960 through to 1988. At the
start of this period the club was a Division One side;
they were subsequently relegated to Division Two in
1971 but returned to the top flight in 1973. A dramatic decline was to follow and by 1985 the club
found itself entrenched in Division Four – the title is
an ironic comment on the slide of a once great side
into the lower reaches.

162 Burnley FC: the 25 year record / editor, Michael
Robinson. Cleethorpes: Soccer Book Publishing, 1994.
63p; pbk
ISBN: 0-947808-45-0

Bury

163 Let's talk about Bury Football Club: including football
personalities and points of interest / Tom Morgan.
London: Sentinel, 1948.
32p; illus; pbk
(Football handbooks. Series 3; no. 51)

Part of an extensive series but extremely lightweight
in content.

164 Bury FC 1885-1985 / Peter Cullen and Paul Greenlees.
Bury?: Civic Publicity, 1985.
80p; illus; pbk

For a club lacking in serious historical studies, researchers may need to be content with this
centenary brochure publication with its brief history
and excellent photographs.

Cambridge United

165 United in endeavour: a history of Abbey United:
Cambridge United Football Club 1912-1988 / written
and researched by Paul M. Daw. Cambridge: Dawn
Publications, 1988.
202p; illus; pbk
ISBN: 0-9514108-0-6
BL: YK.1991.b.9073

The author, a former secretary of Cambridge United,
offers the first in-depth study of the club. They were
officially founded in 1919 as Abbey United and changed
their name to Cambridge United in 1949. This study
is a good starting point for any research project.

166 Cambridge United FC: first team match statistics,
1913-1991 / compiled and researched by Paul M. Daw.
Cambridge: Dawn Publications (Bar Hill), 1991.
70p; pbk

Limited ed.
ISBN: 0-9514108-2-2

A full statistical record covering every competitive match since 1913. The club were late entrants to the Football League, taking the place of Bradford Park Avenue in 1970. Only fifty copies of this authoritative work were published, so it is becoming scarce.

167 On the up: a history of Cambridge United Football Club 1988-1991 / written and researched by Paul M. Daw. Cambridge: Dawn Publications (Bar Hill), 1991.
48p; illus; pbk   ISBN: 0-9514108-1-4
                           BL: YK.1993.b.586

Complete statistical coverage for this limited period backed up by summaries of the matches played.

Cardiff City

168 Let's talk about Cardiff City Football Club: including football personalities and points of interest / Tom Morgan. London: Sentinel, 1946.
32p; illus; pbk
(Football handbooks. Series 1; no. 14)   BL: W.P.1144/14

Interesting as a collector's item but lacks detail.

169 A short history of Cardiff City AFC / 'Citizen'. Cardiff: Western Mail & Echo, 1947.
40p; pbk

Author is Dewi Lewis

Extremely scarce ephemeral item.

170 Cardiff City cavalcade. Cardiff, 1952.

171 The Cardiff City story / Peter Jackson. Barry?: S. A. Brain, 1974.
96p; pbk

172 Cardiff City chronology 1920-86 / written and compiled by John Crooks. Abergavenny: The author, 1986.
164p; illus; pbk   ISBN: 0-9511984-0-8
                           BL: YK.1989.b.3760

173 The Bluebirds: who's who of Cardiff City Football League players / John Crooks. Abergavenny: The author, 1987.
165p; illus; pbk   ISBN: 0-9511984-1-6

This is without a doubt the best publication for any study of the Cardiff players throughout their history.

174 Wembley 1927: the Cardiff-Arsenal FA Cup Final 1927 / Derrick Jenkins and Ceri Stennett. Cardiff?: The authors?, 1987.
45p; illus; pbk   BL: YK.1990.a.6154

It is seldom that a single match can prompt a retrospective study in its own right but the 1927 FA Cup Final was just such a game. Cardiff's 1-0 victory over the mighty Arsenal took the Cup out of England for the first and only time to date. Cynics have remarked that the Welsh club's side on the day actually com-

prised only three Welshmen, supported by one Englishman, three Scots and four Irishmen.

☞ Also listed at: B31

175 Cardiff City Football Club: the official history of 'The Bluebirds' / John Crooks. Harefield: Yore: 1992.
320p   ISBN: 0-9513321-8-X
                           BL: YK.1992.b.5840

The essential definitive history – required reading.

Carlisle United

176 The Carlisle United story: Shaddongate to Division One / Ronald Cowing, Martin Lawson, Bill Willcox. Carlisle: Lakescene Publications, 1974.
2, 80p; illus; pbk   ISBN: 0-9502120-5-9

The club was formed in 1903 – this work is worth consulting for a general overview of its history.

177 Carlisle United 50 seasons on / Keith A. Wild. 1984.
170p

Published privately

Carlisle United joined the League in 1928 to play in the Third Division (North). This book charts their League years including a golden era in the 1970s when they briefly found themselves topping the First Division.

178 Carlisle United: sixty glorious years. Carlisle: Scenic Publications, 1988.
118p; pbk

Souvenir publication celebrating the 60th anniversary of the club's entry into the League.

Charlton Athletic

179 History of Charlton Athletic 1903-1936 / 'Charltonian'. 1937.
32p; pbk

Rare ephemeral item – covers the club's 1905 foundation from a merger of several local sides.

180 History and highlights of Charlton Athletic FC 1903-1946 / Charles Cooper. 1946?

Coverage up to the year in which Charlton appeared in the FA Cup Final, losing 4-1 to Derby County.

181 Let's talk about Charlton Athletic Football Club: including football personalities and points of interest / Tom Morgan. London: Sentinel, 1946.
32p; illus; pbk
(Football handbooks. Series 1; no. 15)   BL: W.P.1144/15

An interesting series but without any detailed content.

182 Don Welsh introduces the Charlton Cup Final team: souvenir issued by the players of Charlton Athletic FC. London: Charlton Athletic Football Club, 1947.
16p; illus; pbk   BL: 7918.a.55

Following disappointment in 1946, Charlton were to triumph over Burnley in the 1947 Cup Final.

183 Charlton Athletic FC official handbook. London: Charlton Athletic Football Club, 1949-
                                               BL: P.P.2489.wkl

184 Charlton Athletic Football Club / Anthony Bristowe. London: Convoy, 1951.
122p; illus; pbk
(Famous football clubs); (Football club series)
                                               BL: 7923.f.14/1

Early and laudable attempt at a club history later to be eclipsed by more substantial works.

185 Charlton Athletic jubilee handbook 1905-1955. London: Charlton Athletic Football Club, 1955.

186 Charlton Athletic Supporters' Club annual official handbook, 1957-58. London: Charlton Athletic Supporters' Club, 1957-   BL: P.P.2489.wlh

187 Charlton Athletic FC league golden jubilee handbook 1921-1971 / Morley Farror and Harold Palmer. London?: Sprits Publications, 1971.
142p

188 The long Good Friday: the story of Charlton Athletic 1905-1990 / Richard Redden. Derby: Breedon Books, 1990.
255p; illus

Bibliography: p255   ISBN: 0-907969-67-4
                              BL: YK.1992.b.402

Extremely comprehensive and interesting study.

189 Battle for the Valley / Richard John Everitt. Welling: Voice of the Valley, 1991.
256p; illus   ISBN: 0-9518125-0-5

In 1985 Charlton vacated their long-standing ground, the Valley, to share with Crystal Palace at Selhurst Park, then later Upton Park. The arrangement was not at all popular with fans and after a hard fought battle over a number of years the club finally moved back, in 1991. This heartfelt and detailed coverage tells the full story, illustrating only too well the passions which can be stirred amongst supporters when 'moving home' is enforced. An excellent and original work.

190 The valiant 500: biographies of Charlton Athletic players past and present / Colin Cameron. Sidcup: The author, 1991.
x, 454p; illus   ISBN: 0-9517729-0-2

514 biographies of Charlton players including over 300 photographs – an excellent example of the 'who's who' style publication.

191 Home and away with Charlton Athletic, 1920-1992: a comprehensive record of line-ups, scorers and attendances of first class matches played by Charlton Athletic FC for the period 1920/21 to 1991/92 inclusive / Colin Cameron. Sidcup: The author, 1992.
vi, 446p; illus   ISBN: 0-9517729-1-0
                              BL: YK.1994.b.82

Strong on statistical content.

192 The history of Charlton Athletic: Valley of tears, Valley of joy / Richard Redden. West Wickham: Print Coordination, 1994.
272p; illus   ISBN: 0-9522652-0-6

Excellent starting point for research.

Chelsea

193 Official handbook (history) and list of fixtures 1906/07-1912/13; 1951/52-. London: Chelsea Football Club, 1906-1912; 1951-   BL: P.P.2489.wfm

Despite their current status as a 'big club', Chelsea were not around in the last century – they were not founded until 1905. These early examples of handbooks can prove hard to come by for the collector.

194 Chelsea: the story of Chelsea Football Club / Reg Groves. London: Newservice, 1947.
40p; pbk
(Famous football clubs)   BL: 7922.k.15/1

Relatively lightweight coverage eclipsed by more recent substantial publications.

195 Let's talk about Chelsea Football Club: including football personalities and points of interest / Tom Morgan. London: Sentinel, 1947.
32p; illus; pbk
(Football handbooks. Series 2; no. 37)

Interesting to the completist collector but of little value otherwise.

196   Chelsea, champions!: the story of the 1954-5 Football League champions from 1905 to their jubilee year / Albert Sewell. London: Phoenix Sports Books, 1955.
176p; illus   BL: 7921.e.123

The golden jubilee year conveniently coincided with Chelsea's only League Championship triumph. This volume celebrates both and includes narrative history and statistics – results, line-ups, appearances and goalscorers for the club's first fifty years.

197   London's Cup Final, 1967: how Chelsea and Spurs reached Wembley / Ralph Leslie Finn. London: Hale, 1967.
188p; illus   BL: X.449/2830

Whilst the rest of the country tend not to be over fond of all-London affairs, interest in the Capital is usually very high, hence this publication. Chelsea were beaten.

☞   Also listed at: B791; D12

198   A history of Chelsea Football Club / Ralph L. Finn. London: Pelham, 1969.
148p; illus   ISBN: 0-7207-0261-5

199   The Chelsea football book / edited by Albert Sewell; foreword by Dave Sexton. London: Stanley Paul, 1970.
128p; illus   ISBN: 0-09-103320-9
     BL: X.620/1721

This series ran to five volumes; each volume is in effect an account of the previous season and as such reveals details which the more general studies may lack.

200   A history of Chelsea Football Club / Ralph Leslie Finn. London: Pelham, 1970.
148p; illus   ISBN: 0-7207-026-5
     BL: X.449/3614

Rather weak on the early period – heavy concentration on post-war which is admirably covered.

201   The Chelsea football book no. 2 / edited by Albert Sewell. London: Stanley Paul, 1971.
128p; illus   BL: X.620/1721

202   The Chelsea football book no. 3 / edited by Albert Sewell. London: Stanley Paul, 1972.
128p; illus   BL: X.620/1721

203   The Chelsea football book no. 4 / edited by Albert Sewell. London: Stanley Paul, 1973.
128p; illus   BL: X.620/1721

204   The Chelsea football book no. 5 / edited by Albert Sewell. London: Stanley Paul, 1974.
128p; illus   BL: X.620/1721

205   The Chelsea story / John Moynihan; foreword by Sebastian Coe. London: Arthur Barker, 1982.
x, 173p; illus   ISBN: 0-213-16823-5
     BL: X.622/13598

Concentrates on the high spots and famous personalities from the club's history.

206   Chelsea: the real story / Brian Mears. London: Pelham, 1982.
175p; illus   ISBN: 0-7207-1425-7
     BL: X.629/18673

Unusual approach herewith presented by the Chairman of the club – very much an insider's account.

207   Chelsea FC: the first ten years 1905-1915 / Neil F. Jensen. London: Chelsea Statistics Club, 1984.
44p; pbk

A statistical record of the club's earliest days.

208   Chelsea Football Club: the full statistical story 1905-1985 / Scott Cheshire, Ron Hockings. London: R. Hockings, 1985.

This book won the Association of Football Statisticians Book of the Year award for 1985. All attendances, results, line-ups, and scorers are given for each season along with pen pictures of every player. Extremely comprehensive.

☞   Subsequent ed. B209

209   Chelsea Football Club: the full statistical story 1905-1986 / Scott Cheshire, Ron Hockings. 2nd ed. London: R. Hockings, 1986.
216p; illus   ISBN: 0-9511640-0-7
     BL: YK.1988.b.5360

☞   Previous ed. B208; subsequent ed. B210

210   Chelsea Football Club: the full statistical story, 1905-1988 / Scott Cheshire, Ron Hockings. 3rd ed. Wembley: R. Hockings, 1988.
232p; illus   ISBN: 0-9511640-1-5
     BL: YK.1989.b.4924

☞   Previous ed. B209

211   The Bridge: the history of Stamford Bridge football ground, home of Chelsea Football Club/ Colin Benson. London: Chelsea FC, 1987.
208p   ISBN: 0-9509798-1-3

Few books have been published taking one particular ground as their subject. As most clubs now have their exhaustive histories chronicled, this could become a soccer publishing trend. This is an excellent example of how it should be done – Chelsea have more material to draw from in this department than most and other club historians following suit may find their final results somewhat slimmer.

212   Chelsea FC players who's who / Scott Cheshire; photographs Ron Hockings. Stoke-on-Trent: The author, 1987.
iv, 272p; illus; pbk   ISBN: 0-9512715-0-4
     BL: YK.1990.a.4320

Comprehensive who's who – a photograph of almost every player to have made a first team appearance together with full career details.

213 Chelsea: a complete record 1905-1991 / Scott Cheshire. Derby: Breedon Books, 1991.
416p; illus
ISBN: 0-907969-87-9
BL: YK.1993.a.9227

Essential and authoritative reference text.

214 Chelsea: player by player / Peter Lovering. Enfield: Guinness, 1993.
176p; illus
ISBN: 0-85112-510-7
BL: YK.1993.b.14446

Coverage of the leading names only.

215 Chelsea: an illustrated history / Scott Cheshire. Derby: Breedon Books, 1994.
159p; illus
ISBN: 1-873626-91-6

Chester City

216 Chester FC 1885-1935. 1936.

Extremely scarce item mainly containing reminiscences of the pre-league era.

217 Keep the flag flying: Chester City 1931-52. Chester: Chester City FC, 1952.
32p; pbk

Although the club was founded in 1884, it did not enter the League until 1931 – this covers their League years rather than the early history.

218 Chester Football Club Limited celebrates fifty years of league football 1931-1981 / Terry Vickers. Chester: Chester City FC, 1981.
64p; pbk

Results of all games – strictly statistical.

Chesterfield

219 History of Chesterfield FC / Stewart Basson.

Chesterfield have a long history – their origins can be traced back to 1866 although they did not turn professional until 1891. Unfortunately they are rather poorly chronicled in print.

220 Pictures of Chesterfield's championship winning season 1984-85. Chesterfield: Chesterfield FC, 1985.
20p; illus; pbk

No text but over 30 photos.

Colchester United

221 Reminiscences of Colchester Town / Clark. 1924.

Scarce item. Colchester United were founded in 1937 as successor to the amateur club Colchester Town. This item covers the Town club. Later reprinted in facsimile in 1994.

☞ See also: B225

222 Up the City: the story of Chelmsford City FC: the story of Chelmsford City and the meteoric rise of Colchester United FC / R. A. F. Handley. Chelmsford?: Thompson, Hansley & Spurgeon, 1948.
64p; pbk

Colchester warrant 16 pages in this scarce publication, sharing coverage with Crittall Athletic, Maldon Town, and Heybridge Swifts.

☞ Also listed at: B963

223 Colchester United 1950-1990: a statistical record / Frank Grande. Norwich: Stateside Sports, 1990.
72p

Although Colchester United were formed in 1937, they did not enter the Football League until thirteen years later. This statistical record gives a season-by-season breakdown from 1950.

224 Colchester United: the official history of 'The Us' / Hal Mason. Harefield: Yore, 1993.
239p; illus
ISBN: 1-874427-50-X
BL: YK.1994.b.8468

The definitive history – essential reading.

225 Reminiscences of Colchester Town. Harefield: Yore, 1994.
40p; pbk

Facsimile reprint of the scarce 1924 booklet.

☞ See also: B221

Coventry City

226 Souvenir and brief history, with photographs, of the Coventry Football Club, past and present / Herbert Coulson. Coventry: Coventry Football Club Supporters' Association, 1920.
40p; pbk
BL: D

Scarce early historical item.

227 Let's talk about Coventry Football Club: including football personalities and points of interest / Tom Morgan. London: Sentinel, 1948.
32p; illus; pbk
(Football handbooks. Series 3; no. 55)

Part of a well-known series – lacks detail.

228 Miracle in sky blue / Marshall Stewart. Leamington Spa: Instant Publications, 1967.
85p
BL: X.619/9674

One of the less common books on Coventry published at a time when the club was at the forefront of innovatory ideas in the way football was run, presented and sold.

229 The Sky Blues: the story of Coventry City FC / Derek Henderson. London: Stanley Paul, 1968.
128p ISBN: 0-09-087480-3

Very much a tribute to the reign of Jimmy Hill as Coventry manager — little early history but concentrated coverage of the 1961-1968 era.

230 The Coventry City football book / Derek Henderson; foreword by Noel Cantwell. London: Stanley Paul, 1970.
128p; illus ISBN: 0-09-103250-4

231 Coventry City: the complete history of the club / Neville Foulger. Norwich: Wensum, 1979.
112p; illus ISBN: 0-903619-29-6

Written by the chief sports writer of the *Coventry Evening Telegraph*. Lacking in very early history but strong on post-1961 material.

232 Singers to Sky Blues: the story of Coventry City Football Club / David Brassington, Rod Dean & Don Chalk. Buckingham: Sporting & Leisure, 1986.
132p; illus; 1 plan; index ISBN: 0-86023-259-X
BL: YK.1988.b.1232

The three authors evidently have a serious love of the 'Sky Blues' — they are all members of Coventry's London-based supporters' club. Excellent balanced coverage of all eras. The curious title reflects the fact that the club was formed in 1883 by workers at the Singer bicycle factory.

233 Coventry City: a complete record 1883-1991 / Rod Dean and others. Derby: Breedon Books, 1991.
416p; illus ISBN: 0-907969-88-7
BL: YK.1993.a.9601

One of a highly regarded series — essential reading.

234 Coventry City footballers, 1908-1993: the complete who's who / Martin and Paul O'Connor. Harefield: Yore, 1993.
223p; illus ISBN: 1-874427-45-3
BL: YK.1994.b.8158

This is the best research volume for coverage of the players from all eras.

Crewe Alexandra

235 Crewe Alex: 100 years up. Crewe?: Rolls Royce Motors Ltd, 1977.
28p; pbk

Disappointingly light for a centenary publication — heavy concentration on the current season and many advertisements.

Crystal Palace

236 Let's talk about Crystal Palace Football Club: including football personalities and points of interest / Tom Morgan. London: Sentinel, 1948.
32p; illus; pbk
(Football handbooks. Series 3; no. 58)

Lacks serious research content.

237 Crystal Palace jubilee handbook 1954-55. London: Crystal Palace FC, 1954.

238 The Crystal Palace story / Roy Peskett. London: Roy Peskett, 1969.
144p; illus ISBN: 0-9501039-0-X
BL: X.441/1348

Earliest attempt at a history of the club written to coincide with winning promotion to the First Division.

239 Crystal Palace official annual / edited by Harry Harris. Ilford: Circle Publications, 1979-1980.
107p; illus ISSN: 0261-6882
BL: P.441/935

Particularly high on illustrative content.

240 There and back again: Crystal Palace 1969-1979. London: Crystal Palace FC, 1979.
48p; pbk

The title reflects the club's mixed fortunes during this period — from the First Division they slumped to the Third, then back again in 1979.

241 Crystal Palace: a complete record 1905-1989 / Mike Purkiss. Derby: Breedon Books, 1989.
416p; illus ISBN: 0-907969-54-2

Excellent definitive study. The start date of 1905 represents the foundation date of the modern club, although the first Crystal Palace team was actually founded back in 1861 by staff working at the Great Exhibition in Joseph Paxton's celebrated Crystal Palace structure.

242 Crystal Palace FC, 1969-1990: a biased commentary / written and illustrated by Chris Winter. London: Red Post, 1990.
95p; illus; pbk

ISBN: 0-9516636-0-7
BL: YK.1992.b.4061

Includes line drawings of leading players and personalities.

243 Crystal Palace Football Club: the A-Z / Nigel Sands. Buckingham: Sporting and Leisure, 1990.
108p; illus; index

ISBN: 0-86023-483-5
BL: YK.1991.b.5289

Reverend Nigel Sands is one of Crystal Palace's most loyal and celebrated fans, also their most prolific historian of recent years. This is an interesting mixture of trivia, records and other oddments.

244 No fishcakes on matchdays: the inside story of Crystal Palace's remarkable 1989-90 season / Deano Standing. London: Rosters, 1990.

A delightfully titled study of the season in which Palace regained their First Division status yet again, this time under manager Steve Coppell. Quite why the said fishy comestibles were declared unavailable remains a mystery – pea mixes all round no doubt!

245 The Palace centurions: the players with 100+ first-class appearances / Nigel Sands. Buckingham: Sporting & Leisure, 1991.
126p; illus; index

ISBN: 0-86023-497-5
BL: YK.1991.b.8230

Excellent study of all the leading players from the club's long history.

246 The Coppell campaigns 1984-1992 / Nigel Sands. Whittlebury: Sporting & Leisure, 1992.
132p; illus; index

ISBN: 0-86023-501-7
BL: YK.1993.b.1190

The writing Reverend knows his Palace history backwards and a shrewd eye for market segmentation has enabled him to publish on an ongoing basis, taking a slightly different approach each time. This covers the years under Steve Coppell's management up to the year in which the club played in the first ever Premier League prior to speedy relegation at the end of their first campaign.

247 Palace promotions: the club's eight promotion seasons, 1905-06 to 1988-89 / Nigel Sands. Whittlebury: Sporting & Leisure, 1993.
160p; illus; index

BL: YK.1993.b.14445

Concentrates on Palace's triumphs throughout their history – unfortunately the club has something of the yo-yo tendency in its make-up and the odd reference to relegation inevitably creeps in from time to time. Despite the optimistic title, neutral observers would be wrong to assume that the club now plays in the Nirvana League.

248 We all follow the Palace / edited and designed by Tony Matthews. London: Eagle Eye, 1993.
331p; pbk

ISBN: 0-9522221-0-8
BL: YK.1994.b.13345

Essential reference work best used in conjunction with other key texts.

249 Palace parade: the most memorable matches 1984-1994 / Nigel Sands. Whittlebury: Sporting & Leisure, 1994.
160p; illus; index
Coverage of an eventful decade.

250 Crystal Palace FC 1905-1995 / Nigel Sands. Whittlebury: Sporting & Leisure Press, 1995.

This sixth offering from Palace's 'celebrity' supporter covers the entire history of the club and is an essential reference work.

Darlington

251 Darlington 1883-1983 / Frank Tweddle. 1983?

Darlington are one of the less chronicled clubs. They were founded in 1883 and for many years played as a leading amateur side before joining the League in 1921. This is their centenary publication.

Derby County

252 The Derbyshire football guide for seasons 1884-1888 / edited by Robert J. Smith and 'Argus'. Derby, 1884-1887.
BL: P.P.2489.wgd
Very scarce early publications which first appeared in 1884, the year Derby County was formed. These may yield some lesser known material.

253 The annual Athletic Festival: programme. Derby: Derby County Football Club 1887-
BL: D
Extremely scarce ephemeral item of interest to the completist collector.

254 Derbyshire football guide . . . season 1910-11- / edited by Edmund F. Hind. Chesterfield: 1910-
BL: P.P.2489.wgk

255 Derby County: cup winners autographed souvenir brochure. Derby: Derby County Football Club, 1946.
11p; pbk
Slimline brochure published to celebrate the club's 1946 FA Cup Final victory. Scarce but certainly obtainable from time to time via specialist dealers' catalogues.

256 Let's talk about Derby County Football Club: including football personalities and points of interest / Tom Morgan. London: Sentinel, 1946.
32p; illus; pbk
(Football handbooks. Series 1; no. 1)   BL: W.P.1144/1
Tom Morgan, sports editor of The People chose Derby County as number one in this extensive series of booklets. The item is curious as a collector's piece but extremely limited in content.

257 The Derby County football book no. 1 / edited by George Edwards. London: Stanley Paul, 1970.
128p; illus
ISBN: 0-09-103260-1

258 The Derby County football book no. 2 / edited by George Edwards. London: Stanley Paul, 1971.
128p; illus
ISBN: 0-09-108330-3

259 Champions again!: Derby County 1967-75 / Gerald Mortimer. Manchester: Derek Hodgson, 1975.
2, 78p; illus; pbk
ISBN: 0-9502837-3-8
BL: X.619/16963
In 1967 Brian Clough and Peter Taylor arrived as managers to spark off an exciting era. The League Championship season of 1972 is covered here and the book concludes with another title under the management of Dave Mackay in 1975.

260 The Derby County story / Anton Rippon. Derby: Breedon Books, 1983.
104p; illus; pbk
ISBN: 0-907969-03-8
Good illustrated history.

261 Derby County: the complete record, 1884-1984 / Gerald Mortimer. Derby: Breedon Books, 1984.
352p; illus
ISBN: 0-907969-04-6
Whilst this is undoubtedly an important and essential item for Derby County historians, its true significance lies in a publishing sense. This was the first in the Complete Record series from Breedon Books – not only did it spawn many more excellent titles in the same series, but it also prompted a veritable boom in the number of historically-based soccer books created. In this way, 1984 was a most important year in football publishing.

262 There was some football too: 100 years of Derby County / Tony Francis. Derby: Derby County Football Club, 1984.
223p
This is a substantial but relatively scarce publication written from an interesting angle – whilst it touches on the achievements of the team, it favours specific coverage of behind the scenes activity and boardroom politics. Derby County provide more material than most in this respect!

263 Derby County: the complete record 1985 supplement / Gerald Mortimer. Derby: Breedon Books, 1985.
112p
ISBN: 0-907969-11-9

264 Derby County: a complete record 1884-1988 / Gerald Mortimer. Derby: Breedon Books, 1988.
448p; illus
ISBN: 0-907969-39-9
BL: YK.1992.a.8192

265 The Derby County story told in pictures / David Thornton. Leeds: D. & J. Thornton, 1989.
16p; chiefly illus; pbk
ISBN: 0-907339-31-X
BL: YK.1990.a.6425
A rather unusual publication aimed effectively at the juvenile market. The history of the club is told entirely through cartoon strips. The narrative is rather more accurate than some of the artistic representations.

266 The fall and rise of Derby County FC throughout the 1980s. Derby: Derbyshire Sport, 1989.
44p; pbk
Extremely lightweight.

267 The Derby County quiz book / P. Whyte. London: Rosters, 1990.
160p; illus; pbk   ISBN: 0-948032-19-7

268 The Derby County story, 1884-1991 / Gerald Mortimer. Derby: Breedon Books, 1991.
256p; illus   ISBN: 0-907969-97-6
Very well informed coverage from the chief sports writer of the *Derby Evening Telegraph*.

269 The who's who of Derby County / Gerald Mortimer. Derby: Breedon Books, 1992.
256p; illus   ISBN: 1-873626-31-2
                               BL: YK.1994.b.4799
Definitive study of players and personalities.

270 The great days of Derby County / edited by Anton Rippon; research by Pip Southall. Derby: Breedon Books, 1993.
240p; illus   ISBN: 1-873626-58-4
Includes material not previously featured in earlier volumes.

271 The book of Derby County / edited by Anton Rippon. Derby: Breedon Books, 1994.
182p; illus   ISBN: 1-873626-89-4
Another publication from the Breedon stable presenting much of the same along with some new material.

Doncaster Rovers

272 The story of Doncaster Rovers Football Club 1879-1949 / J. C. Morris. Doncaster: Doncaster Rovers Supporters' Club, 1949.
34p; illus; pbk
Includes numerous team photos in a concise history.

273 Doncaster Rovers facts and figures: a statistical history / compiled by Leigh Edwards and Ernest Wiles. Doncaster?: The authors, 1989.
76p; pbk

274 When Doherty was king / Paul Gilligan. Doncaster?: The author, 1989.
72p; pbk
    Limited ed of 500 copies
Covers the 1949/50 season when the club won promotion from Division Three (North) under the management of Peter Doherty. Includes a pull-out team photo.

275 The winter of '47 / Paul Gilligan. 1989.
68p
Story of the club's 1946/47 Third Division (North) title winning campaign when they amassed 72 points — they won 18 out of 21 away fixtures and kept a clean sheet in 20 games. Includes a pull-out team photograph.

276 Donny: the official history of Doncaster Rovers FC / Tony Bluff and Barry Watson. Harefield: Yore, 1994.
240p; illus   ISBN: 1-874427-55-0
                               BL: YK.1995.b.5114
Substantial definitive history covering all eras from the club's foundation in 1879 — an essential reference work.

277 Rovers in focus 1879-1994 / Paul Gilligan. Doncaster?: The author, 1994.
96p; illus; pbk
Concentrates on pictorial representations of the club's history supported by narrative.

Everton

278 History of the Everton Football Club, 1878-9-1928-9 / Thomas Keates. Liverpool: Thomas Brakell, 1929.
xiv, 155p; illus   BL: 7921.bb.14
Very few clubs were the subject of substantial early histories — Everton were one of the exceptions. This is well worth consultation and is a scarce, keenly sought, collector's item.

279 Let's talk about Everton Football Club: including football personalities and points of interest / Tom Morgan. London: Sentinel, 1946.
32p; illus; pbk
(Football handbooks. Series 1; no. 4)   BL: W.P.1144/4
Written to the standard format typical of this series — little in the way of original content.

280　Everton Football Club: League champions 1962-63,
　　contenders for the European Cup 1963-64. Liverpool:
　　Everton Football Club?, 1963?
　　60p; pbk

　　　Published to celebrate Everton's 1962-63 Champion-
　　　ship success and their entry into the European Cup
　　　at a time when travelling to overseas games was re-
　　　garded as something of a novelty.

281　Football on Merseyside / Percy Marshall Young.
　　London: Stanley Paul, 1963.
　　215p; illus　　　　　　　　　　　　　BL: 7926.n.47

　　　A detailed history of Everton, Liverpool, Tranmere,
　　　and New Brighton

　　☞　Also listed at: B386, B818, B1019

282　The Everton football book / Derek Hodgson. London:
　　Stanley Paul, 1970.
　　128p; illus　　　　　　　　　　ISBN: 0-09-103220-2

283　The Daily Express A-Z of Mersey soccer / John Keith
　　and Peter Thomas. London: Beaverbrook Newspapers,
　　1973.
　　141p; illus

　　　Covers Everton as well as the other Merseyside
　　　teams.

　　☞　Also listed at: B388, B819

284　Everton FC official annual. Ilford: Circle Publications,
　　1978-
　　illus　　　　　　　　　　　　　BL: P.441/915

285　Everton: the official centenary history / John Roberts;
　　foreword by Joe Mercer. London: Mayflower, 1978.
　　240p; illus; index; pbk　　　　ISBN: 0-583-12832-7
　　　　　　　　　　　　　　　　　　BL: X.619/18974

　　　The definitive work at the time of publication – still
　　　worthy of consultation.

286　The Everton story / Derek Hodgson. London: Arthur
　　Barker, 1979.
　　143p; illus　　　　　　　　　ISBN: 0-213-16716-6
　　　　　　　　　　　　　　　　　BL: X.620/18767

287　The Blues and the Reds: a history of the Liverpool and
　　Everton football clubs / Tony Mason. Liverpool:
　　Historic Society of Lancashire & Cheshire, 1985.
　　24p; pbk

　　　Short but scholarly.

　　☞　Also listed at: B399

288　Everton: a complete record 1878-1985 / Ian Ross.
　　Derby: Breedon Books, 1985.
　　400p; illus　　　　　　　　　ISBN: 0-907969-10-0

　　　Definitive coverage, later updated.

289　Everton / Matthew Graham. Twickenham: Hamlyn,
　　1986.
　　124p; illus, coat of arms; index　　　ISBN: 0-600-50238-4
　　　　　　　　　　　　　　　　　　　BL: YK.1987.b.6340

　　☞　Subsequent ed. B290

290　Everton / Matthew Graham. Enlarged 1987
　　championship ed. Twickenham: Hamlyn, 1987.
　　140p; illus, coat of arms; index　　　ISBN: 0-600-55633-6
　　　　　　　　　　　　　　　　　　　BL: YK.1988.b.1472

　　☞　Previous ed. B289

291　The Everton quiz book / compiled by Alex Hosie.
　　Edinburgh: Mainstream, 1987.
　　176p; illus; pbk　　　　　　　　ISBN: 1-85158-093-X
　　　　　　　　　　　　　　　　　BL: YK.1989.a.3661

　　　1,001 questions and answers

292　Forever Everton: the official illustrated history of
　　Everton FC / Stephen F. Kelly. London: Macdonald,
　　1987.
　　192p; illus; index
　　　Bibliography: p92　　　　　　ISBN: 0-356-15055-0
　　　　　　　　　　　　　　　　　BL: YK.1988.b.7

　　　Very strong on photographic content.

293　Everton: a complete record 1878-1988 / Ian Ross &
　　Gordon Smailes. Derby: Breedon Books, 1988.
　　400p; illus　　　　　　　　　ISBN: 0-907969-43-7
　　　　　　　　　　　　　　　　　BL: YK.1991.a.10598

　　　Update of an essential work.

294　The great 1962-1988 derbies Everton v Liverpool: a
　　celebration of the Merseyside Derby / Brian Barwick,
　　Gerald Sinstadt. London: BBC Books, 1988.
　　156p; illus; index　　　　　　ISBN: 0-563-20678-0
　　　　　　　　　　　　　　　　　BL: YK.1990.b.1535

　　　Everton v Liverpool has long been regarded as one of
　　　the truly classic fixtures, although it has produced
　　　its fair share of stalemate 0-0 draws for the TV
　　　cameras. This is a focused study of the history of
　　　the fixture from 1962.

　　☞　Also listed at: B408

295　Everton / David Prentice and Craig Warwick. London:
　　Purnell, 1989.
　　96p; illus
　　　　ISBN: 0-361-08510-9 (cased) ● ISBN: 0-361-08511-7 (pbk)
　　　　　　BL: YK.1990.a.162-1 ● BL: YK.1989.a.4064

296　Everton greats / Ken Rogers. Edinburgh: Sportsprint in
　　association with Liverpool Echo, 1989.
　　v, 170p; illus; pbk　　　　　　ISBN: 0-85976-274-2
　　　　　　　　　　　　　　　　　BL: YK.1990.a.3364

　　　Pieces on selected greats from Everton's history,
　　　rather than a comprehensive who's who.

297 Everton: player by player / Ivan Ponting. Enfield:
Guinness, 1992.
176p; illus

ISBN: 0-85112-567-0
BL: YK.1993.b.3502

The players since 1958/59.

298 One hundred years of Goodison glory: the official centenary
history / Ken Rogers. Derby: Breedon Books, 1992.
239p; illus

ISBN: 1-873626-11-8
BL: YK.1993.b.8886

299 Everton: a complete record 1878-1993 / Ian Ross &
Gordon Smailes. Derby: Breedon Books, 1993.
416p; illus

ISBN: 1-873626-43-6
BL: YK.1994.a.3691

300 Three sides of the Mersey: an oral history of Everton,
Liverpool and Tranmere Rovers / Rogan Taylor and
Andrew Ward, with John Williams. London: Robson,
1993.
290p; illus

ISBN: 0-86051-871-X
BL: YK.1995.b.1019

An original approach presenting material which the
standard works don't reveal.

☞ Also listed at: B430; B822

Exeter City

301 Exeter City: a complete record 1904-1990 / Maurice
Golesworthy, Garth Dykes, Alex Wilson. Derby:
Breedon Books, 1990.
384p; illus

ISBN: 0-907969-68-2
BL: YK.1992.a.9820

An essential work of reference which demonstrates
how smaller clubs may, through dedicated research,
be chronicled in detail. Unfortunately, Alex Wilson died
before he could see the final result but he would have
had justifiable cause to be proud of his and his col-
leagues' efforts. Published in the year in which the
club won the Division Four Championship.

302 Exeter City: a file of fascinating football facts / Mike
Blackstone. Exeter: Obelisk, 1992.
112p; illus; pbk

ISBN: 0-946651-53-1
BL: YK.1992.a.11187

A rather more light-hearted study and an excellent
companion volume to the 'Complete Record'. The A-Z
format presents numerous entertaining anecdotes
from 'Abandoned matches' to 'Zider', all well illustrated with photographs. The author was editor of
the award-winning programme of Exmouth Town and
here uses his trained eye to excellent effect.

Fulham

303 Let's talk about Fulham Football Club: including football
personalities and points of interest / Tom Morgan.
London: Sentinel, 1947.
32p; illus; pbk
(Football handbooks. Series 2; no. 24)
Ephemeral booklet short on serious content.

304 Foundation history of the Fulham Football Club and
record of ex-players, local clubs and reminiscences / H.
D. Shrimpton. London: J. B. Shears, 1950.
27p; pbk

As early efforts at club histories generally go, this
example is above average. It was probably helped by
the fact that Shrimpton was an ex-player and secretary of the club. The history covers the club's
formation and early years using an informal chatty
style with a number of anecdotal interludes. Likely to
bear fruit for all researchers of the club's formative
days. If only every club was given a similar treatment . . .

305 Fulham we love you: a supporter's history of Fulham FC
/ Morgan D. Phillips. London: The author, 1976.
52p; illus; pbk

Bibliography: p51

ISBN: 0-9505355-0-8
BL: X.619/17180

Relatively lightweight but rightly claims to be the first complete history of the club. Later to be eclipsed by more substantial studies.

306 A history of Fulham Football Club 1879-1979 / Dennis Turner. London: Fulham Football Club, 1979.
203p; illus   BL: X.629/22119

Certainly comprehensive to the date of publication but the same author's 'Complete Record' would be a better starting point for most research projects.

307 Fulham: a complete record 1879-1987 / Dennis Turner & Alex White. Derby: Breedon Books, 1987.
432p; illus   ISBN: 0-907969-28-3
                                 BL: YK.1991.a.12515

Ideal for use as a key historical text — extremely comprehensive.

308 Fulham's golden years: a pictorial memoir of Fulham Football Club 1958-1983 / Ken Coton. Twickenham: Ashwater, 1992.
288p; illus   ISBN: 0-9515217-2-1
                                 BL: YK.1993.b.8497

Adds a visual flavour to the historical narrative found in other books — well worth consulting.

309 Cottage chronicles: an anecdotal history of Fulham Football Club / edited by Dennis Turner. London?: Northdown, 1994.
288p; illus

Very entertaining — includes an abundance of fascinating material, fun items and lesser known episodes from the club's history.

Gillingham

310 Gillingham Football Club / Roger Triggs. Gillingham: Gillingham Public Libraries, 1973.
31p; pbk   ISBN: 0-903316-07-2

Part of a series of local study publications from Gillingham Library. The same author went on to publish more definitive accounts of the club — 'giant oaks from little acorns grow'.

311 The 'Gills' / Tony Conway; photographs by Roger Hills with Alan Cuff and Tess May; statistics provided by Roger Triggs. Gillingham: Meresborough, 1980.
88p; illus   ISBN: 0-905270-26-6
                                 BL: X.622/17011

312 Gillingham Football Club: a chronology 1893-1984 / compiled by Roger Triggs. Maidstone: Kent County Library, 1984.
62p; illus; pbk
(Gillingham local history series; no. 13)
                                 BL: YK.1990.b.5533

313 Priestfield profiles: a who's who of Gillingham's Football League players 1950-1988 / Roger Triggs. Gillingham: The author, 1988.
145p; illus; pbk   ISBN: 0-9514092-0-4
                                 BL: YK.1992.a.9695

Definitive study of players and personalities.

314 Home of the shouting men: the complete history of Gillingham 1893-1993 / Andy Bradley and Roger Triggs. Gillingham: Gillingham FC, 1994.
450p   ISBN: 0-9523361-0-3

An essential research volume. Traces the club's beginnings as Excelsior in 1893, their turn to professionalism as New Brompton in 1894, and their final transformation to Gillingham in 1913.

Grimsby Town

315 Let's talk about Grimsby Town Football Club: including football personalities and points of interest / Tom Morgan. London: Sentinel, 1947.
32p; illus; pbk
(Football handbooks. Series 2; no. 38)

One of a well known series by the sports editor of The People — very little detail.

316 Grimsby Town FC centenary brochure 1878-1978 / edited by Charles Ekberg. Grimsby: Grimsby Town FC, 1978.
48p; illus; pbk

Includes a brief history and rather a lot of advertising. Later works give a much better overview.

317 The Mariners: the story of Grimsby Town Football Club / Charles Ekberg & Sid Woodhead. Buckingham: Sporting and Leisure, 1983.
148p; illus; index   ISBN: 0-86023-176-3
                                 BL: X.622/16772

Well illustrated text with good material on the early years. The club were founded in 1878 as Grimsby Pel-

ham but changed their name to Grimsby Town a year
later; they joined the League in 1892.

318   A who's who of Grimsby Town AFC 1890-1985 /
Douglas Lamming. Beverley: Hutton, 1985.
202p; illus; pbk
                              ISBN: 0-907033-34-2
                              BL: YK.1987.a.2908

Extremely comprehensive coverage of players and
personalities from the club's history — 756 pen pictures in all.

319   Grimsby Town: a complete record 1878-1989 / Les
Triggs with David Hepton and Sid Woodhead. Derby:
Breedon Books, 1989.
416p; illus
                              ISBN: 0-907969-46-1
                              BL: YK.1993.a.104

The usual excellent coverage from the 'Complete Record' series — an essential work of reference.

320   Grimsby Town Football Club: a pictorial history / Geoff
Ford. Runcorn: Archive, 1989.
132p; illus; pbk
                              ISBN: 0-948946-62-8

200 photographs with little text — the bias is very
much towards the post-war era.

321   Grimsby Town quiz book / Sid Woodhead and Robert
Briggs. Ipswich: Almeida, 1991.
36p; illus; pbk

This is the first in a series which was later to cover a
number of clubs.

322   Two great years of the Mariners: 1989-91 / Neville J.
Sullivan. Newark: Partners, 1991.
36p; illus; pbk

Promotion to Division Three, then Division Two and finally to Division One in 1991/92 marked an excellent
period for the club.

323   Grimsby Town seasons 1983-84 to 1992-93:
season-by-season commentary / Rob Briggs; statistics
and history Mike Ross; editors, Michael Robinson, John
Robinson & Philip Norminton. Cleethorpes: Soccer
Book Publishing, 1993.
52p; illus; pbk
(The 10 seasons series)
                              ISBN: 0-94708-29-9
                              BL: YK.1994.a.3340

Part of a series covering the last ten seasons of a
number of clubs — good statistical content.

Hartlepool United

324   Hartlepool United / Ed Law. Derby: Breedon Books,
1989.
129p; illus
                              ISBN: 0-907969-57-7
                              BL: YK.1992.b.9261

The club were founded as Hartlepools United and retained that name until 1968, becoming simply

Hartlepool until 1977. They joined the League in 1921
and have spent almost their entire life in the bottom
reaches. This is the definitive work on the club.

Hereford United

325   Hereford United FC: 30 years of Southern League
football / Dave Hornsby. Hereford: Hereford United
FC, 1968.
32p; pbk

Whilst the club were formed in 1924, they only gradu-
ated to league football in 1972 — this publication
covers their non-league days only.

326   Hereford United for League status. Hereford: Hereford
United FC, 1970.
12p; pbk

Effectively a prospectus staking their claim for a
place in the Football League.

327   Hereford United giantkillers / Berry Griffiths and Peter
Manders. Hereford: Hereford United FC, 1972.
20p; pbk

During the 1971/72 season the club became one of the
most famous giantkillers of the modern era when
they beat Newcastle United 2-1 in the third round of
the FA Cup. Mass exposure on BBC's Match of the
Day has ensured this will remain an enduring image.

328   The Hereford United story: fifty years at Edgar Street /
John Williamson. Hereford: Hereford Printing Co., 1974.
160p

Coverage of all eras is presented in this essential work.
The club were formed in 1924 and played minor league
football until election to the Football League in 1972.

Huddersfield Town

329   Huddersfield Town: a history of the club and the life
story of Billy Smith. 1924.

The club were formed in 1908, which was unusually
late for a team which was later to become one of the
legends of football. Billy Smith scored the winning
goal in the 1921-22 FA Cup Final from a penalty — the
first spot-kick to decide a cup final. This scarce item
covers the tenure of Herbert Chapman as manager
from 1921 to 1925, a period which effectively made
the club into a great one. Billy Smith himself played
520 times for the club between 1914 and 1934.

330   Huddersfield Town souvenir brochure. Huddersfield:
Huddersfield Town FC, 1926.

Extremely scarce ephemeral publication celebrating
the club's magnificent feat in winning the Football
League Championship three times in a row.

331 Huddersfield Town FC: coming of age souvenir.
Huddersfield: Huddersfield Town FC, 1930.

Covers the seasons 1908/09 to 1929/30.

332 Let's talk about Huddersfield Town Football Club:
including football personalities and points of interest /
Tom Morgan. London: Sentinel, 1946.
32p; illus; pbk
(Football handbooks. Series 1; no. 11)   BL: W.P.1144/11

*Not for the serious historian, but an interesting col-
lector's item nonetheless.*

333 Huddersfield Town FC: the wonder club of football /
Robert Arnott. 1953.
68p

*The club were a First Division side from 1920 to 1952,
winning the Championship three years in a row during
the 1920s. This publication effectively marked the beginning of a period of decline.*

334 Huddersfield Town May 1951 to August 1954: the
complete record / Bill Carter. Huddersfield?: The
author, 1954.
64p

*Commentary and statistics. The use of the term
'complete record' in the title was uncommon at the
time and presaged one of the best known series of recent years.*

335 Huddersfield Town AFC Ltd: jubilee year 1958
brochure. Huddersfield: Huddersfield Town Supporters
Association, 1958.
68p; pbk

336 Huddersfield Town Association Football Club.
Huddersfield: Kirklees Libraries & Arts Division, 1984.
4p; illus; unbound
(Information sheet / Kirklees Libraries; no. 5)
BL: X.805/6956

Curious ephemeral item.

337 Huddersfield Town 75 years on: a history of one of the
country's greatest football clubs / George S. Binns.
Huddersfield Town AFC, 1984.
434p

*Excellent work – this volume won the 1984 AFS
award. An essential reference text.*

338 Huddersfield Town: a complete record 1910-1990 /
Terry Frost. Derby: Breedon Books, 1990.
416p; illus   ISBN: 0-907969-64-X
BL: YK.1992.a.10720

Definitive work of reference.

339 Leeds Road: home of my dreams / Ian M. C. Thomas.
Huddersfield: Huddersfield Town FC, 1994.
114p; illus

*Published to commemorate the last game at Leeds
Road. Includes many photos of the ground itself.*

Hull City

340 Let's talk about Hull City Football Club: including
football personalities and points of interest / Tom
Morgan. London: Sentinel, 1948.
32p; illus; pbk
(Football handbooks. Series 3; no. 60)

Early item of interest but short on detail.

341 A who's who of Hull City AFC 1904-1984 / Douglas
Lamming. Beverley: Hutton, 1984.
146p; illus; pbk   ISBN: 0-907033-20-2
BL: YK.1987.a.1793

*An excellent study of the players. The numerous pen
pictures are supported by photographs and line
drawings.*

342 Hull City: a complete record, 1904-1989 / Chris Elton.
Derby: Breedon Books, 1989.
416p; illus   ISBN: 0-907969-49-6
BL: YK.1992.a.10153

*Essential definitive study charting the club's growth
in the midst of a rugby stronghold from the year of
formation to the present.*

Ipswich Town

343 Ipswich Town quiz book / John Eastwood.

344 Up the town: an illustrated history of Ipswich Town
Football Club / Ken Rice. Norwich: Wensum, 1973.
112p; illus   ISBN: 0-903619-05-9

*Earliest study of the club – now relatively difficult to
obtain through specialist dealers.*

345 Ipswich Town football book no. 1. / edited by Ken Rice & Neal Manning. Norwich: Wensum, 1974.
96p; illus; pbk   ISBN: 0-903619-12-1

346 Ipswich Town annual / Mel Henderson. Hainault: Circle, 1977-
96p; illus; pbk   ISSN: 0141-156X
         BL: P.441/846

347 The men who made the Town: the official history of Ipswich Town FC since 1878 / John Eastwood and Tony Moyse. Ipswich: Almeida Books, 1986.
352p

> *Annual supplements issued by Ipswich Town FC 1987-1993 with editorial assistance from Bryan Knights and Dave Allard*

This excellent study won an award from the Association of Football Statisticians. It includes a 200 page season-by-season history followed by a detailed who's who and a comprehensive statistical record — essential reference reading.

348 Ipswich Town: back in the big time / edited by Mike Noye. Ipswich: Ipswich Town FC, 1992.
48p; pbk

After a period of exile in Division Two from 1986-1992, the club regained their place in the top flight — hence the title of this publication.

Leeds United

349 Let's talk about Leeds Football Club: including football personalities and points of interest / Tom Morgan. London: Sentinel, 1947.
32p; illus; pbk
(Football handbooks. Series 2; no. 31)
Scarce but very limited in content.

350 Leeds United book of football no. 1. London: Souvenir, 1969.
144p; illus   ISBN: 0-285-50265-4
Includes contributions from the playing squad.

351 Leeds United & Don Revie / Eric Thornton. London: Hale, 1970.
185p; illus   ISBN: 0-7091-1873-2
Coverage of the entire Don Revie era to this date.

352 Leeds United book of football no. 2. London: Souvenir, 1970.
138p; illus   ISBN: 0-285-50287-5

353 The Leeds United story / Jason Tomas. London: Arthur Barker, 1971.
117p; illus   ISBN: 0-213-00498-4
The story of the club largely through the 1960s.

354 12 at the top: the story in words and pictures of Leeds United's great years / Colin S. Jeffrey. 1977.
28p; pbk

Leeds were League champions in 1968/69 and 1973/74, FA Cup winners in 1972 and League Cup winners in 1967/68. European appearances and trophies complete a most successful era for the club. This small publication celebrates this period.

355 Leeds United: the official history of the club / Don Warters. Norwich: Wensum, 1979.
90p; illus   ISBN: 0-903619-32-6
Informative coverage with statistics and photographs.

356 Leeds United (including Leeds City), 1905-1978: results, league tables, would you believe it items / Norman Lovett. Hull: British Programme Collectors Club, 1980.
84p; pbk
(Facts and figures on the Football League clubs; no. 1)
     ISBN: 0-9504273-2-2
     BL: X.0629/552(1)

Essentially a season-by-season statistical compilation — one of an idiosyncratic little series.

357 Leeds United: a complete record, 1919-1986 / Martin Jarred, Malcolm Macdonald. Derby: Breedon Books, 1987.
432p; illus   ISBN: 0-907969-17-8
     BL: YK.1990.a.2330

Definitive study of the club. Includes coverage of Leeds City, formed in 1904 and disbanded by order of the FA in 1919 following allegations of illegal payments. Leeds United were formed in 1919 and joined Division Two of the Football League in 1920.

358 Leeds United: a complete record 1919-1989 (includes Leeds City 1904-1919) / Martin Jarred & Malcolm Macdonald. Derby: Breedon Books, 1989.
416p; illus   ISBN: 0-907969-50-X
     BL: YK.1992.a.3537

Update of an essential work.

359 Leeds United: a complete record 1919-1990 (includes Leeds City 1904-1919) / Martin Jarred, Malcolm Macdonald. Derby: Breedon Books, 1990.
416p; illus   ISBN: 0-907969-78-X
     BL: YK.1991.a.13077

360 The Leeds United cup book / Martin Jarred & Malcolm Macdonald. Derby: Breedon Books, 1992?
256p; illus   ISBN: 0-907969-99-2
     BL: YK.1993.b.13398

Covers every FA Cup game from 1904 plus all the League Cup matches.

361 Leeds United: player by player / Andrew Mourant. Enfield: Guinness, 1992.
160p; illus   ISBN: 0-85112-568-9
     BL: YK.1992.b.8424

All the players from 1961 to date.

362 The Leeds United story / Malcolm Macdonald & Martin Jarred. Derby: Breedon Books, 1992.
251p; illus   ISBN: 1-873626-13-4
                                BL: YK.1993.b.7460

Excellent recent study worthy of consultation.

363 Leeds United: the return to glory / Ian Ross. Edinburgh: Mainstream, 1992.
174p; illus   ISBN: 1-85158-508-7
                                BL: YK.1993.b.10942

364 The origin and development of football in Leeds / Mike Green. Leeds?: The author, 1992.
40p; illus, maps; pbk

Covers the early years up to 1905. A scholarly look at how football developed in this essentially rugby stronghold, backed up by maps, pictures, photographs and other memorabilia.

365 Leeds United: seasons, 1983-84 to 1992-93 / season-by-season commentary by Don Warters; statistics and history by Mike Ross; editors, Michael Robinson, John Robinson & Philip Norminton. Cleethorpes: Soccer Book Publishing, 1993.
52p; illus; pbk
(The 10 seasons series)
                                ISBN: 0-947808-31-0

366 The Elland Road encyclopedia: A-Z of Leeds United FC / Paul Harrison. Edinburgh: Mainstream, 1994.
192p; pbk   ISBN: 1-85158-675-X

368 Let's talk about Leicester City Football Club: including football personalities and points of interest / Tom Morgan. London: Sentinel, 1948.
32p; illus; pbk
(Football handbooks. Series 3; no. 49)
Lightweight content only.

369 A history of Leicester City Football Club / Robert Folliard. Hornchurch: Ian Henry, 1980.
30p; illus; pbk   ISBN: 0-86025-700-2
                                BL: X.629/14803

Relatively lightweight with idiosyncratic observations.

370 Leicester City centenary brochure. Leicester: Leicester City Football Club?, 1984.
50p

371 Leicester City Football Club centenary 1884-1984 / Julian Baskomb, Mark Chaplin and Steve Lambden; edited by Julian Baskomb. Leicester: The Club, 1984.
144p; illus
Well-informed study with many photographs.

372 Of fossils & foxes: the official history of Leicester City Football Club / Dave Smith and Paul Taylor. Leicester: ACL Colour Print & Polar, 1989.
384p; illus   ISBN: 0-9514862-0-9
                                BL: YK.1992.b.4928

First class definitive study including a complete who's who section – an essential research tool.

Leicester City

Leyton Orient

367 From Fosse to City: a comprehensive and pictorial record of Leicester's senior soccer club from 1884 to 1948 / Noel Tarbottom. Leicester: Leicester Evening Mail, 1948.
160p; illus

Rare item – traces the club's history from their formation as Leicester Fosse to the early post-war years.

373 Orient FC: a pictorial history / Neil Kaufman and Alan Ravenhill. London: Jupiter Books, 1974.
116p; illus   ISBN: 0-904041-10-7
                                BL: X.620/8061

Excellent on pictorial content but also contains detailed statistics.

374 One hundred years of Orient: centenary handbook 1881-1981 / Neil Kaufman. London: Leyton Orient Football Club, 1981.
48p; pbk

375 Leyton Orient: a complete record 1881-1990 / Neil Kaufman, Alan Ravenhill. Derby: Breedon Books, 1990.
400p; illus
ISBN: 0-907969-66-6
BL: YK.1992.a.8962

The club are one of the less chronicled sides but this volume alone provides the researcher with all the relevant information. From the 1881 formation out of the Glyn Cricket Club at Homerton Theological College, the club developed into the Orient Football Club in 1888 due to close connections amongst certain of the players with the Orient Shipping Line. In one of the game's more complicated tales of nomenclature the titles Clapton Orient, Leyton Orient and simply Orient will all be referred to in this excellent work.

Lincoln City

376 Some recollections of former players of Lincoln City FC. 1915.

Extremely scarce early ephemeral publication, likely to be of great interest to those chronicling the very early years – if they can find a copy.

377 Cock o' the North: an account of Lincoln City FC's career in the Northern Section [of the Third Division of the Football League] / Benny Dix. Lincoln: W. H. Smith, 1932.
62p; pbk

Benny Dix is pseudonym for G. H. Grosse
BL: Mic.A.10554(14) (microfilm copy)
A rare item charting the years 1921-32.

378 Down the years with Lincoln City / J. J. Sawyer. Lincoln: G.W. Betton, 1954.
52p; pbk

Another scarce item. It is surprising how the smaller clubs were often the subject of early ephemeral studies whilst the larger clubs were neglected.

379 The Imps Supporters' Club official magazine. Lincoln: The Supporters' Club, 1967-
BL: P.441/106

☞ Also listed at: L262

380 Promotion book. Lincoln: Lincoln City Football Club, 1977-
BL: P:621/772

381 Lincoln City centenary souvenir 1883-1983 / Geoff O'Neill and John Holliday. Lincoln: Lincoln City Football Club and Lincolnshire Standard, 1983.
52p; pbk

Includes 19 pages of history, pen pictures of the current staff and a profile of a 75 year old supporter!

382 Lincoln City bygones. Lincoln: Lincolnshire Echo, 1991.
24p; illus; pbk

A brief history, early match reports, pen pictures in a special issue of the *Lincolnshire Echo* on 5 October 1991.

383 Who's who of Lincoln City, 1892-1994 / Donald and Ian Nannestad. Harefield: Yore, 1994.
180p; illus; pbk
ISBN: 1-87442790-9

Definitive coverage of players and personalities from the club's long history.

Liverpool

384 The progress of Liverpool. 1918.

The club were founded in 1892 following a dispute in which Everton quit Anfield to move to Goodison Park. This is a scarce early item.

385 Let's talk about Liverpool Football Club: including football personalities and points of interest / Tom Morgan. London: Sentinel, 1947.
32p; illus; pbk
(Football handbooks. Series 2; no. 33)

One of a well-known series of booklets – interesting but limited original material.

386 Football on Merseyside / Percy Marshall Young. London: Stanley Paul, 1963.
215p; illus   BL: 7926.n.47

Well-informed study including coverage of Liverpool and other Merseyside clubs.

☞ Also listed at: B281, B818, B1019

387 Come on the Reds!: the story of Liverpool FC / David Robert Prole. London: Hale, 1967.
192p; illus   BL: X.449/2835

The first detailed history of the club.

388 The Daily Express A-Z of Mersey soccer / John Keith and Peter Thomas. London: Beaverbrook Newspapers, 1973.
141p

Useful quick reference source.

☞ Also listed at: B283, B819

389 Liverpool Football Club / Stan Liversedge. London: Vantage Books, 1976.
8, 104p; illus
        ISBN: 0-904545-05-9 (cased) • ISBN: 0-904545-06-7 (pbk)
                BL: X.629/10859 • BL: X.619/17127

390 Journey to Wembley: the story of the 1976-77 FA Cup competition and Liverpool's bid for the treble: a football odyssey from Tividale to Wembley / Brian James. London: Marshall Cavendish, 1977.
225p; illus
        ISBN: 0-85685-307-0 (cased) • ISBN: 0-85685-321-6 (pbk)
                BL: X.620/17548

The club reached Wembley in 1977 but lost 2-1 to Manchester United.

☞ Also listed at: D17

391 Liverpool, champions of Europe: the players' official story / John Keith; foreword by Ian Callaghan; colour photography by Harry Ormesher. London: Duckworth; Liverpool: Elmwood, 1977.
3-62p; illus, 1 map

        Includes contributions by others   ISBN: 0-7156-1270-0
                BL: X.622/6072

The club won the European Cup in both 1976/77 and 1977/78.

392 Liverpool FC official annual / edited by John Keith and Harry Ormesher. Hainault: Circle, 1977-
96p; illus; pbk   ISSN: 0141-1578
                BL: P.441/847

393 The Liverpool story / Derek Hodgson. London: Arthur Barker, 1978.
152p; illus   ISBN: 0-213-16681-X
                BL: X.620/17930

☞ Subsequent ed. B395

394 Bob Paisley's Liverpool scrapbook / Bob Paisley. London: Souvenir, 1979.
144p; chiefly illus   ISBN: 0-285-62402-4

Largely pictorial presentation from one of the club's most successful managers.

395 The Liverpool story / Derek Hodgson. Rev. and updated ed. London: Mayflower, 1979.
176p; illus; pbk   ISBN: 0-583-13127-1
                BL: X.619/22236

☞ Previous ed. B393

396 Liverpool 1893-1978: results, league tables, would you believe it items / Norman Lovett. Hull: British Programme Collectors Club, 1980.
96p; pbk
(Facts and figures on the Football League clubs (1888-1978); no. 3)   ISBN: 0-9504273-5-7
                BL: X.0629/552(3)

Season-by-season statistics – part of an idiosyncratic little series covering several of the top clubs.

397 The story of Liverpool FC / Anton Rippon. Ashbourne: Moorland, 1980.
96p; illus   ISBN: 0-903485-98-2
                BL: X.622/9552

398 Liverpool / Matthew Graham. Feltham: Hamlyn, 1984.
124p; illus, 1 coat of arms; index   ISBN: 0-600-34722-2
                BL: X.622/23792

A history of the club mainly from Shankly onwards.

☞ Subsequent ed. B400

399 The Blues and the Reds: a history of the Liverpool and Everton football clubs / Tony Mason. Liverpool: Historic Society of Lancashire & Cheshire, 1985.
24p; pbk

Concentrates on financial and business matters.

☞ Also listed at: B287

400 Liverpool / Matthew Graham. Rev. ed. Twickenham: Hamlyn, 1985.
124p; illus, 1 coat of arms; index   ISBN: 0-600-50254-6
                BL: YC.1986.b.1288

☞ Previous ed. B398; subsequent ed. B401

401 Liverpool / Matthew Graham. 2nd rev. edition. Twickenham: Hamlyn, 1986.
125p; illus, 1 coat of arms; index   ISBN: 0-600-50339-9
                BL: YK.1988.b.1702

☞ Previous ed. B400

402 Liverpool: a complete record 1892-1986 / Brian Pead. Derby: Breedon Books, 1986.
432p; illus   ISBN: 0-907969-15-1
                BL: YK.1988.a.1831

Definitive study – an essential work of reference later updated.

403   Liverpool FC: season 1959-60 / compiled by Eddie
Marks. Crosby: Marksport, 1986.
175p; illus; pbk
(Eddie's golden years scrapbooks)   ISBN: 1-869951-00-X
BL: YK.1987.b.1892

*Covers a rare period during which Liverpool played in
Division Two. Undoubtedly the season in question was
a golden one for Eddie – whether it was for anybody
else is a debatable point. An unusual treatment but
well worth a look.*

404   Liverpool supreme: the official Liverpool FC publication
celebrating their league championship and FA Cup
double / edited by John Keith. London: Cockerel
Books, 1986.
124p; illus; pbk   ISBN: 1-869914-03-1
BL: YA.1990.b.62

*A match-by-match celebration of the 1985/86 sea-
son*

405   Bob Paisley's personal view of the Liverpool First Team
Squad of 1986-1987 / Bob Paisley. Liverpool: Cablestar,
1987.
84p; pbk   ISBN: 0-9513061-0-3

*The club were Division One runners-up in this season.
Here their former manager appraises the players.*

406   The Liverpool quiz book / compiled by Alex Hosie.
Edinburgh: Mainstream, 1987.
176p; illus; pbk   ISBN: 1-85158-094-8
BL: YK.1989.a.3767

1,001 questions and answers

407   You'll never walk alone: the official illustrated history of
Liverpool FC / Stephen F. Kelly. London: Macdonald,
1987.
208p; illus; index
    Bibliography: p208   ISBN: 0-356-14230-2
BL: YK.1987.b.2225

Excellent photographic content.

☞ Subsequent ed. B414

408   The great 1962-1988 derbies Everton v Liverpool: a
celebration of the Merseyside Derby / Brian Barwick,
Gerald Sinstadt. London: BBC Books, 1988.
156p; illus; index   ISBN: 0-563-20678-0
BL: YK.1990.b.1535

History of the Liverpool v Everton derby

☞ Also listed at: B294

409   Inside Anfield / John Aldridge with Brian Woolnough.
Edinburgh: Mainstream, 1988.
190p; illus
    ISBN: 1-85158-191-X (cased) • ISBN: 1-85158-192-8 (pbk)
BL: YK.1989.b.2321

Observations from one of their leading players.

☞ Also listed at: C2

410   Liverpool / Bill Day; illustrated by Craig Warwick.
London: Purnell, 1988.
96p; illus
    ISBN: 0-361-08490-0 (cased) • ISBN: 0-361-08491-9 (pbk)
BL: YK.1989.a.825

411   Liverpool: a complete record 1892-1988 / Brian Pead.
Derby: Breedon Books, 1988.
432p; illus   ISBN: 0-907969-44-5
BL: YK.1992.a.3403

412   Liverpool – club of the century: a special tribute to
Liverpool FC's 17 championship winning seasons / Ian
Hargraves, Ken Rogers and Ric George. Liverpool:
Liverpool Echo, 1988.
192p

*Liverpool's record is a truly remarkable one. This book
celebrates their championships to date.*

413   The Liverpool year / Kenny Dalglish with John Keith.
London: Willow, 1988.
162p; illus   ISBN: 0-00-218337-4
BL: YK.1989.b.533

*The manager's account of the 1987/88 season in
which Liverpool won yet another League championship.*

414   You'll never walk alone: the official illustrated history of
Liverpool FC / Stephen F. Kelly. Rev. ed. London:
Macdonald, 1988.
223p; illus; index
    Bibliography: p223   ISBN: 0-356-17264-3
BL: YK.1989.b.719

☞ Previous ed. B407; subsequent ed. B423

415   Liverpool greats / Ian Hargraves; foreword, Bob Paisley.
Edinburgh: Sportsprint in association with Liverpool
Echo, 1989.
viii, 219p; illus; pbk   ISBN: 0-85976-273-4
BL: YK.1990.a.3365

Selected players from the club's history.

416   Ray Houghton's Liverpool notebook: inside Anfield
1988-89 / Ray Houghton. London: Macdonald, 1989.
176p; illus   ISBN: 0-356-17649-5
BL: YK.1990.b.2942

Observations from one of the playing squad.

417   Who's who of Liverpool 1892-1989 / Doug Lamming.
Derby: Breedon Books, 1989.
160p; illus; pbk   ISBN: 0-907969-55-0
BL: YK.1991.a.9832

*Excellent survey of the players and personalities from
all eras.*

418   Liverpool: a complete record 1892-1990 / Brian Pead.
Derby: Breedon Books, 1990.
432p; illus   ISBN: 0-907969-76-3
BL: YK.1991.a.12996

Update of an essential work.

419 Liverpool: champions of champions / Brian Pead;
     foreword by Bob Paisley. Derby: Breedon Books, 1990.
     255p; illus   ISBN: 0-907969-74-7
                                                   BL: YK.1992.b.158

420 Liverpool: player by player / Ivan Ponting. Swindon:
     Crowood, 1990.
     176p; illus   ISBN: 1-85223-526-8
                                                   BL: YK.1991.b.2361

     The emphasis is on more recent years.

421 My 50 golden reds / Bob Paisley. Warrington: Front
     Page, 1990.
     128p; illus   ISBN: 0-948882-06-9
                                                   BL: YK.1992.b.913

     Ex-manager Bob Paisley selects his 50 best players.

422 Liverpool: the official centenary history, 1892-1992 /
     Stan Liversedge; foreword by Bob Paisley. London:
     Hamlyn, 1991.
     224p; illus; index   ISBN: 0-600-57308-7
                                                   BL: YK.1992.b.8738

     Very useful work of reference.

423 You'll never walk alone: the official illustrated history of
     Liverpool FC / Stephen F. Kelly. Centenary ed. London:
     Macdonald, 1991.
     239p; illus; index
          Bibliography: p239   ISBN: 0-356-19594-5
                                                   BL: YK.1991.b.9220

     ☞ Previous ed. B414

424 Liverpool: a pictorial history / Neal Simpson. Derby:
     Breedon Books, 1992.
     240p; chiefly illus   ISBN: 1-873626-23-1
                                                   BL: YK.1994.b.4184

425 Liverpool in Europe / Steve Hale & Ivan Ponting.
     Enfield: Guinness, 1992.
     208p; illus   ISBN: 0-85112-569-7
                                                   BL: YK.1993.b.8379

426 Liverpool in Europe: the complete record from 1964 /
     Stephen F. Kelly. London: CollinsWillow, 1992.
     175p; illus; index   ISBN: 0-00-218421-4
                                                   BL: YK.1993.b.417

     *A review of Liverpool in Europe from their first ap-
     pearance in 1964.*

427 The official Liverpool centenary yearbook / Stan
     Liversedge; foreword by Mark Wright. London: Hamlyn,
     1992.
     61p; illus; pbk   ISBN: 0-600-57688-4
                                                   BL: YK.1994.b.1055

428 The Anfield encyclopedia: an A-Z of Liverpool FC /
     Stephen F. Kelly. Edinburgh: Mainstream, 1993.
     224p; illus   ISBN: 1-85158-568-0
                                                   BL: YK.1994.b.14958

*Original alphabetical format covering not only well-
known material but also more bizarre and anecdotal
revelations.*

429 Ee aye addio – we've won the Cup!: Liverpool in the FA
     Cup 1892-1993 / Brian Pead with illustrations by Neil
     Cowland. Sidcup: Champion, 1993.
     ix, 533p; illus   ISBN: 1-898058-00-8
                                                   BL: YK.1994.b.5251

     *Includes 5 victories and many a stirring encounter –
     this massive survey is the definitive work on this subject.*

430 Three sides of the Mersey: an oral history of Everton,
     Liverpool and Tranmere Rovers / Rogan Taylor and
     Andrew Ward, with John Williams. London: Robson,
     1993.
     290p; illus   ISBN: 0-86051-871-X
                                                   BL: YK.1995.b.1019

     *Original approach presenting anecdotal observations
     and reminiscences.*

     ☞ Also listed at: B300, B822

431 Liverpool: 10 seasons at Anfield 1984/85 to 1993/94 /
     season-by-season write-ups by Stan Liversedge; editor,
     Michael Robinson. Cleethorpes: Soccer Book Publishing,
     1994.
     72p; illus; pbk
     (The 10 seasons series)   ISBN: 0-947808-41-8

*Luton
Town*

432 Luton Town: a pictorial celebration of their cup history
     / Timothy Collings. Luton: Luton Town Football Club,
     1985.
     108p   ISBN: 0-951067-91-5

     *Full coverage of the FA and League Cups; best used
     in conjunction with the following entry.*

433 The Luton Town story 1885-1985 / Timothy Collings.
Luton: Luton Town Football Club, 1985.
355p   ISBN: 0-951067-90-7
  *Extremely comprehensive coverage; an essential text
  for all research projects.*

Manchester
City

434 Manchester City Football Club: souvenir history / Fred
Johnson. Manchester: Holt, 1930.
116p
  Scarce early history well worth consultation.

435 Let's talk about Manchester City Football Club:
including football personalities and points of interest /
Tom Morgan. London: Sentinel, 1947.
32p; illus; pbk
(Football handbooks. Series 3; no. 35)
  Short on historical detail.

436 Manchester City / David Williams. London: Newservice,
1947.
36p; pbk
(Famous football clubs)   BL: 7922.k.15/4
  Generally rather lightweight.

437 The Manchester City football book / edited by Peter Gardner;
foreword by Joe Mercer. London: Stanley Paul, 1969.
127p; illus   SBN: 09-097850-1
                                 BL: X.0620/106
  *This book and its later updates generally cover the
  season immediately prior to publication.*

438 Manchester City: Meredith to Mercer – and the Cup /
Eric Thornton. London: Hale, 1969.
191p; illus   ISBN: 0-7091-1064-2
                                 BL: X.449/3869
  *Billy Meredith captained the 1904 Cup winning side;
  Joe Mercer managed the club from 1965 to 1971. This
  study effectively covers this entire period.*

439 The Manchester City football book no. 2 / edited by
Peter Gardner; foreword by Joe Mercer. London: Stanley
Paul, 1970.
128p; illus   ISBN: 0-09-108310-9
                                 BL: X.0620/106

440 The Manchester City football book no. 3 / edited by
Peter Gardner; foreword by Joe Mercer. London: Stanley
Paul, 1971.
128p; illus   ISBN: 0-09-108310-9
                                 BL: X.0620/106

441 The Manchester City football book no. 4 / edited by
Peter Gardner. London: Stanley Paul, 1972.
128p; illus   ISBN: 0-09-112600-2
                                 BL: X.0620/106

442 Manchester City Football Club: official record handbook
commencing 1892 / Bill Miles. Manchester: Manchester
City Football Club, 1976.
56p; pbk

443 The A-Z of Manchester football: 100 years of rivalry
1878-1978 / Derek Brandon. London: Boondoggle, 1978.
251p   ISBN: 0-86148-001-7
  Very useful quick reference work.

  ☞ Also listed at: B489

444 The Manchester City football book no. 5 / edited by
Peter Gardner. London: Stanley Paul, 1979.
95p; illus   ISBN: 0-09-139290-X
                                 BL: X.0620/106

445 Manchester City (including Ardwick) 1892-1980: results,
league tables, would you believe it items, facts & figures
/ Norman Lovett. Hull: British Programme Collectors
Club, 1981.
101p; pbk
(Facts and figures on the Football League clubs; no. 32)
                                 ISBN: 0-907263-01-1
                                 BL: X.0629/552(32)

  *Curious item presenting statistics and other trivia in
  a rather idiosyncratic fashion – part of a series covering a number of leading clubs.*

446 The Manchester City story / Andrew Ward. Derby:
Breedon Books, 1984.
96p; illus; pbk   ISBN: 0-907969-05-4
                                 BL: YK.1986.b.845

  Rather lightweight coverage eclipsed by later works.

447 Manchester City / Neville Sullivan. York: Longman, 1986.
28p; illus; pbk
(Inside football)

448 Manchester City: a complete record 1887-1987 / Ray
Goble. Derby: Breedon Books, 1987.
400p; illus   ISBN: 0-907969-24-0
                                 BL: YK.1988.a.2307

  Definitive work; an essential reference item.

449 The Manchester City quiz book / John Maddocks;
foreword by Colin Bell. Edinburgh: Mainstream, 1988.
142p; illus; pbk   ISBN: 1-85158-196-0
                                    BL: YK.1989.a.3948

   1,000 questions and answers

450 City: the untold story of a club that went bananas / Peter
Oakes assisted by Gordon Burnett. Warrington: Front
Page Books, 1989.
224p; illus   ISBN: 0-948882-02-6

   *A highly original treatment best used in conjunction
   with the more serious historical studies. The reference to bananas relates to the bizarre habit started
   by City fans during the late 1980s, of taking oversize
   inflatable mascots to matches. The banana was
   adopted by City fans and brandished aloft to the TV
   theme tune of the Banana Splits – bizarre stuff!*

451 From Maine Road to Banana Citizens: pictorial
milestones of Manchester City FC / Gary James and
Keith Mellor. Nottingham: Temple, 1989.
136p; illus   ISBN: 1-870010-08-6

   *Pictorial history, though relatively lightweight on the
   early years.*

452 The pride of Manchester: a history of the Manchester
derby matches / Steve Cawley and Gary James.
Leicester: ACL Colour Print & Polar Publishing, 1991?
352p; illus   ISBN: 0-9514862-1-7
                                    BL: YK.1992.b.518

   *A complete history of the Manchester derby. In keep-
   ing with Liverpool versus Everton, and Celtic versus
   Rangers games this is one of the key football fixtures
   irrespective of the relative positions of the teams.*

   ☞ Also listed at: B519

453 Manchester City: moments to remember / John
Creighton. Wilmslow: Sigma Leisure, 1992.
150p; illus; pbk   ISBN: 1-85058-260-2
                                    BL: YK.1993.a.4700

454 Manchester City: a complete record 1887-1993 / Ray
Goble with Andrew Ward. Derby: Breedon Books, 1993.
416p; illus   ISBN: 1-873626-41-X
                                    BL: YK.1994.a.4220

455 The battle for Manchester City / Alec Johnson.
Edinburgh: Mainstream, 1994.
187p; illus   ISBN: 1-85158-654-7

   *A bitter battle for control of the club ended with fa-
   mous ex-player Francis Lee taking the helm on a tidal
   wave of support from the fans.*

456 The Kippax: a celebration / editor: Noel Bayley.
Wythenshawe: Electric Blue, 1994.
59p; pbk

   *Reminiscences of the famous Kippax standing area
   which had to be converted to seating to comply with
   the Taylor Report.*

Manchester United

457 Let's talk about Manchester United Football Club:
including football personalities and points of interest /
Tom Morgan. London: Sentinel, 1946.
32p; illus; pbk
(Football handbooks. Series 1; no. 20)   BL: W.P.1144/20

   *Scarce collector's item but lacks any really detailed
   coverage.*

458 Manchester United / Alf Clarke. London: Newservice,
1948.
40p; illus
(Famous football clubs)   BL: 7922.k.15/8

   Another somewhat lightweight study.

459 Manchester United Football Club / Alf Clarke. London:
Convoy, 1951.
112p; illus; pbk
(Famous football clubs) ; (Football club series)
                                    BL: 7923.f.14/2

   *Rather more thorough than the Sentinel and
   Newservice publications; the first detailed history.*

460 The Reds reviewed 1946-1958 / Roy Cavanagh.

   *A history of the club over this period as seen through
   the pages of 'United Review', the club programme.*

461 Babes in arms: countdown to Munich / David
Thompson.

   *At four minutes past three on the afternoon of
   Thursday 6 February 1958, the aircraft carrying the
   Manchester United side back from Yugoslavia came
   to grief taking off from Munich after a refuelling stop.
   Eight of the team, known as the Busby Babes, died in
   the tragedy. Material from the programmes for that
   fateful season leading up to the disaster is reprinted
   here. It is an eerie and moving experience reading it
   with the benefit of hindsight.*

462 Charles Buchan's salute to Manchester United. London:
1959.
63p; illus; pbk   BL: 7925.c.5

463 The day a team died / Frank Taylor. London: Stanley
Paul, 1960.
160p; illus   BL: 7925.bb.43

   *An account of the Munich disaster by one of the sur-
   vivors.*

   ☞ Subsequent ed. B465

464 Manchester United / Percy Marshall Young. London:
Heinemann, 1960.
xiv, 242p; illus   BL: 7925.f.8

   *One of football's best writers here presents the first
   comprehensive study of one of the world's greatest
   clubs.*

465 The day a team died / Frank Taylor. London: World
     Distributors, 1963.
     157p; illus
     (Consul books; no. 780)   BL: 7926.f.14
       ☞ Previous ed. B463; subsequent ed. B497

466 Champions again: Manchester United, 1957 and 1965 /
     Ralph Leslie Finn. London: Hale, 1965.
     207p; illus   BL: X.441/474
     Coverage of two championship seasons.

467 The Manchester United football book / edited by David
     Meek. London: Stanley Paul, 1966.
     128p; illus   BL: X.0444/22
     *Part of a series – effectively covers the season just
     prior to publication.*

468 The Manchester United football book no. 2 / edited by
     David Meek. London: Stanley Paul, 1967.
     128p; illus   BL: X.0444/22

469 The Manchester United football book no. 3 / edited by
     David Meek. London: Stanley Paul, 1968.
     128p; illus   BL: X.0444/22

470 Manchester United in Europe / Roger MacDonald.
     London: Pelham, 1968.
     144p; illus   BL: X.449/3384
     *A detailed account of the club in the European Cup
     written during the season in which they won the tro-
     phy in a memorable triumph over Benfica at Wembley
     Stadium.*

471 The Manchester United football book no. 4 / edited by
     David Meek. London: Stanley Paul, 1969.
     128p; illus   BL: X.0444/22

472 Manchester United: the religion / Tom Tyrrell. London:
     Kaye & Ward, 1969.
     *Whilst the title may seem a little overstated, it is a
     fair comment. Such is the commitment and fervour
     that many followers give to their club, that there are
     distinct parallels between 'fandom' and religious wor-
     ship.*

473 The Manchester United football book no. 5 / edited by
     David Meek. London: Stanley Paul, 1970.
     128p; illus   BL: X.0444/22

474 The Red Devils' disciples / Tom Tyrrell; photographs by
     Graham Collin. London: Kaye & Ward, 1970.
     96p; illus   SBN: 7182-0838-2
                                                BL: X.629/2826

475 Manchester United: Barson to Busby / Eric Thornton.
     London: Hale, 1971.
     169p; illus   ISBN: 0-7091-2499-6
                                                BL: X.629/3675
     *Frank Barson, one of the toughest defenders of his
     era, signed for United in August 1922. Matt Busby*

*was the legendary United manager from 1945 to
1970. This work covers the years spanned by two of
the club's most famous personalities.*

476 The Manchester United football book no. 6 / edited by
     David Meek. London: Stanley Paul, 1971.
     128p; illus   BL: X.0444/22

477 The Manchester United football book no. 7 / edited by
     David Meek. London: Stanley Paul, 1972.
     128p; illus   BL: X.0444/22

478 The Manchester United football book no. 8 / edited by
     David Meek. London: Stanley Paul, 1973.
     128p; illus   BL: X.0444/22

479 Munich air disaster: Captain Thain's ordeal / Stanley
     Williamson. Oxford: Cassirer, 1973.
     280p; illus   ISBN: 0-85181-005-5
     *Thain should have been the pilot of the ill-fated air-
     craft, but when his scheduled co-pilot withdrew at
     the last moment and was replaced by Kenneth Ray-
     ment, fate took a turn. Rayment was regarded as a
     senior pilot to Thain, so he took the main seat. Al-
     though officially in charge of the flight, James Thain
     therefore took the co-pilot's seat. This excellent
     study is a full analysis of everything that followed. An
     essential work for anyone researching the Munich dis-
     aster.*

480 The history of United / Tony Pullein. Manchester:
     Manchester United Football Club, 1974.
     49p; pbk
     Lightweight presentation only.

481 The Manchester United football book no. 9 / edited by
     David Meek. London: Stanley Paul, 1974.
     128p; illus   BL: X.0444/22

482 The Manchester United football book no. 10 / edited by
     David Meek. London: Stanley Paul, 1975.
     128p; illus   BL: X.0444/22

483 The team that wouldn't die / John Roberts. London:
     Arthur Barker, 1975.
     ix, 180p; illus   ISBN: 0-213-16530-9
                                                BL: X.629/7126
     *Following the destruction of the Busby Babes in the
     1958 Munich air disaster, the club began a rebuilding
     exercise which was to culminate in a 1968 European
     Cup triumph. This is a retrospective study of the
     Busby Babes, the disaster and the subsequent re-
     building. Essential reference work.*
       ☞ Subsequent ed. B485

484 The Manchester United football book no. 11 / edited by
     David Meek. London: Stanley Paul, 1976.
     128p; illus   BL: X.0444/22

485 The team that wouldn't die: the story of the Busby Babes / John Roberts; introduction by Sir Matt Busby. St Albans: Mayflower, 1976.
189p; illus; pbk　ISBN: 0-583-12735-5
BL: X.619/17102

☞ Previous ed. B483

486 Manchester United FC official annual / Peter Fitton, John Keith and Harry Ormesher. Hainault: Circle, 1977-
96p; illus; pbk　ISSN: 0141-1586
BL: P.441/848

487 The Manchester United football book no. 12 / edited by David Meek. London: Stanley Paul, 1977.
128p; illus　BL: X.0444/22

488 The Manchester United story / Derek Hodgson. London: Arthur Barker, 1977.
149p; illus　ISBN: 0-213-16631-3
BL: X.622/5974

☞ Subsequent ed. B493

489 The A-Z of Manchester football: 100 years of rivalry 1878-1978 / Derek Brandon. London: Boondoggle, 1978.
251p　ISBN: 0-86148-001-7

Material here on United and their great rivals, City.

☞ Also listed at: B443

490 The Manchester United football book no. 13 / edited by David Meek. London: Stanley Paul, 1978.
128p; illus　BL: X.0444/22

491 There's only one United / Geoffrey Green. London: Hodder and Stoughton, 1978.
352p; illus; index　ISBN: 0-340-22895-4

One of the game's truly respected writers presents a substantial study. Well worth consultation.

492 The Manchester United football book no. 14 / edited by David Meek. London: Stanley Paul, 1979.
128p; illus　BL: X.0444/22

493 The Manchester United story / Derek Hodgson. New ed. London: Arthur Barker, 1979.
156p; illus　ISBN: 0-213-16731-X
BL: X.620/18917

☞ Previous ed. B488

494 The Manchester United football book no. 15 / edited by David Meek. London: Stanley Paul, 1980.
128p; illus　BL: X.0444/22

495 Manchester United (including Newton Heath) 1892-1978: results, league tables, would you believe it items / Norman Lovett. Hull: British Programme Club, 1980.
96p; pbk
(Facts and figures on the Football League clubs, (1888-1978); no. 2)　ISBN: 0-9504273-4-9
BL: X.0629/552(2)

Rather idiosyncratic little publication – part of a series covering some of the leading clubs.

496 Matt Busby's Manchester United scrapbook / Sir Matt Busby. London: Souvenir, 1980.
144p; illus
ISBN: 0-285-62469-5 (cased) • ISBN: 0-285-62456-3 (pbk)
BL: X.622/14044

Busby's contribution to the history of United cannot be overestimated – from his appointment as manager in 1945 through to his death in 1994, he was always a highly respected figure, and was knighted for his services to football in 1968. This publication presents reminiscences of his time at the club up to 1980.

497 The day a team died / Frank Taylor. Rev ed. London: Souvenir, 1983.
192p; illus　ISBN: 0-285-62563-2
BL: X.629/20038

☞ Previous ed. B465

498 The Manchester United air crash / Max Arthur. London?: Aquarius, 1983.

Another retrospective study of the Munich disaster published twenty-five years after that fateful day.

499 Manchester United / Tom Tyrrell. Feltham: Hamlyn, 1984.
123p; illus; index　ISBN: 0-600-38550-7
BL: X.622/23796

☞ Subsequent ed. B500

500 Manchester United / Tom Tyrrell. Rev. ed. Twickenham: Hamlyn, 1985.
131p; illus; index　ISBN: 0-600-50253-8
BL: YC.1986.b.1287

☞ Previous ed. B499; subsequent ed. B503

501 Manchester United who's who, 1945-1986 / Tony Matthews. Derby: Breedon Books, 1985.
104p; illus; pbk　ISBN: 0-907969-09-7

Pen pictures of the players and staff for the period stated.

502 Winners and champions: the story of Manchester United's 1948 Cup Final and 1952 League Championship winning teams / Alec Shorrocks. London: Arthur Barker, 1985.
246p; illus; index　ISBN: 0-213-16920-7
BL: YC.1986.a.148

503 Manchester United / Tom Tyrrell. Rev. ed. Twickenham: Hamlyn, 1986.
133p; illus; index　ISBN: 0-600-50338-0
BL: YK.1988.b.1233

☞ Previous ed. B500

504 Manchester United: a complete record 1878-1986 / Ian Morrison & Alan Shury. Derby: Breedon Books, 1986.
432p; illus
ISBN: 0-907969-16-X
BL: YK.1988.a.2325

Essential work of reference later to be updated.

505 Manchester United: pictorial history and club record / Charles Zahra and others. Subscribers' limited ed. Nottingham: Temple Nostalgia, 1986.
296p; illus
ISBN: 1-870010-01-9
BL: YK.1988.b.5299

Excellent source of photographs.

506 Heathens and red devils: pictorial milestones of Manchester United / Keith Mellor. Nottingham: Temple Nostalgia, 1987.
112p; illus
ISBN: 1-870010-05-1

507 The Manchester United quiz book / compiled by Cliff Butler. Edinburgh: Mainstream, 1987.
188p; illus; pbk
ISBN: 1-85158-095-6
BL: YK.1989.a.3949

1,000 questions and answers.

508 Manchester United / Bill Day; illustrated by Craig Warwick. London: Purnell, 1988.
96p; illus
ISBN: 0-361-08492-7 (cased) • ISBN: 0-361-08493-5 (pbk)
BL: YK.1989.a.826

509 Manchester United: the official history / Tom Tyrrell & David Meek. London: Hamlyn, 1988.
240p; illus; index
ISBN: 0-600-55703-0
BL: YK.1989.b.1301

Worthwhile reference source.

☞ Subsequent ed. B534

510 Red devils in Europe: the complete history of Manchester United in European competition / David Meek. London: Cockerel, 1988.
271p; illus
ISBN: 1-869914-04-X
BL: LB.31.b.9

The club have played many dramatic games in European competition – this substantial work covers them in detail.

511 Manchester United greats / David Meek; foreword by Sir Matt Busby. Edinburgh: Sportsprint, 1989.
177p; illus; pbk
ISBN: 0-85976-276-9
BL: YK.1990.b.7974

A selection of the greatest players to have represented the club.

512 Manchester United: player by player / Ivan Ponting. Marlborough: Crowood, 1989.
176p; illus
ISBN: 1-85223-256-0
BL: YK.1990.b.8532

Potted biographies of many of their leading players.

☞ Subsequent ed. B536

513 Manchester United: the betrayal of a legend / Michael Crick & David Smith. London: Pelham, 1989.
viii, 246p; illus, 1 geneal. table; index
Bibliography: p237-239
ISBN: 0-7207-1783-3
BL: YK.1989.b.4935

Concentrates on financial and boardroom problems.

514 Back page United: a century of newspaper coverage of Manchester United / Stephen F. Kelly. London: Queen Anne Press, 1990.
207p; illus
ISBN: 0-356-17648-7
BL: YK.1990.b.9872

An original idea well worth consulting – stories as presented by the press often throw up material which no serious history would cover.

☞ Subsequent ed. B530

515 Manchester United: a complete record 1878-1990 / Ian Morrison and Alan Shury. Derby: Breedon Books, 1990.
432p; illus
ISBN: 0-907969-80-1
BL: YK.1992.a.3396

Update of a key historical text.

516 Manchester United: the Irish connection / Stephen McGarrigle. Dublin: Blackwater, 1990.
112p
ISBN: 0-361-21365-3

Many Irish players have turned out for the club over the years. This is the definitive work chronicling this connection.

517 The official Manchester United FA Cup review. Grimsby: McKinnon Farmer in association with Manchester United Football Club, 1990.
64p; illus; pbk
ISBN: 0-9514711-5-5
BL: YK.1991.b.6733

The club won the Cup in this year, beating Crystal Palace 1-0 in a replay, after a 3-3 draw in the first game.

518 Manchester United: moments to remember / John Creighton. Wilmslow: Sigma Leisure, 1991.
88p; illus; pbk
ISBN: 1-85058-259-9
BL: YK.1993.b.147

519 The pride of Manchester: a history of the Manchester derby matches / Steve Cawley and Gary James. Leicester: ACL Colour Print & Polar Publishing, 1991?
352p; illus
ISBN: 0-9514862-1-7
BL: YK.1992.b.518

United versus City – one of the great fixtures in world football.

☞ Also listed at: B452

520 Manchester United: a complete record 1878-1992 / Alan Shury, Ian Morrison. Derby: Breedon Books, 1992.
448p; illus
ISBN: 1-873626-22-3
BL: YK.1993.a.10465

A further update of this key historical text.

521 Manchester United: a pictorial history / compiled by
Neal Simpson. Derby: Breedon Books, 1992.
256p; illus   ISBN: 1-873626-24-X
                                          BL: YK.1993.b.12366

 Excellent source of illustrative material.

522 Manchester United: a portrait in old picture postcards /
compiled by James Thomas and John Edminson.
Seaford: S. B. Publications, 1992.
viii, 88p; chiefly illus; pbk
(A portrait in old picture postcards)
                                          ISBN: 1-85770-026-0

 A delightful idea, full of nostalgia from the early days.

523 Manchester United in pictures / Cliff Butler.
Manchester: Manchester United Football Club, 1992.
illus   ISBN: 0-9520509-0-0

524 United remembered: a personal history of Manchester
United. Part 1: From the Busby Babes to champions of
Europe 1952-68 / Peter Woodhead. Houghton-on-the-
Hill: The author, 1992.
38p; illus; pbk   ISBN: 0-9520346-0-3
                                          BL: YK.1993.a.11602

 Idiosyncratic observations – worth consulting.

525 Champions: Manchester United / Tommy Docherty.
London: Sidgwick & Jackson, 1993.
144p; pbk   ISBN: 0-283-06200-2

 Ex-manager Tommy Docherty gets in on the act with
 another championship celebration.

526 Champions: the 26 year quest for glory: the story of
Manchester United's winning season / compiled by
Frank Malley. London: Simon & Schuster, 1993.
159p; illus; pbk   ISBN: 0-671-85264-7
                                          BL: YK.1995.b.1146

 Celebrates their 1992/93 Premier League triumph.

527 Just champion! / Alex Ferguson with Peter Fitton.
Manchester: Manchester United Football Club, 1993.
150p; illus; pbk   ISBN: 0-9520509-1-9

 No prize for original titles as manager Alex Ferguson
 lapses into Lancashire vernacular to review his triumph.

528 Manchester United champions at last: the official story /
Tom Tyrrell. London: Partridge, 1993.
172p; illus   ISBN: 1-85225-226-X

 It is unusual for one single event to spawn so many
 publications – it is probably a measure of the pent-up
 sense of expectation and sublime relief that accompanied United's title win after such a long wait.

529 The Old Trafford encyclopedia: an A-Z of Manchester
United / Stephen F. Kelly. Edinburgh: Mainstream, 1993.
207p; illus   ISBN: 1-85158-569-9
                                          BL: YK.1995.b.1685

 Very useful reference work when used in conjunction
 with more general historical and statistical works.

530 Back page United: a century of newspaper coverage of
Manchester United / Stephen F. Kelly. Rev. ed. London:
Queen Anne Press, 1994.
224p; illus; pbk   ISBN: 1-85291-553-6

 ☞ Previous ed. B514

531 Champions again / Bryan Robson with Tom Tyrrell.
London: Partridge, 1994.
205p; illus   ISBN: 1-85225-238-3

532 Champions: Manchester United review of the 1993/94
season. London: Virgin, 1994.
160p; illus; pbk   ISBN: 0-86369-891-3

 After waiting 26 years to win the title in 1992/93,
 United did it again the following season to stake their
 claim as the team of the nineties.

533 Gibson guarantee: Manchester United, 1931-1951 /
Peter Harrington; illustrated by George Butterworth.
York: Questions Answered, 1994.
128p; illus   ISBN: 0-9515972-4-8

 In 1930 America suffered the Wall Street crash which
 sent reverberations around the world. Businesses
 and institutions which might have been rocky were
 pushed over the edge. Manchester United found
 themselves in deep financial trouble. Only the inter-
 vention of James Gibson and his 'guarantee' for the
 club's future was able to ensure continuity. This book
 presents the full story and reminds us just how vital
 a role the club chairman can play.

534 Hamlyn illustrated history of Manchester United
1878-1994 / Tom Tyrrell and David Meek; foreword by
Bobby Charlton. Rev. and enlarged ed. London:
Hamlyn, 1994.
272p; illus   ISBN: 0-600-58399-6

 ☞ Previous ed. B509

535 Manchester United: a celebration 1993-94. London:
Simon & Schuster, 1994.
160p; illus; pbk   ISBN: 0-671-71369-8

536 Manchester United: player by player / edited by Ivan
Ponting. 2nd ed. Taunton: T. Williams Publications,
1994.
208p; illus   ISBN: 1-869833-29-5

 ☞ Previous ed. B512

537 Manchester United: 10 seasons at Old Trafford
1984/85-1993/94 / season-by-season write-ups, Cliff
Butler; editor, Michael Robinson. Cleethorpes: Soccer
Book Publishing, 1994.
72p; illus
(The 10 seasons series)   ISBN: 0-947808-42-6

538 The United alphabet: a complete who's who of
Manchester United FC / Garth Dykes. Leicester: ACL &
Polar Publishing, 1994.
423p; illus   ISBN: 0-9514862-6-8

Covers all the players from every era of the club's history – an essential reference work detailing over 700 personalities from 1896 onwards.

539 United: the story of Manchester United in the FA Cup / Steve Cawley. Sidcup: Champion Press, 1994.
224p; illus   ISBN: 1-898058-05-9

540 United we stood: the unofficial history of the Ferguson years / Richard Kurt. Wilmslow: Sigma, 1994.
183p; pbk   ISBN: 1-85058-432-X

A fan's eye view of the club's recent triumphs.

541 Are you watching, Liverpool? / Jim White. London: Heinemann, 1995.
291p; illus   ISBN: 0-434-00115-5

Chronicles the 1993-94 League and Cup double.

Mansfield Town

542 Stags 50 years / edited by Stan Searl. Mansfield: Mansfield Town Football Club, 1981.
50p; pbk

The 50 years date from their first League game in 1931, rather than their foundation in 1910. This slim volume lists all their League results and includes articles on their history, managers and top marksmen.

543 Mansfield Town: a complete record 1910-1990 / Stan Searl. Derby: Breedon Books, 1990.
416p; illus   ISBN: 0-907969-70-4
    BL: YK.1992.a.9143

Excellent work and the obvious starting point for all research projects.

Middlesbrough

544 Let's talk about Middlesbrough Football Club: including football personalities and points of interest / Tom Morgan. London: Sentinel, 1948.
32p; illus; pbk
(Football handbooks. Series 3; no. 53)

Curious collector's item – short on historical content.

545 Middlesbrough quiz book / Nigel Gibb.

546 Middlesbrough: a complete record, 1876-1989 / Harry Glasper. Derby: Breedon Books Sport, 1989.
416p; illus

Limited edition of numbered copies   ISBN: 0-907969-53-4
    BL: YK.1993.a.2258
Essential work of reference from foundation.

547 Middlesbrough Football Club / Eric Paylor. Runcorn: Archive, 1989.
128p; illus; pbk   ISBN: 0-948946-32-6

548 Up the 'Boro!: the diary of Middlesbrough Football Club's promotion season 1991-1992 / Stuart Carr; foreword by Michael McGeary. Ayr: Fresh Ayr Books, 1992.
96p; illus   ISBN: 1-897770-05-7
    BL: YK.1993.a.16891

Celebrating promotion into the Premier League.

549 Middlesbrough: a complete record / Harry Glasper. Derby: Breedon Books, 1993.
256p; illus   ISBN: 1-873626-46-0
    BL: YK.1995.b.288

Update of this essential reference work.

Millwall

550 Let's talk about Millwall Football Club: including football personalities and points of interest / Tom Morgan. London: Sentinel, 1948.
32p; illus; pbk
(Football handbooks. Series 3; no. 54)

Collectable ephemeral booklet though it lacks detail.

551 Lions through the lens / Ted Wilding. Nottingham: Temple Nostalgia.
140p; chiefly illus

Mainly photographs.

552 Millwall: lions of the South / James Murray. Wellingborough: Indispensable Publications and Millwall FC, 1988.
288p; illus, 2 maps; index

Limited edition of 200 copies
ISBN: 1-871220-01-7 (leather) • ISBN: 1-871220-00-9 (pbk)
    BL: YK.1989.b.703

The first substantial history takes a season-by-season approach with a good balance from all eras — strong on illustration but little in the way of statistics.

553 Millwall: a complete record 1885-1991 / Richard Lindsay. Derby: Breedon Books, 1991.
416p; illus   ISBN: 0-907969-94-1
                               BL: YK.1993.a.8940

Best used in conjunction with the previous entry. An essential starting point for all projects.

Newcastle United

554 Newcastle United: souvenir record season 1926-27. Newcastle?: R.L. Rutter, 1927.
14p; illus; pbk

Scarce ephemeral item celebrating Newcastle's championship success during this particular season.

555 United's fight for the Cup / Evening Chronicle staff. Newcastle: Newcastle United FC, 1932.
32p; illus; pbk

Newcastle won the FA Cup in this year, beating Arsenal 2-1.

556 Let's talk about Newcastle United Football Club: including football personalities and points of interest / Tom Morgan. London: Sentinel, 1946.
32p; illus; pbk
(Football handbooks. Series 1; no. 17)
                               BL: W.P.1144/17

Limited historical content.

557 Newcastle United's promotion souvenir 1948-49. Newcastle: Evening Chronicle, 1948.
32p; illus; pbk

Celebrates promotion from Division Two to Division One by presenting a brief history and record along with the fixtures for the forthcoming campaign.

558 The cup romance of Newcastle United / Tom Hall. Newcastle: Evening Chronicle, 1952.
59p; illus; pbk

Mainly contemporary in its coverage — the club won the FA Cup in 1951 and 1952.

559 Newcastle United's Cup Final souvenir / Evening Chronicle staff. Newcastle: Newcastle United Players Pool, 1955.
32p; illus; pbk

Yet another Cup Final victory came in 1955.

560 The Magpie review about Newcastle United. Newcastle?: Guiness & Rawson, 1967.
48p; illus; pbk

Mainly player biographies.

561 The Magpie review about Newcastle United. Newcastle?: Guiness & Rawson, 1968.
32p; illus; pbk

562 Newcastle United FC official booklet. Newcastle: Newcastle United FC, 1968.
32p; illus; pbk

563 The Magpie review about Newcastle United. Newcastle?: Guiness & Rawson, 1969.
28p; illus; pbk

564 The Newcastle United FC story / John Gibson. London: Pelham, 1969.
156p; illus   SBN: 7207-0281-X

565 Newcastle United official brochure. Newcastle: Newcastle United FC, 1969.
48p; illus; pbk

566 Our fabulous Fairs Cup. Newcastle: Newcastle United Players Pool, 1969.
40p; illus; pbk

Written by the players who won the Cup

Newcastle beat Ujpest Dozsa over two legs — 60,000 people witnessed the 3-0 home leg win at St James Park.

567 Newcastle United FC official brochure. Aldershot: Gale & Polden, 1970.
32p; illus; pbk

Review of the 1969/70 season.

568 The Newcastle United FC story no. 2 / John Gibson. London: Pelham, 1970.
157p; illus   ISBN: 0-7207-0419-7

569 The Newcastle United FC story no. 3 / John Gibson. London: Pelham, 1972.
125p; illus   ISBN: 0-7207-0525-8

570 The supporter / Newcastle Supporters Association.
Newcastle upon Tyne: N.S.A, 1978-
illus
ISSN: 0142-6788
BL: P:2000/657

☞ Also listed at: L343

571 The Inkerman history of Newcastle United / Paul
Joannou. Newcastle?: Inkerman, 1980.
84p; illus; pbk
Joannou's first Newcastle United book – he went on
to write a number of key historical texts.

☞ Subsequent ed. B574

572 Jackie Milburn's Newcastle United scrapbook / Jackie
Milburn. London: Souvenir, 1981.
128p; chiefly illus
ISBN: 0-285-62492-X
Milburn first appeared for Newcastle in 1946 and
achieved cult status during the 1950s, scoring a career total of 179 goals in 354 League games. This
takes a retrospective look at his time with the club.

573 A complete who's who of Newcastle United / Paul
Joannou. Newcastle: Newcastle United Supporters Club,
1983.
208p; illus
ISBN: 0-9508876-1-7 (cased) • ISBN: 0-9508876-0-9 (pbk)
Definitive coverage of the players and personalities.
An essential text for any research work.

574 The history of Newcastle United 1882-1984 / Paul Joannou.
Newcastle: Newcastle United Supporters Club, 1984.
80p; illus
ISBN: 0-9508876-3-3 (cased) • ISBN: 0-9508876-2-5 (pbk)

☞ Previous ed. B571

575 The Newcastle United story / John Gibson. London:
Arthur Barker, 1985.
192p; illus
ISBN: 0-213-16919-3

576 Newcastle United: a complete record 1882-1986 / Paul
Joannou. Derby: Breedon Books, 1986.
432p; illus
ISBN: 0-907969-18-6
BL: YK.1988.a.2218
Key historical text by the author justifiably known in
football publishing circles as 'Mr Newcastle'. An es-
sential work of reference, later updated.

577 Newcastle United Football Club: a pictorial history /
John Gibson. Runcorn: Archive, 1988.
128p; illus; pbk
ISBN: 0-948946-30-X
Good source of illustrations but concentration is on
the modern era.

578 The Newcastle United quiz book / Paul Joannou.
Edinburgh: Mainstream, 1988.
160p; pbk
ISBN: 1-85158-142-1
1,020 questions and answers.

579 Ha'way the lads!: the illustrated story of Newcastle
United / illustrated by Tommy Canning; assisted by
Patrick Canning; story by Paul Joannou; design by Paul
Joannou, Patrick & Tommy Canning. Edinburgh:
Mainstream, 1989.
147p; illus; pbk
ISBN: 1-85158-257-6
BL: YK.1991.b.1891
Interesting pictorial coverage of all eras.

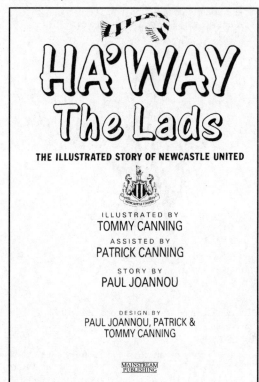

580 Newcastle United / Graham Robinson and Craig
Warwick. Maidenhead: Purnell, 1989.
96p; illus
ISBN: 0-361-08512-5 (cased) • ISBN: 0-361-08513-3 (pbk)
BL: YK.1990.a.1620 • BL: YK.1989.a.3588

581 Newcastle United greats / John Gibson. Edinburgh:
Sportsprint, 1989.
v, 154p; illus; pbk
ISBN: 0-85976-265-3
BL: YK.1990.b.7971

582 Newcastle United story: told in pictures / David
Thornton. Leeds: D. & J. Thornton, 1989.
16p; chiefly illus; pbk
ISBN: 0-907339-29-8
BL: YK.1990.a.3321
Unusual approach directed at the juvenile market.

583 Newcastle United: a complete record 1882-1990 / Paul Joannou, Bill Swann, Steve Corke. Derby: Breedon Books, 1990.
432p; illus
ISBN: 0-907969-79-8
BL: YK.1992.a.9144

584 Newcastle United: a portrait in old picture postcards / compiled by John Edminson. Loggerheads: S. B. Publications, 1990.
viii, 80p; chiefly illus; pbk
(A portrait in old picture postcards)

Includes bibliography
ISBN: 1-870708-52-8
BL: YK.1992.a.10566

Pure nostalgia; an excellent source of illustrations.

585 The all time great matches / Paul Tully. Newcastle: Evening Chronicle, 1991.
104p; illus; pbk

Covers both Newcastle United and Sunderland.

☞ Also listed at: B754

586 The all time greats / Paul Tully. Newcastle: Evening Chronicle, 1991.
104p; illus; pbk

Again covers both Newcastle United and Sunderland.

☞ Also listed at: B755

587 United – the first 100 years: the official centenary history of Newcastle United / Paul Joannou. Leicester: ACL Colour Print & Polar Publishing, 1991.
416p; illus

A 4p update supplement was issued in 1992 for insertion into the original
ISBN: 0-9514862-4-1
BL: YK.1992.b.2854

Best used in conjunction with the 'Complete Record' – comprehensive and essential historical text.

588 Newcastle United review 1993 / edited by Paul Tully. Warley: Sports Projects, 1993.
160p; illus
(Match by match)
ISBN: 0-946866-10-4

In 1992/93 the club won the First Division to claim a place in the Premiership. Formed in 1881, and as one of the great football clubs over many years, there was a general consensus of opinion that Newcastle had regained their rightful status after a number of years in the wilderness.

589 Newcastle United: seasons 1983-84 to 1992-93 / season-by-season commentary by John Gibson; statistics and history by Mike Ross; editors, Michael Robinson, John Robinson & Philip Norminton. Cleethorpes: Soccer Book Publishing, 1993.
52p; illus; pbk
(The 10 seasons series)
ISBN: 0-947808-33-7

Season-by-season review of a decade of mixed fortunes for the club.

590 Geordie passion: a lifetime love of Newcastle United / Mark Hannen. South Woodham Ferrers: Publishing Corporation, 1994.
illus
ISBN: 1-897780-66-4

591 Toons of glory / Joe Bernstein. London: Souvenir, 1994.
96p; illus; pbk
ISBN: 0-285-63236-1

Northampton Town

592 The Cobblers: the story of Northampton Town Football Club / Frank Grande; assisted by John Harley. Buckingham: Sporting & Leisure, 1985.
152p; illus, 1 coat of arms; index
ISBN: 0-86023-252-2
BL: YK.1986.b.1149

Excellent era-by-era study of the club from its foundation in 1897.

593 Who's who – the Cobblers: the story of the players 1920-1988 / Frank Grande; assisted by John Harley. Buckingham: Sport & Leisure, 1988.
112p; illus, 1 coat of arms; index
ISBN: 0-86023-427-4
BL: YK.1990.b.7576

Covers the club's history from 1920 when 'The Cobblers' were founder members of the Third Division.

*Norwich
City*

*Nottingham
Forest*

594 Norwich City football promotion souvenir handbook.
London: Pyramid Press, 1960-   BL: P.P.7613.kf

595 On the ball City: an illustrated history of the Norwich
City Football Club / Ted Bell. Norwich: Wensum
Books, 1972.
112p; illus   BL: X.622/2004

Good early attempt at a comprehensive coverage
with all eras well chronicled.

596 Canary crusade. 1974.
32p; pbk

Lightweight coverage only – concentrates on the club's
highlights with particular reference to the FA Cup.

597 Canary Citizens: the official history of Norwich City FC
/ John Eastwood and Mike Davage. Ipswich: Almeida,
1986.
352p

Essential definitive text covering every element of the
club's history and development.

598 Norwich City: a portrait in old picture postcards / Dick
Middleton and Paul Standley; foreword by Dave
Stringer. Seaford: S.B. Publications, 1992.
80p; chiefly illus; pbk   ISBN: 1-85770-033-3
                                 BL: YK.1994.a.14057

A number of clubs have been made the subject of this
original treatment – the result is an excellent source
of illustrative material.

599 Norfolk 'n' good: a supporter's view of Norwich City's
best-ever season / Kevin Baldwin. London: Yellow Bird,
1993.
306p; pbk   ISBN: 0-9522074-0-0
                   BL: YK.1994.a.1043

Original approach, very readable – contributions by
literate supporters may become a distinctive trend in
football publishing. Worthwhile and easy reading – the

hardest bit may perhaps be explaining the title to
your ten year old son!

600 Glorious Canaries past and present, 1902-1994 / Mike
Davage. Norwich: Norwich City Football Club, 1995.
448p; illus   ISBN: 0-9523857-0-8

601 Let's talk about Nottingham Forest Football Club:
including football personalities and points of interest /
Tom Morgan. London: Sentinel, 1946.
32p; illus; pbk
(Football handbooks. Series 1; no. 19)   BL: W.P.1144/19

Part of a popular series – interesting but without detailed coverage.

602 The Forest cup story: the background to Wembley 1959.
Nottingham: Peter Skinner, 1959.
36p; illus; pbk   BL: 7924.c.22

Forest were victorious in the FA Cup in this year –
their first triumph in the competition since 1898.
Rather quaint coverage including player comments
and a number of adverts which very much capture the
flavour of the era.

603 The hundred years story of the Nottingham Forest FC
1865-1965 / A. J. Turner. Nottingham: Nottingham
Forest FC, 1965.
195p

Particularly strong on early history.

604 Forest, 1865-1978 / cover photo by Keith Gibson;
written by John Lawson; edited & designed by Michael
Shaw. Norwich: Wensum, 1978.
111p; illus   ISBN: 0-903619-24-5
                     BL: X.620/18234

Despite the title, most of the detailed coverage is
post-war.

☞ Subsequent ed. B606

605 Nottingham Forest FC official annual. Ilford: Essex
Circle, 1978-
BL: P.441/916

606 Forest, 1865-1978 / John Lawson; with an introduction
by Brian Clough. London: Mayflower, 1979.
189p; illus; pbk   ISBN: 0-583-13170-0
BL: X.619/19687

☞ Previous ed. B604

607 Forest: kings of Europe. Nottingham: Nottingham
Evening Post, 1979.
63p; illus; pbk
Celebrating the club's first European Cup triumph.

608 Forest: the 1979 season / John Lawson. Norwich:
Wensum, 1979.
111p

609 Forest: the 1980 season / John Lawson. Norwich:
Wensum, 1980.
104p
Forest beat Hamburg to win the European Cup in successive seasons – a remarkable feat for a club which had hitherto struggled in its quest for honours. This is a full study of a memorable season.

610 The story of Nottingham football. Nottingham: Castle
Museum, 1983.
32p; illus; pbk   BL: X.622/16081
Published to coincide with an exhibition at the Castle Museum.

☞ Also listed at: B621

611 The Garibaldi Reds: the pictorial history of Nottingham
Forest Football Club / Keith Mellor. Buckingham:
Sporting and Leisure, 1984.
180p; illus; index   ISBN: 0-86023-224-7
BL: X.622/24140
Extremely well illustrated on a season-by-season basis – particularly evocative in its use of memorabilia from the author's own collection.

612 Forest Road: pictorial milestones of the Garibaldi Reds /
Keith Mellor. Nottingham: Temple Nostalgia, 1986.
96p; illus; pbk   ISBN: 1-870010-00-0
Over 200 photographs including many of historic documents from the club's archives.

613 Nottingham Forest Football Club: 30 years in
photographs / Duncan Hamilton. Runcorn: Archive,
1988.
128p; illus; pbk   ISBN: 0-948946-36-9
Over 200 pictures cover the years from the 1959 Wembley triumph to the glory years under Brian Clough.

614 Nottingham Forest: a complete record 1892-1991 / Pete
Attaway. Derby: Breedon Books, 1991.
416p; illus   ISBN: 0-907969-95-X
BL: YK.1994.a.13147

An essential work – the ideal starting point for researchers of the club.

615 Forest: the first 125 years / Ken Smales. Nottingham:
Temple, 1992.
265p; illus   ISBN: 1-870010-09-4
Each season is given one full page. Overlaps with the 'Complete Record' volume but still useful in its own right. The author was a former Nottinghamshire cricketer and secretary of Nottingham Forest from 1961-1987.

616 Nottingham Forest FC: the 25 year record / edited by
Michael Robinson. Cleethorpes: Soccer Book Publishing,
1994
60p; pbk   ISBN: 0-947808-43-4

Notts County

617 The story of Notts County Association Football Club /
J. Cantrell. Liverpool: Ports & Cities Publishing, 1927.
xvi p   BL: D
Extremely scarce ephemeral publication very rarely seen in specialist dealers' catalogues.

618 Let's talk about Notts County Football Club: including
football personalities and points of interest / Tom
Morgan. London: Sentinel, 1948.
32p; illus; pbk
(Football handbooks. Series 3; no. 59)
Part of a well known series – uncommon, but of limited interest.

619 Centenary handbook, 1862-1962 / Notts County
Football Club. London: Pyramid Press, 1962.
51p   BL: X.441/414
This can claim to be the earliest centenary history of a Football League club by virtue of the fact that Notts County are the oldest club in the League. Rather lightweight, including adverts, but offers some interesting photographs.

620 Flyaway Magpies: the story behind Notts County's climb back to the First Division / Terry Bowles. Nottingham: Notts County FC, 1981.
44p; pbk
Mostly covers the 1980-81 season.

621 The story of Nottingham football. Nottingham: Castle Museum, 1983.
32p; illus; pbk   BL: X.622/16081
Published to coincide with an exhibition at the Castle Museum.
☞ Also listed at: B610

622 The Magpies: the story of Notts County Football Club, the oldest Football League club in the world founded in 1862 / Keith Warsop; assisted by Paul Wain. Buckingham: Sporting and Leisure, 1984.
192p; illus; index   ISBN: 0-86023-214-X
    BL: X.622/20670
Limited edition — a comprehensive treatment and valuable work of reference.

623 Notts County / Neville Sullivan. York: Longman, 1986.
28p; illus; pbk
(Inside football)   BL: YK.1988.b.4170
Unusual item — effectively an insight into the running of a football club with particular reference to match-day procedures.

624 Notts County Football Club / Dave McVay. Runcorn: Archive, 1988.
128p; illus; pbk   ISBN: 0-948946-37-7
Weighted towards the post-war years.

Oldham Athletic

625 Oldham Football Club handbook: scores, results, and records, fixtures for 1903-4. Oldham: Oldham Athletic Football Club, 1903.
    BL: Mic.A.11038(19) (microfilm copy)

This is a scarce item from one of the club's early seasons — they were formed in 1895 as Pine Villa and became Oldham Athletic in 1899.

626 History of Oldham Athletic Football Club. Clebar Publishing, 1933.
Scarce pamphlet commissioned by the *Oldham Chronicle*.

627 The team from a town of chimneys: chronicle of Oldham Athletic Association Football Club / compiled & produced by Stewart W. Beckett. Oldham: The author, 1982.
223p; illus   BL: YA.1991.a.21933
Profusely illustrated. Best used in conjunction with the following book.

628 Oldham Athletic: complete record 1899-1988 / Garth Dykes. Derby: Breedon Books Sport, 1988.
416p; illus   ISBN: 0-907969-36-4
    BL: YK.1992.a.6871
The definitive publication — essential reading.

629 The team from a town of chimneys revisited: the official chronicles of Oldham Athletic AFC Ltd 1897-1990 / Stewart W. Beckett; edited by Bob Young; illustrations by A. S. Mellor. Manchester: Comprehensive Art Services, 1990.
288p; illus; pbk   ISBN: 0-9516497-0-1
An essential research text.

630 Keeping the dream alive / Stewart W. Beckett; edited by Eric Krieger; illustrations by A. S. Mellor. Manchester: Comprehensive Art Services, 1991.
288p; illus; pbk   ISBN: 0-9516497-1-X
The years 1923 to 1991 are chronicled in detail — this is the period when the club languished outside the First Division, their exile finally ending with their 1990/91 promotion.

631 First Division days / Stewart W. Beckett. Manchester: Comprehensive Art Services, 1992.
128p; pbk   ISBN: 0-9516497-2-8
This complements the above book by covering the club's two spells in the First Division, namely 1910-1923 and 1991 to publication date.

632 Oldham Athletic: an A-Z / Dean Hayes. Preston: Palatine Books, 1994.
160p; illus; pbk
(Carnegie soccer A-Z; v.2)   ISBN: 1-874181-12-8

Oxford United

633 Anatomy of a football club: the halcyon years of Headington/Oxford United / Vic Couling. Bognor Regis: New Horizon, 1983.
134p   ISBN: 0-86116-828-3
    BL: X.629/20880

Original approach charting the inside story of the club – the author has been associated with Oxford United since 1947.

634 Oxford United 1983-84 official souvenir brochure: a year to remember / edited by M. A. Brown. Oxford: Oxford United Football Club, 1984.
48p; pbk

This was the season in which the club won the Third Division title and reached the fifth round of the FA and League Cup competitions.

635 Rags to riches: the rise and rise of Oxford United / John Ley. London: Macdonald, 1985.
64p; illus; pbk   ISBN: 0-356-12158-5
                                   BL: X.622/25240

Centres on the period 1981-1985. The foreword is by Robert Maxwell and he features in many of the photographs – not surprising since the book was commissioned by him and given as a gift to the employees of one of his many companies.

636 Oxford United: a complete record, 1893-1989 / Andy & Roger Howland. Derby: Breedon Books, 1989.
400p; illus   ISBN: 0-907969-52-6
                                  BL: YK.1992.a.10154

An essential text and the ideal starting point for any study. This volume was not sponsored by the club's benefactor Robert Maxwell – hence he is featured in just two of the many excellent photographs.

637 Oxford's hundred: Oxford United's official centenary publication / edited by Mark Shanahan. Oxford: Oxford United Football Club Ltd, 1993.
48p; pbk   ISBN: 0-9522818-0-5

The club were founded in 1893 as Headington – this is the centenary publication.

Peterborough United

638 Never so posh / Paul Mowforth. 1960.
64p; pbk

Describes the foundation and early history of the club – to the uninitiated, 'Posh' is their nickname.

639 The Peterborough United success story. Peterborough: Peterborough Advertiser, 1960.
16p; pbk

A newspaper supplement from 19 August 1960 giving a brief history of the club and celebrating their election to the Football League in that year.

640 Champions first time. Peterborough: Peterborough FC, 1961.
pbk

The club won the Fourth Division title at the first attempt.

641 Posh: the success story of Peterborough United Football Club / edited by Paul Mowforth. Peterborough: Peterborough United FC, 1974.
102p

Laudable effort at a complete history and record, later to be eclipsed by the following more comprehensive publication.

642 Peterborough United Football Club: the official history of 'The Posh' / Andy Groom & Mick Robinson. Harefield: Yore, 1992.
illus   ISBN: 1-874427-15-1
                                  BL: YK.1994.b.893

An excellent definitive history from the club's foundation in 1934 – an essential text.

Plymouth Argyle

643 Let's talk about Plymouth Argyle Football Club: including football personalities and points of interest / Tom Morgan. London: Sentinel, 1947.
32p; illus; pbk
(Football handbooks. Series 2; no. 21)

Collectable ephemeral booklet but of little value to the serious researcher.

644 Plymouth Argyle: golden jubilee 1903-1953 / Henry P. Twyford. 1953.

Scarce ephemeral commemorative.

645 All about Argyle 1903-1963 / W. S. Tonkin. Plymouth: Plymouth Argyle Football Club, 1963.
128p

A laudable effort at a detailed club history long before many other clubs had bothered – records, statistics and many photographs are included but the content is eclipsed by later publications.

646 Dave Smith's promotion diary / Harley Lawer. Plymouth: Green Books, 1986.

Manager Dave Smith presents a match-by-match account of the 1985/86 season in which promotion was achieved from Division Three.

647   Harley Lawer's Argyle classics: memorable moments in Plymouth Argyle's league and cup history. Plymouth: Green Books, 1988.
350p; illus; index   ISBN: 0-9513817-0-9
                                  BL: YK.1992.b.3705

An original approach with over 300 match reports interspersed with photographs, cigarette cards and cartoons.

648   Plymouth Argyle: a complete record 1903-1989 / Brian Knight. Derby: Breedon Books Sport, 1989.
416p; illus   ISBN: 0-907969-40-2
                                  BL: YK.1992.a.11902

Although the club were founded in 1886 in an area which was very fond of rugby, support from local servicemen helped develop the game quickly. The club turned professional in 1903 and this is generally taken as the start date for historical studies of the club. This is an indispensable text for researchers.

649   Plymouth Argyle: a file of fascinating football facts / Mike Blackstone. Exeter: Obelisk, 1993.
96p; illus; pbk   ISBN: 0-9466516-5-5
                                  BL: YK.1993.a.5756

Adopts a more light-hearted approach – this selection of anecdotal material is likely to reveal the lesser known and more bizarre stories about the club.

Port Vale

650   The story of Port Vale 1876-1950 / Norman Gosling. Stoke-on-Trent: Port Vale FC, 1950.
36p; illus; pbk

Published to mark the opening of their new ground, Vale Park, this scarce item presents a brief history from the 1876 foundation and takes in the years 1884 to 1911 when they were known as Burslem Port Vale. It includes many photographs of the ground under construction and an artist's impression of how the so-called 'Wembley of the North' would look.

651   Port Vale promotion 69/70. 1970.
72p; illus; pbk

Celebrates promotion from the Fourth to the Third Division.

652   Back to where we once belonged!: Port Vale promotion chronicle 1988-1989 / Jeff Kent. Alsager: Witan, 1989.
101p; illus; pbk   ISBN: 0-9508981-3-9

Promotion from Division Three to Division Two.

653   The Valiants' years: the story of Port Vale / Jeff Kent. Alsager: Witan, 1990.
305p; illus; pbk   ISBN: 0-9508981-4-7
                                  BL: YK.1991.a.4252

A substantial work and an essential reference tool from 'Mr Port Vale'. Works of this type illustrate only too well how the dedication of a keen historian-supporter can ensure that the smaller clubs are well chronicled for posterity.

654   Port Vale tales: a collection of stories, anecdotes and memories / compiled by Jeff Kent. Stoke-on-Trent: Witan, 1991.
vii, 332 p; illus; pbk   ISBN: 0-9508981-6-3
                                  BL: YK.1992.a.9373

An interesting and original approach – nearly 70 supporters and ex-players tell in a series of stories and anecdotes why they support Port Vale. Stanley Matthews is one of those featured.

655   Port Vale forever / Jeff Kent. Stoke-on-Trent: Witan, 1992.
iii, 21p; illus; pbk   ISBN: 0-9508981-8-X
                                  BL: YK.1994.a.8473

Another unusual item – this is an illustrated song book with accompanying cassette tape of ten folk songs pertaining to the club. It begins with 'Burslem is the only place to be' and continues in similar vein. Certainly a curiosity which all Port Vale completists will want to acquire.

656   The Port Vale record 1879-1993 / Jeff Kent. Stoke-on-Trent: Witan Books, 1993.
vi, 292p; illus; pbk   ISBN: 0-9508981-9-8
                                  BL: YK1994.a.5095

Adopts a season-by-season approach to the coverage of the club throughout its history.

Portsmouth

657   Historical souvenir of the Portsmouth Football Club, 1898-1927. Portsmouth: Portsmouth FC, 1927.
72p; pbk   BL: 07905.ee.70

Scarce item chronicling the club's first 29 years. These years conceal a remarkable story – in 1920

'Pompey' were founder members of the Third Division and by 1927 they had risen to the First, where they remained for the next 32 years. That phenomenal journey has inspired this publication.

658 Let's talk about Portsmouth Football Club: including football personalities and points of interest / Tom Morgan. London: Sentinel, 1946.
32p; illus; pbk
(Football handbooks. Series 1; no. 2)   BL: W.P.1144/2
   One of a well-known but lightweight series.

659 Portsmouth Football Club: golden jubilee handbook 1898-1948 / F. J. H. Young. Portsmouth: Grosvenor, 1948.
64p; illus; pbk
   Ephemeral publication with some interesting original material including the minutes founding the club.

660 Pompey: the history of Portsmouth Football Club / Mike Neasom, Mick Cooper and Doug Robinson. Portsmouth: Milestone, 1984.
256p; illus   ISBN: 0-903852-50-0
                       BL: YC.1986.b.1668
   Essential work of reference achieving a good balance of text, illustrations and statistics.

661 Pompey: season . . . / Mike Neasom. Horndean: Milestone, 1985-1987.
illus
      Published for 3 seasons: 1984/85, 1985/86, 1986/87
                       BL: ZK.9.a.1618

Preston North End

662 Let's talk about Preston North End Football Club: including football personalities and points of interest / Tom Morgan. London: Sentinel, 1947.
32p; illus; pbk
(Football handbooks. Series 2; no. 22)
   Interesting but of limited content.

663 Preston North End / Alex James and Lainson Wood. London: Newservice, 1947.
36p; pbk
(Famous football clubs)   BL: 7922.k.15/2
   Rather limited coverage.

664 Preston North End Football Club: 100 years at Deepdale 1881-1981 / Harry Berry and Geoffrey Allman. 1982. Preston: Preston North End Football Club, 1982.
268p
   Detailed and definitive study up to 1981 – an essential work of reference.

665 Tom Finney's Preston North End scrapbook / Tom Finney. London: Souvenir, 1982.
144p; illus
                       ISBN: 0-285-62549-7
   Well illustrated study fronted by one of the club's greatest servants.

666 Preston North End: 100 years in the Football League / Dave Russell. Preston: University of Central Lancashire Community History Project, Lancashire Polytechnic, 1988.
58p; illus; pbk
                       ISBN: 0-906694-16-7
   25 pages of history alongside a good selection of photographs.

667 North End!: a pictorial history of Preston North End spanning six Preston Guilds / Paul Agnew and Ian Rigby. Manchester: Chase Creative Consultants, 1992.
92p; illus   ISBN: 1-897871-00-7

Queen's Park Rangers

668 The football handbook of the Queen's Park Rangers: season 1899-1900. London: Stead & Co., 1899-
      Contains biographies & portraits   BL: 7912.df
   Scarce early ephemeral item.

669 Football heroes: dedicated to the Queen's Park Rangers / W. J. Brown. London: J. S. Carte, 1910.
1 sheet   BL: 1879.c.12(50)
   Extremely scarce item presented in verse.
   ☞ Also listed at: I182

670 Let's talk about Queen's Park Rangers Football Club: including football personalities and points of interest / Tom Morgan. London: Sentinel, 1947.
32p; illus; pbk
(Football handbooks. Series 2; no. 23)
   Limited content but still of interest to the completist collector.

671 Queen's Park Rangers / Reg J. Hayter. London:
Newservice, 1948.
40p; pbk
(Famous football clubs)   BL: 7922.k.15/6

   Rather lightweight again – adds to the relative prolif-
   eration of early ephemeral QPR publications.

672 Queen's Park Rangers 1947/48 souvenir / edited by W.
G. MacAllister-Batt. London?: Pick Publications, 1948.
32p; pbk

673 The road to glory / editor, Ron Phillips. London:
Queen's Park Rangers Football Club, 1968.
20p; illus

   Photographic record of 1966-68, two of the most
   successful years in the club's history when they won
   the League Cup and gained promotion to the First Division.

674 A history of Queen's Park Rangers FC / Dennis Signy.
London: Pelham, 1969.
151p   ISBN: 0-7207-0239-9

   This is the first history of any substance written to
   coincide with the club's entry into the First Division
   for the first time in their history.

675 The facts about a football club, featuring Queen's Park
Rangers / Alan Road; photographed by Bryn Campbell;
introduction by Bobby Charlton. London: G. Whizzard
Publications Ltd; Deutsch, 1976.
53p; illus
(Fact book)   ISBN: 0-233-96775-3
                              BL: X.622/5813

   QPR are the feature here of a somewhat unique
   treatment that looks at the organisation and administration of a football club.

676 The QPR story: official Queen's Park Rangers souvenir
brochure / Steve Pitts. London: Queen's Park Rangers
Football Club, 1982.
48p; pbk

   Published to mark the club's official centenary and
   achievement in reaching the 1982 Cup Final. Many
   historians put the foundation of the club at 1885
   with the formation of St. Jude's Institute, whereas
   other authorities insist upon 1882 as the moment of
   conception.

677 QPR supporters' review / Tony Incenzo. London?: The
author, 1985.
72p

   The first of a small series – concentrates on the
   1984-85 season.

678 Rangers in action / John Seabright. London: Queen's
Park Rangers FC, 1985.
16p; chiefly illus

679 We love you Rangers we do / Tony Incenzo. London?:
The author, 1985.
72p; pbk

   Concentrates on the 1985-86 season.

680 We're the famous QPR and we're gonna Wem-ber-lee /
Tony Incenzo. London?: The author, 1986.
72p; pbk

   Celebrates the club's League Cup Final appearance –
   a 3-0 reverse was disappointing for Rangers but gave
   Oxford United their finest hour.

681 Come on you R's / Tony Incenzo. London?: The
author, 1987.
72p; pbk

   This time concentrating on the 1986/87 season.

682 The history of Queen's Park Rangers 1882-1990 / Mark
Shaoul. London?: J. T. Design, 1990.
224p; illus

   Excellent study for the most part, but lapses a little
   in the later pages, falling into sketchy statistics and
   adverts. Nonetheless it is a key research text.

683 Queen's Park Rangers: a complete record / Gordon
Macey. Derby: Breedon Books, 1993.
256p; illus   ISBN: 1-873626-40-1
                              BL: YK.1994.b.10086

   Definitive account conveniently avoiding the use of
   dates in the title as the exact origins are in dispute.
   This is likely to give the most authoritative view.

Reading

684 Let's talk about Reading Football Club: including
football personalities and points of interest / Tom
Morgan. London: Sentinel, 1948.
32p; illus; pbk
(Football handbooks. Series 3; no. 43)

   Scarce collector's item – no real historical coverage.

685 Reading FC through the years 1871-1966. Reading:
Reading Evening Post, 1966.
20p; pbk

> Includes a brief history.

686 Biscuits and Royals: a history of Reading FC 1871-1984
/ David Downs. Reading?: Fericon, 1984.
214p   ISBN: 0-9509996-0-1

> Excellent and definitive publication chronicling the
> club's history from foundation – Reading claim to be
> the oldest league club in the South.

> ☞ Subsequent ed. B688

687 An A to Z of Reading Football Club / Alan Sedunary.
Reading: Reading Football Supporters' Club, 1985.
84p; illus; pbk   ISBN: 0-9511082-0-4

> A relatively light-hearted mixture of curious items.

688 Biscuits and Royals: a history of Reading FC 1871-1986
/ David Downs. Rev. ed. Reading?: Fericon, 1986.
234p

> New edition to cover the 1985-86 championship

> ☞ Previous ed. B686

689 Record breaking Royals / compiled and edited by Alan
Porton, David Downs and Ralph Webb. Reading:
Reading Football Club, 1986.
96p; illus; pbk   BL: YK.1988.b.2866

> Published to celebrate the club winning the Third Division
> title in 1986, amassing 94 points in the process.

690 More than a job?: the player's and fan's perspectives /
Roger Titford with Eamon Dunphy. Upavon, Pewsey:
Further Thought Publishing, 1992.
128p; pbk   ISBN: 0-9518771-0-0
                       BL: YK.1993.a.1088

> A look at Reading's 1975-76 season through the eyes
> of Dunphy the player and Titford the fan. Unique in its
> approach, this is of interest to students of the game
> in general rather than Reading historians *per se*.

> ☞ Also listed at: H126

Rochdale

691 Forward with Dale: a history of Rochdale AFC / Brian
Clough. Rochdale: The author, 1981.
38p; pbk

> The author is not 'the' B.C. – this slim volume com-
> prises a history and summary of the club's highlights.

692 The survivors: the story of Rochdale Association
Football Club / Steven Phillipps. Buckingham: Sporting
and Leisure, 1990.
176p; illus; index   ISBN: 0-86023-453-3
                     BL: YK.1991.b.8905

> An essential reference work on one of football's less
> chronicled clubs comprising a season-by-season ac-
> count from the earliest days to the present. The club
> were founded in 1907 following the demise of
> Rochdale Town, which was itself formed seven years
> earlier. As the title suggests, they have had a tough
> life in which the high spots have been few and far be-
> tween.

Rotherham United

693 Rotherham United 1951: Division Two. Rotherham:
Rotherham United Football Club, 1951.
29p; illus

> Celebrates promotion to Division Two for the first
> time with detailed records of the 1950-51 season
> along with all the results from 1923 onwards.

694 Football in Rotherham: the early years 1872-1925 /
Harold Tinkler. Rotherham: Clifton Local History
Group, 1986.
29p; pbk

> *Author's name is a pseudonym*
> Small ephemeral booklet on the club's first 50 or so
> years.

695 Millmoor personalities, 1946-1986 / David Watson.
Rotherham: Department of Libraries, Museum and Arts,
1986.
261p; illus
     ISBN: 0-903666-28-6 (cased) • ISBN: 0-903666-29-4 (pbk)
             BL: YK.1987.b.5306 • BL: YK.1987.b.5307

> Definitive text on the playing and management staff
> of the club – presents over 100 potted biographies.

696 100 years of football in Rotherham: history of
Rotherham United / Richard Finney and P. Baxter.
Rotherham?: The authors, 1988.
48p; pbk

> This slim volume presents a brief history. The club
> were formed in 1884 as Thornhill United, turning pro-
> fessional in 1905 as Rotherham County and
> becoming Rotherham United in 1925.

Scarborough

697 Scarborough AFC Wembley 1973. Scarborough:
Scarborough AFC, 1973.
16p; pbk

> Some years before the club were finally elected to the
> Football League, Scarborough tasted glory as FA
> Trophy winners in 1973.

698 Up for t'cup: the story of Scarborough FC in the FA
Cup 1887-1985 / Steve Adamson. 1985.
38p; pbk

> Studies every FA Cup game the club has ever played,
> including venturing into the third round proper in
> 1931, 1938, 1976 and 1978.

699 Scarborough FC in the FA Challenge Trophy: the
complete record 1969-1987 / Steve Adamson. 1987.
72p; pbk

> Match-by-match record of Scarborough in the Trophy
> – includes victories in 1973, 1976 and again in 1977.

700 The Boro boys / Steve Adamson. 1993.
24p; pbk

> By this time Scarborough had graduated into the
> Football League by becoming, in 1987, the first side
> to benefit from automatic promotion from the Con-
> ference League. This is, however, only a light
> ephemeral item.

Scunthorpe United

701 The history of Scunthorpe United Football Club / John
Staff. Scunthorpe: John Staff Enterprises, 1980.
250p; illus; pbk

BL: X.629/17370

> This book offers a remarkably detailed look at one of
> the smaller clubs in the League, chronicling their be-
> ginnings in 1899 and including the period 1910-1958
> when they were known as Scunthorpe and Lindsey
> United. Well worth consultation.

702 Scunthorpe United Football Club: a pictorial history /
Bob Steels. Runcorn: Archive, 1990.
120p; illus

ISBN: 0-948946-61-X

> Includes some photographs from their pre-league
> days but is largely about the club's league history
> from 1950 onwards.

703 Scunthorpe United: seasons 1983-84 to 1992-93 /
season-by-season commentary by Bob Steels; statistics
and history by Mike Ross; editors Michael Robinson,
John Robinson & Philip Norminton. Cleethorpes:
Soccer Book Publishing, 1993.
52p; illus; pbk
(The 10 seasons series)

ISBN: 0-947808-30-2

Sheffield United

704 The Sheffield Telegraph football guide and annual.
Sheffield & London: Sheffield Telegraph, 1919-

BL: P.P.2489.wfy

> General coverage of Sheffield football; contains some
> material of interest to United supporters.

☞ Also listed at: J49

705 Sheffield Independent football guide. Sheffield: Sheffield
Independent, 1926-
BL: P.P.2489.wfx

☞ Also listed at: J62

706 Let's talk about Sheffield United Football Club:
including football personalities and points of interest /
Tom Morgan. London: Sentinel, 1947.
32p; illus; pbk
(Football handbooks. Series 2; no. 26)

> Written to the standard format typical of this series
> – quaint as part of a collection but containing little
> real substance.

707 Sheffield United / Richard Sparling. London:
Newservice, 1949.
40p; pbk
(Famous football clubs)
BL: 7922.k.15/12

> Somewhat lightweight coverage.

708 Football in Sheffield / Percy Marshall Young. London:
Stanley Paul, 1962.
216p
BL: 7923.ttt.25

> Also covers Wednesday and early football in general
> in Sheffield.

☞ Also listed at: B714

709 Sheffield United FC: portrait of a championship Football
League Div. 4, 1981-2. Sheffield: The Club, 1982?
67p; illus; pbk
ISBN: 0-9508588-0-3
BL: X.622/24656

United were formed in 1889 and spent much of their history in the very top flight. So it was rather a shock for the club to find itself in Division Four for this season. As it happened, they escaped quickly – this is their promotion souvenir.

710 Sheffield United FC: united we rise. Sheffield?: Sheffield United Football Club?, 1984.
52p; pbk

Promotion was achieved again in 1983-84, this time from Division Three to Division Two.

711 Sheffield United centenary history 1889-1989 / Denis Clarebrough. Sheffield: Sheffield United FC, 1990.
272p   ISBN: 0-9508588-1-1

Expertly researched definitive history; the essential text on this club.

Sheffield Wednesday

712 The romance of the Wednesday, 1867-1926 / Richard Sparling. Sheffield: Sir W. C. Leng & Co., 1926.
274p; illus   BL: D

Very few clubs were covered substantially in print in their early years. This highly collectable work is an exception.

713 Let's talk about Sheffield Wednesday Football Club: including football personalities and points of interest / Tom Morgan. London: Sentinel, 1946.
32p; illus; pbk
(Football handbooks. Series 1; no. 10)   BL: W.P.1144/10

Low on detail.

714 Football in Sheffield / Percy Marshall Young. London: Stanley Paul, 1962.
216p   BL: 7923.ttt.25

Excellent study with much material on the formative years of the association game in and around the city – significant Wednesday content.

☞ Also listed at: B708

715 Sheffield Wednesday Football Club 1867-1967 / Richard A. Sparling. Sheffield: Sheffield Wednesday Football Club, 1967.
35p; pbk

Richard Sparling amassed a great deal of research for a major centenary volume but, in the event, the project did not come to fruition. Instead a diluted version was published and this effectively serves as the club handbook for 1967-68 containing brief historical notes, FA Cup results from 1880 and pen pictures of contemporary staff.

716 Wednesday!: the history of Sheffield's oldest professional football club / Keith Farnsworth. Sheffield: Sheffield City Libraries, 1982.
x, 284p; illus
    ISBN: 0-900660-87-2 (cased) • ISBN: 0-900660-88-0 (pbk)
                                          BL: X.809/54799

The club were formed in 1867 by Sheffield Wednesday Cricket Club – this is a definitive historical text best used in conjunction with the following entry.

717 Sheffield Wednesday: a complete record, 1867-1987 / Keith Farnsworth. Derby: Breedon Books, 1987.
384p; illus   ISBN: 0-907969-25-9
                                       BL: YK.1988.a.3972

An essential text presenting statistics from formation of the club to the present, supported by historical narrative.

Shrewsbury Town

718 Up the Blues: into the 2nd Division. Shrewsbury: Shrewsbury Town FC, 1979.
20p; pbk

Celebrates their 1978-79 Division Three championship season.

719 Shrewsbury Town FC centenary souvenir 1886-1986 / Derek Clarke and Roy Williams. Shrewsbury: Shrewsbury Town Football Club, 1986.
34p; illus; pbk

The club were founded in 1886 but did not join the League until 1950. This small booklet presents a brief history.

720 Shrewsbury Town FC facts and figures: a statistical history / compiled by Leigh Edwards. The author, 1989.
60p; pbk

Includes all the league tables from 1890-1950 – as such this is a statistical history of the club's pre-league career. A valuable piece of research.

Southampton

721 The history of the Southampton Football Club / A. E.
Jones. London: G. W. May, 1924.
32p; pbk   BL: Mic.A.8206.(3) (microfilm copy)

A very rare early example covering the club's foundation in 1885 as Southampton St Marys and their
subsequent development as a league club from 1920.

722 Fifty years of football: a golden jubilee souvenir
1885-1935. Southampton: Southampton FC, 1935.
48p; illus; pbk

Equally scarce ephemeral brochure.

723 Let's talk about Southampton Football Club: including
football personalities and points of interest / Tom
Morgan. London: Sentinel, 1947.
32p; illus; pbk
(Football handbooks. Series 2; no. 29)

Scant historical coverage.

724 Southampton / Fred Ward. London: Newservice, 1947.
40p; pbk
(Famous football clubs)   BL: 7922.k.15/5

A brief history but not an important historical source.

725 Handbook of Saints. Southampton: Southampton
Football Club, 1968.
48p

726 Southampton: the official club history / Peter East.
Norwich: Wensum, 1979.
112p; illus   ISBN: 0-903619-30-X

Relative bias towards the post-war years in this first
serious effort at the club's history.

727 Southampton Football Club centenary 1885-1985 /
edited by Jeff Powell. Southampton: Southampton
Football Club, 1986.
64p; pbk

728 Saints: a complete record of Southampton Football Club
1885-1987 / Gary Chalk and Duncan Holley. Derby:
Breedon Books, 1987.
320p; illus   ISBN: 0-907969-22-4
               BL: YK.1988.b.1183

In keeping with all the 'Complete Record' series, this is
an essential reference work.

729 The alphabet of the Saints: a complete who's who of
Southampton FC / Duncan Holley & Gary Chalk.
Leicester: ACL Colour Print & Polar Publishing, 1992.
416p; illus   ISBN: 0-9514862-3-3
               BL: YK.1993.b.9895

No fewer than 725 players are featured – an essential companion volume to the 'Complete Record'
above.

Southend United

730 Southend United Football Club: the official history of
'The Blues' / Peter Mason & David Goody. Harefield:
Yore, 1993.
320p; illus, plans   ISBN: 1-874427-20-8
                  BL: YC.1994.b.125

The one and only text covering the club, but it includes everything one might need to know.

Stockport County

731 The history of Stockport County AFC 1883-1965 /
Simon Myers. Stockport?: The author, 1966.
164p

Despite its relatively recent date, this is a scarce
book. It offers a season-by-season summary of the
club's history.

732 Stockport County centenary 1883-1983 / Tom Turton
and Howard Jones. Stockport: Stockport Football Club,
1983.
36p; pbk
*The full cover title of this small item leaves us in little
doubt regarding the period of coverage – 'Stockport
County 1883-1983 – 100 years centenary'. As you
will gather it covers the club's demi bi-centenary celebrations.*

733 Stockport County: a complete record / Peter Freeman
with assistance from Richard Harnwell. Derby: Breedon
Books, 1994.
256p; illus   ISBN: 1-873626-72-X
Essential work of reference.

Stoke City

734 Let's talk about Stoke City Football Club: including
football personalities and points of interest / Tom
Morgan. London: Sentinel, 1946.
32p; illus; pbk
(Football handbooks. Series 1; no. 12)
     BL: W.P.1144/12
Scarce ephemeral booklet – limited content.

735 Stoke City / R. L. D. Austerberry and W. J. Foster.
London: Newservice, 1949.
44p; pbk
(Famous football clubs)   BL: 7922.k.15/11
*One of a well-known series – generally rather light-
weight.*

736 Stoke City Football Club centenary handbook,
1863-1963: a history of the club over the past one
hundred years / Peter Buxton. London: Pyramid Press,
1963.
76p   ISBN: 0-493-80007-7
     BL: 7926.d.20

*Stoke are the second oldest side in the entire
League: 1863 has been taken as their foundation
year but more recent research by Wade Martin suggests 1868, the year Stoke Ramblers were formed by
local railway workers. No doubt the debate will continue.*

737 A potter's tale: the story of Stoke City Football Club /
Wade Martin. Buckingham: Sporting & Leisure, 1988.
132p; illus; index
     ISBN: 0-86023-407-X
     BL: YK.1989.b.4053

*An excellent study – good coverage of the early
years.*

738 Goalkeepers / Wade Martin. Stoke-on-Trent: Sisyphus,
1991.
48p; pbk
(Master potters of Stoke City)
     ISBN: 1-873716-01-X

*This is the first in a series of six which dissect the
personnel in terms of the roles they played in the club
– an interesting approach, which has also been applied to Wolverhampton Wanderers; this could be a
trend which other club historians may follow.*

739 Goalscorers / Wade Martin. Stoke-on-Trent: Sisyphus,
1991.
48p; pbk
(Master potters of Stoke City)
     ISBN: 1-873716-00-1

740 Central defenders / Wade Martin. Stoke-on-Trent:
Sisyphus, 1992.
48p; pbk
(Master potters of Stoke City)
     ISBN: 1-873716-02-8

741 Midfielders / Wade Martin. Stoke-on-Trent: Sisyphus,
1992.
48p; pbk
(Master potters of Stoke City)
     ISBN: 1-873716-03-6

742 Full backs / Wade Martin. Stoke-on-Trent: Sisyphus,
1993.
48p; pbk
(Master potters of Stoke City)
     ISBN: 1-873716-04-4

743 The managers / Wade Martin. Stoke-on-Trent: Sisyphus,
1993.
48p; pbk
(Master potters of Stoke City)
     ISBN: 1-873716-05-2

Sunderland

744 Let's talk about Sunderland Football Club: including football personalities and points of interest / Tom Morgan. London: Sentinel, 1946.
32p; illus; pbk
(Football handbooks. Series 1; no. 12a)

BL: W.P.1144/12a

Interesting ephemeral item but extremely lightweight coverage. In keeping with the superstition which prevails amongst the football fraternity, the book was numbered 12a, even though it was the thirteenth in the series.

745 Ha'way the lads: the road to Wembley: the story of Sunderland Association Football Club and its supporters 1879-1973, and the FA Cup finals of 1913, 1937 and 1973 / Ceolfrith Arts Centre; edited by Christopher Carrell and Richard Padwick. Sunderland: Ceolfrith Press, 1974.
120p; illus

Published in conjunction with the Sunderland Arts Centre exhibition 'Ha'way the lads – the road to Wembley'
BL: X.619/7953

Excellent evocative study which chronicles the team's Cup Final appearances. This was entirely prompted by Sunderland's 1973 Wembley appearance against Leeds United – their 1-0 triumph was one of the most memorable in the history of the competition.

746 Sunderland and the Cup / Arthur Appleton. Sunderland: Frank Graham, 1974.
80p

General survey of the club's cup history.

747 Sunderland AFC centenary 1879-1979. Sunderland: Sunderland Football Club, 1979.
80p; illus

Lightweight centenary publication.

748 The history of Sunderland AFC: 1879-1986 / Bill Simmons & Bob Graham. Sunderland?: The author, 1986.
522p; illus, maps; pbk

BL: YK.1987.a.5240

Extremely substantial coverage – an essential work of reference.

749 The Sunderland quiz book / Paul Joannou. Edinburgh: Mainstream, 1988.
176p; illus

ISBN: 1-85158-181-2
BL: YK.1989.a.3968

1,000 questions.

750 The Sunderland story / David Thornton. D. & J. Thornton, 1988.
16p; pbk

ISBN: 0-907339-32-8
BL: YK.1990.a.5216

An unusual item telling the history of the club entirely in cartoon form – aimed at the juvenile market.

751 Sunderland greats / Paul Hetherington; foreword, Bob Murray. Edinburgh: Sportsprint, 1989.
ix, 92p; illus; pbk

ISBN: 0-85976-266-1
BL: YK.1990.a.4602

A selection of the best players to have donned the red and white stripes.

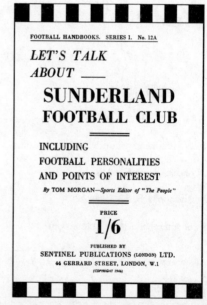

FOOTBALL HANDBOOKS. SERIES 1. No. 12A

LET'S TALK
ABOUT ——
**SUNDERLAND
FOOTBALL CLUB**

INCLUDING
FOOTBALL PERSONALITIES
AND POINTS OF INTEREST
By TOM MORGAN—*Sports Editor of "The People"*

PRICE
1/6

PUBLISHED BY
SENTINEL PUBLICATIONS (LONDON) LTD.
44 GERRARD STREET, LONDON, W.1
(COPYRIGHT 1946)

752 Sunderland AFC 1890-1990: 100 years of league football. Sunderland: Sunderland AFC Supporters Club, 1990.
64p; pbk

The club played their first Football League game on 13 September 1890 – it proved to be an unlucky date as they lost at home to Burnley by 3-2.

753 Sunderland's 100th year in the Football League /
photographs by Charles Biggs & Alice King. Ashbrooke:
Cedar Lodge Marketing, 1990.
xii, 131p; chiefly illus   ISBN: 0-9517016-0-6
   A good source of illustrations.

754 The all time great matches / Paul Tully. Newcastle:
Evening Chronicle, 1991.
104p; illus; pbk
   Coverage of both Sunderland and Newcastle United
   ☞ Also listed at: B585

755 The all time greats / Paul Tully. Newcastle: Evening
Chronicle, 1991.
104p; illus; pbk
   Coverage of both Sunderland and Newcastle United
   ☞ Also listed at: B586

756 Sunderland: seasons, 1983-84 to 1992-93 / season-by-
season commentary by Geoff Storey; statistics and
history by Mike Ross; editors, Michael Robinson, John
Robinson & Philip Norminton. Cleethorpes: Soccer
Book Publishing, 1993.
52p; illus; pbk
(The 10 seasons series)   ISBN: 0-947808-32-9

Swansea City

757 Let's talk about Swansea Football Club: including
football personalities and points of interest / Tom
Morgan. London: Sentinel, 1947.
32p; illus; pbk
(Football handbooks. Series 2; no. 34)
   Limited content.

758 The Swans: a history of the Swansea Town Football
Club / Brinley E. Matthews. Swansea: Uplands
Bookshop, 1967.
131p

   The club were known as Swansea Town until 1970.
   ☞ Subsequent ed. B763

759 The Swansea City story 1912-1972 / Bryn Matthews.
Swansea: Swansea City AFC, 1976.
106p
   *The club were formed as Swansea Town in 1912 and
changed their name to City in 1970. This is a worthwhile general history.*

760 Swansea City AFC official annual / edited by Jim Hill.
Swansea: C. Davies, 1979-
96p; illus; pbk   BL: X.629/13812
   *The first edition of this annual coincided with the
club's promotion to Division Two.*

761 Division One Swansea City FC official souvenir.
Swansea: South Wales Evening Post, 1981.
   *Celebrates the club's promotion to the top flight –
Division One.*

762 Swansea City 1912-1982 / David Farmer. London:
Pelham, 1982.
272p; illus; index   ISBN: 0-7207-1413-3
                               BL: X.809/54335
   *A comprehensive history, particularly strong on the
early years.*

763 The Swans: a history of the Swansea City Football Club
1912-1987 / Brinley E. Matthews. Swansea: Uplands
Bookshop, 1987.
132p; illus
   *An updated version of the author's earlier work. Not
many clubs can include a victory over Real Madrid in
their history – Swansea beat them 3-0 in 1927. Evidently they had to do something to match the FA
Cup Final victory of their great rivals, Cardiff City, in
the same year. This book records this and many
other interesting events.*
   ☞ Previous ed. B758

764 Swansea City Football Club / John Burgum. Runcorn:
Archive, 1988.
128p; illus; pbk
                             ISBN: 0-948946-19-9
   *An interesting photographic study which concen-
trates on recent years.*

Swindon Town

765 Swindon Football Club: Argentine tour, June-July, 1912 / Samuel Henry Allen. London: Daily Chronicle, 1912.
31p; pbk   BL: D

A scarce early item. During the immediate pre-war years the club were flying high in the Southern League, never finishing outside the top five between 1907 and 1914. Their legendary England International, Harold Fleming, was an important influence.

766 Handbook 1948-49 / Swindon Town Football Club. Swindon: The Club, 1949-   BL: P.P.2489.wkc

767 Swindon Town FC 1881-1981 / Paul Plowman. Swindon: Swindon Town Football Club, 1981.
40p; pbk

A centenary magazine style publication containing many adverts and little material which cannot be found in later more substantial works.

768 Swindon Town: first in Wiltshire / Paul Plowman. 1981.

Swindon were founder members of the Third Division in 1920. This covers their Southern League days before that date presenting a statistical record to include all League and Cup appearances, plus results, scorers and pen pictures.

769 Swindon Town in the Third South / Paul Plowman. Swindon: The author, 1983.

Continues the statistical record of the club concentrating on their days in the Third Division (South) between 1921 and 1958.

770 Town through time: Swindon Town goalkeepers 1884-1984 / Paul Plowman. Swindon?: Footprint, 1984.
32p; pbk

An unusual approach concentrating entirely on the 'custodian' breed.

771 Swindon Town to Wembley and beyond / Paul Plowman. 1987.
120p

Continues the author's chronological statistical approach, covering the years 1958 to 1985 with all the line-ups, scorers etc. Plowman is a particularly good example of the breed of club statistician, prepared to undertake painstaking research to present the bare bone figures which complement the flesh and blood of the historical narrative. Barclay, in his fifth eclogue of 1508, evidently presaged the labours of his ilk – 'The sturdie plowman, lustie, strong and bold, overcometh the winter with driving the foote-ball, forgetting labour and many a grievous fall!'

772 The Robins: the story of Swindon Town Football Club / Dick Mattick. Buckingham: Sporting and Leisure, 1989.
128p; illus; index   ISBN: 0-86023-460-6
          BL: YK.1990.b.8184

Unusually, the author of this first major history of the club was a board member when it was written. Half the book relates to the club's history while the balance comprises photographs, documents, cartoons and accounts of great matches – this is the obvious starting point for all researchers.

773 100 years of football in Swindon and district / George Thomas. Swindon: Swindon & District Football League, 1991.
112p; illus; pbk   ISBN: 0-9517389-0-9

Contains material of interest to the Swindon Town historian.

Torquay United

774 Torquay United football annual: golden jubilee number 1948-49.

Includes a history of the club by W. J. Luscombe
         BL: P.P.2489.wkh

This scarce early item includes the club's history from its foundation in 1898 taking in the years between 1910 and 1921, when they played as Torquay Town. Turning professional in 1921, they then acquired their current familiar name.

775 Torquay United: the first 70 years / Laura Joint. Exeter: Obelisk, 1991.
96p; illus; pbk   ISBN: 0-946651-42-6
          BL: YK.1992.a.4396

This is the essential work for researchers interested in this club which has had a very limited coverage in published form. The author is the regular football correspondent for the *Western Morning News* and takes 1921 as the startpoint for her highly informative study.

Tottenham Hotspur

776 Tottenham Hotspur Football Club programme Sept. 16, 1897 / Tottenham Hotspur Football Club. Tottenham: C. Coventry, 1897.   BL: D

The club were formed in 1882. This is a record of a scarce early example of the club programme.

777 The Tottenham Hotspur football handbook. London: Tottenham Hotspur Football Club, 1897-

Not published 1915-1918; 1941-1947   BL: P.P.2489.wfl

778 The White Hart: souvenir of the Spurs entry to the English League. London: J. Cameron, 1908.
48p; pbk

This is an extremely scarce ephemeral publication which effectively offers the first history of the club. The first twelve seasons were covered by 'Two Old Spurs' and the remaining by John Cameron who played from 1898 to 1904 and managed the club from 1899 to 1907, in addition to his duties as club secretary! The White Hart public house at 750 High Road was the address for the club's offices. Spurs entered the League in 1908.

779 A romance of football: the history of the Tottenham Hotspur FC London: Tottenham & Edmonton Weekly Herald, 1921.
36p; pbk

This history originally appeared in the Herald in weekly instalments. This is the revised material published in booklet form. In April 1921 a special 24 page supplement was also produced entitled 'How the Spurs got into the Cup Final'. Both items are extremely scarce.

780 Let's talk about Tottenham Hotspur Football Club: including football personalities and points of interest / Tom Morgan. London: Sentinel, 1946.
32p; illus; pbk
(Football handbooks. Series 1; no. 16)   BL: W.P.1144/16
Little of serious historic value.

781 Tottenham Hotspur Football Club: its birth and progress, 1882-1946 / G. Wagstaffe Simmons. Tottenham: The Club, 1947.
viii, 224p; illus   BL: 7919.b.23

Rare for such a substantial work to be published at this early date. Comprehensive and informative and a collector's item in its own right. The author was a director of the club.

782 Tottenham Hotspur / Fred Ward. London: Newservice, 1948.
36p; illus
(Famous football clubs)   BL: 7922.k.15/10
Lightweight coverage only.

783 Spurs: a history of Tottenham Hotspur Football Club / Julian Holland. London: Phoenix Sports Books, 1956.
224p; illus   BL: 7922.ee.20

Regarded as one of the best books about Spurs. Includes extensive coverage of the amateur and pre-league days.

784 Spurs 1961: the official publication of the Spurs players to mark their achievements in season 1960-61. London: Tottenham Hotspur FC, 1961.
48p; illus; pbk
Illustrated celebratory brochure.

785 Spurs supreme: a review of soccer's greatest-ever side 1960-61 / Ralph Leslie Finn. London: Hale, 1961.
158p; illus   BL: 7925.g.3

Only a great individual eleven could warrant a complete book all to itself. The Spurs double-winning side was worthy of the treatment. All the players are well covered and much of the work comprises reproductions of match reports. Essential reference work for all researchers of this time in the club's history.

786 Spurs: the double / Julian Holland. London: Heinemann in association with Naldrett, 1961.
199p; illus

Effectively an update of Holland's previous work extended to cover Spurs rare feat in winning the double of League Championship and FA Cup.

787 Spurs in action: a pictorial survey of the 1961-62 season. London: Weekly Herald Publications, 1962.
36p; pbk

Yet another ephemeral celebration of a memorable season. Following the double year the club went on to win the FA Cup again and to compete in the European Cup.

788 Spurs go marching on: the European triumph, 1963 / Ralph Leslie Finn. London: Hale, 1963.
192p; illus   BL: 7926.ee.40

Spurs' victory in the European Cup Winners' Cup was a significant one for British football as it was the first major European trophy won by a British side.

789 Spurs in action: a pictorial survey of the 1962-63 season. London: Weekly Herald Publications, 1963.
36p; pbk

Cup winners again and runners-up in the championship.

790 Spurs in action: a pictorial survey of the 1963-64 season. London: Weekly Herald Publications, 1964.
36p; pbk

No major trophies in this campaign.

791 London's Cup Final, 1967: how Chelsea and Spurs reached Wembley / Ralph Leslie Finn. London: Hale, 1967.
188p; illus   BL: X.449/2830

Spurs triumphed in the FA Cup yet again – their fifth success to date at this time.

☞ Also listed at: B197; D12

792 The Tottenham Hotspur football book / Dennis Signy. London: Stanley Paul, 1967-1974.
illus

8 issues published   BL: P.441/164

Noted for its illustrations more than its narrative.

793 Spurs. London: Evening Standard, 1970.
(London football clubs series)

794 Spurs again: the story of the League Cup season 1970-71 / Ralph Leslie Finn. London: Hale, 1971.
190p; illus   ISBN: 0-7091-2770-7
     BL: X.629/3778

Spurs won the League Cup in this year – the only major domestic prize which had eluded them thus far.

795 The Tottenham Hotspur story / Deryk Brown. London: Arthur Barker, 1971.
144p; illus   ISBN: 0-213-99384-8
     BL: X.629/3953

796 The battle of London: Arsenal versus Tottenham Hotspur / Rex Pardoe. London: Tom Stacey, 1972.
xix, 220p; illus   ISBN: 0-85468-150-7
     BL: X.629/4130

An overall history of the rivalry between the two clubs from the 1880s to the 1970s.

☞ Also listed at: B21

797 The glory game / Hunter Davies. London: Weidenfeld and Nicolson, 1972.
xii, 332p; illus; index   ISBN: 0-297-99579-0

A detailed account of Spurs' 1971-72 season in all it's aspects. An unusual 'insider' approach – the author was given unprecedented fly-on-the-wall access to present a view of football and footballers never seen before. As such, this is an important work for the game in general rather than just for Spurs followers.

☞ Subsequent ed. B804

798 Tottenham Hotspur FC: the official history / Ralph L. Finn. London: Hale, 1972.
221p; illus   ISBN: 0-7091-3079-1
     BL: X.629/4904

General history concentrating heavily on particular highlights.

799 Tottenham Hotspur official annual. Hainault: Essex Circle, 1979-1992.
illus

Published by Cockerel Books 1985-1988; not published 1989-1991; published by Tottenham Hotspur FC 1992

800 The Tottenham Hotspur story / Anton Rippon. Ashbourne: Moorland Publishing, 1980.
95p; illus   ISBN: 0-903485-97-4
     BL: X.622/9371

Mostly 1950 to date – rather light on early history.

801 And the Spurs go marching on ... / Phil Soar with Danny Blanchflower and others. London: Hamlyn, 1982.
256p; illus; index   ISBN: 0-600-34664-1
     BL: X.622/13837

The club's centenary history. Superbly presented. An essential research text.

☞ Subsequent ed. B803

802 The Spurs historiette. Basildon: Association of Football Statisticians, 1983-1985.
Note: 29 issues published   BL: P.441/1037

Published monthly from January 1983 to June 1985; a number of issues were entitled 'The Spur and Historiette'.

☞ Also listed at: L546

803 And the Spurs go marching on . . . / Phil Soar with Danny Blanchflower and others. Rev. ed. London: Hamlyn, 1985.
272p; illus; index   ISBN: 0-600-50175-2

☞ Previous ed. B801

804 The glory game / Hunter Davies. New ed. Edinburgh: Mainstream, 1985.
xxxii, 346p; illus; index
     ISBN: 1-85158-002-6 (cased) • ISBN: 1-85158-003-4 (pbk)
     BL: YK.1991.a.2407

☞ Previous ed. B797; subsequent ed. B807

805 The glory, glory nights: the complete history of Spurs in European competition / Colin Gibson and Harry Harris. London: Cockerel, 1986.
272p; illus; pbk   ISBN: 1-869914-00-7

A reprinting of newspaper reports 1961-1986 – reports like these, usually written in the heat of the moment, can add an interesting perspective when compared to the more studied, retrospective accounts of serious historical publications. Well worth consultation.

806 Spurs: a complete record 1882-1988 / Bob Goodwin.
Derby: Breedon Books, 1988.
464p; illus   ISBN: 0-907969-42-9
                           BL: YK.1991.a.9350

An essential work – later updated.

807 The glory game: the new edition of the British football
classic / Hunter Davies. Rev. ed. Edinburgh:
Mainstream, 1990.
346p; illus; index; pbk   ISBN: 1-85158-376-9
                           BL: YK.1991.a.2407

☞ Previous ed. B804

808 Tottenham Hotspur greats / Harry Harris; foreword by
Irving Scholar. Edinburgh: Sportsprint, 1990.
vii, 172p; illus; pbk   ISBN: 0-85976-309-9
                           BL: YK.1990.b.9523

*One of Spurs' greatest managers, Bill Nicholson,
chooses 11 greats from the post-war era. Includes
many quotations and anecdotes.*

809 Heroes and villains: the inside story of the 1990-91
season at Arsenal and Tottenham Hotspur / Alex Fynn
and Lynton Guest. London: Penguin, 1991.
373p; illus; pbk   ISBN: 0-14-014769-1
                           BL: YK.1991.a.9721

*Spurs won the FA Cup in the year in which Arsenal
were League champions.*

☞ Also listed at: B38

810 Spurs: a complete record 1882-1991 / Bob Goodwin.
Derby: Breedon Books, 1991.
416p; illus   ISBN: 0-907969-93-3

Updated version of an essential text.

811 Behind closed doors: dreams and nightmares at Spurs /
Irving Scholar with Mihir Bose. London: Deutsch, 1992.
xiv, 367p; illus   ISBN: 0-233-98824-6
                           BL: YK.1993.b.13867

*A detailed account of boardroom politics which
throws light on the goings-on which most of the public are generally shielded from. This is an essential
work for all Spurs researchers but is also of much
value to football writers in general as many major issues are touched upon.*

☞ Also listed at: C437

812 Sick as a parrot: the inside story of the Spurs fiasco /
Chris Horrie. London: Virgin, 1992.
vii, 293p; illus; pbk
     Bibliography: p292-293
                           ISBN: 0-86369-620-1
                           BL: YK.1993.a.10372

*Amongst other things, the Spurs manager Terry
Venables endured a major wrangle with chairman Alan
Sugar, leading to the manager's sacking in 1993 – a
sad period indeed for a great club involving all manner
of political issues. This work presents a detailed
study of the prevailing chaos.*

813 The Spurs alphabet: a complete who's who of
Tottenham Hotspur FC / Bob Goodwin. Leicester:
ACL & Polar Publishing, 1992.
416p; illus   ISBN: 0-9514862-8-4
                           BL: YK.1993.b.5083

*Substantial work on the players and managers from
all eras in the club's history.*

814 Spurs: a complete record 1882-1993 / Bob Goodwin.
Derby: Breedon Books, 1993.
416p; illus   ISBN: 1-873626-29-0
                           BL: YK.1994.a.4231

Recent update of essential work.

815 Tottenham Hotspur: player by player / Ivan Ponting.
Enfield: Guinness, 1993.
176p; illus   ISBN: 0-85112-717-7
                           BL: YK.1993.b.14660

Covers leading figures rather than every single player.

816 Barcelona to Bedlam: Venables-Sugar – the true story /
Guy Nathan. Woodham Ferrers: New Author
Publications, 1994.
379p; pbk   ISBN: 1-89778-026-5
                           BL: YK.1994.a.11222

*The use of the word 'true' might well be in dispute as
both sides in the acrimonious Venables/Sugar battle
undoubtedly present differing versions. Certainly of
interest to Spurs followers and to anyone researching into football administration and politics.*

Tranmere Rovers

817 Let's talk about Tranmere Rovers Football Club:
including football personalities and points of interest /
Tom Morgan. London: Sentinel, 1948.
32p; illus; pbk
(Football handbooks. Series 3; no. 45)

Lightweight content only.

818 Football on Merseyside / Percy Marshall Young.
London: Stanley Paul, 1963.
215p; illus   BL: 7926.n.47

*Excellent study of all the Merseyside clubs from one
of football's most respected writers. Tranmere are
well covered alongside their more illustrious neigh-
bours, Everton and Liverpool.*

☞ Also listed at: B281, B386, B1019

819 The Daily Express A-Z of Mersey soccer / John Keith
and Peter Thomas. London: Beaverbrook Newspapers,
1973.
141p; illus

*Includes Tranmere Rovers material but is not a key
text.*

☞ Also listed at: B283, B388

820 The A-Z of Tranmere Rovers / Peter Bishop. Tranmere: Tranmere Rovers Football Club, 1990.
94p; illus; pbk

> Tranmere are given the alphabet all to themselves for the first time, unhampered by the other clubs across the river.

821 Tranmere Rovers 1881-1921: a new history / Gilbert Upton. Southport: The author, 1991.
134p; illus; pbk   ISBN: 0-9518648-0-7
BL: YK.1992.a.5458

> An essential work of reference covering the club's early history – 1884 is generally taken as their foundation year when they played under the name Belmont. This work covers their pre-league days – they joined the Third Division (North) in 1921.

822 Three sides of the Mersey: an oral history of Everton, Liverpool and Tranmere Rovers / Rogan Taylor and Andrew Ward, with John Williams. London: Robson, 1993.
290p; illus   ISBN: 0-86051-871-X
BL: YK.1995.b.1019

> Reminiscences and observations on the three Merseyside clubs. On a number of occasions recently Tranmere have come close to joining their near neighbours in the top flight but have missed out so far . . . They will try again in 1995/96.

☞ Also listed at: B300, B430

Walsall

823 Walsall FC 1888-1955 / W.B. Rawlinson ('Philistine'). Walsall: Walsall Observer, 1955.
64p; pbk

> Season-by-season coverage in this scarce booklet.

824 The history of Walsall Football Club 1888-1992 / Tony Matthews and Geoff Allman. Warley: Sports Leisure Concepts, 1992.
272p   ISBN: 1-873171-06-4

> Excellent wide-ranging coverage – this is the essential starting point for students of the club.

Watford

825 Watford and West Hertfordshire: football portraits reprinted from the Watford and Herts Leader. Watford: Watford Printing Works, 1896.
BL: D

> Extremely scarce item of interest to the Watford historian. The club itself was founded in 1891 as Watford Rovers although the exact origins of the club can be debated.

826 Watford Football Club: official handbook 1960-1961 / Watford Football Club. London: Pyramid Press, 1960-
BL: P.P.7613.kc

827 Watford: a tale of the unexpected / Geoff Sweet and Graham Burton. Watford: Burton, 1983.
96p; illus
(Bugle books)   ISBN: 0-9508973-0-2
BL: X.622/17983

> This is effectively an account of Watford's first season in Division One – 1982/83 – in which they finished runners-up.

828 Watford – Wembley '84 FA Cup Final official souvenir brochure produced in conjunction with Benskins. Watford: Watford Association Football Club, 1984.
24p; illus; pbk   ISBN: 0-9509601-0-1
BL: X.622/21934

> The club were runners-up to Everton, losing in the final by 2-0.

829 The official centenary history of Watford FC 1881-1991 / Oliver Phillips. Watford: Watford Football Club, 1991.
304p; illus   ISBN: 0-9509601-6-0

> Very comprehensive coverage – an essential work of reference.

West Bromwich Albion

830 Let's talk about West Bromwich Albion Football Club: including football personalities and points of interest / Tom Morgan. London: Sentinel, 1947.
32p; illus; pbk
(Football handbooks. Series 2; no. 40)

> Of value to the collector rather than the historian in view of its rather lightweight content.

831   West Bromwich Albion / W. Ellery Jephcott. London: Newservice, 1948.
40p; pbk
(Famous football clubs)

Although the 'Famous Football Club' series was promoted as offering an 'official history' of many of the leading clubs, the coverage was in truth rather lightweight.

832   Hawthorns golden jubilee: the story of the West Bromwich Albion football ground 1900-1950 / W. Ellery Jephcott. West Bromwich: West Bromwich Albion Football Club, 1950.
38p; pbk

Concentrates on the history and development of The Hawthorns, the ground of West Bromwich Albion since the start of the century.

833   West Bromwich Albion: soccer in the Black Country, 1879-1965 / Peter Morris. London: Heinemann, 1965.
xviii, 190p; illus   BL: X.449/1456

Well balanced coverage of all eras.

834   The West Bromwich Albion football book / Ray Matts. London: Stanley Paul, 1970.
128p; illus   ISBN: 0-09-103240-7

Contemporary coverage only.

835   Albion through the war: a statistical history of West Bromwich Albion's fortunes during the Second World War / Tony Matthews. West Bromwich: West Bromwich Albion Football Club, 1976.
2, 29p; illus; pbk   ISBN: 0-9505585-0-8
     BL: X.619/17407

Unusual concentration on one particular era from the club's history; comprehensive statistics for the period.

836   Who's who of West Bromwich Albion 1879-1977 / Tony Matthews. Birmingham: West Bromwich Albion Football Club, 1977.
112p; illus

Covers every first team player for the period.

837   1879-1979: West Bromwich Albion Football Club centenary brochure. West Bromwich: West Bromwich Albion FC, 1979.
68p; pbk

838   Albion in China: the first British football tour to China: West Bromwich Albion / introduction and captions by Frank Taylor; photographs by David Kingsley. Oxford: Pergamon for The London Export Corporation, 1979.
64p; chiefly illus; pbk   ISBN: 0-08-024496-3
     BL: X.619/19838

An unusual ephemeral publication resulting from a somewhat bizarre excursion. John Trewick, one of the players lucky enough to be given such an opportunity, was also offered the chance to see the Great Wall in an off-duty moment – his response must surely be one of football's gems – 'No thank you. When you've seen one wall, you've seen the lot'.

839   The centenary A-Z of Albion / Tony Matthews and Colin MacKenzie. West Bromwich?: T. Matthews & J. Osborne, 1979.
310p   ISBN: 0-9505585-1-6

Many interesting items alongside lesser known material.

840   West Bromwich Albion: the first hundred years / G. A. Willmore. London: Hale, 1979.
207p; illus, 1 map   ISBN: 0-7091-7865-4
     BL: X.629/12754

A chapter for each decade.

841   A unique double: FA Cup winners and promoted from Division Two 1930-31 / Tony Matthews. Birmingham: West Bromwich Albion FC, 1981.
32p; illus; pbk   ISBN: 0-9505585-3-2

Retrospective study of a triumphant season.

842   Albion!: a complete record of West Bromwich Albion 1879-1987 / Tony Matthews with Colin Mackenzie. Derby: Breedon Books, 1987.
320p; illus   ISBN: 0-907969-23-2
     BL: YK.1988.b.1184

Essential definitive work on one of football's most famous clubs.

843   Who's who of West Bromwich Albion 1879-1988 / Tony Matthews. Birmingham: Albion News Publications, 1989.
104p; illus   ISBN: 0-9505585-6-7

Features every Albion first team player for the period.

844   The official history of Albion in the Central League / edited by G. A. Willmore. Birmingham?: The author, 1991.
100p

Club historians are ever resourceful in their quest for new angles – this covers the Albion reserve side. Whether this prompts a trend in football publishing remains to be seen. Personally, I think not.

845   FA Cup Final victory: commemorating the 25th anniversary of West Bromwich Albion's Cup Final victory 18th May 1968 / Tony Matthews. Warley: Sports Leisure Concepts, 1993.
32p; illus; pbk   ISBN: 1-873171-09-9

Yet more resourcefulness – this time looking back at Albion's 1-0 extra time win over Everton. The presentation is largely by way of a collection of newspaper reproductions.

846   West Bromwich Albion: a complete record / Tony Matthews. Derby: Breedon Books, 1993.
256p; illus   ISBN: 1-873626-47-9
     BL: YK.1994.b.4015

A complete update of this essential work.

847 West Bromwich Albion: 100 great matches / G. A.
Willmore. Derby: Breedon Books, 1994.
256p; illus   ISBN: 1-873626-96-7

*West Ham
United*

848 The Football Association's English Cup Competition
Final to be played at the Empire Stadium (Wembley) on
April 28, 1923 between Bolton Wanderers and West
Ham United: programme & souvenir. London: W. H.
Smith, 1923.   BL: 7913.c.61
  Although this bibliography excludes programmes, an
  exception has been made for this rare collector's
  item from the first Wembley Cup Final. 'The Hammers'
  lost the game 2-0 amidst alarming crowd scenes,
  the cup fever generating serious overcrowding in and
  around the new stadium.

    ☞ Also listed at: D2

849 Let's talk about West Ham United Football Club:
including football personalities and points of interest /
Tom Morgan. London: Sentinel, 1946.
32p; illus; pbk
(Football handbooks. Series 1; no. 18)   BL: W.P.1144/18
  Curious little booklet – collectable but short on detail.

850 West Ham United / Reg Groves. London: Newservice,
1947.
40p; illus; pbk
(Famous football clubs)   BL: 7922.k.15/3
  Another lightweight early effort at historical coverage.

851 West Ham, 1964: the official publication of the West
Ham players to mark their achievements in the season
1963-1964 / compiled and edited by Ken Jones and
John Bromley. London: The Club, 1964.
47p; illus; pbk   BL: X.449/42
  Marks their victory in the FA Cup Final over Preston
  North End.

852 The West Ham United football book / Dennis Irving.
London: Stanley Paul, 1968.
128p; illus   BL: X.0620/107

853 The West Ham United football book no. 2 / Dennis
Irving. London: Stanley Paul, 1969.
128p; illus   BL: X.0620/107

854 The West Ham United football book no. 3 / Dennis
Irving. London: Stanley Paul, 1970.
128p; illus   BL: X.0620/107

855 West Ham United annual. Hainault: Essex Circle, 1980-
illus
    Cover title: West Ham United official annual
                                          BL: P.441/927

856 Champions! back to the First Division / Harry Harris.
Hainault: Circle Sports, 1981.
48p; illus; pbk

857 Annual / West Ham Statisticians Group. Great Baddow:
The Group, 1983-1985.
    *Three issues published: No 1: 1919-39. 60p; No. 2:
    1946-66. 90p; No. 3: 1966-85. 100p*
                                          BL: ZK.9.a.1689
  Detailed statistical work indeed, covers all line-ups
  and scorers to 1985.

858 The West Ham story / John Moynihan. London: Arthur
Barker, 1984.
viii, 175p; illus   ISBN: 0-213-16912-6
                                          BL: X.622/23045
  Attractive production with many photographs but
  concentrates on highlights rather than offering a
  complete history.

859 West Ham United: the making of a football club /
Charles Korr. London: Duckworth, 1986.
xiii, 257p; illus; index
    ISBN: 0-7156-2143-2 (cased) • ISBN: 0-7156-2126-2 (pbk)
                                          BL: YK.1987.b.6507
  This must be one of the most unusual works ever produced about any football club. The playing side is
  almost entirely ignored in favour of a scholarly history of the ownership and internal management of
  the club. As such, it will be of interest to football researchers across the board and not just West Ham
  followers. Charles Korr was an American researcher
  given full access to the club's minutes and archive records. His motives in producing what was always
  destined to be a work of limited appeal can only be
  guessed at but in its own slightly bizarre way this is
  a valuable addition to football literature.

860 Who's who of West Ham United 1900-1986 / Tony
Hogg and Jack Helliar. London: Helliar & Sons, 1986.
96p; illus; pbk
  A pen picture of every player since 1900 with many
  accompanying photographs.

861 West Ham United: a complete record 1900-1987 includes Thames Ironworks 1895-1900 / John Northcutt and Roy Shoesmith. Derby: Breedon Books Sport, 1987. 432p; illus   ISBN: 0-907969-29-1
      BL: YK.1992.a.3113

The best starting point for any research project.

862 The West Ham quiz book / Tony Hogg. Edinburgh: Mainstream, 1988. 160p; illus; pbk   ISBN: 1-85158-186-3
      BL: YK.1989.a.3865

1,015 questions, thankfully accompanied by answers – difficult is not the word!

863 The official West Ham United quiz book. London: Rosters, 1991. 127p; pbk

Yet more torture and trivia.

864 West Ham United: a complete record: includes Thames Ironworks 1895-1900 / John Northcutt and Roy Shoesmith. Derby: Breedon Books, 1993. 416p; illus   ISBN: 1-873626-44-4
      BL: YK.1994.a.3715

Unlike the earlier 'Complete Record' series, this gives even wider coverage to the club's earliest years playing under the name of Thames Ironworks, a side formed by workers at a shipyard of that name. This amateur club disbanded in 1900 and West Ham United were formed. Whilst generally known as 'The Hammers', the nickname 'The Irons' also prevails to preserve these links with the club's true origins.

865 West Ham United: an illustrated history / John Northcutt and Roy Shoesmith. Derby: Breedon Books, 1994. 192p; illus   ISBN: 1-873626-93-2

866 Who's who, West Ham United: a player by player guide to West Ham United FC / Tony Hogg & Tony McDonald. Centenary ed. London: Independent UK Sports, 1994. 250p; illus

The definitive work on the players and personalities – best used in tandem with the 'Complete Record'.

Wigan Athletic

867 Wigan Athletic Association Football Club: souvenir handbook / C. P. Stuart. Wigan: Wigan Athletic Supporters Club, 1934. 28p; pbk

Scarce item from the club's very early days – they formed in 1932.

868 The league – at last / written and edited by D. Bruce Cherry; research, statistics by Pete Murphy. Burnley?: DBC Enterprises, 1979. 136p; illus; pbk

'The Latics' are one of the later entrants to the Football League, winning election in 1978.

869 Wigan Athletic Football Club 60th anniversary 1932-1992: souvenir brochure / edited and compiled by Steve McIlwham. Ormskirk: Waring Collins Partnership, 1992. 32p; pbk

In 1931 Wigan Borough had disbanded and became the first club ever to resign from the Football League. Wigan Athletic were formed in 1932 to effectively take their place. This brochure covers the club from foundation to the present.

Wimbledon

870 Wimbledon FC diamond jubilee souvenir handbook 1889-90 to 1949-50 / Jack Blanche. London: Wimbledon FC, 1950. 64p; pbk

Although they did not enter the Football League until 1977, the club was actually founded in 1889 as Wimbledon Old Centrals. This scarce publication presents a good history of the club with player biographies.

871 Souvenir handbook / compiled & edited by Peter Miller, assisted by A. Fuce and B. C. Corke. London: Pyramid Press, 1959. 71p; illus   BL: 7923.o.21

872 Mission impossible: the story of Wimbledon Football Club's historic rise from non-league to the First Division / compiled by Leigh Edwards and Andy Watson. London: Dons Outlook, 1986. 51p; illus; pbk   BL: YK.1987.b.3533

The use of the term historic rise is not in this case an overstatement. In 1976 the club were a non-league outfit; in 1986 they reached the First Division proving that there are no true mission impossibles. At the same time they provided a source of inspiration to minor clubs everywhere. This publication is particularly strong on the early history.

873 Wimbledon Football Club: the first 100 years / Michael Lidbury. Wimbledon: Wimbledon Football Club, 1991. 135p; illus

Cover title: Wimbledon FC centenary, 1889-1989
      BL: YK.1991.b.7280

Well balanced account chronicling one of the most remarkable stories in football – by this time the club had captured the FA Cup in 1988 and were about to become founder members of the Premier League in 1992. An essential text for all Wimbledon students.

Wolverhampton Wanderers

874 A history of Wolverhampton Wanderers Football Club
     1877 to 1938 in cartoons / S.S.P.
     40p; pbk
     *Unusual publication chronicling the period through
     cartoons.*

875 Wolves fanfare: a history. 1946.
     Scarce early ephemeral item.

876 Let's talk about Wolverhampton Wanderers Football
     Club: including football personalities and points of
     interest / Tom Morgan. London: Sentinel, 1948.
     32p; illus; pbk
     (Football handbooks. Series 3; no. 57)
     *One of the well-known Tom Morgan series – little in
     the way of detail.*

877 The Wolves: the first eighty years / Percy M. Young.
     London: Stanley Paul, 1959.
     160p; illus   BL: 7922.g.35
     *One of football's most respected writers presents the
     first comprehensive study of the club. It includes a fu-
     turistic portrayal of the ground – interesting to note
     how it compares with the development of Molineux which
     has occurred to such good effect in recent years.*

878 Wolverhampton Wanderers football book / edited by
     Phil Morgan. London: Stanley Paul, 1970.
     128p; illus   ISBN: 0-09-103270-9
     Largely pictorial and contemporary in its coverage.

879 Centenary Wolves / Percy M. Young. Wolverhampton:
     Wolverhampton Wanderers FC (1923) Ltd, 1976.
     12, 209p; illus; index   ISBN: 0-9505245-0-6
                                          BL: X.629/11259
     Effectively an update of the author's previous work.

880 Molineux memories: Molineux, home of
     Wolverhampton Wanderers for a century by the summer
     of 1989: 110 years of the Wolves – 1877-1987, 1988
     update / the North Banker (Michael Slater).
     Wolverhampton?: Slater Books, 1988.
     viii, 166p; illus; pbk   ISBN: 0-9513991-0-1
                                          BL: YK.1990.a.406

     *Each season is given a general review in one of the most
     specifically titled works one is likely to encounter.*

881 The Wolverhampton quiz book / Tony Matthews.
     Edinburgh: Mainstream, 1988.
     176p; illus; pbk   ISBN: 1-85158-198-7
                                          BL: YK.1989.a.3970
     Comprises over 1,000 questions and answers.

882 The Wolves: an encyclopaedia of Wolverhampton
     Wanderers Football Club 1877-1989 / Tony Matthews
     and Les Smith. Paper Plane, 1989.
     304p   ISBN: 1-871872-00-6
     Excellent work; essential reference tool.

883 The goalscorers / compiled by Tony Matthews. Warley:
     Sports Leisure Concepts, 1990.
     42p; illus; pbk
     (Golden greats of Wolverhampton Wanderers; bk. 1)
                                          ISBN: 1-87317-100-5
                                          BL: YK.1993.b.6213

     *First in a series of six 'Golden Greats' books concen-
     trating on personalities in particular playing roles in
     the club throughout its history.*

884 The goalkeepers / compiled by Tony Matthews. Warley:
     Sports Leisure Concepts, 1990.
     44p; illus; pbk
     (Golden greats of Wolverhampton Wanderers; bk. 2)
                                          ISBN: 1-87317-102-1
                                          BL: YK.1994.b.10856

885 Wolverhampton Wanderers greats / David Instone;
     foreword by Graham Turner. Edinburgh: Sportsprint,
     1990.
     vii, 163p; illus; pbk   ISBN: 0-85976-312-9
                                          BL: YK.1990.b.9534

886 The defenders / compiled by Tony Matthews. Warley:
     Sports Leisure Concepts, 1991.
     48p; illus; pbk
     (Golden greats of Wolverhampton Wanderers; bk. 3)
                                          ISBN: 1-87317-103-X
                                          BL: YK.1993.b.4842

887 The inside forwards, wing halves and midfielders /
     compiled by Tony Matthews. Warley: Sports Leisure
     Concepts, 1991?
     48p; illus; pbk
     (Golden greats of Wolverhampton Wanderers; bk. 4)

888 The full backs / compiled by Tony Matthews. Warley:
Sports Leisure Concepts, 1992?
48p; illus; pbk
(Golden greats of Wolverhampton Wanderers; bk. 5)

889 In keeping with the Wolves / Charlie Bamforth.
Lichfield: Pemandos, 1992.
108p; illus; pbk
                ISBN: 0-9520314-0-X
                BL: YK.1993.a.11863

    Covers all Wolves post-war goalkeepers in an interview
    and anecdote format.

890 The managers, coaches, trainers, reserves, secretaries and
back room staff / compiled by Tony Matthews. Warley:
Sports Leisure Concepts, 1992?
48p; illus; pbk
(Golden greats of Wolverhampton Wanderers; bk. 6)

    The final book in this series completing its exhaustive
    coverage. It is rumoured that 'Clicketty-click with the
    Wolves – 66 Great Molineux Turnstile Men' is in
    preparation at this very moment.

891 Old gold: a living history of Wolves and Wolverhampton
/ Tony Ball. Paper Plane, 1992.
122p   ISBN: 1-871872-06-5

    Unusual item offering a highly original method of
    presentation – a series of colour photo montages in
    chronological order showing images of the football
    club juxtaposed with those of the town itself, all ac-
    companied by supporting anecdotes.

892 Wolves: the complete record / Tony Matthews. Derby:
Breedon Books, 1994.
256p; illus   ISBN: 1-859830-00-5

    Wolves are comparative latecomers to the 'Complete
    Record' series of books – this will become an impor-
    tant standard text.

Wrexham

893 Wrexham AFC Shareholders and Supporters Association
souvenir journal 1948-49. Wrexham: Wrexham FC, 1949.

    A scarce ephemeral item celebrating 21 years in the
    Football League.

894 Official handbook, 1962/63- / Wrexham Football Club.
London: The Club, 1962-   BL: P.P.8000.nf

    The first issue of this handbook coincided with the
    club's promotion from Division Four.

895 The Robins story: the official history of Wrexham AFC
/ Anthony Jones. Shrewsbury: Temple, 1974.

    Effectively a yearbook for the 1973-74 season; in-
    cludes only a brief history.

896 Wrexham: a complete record 1873-1992 / Peter Jones.
Derby: Breedon Books, 1992.
432p; illus   ISBN: 1-873626-19-3
                BL: YK.1993.a.15640

    Wrexham are rather light on published works but as
    usual the 'Complete Record' series comes to the res-
    cue in admirable fashion. Essential work of reference.

Wycombe Wanderers

897 Out of the blue: the success story at Wycombe
Wanderers / Pete Lansley. London: Aldridge Press in
collaboration with Wycombe Wanderers Football Club,
1992.
ix, 116p; illus   ISBN: 0-952065-10-X
                BL: YK.1993.a.17483

    Founded in 1884, the club spent 64 years in the Isth-
    mian League from 1921, finally gaining election to the
    Football League in 1993.

898 Wycombe Wanderers in camera / compiled by Philip
Barker. Whittlebury: Quotes, 1992.
80p; illus; index   ISBN: 0-86023-605-6
                BL: YK.1994.a.2151

    Interesting collection of photographs from 1884 to
    the present – many rarities.

York City

899 50th anniversary of York City 1922-1972. York: York
City Supporters Club, 1972.
44p; illus; pbk

    This takes York City's foundation date as 1922 –
    that is indeed correct as far as the modern club is
    concerned, although researchers might like to note
    that an earlier York City were formed in 1903 before
    disbanding during the First World War. This publica-
    tion adopts a season-by-season summary.

900 City go nap as Quakers halt slump / Patrick Barclay;
photographs by Michael Pearson. York: Jackson Wilson,
1985.
24p; chiefly illus; pbk

    An evocation of lower league football. A collection of
    24 high quality photographs published to coincide
    with an exhibition at the Impressions Gallery of Pho-
    tography, York in 1985.

    ☞ Also listed at: H110

901 York City / Neville Sullivan. York: Longman, 1986.
24p; illus; pbk
(Inside football)

    An insight into the running and administration of a

football club along with matchday preparations and a spotlight on a typical day in the life of an apprentice player.

902 A chronological account of a journey: in search of York City / Malcolm Howe. York: Ebor Press, 1987.
44p; illus; pbk   ISBN: 0-9512338-0-7
                               BL: YK.1989.a.1386

Unusual approach – one dedicated fan's account of the grounds and sights he encounters on his travels in support of the 'Minstermen'.

☞ Also listed at: F5

903 The York City Shipton Street quiz book / Chris Forth. York: The author, 1988.
52p; pbk

Proceeds went towards the Shipton Street Roof Appeal – contrary to what one might be tempted to deduce from the title not all the questions are actually about Shipton Street!

904 York City: a complete record 1922-1990 / Dave Batters. Derby: Breedon Books, 1990.
432p; illus   ISBN: 0-907969-69-0
                              BL: YK.1992.a.9150

An excellent full account and an essential work of reference.

Former Members of the Football League

Accrington Stanley

905 Accrington Stanley to Wembley: a personal review of the 1983/84 FA Trophy competition / Tony Incenzo.
60p; pbk

906 Accrington Stanley: a complete record, 1894-1962 / Mike Jackman & Garth Dykes. Derby: Breedon Books, 1991.
416p; illus   ISBN: 0-907969-89-5
                            BL: YK.1993.a.13598

The club, which has acquired mythical status and a place in many a comedian's repertoire, were founder members of the Football League in 1888, resigning amidst financial scandal in 1893, before disbanding in 1896. The team revived, however, as amateur club Stanley Villa, and acquired league status in 1921, before finally dropping out in 1962. The club's name was revived in 1968 in the shape of non-league side Accrington Stanley, who play in the Northern Premier League.

Aldershot

907 Aldershot FC history 1926-1975 / Jack Rollin. FICS, 1971.
121p

One of football's most respected writers presents here an era-by-era study from the club's foundation, taking in their league years from 1932. Researchers of wartime football may find particular material of interest here in view of Aldershot's military connections – their wartime team sheets included a number of famous players posted there on military service.

908 The statistics of Aldershot Football Club. Basildon: Association of Football Statisticians, 1982.
88p; unbound   BL: X.629/19683

Coverage from 1932. The club was a member of the League from then until 1992 but now play in the Isthmian League. Their demise was entirely due to financial reasons – they were the first club since Accrington Stanley to drop out of the League with such difficulties.

909 Thanks for the memory: sixty years of Aldershot FC / Tim Childerhouse. Aldershot: The author, 1986.
76p

Published to mark the club's diamond jubilee. Includes 'The Story of Aldershot', reprinted from the club's 1957 souvenir handbook. The title proved to be somewhat prophetic as 'The Shots' were to resign from the League in March 1992.

910 The rise and rise of Aldershot Town: compilation of Aldershot town's first season / Graham Brookland and Karl Prentice. Adline, 1993.

Let it not be thought that there is no life after league football – this is true 'Phoenix from the flames' material, chronicling the first season of newly resurrected Aldershot Town in the Isthmian League.

Barrow

911 Barrow AFC quizbook.

912 Barrow AFC: the post-war years / Trevor Jones and Darren Gardner. Barrow: Barrow AFC, 1988.
illus; pbk

First of a number of short studies which together offer an excellent overview of Barrow's history.

☞ Subsequent ed. B915

913 Barrow AFC: the match / Darren Gardner; illustrated by Paul Musgrave. Barrow: The authors, 1989.
64p; illus; pbk

A 28 page supplement subsequently published in 1992

914 Barrow AFC facts and figures: a statistical history / compiled by Leigh Edwards and Michael Gardner. 1989.
76p; pbk

915 Barrow AFC: the post-war years / Trevor Jones and
     Darren Gardner. Rev. ed. Barrow: Barrow AFC, 1990.
     136p; illus; pbk

        ☞ Previous ed. B912

916 Barrow AFC: the post-war managers / Darren Gardner.
     Barrow: The author, 1991.
     36p; pbk

917 In the beginning there was the end / Martin Wingfield.
     Worthing?: Worthing Typesetting, 1991.
     44p; pbk

     Founded in 1901, the club joined the League in 1921
     but dropped out in 1972 when their place was taken
     by Hereford United. This is both a history and a par-
     ticular look at the 1989-90 season in which Barrow
     won the FA Trophy.

918 Barrow AFC: the Holker Street greats / Darren Gardner
     and Phil Yelland. Barrow: The authors, 1993.
     32p; pbk

Bootle

919 Bootle Football Club: third time lucky / Tommy Barnes.
     Bootle?: The author, 1988.

     One of the earliest members of the Football League;
     the club resigned in 1893 after just one year, giving
     them the distinction of being the first club ever to
     drop out. Their current exploits are, to a degree, over-
     shadowed by near neighbours Liverpool and Everton.
     The book describes the efforts over the last century
     of three clubs to represent the town of Bootle — pro-
     ceeds from the copies sold went towards their
     floodlight fund.

Bradford Park Avenue

920 Let's talk about Bradford Park Avenue Football Club:
     including football personalities and points of interest /
     Tom Morgan. London: Sentinel, 1947.
     32p; illus; pbk
     (Football handbooks. Series 2; no. 27)

     The club played league football from 1908 to 1970.
     The name was revived in 1988 with the declared long-
     term aim of regaining league status.

921 The Avenue: Bradford Park Avenue pictorial history and
     club record / Malcolm Hartley and Tim Clapham.
     Nottingham: Temple, 1987.
     192p

     Definitive history of the club. This volume attracted
     over 1,000 advance subscribers — testimony indeed
     to the fact that it isn't just the big clubs which foot-
     ball people want to read about.

922 A game that would pay: a business history of
     professional football in Bradford / A. J. Arnold.
     London: Duckworth, 1988.
     xi, 217p; illus; index

        Bibliography: p209-212   ISBN: 0-7156-2506-3
                                          BL: YC.1988.b.6581

     Scholarly and unusual study containing much of in-
     terest to the Park Avenue historian.

        ☞ Also listed at: B124

Gateshead

923 Let's talk about Gateshead Football Club: including
     football personalities and points of interest / Tom
     Morgan. London: Sentinel, 1947.
     32p; illus; pbk
     (Football handbooks. Series 2; no. 25)

     Founded in 1899, the club joined the League in 1919
     but were rather harshly denied re-election in 1960 to
     be replaced by Peterborough United. This lightweight
     publication presents a brief overview to 1947.

924 Requiem for Redheugh: a history of football in
     Gateshead / Goff Esther; with a foreword by Lawrie
     McMenemy. Gateshead: Gateshead Metropolitan
     Borough Council, Libraries, Arts and Shipley Gallery
     Committee, 1984.
     94p; illus; pbk   BL: YK.1987.a.5276

     The team were reincarnated in 1977, and now play in the
     Conference League, from where a return back to the
     Football League is possible. This publication presents a
     full account of the history of football in the town.

Halifax Town

925 Milestones 1911-1937: history and records of Halifax
     Town AFC / T. T. Dickinson. Halifax: National Union
     of Journalists Halifax Branch, 1937.
     118p; illus

     Scarce early publication of considerable substance
     published during a decade in which the club was fighting
     for their very lives due to extreme financial pressures.
     Includes history, records, biographies and photographs.

926 From Sandhall to the Shay / Tony Thwaites. Halifax:
     Halifax Town FC.

     Published in recent years, this is the definitive ac-
     count of the club which was founded in 1911, joined the
     League in 1921 and finally dropped out in 1993.

Maidstone United

927 Maidstone United FC: personalities 1960-61. Maidstone:
     Maidstone United FC, 1961.
     34p; pbk

     Lightweight ephemeral publication presenting pen pictures of contemporary staff in Maidstone's pre-league days.

928 Special investigation: the rise and fall of the Stones. Maidstone: Kent Today, 1993.

Founded in 1897 as successors to Maidstone Invicta, themselves formed in 1891, the club played professionally until 1927 and then as amateurs until 1971, when they joined the Southern League. They finally acquired league status in 1989 but only held it until 1992 when they succumbed to financial pressures. 'Rise and fall' is therefore a most appropriate title.

New Brighton

929 New Brighton Association Football and Athletic Club Company Limited: investigation under section 165(b) of the Companies Act 1948: report / Andrew Rankin and Thomas White for the Department of Trade. London: HMSO, 1977.
2, iv, 112p; pbk

ISBN: 0-11-512028-9
BL: BS.41/1048

An example of the sort of investigation clubs seek to avoid. The arrival of the men from the ministry usually suggests financial difficulty or irregularities.

930 New Brighton: a complete record of the Rakers in the Football League / Garth Dykes. Derby: Breedon Books, 1990.
256p; illus

ISBN: 0-907969-65-8
BL: YK.1992.a.287

New Brighton were members of the Football League from 1923 to 1951, their place being inherited by Workington. Prior to this spell, New Brighton Tower had been League members from 1898 to 1901. This book offers a remarkably full coverage of one of the 'ghosts of the League'.

Newport County

931 Let's talk about Newport County Football Club: including football personalities and points of interest / Tom Morgan. London: Sentinel, 1948.
32p; illus; pbk
(Football handbooks. Series 3; no. 56)
Lightweight early study.

932 The history of Newport County FC 1912-1973 / Richard Shepherd. Newport: Newport County Vice Presidents Club, 1973.
128p

Published to mark the diamond jubilee of the club. They were founded in 1912 and enjoyed two spells in the League: 1921 to 1931 and 1932 to 1988.

933 Newport County 1979-80: a season of triumph / Richard Shepherd. Newport: Newport County FC, 1980.

934 Seventy years of Newport County Football Club: a pictorial history 1912-1982 / Richard Shepherd. Newport: Newport County FC, 1982.

935 The Ironsides: a lifetime in the league: who's who of Newport County 1912-1989 / Tony Ambrosen. Harefield: Yore, 1991.
219p; illus; pbk

ISBN: 0-9513321-7-1
BL: YK.1992.a.3197

An essential work of reference covering the club's entire league history.

936 Amber in the blood: a history of Newport County FC / Tony Ambrosen. Harefield: Yore, 1993.
176p; illus

ISBN: 1-874427-40-2

Best used in conjunction with the above work – an essential reference book.

Northwich Victoria

937 A team for all seasons: a history of Northwich Victoria FC and the story of the Drill Field / K. R. Edwards. Chester: Cheshire Country, 1992.
386p; illus

ISBN: 0-949001-08-2
BL: YK.1994.a.12049

Extremely comprehensive coverage of the club founded in 1874 – they were founder members of the Second Division in 1892 but dropped out after just two seasons. They now play in the Conference League. This excellent work was written by the Club President.

Southport

938 Vintage 'port / compiled by Leigh Edwards. 1989.

Giant oaks from little acorns grow – this effort was the first book about Southport but was not generally well received by knowledgeable historians of the club. As a consequence, a massive work is currently in preparation by Michael Braham and Geoffrey Wilde – they have interviewed an astonishing 621 of the 650 players who represented the club in league football between 1921 and 1978. Followers of Southport should await this with great interest.

939 Southport FC: souvenir brochure / Geoff Wright. Southport: Southport FC, 1993.
40p; pbk

Produced to celebrate the club's elevation to the Vauxhall Conference League from which a direct route back to the Football League is available.

Workington

940 Workington AFC 1884-1984 / Steve Durham. Workington: Workington AFC, 1985.
72p; illus; pbk

Founded in 1884, the club played league football from 1951 to 1977 when they were replaced by Wimbledon.

941 So sad, so very sad: the league history of Workington AFC. Part 1: 1951-1958 / Martin Wingfield. Worthing?: Worthing Typesetting, 1992.
80p; pbk

This is part one of a series which intends to build up to a complete history of the club .

942 So sad, so very sad: the league history of Workington Association Football Club: the pictorial supplement to Part One 1951-58 / Martin Wingfield. Worthing?: Worthing Typesetting, 1992.
32p; illus; pbk

943 So sad, so very sad: the league history of Workington AFC. Part 2: 1958-1964 / Martin Wingfield. Worthing?: Worthing Typesetting, 1993.
76p; pbk

944 So sad, so very sad: the league history of Workington AFC. Part 3: 1964-1965 / Martin Wingfield. Worthing?: Worthing Typesetting, 1993.
40p; pbk

League & Former League Collective Studies

945 Second to none: great teams of post-war soccer / John Motson. London: Pelham, 1972.
167p; illus   ISBN: 0-7207-0605-X
                               BL: X.629/4824

Hungary 1950-56, Brazil 1950, 1958-62, England 1966, Real Madrid 1955-61, Celtic 1967, Spurs 1960-63, Liverpool 1964-66, Arsenal 1970-71, Leeds, and Manchester United.

946 Rejected FC: comprehensive histories of the ex-Football League clubs. Vol. 1 / Dave Twydell. Harefield: The author, 1988.
361p; illus, maps; pbk   ISBN: 0-9513321-0-4
                               BL: YK.1989.a.3753

Aberdare, Ashington, Bootle, Bradford P.A., Burton (Swifts, Wanderers & United), Gateshead, South Shields, Glossop, Loughborough, Nelson, Stalybridge, Workington – all these clubs are covered by Dave Twydell, who has become the acknowledged expert on the ex-League clubs. For all researchers requiring a general overview of the teams which have dropped out of the League over the years, this is truly an essential work of reference.

☞ Subsequent ed. B951

947 Those we have loved. Vol. 1 / David Thompson. London: The author, 1988.
100p; pbk   ISBN: 0-9513841-0-4

The league history of 19 former League clubs – a valuable reference work.

948 Rejected FC: comprehensive histories of the ex-Football League clubs. Vol. 2. / Dave Twydell. Harefield: Yore, 1989.
488p; illus, maps; pbk   ISBN: 0-9513321-2-0

Accrington Stanley, Barrow, New Brighton, Darwen, Durham City, Gainsborough Trinity, Merthyr Town, Northwich Victoria, Thames Association, and Middlesbrough Ironopolis – these are the clubs covered in Twydell's second comprehensive volume. Another essential work of reference.

949 The team now leaving / David Howgate. Southport?: The author, 1990.

A factual survey plus a little added personal comment on the last seasons played in the League by a number of ex-League clubs. The teams covered are those who have dropped out since season 1926/27 – 19 clubs in all.

950 The team now arriving / David Howgate. Southport?: The author, 1991.
60p

The author chronicles the first seasons of new clubs entering the League since 1923, giving all their results with added personal narrative and opinion.

951 Rejected FC: histories of the ex-Football League clubs. Vol. 1 / Dave Twydell. Rev. ed. Harefield: Yore, 1992.
288p; illus, maps; pbk   ISBN: 1-874427-00-3
                               BL: YK.1993.a.13358

☞ Previous ed. B946

Non-League & Amateur Clubs

Awbridge

952 Awbridge FC: the history of a village football club / John Moody. Romsey: The author, 1980.
38p; pbk

Bishop Auckland

953 The Bishops / W. T. D. Reed. Bishop Auckland?: The author, 1985.
72p; pbk

Written by the club's secretary of many years. Founded in 1886, Bishop Auckland emerged as the most successful amateur side in post-war football, winning the Amateur Cup a record number of times.

954 Kings of amateur soccer: the official centenary history of Bishop Auckland FC / Chris Foote-Wood. Bishop Auckland: North Press, 1985.
132p; illus; pbk   ISBN: 0-9510624-0-9

Excellent definitive study of a club now playing in the Northern Premier League.

Bitterne Sports

955 Bitterne football: a glimpse of the past / Ken Prior. 1992.
44p; pbk

Bitterne Sports FC currently represent the area in the Southampton League but in times past local sides competed in the FA Cup. This is a modest but scholarly work of interest to all historians studying the game in its early years in Hampshire.

Blyth Spartans

956 History of Blyth Spartans AFC 1899-1950 / 'Crofter'. Blyth: Blyth Spartans Supporters Club, 1950.
58p; pbk

Author is R. Thompson

Informed study of one of the best known non-league sides famed for their occasional heroic exploits in the FA Cup.

Bromley

957 The history of the Bromley Football Club, 1892-1938, together with complete results and other valuable data / edited and compiled by A. S. Bissmire. Bromley: The Club, 1938.
87p; illus   BL: X.629/14413

Excellent study up to the Second World War.

958 Bromley Football Club 1892-1992: a centenary history / Muriel V. Searle. Bromley: Bromley Football Club, 1992.
150p; illus   ISBN: 0-9519900-0-4
                                  BL: YK.1993.b.11333

Very full definitive account — an essential reference work. It includes all this Diadora League club's results together with all the match dates and scorers from 1960. The club has participated in the Athenian League, Spartan League and Kent League over the years, so historians of these leagues will find material of interest here.

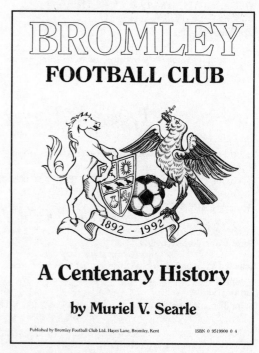

Bromsgrove Rovers

959 Bromsgrove Rovers centenary, 1885-1985: a history of Bromsgrove Rovers Football Club / Bill Kings. Bromsgrove: Bromsgrove Rovers FC, 1985.
157p; illus, 1 map; pbk

Limited ed. of 900 pbk and 100 cased copies
ISBN: 0-9509433-1-2 (cased) • ISBN: 0-9509433-2-0 (pbk)
                                  BL: YC.1987.a.2342

Excellent study of this Conference League club founded in 1885.

960 Old Rover / Arthur Clarke. 1993.

A collection of cartoons charting the club's progress.

Burton Albion

961 Wellington Street to Wembley: Burton Albion the complete history 1950-1990 / Rex Page. 1990.

An excellent study of 'The Brewers', one of the most promising non-league sides outside the Conference. They were founded in 1950 and cherish the ambition of bringing league football back to the brewing capital of the world. Around the turn of the century this small town boasted two league sides, Burton Swifts and Burton Wanderers, who then merged to create Burton's third league name – Burton United.

Cambridge City

962 The City story: the history of Cambridge Town/City FC / edited by Terry Dunn. Cambridge?: NKT, 1992. 200p   ISBN: 0-9517824-0-1

Very detailed coverage of Cambridge City, the club founded in 1908 as Cambridge Town. They adopted their present name in 1958 when they entered the Southern League from the Athenian League. They finished as champions in 1963, three points ahead of rivals Cambridge United who at that time had not yet entered the Football League.

Chelmsford City

963 Up the City: the story of Chelmsford City FC: the story of Chelmsford City and the meteoric rise of Colchester United FC / R. A. F. Handley. Chelmsford?: Thompson, Hansley & Spurgeon, 1948. 64p; pbk

Chelmsford City were formed in 1938 and have spent their entire history in the Southern League. Also covered is Colchester United, Crittall Athletic, Maldon Town, and Heybridge Swifts.

☞ Also listed at: B222

Christchurch

964 Christchurch FC 1885-1985: the first 100 years / Tom Kelly. 1986. 211p

Excellent centenary history of the Dorset club with many photographs and newspaper reports – limited edition.

Clapton

965 Clapton Football Club: seventy-five years of football history, 1878-1953 / edited by Reginald A. J. Ward. London: C. E. Fisher, 1954. 45p; pbk   BL: 7920.b.103

A concise history of this non-league club founded in 1878. They play in the Isthmian League at one of the more bizarrely named grounds in football – the 'Old

Spotted Dog'. The Isthmian League is now known as the Diadora League.

Colne Dynamoes

966 The official history of the Colne Dynamoes Football Club / Philip Terry. Nelson, Lancs.: Hendon, 1990. 64p; illus   ISBN: 0-860671-41-0
                              BL: YK.1991.b.8166

In 1963, eleven Lancashire school friends founded their own club, a side which prospered and improved, going on to win the 1988 FA Vase at Wembley and the HFS Loans League in 1990. Promotion to the Conference and then on to the Football League might surely follow? It was not to be, however, as disputes over their ground led the chairman to dissolve the club in controversial fashion. This is an unusual story indeed – almost a fairy tale, but not quite.

Corinthians

967 Annals of the Corinthian Football Club / edited by B. O. Corbett. London: Longmans, Green., 1906. xiii, 254p; illus   BL: 07906.de.3

The is an excellent history of a celebrated English amateur club founded in 1882 by N. Lane Jackson. The side consisted entirely of amateurs and moulded itself into a highly successful unit. Their name became a by-word for fair play and they often humbled professional sides. This volume includes notes on the players, their foreign tours, a full results record and a chapter on how to play the 'Corinthian Way'.

968 A history of the Corinthian Football Club / Frederick Norman Smith Creek. London: Longmans, Green, 1933. x, 282p; illus   BL: 7916.dd.5

Another definitive work on the club written by one of its playing members – an essential work of reference with some fascinating reminiscences of the game in the early part of the century. This work pre-dates the club's amalgamation in 1939 with 'The Casuals', when they became known as Corinthian-Casuals.

Covies

969 Covies FC: the twenty five years / David Griffin. 1993. 155p

The story of a small Hampshire club which started life in 1967 as Farnborough Covenanters in Division Three of the Woking and District League. A modest rise saw them playing in Division Three of the Hampshire League by 1993. This book shows very well how the history of a club – whether they are Manchester United or Covies – may be chronicled by diligent research. This is a much better publication than some which have been produced for much larger clubs.

Croydon Common

970 Who killed the Cock Robins?: the history of Croydon
Common FC 1891-1917 / Alan Futter. 1991.

This is the only Southern League Division One side
which did not survive the First World War to continue
playing league football. The author presents a painstakingly researched work of this South London side
with accompanying photographs, programmes, cartoons and even an illustration of the 1917 Court
Order which wound the club up (in the legal sense,
that is, although they were no doubt emotionally dis-
traught too). This is a first-class history and a good
example of the type of work which needs to be produced if defunct clubs like Croydon Common are not
to be forgotten forever.

Dover Athletic

971 Dover Athletic 1983-1992 / Chris Roberts. 1992.
56p; pbk

Comprehensive statistical coverage of the first nine
years of this former Beazer Homes League side giving all
the results, attendances, and scorers. The club were
formed following the demise of Dover FC in the summer
of 1983 and now play in the Vauxhall Conference League.

Eastbourne

972 Eastbourne Football Club season 1967-68: official
handbook. Edgware: Sports Publications, 1967-
BL: X.619/11267

Ely City

973 One hundred years of Ely City Football Club, 1885-1985: a
history / compiled by S. C. Lawrence. Ely: The Club, 1985.
42p; illus; pbk   BL: YK.1988.a.3561

A concise account of the Cambridgeshire club.

Finchley

974 One hundred years of playing the game, 1874-1974,
featuring the history of the Finchley Football Club /
Harold Whiddon. London: Hillside, 1974.
232p; illus   ISBN: 0-9503828-0-9
BL: X.620/7950

Very detailed account of a famous old club.

Fleetwood Town

975 Through stormy waters: a history of Fleetwood FC /
Phil Brown. Fleetwood: Rossall Press, 1995.
192p; illus; pbk   ISBN: 0-9525109-0-1

Fordingbridge Turks

976 Fordingbridge Turks Football Club / Norman
Gannaway. Hampshire: Fordingbridge Turks FC, 1994.
520p; pbk

Keen Dorset and Hampshire historian, Norman Gannaway, here presents the 125 year story of this small
Hampshire club, playing in the Bournemouth League Division Four. A most interesting and informative account.

Grays Athletic

977 Grays Athletic: the first 100 years. London: London
Advertising Centre, 1992.
120p

This informative account of the Essex club along with
many anecdotes and reminiscences makes essential
reading for the Grays follower.

Gresley Rovers

978 A history of Gresley Rovers / Rex Page.

Gresley Rovers play their football in Church Gresley
near Swadlincote in Derbyshire. They are one of the
up-and-coming non-league sides and boast a long
and interesting history which is well chronicled here.

Hallam

979 The Countrymen: the story of Hallam FC / J. A. Steele.
1987.

The story of the world's second oldest football club,
particularly of interest to researchers of the game in
the Sheffield area.

Hednesford Town

980 100 years of soccer – Hednesford Town. Hednesford:
Hednesford Town Football Club, 1981.
88p; illus

A good centenary account of 'The Pitmen', the West
Midlands club founded in 1880 currently playing in
the Southern League. The club were champions of the
Premier Division in 1994-95.

Kidderminster Harriers

981 Centenary history of Kidderminster Harriers FC / Colin
C. Youngjohns. 1987.
200p; illus

A definitive history of one of the higher profile non-
league clubs. Founded in 1877, the club now play in the
Vauxhall Conference League which they joined in 1983;
they have firm aspirations to gain a place in the
Football League before too long.

Lancing Athletic

982 Lancing Athletic football review 1948-1950. Brighton: Crabtree, 1948-50. BL: P.P.2489.why

Lawrence Boys' Club

983 A history of Lawrence Boys' Club, Lymington 1928-1988 / Norman Gannaway. Highcliffe: Eon Graphics, 1988.
136p
This interesting study includes appreciable football content.

Leek

984 Football in Leek 1870 to 1892 / Charles Diehl; illustrations by Arthur Diehl. Leek: Churnet Valley Books, 1993.
100p; illus
Facsimile of ed. published: 1893 ISBN: 1-897949-05-7

London Caledonians

985 The story of the London Caledonians Football Club / 'Old Member'. 1924.
26p; pbk
Scarce early item chronicling the history of a side which won the 1923 FA Amateur Cup — this 2-1 victory over Evesham Town at Crystal Palace inevitably prompted the publication.

Lydd

986 Lydd Football Club: lifting the 'Lydd' off 100 years of history / Peter Lindsey. Lydd: Margaret F. Bird & Associates, 1987.
47p; illus; pbk ISBN: 0-9509267-4-4
BL: YK.1988.a.4406
A concise and informative history of the Kent club which represents this small historic town on the fringe of Romney Marsh. Football followers, never having read a history of this type, will find this book most refreshing as a reminder that the large clubs are really just the very tip of the iceberg.

Lymington Town

987 A history of Lymington Football Club 1876-1984 / Norman Gannaway. Highcliffe: Eon Graphics, 1984.
116p
Informative history of the Hampshire coast club presented by one of the area's leading football historians.

Middlesex Wanderers

988 Football all round the world / Robert B. Alaway. London: Newservice, 1948.
viii, 171p; illus BL: 7919.cc.31
Recalls the club's exploits in remote corners of the world, as well as on home soil.

Nantwich Town

989 Centenary Dabbers: a history of Nantwich Town Football Club 1884-1984 / Michael Chatwin with a foreword by Joe Mercer. Faddiley: The author, 1983.
73p; illus; pbk BL: X.629/23587

Newcastle Bohemian

990 History and record of the Bohemian Association Football Club 1895-1926 / Harry Gilbert. Newcastle?: Harry Gilbert Ltd, 1926.
160p
Detailed history of the North East Northern Amateur League champions of 1923-24.

Newmarket

991 Newmarket Town Football Club 1877-1977 / E. J. Wybrew. Newmarket: Jomyra, 1992.
185p; illus; pbk ISBN: 0-9517844-0-4
BL: YK.1993.a.9318
The title is something of a misnomer as the coverage actually extends to 1992. Written by the ex-club secretary, this is one of the best works on a non-league side.

992 Newmarket Town and the FA Cup 1922-1993 / E. J. Wybrew. Newmarket: Jomyra, 1993.
A page is devoted to each of the 96 games played by the club in the FA Cup during this period.

Old Foresters

993 From little acorns: a centennial review of the Old Foresters Football Club and its place in the history of the game / P. C. Adams. Windsor: The author, 1976.
4, 82p; illus; pbk ISBN: 0-9505531-0-7
BL: X.615/1789
An informed history of one of the leading amateur clubs from the game's early history.

Pegasus

994 Pegasus / Ken Shearwood. Oxford: Oxford Illustrated Press, 1975.
x, 245p; illus ISBN: 0-902280-31-7
BL: X.629/10424

A detailed history of the famous Oxford and Cambridge combined universities' side of the fifties. They succeeded Corinthians as the most celebrated amateur club in the country following World War Two. They won the Amateur Cup in 1951 and 1953, capturing the public imagination and playing in front of crowds of 100,000 at Wembley. Founded in 1948, they were finally disbanded in 1963. The author was the club's centre-half for eight years.

Pennington St Marks

995 A history of Pennington St Marks FC 1889-1989 / Norman Gannaway. Pennington: Pennington St Marks FC, 1989.
80p

A concise account of this small Hampshire club.

Penrith

996 True blues: a history of Penrith Football Club / John Hurst. 1994.
124p

Poole Town

997 Poole Town: facts and figures – a statistical history / compiled by Leigh Edwards. The author, 1990.
56p; pbk

Southern League side formed in 1880.

Prescot

998 From Slacky Brow to Hope Street: a century of Prescot football / edited by Neville Walker. Huyton: Metropolitan Borough of Knowsley, Department of Leisure Services, Libraries Division, 1990.
vi, 88p; illus, plans; index; pbk   ISBN: 0-947739-10-6
                             BL: YK.1992.b.5953

Covers football in this small town just north of Liverpool.

Preston Ladies

999 In a league of their own / Gail J. Newsham. Chorley: Pride of Place Publishing, 1994.
180p; illus; pbk   ISBN: 1-874645-18-3

A most interesting study of this pioneering women's football club known as Dick Kerr's Ladies, in reference to the engineering factory in Preston where many of the players worked.

Romsey

1000 Romsey Town FC: history / John Moody. Romsey: The author.

South Liverpool

1001 Holly Park: the lost years / Hyder Gareth Jawad. Liverpool: Eldorado Communications, 1991.
160p; illus   ISBN: 1-873795-00-9

An excellant study of former HFS Loans League side, South Liverpool, which came to grief in the 1991 close season. Amongst the anecdotes and historical memories, is an account of their Welsh Cup victory in 1939 and a tale of exploits in 1949 against a team of barefooted Nigerians in front of a crowd of 13,000.

Sudbury Town

1002 Sudbury Town to Wembley: the 1985/86 FA Cup qualifying competition / Tony Incenzo. London?: The author, 1986.
20p; pbk

Founded in 1898, the club play in the Southern League.

Sutton United

1003 Sutton United Football Club: golden jubilee souvenir handbook 1898-1948 / written and compiled by G. F. Buck. Sutton: Sutton United Football Club, 1948?
132p; illus; pbk

Definitive history to 1948.

1004 Sutton United FC 1898-1973. Sutton: Sutton United Football Club, 1973.
104p; illus

Totton

1005 A 100 years history of Totton Football Club 1885-1985 / Peter Chilcott. Hampshire: Totton FC, 1985.
44p; pbk

Tow Law Town

1006 Tow Law: the first 150 years. 1994.

Trowbridge Town

1007 Trowbridge Town AFC centenary 1880-1980 history of the club / S. H. White. 1980.
36p; pbk

Founded in 1880, 'The Bees' play in the Southern League.

Ware

1008 An intention to play: the history of Ware Football Club, 1892-1992 / Steve King. Ware?: The author, 1992.
ii, 94p; illus, 1 map; pbk

                             BL: YK.1993.a.15377

This scholarly study charts the growth of the town as well as the team and covers all aspects of the club's long history. Ware do not have a suffix to their name which apparently makes them the shortest named affiliate of the Football Association.

Wealdstone

1009 1984-85: the double year / edited by Peter Worby. Wealdstone: Wealdstone Football Club, 1985?
30p; pbk   BL: YK.1990.b.2974

This was the club's finest hour — founded in 1899, they won both the Southern League championship and the FA Trophy in 1984-85.

Wednesbury Old Athletic

1010 The Old 'Uns: the story of Wednesbury Old Athletic 1874-1893 / Steve Carr. 1994.
76p

Whitburn

1011 Whitburn 1882-1989: a soccer history / Brian Hastings. 1989.
32p; pbk

Informed account of this small north-east coastal town club, situated just north of Sunderland.

Willenhall Pickwicks

1012 The Picks: the story of Willenhall Pickwicks Football Club 1884-1916 / Horace Davis and Peter Davis. Bloxwich: Willenhall History Society, 1994.
75p; illus; pbk   ISBN: 0-9523137-0-7

Woking

1013 A season to savour: the story of Woking's giant killing season 1990-91 / Mike Deavin. 1991.
80p

This was an outstanding season — their exploits in the FA Cup made waves well beyond the leafy lanes of Surrey. They were not at this time a Conference League club, which made their 4-2 defeat of West Bromwich Albion in the FA Cup 3rd round, even more remarkable. They exited the competition in the following round, but only to a narrow 1-0 defeat at Everton.

1014 The race for the Conference / Mike Deavin. 1992.
48p; pbk

Founded in 1899, the club gained promotion to the Vauxhall Conference in the 1991/92 season, putting them just one step away from an entry to league football.

Wooldale Wanderers

1015 'Bonnie oodle': celebrating 75 years of Wooldale Wanderers AFC, 1919-1994 / researched, compiled and written by Simon Paul Berry. Holmfirth: The author, 1994.
163p; illus; pbk   BL: YK.1994.a.11323

Non-League & Amateur Collective Studies (England)

1016 Defunct FC: club histories and statistics, Bedford Town, Chippenham United, Guildford City, Pegasus, Symingtons, Market Harborough Town / Dave Twydell. Harefield: The author, 1988?
251p; illus, maps; pbk   BL: YK.1989.a.2299

Histories and statistics of non-league clubs no longer in existence. Includes diagrams of grounds, newspaper reports and anecdotal material compiled in the usual thorough manner by one of football's most determined historians. A limited edition.

1017 More . . . defunct FC: club histories and statistics — Bedford Avenue, Lovell's Athletic, Romford, Rugby Town, Slough Centre, West Stanley / Dave Twydell. Harefield: The author, 1990.
230p; illus, maps; pbk   ISBN: 0-9513321-3-9
                                          BL: YK.1992.a.1396

Another excellent work from the Twydell stable.

Regional & General Studies (England)

1018 Hotbed of soccer: the story of football in the north-east / Arthur Appleton. London: Rupert Hart-Davis, 1960.
219p; illus   BL: 7925.b.79

  Potted histories of the professional clubs in the north-east — Gateshead, South Shields, Middlesbrough, Darlington, Hartlepool, Berwick, Newcastle, and Sunderland.

1019 Football on Merseyside / Percy Marshall Young. London: Stanley Paul, 1963.
215p; illus   BL: 7926.n.47

  Covers Liverpool, Everton, and Tranmere Rovers in the main.

  ☞ Also listed at: B281, B386, B818

1020 Football in London / David Robert Prole. London: Hale, 1964.
208p   BL: X.449/795

  The progress of the 11 London league clubs since 1945.

1021 Soccer in the Midlands / Peter Morris. Bernard Bale, 1969.
30p; pbk

  Histories of 15 Midlands clubs.

1022 Kings of English football / John Bill. London: Janay, 1972.
vii, 74p; illus
  For children   ISBN: 0-323-11008-8
                                               BL: X.622/1420

  Covers Arsenal, Manchester United and Aston Villa.

1023 The Midlands soccer story / John Squires. London: Wayland, 1973.
96p

  A good résumé of the Midlands clubs.

1024 The amateur game in the north-east / W. T. D. Reed. 1980.
60p

  An account of the north-east's contribution to the amateur game.

1025 Great soccer clubs of the north-east / Anton Rippon. Ashbourne: Moorland, 1981.
126p; illus; pbk   ISBN: 0-86190-022-7
                                               BL: X.622/11888

1026 Midlands soccer at war / Tony Matthews. Warley: Sports Leisure Concepts, 1991.
48p; illus; pbk   ISBN: 1-873171-01-3
                                               BL: YK.1992.b.9229

  An unusual study of the wartime era, a period often neglected by club historians.

1027 Soccer city: the future of football in London / Denis Campbell and Andrew Shields. London: Mandarin, 1993.
278p; illus; pbk   ISBN: 0-7493-1651-9
                                               BL: YK.1994.a.14542

  Excellent and scholarly account of the future of football in the capital — useful material here for all researchers interested in how the game is set to develop in the years to come.

Scotland ~ The Football League

Aberdeen

1028 Let's talk about Aberdeen Football Club: including football personalities and points of interest / Tom Morgan. London: Sentinel, 1948.
32p; illus; pbk
(Football handbooks. Series 3; no. 41)

  Lightweight coverage only in this early ephemeral publication.

1029 Aberdeen FC handbook and history 1949-50. Dundee: Simmath, 1949.

  Again relatively lightweight coverage.

1030 The Dons: the history of Aberdeen Football Club / Jack Webster. London: Stanley Paul, 1978.
224p; illus; index   ISBN: 0-09-133730-5
                                               BL: X.620/17889

  The first comprehensive history — definitive at the time, but later eclipsed by more detailed works.

  ☞ Subsequent ed. B1039

1031 Here we go!: an official account of the 1983 double cup winning triumph / Aberdeen Football Club. Warley: Sports Projects, 1983.
96p; illus; pbk   ISBN: 0-946866-00-7
                                               BL: LB.31.a.833

1032 The Aberdeen football companion: a factual history, 1946-86 / Clive Leatherdale. Edinburgh: Published by John Donald in association with Aberdeen Football Club, 1986.

viii, 364p; illus; pbk   ISBN: 0-85976-182-7
     BL: YK.1987.b.2665

An essential work of reference covering the post-war years.

1033 The Dons' quiz book / compiled by Ally Walker. Edinburgh: Mainstream, 1986.

176p; pbk   ISBN: 1-85158-044-1
     BL: YK.1987.a.7620

1,001 questions.

1034 A year in the life of the Dons 1985/86 / Ally Walker. 1986.

32p; pbk

1035 Aberdeen: a complete record 1903-1987 / Jim Rickaby. Derby: Breedon Books, 1987.

368p; illus   ISBN: 0-907969-30-5
     BL: YK.1991.a.12331

The club were formed in 1903 – this is an indispensable work with particular emphasis on statistical coverage.

1036 Aberdeen Football Club: a pictorial history / compiled by A. Guthrie. Runcorn: Archive, 1988.

128p; illus; pbk   ISBN: 0-948946-23-7

A good source of pictoral material.

1037 Aberdeen greats / A. Guthrie. Edinburgh: Sportsprint, 1989.

viii, 160p; illus; pbk   ISBN: 0-85976-278-5
     BL: YK.1990.a.3363

Biographical coverage of some of the club's greatest personalities throughout their history.

1038 Aberdeen: final edition / Robert A. Crampsey. Aberdeen: K. Murray, 1990.

200p; illus; pbk   ISBN: 1-870978-30-7

1039 The Dons: the history of Aberdeen Football Club / Jack Webster. Rev. ed. London: Stanley Paul, 1990.

282p; illus; pbk   ISBN: 0-09-174373-7
     BL: YK.1990.b.8153

Excellent update of the author's first work – essential reading.

☞ Previous ed. B1030

Airdrieonians

1040 Airdrieonians FC: 100 years and more / Bill Marwick. 1992.

Comprehensive coverage of the club formed in 1878 as Excelsior; they became Airdrieonians in 1881 and entered the League in 1894.

Albion Rovers

1041 The boys from the 'Brig: the life and times of Albion Rovers / R. W. Marwick. Coatbridge: Monklands Library Services Department, 1986.

376p; illus; pbk   ISBN: 0-946120-19-6
     BL: YK.1989.a.2000

Written by a club director, this is a comprehensive work which charts the club history from foundation in 1882 to date of publication.

1042 Champion Albion / Robin W. Marwick. Coatbridge: The author, 1989.

107p; illus; pbk   ISBN: 0-9515244-0-2

The club's triumphs have been few and far between – this work celebrates their Second Division championship win of 1988-89.

Alloa

1043 Alloa Athletic through the years. Dundee: Simmath, 1949.

Scarce early ephemeral item – rather lightweight.

1044 1921-1981, 60 years in the Scottish League: Alloa Athletic Football Club / Stuart Latham. Alloa Athletic Football Club, 1982.

64p

Although the club were formed in 1883, they did not join the League until 1921 – this works charts their full league history.

Arbroath

1045 Arbroath FC: story of the Maroons past and present, 1878-1947. Dundee: Simmath, 1947.

A scarce early ephemeral work chronicling the club from its 1878 foundation. Includes inevitable mention of their record-breaking 36-0 victory over Bon Accord in 1885, one of very few occasions when they have hit the headlines.

1046 The Red Lichties / Malcolm Gray and Stephen Mylles. 1978.

The club joined the League in 1921 – this is the most comprehensive modern study of the 'Red Lichties' to date.

Ayr United

1047 The Ayr United story 1910-1960 / Billy Hannah. 1960.

The 'Honest Men' were founded in 1910. This work celebrates fifty years during which they won the Division Two championship five times, but failed to make a real impact in the top flight.

1048 The history of Ayr United. Vol. 1: 1876-1939 / Duncan Carmichael. Ayr: Ayr United FC, 1990.
232p

> Extremely comprehensive coverage which covers their Ayr FC and Ayr Parkhouse origins – an essential work up to the Second World War.

1049 The history of Ayr United. Vol. 2: 1939-1990 / Duncan Carmichael. Ayr: Ayr United FC, 1992.
317p

> Another excellent work from the same author tracing the club's history from World War Two to the present – essential reference.

Berwick Rangers

1050 History and reminiscences of the Berwick Rangers Football Club (1881-1939) / Rupert W. King. 1946.

> Scarce early item covering Berwick's pre-war years from their 1881 foundation. One of their claims to fame is that they are effectively an English club, but they are so near the border that they joined the Scottish League in 1951 after playing in the Northumberland Association – hence their nickname 'The Borderers'.

1051 Berwick Rangers: a sporting miracle 1881-1981 / Tony Langmack. Berwick?: Berwick Rangers Football Club, 1981.
124p

> Essential reading for all students of the club. Despite having only one Second Division championship and a runners-up spot on their honours list, this is a club with a rich history. It is indeed a miracle of sorts that teams of this ilk are able to survive at all in the modern era.

Brechin City

1052 Brechin City through the years / George Cumming. Dundee: Simmath, 1948.

> A scarce early ephemeral publication covering the period from the club's foundation in 1906. At the time this was published, the club had no honours to their name but they have since won the Second Division title on a number of occasions. A satirical profile of the club on Radio Scotland in 1986 suggested that they were the first club to invite sponsorship – 'the people of Brechin offered them money to go to play somewhere else!'.

Caledonian Thistle

> Caledonian Thistle are a 'new' club elected to the Scottish League for the 1994-95 season. The club was formed as a result of a merger between Inverness Caledonian and Inverness Thistle. Entries for these two clubs are in the Scotland ~ Former & Non-League section of this chapter.

Celtic

1053 The story of Celtic / Willie Maley. Glasgow: Villafield, 1939.

> Scarce early history of one of the world's foremost clubs. This was written by one of the greatest personalities from the early days, a man who played in their first ever game and who managed the club for many years until 1938. Well worth seeking out.

1054 Let's talk about Celtic Football Club: including football personalities and points of interest / Tom Morgan. London: Sentinel, 1947.
32p; illus; pbk
(Football handbooks. Series 2; no. 36)

> Lightweight ephemeral item.

1055 The Celtic story: a history of the Celtic Football Club / James Edmund Handley. London: Stanley Paul, 1960.
216p; illus   BL: 7925.bb.68

> The first comprehensive modern coverage of the club.

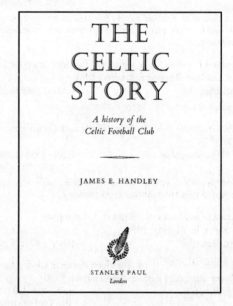

THE CELTIC STORY

A history of the Celtic Football Club

JAMES E. HANDLEY

STANLEY PAUL
London

1056 Celtic triumphant / Ian Alexander Ross Peebles. London: Stanley Paul, 1967.
xi, 99p; illus   BL: X.441/888

> A detailed account of the 1966-67 season when Celtic won everything – the League Championship, the Scottish Cup, the League Cup and the European Cup.

1057 Playing for Celtic / edited by R. Baillie. London: Stanley Paul, 1969-1989.
illus; pbk

> 20 issues published

1058 Glasgow Celtic 1945-1970 / Tom Campbell. Glasgow: Civic Press, 1970.
202p

A comprehensive study; includes 42 pages of statistics.

1059 Celtic / Sir Robert Kelly. Glasgow: Hay, Nisbett & Miller, 1971.
188p

James Kelly was the club's first captain, then director and chairman – this volume is written by his son, who became chairman upon his father's death and was knighted in 1969. Well worth consultation.

1060 An' you'll never walk alone / Gerald McNee. Aberdeen: Impulse Publications, 1972.
ix, 165p; illus   ISBN: 0-901311-37-5
                         BL: X.619/6606

An account from the fan's perspective charting the experience of following Celtic on their European travels.

1061 My team Celtic / Jack Adams. Glasgow: Collins, 1972.
64p; chiefly illus; pbk
(Daily Record specials)   ISBN: 0-00-103313-1

1062 Celtic: World League record holders souvenir. Glasgow: Celtic Football Club, 1975.
illus; pbk

1063 The Celtic joke book / Tom Shields. Alexandria: Famedram, 1978.

1064 Champions Celtic, season 1976-1977. Glasgow: Glasgow Celtic Football Club, 1978.
36p; illus; pbk

'A Celtic player pool publication' – cover   BL: X.611/8730
Celtic were winners of the Premier Division this year.

1065 The story of Celtic: an official history / Gerald McNee. London: Stanley Paul, 1978.
245p; illus; index   ISBN: 0-09-132410-6
                            BL: X.620/17575

Comprehensive coverage from 1888 to 1978. An excellent reference text.

1066 Celtic FC facts and figures 1888-1981 / compiled by P. Woods. Glasgow: Celtic Supporters Association, 1981.
88p; illus; pbk

Bibliography: p87-88   BL: X.629/16350

1067 The Old Firm: sectarianism, sport and society in Scotland / Bill Murray. Edinburgh: John Donald, 1984.
ix, 294p; illus; index; pbk

Bibliography: p282-285   ISBN: 0-85976-121-5
                                BL: X.800/40862

Celtic and Rangers are together regarded as the 'Old Firm'; this scholarly study says much about Scottish football but even more about society and religious divisions. Essential reading.

☞ Also listed at: B1200, H31

1068 The Old Firm guide: Celtic versus Rangers: a background to football's most celebrated contest / Neil McDermott. Alexandria: Famedram, 1985.
112p; pbk   ISBN: 0-905489-24-1

Historical coverage of one of the world's truly great fixtures.

☞ Also listed at: B1201

1069 The Celtic football companion / David Docherty; foreword John C. McGinn. Edinburgh: Published by John Donald with the approval of Celtic FC, 1986.
x, 355p; illus; pbk   ISBN: 0-85976-173-8
                             BL: YK.1987.b.2602

Essential reference work – very comprehensive.

1070 The glory and the dream: the history of Celtic FC 1887-1986 / Tom Campbell & Pat Woods. Edinburgh: Mainstream, 1986.
477p; illus, plans; index
     ISBN: 1-85158-054-9 (cased) • ISBN: 1-85158-055-7 (pbk)
                             BL: YK.1988.b.5845

Yet another extremely thorough work which should not be overlooked by any student of the club.

☞ Subsequent ed. B1072

1071 The Celtic quiz book / compiled by Pat Woods. Edinburgh: Mainstream, 1987.
174p; illus; index; pbk   ISBN: 1-85158-090-5
                                 BL: YK.1989.a.3662

1,001 questions.

1072 The glory and the dream: the history of Celtic FC 1887-1987 / Tom Campbell and Pat Woods. Rev. ed. London: Grafton, 1987.
475p; illus; index; pbk   ISBN: 0-586-20005-3
                                 BL: YK.1988.a.1906

☞ Previous ed. B1070

1073 Celtic / Alex Gordon; illustrated by Craig Warwick. London: Purnell, 1988.
96p; illus; index
     ISBN: 0-361-08488-9 (cased) • ISBN: 0-361-08489-7 (pbk)
                             BL: YK.1989.a.221

1074 Celtic / Ian Archer. London: Hamlyn, 1988.
121p; illus   ISBN: 0-600-55885-1
                     BL: YK.1989.b.2890

1075 Celtic: a century with honour / Brian Wilson. London: Collins, 1988.
224p; illus; index   ISBN: 0-00-218230-0
                            BL: YK.1989.b.4095

Comprehensive centenary coverage.

1076 Celtic, a celebration: the players' own picture story of the centenary league and cup winning season. Edinburgh: The Celtic players in association with John Donald, 1988.
88p; chiefly illus; pbk   ISBN: 0-85976-275-0
                                 BL: LB.31.a.1863

1077 Celtic greats / Hugh Keevins; foreword by John C.
McGinn. Edinburgh: John Donald, 1988.
viii, 160p; pbk   ISBN: 0-85976-238-6
                                   BL: YK.1989.b.426

*Biographies of leading players and personalities from
throughout the club's history.*

1078 Glasgow's giants: 100 years of the Old Firm / Bill
Murray. Edinburgh: Mainstream, 1988.
224p; illus
      ISBN: 1-85158-111-1 (cased) • ISBN: 1-85158-112-X (pbk)
                                   BL: YK.1990.b.3265

☞ Also listed at: B1205

1079 One afternoon in Lisbon / Kevin McCarra and Pat
Woods. Edinburgh: Mainstream, 1988.
240p; illus
      ISBN: 1-85158-117-0 (cased) • ISBN: 1-85158-118-9 (pbk)
                                   BL: YK.1989.b.5009

*Retrospective account of the afternoon in 1967 in
Portugal's capital when Celtic became the first British club to win the European Cup.*

1080 The will to win!: the illustrated story of Glasgow Celtic /
illustrated by Tommy Canning; written by Patrick
Canning; lettering by Alistair Bell. Edinburgh:
Mainstream, 1988.
160p; illus
      ISBN: 1-85158-199-5 (cased) • ISBN: 1-85158-165-0 (pbk)
                                   BL: YK.1990.b.3283

*Celtic certainly have the will to win which many clubs
would love just a hint of – their honours list is phenomenal.*

1081 The great 1949-1989 derbies: Blue & Green, Rangers v
Celtic: a personal look at the Glasgow derby / Archie
Macpherson. London: BBC Books, 1989.
150p; illus; index   ISBN: 0-563-21480-5
                                   BL: YK.1990.b.8437

*Scotland's best known football commentator studies
the post-war derby games.*

☞ Also listed at: B1209

1082 More Celtic greats / Hugh Keevins. Edinburgh: John
Donald, 1990.
vi, 153p; illus; pbk   ISBN: 0-85976-308-0
                                   BL: YK.1991.b.254

1083 Rhapsody in green: great Celtic moments / Tom
Campbell and Pat Woods; foreword by Bobby Murdoch.
Edinburgh: Mainstream, 1990.
369p; illus; pbk
      ISBN: 1-85158-328-9 (cased) • ISBN: 1-85158-340-8 (pbk)
                                   BL: YK.1992.b.8496

*A detailed study of some of the highlights – such is
their record that some of their championship wins
are given scant coverage, being regarded as a matter
of pure routine!*

1084 Faithful through and through: a survey of Celtic's most
committed supporters / Raymond Boyle. 1991.

*Unusual treatment – for once the supporters are
portrayed as the stars of the show.*

1085 The glory of the green: the Celtic trophies / John
Traynor, Douglas Russell. Glasgow: Holmes McDougall,
1991.
112p; illus; pbk
      ISBN: 0-7157-2850-4 (cased) • ISBN: 0-7157-2848-2 (pbk)
                                   BL: YK.1992.b.5698

*Very few clubs could publish a book of this size on
their trophies alone – cover to cover silverware is the
order of the day in this unusual work.*

1086 Celtic: a complete record 1888-1992 / compiled by Paul
Lunney. Derby: Breedon Books, 1992.
288p; illus   ISBN: 1-873626-27-4
                                   BL: YK.1993.b.12107

Definitive statistical coverage to this date.

1087 A Celtic A-Z / Tom Campbell and Pat Woods;
foreword by Billy McNeil. Glasgow: Greenfield, 1992.
viii, 219p; illus   ISBN: 0-9519501-0-X
                                   BL: YK.1993.b.2866

*A useful reference work detailing all manner of sub-
jects connected with the club.*

1088 A season in the sun: Celtic's wonder year of 1966/67 /
John Traynor & Tony Griffin. Lion Books, 1992.
104p; illus   ISBN: 0-9520458-0-X
                                   BL: YK.1994.a.7439

*Detailed account of the European Cup triumph; for
good measure the club also won all three domestic
trophies in the same year.*

1089 An alphabet of the Celts: a complete who's who of Celtic
FC / Eugene MacBride, Martin O'Connor & George
Sheridan. Leicester: ACL & Polar Publishing, 1994.
464p   ISBN: 0-9514862-7-6

*An essential work of reference for all students of the
players and personalities associated with the club.*

1090 Jungle tales: Celtic memories of an epic stand / John
Quinn; foreword by Billy McNeill. Edinburgh:
Mainstream, 1994.
188p; illus   ISBN: 1-85158-673-3

*Varied memories of the covered terracing known as
the 'Jungle' so called because of the lively and unpredictable nature of its indigenous inhabitants. Now it
has finally been equipped with seating, this volume will
stand as a lasting memory of the way watching football used to be.*

1091 Now you know about Celtic / Robert A. Crampsey.
Colintraive: Argyll Publishing, 1994.
160p; pbk   ISBN: 1-874640-16-5

1092 Paradise lost: the struggle for Celtic's soul / Michael
Kelly. London: Canongate, 1994.
160p; illus; pbk   ISBN: 0-86241-506-3

1093 Rebels in Paradise: the inside story of the battle for
Celtic Football Club / David Low and Francis Shennan.
Edinburgh: Mainstream, 1994.
196p; illus   ISBN: 1-85158-677-6

Boardroom politics abounding – detailed study of the
internal wrangling affecting the club at this time.

1094 Sack the board! Celtic: the end of a dynasty / Allan
Caldwell; foreword by Brian Dempsey. Edinburgh:
Mainstream, 1994.
174p; illus   ISBN: 1-85158-682-2

Another comprehensive account concentrating on
the political and administrative issues at stake for a
club built on tradition and family continuity.

Clyde

1095 The Bully Wee: Clyde FC / Tom Greig. Clyde Football
Club, 1978.
124p

Founded in 1878, the club played their first games on
the banks of the River Clyde in Glasgow – hence the
name. This is their centenary brochure publication.

1096 The Shawfield story / Norman Brown and John Taylor.
Glasgow?: Norwood Howe, 1986.
150p

Definitive account of the club which had played at the
Shawfield Stadium for many years prior to a controversial move in 1986 to Firhill Park, home of their
great rivals Partick Thistle.

Clydebank

1097 Clydebank football historian / edited by Alan Urquhart.
August 1990-October 1991.

5 issues published

At the time of compilation no formally published material for this club can be traced. The club were
founded as late as 1965 joining the League in 1966.
Despite this short history, they have been noted as
an innovative club and have enjoyed some measure of
success. They would certainly be worthy of a full club
history publication.

Cowdenbeath

1098 Cowdenbeath in words and pictures / H. B. Boyne.
Dundee: Simmath, 1948.
pbk

A scarce ephemeral publication covering the years
from foundation in 1881.

1099 Black diamonds and the Blue Brazil: a chronicle of coal,
Cowdenbeath and football / Ronald Ferguson. Ellon:
Northern Books, 1993.
191p; illus; pbk   ISBN: 0-905489-53-5
BL: YK.1994.a.15041

Excellent definitive account of the 1992-93 season.
The 'Blue Brazil' is Cowdenbeath, whilst the 'black diamonds' are the nuggets of coal once mined in the
area! Although the coverage is largely of the season
which saw the club relegated to Division Two, it is
nicely interspersed with tales of past Cowdenbeath
teams and the local community.

Dumbarton

1100 Dumbarton FC centenary. Dumbarton: Dumbarton
Football Club, 1972.

Founded in 1872, the club were one of the dominant
sides in the early history of the Scottish League,
joining as founder members of the First Division in
1890 and enjoying a highly successful decade. This is
their centenary publication.

1101 Sons of the rock: the official history of Dumbarton FC /
Jim McAllister and Arthur Jones. Dumbarton?:
J. McAllister, 1992.
76p; pbk

An essential reference work to be used in conjunction
with the above.

Dundee

1102 The dark blues: the story of Dundee FC in words and
pictures / H. B. Boyne. Dundee: Simmath, 1948.
illus

Scarce ephemeral item rather lightweight in content.

1103 Across the great divide: a history of professional football
in Dundee / Jim Wilkie. Edinburgh: Mainstream, 1984.
220p; illus
ISBN: 0-906391-76-8 (cased) • ISBN: 0-906391-77-6 (pbk)
Also covers Dundee United.

☞ Also listed at: B1107

1104 Dundee greats / Jim Hendry; foreword by Craig Brown.
Edinburgh: Sportsprint, 1991.
viii, 182p; pbk   ISBN: 0-85976-347-1
BL: YK.1992.b.9286

Essential reference work for coverage of the players.

1105 Up wi' the bonnets!: the centenary history of Dundee
Football Club / Norrie Price. Aberdeen: The author,
1993.
222p; illus, 1 plan
ISBN: 0-9521426-1-9 (cased) • ISBN: 0-9521426-0-0 (pbk)
BL: YK.1994.b.4068

Definitive essential work – traces the club's history
from formation in 1893.

Dundee United

1106 Dundee United through the years / H. B. Boyne. Dundee: Simmath, 1947.

> Scarce early ephemeral publication.

1107 Across the great divide: a history of professional football in Dundee / Jim Wilkie. Edinburgh: Mainstream, 1984. 220p; illus

> ISBN: 0-906391-76-8 (cased) • ISBN: 0-906391-77-6 (pbk)

> Material of interest to followers of 'The Terrors' as well as rivals Dundee – an essential reference work.

> ☞ Also listed at: B1103

1108 Rags to riches: the official history of Dundee United / Mike Watson. Dundee?: David Winter & Sons, 1985. 304p

> The club were founded in 1909 and joined the League a year later, playing as Dundee Hibernian until 1923 when they adopted their present name. The book's title is very apt – their early days were relatively undistinguished but during the 1980s in particular, they became a highly admired and successful side providing inspiration to all followers of under-achieving clubs.

1109 The view from the ground / Martha Gellhorn. London: Granta in association with Penguin, 1989. 459p; pbk

> ISBN: 0-14-014001-8
> BL: YC.1991.a.1820

> Essential material for all researchers of Dundee United in this comprehensive work.

Dunfermline Athletic

1110 Black and white magic 1959-1970 / Jim Paterson and Douglas Scott. 1985.

> The 1960s was the first truly successful era for 'The Pars' – they won the Scottish Cup in 1961 and 1968 and played regularly in Europe. This retrospective study covers a particularly memorable decade.

1111 Dunfermline Athletic Football Club: a centenary history, 1885-1985 / John Hunter. Dunfermline: The author, 1985. 192p; illus; pbk

> ISBN: 0-951083-00-7

> Excellent definitive history – essential work of reference.

1112 Leishman's lions: the roaring success story / Robert Fraser. 1987. 158p

> Concentrates on the 1985 and 1986 seasons, when manager Leishman took the club to the Second Division championship followed immediately by a runners-up spot in the First Division – a remarkable turn round in such a short period.

1113 Premier bound: the story of Dunfermline Athletic's return to the big time / John Hunter. Edinburgh: John Donald, 1987.
xii, 188p; illus; pbk

> ISBN: 0-85976-203-3
> BL: YK.1988.b.2623

> Concentrates again on the 1985-86 and 1986-87 seasons – essential reference work for that period.

East Fife

1114 East Fife through the years / William Phenix. Dundee: Simmath, 1948.

> Early ephemeral item covering the club's foundation in 1903, entry into the League in 1921 and a successful period from 1938, when they won the Scottish Cup.

1115 Black and gold heroes / Andrew Wilkie and Jim Stewart. Methil: East Fife Football Club, 1991. 51p; illus

> The club's distinctive black and gold strip gives this short study its title. They are one of the less chronicled Scottish clubs.

East Stirling

1116 Showing in black & white only / Alan McMillan. Kilsyth: Garrell, 1981. 45p; illus; pbk

> BL: X.805/2913

> Short but informative centenary publication.

Falkirk

1117 Falkirk through the years. Dundee: Simmath, 1948?

> Charts the club's history from foundation in 1876, and their entry into the League in 1902. Scarce publication.

1118 The Bairns / W. McFarlane. 1976.

> Published in the year in which the club played again in the First Division after their 1974-75 Second Division championship success.

1119 On wi' the gemme. Falkirk: Falkirk Football Club, 1976.

1120 The season that started in February / Michael White. 1988.

1121 The Brockville bairns. Vol 1: 1946-1969 / Michael White. 1991.

> Published in the year in which the club won the First Division championship; contains notable coverage of the post-war era.

Forfar Athletic

1122 The history of Forfar Athletic. Dundee: Simmath, 1948. 32p; illus

> Lightweight early ephemeral publication.

1123 Forfar Athletic Football Club: a centenary history /
Douglas Soutar and David McGregor. Forfar: The
Club?, 1985.
73p; illus   BL: YK.1990.b.7784

> The club were founded in 1885 and joined the League
> in 1921; this is the best account of their history.

Greenock Morton

1124 Morton 1874-1974 / Tom Robertson. 1974.

> Definitive coverage of Morton – or Greenock Morton,
> as they are currently known – from their 1874 foun-
> dation to date. The club claimed the Scottish Cup in
> 1922 and suffered many barren years until the 1950
> Second Division title sparked off a brighter period
> over the next few decades. I do not know of any re-
> cently published comprehensive history and so this
> entry is an essential reference work despite not being
> up to date.

Hamilton Academical

1125 Hamilton Academical centenary handbook. Hamilton?:
MacLellan, 1975.

> *Limited edition*

> 'The Accies' were founded in 1875 at Hamilton, near
> Glasgow. This centenary handbook includes a brief
> history. It appears that a substantial history of the
> club has yet to be written.

Heart of Midlothian

1126 The Hearts and the Great War / John McCartney. 1918.

> Unusual study covering the First World War period –
> the club themselves provided the nucleus of a whole
> battalion in the Royal Scots and many of them lost
> their lives in combat.

1127 Story of the Hearts 1874-1924 / William Reid.
Edinburgh: Hearts Football Club, 1924.
111p

> The Hearts were formed in 1874, their romantic name
> being derived from an old Edinburgh prison immortal-
> ised in Sir Walter Scott's novel, *The Heart of
> Midlothian*. This is a scarce and highly collectable
> early history.

1128 Tales from Tynecastle. Dundee: Simmath, 1928.
32p; pbk

> Scarce early publication reviewing the 1928-29 season.

1129 Let's talk about Heart of Midlothian Football Club:
including football personalities and points of interest /
Tom Morgan. London: Sentinel, 1946.
32p; illus; pbk
(Football handbooks. Series 1; no. 9)   BL: W.P.1144/9

> Ephemeral booklet of lightweight content.

1130 The history of the Heart of Midlothian FC. Dundee:
Simmath, 1948.
40p; pbk

1131 Heart of Midlothian official annual. Edinburgh: Scott
Hamilton, 1955-

1132 The Hearts: the story of the Heart of Midlothian FC /
Albert Mackie. London: Stanley Paul, 1959.
208p   BL: 7922.c.51

> This is the first substantial history of the Edinburgh
> club published in the season when they were to go on
> to win both the Championship and the League Cup.

1133 Heart of Midlothian FC: a centenary history. Edinburgh:
Heart of Midlothian FC, 1974.
24p; pbk

1134 The Heart of Midlothian Football Club: a pictorial
history 1874-1984 / David Speed, Bill Smith and
Graham Blackwood. 1984.
186p; illus

> Excellent source of illustrations.

1135 Glorious Hearts: the story of an incredible season /
edited by Mike Aitken; foreword by Tommy Walker.
Edinburgh: John Donald, 1986.
ix, 170p; illus
ISBN: 0-85976-181-9 (cased) • ISBN: 0-85976-180-0 (pbk)
                                           BL: YK.1987.b.227

> In the 1985-86 season the club led the Premier
> League for months, only to finally lose it on goal dif-
> ference. This book follows that glory trail which ended
> in heartbreak, giving a match report and full statis-
> tics for every game.

1136 The talk of the toon are the boys in maroon, Heart of
Midlothian: the authorised inside story of an
unforgettable season / John Fairgrieve; introduction by
Wallace Mercer. Edinburgh: Mainstream in conjunction
with Heart of Midlothian Football Club, 1986.
160p; illus
ISBN: 1-85158-048-4 (cased) • ISBN: 1-85158-049-2 (pbk)
                                           BL: YK.1989.a.3704

> Another comprehensive celebration of a season of
> mixed feelings. This is the club's authorised version.

1137 The Hearts quiz book / compiled by Graham
Blackwood, Bill Smith and David Speed. Edinburgh:
Mainstream, 1987.
176p; illus; pbk   ISBN: 1-85158-092-1
                              BL: YK.1989.a.5195

> 1,025 questions.

1138 Heart to heart: the anatomy of a football club / Mike
Aitken and Wallace Mercer. Edinburgh: Mainstream,
1988.
200p; illus
ISBN: 1-85158-140-5 (cased) • ISBN: 1-85158-141-3 (pbk)
                                           BL: YK.1989.b.2351

Chairman Wallace Mercer conveys many of the inner workings of the club in this refreshing approach.

☞ Also listed at: C370

1139 Hearts greats / Brian Scott. Edinburgh: John Donald, 1988.
vi, 154p; illus; pbk

ISBN: 0-85976-240-8
BL: YK.1989.b.2494

Comprehensive coverage of the better known players and personalities from the club's history.

1140 Hearts stat attack August 1975 to May 1990 / Craig Young. 1990.

An enthusiastic presentation of statistics.

1141 Ten of Hearts: the Heart of Midlothian story 1980-1990 / Ray Hepburn. Edinburgh: Mainstream, 1990.
174p; illus

ISBN: 1-85158-392-0
BL: YK.1991.b.7932

Hibernian

1142 Let's talk about Hibernian Football Club: including football personalities and points of interest / Tom Morgan. London: Sentinel, 1947.
32p; illus; pbk
(Football handbooks. Series 2; no. 28)

Collectable ephemeral item light on coverage.

1143 Hibernian FC in word and picture. Dundee: Simmath, 1948.

Relatively lightweight coverage in this early ephemeral booklet.

1144 100 years of Hibs, 1875-1975 / Gerry Docherty and Phil Thomson. Edinburgh: John Donald, 1975.
128p; illus

ISBN: 0-85976-007-3
BL: X.620/7942

The club were formed in 1875 by Irish immigrants to Edinburgh, hence the name Hibernian from the ancient name for Ireland. This is the first comprehensive history.

1145 The Hibees: the story of Hibernian Football Club / John R. Mackay; foreword by Kenneth Waugh. Edinburgh: John Donald, 1986.
ix, 277p; illus, 2 maps; index

ISBN: 0-85976-152-5

Comprehensive coverage – an essential work of reference.

1146 Hibernian greats / Stewart Brown; foreword by Bernard Gallacher. Edinburgh: John Donald, 1987.
vii, 115p; illus

ISBN: 0-85976-192-4
BL: YK.1988.b.4121

Good coverage of the most noted players and personalities from the club's history – the players covered are Gordon Smith, Lawrie Reilly, Tommy Younger, Joe Baker, Pat Stanton, Willie Hamilton, John Brownlie, George Best and Alan Rough.

1147 The Hibs quiz book / Jim Hossack. Edinburgh: Mainstream, 1988.
174p; illus; pbk

ISBN: 1-85158-183-9
BL: YK.1989.a.3864

1148 Bile and guile in the Emerald Isle / Hibbie Hippie. 1990.

First in a series of curiously titled personal studies from the equally curious sounding Hibbie Hippie. The author is actually called Sandy McNair.

1149 Hibernian: the complete story / John R. Mackay; foreword by The Proclaimers. Edinburgh: Sportsprint, 1990.
vii, 229p; illus, maps; index; pbk

ISBN: 0-85976-321-8
BL: YK.1991.b.1708

Comprehensive history to 1990 with a celebrity supporter foreword by musical duo, The Proclaimers.

1150 Hibees history: the story of the Drybrough Cup 1972-82 / Hibbie Hippie. 1991.

The lesser known Drybrough Cup was a short-lived and curious Scottish competition involving the highest-scoring teams in the Scottish League. It was first contested in 1971 and abandoned in 1982.

1151 Grumpy Gibby's mightiest moans / Hibbie Hippie. 1992.

1152 Hibbies history: the League Cup 1972 / Hibbie Hippie. 1993.

1153 Bring on the Albanians by the score: Hibs in Europe 1970-73 / Hibbie Hippie. 1994.
34p; pbk

1154 Hibernian FC the war years 1939-1946: a complete record of games played by Hibernian FC during the Second World War / Brian Mark. Edinburgh: Archways Promotions, 1994.
52p; illus
(Edinburgh: football heritage series; no. 1)

ISBN: 1-899061-00-2

Unusual retrospective approach covering the war years, including the 1939-40 season, abandoned after only five games due to the outbreak of war.

Kilmarnock

1155 Kilmarnock FC past and present. 1898.

Extremely scarce early item covering the years from foundation in 1869; Kilmarnock are Scotland's second oldest club.

1156 Kilmarnock through the years. Dundee: Simmath, 1949.

Scarce ephemeral booklet, lightweight on content.

1157 Go, fame: the story of Kilmarnock FC 1869-1969 / Hugh Taylor. Kilmarnock: Kilmarnock Football Club, 1969.
98p

Short centenary history.

1158 Who's who of Kilmarnock FC / Bill Donnachie.
Edinburgh: Mainstream, 1989.
263p
  Definitive coverage of the players and personalities.

1159 We were the champions, season 1964-65 / J.
Livingstone. 1990.
  *Retrospective study of the season in which the club
  won Division One.*

1160 Killie – the official history: 125 years of Kilmarnock FC
/ David Ross. Harefield: Yore, 1994.
255p; illus   ISBN: 1-874427-75-5
  Excellent history and an essential reference work.

Meadowbank Thistle

  *No formal publications for the 'Wee Jags' were traced
  at the time of compilation.*

Montrose

1161 The history of Montrose. Dundee: Simmath, 1948.
pbk
  *An early ephemeral publication which includes a brief
  history from the club's foundation in 1879.*

1162 The official history of Montrose FC 1879-1991 / David
Smith. 1991.
  *Essential work of reference published in the year in
  which the club gained promotion to the First Division
  for only the second time in their history.*

Motherwell

1163 Let's talk about Motherwell Football Club: including
football personalities and points of interest / Tom
Morgan. London: Sentinel, 1947.
32p; illus; pbk
(Football handbooks. Series 2; no. 39)
  Collectable item though lightweight in content.

1164 Motherwell Football Club: a history of 'The Steelmen',
1886-1986 / John Swinburne. Motherwell: Motherwell
Football Club, 1986.
192p; illus   ISBN: 0-9511029-0-7
  *The first detailed history was not published until the
  club's centenary year – essential work of reference.*

1165 'Well worth the wait: the story of Motherwell's epic cup
triumph / John Swinburne. Edinburgh: Mainstream,
1991.
202p; illus; pbk   ISBN: 1-85158-447-1
                      BL: YK.1993.b.12685
  *Published to celebrate Motherwell's victory in the
  Scottish Cup in 1991, their first since 1952.*

Partick Thistle

1166 The history of Partick Thistle / R. M. Connell. 1927.
  *Scarce early history of the club that were founded in
  1876 and joined the League in 1893.*

1167 The Jags: the centenary history of Partick Thistle
Football Club / Ian Archer. Glasgow: Molendinar, 1976.
95p; illus   ISBN: 0-904002-19-5
                    BL: X.629/10995

  The first substantial history from the modern era.

1168 Partick Thistle: the people's club / text compiled by
Colin Menabney, Janet Darling; artwork, Andrew
Crossan, Alan Wilson. Glasgow: Maryhill Community
Central Hall, 1986.
36p; illus; pbk   ISBN: 1-870230-00-0
                      BL: YK.1990.a.1487

  Slight but nonetheless interesting study.

Queen of the South

1169 The Queens 1919-1969 / W. Jardine. 1969.
  *Founded in 1919, the club were named after the tradi-
  tional nickname of their home town Dumfries. This is
  their fiftieth anniversary history.*

Queen's Park

1170 History of the Queen's Park Football Club, 1867-1917 /
Richard Robinson. Glasgow: Hay Nisbet, 1920.
vi, 446p; illus   BL: 7918.c.1
  *This is one of the most comprehensive of the early
  football club histories and is a collector's item in its
  own right. Queen's Park, formed in 1867, are not only
  Scotland's oldest football club but have also retained
  their amateur status throughout their history. This
  scarce item chronicles their early history, covering
  the last two decades of the nineteenth century when
  they dominated the Scottish Cup for an unbeaten
  run of 7 years. This is a volume which must be consulted by all Queen's Park historians, and one which
  will serve the general football historian equally well.*

1171 Queen's Park Football Club / Richard Robinson.
London: G. W. May, 1924.
36p; illus   BL: 7911.dd.24
  Scarce ephemeral publication, but an essential one.

1172 Souvenir of Greater Hampden Park. Glasgow: Queen's
Park Football Club, 1938.
  *Hampden Park has been the club's home ground since
  1903. They had already vacated two grounds prior to
  their move to what was, in effect, the third Hampden
  Park. Their present ground, which has served as the
  national stadium for many years, has its own very
  personal history of triumph and tragedy.*

History
of the
Queen's Park Football Club
1867—1917

By

RICHARD ROBINSON

HAY NISBET & CO. LTD., GLASGOW
PRINTERS AND PUBLISHERS
1920

CONTENTS

Title Page and Extensive Contents of the Earliest Work on Queen's Park

1173 The game for the game's sake: the history of Queen's
Park Football Club, 1867-1967 / R. A. Crampsey.
Glasgow: The Club, 1967.
402p; illus   BL: X.620/8466
Excellent centenary work and an essential reference
work.

1174 The men with the educated feet / edited by Forrest H.
C. Robertson. Glasgow: Queen's Park Supporters'
Association, 1984.
☞ Subsequent ed. B1175

1175 The men with the educated feet / edited by Forrest H.
C. Robertson. 2nd ed. Glasgow: Queen's Park
Supporters' Association, 1985.
☞ Previous ed. B1174; subsequent ed. B1177

1176 Report of the public local inquiry into its appeal by
Queen's Park FC. Edinburgh: Scottish Office, 1990.
pbk

1177 The men with the educated feet / edited by Forrest H.
C. Robertson. 3rd ed. / updated by Hector S. Cook.
Glasgow: Queen's Park Football Club, 1992.
160p; illus
ISBN: 0-9510047-0-0 (cased) • ISBN: 0-9510047-1-9 (pbk)
☞ Previous ed. B1175

Raith Rovers

1178 The history of the Raith Rovers Football Club / R. M.
Connell. London: G. W. May, 1924.
32p; pbk   BL: Mic.A.10411(5) (microfilm copy)
Relatively lightweight but interesting club history.

1179 Raith Rovers FC: the story of the club in words and
pictures / Peter S. Napier. Kirkcaldy: Raith Rovers
Supporters' Club, 1948.
76p; pbk
Another scarce publication extending the story to 1948.

1180 Raith Rovers FC: a centenary history / John Litster.
Kirkcaldy: Raith Rovers FC, 1983.
88p; pbk

Although the earlier works are more collectable by nature, this gives the full centenary history.

1181 Raith Rovers: a promotion diary / John Litster.
Kirkcaldy: Raith Rovers FC, 1987.
60p; pbk

Celebrates promotion from the Second Division.

1182 A history of Raith Rovers / John Litster. Kirkcaldy:
Raith Rovers FC, 1988.
84p

Rangers

1183 The story of Rangers 1873-1923 / John Allan. 1923.
328p

Very few clubs were accorded such comprehensive historical works as early as this – this 50th anniversary publication is a superb exception and a scarce collector's item followed up by others from the same author. Rangers are probably the best chronicled club when judged by the quality of pre-World War Two books. This one contains extremely interesting material.

1184 Eleven great years: the Rangers 1923-34 / John Allan.
1934.
100p

Another scarce item – Rangers dominated the League Championship during this period and also won the Scottish Cup a few times for good measure.

1185 Let's talk about Glasgow Rangers Football Club:
including football personalities and points of interest /
Tom Morgan. London: Sentinel, 1946.
32p; illus; pbk
(Football handbooks. Series 1; no. 6)   BL: W.P.1144/6

Small ephemeral publication of lightweight content.

1186 Rangers: 18 eventful years 1934-1951 / John Allan.
Glasgow: Rangers Football Club, 1951.
147p

John Allan here extends his detailed coverage of the club over a period in which the honours continued to flow.

1187 Salute to Rangers: a tribute in words and pictures /
Glasgow Rangers Football Club. London: Charles
Buchan's Publications, 1959.
63p; illus   BL: 7925.c.23

The club won the championship in 1958-59.

1188 We will follow Rangers / Hugh Baird Taylor. London:
Stanley Paul, 1961.
128p; illus

BL: 7924.bbb.30

1189 Rangers: the player's story. 1962.

1190 Rangers FC: European Cup book. 1963.

1191 Playing for Rangers / edited by Ken Gallacher. London:
Stanley Paul, 1964.
144p; illus   BL: X.441/183

1192 The Rangers: a complete history of Scotland's greatest
football club / John Fairgrieve. London: Hale, 1964.
189p; illus   BL: X.449/499

The first comprehensive history of the club to be published in the modern era.

1193 Rangers, the new era, 1873-1966 / William Allison.
Glasgow: Glasgow Rangers Football Club, 1966.
xiii, 410p; illus   BL: X.622/10586

Extremely comprehensive; a valuable research text.

1194 Playing for Rangers / edited by Ken Gallacher. London:
Stanley Paul, 1969.
128p; illus   ISBN: 0-09-098770-5
BL: X.0620/118

1195 My team Rangers / Jack Adams. 1972.

1196 The road to Barcelona. 1972.

Rangers beat Dynamo Moscow in Barcelona to win the European Cup Winners' Cup – the victory was severely marred by crowd disorder.

1197 Growing with glory / Ian Peebles. Glasgow: Rangers
Football Club, 1973.
260p; illus   BL: YA.1989.a.6414

Comprehensive centenary history.

1198 A glorious treble. 1976.

Celebrates winning the Premier Division Championship, Scottish Cup and League Cup.

1199 The Rangers news annual. Glasgow: Peebles
Publications, 1983-   BL: ZK.9.a.816

1200 The Old Firm: sectarianism, sport and society in
Scotland / Bill Murray. Edinburgh: John Donald, 1984.
ix, 294p; illus; index; pbk

Bibliography: p282-285   ISBN: 0-85976-121-5
BL: X.800/40862

Discusses both Rangers and Celtic and the religious differences which have traditionally and symbolically encapsulated the rivalry between these great clubs.

☞ Also listed at: B1067; H31

1201 The Old Firm guide: Celtic versus Rangers: a
background to football's most celebrated contest / Neil
McDermott. Alexandria: Famedram, 1985.
112p; pbk   ISBN: 0-905489-24-1

Detailed coverage of all the big derby games.

☞ Also listed at: B1068

1202 The Rangers football companion / David Docherty; foreword by Willie Waddell. Edinburgh: John Donald in association with Rangers Football Club, 1986.
ix, 388p; illus; pbk   ISBN: 0-85976-172-X
                                        BL: YK.1989.b.224

   Extremely comprehensive reference work – all the facts for the post-war period.

1203 The Rangers quiz book / compiled by Alex Hosie. Edinburgh: Mainstream, 1987.
158p; illus; pbk   ISBN: 1-85158-091-3
                                        BL: YK.1989.a.3897

   1,001 questions.

1204 Rebirth of the blues: the story of a Rangers revolution / Chick Young; foreword by Jim Baxter. Edinburgh: Mainstream, 1987.
164p; illus; pbk   ISBN: 1-85158-103-0
                                        BL: YK.1989.b.2849

   Following their 1963-64 championship success, Rangers were to win the title only three times in the next 26 years – an extremely barren period for a club used to regular success. Their 1986-87 championship win heralded a renewed period of triumph, hence the title of this useful volume which concentrates on the last decade.

1205 Glasgow's giants: 100 years of the Old Firm / Bill Murray. Edinburgh: Mainstream, 1988.
224p; illus
      ISBN: 1-85158-111-1 (cased) • ISBN: 1-85158-112-X (pbk)
                                        BL: YK.1990.b.3265

   One of a number of studies of the Rangers versus Celtic derby classics, this one extremely thorough.

   ☞ Also listed at: B1078

1206 Rangers / Ian Morrison. London: Hamlyn, 1988.
125p; illus; index   ISBN: 0-600-55886-X
                                        BL: YK.1989.b.2891

1207 Rangers greats / Dixon Blackstock; foreword by Andy Cameron. Edinburgh: John Donald, 1988.
viii, 179p; illus; pbk   ISBN: 0-85976-239-4
                                        BL: YK.1990.b.1471

   A study of just some of the leading personalities from the club's history.

1208 Champions: Rangers' 1988-89 championship season / Alan Fairley. Edinburgh: Forth Sports Marketing, 1989.
96p; illus; pbk   ISBN: 1-872201-00-8

1209 The great 1949-1989 derbies: Blue & Green, Rangers v Celtic: a personal look at the Glasgow derby / Archie Macpherson. London: BBC Books, 1989.
150p; illus; index   ISBN: 0-563-21480-5
                                        BL: YK.1990.b.8437

   One of Scottish football's leading television commentators offers his view of the great post-war derby games.

   ☞ Also listed at: B1081

1210 Rangers: the official illustrated history / Stephen Halliday; foreword by Graeme Souness. London: Arthur Barker, 1989.
158p; illus   ISBN: 0-213-16924-X
                                        BL: YK.1990.b.4877

   Good source of pictures.

1211 Glasgow Rangers: player by player / Bob Ferrier and Robert McElroy. Swindon: Crowood, 1990.
144p; illus   ISBN: 1-85223-404-0
                                        BL: YK.1991.b.3545

   Essential reference work for any study of the players.

1212 Seven years on: Glasgow Rangers and Rangers supporters, 1983-1990 / John Williams with T. Bucke. Leicester: Sir Norman Chester Centre for Football Research, 1990.

   Concentrates on supporter behaviour.

   ☞ Also listed at: H71

1213 Blue heaven: the Ibrox trophy room / Willie Thornton. Glasgow: Holmes McDougall, 1991.
112p
      ISBN: 0-7157-2849-0 (cased) • ISBN: 0-7157-2847-4 (pbk)
                                        BL: YK.1992.b.2089

   Published in the same year as the volume on Celtic's trophy room – perhaps for the avoidance of controversy, the pagination is identical in each case.

1214 More Rangers greats / Dixon Blackstock; foreword by John Greig. Edinburgh: Sportsprint, 1991.
vii, 151p; illus; pbk   ISBN: 0-85976-310-2
                                        BL: YK.1991.b.2980

   Includes additional subjects to those covered in the 1988 volume.

1215 A question of Rangers / foreword by Derek Johnstone. London: CollinsWillow, 1991.
vii,179p; illus; pbk   ISBN: 0-00-218424-9
                                        BL: YK.1991.a.10552

1216 Rangers in Europe: a 35-year history of Rangers in the three European Cup competitions / Alan Fairley. Edinburgh: Forth Sports Marketing, 1991.
87p; illus; pbk   ISBN: 1-872201-01-6
                                        BL: YK.1994.b.642

   Excellent coverage of their non-domestic experiences.

1217 Double champions: Rangers' League and Cup winning season 1991/92 / Alan Fairley. Edinburgh: Forth Sports Marketing, 1992.
96p; illus; pbk   ISBN: 1-872201-02-4

1218 Rangers season by season: the light blue facts & figures book / Robert McElroy. Glasgow: True Blue Publications, 1992.
148p; illus; pbk   ISBN: 0-9520270-0-3
                                        BL: YK.1993.a.15232

1219 The official Rangers book 1994-. Edinburgh:
Mainstream, 1993-
illus

1220 The Rangers treble reports. 1993.

> *Yet another treble from the club, underlining their increasing domination over their Celtic rivals in the nineties.*

1221 Now you know about Rangers / Robert A. Crampsey.
Colintraive: Argyll Publishing, 1994.
160p; pbk   ISBN: 1-874640-11-4

Ross County

> This former Highland League club were elected to the newly re-structured Scottish League for the 1994-95 season. At the time of compilation no formal publications covering the club could be traced.

St Johnstone

1222 St Johnstone through the years. Dundee: Simmath, 1948.

> *Scarce ephemeral item – rather lightweight content.*

1223 Saints alive! / Gordon Bannerman; foreword by Alex
Totten. Edinburgh: Sportsprint, 1991.
vii, 148p; illus; pbk   ISBN: 0-85976-346-3
BL: YK.1992.b.5609

> *Good general reference work covering the club's history from its 1884 foundation. Based in Perth, they joined the Scottish League in 1911.*

1224 Who's who of St Johnstone 1946-1992 / Jim Slater. 1993.

> *Definitive work on the players and personalities from the club's history.*

St Mirren

1225 The history of the St Mirren Football Club / R. M.
Connell. London: G. W. May, 1924.
40p; pbk
BL: Mic.A.10411(4) (microfilm copy)

> *One of a series of similar booklets covering a number of clubs – a scarce ephemeral item albeit only a short study covering the early history from the club's foundation in 1877 by cricket and rugby players from Paisley.*

1226 The Saints / Willie Hunter. 1977.

1227 St Mirren FC centenary brochure: 1877-1977. Paisley:
The Club, 1978.
76p; illus; pbk   BL: X.622/9955

1228 Love affair: some saints / Bill McEwan. 1981.

1229 The black and white years / Alex Bell. 1982.

Stenhousemuir

1230 The warriors: a centenary history of Stenhousemuir
Football Club / written and edited by Peter Moulds.
Larbert: The Club, 1984.
x, 101p; illus, 1 coat of arms, 1 map, 2 plans; pbk
ISBN: 0-9509322-0-5
BL: X.622/20851

> *A good centenary history and an essential reference work.*

Stirling Albion

1231 40 years in the Scottish League: Stirling Albion / Allan
Grieve and John Turnbull. 1986.
40p; pbk

> *Very much a latecomer to the Scottish League, the club were founded in 1945 following the demise of King's Park, whose ground suffered such severe bomb damage during the war that they were disbanded. A new club, Stirling Albion, was then formed; they entered the League in 1947. This is an essential reference work.*

1232 Stirling Albion FC 1945-1988 / Allan Grieve and John
Turnbull. 1988.

> *Updated version of the previous item.*

Stranraer

1233 Stranraer Football Club centenary 1870-1970 / John S.
Boyd. Stranraer?: Free Press, 1970.
56p; pbk

> Fairly lightweight centenary publication but an essen-
> tial work of reference in the absence of anything more
> recent. The club were founded in 1870 and are the
> third oldest club in the Scottish League, which they
> joined in 1949.

Scotland ~ Former League & Non-League

Abercorn

1234 Abercorn: a history / John Byrne. 1985.

> Abercorn were founder members of the Scottish
> League but dropped out in 1915.

Armadale

1235 The Dale: a history of Armadale FC / Stuart
Borrowman. 1990.

> Armadale joined the Scottish League in 1921 and
> dropped out in 1932.

Arniston Rangers

1236 The recorded history of Arniston Rangers Football Club,
1883-1988 / A. C. Smith. Arniston: Arniston Rangers
FC, 1991.
211p; illus; spiral

> *Cover title: The history of Arniston Rangers FC*
> ISBN: 0-9518790-1-4

Arthurlie

1237 A game of two halves: a history of Arthurlie Football
Club / John Byrne.

Ashfield

1238 Ashfield FC centenary / C. McCulloch. 1991.

Auchinleck Talbot

1239 The history of Auchinleck Talbot / James McAuley. 1989.

Back

1240 A history of Back FC 1933-1983. Back Football Club, 1983.

Bathgate Thistle

1241 Bathgate Thistle Junior Football Club: a history / Ian
Anderson. Dechmont: Sam's Publishing Corporation,
1993.
x, 251p; illus, 1 map; pbk   ISBN: 0-9521941-0-4
BL: YK.1994.a.12213

> Extremely comprehensive coverage of a relatively
> small club – Bathgate joined the League in 1921 but
> dropped out in 1928.

Beith

1242 A history of Beith FC. 1927.

> Beith joined the League in 1923 and dropped out in
> 1926.

Blantyre Victoria

1243 Blantyre Victoria: a pocket history / Robert Pickering.
1938.

1244 Blantyre Victoria: 50 years in football / George Manson.
1950.

Buckie Thistle

1245 Happy times at the Old Vic: a history of Buckie Thistle
FC / Easton Thain. Buckie: E. R. Thain, 1993.
111p; illus

Burntisland Shipyard

1246 A short history of Burntisland Shipyard Amateurs /
George Campbell. 1991.

Carmunnock Ladies

1247 Didn't we almost make it?: history of Carmunnock
Ladies FC 1981-1985 / T. Malcolm. 1992.
40p; pbk

Rather a rarity in this bibliography – a history of a
women's club. The Glasgow club were formed from the
ashes of Vale of Clyde and this relates the serious
story of their growth and subsequent early demise.
Certainly essential reading for any researcher chronicling the women's game.

Clachnacuddin

1248 The Lilywhites: a centenary history of Clachnacuddin FC
/ Rod Clyne. Clachnacuddin Football Club, 1986.
88p; illus

Rod Clyne was a former player with Inverness Thistle,
Inverness Caledonian, Elgin City and Nairn County.
Here he presents an excellent history which has nu-
merous photographs along with all the Highland
League final tables from 1913/14 to date.

Clackmannan

1249 The county lads: a history of Clackmannan 1885-1931 /
David Allan. The author, 1993.
28p; pbk

Clackmannan played in the League from 1921 to 1926.
Their end was not a happy one – after an 11-2 loss
against Ayr United in the Scottish Cup in 1931, they
decided enough was enough and never played again.

Clydebank Juniors

1250 Clydebank Juniors FC 1899-1964 / Alun Urquhart. 1991.

The Scottish League club Clydebank were formed in
1965 and as such are a separate club from Clydebank Juniors. However, historians of both clubs
inevitably associate the two – this study covers the
early history of the Juniors up to the foundation of
Clydebank itself which joined the League in 1966.

Cowlairs

1251 A history of Cowlairs Football Club 1876-1896 / John
Weir. Renfrew: Scottish Non-League Review, 1991.
56p; pbk

Formed in 1876, the club only played for twenty
years. One of the founder members of the Scottish
League in 1890, they finished bottom in their first
season and dropped out of the League in 1895.

Cumberland United

1252 Cumberland United / M. Murphy and R. Parker. 1975.

Deveronvale

1253 Deveronvale FC: the first 50 years / Alistair Bruce. 1991.
64p; pbk

Dunipace Juniors

1254 100 years of football: Dunipace Juniors 1888-1988 /
Duncan Buchanan. 1988.
48p; pbk

Edinburgh City

1255 City on a downward slope and revival / George
Campbell. 1990.
44p; pbk

The club were first formed in 1928 with great ambitions,
though they only survived in the League until 1949 before disbanding in 1955. Reference in the title to their
revival comes from their effective re-formation in 1986
by the Post Office side Postal United – they changed
their name to Edinburgh City and adopted the former
black and white colours of that club.

Edinburgh St Bernards

1256 Historic saints of Edinburgh: the history of St Bernards
Football Club 1878-1943 / George Campbell. 1987.
116p

The author has done a great service to Scottish
football history in this and a number of other works.
St Bernards were members of the Scottish League
from 1893 until the Second World War; they won the
Scottish Cup in 1895. This book presents a full history.

Elgin City

1257 Seeing things in black and white: a celebration of
1989-90 / Ron Grant. Edinburgh?: J. Weir, 1990.

Celebrates a treble for Elgin City – Highland League
champions and winners of the Qualifying Cup and the
North of Scotland Cup.

1258 The paths of glory / Douglas Grant. Edinburgh?: J.
Weir, 1993.
16p; pbk

Celebrates the 25th anniversary of the club's run to
the Scottish Cup quarter-final, a year in which they
won the Highland League, the Qualifying Cup and the
North of Scotland Cup.

Forres Mechanics

1259 Forres Mechanics: the first hundred years / Colin G.
Watson. Forres: Forres Mechanics FC, 1985?
108p; illus; pbk   BL: YK.1988.a.4092

Glenbuck

1260 The Cherrypickers: Glenbuck, nursery of footballers /
M. H. Faulds and Wm. Tweedie, Jnr. Muirkirk: Muirkirk
Advertiser and Douglasdale Gazette, 1951.
20p; illus; pbk

☞ Subsequent ed. B1261

1261 The Cherrypickers: Glenbuck, nursery of footballers /
M. H. Faulds and Wm. Tweedie, Jnr. New ed. Cumnock:
Cumnock and Doon Valley District Council, 1981.
20p; illus; pbk   ISBN: 0-9506568-1-X
BL: X.808/35352

☞ Previous ed. B1260

Greenock Wanderers

1262 Greenock Wanderers: the first hundred years 1873-1973
/ J. L. M. Forster. Scotland: The author, 1974?
305p; illus   BL: X622/13270

Inverness Caledonian

1263 Caley all the way / Alex Main. 1987.
136p

Written by a former player and manager. The club
were founded in 1886 and enjoyed a great measure of
success in the Highland League before amalgamating
in 1994 with Inverness Thistle to form Caledonian
Thistle, newly elected to the Scottish League for the
1994-95 season.

Inverness Citadel

1264 Inverness Citadel FC / George Campbell. 1990.

Inverness Thistle

1265 The hub of the hill – Inverness Thistle FC: the first 100
years. 1987.
32p; pbk

In 1994 the club amalgamated with Inverness Caledonian to form Caledonian Thistle, newly elected to the
Scottish League for season 1994-95.

Irvine Meadow

1266 The history of Irvine Meadow / J. F. Delury. 1960.

Kilwinning Rangers

1267 A history of Kilwinning Rangers 1899-1950 / James
Ness. 1950.

Kirkintilloch Rob Roy

1268 A history of Kirkintilloch Rob Roy.

This unusually named club served as a nursery team
for the great Glasgow Rangers. This item was published during the late 1930s.

Linlithgow Rose

1269 Linlithgow Rose: 100 years 1889-1989 / David Roy.
1989.

Lochgelly United

1270 Fifeshire football memories / David A. Allan. Dumfries:
The author, 1991.
60p

Includes bibliographical references   BL: YK.1993.a.319

Includes material of interest to the Lochgelly United
historian – the club were members of the Scottish
League from 1914 to 1926.

☞ Also listed at: B1298

1271 There was a happyland: Lochgelly United FC, 1890-1928
– a history / David A. Allan. Dumfries: The author,
1991.
60p; illus, 1 map   BL: YK.1992.a.9309

Definitive history of the Cowdenbeath based club.

Moorpark Amateurs

1272 When jackets were the goalposts: 70 years of Moorpark
Amateurs / R. B. Wilson. 1977.

Peterhead

1273 Peterhead FC centenary 1891-1991 / B. Campbell. 1991.

Renfrew

1274 Renfrew FC: a short history / edited by Stewart
Davidson. 1990.

Royal Albert Juniors

1275 The boys in black and white: the history of Royal Albert
Juniors / S. Irvine. 1988.

Royal Albert were Scottish League members from
1923 to 1926.

Third Lanark

1276 Let's talk about Third Lanark Football Club: including
football personalities and points of interest / Tom
Morgan. London: Sentinel, 1948.
32p; illus; pbk
(Football handbooks. Series 3; no. 52)

> Lightweight item – includes a brief history of one of
> the better known ex-Scottish League clubs. The Glasgow
> based club were founder members of the Scottish FA
> in 1873 and of the Scottish League in 1890.

1277 Third Lanark Athletic Club Limited: investigation under
section 165(b) of the Companies Act 1948 / report by
John Moncrieff Turner and Henry Shanks Keith
(inspectors appointed by the Board of Trade). London:
HMSO, 1968.
29p; illus   ISBN: 0-11-510100-4
                                            BS41/447

> Third Lanark disappeared from the Scottish League
> at the end of the 1966-67 season. Endless investi-
> gations by the Board of Trade helped speed their
> demise. This report highlights some of the financial
> ills experienced by the club.

1278 Who killed Third Lanark? / David Docherty.
Edinburgh: Polygon, 1992.
200p; pbk   ISBN: 0-7486-6076-3

> Detailed coverage of the club's history – an essential
> work of reference. It is likely that some of the prime
> suspects in the murder enquiry are members of the
> board, as mismanagement is generally quoted as the
> main reason for their fall.

Vale of Leithen

1279 Vale of Leithen FC 1891-1991 / E. B. Sanderson. 1991.

Vale of Leven

1280 Vale of Leven FC cup-tie history / Allan MacLean. 1925.

> Scarce early publication detailing the cup history of
> this former Scottish League club.

1281 The old Vale and its memories / compiled by
J. Ferguson and J. G. Temple. London: printed for
private circulation, 1927.
130p; illus

> Another scarce early item published to mark the end
> of the club's stay in the League – they were members
> from 1890 to 1926 and were once regarded as one of
> the most formidable teams in Scotland.

Epilogue

to

" The Old Vale and
its Memories "

Compiled by
JAMES FERGUSON
and
JAMES GRAHAM TEMPLE

*Printed for Private Circulation only
and published 31st August* 1929

1282 Epilogue to The old Vale and its memories / compiled
by J. Ferguson and J. G. Temple. London: Hazell,
Watson & Viney, 1929.
225p; illus

> *Printed for private circulation*
>   BL: 10370.v.27

> Detailed retrospective study – essential reference
> work for all Vale historians.

Scotland ~ Collective Studies

1283 Scottish League records of the ex-league clubs / Mike
Watson. 1985.

Informative statistical coverage.

1284 Scottish non-league football histories / George
Campbell, David Allan, John Weir; edited by Stewart
Davidson. Renfrew: Scottish Non-League Review,
1990-1992.
3 vols

Histories, records, anecdotes – many of the lesser
known clubs are chronicled here in a 3 volume series,
each of around 50 pages. Amongst those covered
are Gretna who have played in the English FA Cup.

1285 Rejected FC of Scotland: histories of the ex-Scottish
League clubs. Vol. 1: Edinburgh and the south / Dave
Twydell. Harefield: Yore, 1992.
288p; illus, maps; pbk   ISBN: 0-9513321-9-8
                                  BL: YK.1993.a.11095

Following the great success of his English works, the
author now applies the same principles to Scotland in
a most valuable work. The clubs covered are: Mid-Annandale, Solway Star, Nithsdale Wanderers,
Armadale, Bathgate, Broxburn United, Peebles Rovers, Edinburgh City, Leith City, and Edinburgh St
Bernards.

1286 The Scottish Football League: past members. Part 1:
Abercorn, Armadale, Arthurlie, Ayr, Ayr Parkhouse /
compiled by Norman Nicol. Renfrew: Stewart Davidson,
1992.
47p; pbk

All the league and cup results for each of these past
members is presented in this essentially statistical
work planned to run to several parts.

1287 Rejected FC of Scotland: histories of the ex-Scottish
League clubs. Vol. 2: Glasgow and district / Dave
Twydell. Harefield: Yore, 1993.
240p; illus, maps; pbk   ISBN: 1-874427-30-5
                                  BL: YK.1994.a.5963

Essential reference work for all historians interested
in the ex-league clubs of Scotland. This volume covers
Abercorn, Arthurlie, Beith, Cambuslang, Clydebank,
Cowlairs, Johnstone, Linthouse, Northern, Third Lanark and Thistle.

1288 The Scottish Football League: past members. Part 2:
Bathgate, Beith, Bo'ness, Broxburn United, Cambuslang,
Clackmannan, Clydebank, Cowlairs, Dumbarton Harp,
Dundee Hibernian, Dundee Wanderers, Dykehead /
compiled by Norman Nicol. Renfrew: Stewart Davidson,
1993.
130p; pbk

Essential statistical work covering the full records of
twelve ex-league clubs.

1289 The Scottish Football League: past members. Part 3:
Edinburgh City, ES Clydebank, Galston, Helensburgh,
Johnstone, Kings Park, Leith, Leith Athletic / compiled
by Norman Nicol. Renfrew: Stewart Davidson, 1993?
pbk

1290 The Scottish Football League: past members. Part 4:
Linthouse, Lochgelly United, Mid-Annandale, Nithsdale
Wanderers, Northern, Peebles Rovers, Port Glasgow
Athletic, Renton, Royal Albert / compiled by Norman
Nicol. Renfrew: Stewart Davidson, 1993?
pbk

1291 The Scottish Football League: past members. Part 5:
Edinburgh St Bernards, Solway Star, Thistle, Third
Lanark, Vale of Leven / compiled by Norman Nicol.
Renfrew: Stewart Davidson, 1994?
pbk

Scotland ~ Regional Studies

1292 Football in Perthshire past and present / Peter Baxter.
1898.

Extremely scarce item on primitive football forms as
well as the game in the late nineteenth century.

1293 The defunct soccer clubs of Edinburgh / B. Hunter and
S. McPhie. 1969.

Interesting study of the clubs based in and around
Edinburgh over the years.

1294 A history of Ayrshire junior football / Drew Cochrane.
1976.

Updated ed. published 1989

1295 A century of soccer in Selkirk / Graham Bateman. 1980.

1296 Ball-Coise: football in the Western Isles / Iain
MacDonald and Donald Smith. 1985.

The only study I know to cover this footballing outpost.

1297 The history of Shetland football, 1887-1987 / James P. Peterson. Shetland Football Association, 1988.
122p; illus   BL: YK.1994.b.3139

    Definitive history of the game in the Shetland Isles.

1298 Fifeshire football memories / David A. Allan. Dumfries: The author, 1991.
60p

     Includes bibliographical references   BL: YK.1993.a.319

    ☞ Also listed at: B1270

1299 The Rangers, Rovers and good old Bluebell: juvenile football in Auchinleck 1900-1945 / James McAuley. 1992.

This is something of a rarity as it actually deals with juvenile football in Scotland as opposed to the non-league junior scene.

1300 Dumfrieshire football memories / David A. Allan. Dumfries: The author, 1993.

     Includes bibliographical references

David Allan has made many important contributions to Scottish football history. This work covers the southern area of Scotland around the Solway Firth. Amongst the clubs charted are Queen of the South Wanderers, 5th Kirkcudbrightshire Rifle Volunteers, and Dumfries FC.

Wales

Aberystwyth Town

1301 The history of the Aberystwyth & District Football League 1934-1984 = Hanes Cynghrair Pêl-Droed Aberystwyth a'r Clych, 1934-1984 / Gwyn Jenkins; sponsored by Y Ganolfan Chwaraeon Aberystwyth. Aberystwyth: The League, 1984.
72p; illus; pbk

     Includes one chapter in Welsh   ISBN: 0-9509843-0-2
                                     BL: X.805/7356

Includes material of interest not only to Aberystwyth Town supporters but also to followers of other clubs in this western outpost.

1302 The old black and green: Aberystwyth Town Football Club 1884-1984 / Peter Parry and Brian Lile with Donald Griffiths. Aberystwyth: Aberystwyth Town FC, 1987.
x, 285p; illus; index   ISBN: 0-9512172-0-8
                                     BL: YK.1988.a.4621

A detailed account rich in statistics, player profiles and supporting photographs.

Barry Town

1303 The Linnets: an illustrated, narrative history of Barry Town AFC 1888-1993 / Jeff McInery with contributions from A. J. Last and photographs by Peter Wilson. Barry: Nomad Publications, 1993.
151p; illus; pbk   ISBN: 0-9522846-0-X

This detailed history had a print run of just 1,000 copies. Barry were members of the Southern League before the First World War and had aspirations for Football League status, but their 1921 application was unsuccessful. This is a colourful history of a club which has had a roller-coaster life.

Borough United

1304 Heroes all: the wonderful story of Borough United. Borough: Borough United FC, 1964.
32p; illus; pbk

    ☞ Subsequent ed. B1305

United's remarkable feat in winning the Welsh Cup in 1963 qualified the team to play in Europe where they held Slovan Bratislava to a respectable 4-0 scoreline over two legs. These heroics inspired this publication.

1305 Heroes all: the wonderful story of Borough United and their four cup successes. Llandudno Junction?: North Wales Weekly Newspapers, 1994.
35p; illus; pbk

     Republished with additional material

    ☞ Previous ed. B1304

Caernarfon Town

1306 The Canaries sing again: a history of Caernarfon Town Football Club / Ian Garland and Wyn Gray-Thomas. Caernarfon: The authors, 1986.
154p; illus; pbk   ISBN: 0-9511631-0-8
                                     BL: YK.1987.a.4471

A detailed history of the yellow-shirted club founded in 1876. This work was highly acclaimed by the AFS when it was published and is a good example of what can be achieved for the smaller clubs by diligent research.

Cardiff City See FA Premiership & Football League

Colwyn Bay

1307 A history of Colwyn Bay FC. Colwyn Bay FC, 1947.

> Founded in 1885 this Welsh non-league club now play in the Northern Premier League.

Connah's Quay Nomads

1308 Juniors to Nomads: Connah's Quay Nomads AFC: coronation souvenir / W. T. Hughes and F. H. Roberts. Connah's Quay Nomads AFC, 1953?

> Beating Cardiff in the 1929 Welsh Cup Final was perhaps this side's finest hour.

Llanberis

1309 Y Darans / Arwel Jones. Llanberis: Clwb Pêl-droed Llanberis, 1991.
245p; illus; pbk

> *Cover title: Y Darans, Clwb Pêl-droed Llanberis, 1890-91-1990-91*

Machynlleth Maglonians

1310 The Maglonians: 100 years of football in Machynlleth 1885-1985 / D. W. Davies. 1985.

Merthyr Tydfil

1311 Magic moments of Merthyr Tydfil AFC / compiled by David Watkins. Merthyr Tydfil: The author, 1985?
142p; illus; pbk   ISBN: 0-951031-0-4
                                BL: X.622/25743

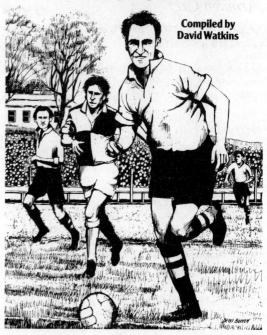

Magic Moments of Merthyr Tydfil A.F.C.

Compiled by David Watkins

Newport County See Former Members of the Football League

Rhosllanerchrugog

1312 From pit to pitch: a pictorial history of football in Rhos / John E. Matthews. Rhosllanerchrugog: Revloc, 1991.
48p; illus; pbk   ISBN: 0-9518440-0-8
                                BL: YK.1993.a.1779

> Includes a number of evocative images.

Rhyl

1313 Rhyl Football Club Ltd: diamond jubilee booklet. Rhyl: The Club, 1988.

> Celebrates sixty years of 'The Lilywhites'.

Spa

1314 100 years of Spa football 1883-1983 / C. Barrett and R. Davies. Spa FC, 1993.

Swansea City See FA Premiership & Football League

Tregaron

1315 The Turfs: a brief history of Tregaron Football Club / Vernon A. Jones. Tregaron: Tregaron Football Club, 1994.
45p; illus

Wrexham See FA Premiership & Football League

Northern Ireland

Armagh City

1316 Armagh City 1964-1989 / Brian Weir. Armagh: The author, 1990.
24p; illus; pbk

Booklet to mark 25 years of this Irish club — narrative and statistics are supported by 25 photographs.

Belfast Celtic

1317 Belfast Celtic / Mark Tuohy. Belfast: Blackstaff Press, 1978.
10, 82p; illus, 1 map; pbk　　　ISBN: 0-85640-139-0
　　　　　　　　　　　　　　　BL: X.619/18850

This former Northern Irish football club was once a powerful force in the land winning the Irish League 14 times. They eventually resigned from the League, however, in 1949 following a game with rivals Linfield which degenerated into a riot. This study relates the full and sorry tale.

1318 Belfast Celtic / John Kennedy; foreword by Bill McKavanagh. Belfast: Pretan, 1989.
x, 109p; illus; pbk　　　ISBN: 0-948868-12-0
　　　　　　　　　　　　BL: YK.1993.a.17458

Bessbrook

1319 A century of Bessbrook football 1893-1993 / Eddie McKee. 1993.
76p

Cliftonville

1320 Cliftonville – the centenary reds 1879-1979: the official history of Cliftonville FC / W. S. Beckett. 1979. Belfast: Cliftonville FC, 1979.
32p; pbk

Short history of the Belfast club. Cliftonville played their first game on 11 October 1879; they are generally regarded as Ireland's first soccer club. The inspiration for their formation came from Mr John McAlery who watched a game of football whilst on holiday in Scotland and decided to take the idea back to the Emerald Isle. His is a shining example to all dedicated 'soccerphiles' as he was actually on honeymoon at the time.

Derry City See Republic of Ireland

Glenavon

1321 Glenavon Football Club: 100 years / Malcolm Brodie. Lurgan: Glenavon FC, 1989.
125p; illus; pbk

Detailed history of this Lurgan based club.

Glentoran

1322 A history of Glentoran 1882-1982 / Malcolm Brodie. Belfast: Glentoran FC, 1982.
176p; pbk

Detailed history of the Belfast club known as the 'Cock and Hens' – rivals of Linfield, they are one of the most successful Irish sides.

Larne

1323 A short history handbook / Brian Blair and Jim Bell. Larne: East Antrim Business Services.
80p; pbk

Linfield

1324 Linfield: 100 years of Linfield Football and Athletic Club / Malcolm Brodie. Belfast: Universities Press, 1985.
230p; illus

Northern Irish club formed in 1886; based at Windsor Park they have enjoyed a long-standing link with the Glasgow club, Rangers.

Tandragee Rovers

1325 The Rovers 80 years: a history of Tandragee Rovers Football Club, 1909-1989 / George Black. Tandragee: Tandragee Rovers Football Club, 1989?

This small club currently play in the Mid-Ulster League.

Republic of Ireland

Athlone Town

1326 A history of Athlone Town FC: the first 101 years /
Frank Lynch. Athlone: The author, 1991.
400p; illus; pbk

> Highly detailed work on one of the South's oldest
> clubs.

Bective Rangers

1327 Bective Rangers Football Club: 75th anniversary,
1881-1956. Blackrock: Mount Salus Press, 1956.
67p; illus   BL: 7923.b.17

Bohemian AFC

1328 Bohemian AFC: official club history, 1890-1976 /
compiled and edited by Tony Reid. Dublin: Tara
Publishing for Bohemian Association Football Club,
1977.
64p; illus; pbk   BL: X.611/7818

> Informative history of the Dublin based club generally
> known simply as Bohemians.

1329 Bohemian times: an outline history of Bohemian
Football Club & Dalymount Park, 1890-1993 / Phil
Howlin. Dublin: The author, 1994.
62p; illus

Cork City

1330 Honour to Cork: a tribute to the victors from County
Cork. Dublin: Parkside, 1945.
52p   BL: 7918.b.16

> Covers both hurling and football

Derry City

1331 The Derry City FC story 1928-86 / Frank Curran.
Londonderry?: Wholesale Newspaper Services, 1986.
172p; illus; pbk

> Derry City are possibly the only team to have played
> in Leagues on both sides of the border.

1332 A history of Derry City Football and Athletic Club
1929-1972. / W. H. W. Platt. Coleraine: The author,
1986.
204p; illus; pbk   ISBN: 0-9501953-2-4

There were just 2,000 copies of this excellent history
produced — abundant statistics and photographs
accompany a general history of the Londonderry club.

1333 Oakboys: Derry's football dream come true / Eoghan
Corry. Dublin: Torc, 1993.
256p; illus; pbk

ISBN: 1-898142-10-6

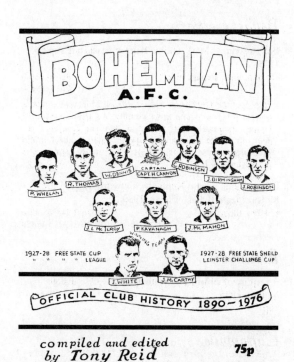

Limerick United

1334 The end of an era: a history of Limerick Senior Soccer at
the Markets Field 1937-84 / edited by Aidan Corr.
80p; pbk

Shamrock Rovers

1335 The Hoops: a history of Shamrock Rovers / Paul
Doolan and Robert Goggins. Dublin: Gill & Macmillan,
1993.
388p   ISBN: 0-7171-2121-6

> Founded in 1899 and based in Dublin, Shamrock Rov-
> ers are regarded as the most successful team in the
> Republic of Ireland. This is a well researched and de-
> tailed work.

Shelbourne

1336 Shelbourne Football Club golden jubilee, 1895-1945:
official souvenir. Dublin: Parkside Press, 1945.
47p   BL: 7918.b.13

> A scarce item covering the early history of this Dublin
> based Southern Irish club.

Ireland ~ Collective Studies

1337 Bass book of Irish soccer / Seán Ryan and Noel Dunne.
Dublin: Mercier, 1975.

Isle of Man

Peel

1338 Triumph and controversy: Peel AFC 1888-1988 / Colin
Moore. The author?, 1988.

> The club's assistant secretary here celebrates 100
> years of the club's history. Peel have certainly domi-
> nated Manx football, winning the championship no
> less than 26 times between 1890 and 1990. This is
> an excellent and well-researched study.

St Mary's

1339 From the Boys' Guild to the Bowl: a centenary history of St
Mary's AFC 1893-1993 / Colin Moore and Eric Clague.
62p

> In this joint effort Colin Moore covers the period from
> 1945 whilst Eric Clague chronicles the pre-war era. St
> Mary's may not be the most successful club on the
> Isle of Man, but their history is a good one — essen-
> tial reading for anyone interested in Manx football.

Isle of Wight

Cowes Sports

1340 Cowes Sports Football Club: souvenir and official history. Cowes Sports FC, 1987.
32p; pbk

It's not all yachting! Informed summary of the coastal club in a town where 'keeping it on the deck' need not necessarily refer to football.

Newport

1341 Newport (IOW) Football Club: the first hundred years 1888-1988 / Percy Ranger. Newport: Newport FC, 1988.
92p

A Southern League team founded in 1888.

Ryde Sports

1342 Ryde for pride / Mike Bull. Ryde: Ryde Sports Club, 1988.
56p; pbk

Short well-informed account.

Club Histories League Table

1st	Manchester United	. . . . 85 books
2nd	Liverpool	. . . . 48 books
3rd	Arsenal	. . . . 45 books
4th	Celtic	. . . . 42 books
5th	Tottenham Hotspur	. . . 41 books
6th	Rangers	. . . . 39 books
7th	Newcastle	. . . . 38 books
=8th	Everton	. . . . 23 books
=8th	Manchester City	. . . . . . 23 books
10th	Chelsea	. . . . 22 books

Personalities

READING ABOUT THE LIVES OF FOOTBALLERS and others involved in the game can be hugely entertaining as well as informative. Cheap jibes about cliché-ridden autobiographies are all very well but few of the authors listed here are professional writers. The biographies and autobiographies listed in this section are of real worth and interest – true, many follow a typical 'working-class-boy made good' formula which often ignores the background detail, but then there are plenty of other books to give us that. At its best, this genre can give some genuine insights into the lives of those who make their living in the world of professional football. Underneath the glamorous veneer, there are aspects of everyday footballing life it would be easy to forget. Footballers have the normal problems of life just like the rest of us but also suffer from those unique to their profession – the demands of training, difficulties with contracts, injuries, huge successes and tragic failures. Against the background of the time in which they were written, these works can serve as a useful measure of the changes which have taken place in association football over the years.

It is a great pity that the inter-war period and the late nineteenth century are covered so scantily with very few detailed accounts of what it was really like to be a footballer in those early days. Students of this era though would do well to consult the early works by two of the great administrators of the game. Sir Frederick Wall [C496] and William Pickford [C412] were two of the 'grand old men' of football able to write memoirs which included first hand accounts of the game before the turn of the century. Those by C. B. Fry [C191] too, and Nicholas 'Pa' Jackson [C273] give a taste of the true flavour of the game as it was played by the Victorian and Edwardian gentleman.

Following the Second World War, and especially in the 1950s, players and their life-style attracted more and more media attention. The number of biographies and autobiographies rose accordingly, to the point at which even relatively minor footballing celebrities were putting pen to paper. Most of the great Internationals of the past forty years are thus represented along with the leading personalities in management and administration. With a growing interest in sport and leisure pursuits, the footballer's life became a popular 'read' during the 1960s. There was certainly no shortage of subjects willing to put themselves under the spotlight to supplement their income.

Within this chapter there are a number of specialist categories. The refereeing fraternity is represented by such well-known names as Jack Taylor [C478], Clive Thomas [C481] and Pat Partridge [C404]. For a comparative study of the role of the men in black in earlier times, the works of Arthur Ellis [C165] and Mervyn Griffiths [C231] are interesting whilst the memoirs of J. M. Wiltshire in *Play to the Whistle* [C507] take us back well before the last war.

It might be surprising to find some female authors in this chapter but if you happen to be the mother of boys called Bobby and Jack then that's surely something to write about. Certainly Cissie Charlton [C95] must be regarded as football's most famous mum! As for the group generically labelled 'players' wives', they have for the most part remained silent, with the exception of Penny Watson [C499] and Beattie Fry [C194] who spill the beans on Dave and Charles respectively, whilst Paul Gascoigne has his card marked, not by his other half, but by Jane Nottage [C205], his former personal assistant.

One might expect biographies to record their subjects' tales of triumph rather than otherwise and on the whole this is indeed the case. A number of players though have been honest enough to chart the difficult times which came following the end of a distinguished career. Anyone needing to research this downside to stardom should certainly consult the twilight publications of Jimmy Greaves [C224], George Best [C37] Tommy Lawton [C309] and even Stanley Matthews [C359]. Whilst all of these suffered to a greater or lesser degree a fall from the heady heights, there is another breed who would never dream of claiming superstar status yet who have nonetheless penned autobiographies of disarming frankness and humour and with no small degree of success. Eamon Dunphy's diary of a professional footballer, *Only a Game?* [C158] is regarded as a classic piece of football writing from one of the most eloquent players in soccer whilst the Fred Eyre series [C168-172] was described as 'hilarious' by contemporary reviewers. *Who the Hell was Dudley Kernick?* [C298] is an apt enough title for another informative yet humorous piece which concentrates on life in football out of the fast lane. This type of biography is numerically disproportionate to the breed it represents, for there are undoubtedly more 'ordinary' footballing lives than there are superstars and it is to the credit of the three highlighted authors that they had the enthusiasm, willingness and ability to place the truth on record.

At the opposite end of the scale, personalities emerge whose draw is so strong that they become worthy of biographical treatment outside their countries of origin. Good examples of these are Pelé [C407-409], Eusébio [C167], Cruyff [C130] and

Puskas [C414]. Players of this status had such natural ability that they were destined for worldwide exposure while the close attention of the media helped make them into household names in this country. On occasions, the writers and broadcasters themselves become so closely associated with the game they cover that they almost unwittingly achieve star status in their own right. For a study of the world of commentary and presentation, Kenneth Wolstenholme [C509], Frank Bough [C55] and Archie MacPherson [C352] give a true professional's view whilst the quality journalists are ably represented by Don Davies [C137] and Geoffrey Green [C227].

Once in a while a book appears that does not fit into the usual categories. Harold Shepherdson, in *The Magic Sponge* [C446], is probably the only run-on trainer to have been well enough known to warrant two hundred pages of life story, whilst books by Gary Mabbutt [C322] and Ray Kennedy [C297] transcend football itself by dint of special circumstances. Mabbutt, apart from being an excellent player, is known as one of the few diabetics playing at the highest level whilst Kennedy, after a highly successful career, was stricken with Parkinson's disease when only thirty-five. Both have used books with a footballing theme to share their stories and undoubtedly give inspiration to many ordinary people in parallel situations.

Unique in this section must be the two works by David Icke [C271-272], the only entrant here who can lay claim to being player, broadcaster and messiah in a highly varied career. Although Brian Clough followers might seek to match this unusual bid, it is probably fair to say that Clough, despite many television appearances, could not truly be regarded as a broadcaster. Those who know Icke's story must ponder whether he wore a turquoise jersey whilst keeping goal for Hereford – to read his early and later work back to back might be as near to a surreal experience as it is possible to come in the world of football literature! Who said 'Goalkeepers are crazy'?

The cricketer/footballer entries in this section will prove fruitful to researchers interested in this special (and dying) breed. Whilst there are still footballers around who are highly proficient in the willow and leather department, it is no longer realistically possible to combine the two careers – Willie Watson's *Double International* [C500] is an excellent evocation of how it used to be done but it is almost certain that nothing of the same ilk will ever be written again.

The 'collective' biographies which follow present general studies of specific areas: goalscorers, managers, black footballers, league chairmen, centre forwards – there are single volumes covering all these for researchers making a comparative study or seeking an overview without wishing to consult a large number of individual volumes. This section also includes the invaluable 'who's who' style of publication which provides extremely useful potted biographies of a great number of players from all eras.

Biographies and autobiographies must surely then have something valid to say to the football student, no matter how experienced. Although they glory in the corniest of titles – and one must suspect that Ian Ure might never have entered the publisher's office but for the splendidly fortuitous *Ures Truly* [C487], – the volumes in this section of the bibliography should not be overlooked as a valuable 'snapshot' source for researchers into many aspects of the game.

Personalities ~ Contents

Biographies & Autobiographies

Aitken, Roy

1 Feed the bear!: the Roy Aitken story / Roy Aitken and Alex Cameron. Edinburgh: Mainstream, 1987.
191p; illus
    ISBN: 1-85158-073-5 (cased) • ISBN: 1-85158-074-3 (pbk)
Much of interest on Celtic and Scotland from this long-serving midfielder.

Aldridge, John

2 Inside Anfield / John Aldridge with Brian Woolnough. Edinburgh: Mainstream, 1988.
190p; illus
    ISBN: 1-85158-191-X (cased) • ISBN: 1-85158-192-8 (pbk)
    BL: YK.1989.b.2321
Mainly Liverpool, but with some reference to his earlier clubs, Oxford United and Newport County, from the Republic of Ireland striker.

☞ Also listed at: B409

Allen, Clive

3 There's only one Clive Allen: an autobiography / Clive Allen with Steve Stammers. London: Arthur Barker, 1987.
x, 142p; illus
    ISBN: 0-213-16953-3
    BL: YK.1988.a.3438
This covers the career to date of this much travelled striker, including Queen's Park Rangers, Crystal Palace and Spurs.

Allen, Ronnie

4 It's goals that count / Ronnie Allen. London: Stanley Paul, 1955.
152p; illus
    BL: 7921.e.130
Scoring for Port Vale and West Bromwich Albion was just a matter of routine by the time this book was published – good coverage of both clubs.

Allison, George

5 The inside story of football / George Allison. Southall: Quaker Oats, 1938.
127p; illus
    BL: X.449/3576
Secretary-manager of Arsenal from 1934 to 1947. This first volume covers Arsenal's championships in 1935 and 1938 along with their FA Cup win of 1936, a glorious period for 'The Gunners'. This flamboyant character writes well and offers a rare insight into 1930's football in one of the earliest examples of autobiography.

6 Allison calling: a galaxy of football and other memories / George Allison. London: Staples Press, 1948.
240p; illus
    BL: 7919.de.63
Allison's second book embraces the war years at Highbury and includes interesting material on his career as a pioneer broadcaster of football for TV and radio. He was narrator for the first TV documentary about the game, 'Soccer at Arsenal', broadcast in September 1937.

Allison, Malcolm

7 Colours of my life / Malcolm Allison written with James Lawton. London: Everest, 1975.
190p; illus; index
    ISBN: 0-903925-55-9
    BL: X.629/10553
A colourful character indeed! His coaching and management days overshadow his professional career with Charlton and West Ham from 1945 to 1958 when the onset of tuberculosis forced him to step down. There is much material here on 'Big Mal's' inspired views on coaching and his successful management years with Joe Mercer at Manchester City followed by a difficult period before his move to Crystal Palace in 1973.

Ames, L. E. G.

8 Close of play / L. E. G. Ames. London: Stanley Paul, 1953.
208p; illus
    BL: 7921.c.44
The Kent cricketer makes a number of references to his handful of games for Clapton Orient and Gillingham between 1926 and 1932. He is one of the better known cricketer-footballers but his abilities were very much weighted to the summer game.

Anderson, Viv

9 Viv Anderson / Andrew Longmore. London: Heinemann Kingswood, 1988.
xv, 110p; illus
    ISBN: 0-434-98153-2
    BL: YK.1990.b.390
Covers the distinguished career of the England International right-back during his playing days from 1974, largely with Nottingham Forest and Arsenal before his 1987 move to Manchester United. This publication pre-dates his time with Sheffield Wednesday and subsequent move into management.

Ardiles, Ossie

10 Ossie: my life in football / Osvaldo Ardiles with Mike Langley. London: Sidgwick & Jackson, 1983.
173p; illus; index
    ISBN: 0-283-98872-X
    BL: X.950/26178

World Cup winner with Argentina in 1978, then a Spurs midfield favourite. Ardiles missed the 1982 FA Cup Final because of the Falklands crisis, an occasion when world politics and English football truly crossed paths creating moral dilemmas for supporters and players alike.

Arlett, Reg

11 Reg Arlett: the Henley Meteor / J. F. Bailey. Henley?: The author, 1994.
16p; pbk

> *Limited edition of 100 copies*
> Heartening tale of this Henley Town folk hero.

Armfield, Jimmy

12 Fighting back: an autobiography / James Christopher Armfield. London: Stanley Paul, 1963.
127p; illus   BL: 10924.c.2

> Long before his current status as journalist and broadcaster, 'Gentleman Jim' achieved fame as Blackpool and England's full-back, signing professional in 1954. He was voted the 'best right-back in the world' after the 1962 Chile World Cup finals. This book pre-dates his management career with Bolton Wanderers and Leeds United.

Astle, Jeff

13 Striker! / Jeff Astle; edited by Philip Osborn. London: Pelham, 1970.
157p; illus   ISBN: 0-13-056008-1
                                             BL: X.629/2925

> Although playing for Notts County from 1959 to 1964, Astle's name is synonymous with West Bromwich Albion, for whom he scored the winning goal against Everton in the 1968 FA Cup Final. This centre forward had a short and inglorious England career and retired from league football in 1973 to pursue a life away from the game. He is now something of a cult figure and is currently making wonderfully surreal guest appearances on TV's 'Fantasy Football League' as a budding recording artist!

Atkinson, Ron

14 United to win / the autobiography of Ron Atkinson with Joe Melling. London: Sidgwick & Jackson, 1984.
170p; illus; index   ISBN: 0-283-99130-5
                                             BL: X.950/42360

> One of football's larger than life personalities, 'Big Ron' had a playing career with Oxford United from 1959 to 1971. This autobiography was written largely though on the strength of his managerial career with Manchester United from 1981 and includes the 1983 FA Cup win over Brighton. He is still making news over a decade later!

Baird, Archie

15 Family of four: the extraordinary autobiographical tale of one man's escape from wartime imprisonment and his 'adoption' by an Italian peasant family / Archie Baird. Edinburgh: Mainstream, 1989.
160p; illus   ISBN: 1-85158-235-5
                                             BL: YK.1995.b.1748

> Unique story of this pre-war Aberdeen player.

Ball, Alan

16 Ball of fire / Alan Ball. London: Pelham, 1967.
144p; illus   ISBN: 0-17-301015-6
                                             BL: X.449/2690

> Autobiography titles come as easily as playing for one of England's greatest midfielders. This first volume covers his playing career at Blackpool and early days at Everton from 1966, the year in which he helped inspire England to World Cup triumph.

17 It's all about a ball: an autobiography / Alan Ball. London: W. H. Allen, 1978.
177p; illus   ISBN: 0-491-02204-2
                                             BL: X.629/12016

> Ball's story is updated to include his League Championship days with Everton in 1969/70, six years with Arsenal from 1971 and two years with Southampton, all pre-dating his still continuing management career.

Banks, Gordon

18 Banks of England / Gordon Banks. London: Arthur Barker, 1980.
ix, 164p; illus; index   ISBN: 0-213-16730-1
                                             BL: X.629/12834

> The most famous goalkeeper of all time? Chesterfield, Leicester and Stoke were his clubs, but it is as England's 1966 World Cup winning keeper that he achieved universal acclaim.

Barnes, John

19 'Out of his skin': the John Barnes phenomenon / Dave Hill. London: Faber, 1989.
xv, 204p; illus; index

> *Bibliography: p197-198*
> ISBN: 0-571-14256-7 (cased) ● ISBN: 0-571-15472-7 (pbk)
>   BL: YK.1990.a.1626

> Watford, Liverpool and England are all covered here, with much significant material on the place of black players in British football during the 1980s.

Barnes, Walley

20 Captain of Wales / Walley Barnes. London: Stanley Paul, 1953.
208p; illus   BL: 10864.aa.15

A full-back stalwart for Arsenal from 1943 to 1955 with 22 caps for his country. One of the most famous figures in Wales' footballing history.

Bartram, Sam

21 Sam Bartram: his autobiography / Sam Bartram. London: Burke, 1956.

159p; illus   BL: 7923.ff.7

A colossus of a goalkeeper, Bartram spent 22 years with Charlton Athletic between 1934 and 1956. He also guested for no fewer than ten different clubs during World War Two and his autobiography, published at the end of his playing career, contains some interesting material on this element of the game.

Bastin, Cliff

22 Cliff Bastin remembers / an autobiography in collaboration with Brian Glanville and others. London, Edinburgh: Ettrick Press, 1950.

211p; illus   BL: 7920.l.15

Spotted playing for Exeter City by the legendary Herbert Chapman, Bastin signed for Arsenal in 1929 and became a classic footballing forward of the 1930s, winning cup and championship medals as a matter of general routine. 229 wartime appearances and 21 appearances for England preceded his 1947 retirement.

Bauld, Willie

23 Willie Bauld: my story.

Scorer of a winning hat-trick for Heart of Midlothian in the 1955 Scottish League Cup, 2 more goals in the 1959 final, a memorable Scottish Cup win against Celtic in 1956 and a Championship medal in 1960 – Bauld's story certainly coincides with a very successful spell for the Edinburgh club.

Baxter, Jim

24 Baxter, the party's over: an autobiography / Jim Baxter with John Fairgrieve. London: Stanley Paul, 1984.

142p; illus   ISBN: 0-09-158450-7
                         BL: X.629/25626

This is one of Scottish football's most famous names in the 1960s. Most closely associated with Rangers, then Sunderland and Nottingham Forest in England.

Beardsley, Peter

25 Proud to be a Geordie / Peter Beardsley with Tony Hardisty. London: Knight Fletcher, 1986.

60p; illus; pbk

Much on his home team by the Newcastle born star.

26 Beardsley: an autobiography / Peter Beardsley with Andy Cairns. London: Stanley Paul, 1988.

156p; illus   ISBN: 0-09-173877-6
                         BL: YK.1989.a.918

Published during the Liverpool years of this popular England International.

Beasant, Dave

27 Tales of the unexpected: the Dave Beasant story / Dave Beasant with Dave Smith. Edinburgh: Mainstream, 1989.

192p; illus   ISBN: 1-85158-220-7
                         BL: YK.1993.b.5314

The goalkeeper's rise to fame from Wimbledon to Chelsea, with Newcastle as a short interlude.

Bentley, Roy

28 Going for goal / Roy Bentley. London: Museum Press, 1955.

127p; illus   BL: 7921.e.121

Captaining Chelsea's 1955 championship side as centre forward was inevitably a cue for this England International to go into print.

Best, George

29 Best of both worlds / George Best. London: Transworld Publishers, 1968.

173p; illus   ISBN: 0-274-58018-7
                         BL: X.449/3358

A footballing phenomenon who has, not surprisingly, been the subject of a variety of publications. This first covers his early years and first five seasons at Manchester United.

30 George Best: the inside story of soccer's super-star. London: Clipper, 1969.

48p; chiefly illus; pbk   ISBN: 0-85108-002-2

A lightweight study of Belfast's most famous sporting son.

31 Anatomy of a football star: George Best / David Meek. London: Arthur Barker, 1970.

138p; illus   ISBN: 0-213-00242-6

The first in-depth Best biography.

32 On the ball / George Best. London: Pelham, 1970.

120p; illus   SBN: 7207-0407-3
                         BL: X.622/830

33 George Best / Derek Hodgson. London: Wolfe, 1971.

64p; illus; pbk
(Giants of football; 1); (Hall of Fame books)
                         ISBN: 0-02-340452-6

34 George Best: fall of a superstar / John Roberts. Manchester: Hodgson, 1973.

88p; illus; pbk   ISBN: 0-9502837-2-X

Published in the year George Best left Manchester United – as the title suggests 'life after superstardom' can be fraught with problems. This is probably one of the first 'warts and all' treatments of a professional player.

35 Best: an intimate biography / Michael Parkinson.
London: Hutchinson, 1975.
144p; illus   ISBN: 0-09-123420-4
                                               BL: X.629/7003

*One of those occasions in which the author is as well
known as his subject. Best himself had been a guest
on Parkinson's famed television chat show – a friend-
ship was forged and this 'intimate' study resulted.*

36 Where do I go from here? / George Best and Graeme
Wright. London: Queen Anne Press, 1981.
206p; illus   ISBN: 0-362-00556-7
                                               BL: X.622/11302

*Spells with Stockport County, Fulham and in the
United States are covered in yet another update.
Bournemouth is the answer to the title question, as
five games for them were to follow shortly!*

37 The good, the bad and the bubbly / George Best with
Ross Benson. London: Simon & Schuster, 1990.
185p; illus   ISBN: 0-671-71026-5
                                               BL: YK.1991.b.1714

*The final overview? All manner of problems, drink
among them, make being a football 'great' a most difficult business, and ceasing to be one even harder.*

Bingham, Billy

38 Soccer with the stars / Billy Bingham. London: Stanley
Paul, 1962.
191p; illus   BL: 7920.f.58

*This first study covers Bingham's playing career as
Northern Ireland International and skilful winger with
Glentoran, Sunderland, Luton and Everton.*

39 Billy: a biography of Billy Bingham / Billy Bingham with
Robert Allen. Hardmondsworth: Viking, 1986.
198p; illus   ISBN: 0-670-81282-X
                                               BL: YA.1993.b.11156

*This much later update takes in his last playing days
with Port Vale but the greatest concentration is on
his role in management. Southport, Linfield, the
Greek national side, Everton, Salonika, Mansfield
Town and Plymouth: all have a place, but Bingham as
manager of Northern Ireland will be the enduring image.*

Blanchflower, Danny

40 The double and before: the autobiography of Danny
Blanchflower. London: Nicholas Kaye, 1961.
viii, 183p; illus   BL: 010609.b.4

*The thinking man's footballer is no longer with us but
all his glory days with Spurs are recalled, not forgetting humbler times at Glentoran, wartime Swindon,
Barnsley and Aston Villa from one of Northern Ireland's greatest Internationals. All told in the
inimitable style of perhaps soccer's greatest
wordsmith.*

Bonds, Billy

41 Bonzo: an autobiography / Billy Bonds. London: Arthur
Barker, 1988.
192p; illus   ISBN: 0-213-16960-6
                                               BL: YK.1989.a.1047

*Twenty-one years with West Ham from 1967 earned
the ultimate recognition when Bonds was awarded
the MBE. This book was written on his retirement
from playing prior to becoming manager. It provides a
unique record of the changing face of football over
the last thirty years.*

Bonetti, Peter

42 Leaping to fame / Peter Bonetti. London: Stanley Paul,
1968.
149p; illus   ISBN: 0-371-41002-9
                                               BL: X.449/3320

*Aptly titled account of the goalkeeping exploits of
'The Cat' with Chelsea and England. 600 league
games make him one of soccer's most loyal subjects.*

Botham, Ian

43 Ian Botham / Bob Farmer. London: Hamlyn, 1979.
160p; illus; index   ISBN: 0-600-34917-9
                                               BL: X.620/18819

*Scunthorpe United haven't fielded many superstars
in their history but Ian Botham was one of them. He
is certainly one of the most famous of the rare foot-
baller-cricketer breed but his prowess was heavily
weighted to the summer game. Indeed, his handful of
Football League appearances between 1979 and 1984
had an element of circus about them, and helped to
put a few onto the Scunthorpe gate. The entries below are included as they may present occasional
references to the winter game of use to researchers
studying the phenomenon of 'crickballers', or be of interest to the desperate Scunthorpe historian.*

44 Ian Botham: the great all-rounder / Dudley Doust.
London: Cassell, 1980.
xiii, 138p; illus; index   ISBN: 0-304-30606-1
                                               BL: X.622/8516

   ☞ Subsequent ed. C45

45 Ian Botham: the great all-rounder / Dudley Doust.
Updated ed. London: Granada, 1981.
272p; illus; index; pbk   ISBN: 0-583-13452-1
                                               BL: X.629/15452

   ☞ Previous ed. C44

46 Ian Botham / Andrew Langley; illustrated by Karen
Heywood. London: Hamilton, 1983.
64p; illus
(Profiles)   ISBN: 0-241-11031-9
                                               BL: X.629/22944

47 Botham / photographs and captions by Patrick Eagar; text by Graeme Wright. Kingswood: Kingswood Press, 1985.
159p; illus   ISBN: 0-434-98063-3
                                             BL: YL.1990.b.115

48 Botham / Don Mosey; foreword by Trevor Bailey. London: Methuen, 1986.
224p; illus; index   ISBN: 0-413-40780-2
                                             BL: YK.1986.a.1977

☞ Subsequent ed. C50

49 It sort of clicks / Ian Botham talking to Peter Roebuck. London: Willow Books, 1986.
153p; illus; index   ISBN: 0-00-218240-8
                                             BL: YK.1987.b.293

50 Botham / Don Mosey; foreword by Trevor Bailey. Rev. and updated ed. London: Sphere, 1987.
266p; illus; index; pbk   ISBN: 0-7221-6167-0
                                             BL: YK.1987.a.7357

☞ Previous ed. C48

51 Living with a legend / Kathy Botham. London: Grafton, 1987.
224p; illus   ISBN: 0-246-13221-3
                                             BL: YK.1987.a.6309

52 Botham: a biography / Patrick Murphy. London: Dent, 1988.
xii, 236p; illus; index   ISBN: 0-460-04725-6
                                             BL: YK.1988.b.5103

53 Ian Botham / Andrew Ward. London: Scholastic, 1993.
48p; illus; pbk
(Sports shots; 8)   ISBN: 0-590-55184-1

54 My autobiography: don't tell Kath / Ian Botham and Peter Hayter. London: CollinsWillow, 1994.
416p; illus   ISBN: 0-00-218316-1

Bough, Frank

55 Cue Frank! / Frank Bough. London: Queen Anne Press, 1980.
191p; illus   ISBN: 0-362-00519-2
                                             BL: X.981/22497

For many years the unflappable front man for BBC sports programmes – this autobiography contains many footballing references and a keen insight into the broadcasting of the game before it became thoroughly hi-tech.

Brady, Liam

56 So far, so good: a decade in football / Liam Brady. London: Stanley Paul, 1980.
215p; illus; index   ISBN: 0-09-141790-2
                                             BL: X.629/13030

As eloquent in speech as he was with his feet – this work was written at the end of his seven years with Arsenal prior to an Italian sojourn and a later spell with West Ham. Some thought provoking comment from one of Eire's greatest Internationals.

Bremner, Billy

57 You get nowt for being second / Billy Bremner. London: Souvenir Press, 1969.
126p; illus   BL: X.449/3941

Typically gritty title choice from a player who seemingly disliked losing more than most. The concentration here is on his long career with Leeds and Scotland. The title was to prove horribly prophetic on more than one occasion, much to the delight of all but the committed 'Bremnerphile'.

Brooking, Trevor

58 Trevor Brooking / Trevor Brooking with the assistance of Brian Scovell. London: Pelham, 1981.
189p; illus   ISBN: 0-7207-1374-9
                                             BL: X.629/16767

The gentlemanly England and West Ham midfielder enjoyed a career, like team-mate Billy Bonds, spanning three decades. Here he covers the majority of his playing life prior to his entry into the world of broadcasting and expert analysis.

Bruce, Steve

59 Heading for victory: an autobiography / Steve Bruce. London: Bloomsbury, 1994.
182p; illus   ISBN: 0-7475-1780-0
                                             BL: YK.1995.b.4486

Covers mostly Manchester United with some references to his two previous clubs, Gillingham and Norwich City.

Buchan, Charles

60 A lifetime in football / Charles Murray Buchan. London: Phoenix House, 1955.
224p; illus   BL: 7922.b.44

He of 'Football Monthly' fame enjoyed a distinguished career with Sunderland and Arsenal from 1910 to 1928 before becoming a sportswriter and BBC radio broadcaster, noted for his 7.25 evening summaries of the Saturday's play. Few autobiographies speak with such authority about football prior to World War One and into the twenties; this is a very informative work.

Bull, Steve

61 Bully: authorized biography of Steve Bull / Steve Bull with Rob Bishop. 1992.
Appropriately titled study of the fearsome Wolves and England striker.

Burgess, Ron

62 Football: my life / Ron Burgess. London: Souvenir
Press, 1952.
179p; illus   BL: 7920.aaa.80

Written as one of the Spurs' senior players and captain, the Welsh International left-half was the first
Welshman to play for the Football League XI.

Burns, Tommy

63 Twists and turns: the Tommy Burns story / as told to
Hugh Keevins; foreword by Roy Aitken. Edinburgh:
Sportsprint, 1989.
ix, 149p; illus; index; pbk   ISBN: 0-85976-286-6
                                     BL: YK.1990.a.3353

The full career story of this long-serving Celtic midfielder.

Burtenshaw, Norman

64 Whose side are you on, ref? / Norman Burtenshaw;
foreword by Brian Clough. London: Arthur Barker, 1973.
xii, 186p; illus   ISBN: 0-213-16437-X

Informative insight into the art of refereeing from one
of the leading exponents of the sixties and seventies.

Busby, Matt

65 My story / Matt Busby as told to David R. Jack.
London: Souvenir Press, 1957.
219p; illus   BL: 10864.g.43

The early story of one of the greatest managers of all
time, taking in his playing days with Manchester City
and Liverpool before he guested for a host of clubs
during World War Two. His management of Manchester United is covered from 1945.

☞ Subsequent ed. C66

66 My story / Matt Busby as told to David R. Jack. 2nd ed.
London: Souvenir Press, 1958.
228p; illus

Tragic events made it necessary to publish this re-
vised second edition. A new chapter covers the
Manchester United Munich air disaster which Matt
Busby so courageously survived.

☞ Previous ed. C65

67 Matt . . . United . . . and me / Jimmy Murphy, as told to
Frank Taylor. London: Souvenir Press, 1968.
186p; illus   BL: X.449/3254

As much about Jimmy Murphy as Matt Busby. Murphy was a key figure in the United scouting system of
the 1950s which was largely responsible for bringing
together the famous 'Busby Babes'.

☞ Also listed at: C392

68 Father of football: the story of Sir Matt Busby / David
Miller. London: Stanley Paul, 1970.
190p; illus   SBN: 09-104650-5
                                         BL: X.629/2926

Includes Manchester United's European Cup triumph
of 1968, the year in which Matt Busby received a
knighthood.

☞ Subsequent ed. C72

69 Soccer at the top: my life in football / Sir Matt Busby.
London: Weidenfeld and Nicolson, 1973.
xiii, 178p; illus   ISBN: 0-297-76680-5
                                     BL: X.629/5805

Includes his second spell in charge at United from
late 1970 to mid 1971, following his 1969 retirement.

70 A strange kind of glory: Sir Matt Busby & Manchester
United / Eamon Dunphy. London: Heinemann, 1991.
405p; illus; index   ISBN: 0-434-21616-X
                                     BL: YK.1991.b.7234

One of the most highly acclaimed football biographies
ever written. Dunphy was an apprentice at United in
the early sixties and after a playing career went on to
become one of the few truly accomplished writers
from the playing ranks.

71 Busby: epitaph to a legend / Stan Liversedge.
Cleethorpes: Soccer Book Publishing, 1994.
144p; illus; pbk   ISBN: 0-947808-35-3
                                     BL: YK.1994.a.16415

This is surely the book which everybody wished might
never have to be written – Busby's death was noted
with sadness throughout the entire football world.

72 Father of football: the story of Sir Matt Busby / David
Miller; foreword by Bobby Charlton. Rev. ed. London:
Pavilion, 1994.
183p; illus   ISBN: 1-857934-73-3

☞ Previous ed. C68

73 Sir Matt Busby: a tribute / Chris Maume; foreword by
George Best. London: Virgin, 1994.
240p; illus   ISBN: 1-85227-464-6

Butcher, Terry

74 Both sides of the border / Terry Butcher with Andy
Cairns. London: Arthur Baker, 1987.
186p; illus   ISBN: 0-213-16950-9
                                     BL: YK.1989.a.1276

In July 1986 Terry Butcher signed for Glasgow Rangers following ten years with Ipswich Town. The
autobiography of the England defender offers interesting observations on the differences in the game in
England and Scotland.

Byrne, Johnny

75 The strategy of soccer / Johnny Byrne. London: Pelham, 1965.
106p; illus   BL: X.449/1599

This England International centre-forward is most closely associated with Crystal Palace and West Ham in the fifties and sixties. This is both autobiographical and instructional.

☞ Also listed at: G109

Callaghan, Ian

76 The Ian Callaghan story / Ian Callaghan and John Keith. London: Quartet Books, 1975.
117p; illus; pbk
                                         ISBN: 0-7043-1225-5

Written as one of the Liverpool 'greats', the England International winger was one of the classiest players of his time.

☞ Subsequent ed. C77

77 Cally, a football phenomenon: the story of Ian Callaghan. Augmented ed. / John Keith. London: Duckworth, 1977.
175p; illus   ISBN: 0-7156-1290-5
                                         BL: X.611/8047

This revised edition appeared on Callaghan's retirement from Liverpool after 637 league games.

☞ Previous ed. C76

Cantona, Eric

78 Cantona, my story / Eric Cantona. London: Headline, 1994.
161p; illus; index
    Translation of: Un rêve modeste et fou
                                         ISBN: 0-7472-1040-3
                                         BL: YK.1995.b.1537

Seldom has any overseas import made such an impact as this Frenchman. Manchester United and Leeds United are amply covered as well as his club days in France.

79 La philosophie de Cantona / Eric Cantona; edited by Michael Robinson. London: Ringpull, 1995.
124p; illus
    Text in English and French   ISBN: 1-898051-39-9

Cantwell, Noel

80 United we stand / Noel Cantwell. London: Stanley Paul, 1965.
127p; illus   BL: X.449/931

West Ham and Manchester were the two 'Uniteds' to benefit from the playing services of this attacking full-back who won 36 caps for the Republic of Ireland and also played for Ireland at cricket.

Carter, Raich

81 Footballer's progress: an autobiography / Horatio Stratton Carter; edited by Edward Lanchbery. London: Sporting handbooks, 1950.
237p; illus   BL: 7917.a.96

A professional from 1931 to 1951, Carter was one of England's greatest ever inside-forwards. His autobiography covers his playing days with Sunderland, Derby County and Hull City as well as his management of the latter club. One chapter is entitled 'Cricket against the Australians' – Carter played for Durham and Derbyshire and was dubbed by the local press as 'The Gilbert Jessop of Durham Cricket'. A highly informative work.

Channon, Mike

82 Home and away: an autobiography / Mike Channon with Neil Ewart. London: Stanley Paul, 1977.
123p; illus   ISBN: 0-09-131290-6
                                         BL: X.629/11573

When this first volume was published Channon had 388 league games for Southampton behind him and was about to move to Manchester City . . .

83 Man on the run / Mike Channon. London: Arthur Barker, 1986.
187p; illus   ISBN: 0-213-16930-4
                                         BL: YK.1987.a.1125

By the time this update appeared on his retirement from the game he had enjoyed a second spell with Southampton followed by Newcastle, Bristol Rovers, Norwich and Portsmouth! Perhaps that explains the title chosen by this much-travelled England forward.

Chapman, Herbert

84 Herbert Chapman on football / edited by John Graves. London: Garrick Publishing, 1934.
xi, 178p   BL: 2271.d.21

One of the earlier examples of football autobiography from a legendary figure who changed the face of football in the 1920s and 1930s. Includes his management days at Northampton, Leeds City, Huddersfield Town and Arsenal as well as his early playing career from 1897. Certainly a superb coverage of the whole period – this is essential reading for students of this era and a most important work for the game.

85   Herbert Chapman: football emperor: a study in the origins of modern soccer / Stephen Studd; foreword by Sir Stanley Rous. London: Peter Owen, 1981.
160p; illus; index

   Bibliography: p154-155   ISBN: 0-7206-0581-4
                                       BL: X.629/16392

If consulting the previous entry on Chapman proves difficult, then this is an admirable alternative. The extended title says it all – his tactical methods and other innovative ideas had a far-reaching effect on the game. His death from pneumonia in 1934 was premature but today his bust stands in the main entrance hall at Arsenal as an epitaph to one of the greatest managers in football.

Chapman, Lee

86   More than a match: a player's story / Lee Chapman. London: Stanley Paul, 1992.
156; illus; index   ISBN: 0-09-177502-7
                                       BL: YK.1993.b.7146

Chapman's easy manner and verbal eloquence off the pitch are in no way indicative of his style on the field of play where he is as tough a forward as most. A good account of the modern game including much of interest to followers of Stoke, Sheffield Wednesday and Leeds, who share the bulk of his league appearances.

Charles, John

87   King of soccer / William John Charles. London: Stanley Paul, 1957.
159p; illus   BL: 7923.r.20

This first study concentrates on the great Welshman's career with Leeds United culminating in promotion to the First Division in 1955-56.

88   The gentle giant / William John Charles. London: Stanley Paul, 1962.
175p; illus   BL: 10710.k.56

In 1957 'King John' was transferred to the Italian club Juventus, where he became a great success as their 'Gentle Giant'. This work includes that era and is one of the first to chronicle the career move abroad.

Charlton, Bobby

89   My soccer life / Bobby Charlton. London: Pelham, 1964.
125p; illus   BL: X.449/381

One of football's greatest ambassadors tells his early story including the first part of his Manchester United career and the 1958 Munich air crash.

90   Forward for England: an autobiography / Bobby Charlton. London: Pelham, 1967.
184p; illus   BL: X.449/2770

This update includes much on Charlton's England career including the World Cup win of 1966.

91   This game of soccer / Bobby Charlton. London: Cassell, 1967.
117p; illus   BL: X.441/869

92   Bobby Charlton / Ken Jones. London: Wolfe, 1971.
64p; illus; pbk
(Giants of football; 3); (Hall of Fame books)
                                     ISBN: 0-7234-0454-2

93   Bobby Charlton's most memorable matches / Bobby Charlton with Ken Jones; cartoons by Roy Ullyett. London: Stanley Paul, 1984.
125p; illus   ISBN: 0-09-153580-8
                                       BL: X.629/24688

An interesting slant on autobiography in which Charlton chronicles his most memorable games from a magnificent career.

Charlton, Bobby & Jack

94   The Charlton brothers / Norman Harris. London: Stanley Paul, 1971.
118p; illus   ISBN: 0-09-109660-X
                                       BL: X.629/3998

One of a handful of double biographies – this one chronicles the careers of English football's most famous brothers.

95   Cissie: football's most famous mother / Cissie Charlton tells her story with Vince Gladhill. Morpeth: Bridge Studio, 1988.
183p; illus   ISBN: 0-9512630-4-8
                                       BL: YK.1990.a.172

Giving birth to football's most famous brothers inevitably brings with it the title of football's most famous mother. One of just a handful of books featuring women and their part in the game.

Charlton, Jack

96   For Leeds and England / Jackie Charlton. London: Stanley Paul, 1967.
176p; illus   BL: X.449/2838

This study of 'Big Jack' concentrates on his long career as centre-half for Leeds United and takes in England's 1966 World Cup triumph.

97 Big Jack: the life and times of Jack Charlton / Stan
Liversedge. South Woodham Ferrers: Publishing
Corporation, 1994.
208p; illus ISBN: 1-897780-81-8

98 The legend of Jack Charlton / Tom Humphries.
London: Weidenfeld & Nicolson, 1994.
95p; illus ISBN: 0-297-83466-5

Since managing the Republic of Ireland Charlton has
been accorded legendary status, much, one suspects,
to his own surprise.

Clarke, Allan

99 Goals are my business / Allan Clarke assisted by Steve
Richards. London: Pelham, 1970.
191p; illus ISBN: 0-7207-0401-4
BL: X.629/2793

One of a famous footballing family, 'Sniffer' Clarke
had an instinctive nose for goals. His career at Walsall, Fulham, Leicester and Leeds is covered, prior to
his best days at the latter club.

100 Soccer: how to become a champion / Allan Clarke;
edited by David Jones. London: Luscombe, 1975.
124p; illus
ISBN: 0-86002-036-3 (cased) • ISBN: 0-86002-131-9 (pbk)
BL: X.629/7236

This update includes his prime years at Elland Road.

Clayton, Ronnie

101 A slave to soccer / Ronnie Clayton. London: Stanley
Paul, 1960.
132p; illus BL: 7925.bb.66

Much of interest to the Blackburn Rovers follower –
the England wing-half played 579 league games for
the club from 1950 to 1968. This book gives a particularly good evocation of the fifties era.

Close, Brian

102 Close on cricket / Brian Close. London: Stanley Paul,
1966.
119p; illus BL: X.449/1939

On the books of Leeds and Arsenal, a representative
of the England youth team and six games at centre
forward for Bradford City in 1952 – this is the footballing side to the tough Somerset, Yorkshire and
England cricketer.

103 Close to cricket / Brian Close as told to Frank Taylor.
London: Stanley Paul, 1968.
152p; illus SBN: 09-088000-5

104 I don't bruise easily: the autobiography of Brian Close /
written in association with Don Mosey. London:
Macdonald and Jane's, 1978.
10, 253p; illus ISBN: 0-354-08521-2
BL: X.620/17629

Clough, Brian

105 Clough: the man most likely. Chimera-Posner, 1978.
32p; illus; pbk
(C. P. newsbook; no. 1)

A lightweight early treatment of one of the greatest
and most outspoken managers in the modern game –
includes 41 photographs.

106 With Clough by Taylor / Peter Taylor with Mike
Langley. London: Sidgwick and Jackson, 1980.
205p; illus; index ISBN: 0-283-98667-0
BL: X.622/8473

Peter Taylor formed a formidable management team
with Clough and knew him better than anyone in football. This study covers their early days together at
Hartlepool United followed by the better known associations at Derby, Brighton and Nottingham Forest.
The first in-depth work on a fascinating character.

☞ Subsequent ed. C107

107 With Clough / Taylor (with Mike Langley). Rev. ed.
Sevenoaks: New English Library, 1981.
170p; illus; index; pbk ISBN: 0-283-98795-2
BL: X.629/16304

This was the year in which an acrimonious split between Clough and Taylor occurred. Part of the reason
was attributed to certain of Taylor's observations in
this book.

☞ Previous ed. C106

108 Clough: a biography / Tony Francis. London: Stanley
Paul, 1987.
237p; illus; index ISBN: 0-09-171420-6
BL: YK.1987.a.6807

This biography embraces a further seven years at
Nottingham Forest and includes material on Clough's
prolific goal-scoring career as a player with Middlesbrough and Sunderland.

☞ Subsequent ed. C109

109 Clough: a biography / Tony Francis. Rev. ed. London:
Stanley Paul, 1989.
240p; illus; index; pbk ISBN: 0-09-174062-2
BL: YK.1990.a.1067

☞ Previous ed. C108; subsequent ed. C110

110 Clough: a biography / Tony Francis. Rev. ed. London:
Stanley Paul, 1993.
254p; illus; index; pbk ISBN: 0-09-178223-6
BL: YK.1993.a.11533

☞ Previous ed. C109

111 His way: the Brian Clough story / Patrick Murphy.
London: Robson Books, 1993.
viii, 239p; illus; index ISBN: 0-86051-889-2
BL: YK.1994.b.13260

Clough is a Sinatra fan and has been known to sing a few bars of 'My Way' for the cameras. This is an apt title for a full summary of a true individualist's career on his retirement.

112 Clough: the autobiography / Brian Clough with John Sadler. London: Partridge, 1994.
326p; illus; index   ISBN: 1-85225-198-0

This controversial autobiography sees Clough expounding on many aspects of the game as he reflects during his well-earned retirement in his own inimitable way.

Comfort, Alan

113 Never walk alone / Gavin Peacock and Alan Comfort; edited by Alan MacDonald. London: Hodder, 1994.
illus; pbk   ISBN: 0-340-60675-4

An excellent insight into the traumas of a career ruined by injury. Comfort suffered a knee problem which forced his retirement in 1989 whilst playing for Middlesbrough. The support of his friend and fellow professional, Gavin Peacock, was never in doubt and never more needed.

☞ Also listed at: C406

Compton, Denis

114 Denis Compton: a cricket sketch / Ernest William Swanton. London: Sporting Handbooks, 1948.
79p   BL: 10862.a.23

A full list of Compton material is included here as some of these publications yield references to his 54 league games for Arsenal from 1936 to 1950, largely as an outside-left. One of the best known examples of a cricketer-footballer, Middlesex and England inevitably creep into most of these works from time to time!

☞ Subsequent ed. C116

115 Playing for England / Denis Charles Scott Compton. London: Sampson Low, Marston, 1948.
xi, 231p; illus   BL: 7919.aaa.26

☞ Subsequent ed. C119

116 Denis Compton / Ernest William Swanton. 2nd ed. London: Playfair Books, 1949.
95p   BL: 7920.aaa.42

☞ Previous ed. C114

117 Denis Compton: our greatest all-round sportsman / John Allen. London: Pitkin Pictorials, 1949.
28p; illus   BL: 7920.b.24

Includes particular reference to Compton's footballing prowess.

118 Focus on Denis Compton / Denis Foster. London: Background Books, 1949.

119 Playing for England / Denis Charles Scott Compton. New ed. London: Sampson Low, Marston, 1949.
xi, 241p; illus   BL: 7917.f.11

☞ Previous ed. C115

120 End of an innings / Denis Compton. London: Oldbourne, 1958.
207p; illus   BL: 10864.r.49

121 Denis Compton: a great sportsman / Charles Wyndham. Exeter: Haldon Books, 1967.
37p; illus
(They reached the top series)
For children   BL: X.0449/47

122 Denis Compton: the generous cricketer / Ian A. R. Peebles. London: Macmillan, 1971.
127p; illus   SBN: 333-11298-9
          BL: X.629/3514

123 Denis Compton: cricketing genius / Peter West. London: Stanley Paul, 1989.
viii, 184p; illus; index   ISBN: 0-09-173788-5
          BL: YK.1990.b.7727

Cooke, Charlie

124 For Chelsea and Scotland / Charlie Cooke. 1969.

Largely covers just what the title suggests, but with some reference to Cooke's earlier days at Aberdeen and Dundee. One of the classic Scottish ball players, enigmatic, a folk hero – this is an interesting study of a thoughtful personality.

Cooper, David

125 True blue: the Davie Cooper story / David Cooper with Graham Clark. Edinburgh: Mainstream, 1987.
192p; illus
          ISBN: 1-85158-069-7 (cased) • 1-85158-071-9 (pbk)

Mostly Rangers, but with some reference to his first club, Clydebank. His tragic death in 1995 prompted many genuine tributes.

Coppell, Steve

126 Touch and go / Steve Coppell with Bob Harris. London: Willow, 1985.
181p; illus   ISBN: 0-00-218146-0
          BL: X.950/44673

Extensive material on his Manchester United career along with references to early days at Liverpool University and Tranmere Rovers. The England International also chronicles his first management years at Crystal Palace – when he took over in 1984 he became the youngest manager in the league.

Craigmyle, Peter

127 A lifetime of soccer / Peter Craigmyle. The author, 1949.
64p; pbk

A scarce study of early refereeing from a famous international Scottish official.

Crerand, Pat

128 On top with United / Pat Crerand, as told to Ian Peebles; foreword by Sir Matt Busby. London: Stanley Paul, 1969.
111p; illus
ISBN: 0-09-099180-X
BL: X.449/3944

A key figure in Manchester United's side during the sixties. Also includes references to his earlier Celtic career.

Croker, Ted

129 The first voice you will hear is— : an autobiography / Ted Croker. London: Collins, 1987.
253p; illus
ISBN: 0-00-218086-3
BL: YK.1987.a.6128

Secretary of the Football Association from 1973 to 1989, Croker was the first former professional footballer to hold that position. He was largely responsible for shaping FA policy in response to the Bradford City fire disaster and the Heysel Stadium tragedy. His autobiography includes some frank revelations about English soccer at that time.

Cruyff, Johann

130 Johann Cruyff, superstar / Jacques Thibert and Max Urbini; translated from the French by Helen Paniguian. London: Pelham, 1975.
96p; illus
(A sporting print)

Translation of: 'Cruyff, super star'. Paris: Calmann-Levy, 1974
ISBN: 0-7207-0787-0 (cased) ● ISBN: 0-7207-0873-7 (pbk)
BL: X.619/15177

One of the most talented overseas players of his time, very much representative of the easy and fluid style which has come to be associated with Dutch football.

Cullis, Stanley

131 All for the Wolves / Stanley Cullis. London: Rupert Hart-Davis, 1960.
226p; illus
BL: 7925.c.35

Player for Wolverhampton Wanderers from 1934, becoming assistant manager in 1947, then manager from 1948 – this is an aptly titled study of the England International and Wolves 'great'.

Dalglish, Kenny

132 King Kenny: an autobiography / Kenny Dalglish with Ken Gallacher. London: Stanley Paul, 1982.
134p; illus
ISBN: 0-09-147730-1
BL: X.629/18442

A rare opportunity to learn something of the personal side of one of football's more private characters. Celtic, Liverpool and Scotland are given an understandably high profile.

☞ Subsequent ed. C133

133 King Kenny: an autobiography / Kenny Dalglish with Ken Gallacher. Rev. ed. London: Panther, 1984.
160p; illus; pbk
ISBN: 0-586-06394-3
BL: X.629/26615

☞ Previous ed. C132

134 Dalglish / Stephen F. Kelly. London: Headline, 1992.
viii, 280p; illus; index
ISBN: 0-7472-0717-8
BL: YK.1993.b.1412

Following a shock resignation from the game in 1991, Dalglish was to return in 1992 as manager of Blackburn Rovers. This study covers both his management of this club and of Liverpool.

Davies, Dai

135 Hanner cystal â 'nhad hunangofiant gôlgeidwad rhyngwladol / Dai Davies gyda Nic Parry. Yr Wyddgrug: Siop y Siswrn, 1985.
164p; illus; pbk
ISBN: 0-948483-00-8
BL: X.629/27728

One of only a few books in the bibliography to give full satisfaction to Welsh language students with a love of football. The international keeper is most closely associated with Swansea, Everton, Wrexham and Tranmere.

136 Never say Dai: based on Hanner cystal â 'nhad by Dai Davies / translation by Iorwerth Roberts. Mold: Siop y Siswrn, 1986.
222p; illus; pbk
Translated from Welsh
ISBN: 0-948483-01-6
BL: YK.1987.a.3058

This will come as a relief to Dai's English fans . . .

Davies, Don

137 Don Davies: 'an old international' / John Roberts Cox. London: Stanley Paul, 1962.
224p; illus
BL: X.449/161

The biography of the distinguished Manchester Guardian sports journalist who perished in the 1958 Munich air crash.

Davies, Hunter

138 My life in football / Hunter Davies. Edinburgh:
Mainstream, 1990.
224p
ISBN: 1-85158-302-5
BL: YK.1991.b.1913

Anecdotal reminiscences of the author with a particular liking of football, best known for his fly on the
wall study of Spurs. Not fully autobiographical, more
a selection of his writing and observations on the
game.

Dawson, Jerry

139 Jerry Dawson: memoirs 1929-1949. 1949.

Dean, Dixie

140 Dixie Dean: the life story of a goal scoring legend / Nick
Walsh. London: Macdonald and Jane's, 1977.
221p; illus
ISBN: 0-354-08515-8
BL: X.629/11555

William Ralph Dean was one of the game's greatest
goal-scoring centre forwards throughout the twenties and thirties. Tranmere, Everton and Notts
County all figure in his story.

141 The fabulous 'Dixie' / Phil Thompson. Wirral: Quarry,
1990.
73p; illus; pbk

Bibliography: p72
ISBN: 0-9515519-0-6
BL: YK.1992.a.7945

142 Dixie Dean of Tranmere Rovers, 1923-1925 / Gilbert
Upton. Southport: The author, 1992.
98p; illus; pbk

Bibliography: p98
ISBN: 0-9518648-1-5
BL: YK.1993.a.9236

Dean made his debut for Tranmere in 1923 at the age
of 15. This unusual biographical treatment concentrates on those early days before he achieved
folkhero status at Everton.

Dickinson, Jimmy

143 Pompey's Gentleman Jim / Peter Jeffs. Derby: Breedon
Books, 1988.
96p; illus

Bibliography: p96
ISBN: 0-907969-45-3
BL: YK.1992.b.5682

One of several 'Gentleman Jims' in the game, Dickinson was never cautioned by a referee in 764 league
appearances for Portsmouth. The England International's entire career as player and manager with one
club is admirably covered.

Dixon, Kerry

144 Kerry: the autobiography / Kerry Dixon. London:
Macdonald, 1986.
192p; illus; index
ISBN: 0-356-12355-3
BL: YK.1986.a.2026

It used to be only the true 'greats' who wrote their
autobiography. Kerry at twenty-five had a lot of
games for Reading and Chelsea behind him but this
book probably says as much about the commerciali-
sation of players' careers during the eighties as it
does about being a footballing star of true quality.

Docherty, Tommy

145 Soccer from the shoulder / Tommy Docherty. London:
Stanley Paul, 1960.
144p; illus; index
BL: 7925.e.17

'More clubs than Jack Nicklaus' is the struggling stag
comedian's standard one-liner about one of the
game's great characters, but when this first work
was published Docherty was only just starting. His
playing days at Celtic, Preston and Arsenal are the
mainstay of this volume.

146 Tommy Docherty speaks / Thomas Henderson
Docherty as told to Roy Peskett. London: Pelham, 1967.
192p; illus
BL: X.449/2836

Seven eventful years of management with Chelsea are
included in this update.

147 Call the Doc / Tommy Docherty with the assistance of
Derek Henderson. London: Hamlyn, 1981.
192p; illus
ISBN: 0-600-34672-2
BL: X.629/17216

Yet another update chronicles management ups and
downs at Rotherham, Queen's Park Rangers, Aston
Villa, Oporto, Hull City, Manchester United, Derby
County and with the Scotland team.

148 Dinner with the Doc / Tommy Docherty with Barry
Roberts. Liverpool: Mediaword, 1988.
87p; illus
ISBN: 0-9514056-0-8

149 Docherty: a biography of Tommy Docherty / Brian
Clarke. London: Kingswood, 1991.
184p; illus
ISBN: 0-413-64730-7
BL: YK.1991.b.8933

Still a few more clubs to go . . . Preston, a spell 'down
under', Wolves, Altrincham and finally retirement to
the hectic world of after-dinner speaking.

Doherty, Peter

150 Spotlight on football / Peter Doherty. London,
Glasgow: Arts & Educational Publishers, 1948.
118p; illus
BL: 7919.cc.39

Written whilst with Huddersfield Town, the famous
Northern Ireland International also covers his playing
years with Glentoran, Blackpool, Manchester City

and Derby as well as putting forward his ideas for the future of the game. A fine study of the period.

Dollery, Tom

151   My life story / Horace Edgar Dollery. Birmingham: Birmingham Gazette, 1950.
23p; illus; pbk

'Tom' Dollery is included here as a cricketer-footballer subject although his appearances for Warwickshire rather outweigh his one game for Reading in 1935/36. Historians of that club may find something of interest in this and the following larger volume.

152   Professional captain / Horace Edgar Dollery. London: Stanley Paul, 1952.
192p; illus   BL: 7921.c.19

Dougan, Derek

153   The sash he never wore / Derek Dougan. London: Allison and Busby, 1972.
176p; illus   ISBN: 0-85031-070-9
                           BL: X.629/4644

Words of wisdom from one of soccer's thinkers who was prolific with the pen and a true all-rounder off the field. Certainly one of football's great characters.

154   On the spot: football as a profession / Derek Dougan and Percy Marshall Young. London: Stanley Paul, 1974.
172p; illus   ISBN: 0-09-121340-1
                           BL: X.629/6358

Part-autobiographical but effectively a look at the wider subject of being a footballer.

155   'Doog'. Wolverhampton: All Seasons Publishing, 1980.
149p; illus   ISBN: 0-907043-00-3
                           BL: YA.1992.a.15275

This is the definitive work on the much travelled Northern Ireland International. Wolves loom very large but Portsmouth, Blackburn, Aston Villa, Peterborough and Leicester receive a share of the coverage in this retrospective of a long career.

156   How not to run football / Derek Dougan. Wolverhampton: All Seasons, 1981.
148p   ISBN: 0-907043-01-1
                           BL: YA.1990.a.17319

As Chairman of the Professional Footballers' Association, Dougan had much to say on how the game should best be run. This book presents his ideas.

Doyle, Mike

157   Manchester City, my team / Mike Doyle. London: Souvenir Press, 1977.
173p; illus   ISBN: 0-285-62306-0
                           BL: X.629/11521

Self-explanatory study of his playing days at Maine Road.

Dunphy, Eamon

158   Only a game?: the diary of a professional footballer / Eamon Dunphy; edited, and with a postscript, by Peter Ball; with a preface by Brian Glanville. Harmondsworth: Kestrel Books, 1976.
191p; illus; index   ISBN: 0-7226-5241-0
                             BL: X.629/10861

How does a professional really view the game from which he earns a living? Dunphy, a fine writer, enlightens us during his days at Reading in highly original format.

Eastham, George

159   Determined to win / George Eastham. London: Stanley Paul, 1964.
123p; illus   BL: X.449/760

Written relatively early in Eastham's playing career, this covers his Newcastle and Arsenal days before his long association with Stoke City.

Edrich, W. J.

160   Cricket heritage / William John Edrich. London: Stanley Paul, 1948.
224p; illus   BL: 7919.c.31

The great Middlesex and England cricketer made twenty appearances for Spurs between 1935 and 1937. Club historians may find some material of interest in these entries.

161   Great batsmen photo-analysed: W. J. Edrich / D. S. Davis; action photos by Eric Joysmith. London: Photo Instruction Books, 1949.
31p; illus   BL: W.P.1109

162   Cricketing days / William John Edrich. London: Stanley Paul, 1950.
231p; illus   BL: 7920.l.2

163   Round the wicket / William John Edrich. London: Frederick Muller, 1959.
viii, 202p; illus   BL: 7922.m.17

Edwards, Duncan

164   Duncan Edwards / Iain McCartney and Roy Cavanagh. Nottingham: Temple, 1988.

'Thanking God for the life of Duncan Edwards, died at Munich, February 1958' – so reads the memorial stained glass window in Dudley Church. This biography tells the full story of the England and Manchester United prodigy so tragically killed at the age of 21.

Ellis, Arthur

165   Refereeing round the world / Arthur Edward Ellis; edited by Kenneth Wolstenholme. London: Hutchinson, 1954.
196p; illus   BL: 7920.g.40

Long before his 'two points for Weston-super-Mare'
days as referee of BBC's 'It's a Knockout', Arthur Ellis
did the job for real as one of the world's leading officials.
This is the best study of refereeing for this era with
many inside observations on the continental game.

166 The final whistle / Arthur Edward Ellis as told to Steve
Richards. London: Stanley Paul, 1962.
173p; illus   BL: 7923.ttt.26

This update includes further observations on the
1958 and 1962 World Cup competitions.

Eusébio

167 My name is Eusébio / Eusébio da Silva Ferreira, assisted
by Fernando F. Garcia; translated by Derrik Low.
London: Routledge & Kegan Paul, 1967.
166p; illus

Originally published as: Meu nome é Eusébio
BL: X.449/2449

When Eusébio left England following the 1966 World
Cup his waxen image remained behind in Madame Tus-
sauds, such had been his impact. Sporting Lisbon,
Benfica and the Portuguese national side figure
largely in this rare example of an overseas player's
autobiography translated into English.

Eyre, Fred

168 A breath of Fred Eyre. Glossop?: The author?, 1980?
pbk

20 clubs in 20 years, playing under 29 managers and
82 coaches — Eyre has seen it all in the lower echelons of the game.

169 Kicked into touch / Fred Eyre. Glossop: Senior
Publications, 1981.
206p; illus; pbk   ISBN: 0-903839-63-6
BL: YK.1992.a.7894

We can't all be superstars, so why not shout about
the glory of being ordinary? This is precisely what
Fred Eyre does in his series of very humourous works
covering his varied life in football. Unusual books,
frank observations, well worth reading.

170 Another breath of Fred Eyre. Glossop: Senior
Publications, 1982.
186p; illus
ISBN: 0-903839-90-3 (cased) • ISBN: 0-903839-85-7 (pbk)

171 What a game / Fred Eyre; edited by Roy Cavanagh.
Glossop: Transport Publishing, 1983.
192p; illus
ISBN: 0-86317-106-0 (cased) • ISBN: 0-86317-101-X (pbk)

A somewhat different approach adopted here as Eyre
commissions celebrity pieces on memorable games —
the majority of the material relates to Manchester
City and Manchester United. Contributors include
John Motson, Stuart Hall, Les Dawson, Sid Little,
Eddie Large, and artist Harold Riley.

172 Taking the mike / Fred Eyre. London: Futura, 1991.
186p; illus; pbk   ISBN: 0-7088-4993-8
BL: YK.1991.a.12645

Farmer, Ted

173 The heartbreak game / Ted Farmer. Wolverhampton:
Hillburgh, 1987.
110p; illus; pbk   BL: YK.1988.a.3971

The title echoes the disappointment of careers pre-
maturely ended. Farmer was an England under-23
International and played 57 league games for Wolves,
scoring a prolific 44 goals between 1960 and 1963.
There, at the age of only 23, his playing days finished.

Fenton, Ted

174 At home with the Hammers: on West Ham United
Football Club / Ted Fenton. London: Nicolas Kaye,
1960.
160p; illus   BL: 7925.bb.63

Pre-war playing days with West Ham, then manager
of Colchester United and back to Upton Park to take
the Hammers back to Division One in 1958.

Fenwick, Terry

175 Earning my spurs / Terry Fenwick with Brian
Woolnough. Edinburgh: Mainstream, 1989.
168p; illus   ISBN: 1-85158-222-3
BL: YK.1991.b.3110

A late career with Tottenham but 318 games for former clubs, Queen's Park Rangers and Crystal Palace
. . . evidently the title was just too easy to resist!

Ferguson, Alex

176 Light in the north: seven years with Aberdeen / Alex
Ferguson. Edinburgh: Mainstream, 1985.
176p; illus
ISBN: 1-85158-007-7 (cased) • ISBN: 1-85158-008-5 (pbk)

Straight to the point with one of the great managers
during his triple championship days with Aberdeen.

177 Alex Ferguson: 6 years at United / Alex Ferguson with
David Meek. Edinburgh: Mainstream, 1992.
159p; illus   ISBN: 1-85158-444-7
BL: YK.1993.b.12950

More of the same, this time at Manchester United,
to ensure Ferguson's immortality.

Finney, Tom

178 Football round the world: reminiscences / Tom Finney.
London: Museum Press, 1953.
112p; illus   BL: 7917.bbb.46

One club from 1946-1959 for this legendary England
forward. Preston North End take centre stage.

179 Finney on football / Tom Finney as told to David R.
Jack with 37 photographs. London: Nicholas Kaye, 1958.
156p; illus   BL: 7923.b.47

     . . . the update just prior to Finney's retirement.

180 Finney: a football legend / by Paul Agnew. Preston:
Carnegie Press, 1989.
272p; illus; index   ISBN: 0-948789-29-8
                                BL: YK.1992.a.5307

     . . . and the complete retrospective overview.

Firmani, Eddie

181 Football with the millionaires / Eddie Firmani. London:
Stanley Paul, 1959.
118p; illus   BL: 010608.l.51

     The money men in question are Sampdoria and Inter
     Milan where Firmani played after earlier years with
     Charlton Athletic. Excellent insight into the pros and
     cons of being an overseas export from an Italian In-
     ternational born in South Africa.

Flowers, Ron

182 For Wolves and England / Ron Flowers. London:
Stanley Paul, 1962.
128p; illus   BL: 7923.ttt.22

     Wolves in the fifties: three Championships and a
     1960 Cup Winners medal. This simple title was cho-
     sen in favour of 'Ascent of Flowers' by one of the
     game's straightforward players.

Ford, Trevor

183 I lead the attack / Trevor Ford. London: Stanley Paul,
1957.
160p; illus   BL: 7923.m.8

     Swansea, Villa, Sunderland and Cardiff are all covered
     by the famed Welsh International centre forward.

Foulkes, Bill

184 Back at the top / Bill Foulkes as told to Ben Wright.
London: Pelham, 1965.
123p; illus   BL: X.441/578

     This story of Manchester United might never have
     been told – Foulkes was one of the survivors of the
     Munich air crash.

Francey, David

185 And it's all over— / David Francey with Phil McEntee.
Edinburgh: John Donald, 1988.
ix, 120p; illus; index; pbk   ISBN: 0-85976-221-1
                                BL: YK.1988.b.5311

     A well-known line from the commentators' armoury
     prefaces a revealing study from one of the men who
     bring football into our living rooms, with many obser-
     vations on the game in Scotland.

Francis, Trevor

186 Trevor Francis: anatomy of a £1 million player / Rob
Hughes with Trevor Francis. Tadworth: World's Work,
1980.
169p; illus   ISBN: 0-437-06900-1
                                BL: X.622/8187

     Moving from Birmingham City to Nottingham Forest
     in 1979, Francis – the boy wonder – became Britain's
     first million plus transfer. Both clubs are well chron-
     icled.

187 The world to play for / Trevor Francis with David
Miller. London: Sidgwick & Jackson, 1982.
209p; illus   ISBN: 0-283-98825-8
                                BL: X.629/19545

     Manchester City and a move to Sampdoria of Italy
     update the story . . .

Franklin, Neil

188 Soccer at home and abroad / Neil Franklin. London:
Stanley Paul, 1956.
164p; illus   BL: 7922.f.16

     Cornelius F. Franklin may sound like a cross between
     an American president and a Groucho Marx charac-
     ter but he was in fact an accomplished England
     International who tells an interesting tale of early
     days at Stoke, wartime football, a spell in Bogota,
     then back to the less glamorous confines of Hull and
     Crewe.

Fry, Charles Burgess

189 Mr C. B. Fry / Albert Craig. London?: Wright, 1906.
A card folded in 4; illus

     . . . a rare early ephemeral item relating to one of
     sport's true all-rounders.

190 C. B. Fry: the man and his methods / A. W. Myers; with
a preface by G. H. R. Dabbs. Bristol: J. W. Arrowsmith,
1912.
xi, 189p   BL: 010854.de.31

     Respected tennis writer Myers here produces the
     first serious study of the Victorian-Edwardian super-
     star. Right-back for Southampton in the 1902 Cup
     Final and a first class cricketing century just a week
     later for the world long jump record holder!

191 Life worth living: some phases of an Englishman / C. B.
Fry. London: Eyre & Spottiswoode, 1939.
423p; illus   BL: 10859.d.5

     This definitive autobiographical work is the one to
     consult for all researchers interested in C. B. With
     the Corinthians, he played against most of the best
     professional clubs from 1888 to 1902 – Chapter XIII
     deals entirely with football, offering one of all too few
     eyewitness accounts of Victorian footballers at play.

     ☞ Subsequent ed. C195

LIFE WORTH LIVING

SOME PHASES OF AN ENGLISHMAN

BY

C. B. FRY

LONDON
EYRE & SPOTTISWOODE
1939

192 C. B. Fry / Denzil Batchelor. London: Phoenix House, 1951.
64p; illus
(Cricketing lives)   BL: X.629/3574(3)

Concentrates on the Sussex and Hampshire careers of the cricketer-footballer from 1894 to 1921 with some inevitable football references.

193 C. B.: the life of Charles Burgess Fry / Clive Ellis. London: Dent, 1984.
x, 294p; illus; index
Bibliography: p277-278   ISBN: 0-460-04654-3
                                      BL: X.950/34764

194 The captain's lady / Ronald Morris. London: Chatto & Windus, 1985.
178p; illus; index
Bibliography: p167   ISBN: 0-7011-2946-8
                                      BL: X.800/41837

This is a biography of Beattie Fry, the wife he called 'Madame'. One of very few works in which it is possible to consider the role of a wife in the life of an early sportsman. Whether or not she washed his muddy kit is not revealed, but all students of C. B. would do well to read this study in tandem with the more obvious research.

195 Life worth living: some phases of an Englishman / C.B. Fry; introduction by Alan Ross. London: Pavilion, 1986.
v, 423p; illus; index
ISBN: 1-85145-026-2 (cased) • ISBN: 1-85145-027-0 (pbk)
                                      BL: YK.1988.a.2220

☞ Previous ed. C191

Gabbiadini, Marco

196 Marco Goalo / Tim Taylor and Marco Gabbiadini. Sunderland?: Gabbiadini Entreprises, 1989.
16p; pbk

Marco bustles his way into the affections of Sunderland followers with a typical piece of publishing opportunism.

Gallacher, Hughie

197 The Hughie Gallacher story / Paul Joannou. Derby: Breedon Books, 1989.
119p; illus
Bibliography: p119   ISBN: 0-907969-58-5
                                      BL: YK.1992.b.5004

Triumph and tragedy for one of the very greatest inter-war players: 463 goals in 624 games for Queen of the South, Airdrie, Newcastle United, Chelsea, Derby County, Notts County, Grimsby and Gateshead before the 'bad boy' of Scottish football threw himself under a train at Dead Man's crossing. The *Newcastle Journal* headline simply declared, 'Hughie of the Magic Feet is Dead'.

Gascoigne, Paul

198 Gazza! / Paul Gascoigne; edited by R. Bickersteth. London: Cockerel, 1989.
61p; illus; pbk   ISBN: 1-869914-09-0
                                      BL: YK.1992.b.24

Gazza is a product, the marketing man's dream, as much as a rare footballing talent. Some very lightweight glossy treatments of the Newcastle and Tottenham star mingle with other more serious and definitive studies.

199 Gazza: daft as a brush? / Paul Gascoigne. London: Queen Anne Press, 1989.
96p; illus; pbk   ISBN: 0-356-17977-X
                                      BL: YK.1990.a.6435

200 Gazza!: a biography / Robin McGibbon. London: Penguin, 1990.
204p; illus; pbk   ISBN: 0-14-014868-X
                                      BL: YK.1991.a.3017

The first detailed study . . .

201 Gazza: my life in pictures / Paul Gascoigne and Mel Stein. London: Stanley Paul, 1990.
128p; illus; pbk   ISBN: 0-09-174869-0
                                      BL: YK.1991.b.1902

202 Good on ya Gazza! London: Dennis Oneshots, 1990.
14p; pbk   ISBN: 1-85504-084-0
                                      BL: YK.1993.b.9218

203 Gazza's football year / Paul Gascoigne and Mel Stein. London: Stanley Paul, 1991.
95p; illus; pbk   ISBN: 0-09-174963-8
                                      BL: YK.1991.b.6544

204 Gazza agonistes / edited by Bill Buford. London: Granta Books, 1993.
256p; pbk   ISBN: 0-14-014064-6

205 Paul Gascoigne: the inside story / Jane Nottage. London: CollinsWillow, 1993.
220p; illus; index; pbk   ISBN: 0-00-218537-7

Interesting account of the circumstances which helped to shape the career of this colourful personality, written by his former personal assistant.

206 Gazza Italia / Ian Hamilton. Harmondsworth: Penguin, 1994.
192p; pbk   ISBN: 0-14-014073-5

Gascoigne's much publicised transfer to Lazio was intended to set the Italians alight. This study of what went wrong throws much light on the pressures of life in the media spotlight.

207 Ha'way the lad: the authorised biography of Paul Gascoigne / Mel Stein. London: Partridge, 1994.
305p; illus   ISBN: 1-85225-220-0

208 Paul Gascoigne / Andrew Ward. London: Hippo, 1994.
48p; illus; pbk
  For children   ISBN: 0-590-55469-7

Geldard, Albert

209 The life and times of a professional footballer / Albert Geldard and John K. Rowlands. Newbury?: Countryside, 1990.
48p; pbk

An unusual retrospective treatment, for Geldard died in 1989 and had played from the twenties, the first Bradfordian to play for England. Bradford Park Avenue, Everton and Bolton all figure largely in the winger's memories. Shortly after his retirement following the war, Geldard actually prepared his autobiography to be entitled 'Soccer Sorcerer' but it never saw the light of day. Much of that material is to be found here.

Gemmel, Mattha

210 Mattha Gemmel o' Clyde: an intimate and humorous account from fifty years of football in the life of . . . Mattha Gemmell / written by his friend 'Solly'. Glasgow: W. Hay, 1943.
45p
  Pseudonym of M. McHugh   BL: 7917.a.66

An unusual item – interesting observations on Scottish football from the Victorian era to the war.

Gemmell, Tommy

211 The big shot / Tommy Gemmell. London: Stanley Paul, 1968.
96p; illus   BL: X.449/3311

The equalising goal for Celtic in their 1967 European Cup win over Inter Milan gave this extrovert full-back the perfect platform and title for this short autobiography.

George, Charlie

212 Charlie George / Jason Tomas. London: Wolfe, 1971.
64p; illus; pbk
(Giants of football; 2); (Hall of Fame books)
                                         ISBN: 0-7234-0453-4

Written during the Arsenal years of one of the game's folk heroes. One cap for England did not do justice to the skill and vision of a player who had spectators purring.

Giggs, Ryan

213 Ryan Giggs: my story. London: Virgin, 1994.
128p; illus   ISBN: 1-85227-459-X

Set to become one of the greatest Welsh footballers of all time – only 21 when this was published; mostly about Manchester United.

Giles, Johnny

214 Forward with Leeds / Johnny Giles as told to Jason Tomas. London: Stanley Paul, 1970.
128p; illus   ISBN: 0-09-103380-2
                                         BL: X.629/2966

The Republic of Ireland International tells mostly of his anchorman days in midfield for Leeds United with some additional references to his earlier career with Manchester United.

Goram, Andy

215 Scotland's for me / Andy Goram as told to Simon Pia. Edinburgh: Sportsprint, 1990.
134p; illus; index; pbk   ISBN: 0-85976-315-3
                                         BL: YK.1991.b.4602

Mostly Hibernian from the Scotland goalkeeper

Gough, Richard

216 Field of dreams: my Ibrox years / Richard Gough with Ken Gallacher. Edinburgh: Mainstream, 1993.
153p; illus   ISBN: 1-85158-570-2
                                         BL: YK1994.b.4586

Concentrates on the Rangers years of the Scotland International, with some reference to Dundee United and Spurs.

Gowling, Alan

217 Football inside out / Alan Gowling. London: Souvenir Press, 1977.
176p; illus   ISBN: 0-285-62307-9
                                               BL: X.629/11618

Manchester University to Manchester United, then Huddersfield Town and Newcastle, all nicely written by one of the soccer 'Brains Trust'.

Graham, George

218 George Graham: the wonder years / Jeff King and Tony Willis. London: Virgin, 1995.
240p; illus   ISBN: 1-85227-580-4

Largely covers Graham's career as high profile manager of Arsenal – the publication date was timely if not a little embarrassing, as it coincided with Graham's undignified dismissal from the club amidst accusations of alleged financial irregularities.

Gray, Andy

219 Shades of Gray / Andy Gray. London: Macdonald, 1986.
208p; illus; index   ISBN: 0-356-12222-0
                                               BL: YK.1986.a.1605

The much travelled Scotland forward takes us on a lively journey looking back on Villa, Everton, Wolves and Dundee United.

Gray, J. R.

220 J. R. Gray: a biographical note / L. T. J. Arlott. Southampton: Hampshire County Cricket Club, 1960.
12p; illus

Limited ed. of 30 signed copies; first appeared in Hampshire County Cricket Club handbook, 1960.

On the books of Arsenal but never got a first team game, Gray is another of those cricketer-footballers whose propensity for run scoring and taking wickets with Hampshire rather overshadowed his footballing talents.

Greaves, Jimmy

221 A funny thing happened on my way to Spurs / Jimmy Greaves as told to Clive Taylor. London: Nicholas Kaye, 1962.
151p; illus   BL: X.449/408

The funny thing in question is a most unhappy spell with AC Milan in 1961 after his successful years with Chelsea. This covers those events along with his early days at Spurs from one of England's most prolific marksmen, with a matching yen for the world of publishing.

222 My world of soccer / Jimmy Greaves. London: Stanley Paul, 1966.
126p; illus   BL: X.449/1767

A full update once he had become established as a Spurs 'great'.

223 Let's be honest / Jimmy Greaves and Reg Gutteridge. London: Pelham, 1972.
144p; illus   ISBN: 0-7207-0517-7
                                               BL: X.629/4348

On his retirement in 1971 Greaves looks back on his career and makes some harsh observations on the current state of the game. Includes his late years with West Ham United.

224 This one's on me / Jimmy Greaves. London: Arthur Barker, 1979.
152p; illus; index   ISBN: 0-213-16701-8
                                               BL: X.629/12368

Retirement brings its difficulties as perhaps the title suggests . . . Greaves made no secret of his alcoholism and discusses the subject frankly in this work. Indeed, on the front of this volume is one of football's truly stark statements: 'My name is Jimmy Greaves. I am a professional footballer. And I am an alcoholic.'

225 Stop the game: I want to get on! / Jimmy Greaves with Norman Giller; illustrations by Roy Ullyett. London: Harrap, 1983.
96p; illus; pbk   ISBN: 0-245-54010-5
                                               BL: X.622/18535

The illustrations are by the famous Daily Express cartoonist.

☞ Also listed at: K18

226 It's a funny old life / Jimmy Greaves. London: Arthur Barker, 1990.
viii, 184p; illus; index   ISBN: 0-213-85002-8
                                               BL: YK.1990.b.6952

By now re-established in the game's hierarchy as a television pundit renowned for his disarming approach, Greaves may be physically unrecognisable from the slight and nimble figure we like to recall but he is still speaking good common sense about a game he understands more than most with, as ever, a liberal dash of impish humour.

Green, Geoffrey

227 Pardon me for living / Geoffrey Green. London: Allen & Unwin, 1985.
x, 207p; illus; index   ISBN: 0-04-796100-7
                                               BL: X.950/42959

If the word 'doyen' is to be used just once in this bibliography, it might fairly be ascribed to the writing talents of one of football's senior high journalists. A Cambridge soccer blue in his youth, this is Green's story with much to say on association football as well as cricket – he was *The Times* correspondent for both sports.

Greenwood, Ron

228 Yours sincerely / Ron Greenwood with Bryon Butler.
London: Willow, 1984.
240p; illus; index   ISBN: 0-00-218074-X
BL: X.622/20965

Sincere indeed he was – Chelsea, Bradford Park Avenue, Brentford and Fulham all remember Greenwood
the stylish centre half, but it is as West Ham and
England manager that he is most often recalled. His
coaching brain is well respected – Oxford University
and Walthamstow Avenue figure in a long career
which has been influential at all levels.

Gregg, Harry

229 Wild about football: his own story / Harry Gregg.
London: Souvenir Press, 1961.
136p; illus   BL: X.449/465

Coleraine, Manchester United and Northern Ireland all
have their place in this international goalkeeper's
story, which might never have been told but for his
heroic survival of the 1958 Munich air crash.

Greig, John

230 A captain's part / John Greig. London: Stanley Paul,
1968.
112p; illus   BL: X.449/3322

Glasgow Rangers and Scotland are well chronicled.

Griffiths, Mervyn

231 The man in the middle: reminiscences of an association
football referee / Mervyn Griffiths. London: Stanley
Paul, 1958.
152p; illus   BL: 7923.n.22

Linesman in the 1954 World Cup final, between West
Germany and Hungary, Griffiths flagged offside a
late equaliser by Puskas to give Germany the trophy.
The Welsh official tells this and many other stories.

Grobbelaar, Bruce

232 More than somewhat / Bruce Grobbelaar with Bob
Harris. London: Willow, 1986.
vi, 185p; illus   ISBN: 0-00-218188-6
BL: YC.1986.a.547

Vancouver Whitecaps, Crewe Alexandra and Liverpool
all experienced the antics of the eccentric Zimbab-
wean international goalkeeper – a great character
tells his unique story.

☞ Subsequent ed. C233

233 Bruce Grobbelaar: an autobiography / Bruce Grobbelaar
with Bob Harris. Sevenoaks: Coronet, 1988.
277p; illus; pbk   ISBN: 0-340-42645-4
BL: YK.1988.a.3304

☞ Previous ed. C232

Gunn, William

234 William Gunn / Albert Craig. London: All England
Athletic Publishing, 1899.
A card folded in 4; illus

Early ephemeral item on this Victorian cricketer-footballer.

235 The Trent Bridge battery: the story of the sporting
Gunns / Basil Haynes & John Lucas. London: Willow,
1985.
208p; illus
Bibliography: p207-208   ISBN: 0-00-218175-4
BL: X.622/24194

William Gunn played county cricket for Nottinghamshire and also at Test level, whilst his footballing
exploits took in both Notts County and England. This
interesting study offers a rare insight into the world
of Victorian sport.

Guthrie, Jimmy

236 Soccer rebel: the evolution of the professional footballer
/ Jimmy Guthrie with Dave Caldwell. Pinner: Pentagon,
1976.
180p; illus   ISBN: 0-904288-08-0
BL: X.629/10754

The captain of Dundee and then Portsmouth for their
1939 FA Cup win is probably better remembered as
an outspoken chairman of the Players' Union. Today's
players owe a debt of gratitude to the sterling work
of this determined Scot in the early post-war years –
this volume traces the key developments in the
status of the footballer during Guthrie's years.

Hacket, Keith

237 Hacket's law / Keith Hacket. London: Willow, 1986.

Informed observations on the game and refereeing
from one of the modern game's best known officials.

Hammond, Wally

238 Cricket my destiny / Walter R. Hammond. London:
Stanley Paul, 1946.
156p; illus   BL: 7917.bb.22

One of Gloucestershire and England's greatest cricketers, Hammond also played 20 games for Bristol
Rovers between 1921 and 1924. These studies contain
scattered footballing references of interest to soccer research students.

239 Cricket my world / Walter R. Hammond. London:
Stanley Paul, 1948.
192p; illus   BL: 7918.bb.31

240 Walter Hammond: a biography / Ronald C. Mason.
London: Hollis & Carter, 1962.
224p; illus   BL: 10632.v.49

241 Walter Hammond / Gerald Howat. London: Allen & Unwin, 1984.
xvi, 160p; illus; index

ISBN: 0-04-796082-5
BL: X.622/21198

Hand, Eoin

242 Eoin Hand story / Eoin Hand and Peter O'Neill. Dublin: Brophy Books, 1986.
144p; illus; pbk

ISBN: 0-907960-48-0

Concentrates on his career as Republic of Ireland manager from 1980 to 1985 before Jack Charlton took over. Refers also to his playing days with Dundalk, Drumcondra, Portsmouth and Limerick United.

Hansen, Alan

243 Tall, dark and Hansen: ten years at Anfield / Alan Hansen with Ken Gallacher. Edinburgh: Mainstream, 1988.
208p; illus; index

ISBN: 1-85158-089-1 (cased) • ISBN: 1-85158-104-9 (pbk)
BL: YK.1990.b.3327

Partick Thistle, Liverpool and Scotland all figure in this cool defender's story.

Hapgood, Eddie

244 Football ambassador / Edris Anthony Hapgood. London: Sporting Handbooks, 1944.
154p; illus

BL: 7916.eee.68

One of the great defenders for Arsenal and England, this first part of Eddie Hapgood's tale includes observations on wartime soccer.

☞ Subsequent ed. C245

245 Football ambassador / Edris Anthony Hapgood; edited by Roy Peskett. Rev. ed. London: Sporting Handbooks, 1951.
186p; illus

BL: 7921.aaa.37

This update includes Hapgood's post-war management years with Blackburn, Watford and Bath City.

☞ Previous ed. C244

Hardaker, Alan

246 Hardaker of the League / Alan Hardaker with Bryon Butler. London: Pelham, 1977.
238p; illus

ISBN: 0-7207-1015-4
BL: X.629/11680

Secretary of the Football League for more than 20 years and a great influence in the shaping of the game.

Harris, Ron

247 Soccer the hard way / Ron Harris. London: Pelham, 1970.
128p; illus

ISBN: 0-7207-0290-9
BL: X.629/2528

'Chopper' Harris writes in his heyday with Chelsea.

Harvey, Joe

248 The Joe Harvey story. Newcastle: Newcastle United FC, 1977.
28p; illus; pbk

Long-serving player and manager of Newcastle United – contains some material of interest to Barrow and Workington followers where Harvey also managed.

Hateley, Mark

249 Mark Hateley: home and away / with Tony Francis. London: Stanley Paul, 1986.
180p; illus

ISBN: 0-09-163870-4
BL: YC.1986.a.4351

Coventry, Portsmouth and AC Milan explain the cryptic title.

250 Top Mark!: an autobiography / Mark Hateley with Ken Gallacher. Edinburgh: Mainstream, 1993.
153p; illus

ISBN: 1-85158-593-1
BL: YK.1994.b.13916

A controversial book; Hateley reveals the differences between the game in England, Scotland and on the Continent, one of few players truly qualified to do this.

Hawtin, Walter

251 An Old Centrals man: a belated tribute to Walter Ernest Hawtin, 1876-1916 / Gillian Hawtin. The author, 1993.
29p; illus; pbk

Alternative title: The first years of the Wimbledon Football Club

BL: YK.1994.a.15793

From 1899-1905 Wimbledon played under the name Wimbledon Old Centrals as they were formed by the Old Boys of Central School – Walter Hawtin was one of them.

Hay, David

252 Paradise lost: the David Hay story / David Hay with Ken Gallacher. Edinburgh: Mainstream, 1988.
160p; illus

ISBN: 1-85158-132-4 (cased) • ISBN: 1-85158-133-2 (pbk)
BL: YK.1990.b.3235

The story of Hay's time as Celtic manager.

Haynes, Johnny

253 Football today / Johnny Haynes. London: Arthur Barker, 1961.
127p; illus

BL: X.441/193

These two studies by the master passer include general observations from the England International along with much significant material on his one and only club, Fulham.

☞ Also listed at: A81

254 It's all in the game / Johnny Haynes. London: Arthur Barker, 1962.
213p; illus   BL: 010662.k.92

Hegarty, Paul

255 Paul Hegarty: heading for glory / Paul Hegarty; foreword by Jim McLean. Edinburgh: John Donald, 1987.
vii, 108p; illus; index   ISBN: 0-85976-206-8
     BL: YK.1988.b.3855

The full story of his many years at Dundee United, with some reference to Hamilton Academical.

Heighway, Steve

256 Liverpool, my team / Steve Heighway. London: Souvenir Press, 1977.
192p; illus   ISBN: 0-285-62305-2
     BL: X.629/12446

Chronicles the career of the Liverpool and Republic of Ireland winger.

Henderson, Willie

257 Forward with Rangers / Willie Henderson. London: Stanley Paul, 1966.
91p; illus   BL: X.449/2272

The extrovert Scottish winger chronicles his winning days with Rangers.

Hendren, Patsy

258 Big cricket / Elias Hendren. London: Hodder & Stoughton, 1934.
160p; illus   BL: 7916.ee.10

Mostly cricket from the famous Middlesex and England man . . .

259 'Patsy' Hendren: the cricketer and his times / Ian A. R. Peebles. London: Macmillan, 1969.
183p; illus   BL: X.449/3846

Hendren was one of the cricketer-footballer breed whose games amounted to more than a handful. His 140 games between 1908 and 1920 included Brentford, Queen's Park Rangers, Manchester City and Coventry; this study includes a number of references to these clubs.

Hill, Gordon

260 Give a little whistle: the recollections of a remarkable referee / Gordon Hill and Jason Tomas. London: Souvenir Press, 1975.
157p; illus   ISBN: 0-285-62187-4
     BL: X.629/10322

Inside stories from a leading referee.

Hill, Jimmy

261 Striking for soccer / Jimmy Hill. London: Peter Davies, 1961.
228p; illus   BL: X.449/135

Long before his TV battles with Terry Venables, Hill was fighting for another cause. This book tells not only of his playing days with Brentford and Fulham but also of his role as chairman of the Professional Footballers' Association and his part in removing the maximum wage restriction.

Hoddle, Glenn

262 Glenn Hoddle: an autobiography / Glenn Hoddle. London: Pelham, 1982.
145p; illus; index   ISBN: 0-7207-1433-8
     BL: X.200/39545

Silken prose of days with Spurs.

263 Spurred to success / Glenn Hoddle with Harry Harris. London: Macdonald, 1987.
176p; illus   ISBN: 0-356-12797-4
     BL: YK.1987.a.2843

The final update on his Spurs career before a move abroad.

Holt, Arthur

264 Arthur Holt: an appreciation / L. T. J. Arlott. Southampton: Hampshire County Cricket Club, 1963.
8p; pbk

Limited ed. of 50 copies; first appeared in the Hampshire County Cricket Club handbook, 1963.

One of Arlott's limited edition monographs covers a particularly good example of a cricketer-footballer, showing how the bat may be taken up that much longer than the boot. Holt played for Hampshire from 1935 to 1948 following a 200 game career with Southampton from 1932 to 1939.

Horton, Henry

265 Henry Horton: a biographical note / L. T. J. Arlott. Southampton: Hampshire County Cricket Club, 1964.
11p; illus

Limited ed. of 50 copies

An even more prolific combined example than Arthur Holt; over 21,000 runs for Hampshire between 1953 and 1967 followed 194 outings with Blackburn, Southampton and Bradford Park Avenue from 1946 to 1954.

Hughes, Emlyn

266 Crazy horse / Emlyn Hughes. London: Arthur Barker, 1980.
vii, 171p; illus   ISBN: 0-213-16747-6
     BL: X.629/14009

Mostly Liverpool and England, but early and late days at Blackpool and Wolves are covered too.

Hughes, Mark

267 Sparky: Barcelona, Bayern and back / Mark Hughes.
London: Cockerel Books, 1989.
200p; illus; pbk   ISBN: 1-869914-10-4

An interesting career path for the powerful Welshman
takes in Bayern München and Barcelona sandwiched
between two spells with Manchester United.

268 Hughesie!: the Red Dragon: an autobiography / Mark
Hughes with David Meek. Edinburgh: Mainstream, 1994.
192p; illus   ISBN: 1-85158-680-6

Hunt, Roger

269 Hunt for goals / Roger Hunt in collaboration with
David Prole. London: Pelham, 1969.
120p; illus   ISBN: 0-7207-0306-9
                                          BL: X.449/3969

Covers the England forward's Liverpool years before
his move to Bolton.

Hurst, Geoff

270 The world game / Geoff Hurst. London: Stanley Paul,
1967.
159p; illus   BL: X.449/2856

His hat-trick in England's 1966 World Cup win was
three more than the runs he scored in one outing
with Essex County Cricket Club in 1962! West Ham
and England are covered in detail.

Icke, David

271 'It's a tough game, son!': the real world of professional
football / David Icke. London: Piccolo, 1983.
128p; illus; pbk   ISBN: 0-330-28047-3
                                          BL: X.629/21718

Icke was already working in journalism and TV when he
wrote this part-autobiographical work. His own career – 37 games for Hereford United as goalkeeper in
1972 – ended at the age of 21 due to rheumatoid ar-
thritis. What followed was to make him more famous
as a personality than he ever was as a player.

272 The truth vibrations / David Icke. London: Aquarian,
1991.
144p; pbk   ISBN: 1-85538-136-2
                                          BL: YK.1991.a.3483

Very few footballers have written works unrelated to
the game. This is a rare example. Icke's visionary ide-
als are laid down here with a few passing football
references. Indeed, he had been playing football on the
beach with his son when he wandered into a
newsagent and picked up a book called Mind to Mind
by Betty Shine. He bought it, read it and took his
first steps towards spiritual healing and beyond. This
book is the result and is probably the most unusual
ever written by an ex-pro!

Jackson, Nicholas Lane

273 Sporting days and sporting ways / Nicholas Lane
Jackson. London: Hurst & Blackett, 1932.
288p; illus; index   BL: 07912.h.53

An important work for anyone studying the early
days of the game – this honorary assistant secretary of the FA was an important administrative
figure in Victorian and Edwardian football, best known
for founding the Corinthians in 1882.

James, Alex

274 Alex James / John Harding. London: Robson, 1988.
214p; illus   ISBN: 0-86051-492-7
                                          BL: YK.1989.a.3332

Painstakingly researched biography of a thirties Arsenal legend including days at Raith Rovers and
Preston. The canny Scot with the voluminous shorts
and flapping shirt typifies a much loved golden era for
football before the last war.

Jardine, Sandy

275 Score and more: the Sandy Jardine story / Sandy Jardine
and Michael Aitken. Edinburgh: Mainstream, 1987.
160p; illus; index
        ISBN: 1-85158-078-6 (cased) • ISBN: 1-85158-106-5 (pbk)
                                          BL: YK.1990.b.3316

Rangers, Hearts and Scotland are all covered.

Jennings, Pat

276 Pat Jennings: an autobiography / Pat Jennings in
association with Reg Drury. London: Willow Books,
1983.
169p; illus   ISBN: 0-00-218069-3
                                          BL: X.629/20649

The Northern Ireland international goalkeeper chronicles his career over three decades with Watford,
Spurs and Arsenal.

Johnston, Craig

277 Walk alone: the Craig Johnston story / Craig Johnston
with Neil Jameson. Lancaster: Fleetfoot, 1990.
255p; illus; pbk

    Originally published: North Ryde, NSW: Collins, 1989
                                          ISBN: 1-85586-001-5
                                          BL: YK.1991.b.3600

There was indeed something of the loner in the make-
up of this thoughtful character. His career with
Middlesbrough and Liverpool is covered before
Johnston asked himself just one question too many
and walked out of the game which provided his living.
A variety of business ventures in Australia have since
given him the kicks which football didn't, including the
development of a revolutionary new boot which may or
may not be a powerful force in the game!

Johnston, Harry

278 The rocky road to Wembley / Harry Johnston. London:
Museum Press, 1954.
112p; illus   BL: 7918.bb.82

> Captaining the Blackpool 1953 Cup winning side must
> surely have prompted this book. His England career
> and Seasider days are admirably covered.

Johnston, Mo

279 Mo: the Maurice Johnston story / Mo Johnston and
Chick Young; foreword by George Best. Edinburgh:
Mainstream, 1988.
158p; illus
     ISBN: 1-85158-159-6 (cased) • ISBN: 1-85158-160-X (pbk)
                                        BL: YK.1989.b.2848

> Partick Thistle, Watford, Celtic and Scotland are all
> covered, with reference also to his spell in France with
> Nantes.

Johnston, Willie

280 On the wing: Willie Johnston / his own story as told to
Alex Hosie. London: Arthur Barker, 1983?
x, 148p; illus   ISBN: 0-213-16889-8
                                        BL: X.629/22181

> A turbulent tale from the Rangers and Scotland win-
> ger including troubles and triumph with the Glasgow
> club, West Bromwich Albion, Vancouver Whitecaps and
> Birmingham City.

Johnstone, Derek

281 Rangers, my team / Derek Johnstone. London: Souvenir
Press, 1979.
188p; illus   ISBN: 0-285-62370-2
                                        BL: X.629/12619

> Full coverage of the Scotland striker's years with
> Rangers.

Johnstone, Jimmy

282 Fire in my boots / Jimmy Johnstone. London: Stanley
Paul, 1969.
109p; illus   ISBN: 0-09-100440-3
                                        BL: X.449/3998

> The fiery Celtic and Scotland winger tells of his win-
> ning years with the Glasgow club.

283 Jinky – now and then: the Jimmy Johnstone story /
Jimmy Johnstone and Jim McCann. Edinburgh:
Mainstream, 1988.
176p; illus
     ISBN: 1-85158-153-7 (cased) • ISBN: 1-85158-154-5 (pbk)
                                        BL: YK.1989.b.2331

> The full retrospective story.

Jones, Cliff

284 Forward with Spurs / Cliff Jones. London: Stanley Paul,
1962.
192p; illus   BL: X.449/305

> Swansea City also get a look in from this Welsh Inter-
> national winger's tales of the double with Tottenham.

Jones, Tommy Eyton

285 Cyw o frid: atgofion newyddiadurwr / Tommy Eyton
Jones; trosiad Mari Ellis. Dinbych: Gwasg Gee, 1985.
163p; illus; pbk   ISBN: 0-7074-0166-6
                                        BL: YC.1986.a.444

> Memoirs of a North Wales journalist with five chap-
> ters on football.

Jones, Vinnie

286 Vinnie: a kick in the grass / Vinnie Jones. Warrington:
Front Page, 1991.
160p; illus   ISBN: 0-948882-01-8
                                        BL: YK.1992.b.1594

> To those who know him, the title says it all. To those
> who don't, Wealdstone, Wimbledon, Leeds and Shef-
> field United are covered in this gentle stroll on the
> greensward with Vincent P. Jones!"

Keegan, Kevin

287 Kevin Keegan / Kevin Keegan. London: Arthur Barker,
1977.
159p; illus   ISBN: 0-213-16647-X
                                        BL: X.622/6126

> This first study of one of football's highest profile
> personalities takes in his Scunthorpe, Liverpool and
> early Hamburg days.

288 Against the world: playing for England / Kevin Keegan
with Mike Langley. London: Sidgwick and Jackson, 1979.
160p; illus; index
     ISBN: 0-283-98539-9 (cased) • ISBN: 0-283-98540-2 (pbk)
                                        BL: X.611/9221

> Includes much on the international scene and his
> later days at Hamburg.

289 Kevin Keegan / Brian Glanville; illustrated by Michael
Strand. London: Hamilton, 1981.
63p; illus
(Profiles)   ISBN: 0-241-10594-3
                                        BL: X.629/15645

> Southampton days are included in this short study.

290 Auf Wiedersehen Kev: tribute to a superstar / Tony
Hardisty. Newcastle: Newcastle United FC, 1984.
illus; pbk

> When Keegan left Newcastle to live in Spain, the New-
> castle club had no idea he would return as manager
> eight years later.

291 Kevin Keegan: portrait of a superstar / John Gibson.
London: W. H. Allen, 1984.
213p; illus   ISBN: 0-491-03363-X
                                   BL: YL.1990.a.513

Playing for Newcastle United made Keegan a legend in
the north-east; yet another update includes that period.

292 Kevin Keegan: black & white / John Moynihan.
London: CollinsWillow, 1993.
224p; illus; index
   Bibliography: p221-222   ISBN: 0-00-218536-9
                                  BL: YK.1994.b.835

It just had to be published — Keegan as Newcastle
manager.

Keeton, G. W.

293 The soccer club secretary / George Williams Keeton.
London: Naldrett, 1951.
ix, 186p   BL: 7921.aaa.51

An unusual work explaining much about this important
role in an era before the aggressive commercialism of
today's game.

THE SOCCER CLUB
SECRETARY

By

PROFESSOR GEORGE W. KEETON,
M.A., LL.D.
Barrister - at - Law

With a Foreword by
SIR STANLEY ROUS, C.B.E.
Secretary of The Football Association

THE NALDRETT PRESS LIMITED
THE THAMES BANK PUBLISHING COMPANY LIMITED

Kelsey, Jack

294 Over the bar . . . / Jack Kelsey as told to Brian Glanville.
London: Stanley Paul, 1958.
164p; illus   BL: 7924.b.8

Welsh international goalkeeper and 'one-club man'
with Arsenal from 1950 to 1962. This covers his first
eight years with the club.

Kendall, Howard

295 Playing for Everton / Howard Kendall. London: Arthur
Barker, 1971.
143p; illus   ISBN: 0-213-00461-5
                                   BL: X.629/3705

Some material on Preston North End in a study
which includes Everton's 1969/70 championship win.

296 Only the best is good enough: the Howard Kendall story
/ Howard Kendall and Ian Ross. Edinburgh:
Mainstream, 1991.
288p; illus   ISBN: 1-85158-486-2
                                   BL: YK.1993.b.8810

This much later update embraces his management
ups and downs with Blackburn, Everton, Athletic Bilbao and Manchester City as well as his last playing
days with Birmingham, Stoke and Blackburn in one of
soccer's most interesting careers.

Kennedy, Ray

297 Ray of hope: the Ray Kennedy story / Andrew Lees and
Ray Kennedy. London: Pelham, 1993.
xii, 352p; illus   ISBN: 0-7207-2019-2
                                   BL: YK.1994.a.142

At the age of 35 this former Arsenal, Liverpool,
Swansea and Hartlepool United player developed
Parkinson's disease. This unusual and inspirational
biography may be the story of an England International, but as a tale of determination in adverse
circumstances it deserves a readership well beyond
football.

Kernick, Dudley

298 Who the hell was Dudley Kernick? / Dudley Kernick.
Crossley, 1988.

This self-deprecating title prefaces fifty years of
Kernick's life in football. Concentrating mainly on his
fifteen years as commercial manager at Stoke City,
it gives an extremely humorous insight into this essential side of the running of the game. Also covers
playing days just after the war from Tintagel to Torquay, Northampton and Birmingham.

Klinsmann, Jürgen

299 Klinsmann / Harry Harris. London: Headline, 1995.
245p; illus   ISBN: 0-7472-1517-0

This stylish German international striker made an
astonishing impact on his arrival at Tottenham
Hotspur. This is a record of his first and only season's outings before his return to Germany.

Knighton, Leslie

300 Behind the scenes in big football / Leslie Knighton.
London: Stanley Paul, 1948.
176p; illus   BL: 7919.cc.41

His minor playing career cut short by an ankle injury, Knighton went on to a long spell in management. Castleford Town, Huddersfield, Manchester City, Arsenal, Bournemouth, Birmingham, Chelsea and Shrewsbury all precede this retirement publication from one who had more to tell than most.

Labone, Brian

301 Defence at the top / Brian Labone. London: Pelham, 1968.
103p; illus

ISBN: 1-81324-019-1
BL: X.449/3268

England and Everton for this 'one-club man'.

Law, Denis

302 Living for kicks / Denis Law as told to Kenneth Wheeler. London: Stanley Paul, 1963.
127p; illus

BL: 10923.r.29

Only six years into his career the great Scottish forward had already played for Huddersfield Town, Manchester City, the Italian club Torino, and Manchester United.

303 The golden boots/ Denis Law. London: Pelham, 1967.
155p

BL: Nov.9798

This first update includes five years at Manchester United.

304 Denis Law: an autobiography / Denis Law in association with Ron Gubba. London: Queen Anne Press, 1979.
175p; illus

ISBN: 0-354-08556-5
BL: X.629/12697

A full retrospective includes his final spell back at Manchester City.

Lawrenson, Mark

305 Mark Lawrenson: the autobiography / Mark Lawrenson with Mike Ellis. London: Macdonald, 1988.
192p; illus

ISBN: 0-356-15285-5
BL: YK.1988.a.2784

Straight treatment of the Republic of Ireland International's career including Preston, Brighton and Liverpool.

Lawton, Tommy

306 Football is my business / Tommy Lawton; edited by Roy Peskett. London: Sporting Handbooks, 1946.
207p; illus

BL: 7919.aa.12

A good early study of the great England centre forward includes Burnley, Everton, wartime and Chelsea.

307 Soccer the Lawton way / Tommy Lawton. London: Nicholas Kaye, 1954.
169p; illus

BL: 7922.b.25

Part-instructional part-autobiographical study from Lawton's Arsenal days.

308 My twenty years of soccer / Tommy Lawton. Heirloom Modern World Library, 1955.
258p

The full career update embraces his years at Notts County, Brentford and Arsenal.

309 When the cheering stopped: the rise, the fall / Tommy Lawton. London: Golden Eagle, 1973.
160p

ISBN: 0-901482-17-X
BL: X.629/5535

Lawton's difficulties in making life work after retirement are well known – this poignant study highlights the vulnerability of even the most talented to the pressures of modern life.

Lee, Francis

310 Soccer round the world: a football star's story – from Manchester to Mexico / Francis Lee. London: Arthur Barker, 1970.
119p; illus

ISBN: 0-213-00241-8
BL: X.629/2899

Indeed, Lee was a star after just ten years in the game with Bolton Wanderers and Manchester City. His World Cup foray to Mexico was simply the preface for much more to come.

Leishman, Jim

311 The giant that awoke: the Jim Leishman story / Jim Leishman with John Lloyd. Edinburgh: Mainstream, 1990.
206p; illus

ISBN: 1-85158-316-5
BL: YK.1992.b.4427

Covers his time as Dunfermline manager.

Lennox, Bobby

312 A million miles for Celtic: an autobiography / Bobby Lennox with Gerry McNee; foreword by Jock Stein. London: Stanley Paul, 1982.
161p; illus

ISBN: 0-09-150240-3
BL: X.629/19581

Mostly on Celtic from one of their greatest servants.

Liddell, Billy

313 My soccer story / William Beveridge Liddell. London: Stanley Paul, 1960.
127p; illus

BL: 7925.c.47

Nearly 500 post-war league outings for Liverpool dominate this Scotland International's story in his retirement volume.

Lineker, Gary

314 Lineker: golden boot / photographs by Bob Thomas; text by Rob Hughes. London: Willow, 1987.
144p; illus; pbk

ISBN: 0-00-218294-7
BL: YK.1987.b.7090

Leicester, Everton and Barcelona occupy the first eight years of the England striker's tale.

315 Gary Lineker / Andrew Ward; designed by Ness Wood. London: Hippo, 1993.
48p; pbk
(Sports shots; 2)

For children

ISBN: 0-590-55186-8
BL: YK.1994.a.10574

316 Gary Lineker: strikingly different – a biography / Colin Malam; foreword by Bobby Charlton. London: Stanley Paul, 1993.
x, 147p; illus; index

ISBN: 0-09-175424-0
BL: YK.1993.b.8978

The full update includes Spurs and a much publicised move to Japan for the model pro.

Little, Brian

317 Starting a wave / Brian Little written in association with Paul Mace. Leicester: Leicester City Football Club, 1993.
153p; illus

ISBN: 0-9504411-1-2

Mostly covers his quest as Leicester City manager to achieve promotion to the Premier League, a goal fulfilled at the expense of Derby County after the book's publication. Leicester were to return immediately to the First Division, being mathematically relegated in early April 1995. Little himself, meanwhile, left the club for Aston Villa earlier in the season under extremely acrimonious circumstances.

Lofthouse, Nat

318 Goals galore / Nat Lofthouse. London: Stanley Paul, 1954.
160p; illus

BL: 7919.a.44

This covers the first half of this England centre forward's great career with Bolton Wanderers.

319 'The lion of Vienna': Nat Lofthouse, 50 years a legend / as told to Andrew Collomosse; foreword by Tom Finney. Edinburgh: Sportsprint, 1989.
ix, 98p; illus; index

ISBN: 0-85976-284-X
BL: YK.1990.b.1815

This full retrospective covers all the England and Bolton years of one of football's loyal servants – he still retains a key administrative role at Burnden Park today.

Lord, Robert William

320 My fight for football / Robert William Lord. London: Stanley Paul, 1963.
158p; illus

BL: 7926.ee.24

Despite ruffling a few feathers along the way, this blunt and controversial Burnley Chairman no doubt always had the best interests of football at heart, and should be regarded as one of the game's great administrators.

Lyall, John

321 Just like my dreams: my life with West Ham / John Lyall with Michael Hart. London: Viking, 1989.
248p; illus

ISBN: 0-670-83234-0
BL: YK.1990.b.1891

A brief playing career with West Ham, followed by one of the longest ever management stints with the same club, are both covered here; the Upton Park stalwart was sadly sacked in the same year this book was published.

Mabbutt, Gary

322 Against all odds / Gary Mabbutt. London: Cockerel, 1989.
200p; illus; pbk

ISBN: 1-869914-11-2

Bristol Rovers, Tottenham and England figure in an apparently straightforward career story but the title hints at something more. Mabbutt is a diabetic who has shown how determination and application can overcome this condition in the physically and emotionally demanding world of football.

Macari, Lou

323 United we shall not be moved / Lou Macari. London: Souvenir Press, 1976.
187p; illus

Contains a chapter by Tommy Docherty

ISBN: 0-285-62260-9
BL: X.629/10970

Manchester United lead in this Scottish International's mid-career story with reference also to his earlier years at Celtic.

McCarthy, Mick

324 Captain Fantastic: my football career and World Cup experience / Mick McCarthy; researched and edited by Matthew Nugent; colour photographs by The Star. Dublin: O'Brien, 1990.
143p; illus; pbk

ISBN: 0-86278-237-6
BL: YK.1991.a.3785

The Republic of Ireland International covers his whole playing career with references to Barnsley, Manchester City, Celtic, Olympic Lyonnais and Millwall.

McCoist, Ally

325 Ally McCoist: my story / Ally McCoist with Crawford Brankin; introduction by Billy Connolly. Edinburgh: Mainstream, 1992.
188p; illus ISBN: 1-85158-500-1
BL: YK.1993.b.12475

Mostly Glasgow Rangers but with some reference to Sunderland and St Johnstone.

326 Ally McCoist / Andrew Ward. London: Hippo, 1994.
48p; illus; pbk
For children ISBN: 0-590-55470-0

327 Ally McCoist: testimonial year 1993-94. Glasgow: Ally McCoist Testimonial Committee, 1993.
20p; illus
Includes information leaflet loosely inserted.

Macdonald, Malcolm

328 Win! / Malcolm Macdonald. London: Pelham, 1977.
157p; illus ISBN: 0-7207-1014-6
BL: X.629/11497

An articulate contribution from the England forward covering his career with Fulham, Luton, Newcastle and Arsenal.

329 Football makes me laugh / compiled by Malcolm Macdonald. London: Pelham; Walton-on-Thames: M. & J. Hobbs, 1979.
96p; illus ISBN: 0-7207-1107-X
BL: X.629/12727

Also listed at: K12

330 Never afraid to miss / Malcolm Macdonald with Brian Woolnough. London: Cassell, 1980.
134p; illus ISBN: 0-304-30639-8
BL: X.629/15625

His later career with Arsenal and a short spell in Sweden are included in this retirement update.

331 Malcolm Macdonald: an autobiography / Malcolm MacDonald as told to Jason Tomas. London: Arthur Barker, 1983.
164p; illus ISBN: 0-213-16879-0
BL: X.629/22492

Management days with Fulham are added to the full playing career.

McGahey, Charlie

332 Cheerful Charlie: a biography of C. P. McGahey the Essex player / Jan Kemp; statistics, Robert Brooke. Great Wakering: J. Kemp, 1989.
152p; illus; index
Bibliography: p143-144
ISBN: 0-9514606-0-9 (cased) • ISBN: 0-9514606-1-7 (pbk)
BL: YK.1990.a.916

Largely the study of a cricketing life but also of interest to Spurs historians.

McGrain, Danny

333 Celtic, my team / Danny McGrain; edited by Bob Patience; foreword by Jock Stein. London: Souvenir Press, 1978.
189p; illus ISBN: 0-285-62369-9
BL: X.629/12127

Much of interest on Celtic and Scotland.

334 In sunshine or in shadow / Danny McGrain with Hugh Keevins; foreword by Kenny Dalglish. Edinburgh: John Donald, 1987.
xiii, 144p; illus; index ISBN: 0-85976-191-6
BL: YK.1988.b.3151

The full update takes in McGrain's entire career.

McGrath, Paul

335 Ooh, aah, Paul McGrath: the black pearl of Inchicore / Paul McGrath with Cathal Dervan; foreword by Bryan Robson. Edinburgh: Mainstream, 1994.
221p; illus ISBN: 1-85158-647-4
BL: YK.1995.b.4945

Much on Manchester United and Aston Villa from the Republic of Ireland defender.

McGrory, Jimmy

336 A lifetime in paradise / Jimmy McGrory and Gerry McNee. Glasgow: Hay, Nisbet & Miller, 1975.
Part of Scottish folklore – in one fifteen season spell with Celtic he averaged over a goal a game! His playing career spanning from 1922 to 1937 is chronicled along with his management days for the Glasgow club and for Kilmarnock. This study was written while he served as Celtic's public relations officer before his death in 1982.

McIlroy, Jimmy

337 Right inside soccer / Jimmy McIlroy as told to David R. Jack. London: Nicholas Kaye, 1960.
128p; illus BL: 7925.l.2

The Northern Ireland International inside-forward chronicles his Burnley days during their championship season and before, with some references to his formative period at Glentoran.

McIlroy, Sammy

338 Manchester United, my team / Sammy McIlroy. London: Souvenir Press, 1980.
171p; illus ISBN: 0-285-62451-2
BL: X.629/14112

Full coverage of his ten years with United before the travel bug bit.

Mackay, Dave

339 Soccer my spur / David Mackay. London: Stanley Paul, 1961.
128p; illus   BL: X.449/702

It is typical of Mackay's inner confidence that just the one autobiography suffices. This Scotland International was one of the great sights on a football field – though Hearts and Spurs are to the fore, he was to go on to even more inspirational achievements.

McKenzie, Duncan

340 One step ahead / Duncan McKenzie. London: Souvenir Press, 1978.
173p; illus   ISBN: 0-285-62368-0
                                  BL: X.629/12138

Typically cocky title from one of football's true entertainers covering Nottingham Forest, Mansfield Town, Leeds, Anderlecht and Everton.

McLean, Jim

341 Jousting with giants: the Jim McLean story / Jim McLean with Ken Gallacher. Edinburgh: Mainstream, 1987.
192p; illus; index   ISBN: 1-85158-088-3
                                  BL: YK.1990.b.3819

Concentrates on his time as Dundee United manager.

McLeish, Alex

342 The Don of an era / Alex McLeish with Alastair Macdonald; foreword by Andy Roxburgh. Edinburgh: John Donald, 1988.
vii, 144p; illus; index; pbk   ISBN: 0-85976-242-4
                                  BL: YK.1989.b.2122

Largely Aberdeen from the Scotland defender.

MacLennan, Sandy

343 Wee Bighead / Sandy MacLennan. Lossiemouth: The author, 1983?
136p; illus; pbk
    Cover title: Leaders in attack   BL: X.629/20715

MacLeod, Ally

344 The Ally MacLeod story: an autobiography / Ally MacLeod. London: Stanley Paul, 1979.
159p; illus   ISBN: 0-09-138720-5
                                  BL: X.629/12675

McLintock, Frank

345 That's the way the ball bounces / Frank McLintock and Terry MacNeill. London: Pelham, 1969.
123p; illus   ISBN: 0-7207-0149-X
                                  BL: X.449/4007

Early days at Leicester City then on to Arsenal for this Scotland International.

McMahon, Steve

346 'Macca can!': the Steve McMahon story / Steve McMahon with Harry Harris; foreword by Graeme Souness. London: Pelham, 1990.
118p; illus   ISBN: 0-7207-1990-9
                                  BL: YK.1991.b.2222

England, Everton, Villa and Liverpool are all featured.

McMenemy, Lawrie

347 The diary of a season: Lawrie McMenemy's account of the 1978-9 season as manager of Southampton Football Club / Lawrie McMenemy; introduced and edited by Brian Scovell. London: Arthur Barker, 1979.
213p; illus   ISBN: 0-213-16724-7
                                  BL: X.629/12766

An unusual autobiographical approach offering a good insight into the day-to-day life of a manager.

McNeill, Billy

348 For Celtic and Scotland / Billy McNeill. London: Pelham, 1966.
122p; illus   BL: X.449/2088

One of Celtic's greatest defenders says much of interest about the period running up to their 1967 European Cup triumph.

349 Back to paradise / Billy McNeill with Alex Cameron. Edinburgh: Mainstream, 1988.
192p; illus
    ISBN: 1-85158-187-1 (cased) • ISBN: 1-85158-188-X (pbk)
                                  BL: YK.1989.b.2804

Mostly covers his second spell as manager of Celtic from 1987 but with some reference to the intervening years in charge of Manchester City and Aston Villa.

Macparland, Peter

350 Going for goal. London: Souvenir Press, 1960.
xi, 131p; illus   BL: 7925.c.101

Mostly Aston Villa from this Northern Ireland International.

McPhail, Bob

351 Legend: sixty years at Ibrox / Bob McPhail with Allan Herron. Edinburgh: Mainstream, 1988.
190p; illus
    ISBN: 1-85158-164-2 (cased) • ISBN: 1-85158-165-0 (pbk)
                                  BL: YK.1990.b.3252

Between 1927 and 1939 McPhail scored 233 league goals for Rangers.

Macpherson, Archie

352 Action replays / Archie Macpherson. London:
Chapmans, 1991.
288p   ISBN: 1-85592-564-8
BL: YK.1992.b.4086

Scotland's well-known commentator and broadcaster
has much to say in his own distinctive style.

Marsh, Rodney

353 Shooting to the top / Rodney Marsh. London: Stanley
Paul, 1968.
128p; illus   BL: X.449/3353

Stylish as ever, Marsh covers the swinging sixties
with Fulham and Queen's Park Rangers.

Marwood, Brian

354 The life of Brian: the Brian Marwood story / Brian
Marwood with Brian Woolnough. Edinburgh:
Mainstream, 1990.
144p; illus   ISBN: 1-85158-367-X
BL: YK.1991.b.7937

Hull, Sheffield Wednesday and Arsenal are covered in
what might best be described as a steady career
from England's one-cap man.

Matthews, Stanley

355 Feet first: autobiographical reminiscences / Sir Stanley
Matthews. London: Ewen & Dale, 1948.
156p; illus   BL: 7920.aaa.18

The world's most famous player? This first of several
studies covers Stoke City and his move to Blackpool
along with his boyhood years.

356 Feet first again / Sir Stanley Matthews. London:
Nicholas Kaye, 1952.
xii, 138p; illus   BL: 7920.b.57

Updated to include more of his Blackpool years but
he has yet to win the FA Cup!

357 The Stanley Matthews story / Sir Stanley Matthews.
London: Oldbourne, 1960.
256p; illus   BL: 10800.bb.10

Includes the famous 1953 Cup Final.

358 Stanley Matthews, CBE / Anthony Davis. London:
Cassell, 1962.
121p; illus
(Red Lion lives; no. 13)   BL: 010600.b.1/13

Back at Stoke City again in a further update.

359 Back in touch / Stanley and Mila Matthews with a
helping hand from Don Taylor. London: Arthur Barker,
1981?
viii, 262p; illus   ISBN: 0-213-16806-5
BL: X.622/11493

One of football's more unusual studies. In 1968 Matthews effectively retired from public view and whilst
touring behind the Iron Curtain he met and fell in love
with Czech Mila Winters. On re-entering a higher profile public life he was persuaded to enlighten his many
followers with an explanation of his lost years.

360 Stanley Matthews: the authorized biography / David
Miller. London: Pavilion, 1989.
x, 230p; illus; index
Bibliography: p222   ISBN: 1-85145-161-7
BL: YK.1990.b.9030

Students looking for a full overview will find Matthew's
management years at Port Vale covered here – this
is an excellent biography but the serious 'Sir Stan'
student should ideally consult all these entries to
fully cover the career of a man who made his league
début in 1932 and played his last game in 1965.

Maxwell, Robert

361 Maxwell / Joe Haines. London: Macdonald, 1988.
ix, 525p; illus, 1 map; index
Bibliography: p491-492   ISBN: 0-356-17172-8
BL: YC.1988.b.4093

Characters from the world of industry and commerce
regularly involve themselves with football clubs but
Maxwell must be regarded as an extreme case of the
genre. Supporters of the clubs he 'financed' invariably
questioned his true motives and affinity for the
game. A selection of works is included here as they do
throw up 'insider' observations on a number of clubs
and issues. Maxwell met his death in mysterious circumstances and it is true to say that few in the
football world, or indeed beyond, genuinely mourned
his passing. Oxford United and Reading are included
in the index of this first work.

362 Maxwell: a portrait of power / Peter Thompson and
Anthony Delano. London: Bantam, 1988.
256p; illus   ISBN: 0-593-01499-5
BL: YC.1994.b.2176

363 Maxwell: the outsider / Tom Bower. London: Aurum,
1988.
374p; illus; index   ISBN: 0-948149-88-4
BL: YC.1988.b.3690

☞ Subsequent ed. C364

364 Maxwell: the outsider / Tom Bower. Updated ed.
London: Heinemann, 1991.
586p; illus; index   ISBN: 0-434-07338-5
BL: YC.1992.b.1085

☞ Previous ed. C363

365 Maxwell stories / Sam Jaffa. London: Robson, 1992.
xi, 190p; pbk   ISBN: 0-86051-829-9
BL: YK.1993.b.14698

366 Maxwell's fall: the appalling legacy of a corrupt man /
Roy Greenslade. London: Simon & Schuster, 1992.
ix, 438p; illus; index; pbk   ISBN: 0-671-71122-9
                                            BL: YK.1993.a.8498

Published after his death, this is the best book to
consult for football snippets – includes several pages
referring to Derby County, Tottenham Hotspur, Oxford United and Reading. The caption to a typical
photograph of Maxwell in baseball cap really says it
all: 'Remember, I own the stadium, you are only the
manager!'.

367 The trade unionist and the tycoon / Allister Mackie;
foreword by Tony Benn. Edinburgh: Mainstream in
conjunction with The Herald, 1992.
224p; illus   ISBN: 1-85158-515-X
                                            BL: YC.1993.b.8647

368 The unknown Maxwell: his astonishing secret lives
revealed by his aide and close companion / Nicholas
Davies. London: Sidgwick & Jackson, 1992.
vi, 346p; index   ISBN: 0-283-06160-X
                                            BL: YK.1994.b.96

Mercer, Joe

369 The authorised biography of Joe Mercer, OBE: football
with a smile / Gary James. Leicester: ACL & Polar, 1993.
304p   ISBN: 0-9514862-9-2
                                            BL: YK.1994.b.3154

'Genial Joe' covers his playing days with Everton and
Arsenal either side of the war, then management with
Sheffield United, Aston Villa, Manchester City, Coven-
try and England.

Mercer, Wallace

370 Heart to heart: the anatomy of a football club / Mike
Aitken and Wallace Mercer. Edinburgh: Mainstream,
1988.
200p; illus
      ISBN: 1-85158-140-5 (cased) • ISBN: 1-85158-141-3 (pbk)
                                            BL: YK.1989.b.2351

The Heart of Midlothian chairman gives an insight
into this important and difficult role.

☞ Also listed at: B1138

Meredith, Billy

371 Football wizard: story of Billy Meredith / John Harding.
Derby: Breedon Books, 1984.
160p; illus; pbk   ISBN: 0-907969-06-2

This is one of rather too few studies looking back on
the careers of great players whose autobiographies
were never written. Meredith was to the early twenties what Matthews was to the fifties, playing to a
ripe old age. A début for Manchester City in 1894, a
legend for Manchester United then back to City to
finish in 1924. Unique material on the Welsh Wizard.

Merrick, Gil

372 I see it all / Gil Merrick. London: Museum Press, 1954.
144p; illus   BL: 7943.fff.11

Goalkeeping days with England and Birmingham City.

Messing, Shep

373 The education of an American soccer player / Shep
Messing. London: Bantam, 1979.

I have not had sight of this item – it is to be assumed it chronicles the experiences of an American
learning the game.

Milburn, Jackie

374 Golden goals / Jackie Milburn. London: Stanley Paul,
1957.
144p; illus   BL: 7923.r.38

Several studies of a true footballing legend begin with
Milburn's own retirement account of his Newcastle
United career.

☞ Subsequent ed. C375

375 Golden goals / Jackie Milburn. Rev. ed. London: Stanley
Paul, 1958.
151p; illus   BL: 7924.b.7

☞ Previous ed. C374

376 Jackie Milburn in black and white: a biography / Mike
Kirkup. London: Stanley Paul, 1990.
xii, 178p; illus; index   ISBN: 0-09-174483-0
                                            BL: YC.1990.b.5797

This retrospective view covers his post-Newcastle
days as well as player-managing at Linfield and at
Southern League Yiewsley before moving on to Ipswich
and Gateshead.

377 Wor Jackie: the Jackie Milburn story / John Gibson.
Edinburgh: Sportsprint, 1990.
ii, 151p; illus; index   ISBN: 0-85976-297-1
                                            BL: YK.1990.b.10397

Miller, Willie

378 The Miller's tale: an autobiography / Willie Miller with
Alastair MacDonald. Edinburgh: Mainstream, 1989.
192p; illus   ISBN: 1-85158-155-3

A study of his long career with Aberdeen and Scotland.

Moncur, Bob

379 United we stand / Bob Moncur, with John Gibson.
London: Pelham, 1971.
125p; illus   ISBN: 0-7207-0435-9
                                            BL: X.629/3716

This covers the Newcastle United period for the
Scotland defender.

Moore, Bobby

380 My soccer story / Bobby Moore. London: Stanley Paul, 1966.
141p; illus   BL: X.449/1815

England's 1966 World Cup winning captain tells of the first half of his career with West Ham United.

☞ Subsequent ed. C381

381 My soccer story / Bobby Moore. Rev. ed. London: Stanley Paul, 1966.
148p; illus   BL: X.449/2186

Includes an additional update chapter entitled 'World Champions'.

☞ Previous ed. C380

382 Bobby Moore: the authorised biography / Jeff Powell. London: Everest, 1976.
192p; illus; index   ISBN: 0-905018-20-6
BL: X.620/16413

This update includes his Fulham years.

383 Bobby Moore: the illustrated biography of a football legend / edited by David Emery. London: Headline, 1993.
160p; illus; pbk   ISBN: 0-7472-7867-9
BL: YK.1993.b.14540

On 24 February 1993, early on a Wednesday morning Bobby Moore died at the age of only 51, sending waves of emotion through the football world. This is the full retrospective biography.

384 Bobby Moore: the life and times of a sporting hero / Jeff Powell. London: Robson, 1993.
281p; illus; index   ISBN: 0-86051-866-3
BL: YK.1993.b.14082

☞ Subsequent ed. C385

385 Bobby Moore: the life and times of a sporting hero / Jeff Powell. New ed. London: Robson, 1994.
296p; illus; pbk   ISBN: 0-86051-906-6

☞ Previous ed. C384

Moores, John

386 The man who made Littlewoods: the story of John Moores / Barbara Clegg. London: Hodder & Stoughton, 1993.
239p; illus, 1 geneal. table   ISBN: 0-340-57479-8

Sir John Moores, former Chairman of Everton, died in 1993 at the age of 97. Builder of the Littlewoods Football Pools empire, a lifelong supporter of Everton and influential in many spheres of the game, this biography includes many interesting references.

Mortensen, Stanley

387 Football is my game / Stanley Mortensen. London: Sampson Low, Marston, 1949.
xiv, 218p; illus   BL: 7920.e.6

This covers the Blackpool career of the England centre forward.

Mullery, Alan

388 In defence of Spurs / Alan Mullery as told to Dennis Signy and Michael Hart. London: Stanley Paul, 1969.
152p; illus   BL: X.449/4014

Covering his playing days at Fulham and Spurs.

389 Alan Mullery / Doug Gardner. London: Wolfe, 1971.
64p; illus; pbk
(Giants of football; 4); (Hall of Fame books)
     ISBN: 0-7234-0455-0

390 Alan Mullery: an autobiography / Alan Mullery with Brian Woolnough. London: Pelham, 1985.
185p; illus   ISBN: 0-7207-1633-0
BL: X.950/46894

This much later update covers his later Spurs years and another spell at Fulham along with management at Brighton, Charlton, Millwall and Queen's Park Rangers.

Murdoch, Bobby

391 All the way with Celtic / Bobby Murdoch; edited by Allan Herron. London: Souvenir, 1970.
128p; illus   ISBN: 0-285-50268-9

Covers Celtic's 1967 European Cup win.

Murphy, Jimmy

392 Matt . . . United . . . and me / Jimmy Murphy, as told to Frank Taylor. London: Souvenir Press, 1968.
186p; illus   BL: X.449/3254

Welsh national team manager and assistant to Matt Busby at Manchester United, Murphy 'missed' the Munich air crash whilst on duty with Wales. He was responsible in the aftermath for keeping the playing side going, winning his first match following the crash with a makeshift side dubbed 'Murphy's Marvels' by the press.

☞ Also listed at: C67

Neal, Phil

393 Attack from the back / Phil Neal. London: Arthur Barker, 1981.
151p; illus   ISBN: 0-213-16783-2
BL: X.629/15456

Northampton Town and Liverpool are featured in the first half of his career.

394 Life at the Kop / Phil Neal. London: Macdonald, 1986.
175p; illus; index   ISBN: 0-356-12335-9
BL: YC.1986.a.4892

On his move to Bolton Wanderers, Neal looks back at his full Liverpool and England career.

Neale, Phil

395 A double life / Phil Neale. Letchworth: Ringpress, 1990.
157p; illus   ISBN: 0-948955-31-7
     BL: YK.1991.b.4675

327 league games for Lincoln City and over 16,000 runs for Worcestershire make Neale one of the last examples of the cricketer-footballer breed. It is unlikely that any future player could possibly match such a record.

Neill, Terry

396 Revelations of a football manager / Terry Neill. London: Sidgwick & Jackson, 1985.
191p; illus   ISBN: 0-283-99222-0
     BL: X.622/25269

A playing career with Arsenal, Hull and Northern Ireland is also covered in this study of his management years with Spurs, Arsenal and the Irish national side, charting many of the difficulties of the job.

Nicholas, Charlie

397 Charlie: an autobiography / Charlie Nicholas with Ken Gallacher. London: Stanley Paul, 1986.
123p; illus   ISBN: 0-09-163820-8
     BL: YC.1986.a.3722

Written during his Arsenal years but including much on Celtic – the move south of the border was to prove a difficult and disappointing one.

Nicholson, Bill

398 Glory glory: my life with Spurs / Bill Nicholson. London: Macmillan, 1984.
224p; illus; index   ISBN: 0-333-36364-7
     BL: X.629/25462

A professional with Spurs from 1938, then manager, advisor and scout for the club which was indeed his life.

O'Leary, David

399 David O'Leary: my story / David O'Leary with Harry Miller. Edinburgh: Mainstream, 1988.
192p; illus
     ISBN: 1-85158-145-6 (cased) • ISBN: 1-85158-146-4 (pbk)
     BL: YK.1989.b.2831

The Republic of Ireland defender tells his Arsenal story from 1975.

Osgood, Peter

400 Ossie the wizard / Peter Osgood. London: Stanley Paul, 1969.
155p; illus   ISBN: 0-09-100520-5
     BL: X.449/3999

Tales of Chelsea and the swinging sixties.

401 Peter Osgood / Rob Hughes. London: Wolfe, 1971.
64p; illus; pbk
(Giants of football; 6); (Hall of Fame books)
     ISBN: 0-7234-0457-7

Page, Louis

402 Liverpool's sporting Pages / Phil Jackson. Bromborough: Lechlade, 1991.
viii, 88p; illus, 1 geneal. table; index; pbk
     Bibliography: p78   ISBN: 0-9517048-0-X
     BL: YK.1991.a.12176

A most unusual and well researched work covering four members of the Page Family, written by the daughter of Louis Page who leads the coverage. His clubs included South Liverpool, Stoke, Northampton and others on the playing side, and Newport, Swindon and Chester as manager. There is a short chapter on each of his clubs. Also covered are his footballer brothers Jack, Thomas and William – all four brothers astonishingly were England International baseball players. Of the lesser known clubs, the book also includes references to Merthyr Town, New Brighton and Bideford Town.

Paisley, Bob

403 Bob Paisley: a lifetime in football / Bob Paisley. London: Arthur Barker, 1983.
170p; illus   ISBN: 0-213-16767-0
     BL: X.629/21089

One of the most successful managers in the history of English club soccer; his story includes playing days at Bishop Auckland and Liverpool, his partnership with Bill Shankly and finally the years of success as Liverpool manager in his own right.

Partridge, Pat

404 Oh, ref! / Pat Partridge and John Gibson. London: Souvenir Press, 1979.
189p; illus   ISBN: 0-285-62423-7
     BL: X.620/18974

Reminiscences of a leading referee.

Paul, Roy

405 A red dragon of Wales / Roy Paul. London: Hale, 1956.
111p; illus
(Champion sports books)   BL: X.629/7721(3)

Early days at Ton Pentre; Swansea City, Manchester City and Wales also figure largely.

Peacock, Gavin

406 Never walk alone / Gavin Peacock and Alan Comfort; edited by Alan MacDonald. London: Hodder, 1994.
illus; pbk   ISBN: 0-340-60675-4

A most unusual double biography, charting the different fortunes of two friends who met as youngsters at Queen's Park Rangers. Peacock was to lead New-castle United to glorious promotion in 1993 whilst Comfort's career ended with Middlesbrough through injury in 1989. Peacock's side of the story includes reference to Bournemouth, Gillingham and QPR as well as Newcastle United.

☞ Also listed at: C113

Pelé

407 'King' Pelé: an appreciation / Paul Trevillion. London: Stanley Paul, 1971.
93p; illus

On Edson Arantes do Nascimento, nicknamed Pelé
ISBN: 0-09-108070-3 (cased) • ISBN: 0-09-108071-1 (pbk)
BL: X.629/3668

One of the candidates for the most famous foot-baller of all time. Includes much on the game in Brazil and the World Cups.

408 Pelé: my life and the beautiful game: the autobiography of Pelé / Pelé and Robert L. Fish. London: New English Library, 1977.
255p; illus   ISBN: 0-450-03230-2
BL: X.800/26392

Pelé's own story, with much on his club side, Santos.

409 Pelé, king of football / Noel Machin. London: Longman, 1980.
16p; illus, 1 map; pbk   ISBN: 0-582-52674-4
A language reader for students of English.

Perryman, Steve

410 A man for all seasons / Steve Perryman. London: Arthur Barker, 1985.
240p; illus   ISBN: 0-213-16922-3
BL: YC.1986.a.397

Written at the end of his very long career with Spurs prior to his move to Oxford and Brentford.

Peters, Martin

411 Goals from nowhere! / Martin Peters as told to Peter Corrigan. London: Stanley Paul, 1969.
128p; illus   ISBN: 0-09-098940-6
BL: X.449/3966

Even the manuscript arrived late! Full coverage of West Ham and England, inevitably in ghost-written format, from a key member of the 1966 winning side.

Pickford, William

412 A few recollections of sport / edited by E. M. P. Bournemouth: Bournemouth Guardian, 1939.
179p; illus   BL: Mic.A.11325(1) (microfilm copy)

A scarce, privately printed item by this father figure of football, a member of the FA Council from 1888 to 1938 and elected President of the FA in 1937. He is

in a unique position to chronicle changes in the sport from its Victorian days into the modern era. A very valuable research source.

Protheroe, Gladys

413 Gladys Protheroe: football genius! / Simon Cheetham. Sheffield: Juma, 1994.
220p; pbk   ISBN: 1-872204-10-4

Humorous memoirs of spoof radio pundit Gladys Protheroe known as England's premier football lady.

Puskas, Ferenc

414 Captain of Hungary / Ferenc Puskas; translated by Aranka de Major. London: Cassell, 1955.
xi, 180p; illus   BL: 7921.aaa.59

Few players who have never played league football in the UK could generate the popularity to justify their autobiography being published here. Puskas is one of those few. Hungary's famous wins over England are covered along with club days at Honved.

Ramsey, Alf

415 Talking football / Alf Ramsey. London: Stanley Paul, 1952.
114p; illus   BL: 7920.b.79

Long before his glory days as England manager, Ramsey enjoyed a superb career with Southampton, Tottenham and England. This first study covers that period.

416 Anatomy of a football manager: Sir Alf Ramsey / Max Marquis. London: Arthur Barker, 1970.
145p; illus   ISBN: 0-213-00166-7
BL: X.629/2912

Ipswich Town and England are well covered in this sec-ond study of the 1966 World Cup winning manager.

Ratcliffe, Kevin

417 The Blues and I: an autobiography / Kevin Ratcliffe. London: Arthur Barker, 1988.
146p; illus   ISBN: 0-213-16959-2
BL: YK.1988.a.5120

Everton and Wales in a straightforward treatment.

Raynor, George

418 Football ambassador at large. London: Stanley Paul, 1960.
142p; illus   BL: 7925.b.86

An unusual figure who took his knowledge abroad af-ter a moderate pre-war career with Mansfield, Rotherham, Bury and Aldershot. Manager of the Swedish national side, Juventus, Lazio, Coventry and finally Skegness Town in 1960. Some interesting ma-terial from a very varied life.

Reid, Peter

419   Everton winter, Mexican summer: a football diary /
      Peter Reid with Peter Ball. London: Macdonald, 1987.
      212p; illus; index   ISBN: 0-356-12245-X
                                         BL: YK.1987.a.3156

      Largely Everton and the 1986 World Cup from this
      former Bolton Wanderers stalwart.

      ☞ Subsequent ed. C420

420   An Everton diary / Peter Reid with Peter Ball. Updated
      ed. London: Queen Anne, 1988.
      300p; pbk   ISBN: 0-7088-4007-8
                                         BL: YK.1988.a.5113

      ☞ Previous ed. C419

Revie, Don

421   Soccer's happy wanderer / Don Revie. London:
      Museum Press, 1955.
      110p; illus   BL: 7920.b.111

      Leicester, Hull and Manchester City are all covered on
      his travels in post-war football.

422   Don Revie: portrait of a footballing enigma / Andrew
      Mourant. Edinburgh: Mainstream, 1990.
      167p; illus   ISBN: 1-85158-342-4
                                         BL: YK.1991.b.4456

      Moments of triumph and despair were to come to Re-
      vie during his management years with Leeds United,
      England and the United Arab Emirates. His last play-
      ing days at Sunderland and Leeds are also included.

Roberts, Graham

423   When the going gets tough: the Graham Roberts story /
      Graham Roberts with Steve Stammers. Edinburgh:
      Mainstream, 1988.
      192p; illus
          ISBN: 1-85158-130-8 (cased) • ISBN: 1-85158-131-6 (pbk)
                                         BL: YK.1989.b.2829

      Covers Tottenham, Chelsea and the early days at
      Rangers.

Robson, Bobby

424   Time on the grass / Bobby Robson. London: Arthur
      Barker, 1982.
      xi, 180p; illus   ISBN: 0-213-16845-6
                                         BL: X.629/18742

      This was published on Robson's appointment as Eng-
      land manager as an overview of his career to date;
      references to his playing days at Fulham and West
      Bromwich Albion prior to management with Vancouver
      Royals, Fulham and Ipswich Town are included.

425   So near and yet so far: Bobby Robson's World Cup diary
      1982-86 / Bobby Robson with Bob Harris. London:
      Willow, 1986.
      219p; illus   ISBN: 0-00-218186-X
                                         BL: YK.1986.a.1443

      Even nearer was yet to come in 1990, but here Rob-
      son chronicles the four year run up to the 1986 World
      Cup in Mexico where quarter-final defeat was waiting
      in ambush at the hands of Maradona.

      ☞ Also listed at: E90

426   Against the odds: an autobiography / Bobby Robson
      with Bob Harris. London: Stanley Paul, 1990.
      217p; illus   ISBN: 0-09-174499-7
                                         BL: YK.1990.b.9966

      The full retrospective update; although he received
      much criticism from all quarters, the lasting view of
      him will be as one of the most unlucky England man-
      agers – it wasn't Robson who missed the penalties!

Robson, Bryan

427   United I stand / Bryan Robson with Tim Russon.
      London: Pelham, 1984.
      176p; illus; index   ISBN: 0-7207-1517-2
                                         BL: X.950/31852

      West Bromwich Albion, Manchester United and Eng-
      land are all featured.

      ☞ Subsequent ed. C428

428   United I stand / Bryan Robson with Tim Russon. Rev.
      ed. London: Panther, 1985.
      208p; illus; index; pbk   ISBN: 0-586-06476-1
                                         BL: X.958/32627

      ☞ Previous ed. C427

429   Glory glory Man United! / Bryan Robson, with Martin
      Chilton. London: CollinsWillow, 1992.
      128p; illus; pbk   ISBN: 0-00-218434-6
                                         BL: YK.1993.b.7152

      A full update of Robson's long career at Old Trafford.

Robson, 'Pop'

430   The sporting worlds of Bryan 'Pop' Robson / Bryan
      Robson with Douglas Weatherall. Newcastle-upon-Tyne:
      Oriel, 1970.
      49p; illus; pbk   ISBN: 0-85362-106-3

      Written when he left Newcastle United for West Ham
      after 205 league games.

Rough, Alan

431   Rough at the top / Alan Rough as told to Stuart Brown.
      Edinburgh: John Donald, 1988.
      illus; pbk; index   ISBN: 0-85976-241-6
                                         BL: YK.1989.a.2975

Rous, Stanley

432 Football worlds: a lifetime in sport / Sir Stanley Rous;
with a foreword by Sir Walter Winterbottom. London:
Faber, 1978.
223p; illus   ISBN: 0-571-11194-7
BL: X.629/12066

> Referee of the 1934 Cup Final, FA Secretary, a
> Knighthood and President of FIFA from 1961-1974 –
> a great influence on the game and its administration
> is revealed in this important study of his life and
> work.

Royle, Joe

433 Royle flush / Joe Royle. London: Pelham, 1969.
119p; illus   SBN: 7207-0283-6
BL: X.449/4269

> Written during his Everton heyday.

Rush, Ian

434 Rush: Ian Rush's autobiography / Ian Rush. London:
Arthur Barker, 1985.
189p; illus   ISBN: 0-586-07087-7
BL: YK.1987.a.1605

> Written towards the end of his first spell at Liverpool
> prior to his move abroad. Also includes reference to
> his first club, Chester City, and his international ca-
> reer with Wales.

435 My Italian diary / Ian Rush; with an introduction by
Brian Glanville. London: Arthur Barker, 1989.
150p; illus   ISBN: 0-213-16962-2
BL: YK.1990.a.825

> Rush returned to Liverpool in 1988 after his experi-
> ence with Juventus – this is a particularly good
> reference work for those wishing to chart the difficul-
> ties of playing overseas.

Sammels, Jon

436 Double champions: playing the Arsenal way / Jon
Sammels with Robert Oxby. London: Arthur Barker,
1971.
142p; illus   ISBN: 0-213-00465-8

> Written at the end of his long Highbury career prior
> to his move to Leicester City.

Scholar, Irving

437 Behind closed doors: dreams and nightmares at Spurs /
Irving Scholar with Mihir Bose. London: Deutsch, 1992.
xiv, 367p; illus   ISBN: 0-233-98824-6
BL: YK.1991.b.13867

> Much on boardroom politics and the financial side of
> running a club from the Spurs chief.

  ☞ Also listed at: B811

Schumacher, Toni

438 Blowing the whistle / Toni Schumacher; translated by
Chris Morris. London: W. H. Allen, 1988.
214p; illus; pbk
   Translation of: Anpfiff   ISBN: 0-352-32194-6
BL: YK.1989.a.723

> Promoted as 'a sensational exposé of European football'
> by this well-known German international goalkeeper.

Seed, Jimmy

439 Soccer from the inside / Jimmy Seed. London:
Thorsons, 1947.
112p
(Let's talk it over; no. 1)   BL: W.P.2013/1

> The famous Charlton Athletic manager covers his ca-
> reer to this date.

440 The Jimmy Seed story: forty-three years in first-class
football as player and manager / Jimmy Seed. London:
Phoenix Sports Books, 1957.
127p; illus   BL: 10864.f.26

> This later work is the definitive one for a full overview.
> It includes much on Charlton Athletic of course, but
> Seed's playing career is also discussed – Whitburn,
> Sunderland, Mid-Rhondda, Spurs and Sheffield
> Wednesday are all referred to in one of football's best
> known autobiographies.

Shackleton, Len

441 Len Shackleton, clown prince of soccer: his
autobiography / Leonard Francis Shackleton; edited by
David R. Jack; with pen-and-ink sketches by Mickey
Durling. London: Nicholas Kaye, 1955.
157p; illus   BL: 7922.bb.44

> Renowned for his impish and anarchic humour – defi-
> nite hints of this in a work covering Sunderland for
> the main part but with earlier references to Bradford
> Park Avenue and Newcastle. It contains the famous
> Chapter 9 covering only one page. Page 78 is headed:
> 'The Average Director's Knowledge of Football' and is
> completely blank save for a publisher's note – 'This
> chapter has deliberately been left blank in accordance
> with the author's wishes'!

Shankly, Bill

442 A legend in his own time: Bill Shankly – a tribute / Bill
Shankly. Chester: J. H. Leeman, 1975.

> *A limited edition of 2,500 copies*

443 Shankly / Bill Shankly. London: Arthur Barker, 1976.
ix, 182p; illus   ISBN: 0-213-16603-8
BL: X.629/10796

> The legendary Liverpool manager expounds on his An-
> field days with background on his playing career too –
> Carlisle, Preston, wartime guesting and Scotland

were followed by management at Carlisle, Grimsby, Workington and Huddersfield before the move to immortality.

444 Shankly / Phil Thompson. Liverpool: Bluecoat, 1993.
96p; illus; pbk   ISBN: 1-872568-11-4

Sharpe, Ivan

445 40 years in football / Ivan Sharpe. London: Hutchinson's Library of Sports & Pastimes, 1952.
224p; illus   BL: W.P.1156/30

This English Amateur International won a gold medal with the Great Britain football team at the 1912 Stockholm Olympics. Playing days with Watford, Glossop, Derby County and Leeds United are covered in a book which is a vital eyewitness link with the really early days of this century. Sharpe is well known as a journalist and editor of *Athletic News* from 1924 – his account is very well written and worth consulting.

Shepherdson, Harold

446 The magic sponge / Harold Shepherdson, with Roy Peskett. London: Pelham, 1968.
200p; illus   BL: X.449/3298

This can claim justifiably to be a unique story. Shepherdson was for many years the England trainer – nowadays we would call him a physio – and he became a familiar sight running on to tend the injured in countless England Internationals. His playing career with Middlesbrough was very modest so he has effectively achieved his immortality without ever kicking a ball!

Shilton, Peter

447 Peter Shilton: the magnificent obsession / Jason Tomas with Peter Shilton. Tadworth: World's Work, 1982.
137p; illus   ISBN: 0-437-17430-1
                                     BL: X.622/12463

Obsession would not be too strong a word to express Shilton's dedication. One of the great England goalkeepers here covers Leicester, Stoke and Nottingham Forest.

Simpson, Ronnie

448 Sure it's a grand old team to play for / Ronnie Simpson; edited by Allan Herron. London: Souvenir Press, 1967.
160p; illus   BL: X.449/2882

. . . especially whilst winning the European Cup in the year of publication. Detailed coverage of Celtic from a veteran of the team of the sixties.

Small, R. Leonard

449 The holy goalie: formerly minister of St. Cuthbert's Parish Church, Edinburgh / R. Leonard Small. Edinburgh: Pentland, 1993.
xiv, 153p; illus   ISBN: 1-85821-037-2
                                     BL: YK.1994.a.6748

An unusual item – the Very Reverend Leonard Small was a leading Scottish churchman and a goalkeeper capped by Scotland as an amateur in 1929. This work was published shortly before his death.

Smith, David Rushworth

450 Off the ball: a sports chaplain at work / David Rushworth Smith; foreword by John Motson. Basingstoke: Marshalls, 1985.
128p; index; pbk
    Bibliography: p124-125   ISBN: 0-551-01194-7
                                     BL: X.208/11217

Footballers encounter many of life's problems and many clubs retain the services of a club chaplain. This is the unique story of one of that breed.

Smith, G. O.

451 Corinthians and cricketers / Edward Grayson. London: Naldrett in association with World's Work, 1955.
248p   BL: 7922.f.1

G. O. Smith is the central figure of this study of the early days of football including much on the Victorian and Edwardian game, university and public schools soccer and, of course, The Corinthians, for whom G. O. was an inspired centre forward. As if that wasn't enough, C. B. Fry says in his introduction: 'By the way, he had curiously fine grey eyes and grey eyelashes such as any girl would envy.'!

☞ Subsequent ed. C452

452 Corinthian-casuals & cricketers / Edward Grayson; with a foreword by C.B. Fry. New & updated ed. Havant: Pallant, 1983.
248p; illus; index; pbk   ISBN: 0-9507141-3-5
                                     BL: X.629/26957

☞ Previous ed. C451

Smith, Jim

453 Bald eagle / Jim Smith and Mark Dawson. Edinburgh: Mainstream, 1990.
144p; illus   ISBN: 1-85158-382-3
                                     BL: YK.1994.b.1391

Concentrates on his management career with Blackburn, Birmingham, Oxford United, Queen's Park Rangers and Newcastle with some reference to playing days at Aldershot, Halifax, Lincoln City, Boston United and Colchester United.

Smith, Tommy

454 I did it the hard way / Tommy Smith. London: Arthur Barker, 1980.
164p; illus   ISBN: 0-213-16766-2
                                     BL: X.629/14169

Many players would testify to the title – Liverpool and Swansea City both feature.

Smith, Walter

455 Mr Smith: the fan who joined the Ibrox legends / Walter
Smith with Ken Gallacher. Edinburgh: Mainstream,
1994.
160p; illus   ISBN: 1-85158-668-7

*The Rangers manager tells the inside story of his
time at Ibrox which was very much the fulfillment of a
personal dream.*

Souness, Graeme

456 No half measures / Graeme Souness with Bob Harris.
London: Willow, 1985.
208p; illus   ISBN: 0-00-218134-7
BL: X.629/27570

*Playing days with Middlesbrough, Liverpool, Scotland,
and Sampdoria.*

☞ Subsequent ed. C457

457 No half measures / Graeme Souness with Bob Harris.
Updated ed. London: Grafton, 1987.
272p; illus; pbk   ISBN: 0-586-07424-4
BL: YK.1987.a.7572

Updated to embrace his move to Rangers.

☞ Previous ed. C456

458 Graeme Souness: a manager's diary / Graeme Souness
with Ken Gallacher. Edinburgh: Mainstream, 1989.
192p; illus   ISBN: 1-85158-224-X
BL: YK.1991.b.2249

*Particular emphasis on Glasgow Rangers during his
tenure as manager.*

459 Graeme Souness: a soccer revolutionary / Stephen F.
Kelly. London: Headline, 1994.
248p; illus; index   ISBN: 0-7472-0978-2
BL: YC.1995.b.1600

St. John, Ian

460 Boom at the Kop / Ian St. John. London: Pelham, 1966.
134p; illus   BL: X.449/1845

*Largely Liverpool from this Scotland International,
with some reference to his earlier days at Motherwell.*

Stanton, Pat

461 'The quiet man', the Pat Stanton story / as told to Simon
Pia. Edinburgh: Sportsprint, 1989.
v, 122p; illus; index   ISBN: 0-85976-288-2
BL: YK.1990.b.9184

*An inspiration to the Hibernian side of the sixties and
seventies.*

Stein, Jock

462 Mr Stein: a biography of Jock Stein CBE, 1922-85 / Bob
Crampsey. Edinburgh: Mainstream, 1986.
192p; illus
ISBN: 1-85158-057-3 (cased) • ISBN: 1-85158-058-1 (pbk)
BL: YK.1989.b.4806

*The story of one of the greatest Scottish managers
of all time. His playing career with Albion Rovers and
Celtic is touched upon here, as is his management of
Dunfermline and a fateful 44 days with Leeds United
– but it is as manager of Celtic and Scotland that he
is best known and there is an abundance of material
here.*

☞ Subsequent ed. C463

463 Jock Stein – the master: a biography of Jock Stein CBE,
1922-85 / Bob Crampsey. Sevenoaks: Coronet, 1987.
224p; illus; pbk   ISBN: 0-340-41425-1
BL: YK.1987.a.7079

☞ Previous ed. C462

464 Jock Stein: the authorized biography / Ken Gallacher;
foreword by Hugh McIlvanney. London: Stanley Paul,
1988.
176p; illus; index   ISBN: 0-09-164410-0
BL: YK.1988.a.2914

Stepney, Alex

465 In safe keeping / Alex Stepney. London: Pelham, 1969.
157p; illus   ISBN: 0-7207-0006-X
BL: X.449/3876

*A straightforward account of goalkeeping days at
Millwall and Manchester United with one game for
Chelsea sandwiched in between.*

466 Alex Stepney / Alex Stepney. London: Arthur Barker,
1978.
152p; illus   ISBN: 0-213-16682-8
BL: X.629/12146

*This book, published upon his retirement, covers all
his Manchester United goalkeeping career and includes a couple of goals from himself for good
measure!*

Steven, Trevor

467 Even Stevens: a season's diary / Gary Stevens and
Trevor Steven with Dave Smith. Edinburgh:
Mainstream, 1988.
200p; illus
ISBN: 1-85158-189-8 (cased) • ISBN: 1-85158-190-1 (pbk)
BL: YK.1989.b.2749

*This joint effort covers the players' time together at
Rangers.*

☞ Also listed at: C468

Stevens, Gary

468 Even Stevens: a season's diary / Gary Stevens and
Trevor Steven with Dave Smith. Edinburgh:
Mainstream, 1988.
200p; illus
  ISBN: 1-85158-189-8 (cased) • ISBN: 1-85158-190-1 (pbk)
  BL: YK.1989.b.2749

☞ Also listed at: C467

Stiles, Nobby

469 Soccer my battlefield / Nobby Stiles; edited by Peter
Keeling. London: Stanley Paul, 1968.
157p; illus
  BL: X.449/3361

Norbert P. Stiles might well have graced a turn of the
century public school side but 'Nobby' is more appropriate for this great competitor whose career began in
1959. Manchester United is the primary subject along
with memories of the 1966 England World Cup win.

470 Nobby Stiles / Peter Keeling. London: Wolfe, 1971.
64p; illus; pbk
(Giants of football; 5); (Hall of Fame books)
  ISBN: 0-7234-0456-9

Stock, Alec

471 Football club manager / Alec Stock; edited by Bryon
Butler. London: Routledge & Kegan Paul, 1967.
161p; illus
  BL: X.449/2887

One of the thinking managers following his pre-war
career with Spurs, Charlton and Queen's Park Rangers. His post-war management of Yeovil Town, Leyton
Orient, Arsenal and AS Roma all get a mention but
Queen's Park Rangers take centre stage from 1959.

472 A little thing called pride: an autobiography / Alec Stock.
London: Pelham, 1982.
172p; illus
  ISBN: 0-7207-1395-1
  BL: X.629/17752

This update includes his management of Luton Town,
Fulham and Bournemouth.

Strachan, Gordon

473 Gordon Strachan: an autobiography / Gordon Strachan
with Jack Webster. London: Stanley Paul, 1984.
183p; illus
  ISBN: 0-09-155170-6
  BL: X.809/60791

Written on his move to Manchester United from
Aberdeen.

474 Strachan style: a life in football / Gordon Strachan with
Ken Gallacher. Edinburgh: Mainstream, 1991.
156p; illus
  ISBN: 1-85158-403-X
  BL: YK.1992.b.8054

This full update includes his Scotland career along
with Manchester United and Leeds United.

Sturrock, Paul

475 Forward thinking: the Paul Sturrock story / Paul
Sturrock with Charlie Duddy and Peter Rundo.
Edinburgh: Mainstream, 1989.
192p; illus
  ISBN: 1-85158-238-X
  BL: YK.1991.b.4455

Covers his long career with Dundee United.

Swift, Frank

476 Football from the goalmouth / Frank Swift; edited by
Roy Peskett. London: Sporting Handbooks, 1948.
190p; illus
  BL: 7920.aaa.24

One of the greatest characters in goalkeeping covers
his one and only club, Manchester City. Ten years after this publication Swift was to die in the Munich air
crash in his line of duty as a reporter.

Taylor, Graham

477 Graham Taylor: when England called / Graham Taylor
with Dennis Shaw. Westone: Pipkin, 1991.
111p; illus; pbk
  ISBN: 1-872840-06-X
  BL: YK.1993.b.10465

Taylor was made England manager in 1990 following
the World Cup finals in Italy. Over the next four years
there was a gradual build up to bitter disappointment – but this was still all to come when this book
setting the scene was published.

Taylor, Jack

478 Jack Taylor, world soccer referee / Jack Taylor with
David Jones. London: Pelham, 1976.
183p; illus
  ISBN: 0-7207-0890-7
  BL: X.629/10517

One of England's toughest referees gives a good overview of his role in the game as an official with
worldwide experience.

479 Soccer refereeing: a personal view / Jack Taylor.
London: Faber and Faber, 1978.
96p; illus
  ISBN: 0-571-11298-6 (cased) • ISBN: 0-571-11299-4 (pbk)
  BL: X.629/12149

☞ Also listed at: G39

Taylor, Tommy

480 Tommy Taylor of Manchester United and Barnsley:
Busby Babe – an illustrated biography / John Kennedy.
Harefield: Yore, 1994.
84p; illus; pbk
  ISBN: 1-874427-85-2

Retrospective study of the Barnsley and Manchester
United centre forward who died in the Munich air
crash when he was just 26.

Thomas, Clive

481 By the book / Clive Thomas. London: Willow, 1984.
203p; illus ISBN: 0-00-218083-9
BL: X.629/23704

The famous referee presents much of interest in a review of his 20 year career. In his early Rhondda Valley days he once played 35 minutes of additional time!

Toshack, John

482 Tosh: an autobiography / John Toshack. London: Arthur Barker, 1982.
165p; illus ISBN: 0-213-16849-9
BL: X.629/19256

A review of the playing career of this well-known Welsh forward covering all his days with Cardiff, Liverpool and Swansea City.

Trautmann, Bert

483 Steppes to Wembley / Bert Trautmann in collaboration with Eric Todd. London: Hale, 1956.
141p; illus
(Champion sports books) BL: X.629/7721(1)

One of football's most unusual characters. The German-born goalkeeper served in the German army as a paratrooper before being captured as prisoner-of-war. This covers his Manchester City years up to the date in which they won the Cup and Trautmann was elected Footballer of the Year.

484 Trautmann: the biography / Alan Rowlands. Derby: Breedon Books, 1990.
256p; illus ISBN: 0-907969-71-2
BL: YK.1992.a.9631

Tully, Charlie

485 Passed to you / the autobiography of Charlie Tully. London: Stanley Paul, 1958.
117p; illus BL: 7943.fff.7

A tale of two Celtics: Glasgow Celtic and Belfast Celtic are both well covered. Particularly of interest to researchers of the Belfast club, 14 times Irish League champions, who left the league in 1949 in circumstances never wholly understood.

Tynan, Tommy

486 Tommy: a life at the soccer factory / Tommy Tynan with Richard Cowdery. Plympton: Bud Books, 1990.
176, 18p; illus ISBN: 0-9516350-0-X
BL: YK.1991.a.10617

An unusual book, for Tynan was never truly a star. A reminder that, for the journeymen of the game, football is very much just a job. Nine clubs are covered, with much on Plymouth Argyle and Newport County.

Ure, Ian

487 Ure's truly / Ian Ure. London: Pelham, 1968.
135p; illus ISBN: 0-7207-0210-0
BL: X.449/3399

Written by the Scottish International centre half during his time with Arsenal, with reference to his early years at Dundee.

Venables, Terry

488 Terry Venables: son of Fred / Fred Venables. London: Weidenfeld and Nicolson, 1990.
viii, 152p; illus ISBN: 0-297-81159-2
BL: YK.1990.b.10602

An unusual approach, father writing about son. Venables was set to become a future England manager but at the time was in charge of Spurs. His management of Queen's Park Rangers, Crystal Palace and Barcelona is covered, along with playing days at Chelsea, Spurs, Queen's Park Rangers and Palace.

FRED VENABLES

TERRY VENABLES:
Son of Fred

WEIDENFELD AND NICOLSON · LONDON

489 Venables: the autobiography / Terry Venables. London: Michael Joseph, 1994.
320p; illus ISBN: 0-7181-3827-9

This much publicised work by the England manager was greeted with some disappointment by the critics. A valuable study, nonetheless, with material of particular interest to followers of the Spurs saga.

490 Venables: the inside story / Harry Harris & Steve Curry. London: Headline, 1994.
313p; illus; index   ISBN: 0-7472-1071-3
                         BL: YK.1994.b.13402

From 1987 to 1991 Venables was Spurs manager, then Chief Executive until 1993 when he was effectivly sacked in very bitter circumstances. This is the full story offering one of the best examples of a 'board-room politics' study involving the man appointed as England manager in place of Graham Taylor.

Waddle, Chris

491 Waddle: the authorised biography of Chris Waddle / Mel Stein. London: Cockerel, 1989.
171p; illus   ISBN: 1-869914-07-4
                   BL: YK.1992.b.9198

Much on Newcastle United and Spurs from this England International along with coverage of his move abroad to Marseille.

Walker, Billy

492 Soccer in the blood / William Henry Walker. London: Stanley Paul, 1960.
128p; illus   BL: 7925.f.16

Aston Villa player from 1919 to 1933, then manager of Sheffield Wednesday, a brief stay with Chelmsford City, followed by twenty-one years in charge at Nottingham Forest. This was written at the end of his tenure and is his full and valuable story.

Walker, Frank

493 Some football reminiscences / Frank Walker. 1920s?

Walker, Tommy

494 Farewell souvenir to Tommy Walker / edited by John Graydon. London: James Truscott, 1949.
illus   BL: 7920.c.41

Memories of playing days with Hearts prior to his spell as manager.

Wall, Bob

495 Arsenal from the heart. London: Souvenir Press, 1969.
192p; illus   BL: X.449/4278

At the age of 16 in 1928, Wall was appointed personal assistant to manager Herbert Chapman. In 1971, when Arsenal won the double, he was still their secretary. This is a valuable account of his time as club administrator.

☞ Also listed at: B14

Wall, Frederick

496 Fifty years of football / Sir Frederick Joseph Wall. London: Cassell, 1935.
viii, 256p   BL: 7915.p.24

Secretary of the FA from 1895 to 1934, Wall looks back on the game in a rare eyewitness account from the very early days. This is an important work to assist in the study of the game's development during this period. Read in conjunction with those by Ivan Sharpe and William Pickford this entire period can be vividly understood.

Wallace, Jock

497 Football is the Wallace religion / edited by Graham Clark. Glasgow: Menard, 1984.
96p; illus; pbk   BL: LB.31.a.2631

A hard taskmaster as manager of Rangers, Leicester City, and Motherwell. This short study also covers his playing years with Workington, Ashton United, Berwick Rangers, Airdrie, West Bromwich Albion and Bedford Town.

Ward, Tim

498 Armed with a football: a memoir of Tim Ward, footballer and father / Andrew Ward. Oxford: Crowberry, 1994.
viii, 151p; pbk   ISBN: 0-9507568-1-4

A poignant work written by a son about his father. Tim Ward spent the last months of his life – he died in 1993 – recording the story of his football career for his son. As a player Tim Ward turned out for Cheltenham Town, Derby County, Hamilton Academical and Barnsley. As manger, he spent just eight days with Exeter City before moving on to Barnsley, Grimsby Town, Derby County and Carlisle United. This is an excellent study of one of the game's true gentlemen, who was twice-capped for England.

Watson, Dave

499 My dear Watson: the story of a football marriage / Penny Watson. London: Arthur Barker, 1981.
134p; illus   ISBN: 0-213-16814-6
                   BL: X.629/16789

A unique and enterprising approach. A football wife tells of the pleasures and difficulties encountered in a role so often unfairly stereotyped. Dave Watson, who played most of his games for Rotherham, Sunderland and Manchester City, is here both centre half and other half.

Watson, Willie

500 Double international / Willie Watson. London: Stanley Paul, 1956.
176p; illus   BL: 7922.f.43

One of the rare breed to be capped by England at both football and cricket, he joined Yorkshire in 1939, played 23 tests and won four full England football caps. Probably the best study of the differing demands of the two sports, covering also his club days at Huddersfield, Sunderland and Halifax where he retired as a player in the year this work was published.

West, Gordon

501   The championship in my keeping / Gordon West.
London: Souvenir, 1970.
157p; illus   ISBN: 0-285-50288-3

> Covers the goalkeeper's winning years at Everton with some early references to Blackpool.

Whittaker, Tom

502   Tom Whittaker's Arsenal story / Tom Whittaker; edited by Roy Peskett. London: Sporting Handbooks, 1957.
351p; illus   BL: 7923.ff.35

> Joined Arsenal as a player in 1919, broke his kneecap in 1925 and was forced to retire. Became the club physiotherapist, then manager and died in 1956 just prior to this publication. An invaluable publication for Arsenal research.

  ☞   Also listed at: B10

Wilkinson, Howard

503   Managing to succeed: my life in football management / Howard Wilkinson with David Walker. Edinburgh: Mainstream, 1992.
174p   ISBN: 1-85158-499-4
     BL: YK.1993.b.11063

> Wilkinson reveals his blueprint for success. His management roles with Notts County, Sheffield Wednesday and Leeds United are all covered.

Williams, Orig

504   Cario'r Ddraig: stori El Bandito / Orig Williams; golygwyd gan Myrddin ap Dafydd. Capel Garmon: Gwasg Carreg Gwalch, 1985.
232p; illus; pbk   ISBN: 0-86381-048-9
     BL: YK.1989.a.2103

> Autobiography of a well-known North Wales character who played football in the fifties and sixties and later became a professional wrestler.

Wilson, Bob

505   Bob Wilson: an autobiography/ Bob Wilson. London: Pelham, 1971.
156p; illus   ISBN: 0-7207-0539-8
     BL: X.629/3804

> Detailed coverage of Arsenal from this Scotland International goalkeeper.

Wilson, Ray

506   My life in soccer / Ray Wilson. London: Pelham, 1969.
160p; illus   ISBN: 0-7207-0233-X

> The England World Cup winning player covers his Huddersfield Town and Everton careers.

Wiltshire, J. M.

507   Play to the whistle! / J. M. Wiltshire in association with H. Roy Wiltshire. London: W. H. Allen, 1948.
127p; illus   BL: 7917.e.31

> The 1947 FA Cup Final referee gives some excellent insights into the role of the official at that time.

Winterbottom, Walter

508   Soccer partnership: Walter Winterbottom and Billy Wright / Bob Ferrier. London: Heinemann, 1960.
230p; illus   ISBN: 1-07-476025-5
     BL: 7925.b.80

> From 1946 these two men were partners in English international football, Winterbottom as manager and Wright as captain. This charts their period together.

  ☞   Also listed at: C516

Wolstenholme, Kenneth

509   Sports special / Kenneth Wolstenholme. London: Stanley Paul, 1956.
160p; illus; index   BL: 7923.k.13

> Ten years on from this work, England's most famous commentator was to achieve icon status as the television voice for England's 1966 World Cup win. He has much to say about early media coverage of the game along with scattered references to the team he truly supports, Bolton Wanderers.

Woodcock, Tony

510   Inside soccer / Tony Woodcock with Peter Ball. London: Macdonald, 1985.
256p; illus; index   ISBN: 0-356-10079-0
     BL: X.622/24096

> Nottingham Forest, Arsenal and FC Köln of Germany feature in the England International's story.

Worthington, Frank

511   One hump or two?: the Frank Worthington story / Frank Worthington with Steve Wells & Nick Cooper; foreword by Bill Maynard. Leicester: ACL Colour Print & Polar, 1994.
256p; illus; pbk

>   *Contains a flicker-vision card-box*
>   ISBN: 1-899538-00-3

'Frankie Wortho' was a cult figure whose career began in 1966 and took in eleven clubs in all. Huddersfield, Leicester, Bolton and Birmingham benefited most from his individualistic skills and flamboyant style. I have not seen the flicker-vision novelty – it should show a wonder goal he once scored for Bolton, but who knows what it might illustrate with Frank around.

Wright, Billy

512 Captain of England / William Ambrose Wright.
London: Stanley Paul, 1950.
192p; illus   BL: 7919.a.22

The career of the England and Wolves legend was
regularly chronicled in a series of works. This first
covers the first half of his playing career with Wolverhampton Wanderers, including wartime games with
Leicester City.

513 Billy Wright's football scrapbook. London: Stanley Paul,
1951.
BL: 7920.cc.37

514 The world's my football pitch / William Ambrose
Wright. London: Stanley Paul, 1953.
176p; illus   BL: 7921.b.51

Includes his travels in the 1950 World Cup.

515 Football is my passport / William Ambrose Wright.
London: Stanley Paul, 1957.
160p; illus   BL: 7923.m.5

Including the 1954 World Cup.

516 Soccer partnership: Walter Winterbottom and Billy
Wright / Bob Ferrier. London: Heinemann, 1960.
230p; illus   BL: 7925.b.80

Wright's relationship with the England manager was a
close one – this covers the period of their time together from 1946, including the 1958 World Cup.

☞ Also listed at: C508

517 One hundred caps and all that / Billy Wright in
collaboration with Bryon Butler. London: Hale, 1962.
191p; illus   BL: X.449/979

Wright was the first player to make 100 appearances
for England. This is a retrospective of his career prior
to his four years of management at Arsenal which
began in the year of publication.

Wright, Ian

518 Inside Wright: my world in pictures / Ian Wright.
London: Hodder & Stoughton, 1994.
96p; illus   ISBN: 0-340-58786-5

Lightweight coverage from the Arsenal and England
star.

Yeats, Ron

519 Soccer with a Mersey beat / Ron Yeats. London:
Pelham, 1966.
111p; illus   BL: X.449/2107

Mostly Liverpool with some reference to earlier days
at Dundee United.

Young, Alex

520 Goals at Goodison / Alex Young. London: Pelham,
1968.
117p; illus   BL: X.449/2944

Mostly Everton, with some early reference to Hearts
from the Scotland International.

Young, George

521 Captain of Scotland / George Lewis Young. London:
Stanley Paul, 1951.
136p; illus   BL: 10857.c.30

Much on Glasgow Rangers from 1946 by the Scotland captain known as 'Corky'.

522 George Young talks football. London: Stanley Paul, 1958.
151p; illus; index   BL: 7923.r.26

After 53 Internationals Young was dropped by Scotland in 1958, a decision which angered him. Soon
afterwards he retired – this is his look back at a
memorable career.

Collective Biographies

523 Scottish Sport's picture gallery: football favourites.
Glasgow: Scottish Sport, 1895-1896.
Only two issues published   BL: 865.a.9(24)

Extremely scarce presentation of characters from
the early years of the game in Scotland.

524 The Sportfolio: portraits and biographies of heroes and
heroines of sport & pastime. London: George Newnes,
1896.
140p; illus; index   BL: Cup.1253.d.18

Includes a number of leading players of the Victorian
era: 38 football subjects in all.

525 Campbell's guide to association football clubs and their
players, 1898-9 / J. and R. Campbell. Southampton: The
authors, 1898.
144p   BL: D

526 The football who's who, and guide to association clubs
and players. London: C. Arthur Pearson, 1901-1903.
BL: P.P.2489.wfd

Who's who publications generally provide thumbnail
sketches or pen pictures of the day. These scarce examples from the beginning of this century were
recently reprinted in facsimile by the AFS.

527 Football who's who / H. R. Brown. 1908.

528 Captains of football / C. E. Wodehouse-Temple and
A. E. Knight. London: Amalgamated Press, 1921.
110p

> Two pages are devoted to each captain: a full page
> photograph on the left and a biographical commen-
> tary with facsimile signature on the right. In all 52
> captains are covered.

529 Sportsfun who's who 1922.
16p; pbk

> *Subsequently published in facsimile by AFS*

530 Sports budget who's who 1925.
39p; pbk

> *Subsequently published in facsimile by AFS*

531 Athletic News who's who in the Football League.
Manchester: Athletic News, 1927-   BL: P.P.2489.whk

532 Topical Times 100 footballers 1930. D. C. Thomson,
1930.
64p; pbk

> *Subsequently published in facsimile by AFS*

533 Topical Times new who's who of 2,000 football stars.
D.C. Thomson, 1933.
40p; pbk

> *Subsequently published in facsimile by AFS*

534 Who's who in football: every famous player's career at a
glance. London: Amalgamated Press, 1934.
94p

> *Subsequently published in facsimile by AFS*

BL: 7916.dd.7

535 The football who's who: a reference work of careers and
records of past and present players and officials of
league clubs and a companion volume to 'The football
encyclopaedia' / edited by Frank Johnston. London:
Associated Sporting Press, 1935.
320p; illus   BL: YA.1994.a.20120

> A particularly good and rather more substantial ex-
> ample of the who's who format than had previously
> appeared. Mr G. Wagstaffe Simmons states in his
> preface that 'here is the book for which votaries of
> soccer have been waiting'. Includes 260 head and
> shoulders portraits and 400 facsimile autographs.
> Excellent source of reference.

> ☞ See also: J179

536 Football Weekly book of 650 football stars. London:
Football Weekly, 1936.
36p; pbk

> *Subsequently published in facsimile by AFS*

THE FOOTBALL WHO'S WHO

*A Reference Work of Careers and Records of Past
and Present Players and Officials of League
Clubs and a Companion Volume to
"The Football Encyclopaedia"*

Edited by
FRANK JOHNSTON
Sports Editor of *The Leader*

With a Preface by
G. WAGSTAFFE SIMMONS
*The prominent Sporting Journalist and
Director of Tottenham Hotspur F.C.*

LONDON : ASSOCIATED SPORTING PRESS Lᵀᴰ.
166 FLEET STREET, E.C.4.

537 1,500 football stars and all about them. D. C. Thomson,
1938.
36p; pbk

> *Subsequently published in facsimile by AFS*

538 Football stars of today. Manchester, 1948.

> *Continued as: The Hotspur book of football stars*

BL: P.P.2489.wkf

> ☞ See also: C542

539 The boy's book of football teams and players. London:
Playfair Books, 1949.   BL: 7920.de.11

540 Football favourites and personalities: portraits and action
studies. Southport: Provincial Sports, 1949.
6 pts; illus; pbk   BL: 7917.bbb.49

541 Football is my goal / Sam Bartram, Johnny Carey, Ron
Burgess, Wilfred Mannion, Tom Finney, Matt Busby;
edited and introduced by Reginald Moore. London:
Phoenix House, 1949.
128p; illus   BL: 7920.aaa.51

542 The Hotspur book of football stars. Manchester, 1949-

> *Continues: Football stars of today*   BL: P.P.2489.wkf

> ☞ See also: C538

543 More stars of football / edited by D. Cole; illustrated by
Tom Kerr. London: Perry Colour Books, 1949.
12p; pbk
(Signature series)   BL: W.P.2686/3

544 Soccer snapshots. Southport: Provincial Sports, 1949-
chiefly illus; pbk

545 Wickets, tries and goals: reviews of play and players in
modern cricket, rugby and soccer / by John Arlott,
Wilfred Wooller, Maurice Edelston. London: Sampson
Low, Marston, 1949.
x, 236p   BL: 7917.f.22
Football shares the stage with rugby and cricket; interesting pieces on several footballers are included.

546 Football favourites annual. Southport: Provincial Sports,
1950-1952.   BL: P.P.2489.wkx

547 Football favourites treasure book of soccer. Southport:
Provincial Sports, 1950.
60p; illus   BL: 7919.b.64

548 Tommy Lawton's all star football book. London:
Sampson Low, Marston, 1950.
188p; illus   BL: 7920.bb.7

549 The Bert Williams all star football book. London:
Sampson Low, Marston, 1951.
155p; illus   BL: 7919.ee.31
The Walsall, Wolves and England goalkeeper heads a
selection of biographical contributions from some of
his leading contemporaries.

550 Football favourites. New series. Southport: Provincial
Sports, 1951-1953.
6 pts; illus; pbk   BL: 7917.bbb.49a

551 Footballer's who's who: 1,400 biographies of present day
players / edited by Brian Glanville. London: Ettrick,
1951.
139p   BL: 7921.dd.26
Excellent who's who covering players from the forties
and fifties – 1,400 subjects are included, making this
an essential reference work for all students of the
period.

552 My greatest game / Ralph Leslie Finn; with
contributions by Ted Ditchburn and others. London:
Saturn, 1951.
144p; illus   BL: 7920.f.49
The contributors are Ted Ditchburn, Eddie Hapgood,
Alf Ramsey, Joe Mercer, Stan Cullis, Ron Burgess,
Tom Finney, Raich Carter, Roy Bentley, Len Shackle-
ton, Stanley Mortensen, Bill Murray and Arthur Ellis.

553 Soccer parade / edited by M. Smith. London: Odhams,
1951.
95p; illus   BL: 7920.f.40

554 Stars of soccer / edited by Cedric Day. Windsor?: The
author, 1952-   BL: W.P.A.212

555 Empire News footballer's who's who. Manchester:
Kemsley Newspapers, 1954-   BL: P.P.2489.wle

556 British footballers / Trevor Hilton. First series. London:
Beverley Books, 1957.
74p; illus
(Beverley sportslives; no. 2)   BL: W.P.14930/2

557 Masters of soccer / Maurice Edelston and Terence
Delaney. London: Naldrett, 1960.
209p; illus   BL: 7925.l.12
Appreciations of twenty leading players from the
1940s and 1950s.

558 The all stars football book. Manchester, 1961-
                                                     BL: P.P.8007.d

559 Soccer top ten / Ivan Sharpe. London: Stanley Paul, 1962.
130p   BL: X.449/45
The author's selection of his 'best players in each position' from the entire history of the game.
Guaranteed to provoke argument.

560 Soccer who's who / compiled by M. Golesworthy.
London: Hale, 1964.
191p; illus   BL: 07926.bb.4
Excellent updated coverage. If used in conjunction
with Frank Johnston from 1935 and Brian Glanville
from 1951, rounded coverage of thirty years of football personalities will be assured.

561 Football champions. London: Purnell, 1965-
Published annually   BL: X.445/51

562 The pro's / Kenneth Wolstenholme. London: Leslie
Frewin, 1968.
223p; illus
BL: X.449/3293
Studies of the world's top players including many
short biographies on the leading continental names.

563 Soccer – the great ones: studies of eight great football
players / editor, John Arlott. London: Pelham, 1968.
160p; illus   ISBN: 0-11-215006-3
                                                     BL: X.449/3338
Arlott selects eight renowned writers to contribute a
piece on a different player. The players chosen are:
Alex James, Tommy Lawton, Stanley Matthews, John
Charles, Duncan Edwards, Danny Blanchflower,
James Woodburn and John Thomson.

564 Champions of soccer / Kenneth Wheeler. London:
Pelham, 1969.
143p; illus   SBN: 7207-0272-0
                                                     BL: X.449/3858
21 different players are discussed.

565 The Clipper annual of who's who in football. London:
Clipper Press, 1969-
Cover title: Who's who in football

566 Soccer: stars of today / edited by Reg Hayter. London: Pelham, 1970.
128p; illus   SBN: 7207-0379-4
                                               BL: X.629/2811

   Chapters on nine great players of the sixties.

567 Soccer who's who: the what, when, where, how and why of football / edited by Harry Brown. London: Arthur Barker, 1970.
157p; illus, coats of arms; pbk   SBN: 213-00170-5
                                               BL: P.445/276

   Interesting miscellany of football facts and trivia with much on the players themselves.

568 Centre-forwards: the great ones / Laurie Mumford. London: Pelham, 1971.
125p; illus
(The great ones series)   ISBN: 0-7207-0362-X
                                               BL: X.629/3888

   Probably the most glamorous position in the game – the studies include Dixie Dean and Ted Drake amongst others.

569 Football stars. Woking: Lutterworth Press, 1971.
32p; chiefly illus; pbk   ISBN: 0-7188-1887-3

570 The team makers: a gallery of the great soccer managers / Peter Morris. London: Pelham, 1971.
160p; illus   ISBN: 0-7207-0427-8
                               BL: X.629/3643

   His selection of the 14 greatest managers, including 'Major' Frank Buckley.

571 The football managers / Tony Pawson. London: Eyre Methuen, 1973.
224p; illus   ISBN 0-413-30370-5
                               BL: X.629/5888

572 All time greats / Phil Soar and Martin Tyler. London: Marshall Cavendish, 1974.
160p

   Detailed appreciations of 67 of the world's greatest players including Lev Yashin, Alfredo di Stefano and Günter Netzer.

573 Who's who in football. Watford: Barnes, Newberry, 1974.
127p; illus   ISBN: 0-903776-01-4

   Excellent coverage of the seventies – check out those hairstyles!

574 Cewri'r b'el-droed yng Nghymru / Geraint H. Jenkins. Llandysul: Gwasg Gomer, 1977.
137p; illus

   Bibliography: p135-137   ISBN: 0-85088-409-8
                                   BL: X.629/11716

   Comprises biographies of leading Welsh players.

575 Who's who of Football League Division One / edited by Peter Oakes & Graham Spiers. Ipswich: Studio Publications, 1977.
144p; illus
(Who's who of sport series)
       ISBN: 0-904584-16-X (cased) • ISBN 0-904584-06-2 (pbk)
                                               BL: X.611/7968

   Comprehensive coverage of the late 1970s.

576 The goalscorers: from Bloomer to Keegan / Tony Pawson; with a foreword by Sir Harold Thompson. London: Cassell, 1978.
xvi, 240p; illus; index   ISBN: 0-304-29855-7
                                      BL: X.629/11907

   Appreciations of the gifted scorers from all eras of the game.

577 Great soccer stars / Jimmy Hill. London: Hamlyn, 1978.
176p; illus   ISBN: 0-600-38334-2
                               BL: X.620/18259

   Appreciations of 100 players chosen from the world-wide football scene from Allchurch to Zoff.

578 The Puffin book of footballers / Brian Glanville. Harmondsworth: Puffin, 1978.
153p; illus; pbk   ISBN: 0-14-030996-9
                               BL: X.619/18577

579 Soccer choice / Bryon Butler and Ron Greenwood. London: Pelham, 1979.
176p; illus   ISBN: 0-7207-1184-3
                               BL: X.629/17008

   The authors' selection of the best players from the post-war era, with a chapter on each position. For the record, their final team selection was Banks, Ramsey, Franklin, Moore, Byrne, Blanchflower, Doherty, Finney, Keegan, Lawton, Best.

580 Famous names in soccer / Jim Bebbington. Hove: Wayland, 1980.
48p; illus; index
   Bibliography: p47   ISBN: 0-85340-790-8
                               BL: X.622/9419

581 Rothmans Football League players records: the complete A-Z 1946-1981 / compiled by Barry J. Hugman; foreword by BBC's John Motson. Aylesbury: Rothmans Publications, 1981.
x, 500p; illus   ISBN: 0-907574-08-4
                               BL: X.622/12039

   This is certainly a landmark publication by Barry Hugman periodically updated in subsequent years. It gives full career records for every single league player from 1946, stirring many memories for the casual reader whilst proving an invaluable source of accurate information for the journalist or statistician.

   ☞ See also: C588, C596, C608

582 Black pearls of soccer / Al Hamilton; foreword by
Jimmy Greaves. London: Harrap, 1982.
72p; illus; index; pbk   ISBN: 0-245-53881-X
   Studies of leading black players.

583 Brian Glanville's book of footballers. Harmondsworth:
Puffin, 1982.
167p; illus; pbk   ISBN: 0-14-031508-X
                                      BL: X.629/17686

584 Black magic: England's black footballers / Brian
Woolnough. London: Pelham, 1983.
186p; illus; index; pbk   ISBN: 0-7207-1476-1
                                      BL: X.629/22199

   *The inclusion of black players in increasing numbers
   throughout the seventies and eighties undoubtedly
   added a new dimension to the game. This is a study
   of the leading names and their influence.*

585 English cricketer-footballers 1888-1939 / Gordon B.
Andrews. London?: Datasport, 1983.
21p; pbk
   *A good checklist for the pre-war years – a useful ref-
   erence for researchers of this 'double breed'.*

   ☞ See also: C589

586 From schoolboy to superstar / Patrick Barclay.
Harmondsworth: Puffin, 1983.
84p; illus; pbk   ISBN: 0-14-031668-X
                                      BL: X.629/22466

   *Interviews with famous players telling how they made
   the step up to the highest level.*

587 Soccer superstars / edited by Stevie Coppell. Bristol:
Purnell, 1983.
61p; illus
   For children   ISBN: 0-86030-413-2

588 Canon League football players: records 1946-1984 /
compiled by Barry J. Hugman. Feltham: Newnes, 1984.
530p; illus   ISBN: 0-600-37318-5
                                      BL: YK.1987.b.1977

   Update of an essential work.

   ☞ See also: C581, C596, C608

589 Datasport English cricketer-footballers 1946-1983 /
Gordon B. Andrews. London?: Datasport, 1984.
   *The second part of this useful checklist covering the
   post-war years.*

   ☞ See also: C585

590 Guinness who's who in soccer / Jack Rollin. Enfield:
Guinness Superlatives, 1984.
305p; pbk   ISBN: 0-85112-418-6
                                      BL: X.629/24048

   *Straightforward biographical and career details of
   current players – the perfect pre-match companion
   for those wishing to be well-informed. Subsequently*

*updated on a regular basis by one of the true stal-
warts of the football publishing world.*

   ☞ Subsequent ed. C593

591 Taking sides: the ten greatest football teams / Jimmy
Greaves with Norman Giller. London: Sidgwick &
Jackson, 1984.
212p; illus
   ISBN: 0-283-99127-5 (cased) • ISBN: 0-283-99128-3 (pbk)
                                      BL: X.629/25265

   *The authors' selections of their best ever sides, with
   a concentration on the individuals that made them up.*

592 Through open doors: football league chairmen reveal
their secrets to Brian Radford. London: Harrap, 1984.
126p; illus; pbk   ISBN: 0-245-54221-3
                                      BL: X.622/21399

   *Chairmen are renowned for talking a lot but rarely
   commit themselves to print. This unusual work offers
   a useful insight into a much maligned but difficult role.*

593 Guinness who's who in soccer / Jack Rollin. Completely
rev. and updated. Enfield: Guinness Superlatives, 1986.
353p; pbk   ISBN: 0-85112-464-X
                                      BL: YC.1986.a.5061

   ☞ Previous ed. C590; subsequent ed. C600

594 Where are they now?: an A-Z of every player who
appeared in the Scottish League from 1975-76 to
1985-86 / Norman Colvin. 1986.
48p; pbk
   *A thorough work of reference but not, as the title
   might suggest, telling us that Sandy McTavish is now
   a financial adviser in the Orkney Islands – more a
   case of presenting career records and moves whilst
   still active in the game. Similar to Barry Hugman's
   1981 publication covering the English game, though
   not as extensive in the number of years covered.*

595 The soccer dragons / Ceri Stennett. Cardiff: The author,
1987.
   Studies of 21 great Welsh footballers from all periods.

596 Football League players: records 1946-1988 / compiled
and edited by Barry J. Hugman. London: Arena, 1988.
576p; illus   ISBN: 1-85443-020-3
                                      BL: YK.1989.b.5081

   ☞ See also: C581, C588, C608

597 Football stars / Rick Ludlam; edited by Jeremy Brown.
Falmouth: Fax-Pax, 1988.
72p; illus; loose-leaf
   For children   ISBN: 1-87314-708-2

598 Trevor Brooking's 100 great British footballers / Trevor
Brooking. London: Macdonald / Queen Anne, 1988.
224p; illus   ISBN: 0-356-14864-5
                                      BL: YK.1989.b.3832

   A page or so on each of his personal selections.

599   The football managers / Johnny Rogan. London: Queen
      Anne, 1989.
      288p; illus   ISBN: 0-356-15902-7
                                                    BL: YK.1990.a.6973

      *A selection of the best managers rather than a com-
      prehensive study of the entire breed; ten in all,
      including Matt Busby, Bill Nicholson, Alf Ramsey, Bill
      Shankly, Don Revie, Jock Stein, Brian Clough, Bobby
      Robson, Bob Paisley and Graham Taylor.*

600   Guinness soccer who's who / Jack Rollin. 3rd ed.
      Enfield: Guinness Superlatives, 1989.
      384p; pbk   ISBN: 0-85112-369-4

      ☞ Previous ed. C593; subsequent ed. C603

601   Private lives. London: Hippo in association with Match,
      1989.
      47p; illus; pbk   ISBN: 0-590-76111-0
                                                    BL: YK.1990.b.6774

      *Favourite food, best film, first car . . . ? Twenty-two of
      today's football stars answer the questions you've
      always wanted to ask. In a hundred years time it
      might well be a valuable social document!*

602   You've got to be crazy: Bob Wilson on goalkeepers and
      goalkeeping. London: Arthur Barker, 1989.
      x, 286p; illus; index

      Bibliography: p279   ISBN: 0-213-16971-1
                                                    BL: YK.1990.b.5159

      *It is often said that goalkeepers are a breed apart.
      Wilson studies the species with specific reference to
      great goalkeepers throughout history.*

603   Guinness soccer who's who / Jack Rollin. 4th ed.
      Enfield: Guinness Superlatives, 1990.
      384p; pbk   ISBN: 0-85112-930-7
                                                    BL: YK.1992.a.883

      ☞ Previous ed. C600; subsequent ed. C605

604   The terrible trio / Brian Scott. Edinburgh: Sportsprint,
      1990.
      ix, 107p; illus; index; pbk   ISBN: 0-85976-306-4
                                                    BL: YK.1991.b.6167

      *Alfie Conn, Willie Bauld and Jimmy Wardhaugh struck
      terror into opposition defences during the fifties,
      scoring almost 1,000 goals between them for Hearts.*

605   Guinness soccer who's who / Jack Rollin. 5th ed.
      Enfield: Guinness Superlatives, 1991.
      384p; pbk   ISBN: 0-85112-965-X

      ☞ Previous ed. C603; subsequent ed. C609

606   The match of my life / edited by Bob Holmes. London:
      Kingswood, 1991.
      xii, 259p; illus; pbk   ISBN: 0-413-66260-8
                                                    BL: YK.1993.a.6753

      Selected personalities choose their best ever game.

      ☞ Subsequent ed. C612

607   FA Carling Premiership: the players: a complete guide to
      every player. Taunton: Tony Williams Publications, 1992-
      illus

      Published annually   ISSN: 1356-8949

608   Football League players: 1945-92 / edited by B. J.
      Hugman. Taunton: Tony Williams Publications, 1992.
      624p; illus   ISBN: 1-869833-20-1

      *Ever expanding and extremely comprehensive; effec-
      tively updates and supercedes Hugman's previous
      editions.*

609   Guinness soccer who's who / Jack Rollin. 6th ed.
      Enfield: Guinness, 1992.
      400p; pbk   ISBN: 0-85112-540-9
                                                    BL: YK.1993.a.1811

      ☞ Previous ed. C605; subsequent ed. C613

610   The Breedon book of football managers / Dennis
      Turner and Alex White. Derby: Breedon Books, 1993.
      256p; illus   ISBN: 1-873626-32-0
                                                    BL: YK.1994.b.12663

      *A superb reference book for all researchers needing
      details of all the personalities who have managed in
      the Football League. Does not include those who have
      managed only in Scotland, Wales, Ireland or overseas.*

611   Don't shoot the manager / Jimmy Greaves and Norman
      Giller. London: Boxtree, 1993.
      256p; pbk   ISBN: 1-85283-414-5

      *The job of England manager can be a thankless task.
      The authors here study all those brave enough to
      take on the role, with a touch of sympathy for the
      less successful.*

612   Fifty football stars describe my greatest game / edited by
      Bob Holmes. Edinburgh: Mainstream, 1993.
      256p; illus; pbk
                                                    ISBN: 1-85158-579-6
                                                    BL: YK.1994.a.5936

      ☞ Previous ed. C606

613   Guinness soccer who's who / Jack Rollin. 7th ed.
      Enfield: Guinness, 1993.
      400p; pbk   ISBN: 0-85112-718-5

      ☞ Previous ed. C609; subsequent ed. C618

614   Premier and Football League players / edited by Barry J.
      Hugman. Taunton: T. Williams Publications, 1993.
      illus; pbk   ISBN: 1-869833-56-2

      *All the current players thoroughly documented in
      typically efficient 'Hugmanesque' fashion.*

615   Premier League, the players 1994 / edited by Barry J.
      Hugman. Taunton: T. Williams Publications, 1993.
      illus; pbk   ISBN: 1-869833-46-5

616 Who's who of the Football League 1888-1915 / Ray
Spiller. Basildon: Association of Football Statisticians,
1993-

The first issue lists all players whose surnames begin
with A and who played in the Football League between
1888 and 1915. Then on to B, etc. progressing into a
full series until hopefully it produces a full listing of
every single player for the period. This is typical of the
painstaking research undertaken by the AFS whose
members are adept at rising to the challenge of even
the most mind boggling tasks.

617 Who's who of the Football League 1919-1939 / Ray
Spiller. Basildon: Association of Football Statisticians,
1993-

A similar treatment to the one above, this time covering the inter-war years. This helps fill a vital gap
not covered by Hugman's excellent publications whose
work is comprehensive only for the post-war years —
at least for the moment.

618 Guinness soccer who's who / Jack Rollin. 8th ed.
Enfield: Guinness, 1994.
400p; pbk   ISBN: 0-85112-777-0

Valuable quick reference source giving career and personal details of all current Premier League and
Football League players — truly the commentators'
and journalists' faithful friend.

☞ Previous ed. C613

619 200 superstars of world football / edited by J. Govaerts.
West Drayton: COMAG, 1994.
4 vols; illus; pbk

620 Non-league players fact file / Steve Whitney.

621 Non-league footballers who's who / edited by Tony
Williams.

622 Where are they now?: life after football / Andrew
Pringle. Southampton: Runnymede, 1995.
224p; illus   ISBN: 0-9525428-0-3

Regional Biographies

623 Great masters of Scottish football / Hugh Baird Taylor.
London: Stanley Paul, 1967.
144p   BL: X.449/2782

Appreciations of Alex James, Billy Steel, Gordon
Smith, John Thomson, Hughie Gallacher, Jimmy Ma-
son, Alan Morton, Patsy Gallagher, Jim Baxter, Denis
Law and George Young.

624 The book of Irish goalscorers / Seán Ryan and Stephen
Burke. Dublin: Irish Soccer Co-op, 1987.
256p; illus; pbk

625 Yorkshire soccer heroes / Keith Farnsworth. Lancaster:
Dalesman, 1988.
72p; illus; pbk

Bibliography: p71-72   ISBN: 0-85206-958-8
                                         BL: YK.1989.a.5174

Yorkshire has produced many great players — this is
a selection of the best.

626 Lancashire footballing greats 1946-1991: a collection of
100 biographies of players who have given splendid
service to Lancashire football / Dean Hayes.
Manchester: Didsbury, 1991.
207p; illus; pbk   ISBN: 1-872325-03-3
                                         BL: YK.1993.a.13963

Interesting that the equivalent Yorkshire publication
has only 72 pages.

UK Cup

Competitions

THERE ARE CERTAIN DAYS IN THE CALENDAR when a football supporter would prefer not to work, go on holiday, get married or indeed do anything which might hinder attendance at the match. Cup days are just such days, when the simple utterance of the words 'It's the Cup' speak volumes to those who know and care whilst provoking profound puzzlement in those who don't. 'Is it something special?' they ask, looking forward to the unbounded joys of an afternoon's shopping or DIY. One never troubles to give more than a cursory answer, for how is it possible to explain to a non-believer the romance, drama, agony and ecstasy that the occasion might generate? There is certainly a finality about any knockout competition which heightens the tension and can leave even the greatest of sides hoping forlornly for a second chance which they know will never come.

When we speak of 'the cup' in England, it is generally the Football Association Challenge Cup, the FA Cup, to which we refer, for it is indeed the most famous of them all and not surprisingly dominates the available literature. For the researcher wishing to study the competition right from its inception in 1871-72, when only fifteen clubs entered, there are some excellent sources. A good starting point would be Geoffrey Green's *Official History of the FA Cup* [D6] covering the years from 1872 to 1949. It is particularly strong on the historical background to the competition and the early years prior to 1923 before the finals were played at Wembley Stadium, a venue now synonymous with the Cup Final. Green's book is regarded as a classic study from one of the great football writers and has been the standard reference work for many of the more recent publications on the same subject. A good follow up to this work is David Prole's *Cup Final Story* [D11] covering the years 1946 to 1965, and thereafter Tony Pawson's *100 Years of the FA Cup: the Official Centenary History* [D16] gives a detailed overview of the first one hundred years.

A number of fully updated histories appeared in 1981 to celebrate the one hundredth FA Cup Final, the most comprehensive of these being the official Football Association publication by David Barber, *We Won the Cup: a Celebration for the 100th FA Cup Final,* [D23]. Worthy of particular mention though is Martin Tyler's *Cup Final Extra* [D20], interesting for its novel approach to the subject. It studies the one hundred finals largely through facsimiles of contemporary newspaper reports and it is possible in a volume such as this to uncover snippets of useful information which a more serious historical study might not touch upon. It also includes colour reproductions of many of the Final programme covers so prized by collectors.

Notwithstanding the availability of the earlier material, such is the quality of recently published works that the research for a general study of the FA Cup might readily be satisfied by consulting one single volume. Mike Collett's *Guinness Record of the FA Cup* [D30] is a particularly strong example while the post-war period is admirably covered by Ivan Ponting [D29].

Thoughts of the Cup inevitably prompt thoughts of 'giantkillers' and it is no surprise to find that a number of books on this topic have appeared. In 1993-94 it was Kidderminster Harriers who became, for a short and glorious time, a household name. Next season it will be someone else and 'Kiddy' will be forgotten by all but the faithful. It is to the memory of such football cavaliers that Bryon Butler's *The Giant Killers* [D24] is addressed and, in similar vein, Goodall's *FA Cup Non-League Giant-killers* [D25]. Both are very worthwhile treatments of the phenomenon of the triumphant underdog which so appeals to the 'famous for fifteen minutes' psyche of the British public.

Aside from the romantic notions of the Cup, those in search of solid statistical information will find the publications by James Wright [D39] and Tony Brown [D41] of great value whilst Ray Spiller, of the Association of Football Statisticians, has been responsible for exhaustive research, especially of the early years [D33-37]. His statistical analysis not only includes all the dates and results but also the full line-ups and scorers along with results for all the qualifying games. Certainly any researcher requiring accurate factual information will find the appropriate publications of the AFS a cast-iron source.

Let it not be thought that Scotland, Ireland and Wales do not have their cups. Indeed they do, but the literary coverage, certainly of the latter two, is rather more sketchy. For the early history of the Scottish Cup the 1946 publication by Chalmers Anderson [D42] is short but informative. Hugh Keevin's *100 Cups* [D43] is an in-depth study bringing the story into more recent times. As for hard facts, the Scottish

Cup has been particularly well covered statistically by the work of the Scottish Non-League Review and the Association of Football Statisticians. Works by John Byrne [D46], Keith Anderson [D45], Tom O'Rourke [D47-48] and Stewart Davidson [D49] have not only covered the main Cup itself but also the early qualifying stages. As for Ireland, the *Gillette Book of the FAI Cup* [D50] is comprehensive to 1985 whilst Wales is admirably served by the recent work of Ian Garland [D52].

It is not only the professionals who have their cups and dramas – the non-league and amateur sides do battle with each other too. Bob Barton, a veritable guru of the lower echelons of the game, has produced an excellent survey of the Amateur Cup [D64] along with a general history of non-league cup football [D66].

The major clubs also involve themselves in other cup competitions. The League Cups in England and Scotland, under their various sponsorship guises, are true knock out contests which nonetheless have never been taken fully to the hearts of the football public and players alike. Exciting as they are, they have assumed an air of diminished importance which is reflected in the relative dearth of literary coverage. For the most part, generalist writers have ignored the competitions and it has been left to the statisticians to make efforts to restore some balance. Ray Spiller is again at the forefront with a range of studies covering the English [D53-57] and Scottish [D59-63] League Cups whilst Tony Brown's use of the word 'ultimate' in his 1992 publication [D58] cannot truly be argued with, such is the detailed coverage.

In summary then, the available literature within the 'UK Cup Competitions' is more than adequate; whilst there is always more to write as the subsequent dramas unfold, the development of the coverage for future years is likely to concentrate on comprehensive updating rather than on further original research. One thing is for sure; sports journalists will never be short of material in this field, and if on occasion they get carried away, there's a more than reasonable excuse for such excesses – what do we expect? It's the Cup!

UK Cup Competitions ~ Contents

Football Association Cup

✳ Histories

1   Football Association Cup winners from 1883 to 1905.
London: Football Association, 1906
1 sheet; chiefly illus   BL: Mic.A.7129(8) (microfilm copy)

Very scarce early item.

2   The Football Association's English Cup Competition
Final to be played at the Empire Stadium (Wembley) on
April 28, 1923 between Bolton Wanderers and West
Ham United: programme & souvenir. London: W. H.
Smith, 1923.   BL: 7913.c.61

*Whilst this bibliography excludes football programmes
an exception has been made for this, the programme
from the very first Wembley final. This is a rare item
keenly prized by collectors.*

☞ *Also listed at: B848*

3   50 years of FA Cup finals 1883-1932 / edited by D.
MacKenzie. London: Wyman, 1932.
64p; illus; pbk

*Each of the large pages includes a team photograph
of every FA Cup winner from 1883 to 1932 together
with a description of the final.*

☞ *See also: D27*

4   All the FA Cup finals / Roland Allen. London: Goulden,
1947.
112p; illus

*Perceptive and sometimes amusing overviews of each
of the finals played at Wembley excluding the finals
from 1872 to 1922, thereby rendering the title rather
misleading. Researchers may find lesser known material here, not least the cartoons by Tom Webster
especially drawn for the book. Also includes accounts
of the wartime finals.*

5   The story of the FA Cup. Windsor: W. D. S., 1947-1950.
4 parts; illus   BL: 7919.ee.2

Concentrates particularly on the years 1947-1950.

6   The official history of the FA Cup / Geoffrey Green.
London: Naldrett Press, 1949.
256p; illus   BL: 7919.c.48

*All students of the subject should consult this clas-
sic and painstakingly researched work. It traces the
growth of the FA Cup competition from its foundation in 1871/72 and is particularly strong on the early
history, allocating over a hundred pages to the pre-
Wembley finals. Most of the later serious histories
are based firmly on Green's initial narrative.*

☞ *See also: D7; subsequent ed. D10*

7   The Cup: the official pictorial record of the FA's
Challenge Cup. London: Naldrett Press, 1949.
64p; illus

*Condensed from: The official history of the FA Cup /
Geoffrey Green*
                                   BL: 7917.b.55

Much truncated version of Green's official history.

☞ *See also: D6, D10*

8   Focus on the FA Cup / Denis Foster. London:
Background Books, 1950.
24p; pbk   BL: 7919.b.50

9   Day & Mason FA Cup annual. Windsor: Day & Mason,
1951-   BL: P.P.2489.wkz

10 The official history of the FA Cup / Geoffrey Green.
New and enlarged ed. London: Heinemann, 1960.
249p   BL: 7925.b.83

Green's study is here updated to 1960.

☞ *Previous ed. D6*

11 Cup Final story, 1946-1965 / David Robert Prole.
London: Hale, 1966.
176p; illus   BL: X.449/1759

*Comprehensive coverage of the post-war years with a
chapter devoted to each of twenty finals.*

12 London's Cup Final, 1967: how Chelsea and Spurs
reached Wembley / Ralph Leslie Finn. London: Hale,
1967.
188p; illus   BL: X.449/2830

*All-London affairs in the Cup Final are anathema to
the football public at large, but for the participating
teams nothing could be better, as illustrated here by
no less than 188 pages charting the route to the final for Chelsea and Spurs. Of much interest to their
club historians. For the record, the headline of the
Sunday Telegraph on 21 May 1967 read: 'Arrogant
and disdainful . . . Spurs saunter to victory'. The
score was 2-1.*

☞ *Also listed at: B197, B791*

13 The story of the 1969 FA Cup. London: Clipper Press,
1969.
34p; chiefly illus; pbk   ISBN: 0-85108-003-0

14 The FA Cup Final 1970: Chelsea v Leeds Utd / edited
by Ken Jones. London: Hamlyn and IPC Newspapers,
1970.
31p; illus; pbk
(A Daily Mirror special)   BL: X.615/194

Special commemorative publication for one of the
most memorable finals of the modern era, the first
Wembley draw. Chelsea won the replay at Old Trafford
by two goals to one.

15 FA Cup centenary gift book for boys 1872-1972 /
Kenneth Wolstenholme. Manchester: World
Distributors, 1972.
96p; illus

This study, written by one of our foremost commentators, is aimed at the younger element.

16 100 years of the FA Cup: the official centenary history /
Tony Pawson. London: Heinemann, 1972.
ix, 299p; illus

ISBN: 0-330-23274-6
BL: X.611/3108

The centenary year prompted a number of publications – this is a comprehensive study of all aspects
of the competition to 1972.

17 Journey to Wembley: the story of the 1976-77 FA Cup
competition and Liverpool's bid for the treble: a football
odyssey from Tividale to Wembley / Brian James.
London: Marshall Cavendish, 1977.
225p; illus
ISBN: 0-85685-307-0 (cased) • ISBN: 0-85685-321-6 (pbk)
BL: X.620/17548

Possibly the longest title in this bibliography illustrating in its own way that the journey to Wembley is
indeed a long one, starting whilst the leading clubs
are still enjoying their summer holidays. An interesting evocation of the Cup in one specific year.

☞ Also listed at: B390

18 FA Cup. London: Harrington Kilbride & Partners,
1980?-
illus
Published annually   ISSN: 0958-2207
BL: ZK.9.b.2935

19 The official FA Cup review 1980 / A. Williams.
Taunton: T. Williams Publications, 1980.
94p

Concentrates largely on the year in question when
Trevor Brooking headed the winner in West Ham's 1-0
win over Arsenal.

A Cup-tie scene of ninety years ago as depicted by Reg Carter

20   Cup Final extra! / Martin Tyler. London: Hamlyn, 1981.
168p; illus   ISBN: 0-600-34661-7
     BL: X.622/10332

A most unusual treatment strong on visual content and a good source of anecdotal material. Each of the one hundred finals to this date is covered through facsimile newspaper reports of the day. Also includes many colour reproductions of programme covers.

21   Cup magic / David Miller. London: Sidgwick & Jackson, 1981.
220p; pbk
     Bibliography: p220   ISBN: 0-283-98754-5
     BL: X.629/15341

An account of 24 great cup matches. Includes examples from the FA Cup but also covers the World Cup, European Cup, League Cup and others.

22   100 FA Cups: the history of soccer's greatest club competition. London: Mirror Books, 1981.
28p; illus; pbk
     At head of title: Soccer Mirror   ISBN: 0-85939-253-8
     BL: L.45/1068

Lightweight publication covering the history of the one hundred Cup Finals to this date. The discrepancy between this date and the centenary celebrations is accounted for by missing out the 'unofficial' wartime finals.

23   We won the Cup: a celebration for the 100th FA Cup Final / David Barber. London: Pan in association with the Football Association, 1981.
203p; illus; pbk
     ISBN: 0-330-26401-X
     BL: X.629/15702

A huge collection of statistics and a report on each of the first ninety-nine finals.

24   The giant killers / Bryon Butler. London: Pelham, 1982.
184p; illus   ISBN: 0-7207-1371-4
     BL: X.629/17453

'David and Goliath' encounters as the tabloids will insist on calling them, are a popular feature of the FA Cup. This covers the most famous examples, from Darwen in 1879 to Exeter in 1982.

25   Goodall's FA Cup non-league giant-killers annual: 1945-1982 / edited by G. R. (Bill) Goodall. London: Goodall, 1982.
352p; illus; pbk
     ISBN: 0-907579-01-9
     BL: X.629/20553

The Cup offers the rare opportunity for lowly non-league teams to compete with the better known sides. Over the years this has resulted in many unexpected scorelines in favour of the minnows much to the delight of the footballing fraternity at large. This publication covers the non-league heroics of the post-war era; 40 of the best examples are included along with club histories of the sides concerned.

26   Up for the Cup. London: Statmill, 1986-
illus
     Published annually   BL: ZC.9.b.318

27   50 years of FA Cup Finals 1883-1932. Cleethorpes: Soccer Book Publishing, 1991.
64p; illus; pbk
(A classic reprint)
     Facsimile of ed. published 1932   ISBN: 0-947808-15-9
     BL: YK.1991.b.5890

Covers all the finals for the stated period.

☞   See also: D3

A
Classic
REPRINT

50 YEARS
OF
F.A. CUP FINALS

1883 — 1932

Blackburn   **Newcastle**
Olympic   **United**

ORIGINAL EDITION
PUBLISHED 1932

28   From casuals to cup-winners: a journey through the FA Cup 1988-89 / Brian Spurrell. London: Eagle Eye, 1991?
51p; illus; pbk   BL: YK.1992.b.7758

29   The FA Cup: a post-war history / Ivan Ponting; edited by Steve Small. Taunton: T. Williams Publications, 1993.
300p; illus   ISBN: 1-869833-36-8
     Very comprehensive coverage of the post-war era.

30   The Guinness record of the FA Cup / Mike Collett. Enfield: Guinness, 1993.
xiii, 625p; illus; index; pbk
     Includes bibliography   ISBN: 0-85112-538-7
     BL: YK.1994.b.1284

Another extremely thorough treatment.

31   The history of the Wembley FA Cup Final / compiled
      by Andrew Thraves. London: Weidenfeld and Nicolson,
      1994.
      viii, 213p; illus

          At head of title: Daily Mail   ISBN: 0-297-83407-X
                                                 BL: LB.31.b.10140

      Essential work of reference — extremely comprehen-
      sive from 1923 onwards.

32   FA Cup giant killers / Geoff Tibballs. London:
      CollinsWillow, 1994.
      192p; illus; pbk   ISBN: 0-00-218481-8

✳ *Statistics*

33   The FA Cup 1871-81 / Raymond John Spiller. Basildon:
      Association of Football Statisticians, 1985.
      52p; pbk   ISBN: 0-946531-22-6

      This series of publications by the AFS gives a com-
      plete and highly detailed statistical coverage of the
      FA Cup competition — dates, results, line-ups,
      scorers and results of all the qualifying rounds are
      included.

34   The FA Cup 1881-91 / Raymond John Spiller. Basildon:
      Association of Football Statisticians, 1985.
      102p; pbk
                                                 ISBN: 0-946531-21-8

35   The FA Cup 1891-1901 / Raymond John Spiller.
      Basildon: Association of Football Statisticians, 1985.
      78p; illus; pbk
                                                 ISBN: 0-946531-31-5

36   The FA Cup 1901-11 / Raymond John Spiller. Basildon:
      Association of Football Statisticians, 1986.
      112p; pbk
                                                 ISBN: 0-946531-56-0

37   The FA Cup 1911-25 / Raymond John Spiller. Basildon:
      Association of Football Statisticians, 1986.
      pbk

38   The AFS book of Cup Final players / P. Marsh.
      Basildon: Association of Football Statisticians, 1992.
      80p; pbk   ISBN: 0-946531-43-9

      The statistical coverage here concentrates on all the
      players who have appeared in FA Cup Finals up to
      1991. Over 2,500 player details are presented.

39   The FA Cup: club by club records / edited by James
      Wright. Taunton: T. Williams Publications, 1993.
      300p; illus   ISBN: 1-869833-41-4

      This massive survey charts all the results of FA Cup
      games since 1945.

40   Football League clubs in the FA Cup / Tony Brown.
      Basildon: Association of Football Statisticians, 1993.
      273p; pbk   ISBN: 0-946531-68-4
                                                 BL: YK.1994.a.9632

      Extremely comprehensive statistical records chart-
      ing all the results throughout the history of the
      competition.

41   The ultimate FA Cup statistics book / Tony Brown.
      Basildon: Association of Football Statisticians, 1994.
      427p

          Limited edition   ISBN: 0-946531-76-5

      This is a supreme example of the sort of material
      which the AFS and its members are wont to produce.
      All forces were mobilised in winkling out over 50,000
      FA Cup results since the start of the competition as
      well as all the FA Cup qualifying results. A tremen-
      dous achievement.

Scottish Cup

✳ *Histories*

42   Scottish Cup football, 1873-1946 / Chalmers Anderson.
      Edinburgh: C. J. Cousland, 1946.
      35p; pbk

          Author also known as 'Custodian'   BL: 7917.bb.20

      Scarce early item which charts the winners and gen-
      eral history from the inception of the Scottish Cup in
      1873.

43   100 Cups: the story of the Scottish Cup / Hugh Keevins
      & Kevin McCarra. Edinburgh: Mainstream in
      conjunction with Scottish Brewers, 1985.
      240p; illus
          ISBN: 0-906391-85-7 (cased) • ISBN: 0-906391-86-5 (pbk)
                                                 BL: YK.1987.b.5603

      Very comprehensive coverage of the subject — an es-
      sential reference work.

❋ *Statistics*

44 Scottish Cup Finals 1874-1984 / John Litster. 1984.

45 North and South Cups: a review of the 1984-85 season in the Scottish Qualifying Cup / Keith Anderson. 1985.

A study of the annual scramble which ensues to gain entry to the Scottish Cup proper.

46 The Scottish Cup 1873-1986 / John Byrne. Basildon: Association of Football Statisticians, 1987.
244p; pbk

A complete statistical coverage completed to the highly reliable standard set by the AFS.

47 The Scottish Association Consolation Cup 1907-1921 / Tom O'Rourke. 1989.

48 The Scottish Association Qualifying Cup 1895-1931 / Tom O'Rourke. 1989.

49 Scottish Qualifying Cup results 1895-1994 / Stewart Davidson. Renfrew: Scottish Non-League Review, 1994.

Lists all the results for the qualifying rounds for the Scottish Cup proper along with many Cup Final line-ups and scorers. Results are also included for the early pre-Qualifying Cup years of the 1890s, when preliminary rounds for the Scottish Cup took place. Victory and Consolation Cup details conclude this very thorough study.

Football Association Cup ~ Ireland

50 The Gillette book of the FAI Cup / Seán Ryan and Terry O'Rourke. Dublin: Irish Soccer Co-op, 1985.
256p

A very detailed history which incudes all the results and reports from 1922 on-wards, an historic date for Irish football as this was the year following official political division of the North and South. In the same year, plans were formulated for Southern Ireland to form its own Football

Association, known as the Football Asso-ciation of Ireland. 1922 therefore became the date for the first FAI Cup which was won by St. James's Gate. Notwithstanding this, the Irish Cup had been played for since 1880 under the auspices of the Irish Football Association. This publica-tion expands on the inevitably complex history of football in Ireland, a history which is inextricably entwined with power-ful political and religious forces.

Football Association Cup ~ Wales

51 The story of the Welsh Cup 1877-1933 / XYZ. Wrexham: Woodall, Minshall, Thomas, 1933.

XYZ is pseudonym for George G. Lerry
A scarce history of the early years.

52 The history of the Welsh Cup, 1877-1993 / Ian Garland. Wrexham: Bridge, 1993.
316p; illus; pbk

ISBN: 1-87242437-6
BL: YK.1994.a.9366

There is a certain romantic mystique attached to the Welsh Cup as viewed by Englishmen — winners such as Druids, Oswestry, Barry Town and Connah's Quay lend the competition a definite quaintness. This is a most comprehensive treatment from the very first fi-nal, won by Wrexham in 1878. It includes essential material for all students of the Welsh game as well as much to interest club historians, including those of English League clubs such as Cardiff, Swansea, Shrewsbury, Crewe, Bristol City, and Tranmere, all of which have trodden the accessible route to silverware as winners of the Welsh Cup.

Football League Cup

53 Football League Cup, 1960-84: 1960-67 / Raymond John Spiller. Basildon: Association of Football Statisticians, 1984.
100p; pbk

> *This extremely thorough series charts dates, results, line-ups, half-time scores and attendances at every League Cup since the competition began – massive and definitive statistical coverage.*

54 Football League Cup, 1960-84: 1967-73 / Raymond John Spiller. Basildon: Association of Football Statisticians, 1984.
100p; pbk   ISBN: 0-946531-11-0

55 Football League Cup, 1960-84: 1973-78 / Raymond John Spiller. Basildon: Association of Football Statisticians, 1984.
96p; pbk   ISBN: 0-946531-25-0

56 Football League Cup, 1960-84: 1978-82 / Raymond John Spiller. Basildon: Association of Football Statisticians, 1984.
100p; pbk   ISBN: 0-946531-40-4

57 Football League Cup, 1960-84: 1982-84 / Raymond John Spiller. Basildon: Association of Football Statisticians, 1984.
100p; pbk

ISBN: 0-946531-55-2

58 The ultimate Football League Cup statistics book / Tony Brown. Basildon: Association of Football Statisticians, 1992.
184p; pbk

ISBN: 0-94651-48-X

> *A thoroughly comprehensive statistical study of the League Cup competition inaugurated in 1960 at the instigation of the Football League secretary, Alan Hardaker. Despite uncertain beginnings when some of the major sides declined to take part, the competition has grown in status with the passing years. Variously known through sponsorship deals as the Milk Cup, Littlewoods Cup, Rumbelows Cup and Coca-Cola Cup, it now enjoys a very high profile – yet for reasons not entirely explainable, it still lacks the popularity and charisma of the FA Cup.*

Scottish League Cup

59 The Scottish League Cup, 1940-84: 1940-51 / Raymond John Spiller. Basildon: Association of Football Statisticians, 1984.
100p; pbk

ISBN: 0-946531-35-8

> *A series of five volumes which include dates, half-time scores, results and scorers for every Scottish League Cup game plus many attendances and match reports. Full line-ups are given for all quarter-finals, semifinals and finals since 1945. A massive statistical study.*

60 The Scottish League Cup, 1940-84: 1951-60 / Raymond John Spiller. Basildon: Association of Football Statisticians, 1984.
100p; pbk

ISBN: 0-946531-50-1

61 The Scottish League Cup, 1940-84: 1960-68 / Raymond John Spiller. Basildon: Association of Football Statisticians, 1984.
100p; pbk

ISBN: 0-946531-60-9

62 The Scottish League Cup, 1940-84: 1968-76 / Raymond John Spiller. Basildon: Association of Football Statisticians, 1984.
100p; pbk

ISBN: 0-946531-80-3

63 The Scottish League Cup, 1940-84: 1976-85 / Raymond John Spiller. Basildon: Association of Football Statisticians, 1985.
80p; pbk

ISBN: 0-946531-95-1

Football Association Amateur Cup

64   Servowarm history of the FA Amateur Cup / Bob
      Barton. Newcastle-upon-Tyne: The author, 1984?
      243p; illus
               ISBN: 0-9508941-1-7 (cased) • ISBN: 0-9508941-2-5 (pbk)
                                                  BL: X.629/24659

> This is the definitive work of one of the most roman-
> tic of the domestic cups. Founded in 1893, it is
> competed for by the amateur clubs. Public school
> sides figured prominently in the early years whilst fa-
> mous sides such as Bishop Auckland, Pegasus and
> Hendon also made a particular mark in the competi-
> tion. From 1949, the final was played at Wembley,
> presenting the finalists with a glorious opportunity
> to enjoy the same high profile as their professional
> counterparts, if only for the day! The 1951 final be-
> tween Pegasus and Bishop Auckland attracted
> 100,000 spectators. The Amateur Cup finally came
> to an end in 1974 when the Football Association ef-
> fectively dropped the distinction between amateur
> and professional. The Cup's place was taken by the
> FA Vase. This work is an extremely valuable source for
> all researches into the amateur game and includes
> many famous names amongst the players and clubs
> represented.

**SERVOWARM
History of the
F.A.
AMATEUR
CUP
Bob Barton**

Football Association Trophy & Football Association Vase

65   The ultimate FA Trophy and Vase book / Tony Brown.
      Basildon: Association of Football Statisticians.

> Full statistical coverage of both these non-league
> cups.

66   Non league: a history of league and cup football / Bob
      Barton. Newcastle upon Tyne: The author, 1983?
      304p; illus; pbk   ISBN: 0-9508941-0-9
                                      BL: X.629/22345

> A definitive history of the non-league scene including
> much on cup football.

☞   Also listed at: A237

67   The FA Trophy: all the results 1969/1983, qualifying
      competition & competition proper / Mike Ford.
      London: Bureau of Non-League Football, 1985?
      35p; pbk   BL: X.629/27196

> The FA Challenge Trophy, founded in 1969, is com-
> peted for by professional and semi-professional sides
> which are not members of the Football League. It now
> attracts an entry of around 200 of the best non-
> league sides with the final played at Wembley.

68   The FA Vase: all the results 1974/1983, qualifying
      competition & competition proper / Mike Ford.
      London: Bureau of Non-League Football, 1985?
      35p; pbk   BL: X.629/27195

> The FA Challenge Vase competition was founded in
> 1974 to replace the Amateur Cup and was effectively
> aimed at the less prominent non-league sides. Hod-
> desdon Town were the first winners and sides such as
> Billericay Town, Stamford, and Halesowen Town have
> figured prominently in later years. This is a compre-
> hensive statistical study.

County Football Association Cups

69 Leicestershire and Rutland County FA Senior Cup: the history / David Kirkby. Shepshed: JSB Publications, 1988.
200p; illus

> *Covers 100 years – 1887/88 to 1987/88*
>
> BL: YK.1992.a.1766

All the County Football Associations hold their own cup competitions for their members, some of which have been charted in detailed histories. This study from Leicestershire is a fine example of what can be achieved by the amateur historian with a deep affection for his subject.

70 The Renfrewshire FA Cup: the first fifty years / John Byrne. Renfrew: Scottish Non-League Review, 1993.

This is the first book published on a Scottish County Cup competition. It contains all the results for the period 1879 to 1929 along with an historical review of the competition since its inception. More than 100 clubs entered during the fifty year period covered.

Scottish Junior Cup

71 The Scottish Junior Cup 1968-1989 / Paul Crankshaw. 1989.

Junior football is a term used in Scottish circles to effectively describe what the English would call the non-league game. It should not be confused with juvenile football, a different matter altogether. 'Senior' football exists only in the form of the Scottish League proper and three regional competitions, namely the East of Scotland League, the South of Scotland League and the Highland League. Below this, junior football thrives in almost every region of mainland Scotland. This publication is the study of the cup competition fought out amongst the junior fraternity.

The International Game

ALTHOUGH ASSOCIATION FOOTBALL WAS CONCEIVED and developed within our own shores, it quickly spread overseas and is now played at some level in almost every country of the world. It is one of the perks of overseas travel that wherever one may roam there is always a game on somewhere, whether it's a first class 'Serie A' game in Italy, a beach game in Rio, a battle between nations in Africa or a kick-about in a forest clearing somewhere in deepest Amazonia. Football has become a truly international language.

It is not surprising therefore that many books have been published which give a worldwide perspective. What is surprising is that every single entry in this chapter dates from the post-war period – indeed the majority emanate from no earlier than the late 1960s. Should this be interpreted to mean that there was no interest in overseas football before that time? Effectively, this is indeed the case. In the pre-war years the English were of course aware that football was played in other countries but tended to regard it as nothing more than a curiosity; we were masters of the football field just as we were of the Empire. Any publisher brave enough to have brought out an entire book on the 'world game' might well have been embarrassed by the number of copies he was obliged to remainder. And yet the post-war years saw an undeniable shift in perspective and a growth of interest in the overseas game. This was prompted by a number of key events which occurred over a period of years.

One of these was the ending of the war. Many young men were freshly returned from their first taste of overseas travel. Their horizons had been broadened and they had seen at firsthand a world beyond the familiar. Coincidentally, the famous Russian club, Dynamo Moscow, toured this country immediately after the end of the war. Russia was still seen as an ally in those days and in a spirit of wartime comradeship, the crowds turned out in great numbers. The tour was a great success though the men from Moscow humbled Cardiff City 10-1, beat Arsenal 4-3 and drew 2-2 with the mighty Glasgow Rangers. When the tour was over they left behind a startled public and a bemused football establishment which realised, perhaps for the first time, that we were no longer the best in the world at the game we had invented.

There is no doubt that the Dynamo tour sparked a new level of interest in the continental game and this allowed publishers to give greater coverage in 'popular' books to the non-domestic game. *Stanley Mortensen's International Soccer Book* [E172] is an early example of this experimental genre. If the reputation of the overseas game required further bolstering, it was soon to be provided from another quarter of Eastern Europe. In 1953 England suffered a shock 6-3 reverse at Wembley against the Hungarians; any thoughts that it might have been a fluke were quickly dispelled in a return game just six months later when England were trounced 7-1 in Budapest by the team dubbed the 'Magnificent Magyars'. It became blindingly obvious that, whilst England had given football to the world, it certainly had lessons to learn from it's former pupils. *Soccer Revolution* [E173], published in 1955, is a key work explaining the rationale behind this conclusion and effectively pinpoints the date from which the footballing public and publishers alike began to expand their sporting horizons. Other books quickly followed and England's 1966 World Cup victory, Manchester United's 1968 European Cup win, the increased propensity for foreign travel, and the ever increasing TV coverage of overseas games all combined to place the game on a truly international footing in the eyes of a traditionally insular British public.

This chapter is arranged according to the major international competitions and begins with the greatest tournament in the world, the World Cup. There is a good range of works covering the history of the competition from its inception in 1930, when just 13 countries took part, right up to the present day, with over 100 nations fighting it out in the qualifying rounds for the right to play in the prestigious final stages.

Brian Glanville and Jerry Weinstein's *World Cup* [E1], from 1958, is the first thorough historical coverage and still well worth consulting. Other detailed historical narratives include those by John Robinson [E12], Andrew Godsell [E15] and Jack Rollin [E17], whilst Ian Morrison's *Complete Record* [E19] presents an extremely comprehensive statistical coverage.

There are many works which chronicle the individual tournaments from 1966, the year of England's triumph, but far fewer before that date. Indeed, I have been unable to trace any work prior to 1954. The fact that England did not play in the competition until 1950 inevitably has much to do with this. Ralph Finn's résumé of

Switzerland 1954 [E24], John Camkin's account of Sweden 1958 [E25] as well as those by Gordon Jeffery [E26] and Donald Saunders [E27] covering Chile 1962 are all excellent but the official equivalent for England 1966 by Harold Mayes [E37] took the concept of detailed coverage to new heights. It is a classic of the genre, and highly collectable to boot.

England's victory itself is well charted in the gloriously titled *England, World Champions* [E31] by Ralph Finn, whilst the works of Martin Tyler [E39] and David Miller [E40] put the individual team members under the microscope to good effect.

Thereafter, each successive competition guaranteed a mixed assortment of works, some of a rather ephemeral nature, hastily compiled under the banner of a newspaper group or sponsor. England, Scotland and the Irish Republic take centre stage, with Northern Ireland grabbing their share of the limelight in 1982 and 1986. Poor old Wales though, who have qualified just once, in 1958, are notable absentees – what would one of the leading Welsh historians give to pen *Wales: Champions of the World*, one wonders; even *France '98: the Travelling Welsh Supporters' Guide* would be a collector's piece in its own right!

Second only to the World Cup as a tournament for the national sides is the European Championship, established in 1960 and known as the European Nations Cup until 1968. The obvious dearth of printed material illustrates only too well how the tournament lags behind the World Cup in capturing the public's imagination. This is a great pity as it has generated some fine moments. The work of John Robinson [E124] presents a detailed historical coverage and the fact that the next competition is to be held in England in 1996 will inevitably generate some additional items. Club competitions, meanwhile, are well covered under the heading of 'European Cup Competitions'. For a thorough overview of all the competitions the work of Ron Hockings [E132] would be a good starting point whilst the jewel in the crown, the European Cup, is particularly well treated by Brian Glanville [E134].

Such is the spirit of nationalistic fervour and rivalry amongst the domestic national sides that books within that section [E139-171] satisfy a well-defined demand. England and Scotland receive the lion's share of the attention but Ireland and Wales, whilst numerically very poorly represented, have both engendered works of real quality; Dónal Cullen [E153] and Clive Leatherdale [E154] present full coverage for the Republic and Gareth Davies and Ian Garland [E171], authorities on Welsh soccer, present a magnificent volume detailing all the personalities who have ever donned the red shirt for Wales.

All the listings referred to thus far have one element in common. In one way or another they deal with the exploits of UK national or club sides, whether on the home front or playing abroad. The items listed from E172 onwards reflect the developing assumption on the part of publishers that there is an audience for books about the overseas game as well. This is more apparent now than ever, with books on the overseas game becoming increasingly common. In the General Studies section the massive *Guinness Record of World Soccer* [E218] must be the best quick reference work whilst on the statistical side the equally weighty tome by Ron Hockings and Keir

Radnedge [E220] leaves no stone unturned in its analysis of all the European national sides. Stephen Wagg [E224], meanwhile, presents a differing slant by studying world football in its broader political and cultural sense in an academic coverage of the subject under the Leicester University banner.

The range of specialist studies on overseas football from E225 onwards begs a particular question – are these books really written in response to a clearly defined demand or simply because works on the domestic game have reached saturation point? The answer is not conclusive either way but certainly there are volumes listed here which seem to provide evidence both ways!

Football Italia [E232] was inevitably published because of an evident growth of interest from this country in the Italian game; *Football in Ecuador* [E244] though, or Dave Twydell's splendid curiosity *The Little Red Book of Chinese Football* [E228] must surely be regarded rather differently. In the final analysis there is a market for all football related material but it is clear that some of the published works are targeted at much smaller special interest groups and will of necessity be accorded smaller print runs and modest cover prices. Even more typical of this category are the ground breaking statistical works produced by Alexander Graham, David Clayton and Jan Buitenga, listed at E245-246. These are essentially home published computer-generated printouts covering all manner of statistical data for the clubs and national sides of all the European nations. While it isn't everybody who needs copies of the Albanian League Tables for 1932 or has to satisfy themselves as to the complete record of the Latvian national side, the fact is that these items do sell; as such they epitomise the all-embracing nature of coverage given to world football in its broadest sense.

Taking a snapshot view of the material available now against that which existed thirty years ago clearly illustrates how far the world of football publishing has come and how it has responded to changes in the way the game is perceived. It will be good for football if the concept of an ever-shrinking world can be extended to the realm of soccer; so by all means tune into a helping of 'Calcio' on Channel 4, follow the vagaries of the Malaysian scene, or whatever else takes your fancy, but let's keep the home fires burning too and firmly remind ourselves, just once in a while, where it all started.

The International Game ~ Contents

The World Cup

✳ Histories

1   World Cup / Brian Lester Glanville and Jerry Weinstein.
London: Hale, 1958.
226p; illus   BL: 7923.n.14

This is the first comprehensive history of the World
Cup. Although many volumes since have covered the
ground in even more detail this particular book is still
well worth consulting. It is extremely well-written and
offers thoughtful contemporary observations.

2   The Dunlop book of the World Cup / David Guiney;
cartoons by George Houghton. Lavenham: Eastland
Press, 1973.
179p; illus   SBN: 903214-03-2
                                               BL: X.629/5920

Over 300 short anecdotal stories about the World
Cup — events, players, matches, history. A good general miscellany.

☞ Subsequent ed. E4

3   Sunday Times history of the World Cup / Brian
Glanville with the co-operation of FIFA. London: Times
Newspapers, 1973.
260p; illus   ISBN 0-7230-0103-0
                                               BL: X.611/3622

Glanville updates the World Cup story in this official
FIFA history.

☞ Subsequent ed. E6

4   The Dunlop book of the World Cup / David Guiney;
cartoons by George Houghton. Rev. ed. Lavenham:
Eastland Press, 1977.
198p; illus   ISBN: 0-903214-10-5
                                               BL: X.629/12160

☞ Previous ed. E2

5   History of the World Cup / Michael Archer. London:
Hamlyn, 1978.
4-93p; illus   ISBN: 0-600-39400-X
                                               BL: X.622/6584

6   The history of the World Cup / Brian Glanville. Rev. ed.
London: Faber, 1980.
255p; illus; index   ISBN: 0-571-11498-9
                                               BL: X.622/12138

☞ Previous ed. E3; subsequent ed. E10

7   World Cup / John P. Baker, designed by Chris Reed.
Loughborough: Ladybird, 1982.
51p; illus; pbk   ISBN: 0-7214-0739-0

An introduction for children.

8   The World Cup: 1930-1982 / Jimmy Greaves; edited by
Norman Giller. London: Harrap, 1982.
139p; illus, forms, 1 map   ISBN: 0-245-53884-4
                                               BL: X.622/13040

An A-Z type history.

9   World Cup handbook 1930-1982 / Paul Marsh.
Basildon: Association of Football Statisticians, 1982.
100p

This largely statistical publication was the first book
to list all World Cup results from the beginning of the
competition in 1930, including all the qualifying tournament games as well as the final stages.

10 The history of the World Cup / Brian Glanville. New
paperback ed. London: Faber, 1984.
286p; illus; index; pbk   ISBN: 0-571-13245-6
                                               BL: X.629/24035

☞ Previous ed. E6; subsequent ed. E20

11 The Puffin book of the World Cup / Brian Glanville.
Harmondsworth: Penguin, 1984.
217p; illus, 1 map; index; pbk   ISBN: 0-14-031706-6
                                               BL: X.629/25895

12 The FIFA World Cup 1930-1986 / John Robinson.
Grimsby: Marksman, 1986.
136p; illus; pbk   ISBN: 0-947808-03-5
                                               BL: YK.1987.a.891

This book builds on those previously written, not only
looking at every competition since the first World Cup
in 1930 but also listing every country's record and its
scorers for the final stages. Comprehensive coverage
indeed at the time of publication, although subsequent books were to build even further on the
content offered here.

☞ Subsequent ed. E13

13 Soccer: the World Cup 1930-1990 / John Robinson.
Cleethorpes: Soccer Book Publishing, 1990.
184p; illus
        ISBN: 0-947808-12-4 (cased) • ISBN: 0-947808-13-2 (pbk)
                                               BL: YK.1991.b.6867

☞ Previous ed. E12

14 World Cup. London: Redwood, 1990-
illus
(BBC sportsyear)   ISSN: 0959-8545
                                               BL: ZK.9.d.603

15 The World Cup / Andrew Godsell. Alton: Nimrod, 1990.
500p

     ISBN: 1-85259-229-X
     BL: YK.1992.a.9694

   Extremely comprehensive coverage up to 1990.

 ☞ Subsequent ed. E16

16 The World Cup / Andrew Godsell. 2nd rev. ed. Alton:
Nimrod, 1990.
563p
(The sports library)   ISBN: 1-85259-252-4
     BL: YK.1991.a.12916

 ☞ Previous ed. E15

17 The World Cup 1930-1990: sixty glorious years of
soccer's premier event / Jack Rollin. Enfield: Guinness,
1990.
191p; illus; index; pbk   ISBN: 0-85112-920-X
     BL: YK.1990.b.1770

   Jack Rollin is a highly respected writer on football
   subjects – as expected this is a very full treatment
   of the subject, later to be updated by the same
   author.

 ☞ Subsequent ed. E18

18 The World Cup, 1930-1994: sixty glorious years of
soccer's premier event / Jack Rollin. 2nd ed. London:
Guinness, 1990.
191p; illus; index   ISBN: 0-85112-925-0
     BL: YK.1990.b.10146

   Both a comprehensive history of the World Cup and a
   detailed preview of the 1994 competition. Detailed
   statistical coverage, player profiles, a special focus
   on the Republic of Ireland and 'well over 100 photographs complete a first class coverage of the
   subject.

 ☞ Previous ed. E17; subsequent ed. E23

19 The World Cup: a complete record 1930-1990 / Ian
Morrison. Derby: Breedon Books, 1990.
464p; illus   ISBN: 0-907969-62-3
     BL: YK.1992.b.115

   Results, reports, line-ups – typically comprehensive
   coverage from one of the foremost publishers of
   authoritative football works.

20 The story of the World Cup / Brian Glanville. Rev. ed.
London: Faber and Faber, 1993.
351p, illus; index; pbk   ISBN: 0-571-16979-1
     BL: YK.1994.a.1975

 ☞ Previous ed. E10

21 The World Cup / Norman Barrett. Hove: Wayland,
1993.
48p; illus; index

 Bibliography: p47   ISBN: 0-7502-0882-1
     BL: YK.1994.b.5266

22 The encyclopedia of World Cup soccer / Orlando
Duarte. London: McGraw-Hill, 1994.
xix, 435p; illus; pbk

   'Portions of this book were previously published in the
   Spanish language edition under the title Todas las Copas del
   Mundo.' – t.p. verso   ISBN: 0-07-017944-1
     BL: YK.1994.b.7264

23 The Guinness record of the World Cup, 1930-1994 /
Jack Rollin. 3rd ed. Enfield: Guinness, 1994.
192p; illus; index; pbk   ISBN: 0-85112-757-6
     BL: YK.1994.b.7276

 ☞ Previous ed. E18

✻ *Tournament Commentaries*

✻ 1954 – SWITZERLAND

24 World Cup / Ralph Leslie Finn; edited by W. Howard
Baker. London: Hamilton, 1954.
112p; illus   BL: 7922.de.11

   This is a scarce publication in collecting circles – it
   gives a full retrospective of an excellent tournament
   which contained two British sides, England and Scotland, for the first time. The tournament was won by
   Germany.

✻ 1958 – SWEDEN

25 World Cup, 1958 / John Camkin. London: Rupert
Hart-Davis, 1958.
viii, 210p; illus   BL: 7924.b.25

   Full account of the tournament in which Brazil triumphed over the host country in a 5-2 final victory.

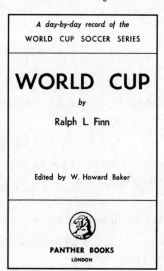

A day-by-day record of the
WORLD CUP SOCCER SERIES

WORLD CUP

by

Ralph L. Finn

Edited by W. Howard Baker

PANTHER BOOKS
LONDON

✱ 1962 – CHILE

26 World Cup '62: the report from Chile / edited by
    Gordon Jeffery, Stratton Smith, Friedebert Becker.
    London: Souvenir, 1962.
    176p   BL: X.449/409

    · Official World Cup summary – very comprehensive
    treatment of the competition which saw Brazil
    triumph yet again.

27 World Cup 1962 / Donald Saunders. London:
    Heinemann, 1962.
    184p; illus   BL: 7917.f.69

    Authoritative alternative coverage of the 1962
    tournament.

✱ 1966 – ENGLAND

28 Daily Express World Cup guide, 1966. London: Daily
    Express, 1965.
    45p; illus   BL: Cup.1255.e.24

    Pre-tournament lightweight guide to the teams and
    venues.

29 The boy's book of the World Cup / Kenneth
    Wolstenholme. Authorised ed. Manchester: World
    Distributors, 1966.
    124p; illus   BL: X.441/732

    Kenneth Wolstenholme and the events of 1966 will al-
    ways be synonymous – his commentary for England's
    victory in the final has earned him a permanent place
    in the broadcasting hall of fame.

30 Dramas of the World Cup / Patrick Greene. London:
    City Magazines, 1966.
    31p; illus   BL: X.445/67

31 England, world champions, 1966 / R. L. Finn. London:
    Hale, 1966.
    xii, 212p; illus   BL: X.449/2195

    If only a volume with the same title could be published
    in 1998 – comprehensive coverage of the whole tour-
    nament and England's victory.

32 England's World Cup / edited by Harry Langton.
    London: Beaverbrook Newspapers, 1966.
    Note: Issued in several parts   BL: Cup.22.a.25

33 England's World Cup triumph / Jack Rollin. London:
    Davies Books, 1966.
    111p; illus   BL: X.449/2327

34 World Cup '66 / edited by Hugh McIlvanney. London:
    Eyre & Spottiswoode, 1966.
    191p; illus   BL: X.449/2181

    Includes contributions by some of the most highly re-
    spected observers from the world of journalism –
    John Arlott, Bob Ferrier, Tony Pawson, and Arthur
    Hopcraft.

35 World Cup football championship, 1966 / Bernard Joy.
    London: Beaverbrook Newspapers, 1966.
    50p; illus

    Evening Standard World Cup special
                                      BL: X.449/1948

    Presented to Evening Standard readers as 'an
    authoritative guide to the 8th World Cup including
    details of teams and matches to be played from July
    11th to July 30th'. This excellent pre-finals survey is
    by one of football's most respected writers.

36 World soccer presents World Cup 1966 digest / Jack
    Rollin. Echo Publications, 1966.

    Includes full statistics of all the qualifying competi-
    tions.

37 World Cup report, 1966 / written and compiled for the
    Football Association by Harold Mayes. London:
    Heinemann, 1967.
    309p; illus   BL: X.441/862

    Essential reading for all students of the subject –
    the official FA report includes much detail about the
    background and organisation of the tournament not
    generally covered in other publications.

38 World Cup winners, 1966. Wrexham: Cambrian Press,
    1967.
    112p; illus   BL: X.445/132

39 Boys of '66: the England team that won the World Cup
    – then and now / Martin Tyler. London: Hamlyn, 1981.
    160p; illus; index   ISBN: 0-600-34660-9
                                      BL: X.622/11402

    This interesting treatment of the subject looks back
    at the 1966 triumph fifteen years on and chronicles
    the fortunes or otherwise encountered by the mem-
    bers of the team since their historic victory.

40 England's last glory: the boys of '66 / David Miller.
    London: Pavilion, 1986.
    192p; illus   ISBN: 1-85145-013-0
                                      BL: YC.1986.b.1638

    Another detailed retrospective of England's victory –
    never having won the tournament since, 1966 will be
    forever in the system. Whilst another England victory
    would not detract from the memory, it is desperately
    needed to turn attention to the future of English
    football – so long as 1966 remains the only triumph
    it is inevitable that we shall always be looking back to
    'better days' rather than moving on.

✱ 1970 – MEXICO

41 David Coleman's World Cup 70 preview / reporter,
    Norman Harris. London: Purnell, 1970.
    64p; illus   SBN: 361-01529-1
                                      BL: X.622/775

    Preview of the Mexico tournament from one of our
    best known commentators.

42 The great World Cup, 1970: a Daily Express special
    report. London: Beaverbrook Newspapers, 1970.

    Issued in several parts   BL: P.803/636

43 Kenneth Wolstenholme's World Cup special. London:
    Sporting Tours & Promotions, 1970.
    55p; illus   BL: X.611/5054

44 Mexico '70 / Martin Peters. London: Cassell, 1970.
    viii, 115p; illus

                                          SBN: 304-93650-2
                                          BL: X.629/3040

    One of the members of England's victorious 1966
    team here gives his impressions.

45 Moore on Mexico: World Cup 1970 / Bobby Moore as
    told to Kevin Moseley. London: Stanley Paul, 1970.
    128p; illus   SBN: 09-103540-6
                                          BL: X.629/2893

    England's 1966 captain also led the side in 1970.
    This is his account of what proved to be a disappoint-
    ing contest for England and an extremely difficult one
    for Moore himself — he was accused of petty theft in
    the notorious 'Bogota incident', fully chronicled here.

46 Shoot's World Cup special. London: Shoot, 1970.
    63p; illus   BL: X.611/5056

47 Wills Whiffs 1970 World Cup preview / edited by Albert
    Sewell. 1970.

    Includes the inevitable wall chart.

48 World Cup '70 / written and edited by Hugh
    McIlvanney and Arthur Hopcraft. London: Eyre &
    Spottiswoode, 1970.
    288p; maps   SBN: 413-27720-8
                                          BL: X.629/3038

    This is the definitive work on one of the best ever final
    series in the World Cup. High quality television cover-
    age left a lasting impression of the glamour and
    excitement which typified the action from Mexico.
    Brazil won the tournament for the third time, beating
    Italy 4-1 in the final, earning them the right to retain
    the Jules Rimet Trophy outright.

49 World Cup, 1970 / edited by Harry Langton. London:
    Beaverbrook Newspapers, 1970.
    Note: Issued in several parts

                                          BL: L.R.430.pp.6

50 World Cup, 1970 / Ralph L. Finn. London: Hale, 1970.
    xii, 164p; illus
                                          ISBN: 0-7091-1766-3

51 World Cup soccer finals: Mexico '70 / edited by Ken
    Jones. London: Hamlyn in association with IPC
    Newspapers, 1970.
    32p; illus
    (A Daily Mirror special)

                                          ISBN: 1-68033-006-3
                                          BL: X.615/195

✱ 1974 – WEST GERMANY

52 Book of the World Cup 1974 / edited by P. Evans.
    London: Knight, 1973.
    128p; illus; pbk
                                          ISBN: 0-340-18056-0

53 David Coleman's World Cup preview / edited by Sam
    Leitch. Maidenhead: Purnell, 1974.
    63p; illus   ISBN: 0-361-02864-4

    Short preview by one of our most well-known commen-
    tators; those who remember the TV coverage from
    this era will fondly recall the ample form of the editor
    whose contribution to the art of broadcasting was
    sadly ended prematurely.

54 World Cup, 1974 / Gordon Jeffery. London: Armada,
    1974.
    128p; illus; pbk

    For children   ISBN: 0-00-690740-7

    One of very few publications on the 1974 tournament;
    host nation, Germany, beat Holland in the final. The
    dearth of material is explained by the fact that Eng-
    land failed to qualify.

55 A report on the World Cup, 1974: the Football
    Association / Allen Wade and Colin E. Murphy.
    London: The Football Association, 1977?
    50p; illus; pbk   BL: X.619/18677

✱ 1978 – ARGENTINA

56 World Cup '78 / Philip Evans. Sevenoaks: Knight
    Books, 1977.
    128p; illus; pbk
                                          ISBN: 0-340-22163-1
                                          BL: X.619/18738

    Again England failed to qualify for the finals but the
    glamour of the venue and the participation of Scot-
    land for the second tournament in a row prompted a
    good number of publications. This one serves as both
    a history and a preview.

    ☞ Subsequent ed. E65

57 Flowers of Scotland: the official book of Scotland's
    World Cup squad / edited by Ken Gallacher. Glasgow:
    Trustee Savings Banks in Scotland, 1978.
    104p; illus, 1 map; pbk   BL: X.619/18883

    Many of the 1978 publications concentrated on
    Scotland's participation – this one takes an in-depth
    look at their squad.

58 The game of the century / Derek Conrad, Robert
    Sidaway, Bob Wilson. London: Fontana, 1978.
    168p; illus; pbk

    At head of title: World Cup '78   ISBN: 0-00-635054-2
                                          BL: X.611/8032

    Both a preview of the 1978 competition and a full his-
    tory published in connection with a lavishly produced
    television series of the same name.

59 The Radio Rentals book of the World Cup '78 / John
    Morgan and David Emery. Cambridge:
    Woodhead-Faulkner, 1978.
    128p; illus, 1 map; pbk   ISBN: 0-85941-087-0
                                       BL: X.619/19986

60 Scotland, Escocia, Schottland: World Cup, Argentina,
    1978 / Scottish Football Association. Glasgow: The
    Association, 1978.
    20p; illus; pbk

        Contains English, Spanish and German text
                                       BL: X.619/22161

61 Scotland the brave: World Cup souvenir, 1978. London:
    Selwood Press, 1978.
    61p; illus; pbk   BL: X.615/2084
        Being brave, regrettably, is not generally enough to
        become world champions – Scotland were no exception.

62 Scotland the greatest: a souvenir handbook / edited by
    John Keith. Ilford: Circle, 1978.
    96p; illus; pbk   BL: X.619/18843

63 Super Scots World Cup 1978 / edited by Alex Cameron.
    1978.

64 World Cup 78 / director of photography, Erich
    Baumann; English edition prepared by Phil Soar;
    translation by Margaret Millership. London: Marshall
    Cavendish, 1978.
    252p; chiefly illus

        Previous German ed.: Zungelsau: Sigloch, 1978
                                       ISBN: 0-85685-480-8
                                       BL: X.622/6927
    Particularly good source of illustrative material.

65 World Cup '78 / Philip Evans. Rev. ed. Sevenoaks:
    Knight Books, 1978.
    3-129p; illus; pbk   ISBN: 0-340-23000-2
                                       BL: X.619/18540

    ☞ Previous ed. E56

66 World Cup Argentina / introduction by Ron
    Greenwood; written by Colin Malam. Glasgow: Collins,
    1978.
    128p; illus; pbk   ISBN: 0-00-411641-0
                                       BL: X.615/2156

67 World Cup diary 1978 / Bob Crampsey. 1978.
        A diary of events seen from the Scotland perspec-
        tive.

68 World Cup: the Argentina story / David Miller. London:
    F. Warne, 1978.
    192p; illus   ISBN: 0-7232-2171-5
                                       BL: X.622/6612

69 Younger's World Cup review, 1978 / editorial John
    Helm. Leeds: Educational Design Limited, 1978.
    48p; illus; pbk

        Includes a 'progress chart' on 2 folded sheets
                                       BL: X.615/2161

✳ 1982 – SPAIN

70 All you need to know about the World Cup: BBC
    Scotland Sportscene / Fraser Elder. Glasgow?: BBC
    Scotland, 1982.

71 Daily Mail World Cup souvenir / edited by Ian Chimes.
    London: Breystand for Harmsworth, 1982.
    48p; illus; pbk

        Contains a chart (59x41cm) stapled into the centre
                                       ISBN: 0-86333-000-2
                                       BL: X.622/13518

72 Disney's family guide to the World Cup 82 / Peter
    Croker & Alex Martin; foreword by Ron Greenwood.
    London: Target, 1982.
    127p; illus, 2 maps; pbk   ISBN: 0-426-20137-X
                                       BL: X.808/36280

73 England World Cup 82 / edited by Bob Harris.
    Manchester: Whitethorn, 1982.
    128p; illus, 1 map; pbk   ISBN: 0-907959-00-8
                                       BL: X.622/18577

        Having missed the last two tournaments, England
        took part again in 1982 – this is a full preview.

74 England!: the 1982 World Cup squad / Hunter Davies.
    London: Macdonald, 1982.
    144p; illus
            ISBN: 0-356-07910-4 (cased) ● ISBN: 0-7088-2200-2 (pbk)
        Respected writer and journalist, Davies, here puts
        the squad under the spotlight.

75 The game of the century: World Cup Spain 1982 /
    David Barnes. London: Sidgwick & Jackson, 1982.
    187p; illus; index
                                       ISBN: 0-283-98846-0
                                       BL: X.622/12576

76 Rothmans presents World Cup '82 / John Morgan &
    David Emery. Aylesbury: Rothmans, 1982.
    128p; illus, 1 map; pbk

    Condensed edition   BL: X.629/17833

77 Rothmans presents World Cup 1982 / John Morgan &
    David Emery. Aylesbury: Rothmans, 1982.
    256p; illus, 1 map; pbk   ISBN: 0-907574-12-2
                                     BL: X.629/17969

78 The Scotsport guide to Spain World Cup '82 / compiled
    and edited by Gordon Brown and Bill Campbell with the
    assistance of Scottish Television. Edinburgh: Mainstream
    in conjunction with STV, 1982?
    95p; illus; pbk   ISBN: 0-906391-25-3
                                     BL: X.629/23473

    Again Scotland took part – this is a guide to the
    event and their squad.

79 Spain '82: the winning of the World Cup / Phil Soar &
    Richard Widdows; photographers Erich Baumann and
    others. London: Hamlyn, 1982.
    240p; illus, 1 map   ISBN: 0-600-34676-5
                                     BL: X.625/796

    This is the most comprehensive coverage of the 1982
    tournament won by Italy for the third time. Essential
    reference work.

80 To Spain, the hard way / Steve Sumner & Bobby
    Almond with Derrick Mansbridge. London: Whitcoulls,
    1982.
    79p; illus; pbk   ISBN: 0-7233-0689-3
                                     BL: X.622/13912

    This publication has an unusual slant – it chronicles
    the progress of New Zealand to the finals for the
    first time ever. Although they suffered three defeats,
    a relatively respectable 5-2 reversal against Scot-
    land effectively prevented the Scots from
    progressing into the quarter-finals.

81 The unofficial World Cup book / Peter Chippindale.
    London: Corgi, 1982.
    96p; illus; pbk

    Contains an illustrated folded sheet as insert
                                     ISBN: 0-552-99003-5
                                     BL: X.622/12948

82 World Cup 82 / Philip Evans. Sevenoaks: Knight Books,
    1982.
    143p; illus, 1 map; pbk   ISBN: 0-340-27747-5
                                     BL: X.629/17619

83 World Cup '82: a complete guide / Nicholas Keith and
    Norman Fox; with photographs by Peter Robinson.
    London: Park Lane Press, 1982.
    128p; illus, 1 map; pbk   ISBN: 0-902935-26-7
                                     BL: X.622/13472

84 World Cup '82: a souvenir guide to football's premier
    competition / written and edited by the Daily Mirror
    Sports Department. London: Mirror Books, 1982.
    26p; illus; unbound
    (A Daily Mirror soccer special) ISBN: 0-85939-314-3
                                     BL: P.2000/557

85 World Cup '82: guide to the competition, the teams &
    the players / Don Howe, Norman Barrett. London:
    Daily Telegraph, 1982.
    130p; illus, 1 map; pbk   ISBN: 0-901684-74-0
                                     BL: X.629/20106

✱ 1986 – MEXICO

86 Mexico '86 / Phil Soar and John Bone. London:
    Windward, 1986.
    240p; chiefly illus

    A pictorial review of the 1986 finals – a colour picture
    on every page.

87 Mexico on fifty dollars a ticket: the unofficial story of the
    1986 World Cup / Mick Worrall. Wallsend: The author,
    1986.
    144p; illus, 1 map; pbk   ISBN: 0-9511742-0-7
                                     BL: YK.1987.a.1253

    Amongst all the preview glossies this work presents a
    refreshing approach, being one travelling supporter's
    personal impressions of his visit to Mexico and the
    experiences – football and otherwise – which he en-
    countered.

88 Off the ball: the football World Cup / edited by Alan
    Tomlinson and Garry Whannel. London: Pluto, 1986.
    174p; pbk   ISBN: 0-7453-0122-3
                                     BL: YK.1987.a.7195

    A series of 12 essays on the tournament all taken
    from differing perspectives – an interesting approach.

    ☞ Also listed at: H42

89 Playfair World Cup: Mexico 1986 / edited by Peter
    Dunk. London: Queen Anne, 1986.
    254p; 1 map; pbk   ISBN: 0-356-10636-5
                                     BL: YC.1986.a.2479

    Extremely comprehensive coverage of the action in
    Mexico. The final was won by Argentina.

90   So near and yet so far: Bobby Robson's World Cup diary
     1982-86 / Bobby Robson with Bob Harris. London:
     Willow, 1986.
     219p; illus   ISBN: 0-00-218186-X
                                          BL: YK.1986.a.1443

     *Four years of build-up culminated in England meeting
     Argentina in the quarter-finals, the first meeting be-
     tween the two nations since the Falklands War of
     1982. Amidst much added tension, England lost the
     game 2-1. Both goals came from Diego Maradona, the
     first being the infamous 'hand of God' hand ball inci-
     dent for which he has never been truly forgiven. Here
     the England manager chronicles all the incidents and
     agonies in an aptly titled coverage.*

     ☞   Also listed at: C425

91   World Cup 86 / John Baker; photographs by George
     Herringshaw. Loughborough: Ladybird, 1986.
     52p; illus; pbk   ISBN: 0-7214-0944-X
     A children's guide.

92   World Cup 86 / Philip Evans. Sevenoaks: Knight, 1986.
     192p; illus; pbk   ISBN: 0-340-39381-5
                                          BL: YC.1986.a.1940

93   The World Cup: essential guide to Mexico '86 / Julie
     Welch. London: Virgin Books, 1986.
     228p; illus; pbk   ISBN: 0-86369-147-1

     *Comprehensive guide to all the venues and participat-
     ing nations from one of England's highly respected
     female journalists.*

✳ 1990 – ITALY

94   All played out: the full story of Italia '90 / Pete Davies.
     London: Heinemann, 1990.
     470p; illus   ISBN: 0-434-17908-6
                                          BL: YK.1991.b.2140

     *This is one of the most highly acclaimed books about
     the World Cup. It is neither a preview nor a standard
     tournament account – it is the personal observa-
     tions of one supporter on the prevailing atmosphere
     and incidents associated with this extremely high
     profile world event. Much unusual material may be
     found here; essential reading.*

95   All-star guide to the World Cup / David Scott. London:
     Beaver, 1990.
     192p; illus, 1 map; pbk   ISBN: 0-09-973940-2
                                          BL: YK.1991.a.7512

96   Italia '90 Scotland: five in a row – the road to Rome /
     Dixon Blackstock. Edinburgh: Sportsprint, 1990.
     96p; illus, 1 map; pbk   ISBN: 0-85976-298-X
                                          BL: YK.1990.a.7248

     *By qualifying to appear in 1990, Scotland completed
     a run of five World Cups – this short study chronicles
     their qualification and the build-up to the finals.*

97   Jack Charlton's World Cup diary / Jack Charlton with
     Peter Byrne; photographs by Billy Stickland. Dublin: Gill
     and Macmillan, 1990.
     171p; illus
       ISBN: 0-7171-1858-4 (cased) • ISBN: 0-7171-1788-X (pbk)
                                          BL: YK.1991.b.7223

     *Jack Charlton, a member of England's 1966 winning
     side, became a cult figure in Ireland after taking the
     Republic to the 1990 finals, where they narrowly
     failed to reach the semi-finals. This is Charlton's full
     account of the tournament from the Irish viewpoint.*

Jack Charlton's
World Cup Diary

with Peter Byrne

Photographs by Billy Stickland

GILL AND MACMILLAN

98   Saint & Greavsie's World Cup special: a match-by-match
     diary of all the matches and most memorable moments
     of Italia '90 / Ian St. John and Jimmy Greaves; edited by
     Norman Giller. London: Stanley Paul, 1990.
     128p; illus, 1 map; pbk   ISBN: 0-09-174629-9
                                          BL: YK.1990.b.7562

99   UAE World Cup Italy 1990: commemorative guide.
     London: EMAP Business Information in conjunction
     with the UAE Football Association, 1990.
     64p; illus; pbk
        Includes a wall chart   BL: YK.1991.b.8267

     *The United Arab Emirates celebrated the most glori-
     ous moment in its footballing history to date by
     qualifying to play in the finals. This short account
     commemorates that achievement.*

100 World Cup 90 / Lorraine Horsley. Loughborough:
     Ladybird, 1990.
     51p   ISBN: 0-7214-1307-2
                                          BL: YK.1990.a.5617

     A short guide for children.

101 World Cup 90 / Philip Evans. London: Hodder and
Stoughton, 1990.
191p; illus, 1 map; pbk   ISBN: 0-340-51735-2
                                 BL: YK.1990.a.3728

> One of the most comprehensive accounts of the tournament won by Germany who defeated Argentina in the final.

102 World Cup 90: souvenir guide / William Hill. London:
William Hill Organization, 1990.
34p; illus   BL: YK.1992.a.9113

103 World Cup '90: official programme. London: Express
Newspapers, 1990.
82p; illus; pbk
At head of title: Sunday Express   ISBN: 0-85079-216-9
                                     BL: LB.31.b.6355

104 World Cup extra. London: Communication Innovations,
1990.
illus
> *Issued in several parts and distributed free*
>   BL: ZK.9.b.2975

105 There we were: Italia '90 / Mary Hunt. Kilpedder,
Wicklow: Sparrow Books, 1991.
277p; illus   ISBN: 1-87245-901-3
                                 BL: YK.1992.b.6720

> A fan's eye view – the 1990 tournament has entered spectator folklore as one of the most enjoyable off-field events in World Cup history. Mary Hunt here views the entire event through Irish eyes which, for the most part, were smiling.

✱ 1994 – USA

106 The greatest show on earth: the World Cup America
1994 / Stewart William Beckett with George Best; edited
by Eric Kreiger. Manchester: Comprehensive Art
Services, 1993.
176p; illus; pbk   ISBN: 0-9516497-3-6

> Serves both as a World Cup preview and as a history of soccer in the USA from its earliest beginnings. Very detailed coverage of all the World Cup venues including, with typical American thoroughness, a guide to the best restaurants and motels! Over 100 photographs, amongst them a real gem of Marilyn Monroe kicking off a game in Brooklyn in 1957.

107 Here we go: US '94 – Republic of Ireland's route to the
World Cup / Mary Hunt. Wicklow: Sparrow Books,
1993.
231p; illus; index; pbk   ISBN: 1-87245902-1
                                 BL: YK.1995.b.4970

> Following her retrospective 'There We Were' in 1990, Mary Hunt looks forward this time to another Irish campaign in the 1994 tournament. Comprehensive coverage, well written and presented.

108 Andy's game: the inside story of the World Cup / Andy
Townsend with Paul Kimmage. London: Stanley Paul,
1994.
192p; illus; pbk   ISBN: 0-09-179012-3

> The Republic of Ireland captain here gives his personal account of the Irish International set-up with particular reference to the World Cup experience of 1994.

109 Cwpan y Byd 94: llyfr posau a sticeri / Norman Barrett;
addasiad Cymraeg: Gwyn Jenkins. Llanrwst: Gwasg
Carreg Gwalch, 1994.
16p; illus, maps; pbk
> *World Cup 1994 sticker activity book*
>   ISBN: 0-86381-280-5

> Wales have only qualified for the World Cup finals once, in 1958. Perhaps when this publication was initially planned, their hopes for 1994 were high. In the event, they again missed out on qualifying at the last gasp, perhaps explaining why this publication is rather a slim one.

110 Dinosaurs World Cup / Keith Brumpton. London:
Orchard, 1994.
32p; illus
    ISBN: 1-85213-380-5 (cased) • ISBN: 1-85213-775-4 (pbk)
> A study for children.

111 FAI World Cup '94 handbook / compiled for and on
behalf of the Football Association of Ireland. Dublin:
Sportsworld, 1994.
160p; illus

112 Going to America: World Cup USA 1994 / Eoghan
Corry. Dublin: Torc, 1994.
368p; illus; pbk
> *Bibliography: p366-368*   ISBN: 1-898142-08-4

> Very comprehensive coverage with much of interest from the Republic of Ireland standpoint.

113 Hosts and champions: soccer cultures, national identities
and the USA World Cup / edited by John Sugden, Alan
Tomlinson. Aldershot: Arena, 1994.
ix, 323p; index
(Popular cultural studies)
> *Includes bibliographies*
>   ISBN: 1-85742-227-9 (cased) • ISBN: 1-85742-228-7 (pbk)
>   BL: YC.1994.a.2652

> Most interesting study considering many elements of the 1994 tournament and the importance of it for surprise hosts, USA. The competition was won by Brazil and generally voted a resounding success by leading observers and fans alike.

114 Jack Charlton's American World Cup diary / Jack
Charlton with Peter Byrne. Dublin: Gill & Macmillan,
1994.
224p; illus
    ISBN: 0-7171-2235-2 (cased) • ISBN: 0-7171-2220-4 (pbk)
> The Republic of Ireland manager chronicles all as-

pects of his team's participation – they made a great impact and many friends along the way.

115 The outrageous guide to the World Cup / Paul Farrell, Graeme Keyes. Dublin: O'Brien, 1994.
96p; illus; pbk   ISBN: 0-86278-398-4

116 Shoot: World Cup '94 / Keir Radnedge. London: Hamlyn, 1994.
63p; illus; pbk   ISBN: 0-600-58320-1
                                         BL: YK.1994.b.6256

117 This is soccer: images of World Cup USA '94 / compiled and edited by Doug Cheeseman and others; principal photographers Peter Robinson and others; foreword by Patrick Barclay. London: Gollancz/Witherby in association with When Saturday Comes, 1994.
96p; illus; pbk   ISBN: 0-575-05892-7
                                         BL: LB.31.b.10401

When Saturday Comes, UK's foremost fanzine style magazine, has become something of a cult publication and has begun to expand its influence into the wider publishing world. This is their photographic record of the 1994 finals, including both the spectacular and delightfully idiosyncratic moments captured by the world's press.

118 The World Cup / David Guiney. Dublin: Sportsworld, 1994.
333p; illus   ISBN: 0-9521698-2-7

119 World Cup / Norman Barrett and David Jefferis. London: Wayland, 1994.
48p; illus; pbk   ISBN: 0-7502-0968-2

120 World Cup 94 / Norman Barrett. Loughborough: Ladybird, 1994.
47p; illus   ISBN: 0-7214-1678-0
                                         BL: YK.1994.a.17846

Children's introduction to the 1994 action.

121 World Cup USA '94: the complete guide to soccer's World Cup and all 24 teams / Glen Phillips and Tim Oldham. London: CollinsWillow, 1994.
280p; illus; pbk
        Originally published: New York: HarperCollins, 1994
                                         ISBN: 0-00-218485-0
                                         BL: H.95/206

Contrary to much speculation that the 1994 tournament would be an almighty flop, it turned into a thoroughly enjoyable event despite England's absence. This is one of a number of comprehensive studies.

122 World Cup: USA 94: the official book / Peter Arnold. London: Stanley Paul, 1994.
80p; illus; pbk   ISBN: 0-09-178612-6
                                         BL: YK.1994.b.6182

The official FIFA preview to the 1994 World Cup finals.

123 More than a game: World Cup diary / Eamon Dunphy. London: Heinemann, 1995.
224p   ISBN: 0-434-00196-1

Highly respected Irish observer Dunphy here presents his personal overview of the 1994 action, including much or relevance to the Irish Republic's participation.

The European Championships

124 The European Championship, 1958-1988 / John Robinson; foreword by John Motson. Cleethorpes: Marksman, 1988.
159p; illus; pbk
        ISBN: 0-947808-09-4 (cased) • ISBN: 0-947808-086 (pbk)
                                         BL: YK.1989.a.2438

The European Championship finals were first played in 1960. It was known as the European Nations Cup until 1968 and thereafter as the European Championships. The competition is held every four years and from the British perspective is second only to the World Cup, having grown in stature with each passing tournament. This is the definitive history and record.

125 The 1992 European Championship / Tony Lynch. London: Boxtree, 1992.
128p; illus   ISBN: 1-85283-733-0
                                         BL: YK.1993.b.10979

Specific coverage of the 1992 tournament which witnessed the greatest moment in the history of Danish football when the national side became the surprise, but thoroughly deserving, winners in one of the most memorable finals in recent history.

126 The European football championships 1958-1992 / John Robinson. Cleethorpes: Soccer Book Publishing, 1992.
189p; illus   ISBN: 0-947808-24-8
                                         BL: YK.1993.a.10406

This updated definitive history of the European Nations Cup includes a country by country record of every game with full statistics and over fifty photographs.

European Cup Competitions

127 European Cup 1963 / edited by Velio Vuolo.
Martspress, 1963.
128p

> This preview publication of the 1963 competition details all the clubs and players involved and includes much on the history of the competition.

128 Football champions / John L. Foster. London: Nelson, 1974.
80p; illus; pbk
(Interest books)   ISBN: 0-17-432036-1

129 The European Cup 1955-1980 / John Motson, John Rowlinson. London: Queen Anne Press, 1980.
335p; illus; index

    Bibliography: p328   ISBN: 0-362-00512-5
                                      BL: X.622/9289

> The top competition for European club sides was founded by UEFA in 1955 to be contested by leading European teams by invitation; it was later open only to the domestic league champions of each nation. and is now played under the banner of the 'Champions Cup'. This extremely detailed history and record covers the event up to 1980.

130 European Cup: the fascinating story of football's most glittering club competition / Anton Rippon. London: Mirror Books, 1980.
v, 201p; illus; pbk

                                 ISBN: 0-85939-209-0
                                 BL: X.629/12933

> A detailed account. The author later set up the Breedon Book Publishing Company which has established a trend for definitive 'complete record' club histories and has elevated the standards of football publishing to new heights.

131 A record of English, Scottish and Welsh clubs in European competitions 1955-1986 / Andrew Cuthew. 1986.
116p

> English, Scottish and Welsh clubs have played many games in Europe over the years – this essentially statistical work gives every line-up, goalscorer, half-time score, result and attendance for every single European Cup, Cup Winners' Cup and Fairs (UEFA) Cup match involving a home-based team.

132 Hockings' European cups: who won which, where, when: European Cup, Cup Winners' Cup, UEFA Cup / Ron Hockings. Emsworth: Mason, 1988.
256p; illus; pbk   ISBN: 0-85937-340-1
                                 BL: YK.1988.a.2987

> Extremely thorough treatment giving results for all the clubs which have taken part in the three major

European cup competitions over the years. Each club's stadium, full name, ground capacity and domestic honours are detailed. An interesting section covers what were described at the time as the 'defunct states' of Latvia and Estonia, prior to the far-reaching political upheavals which were to follow.

133 There we were – Germany '88 / Mary Hunt. Dublin: Sparrow Books, 1989.
176p; illus   ISBN: 1-87245-900-5

134 Champions of Europe: the history, romance and intrigue of the European Cup / Brian Glanville. Enfield: Guinness, 1991.
192p; illus; index

    Includes bibliography   ISBN: 0-85112-948-X
                                   BL: YK.1991.b.6557

> The subtitle hints at the delights to come. Whilst the book inevitably includes the necessary statistics, Glanville's greatest strength is, without doubt, his writing. The book gives a superb account of the triumphs, tragedies and controversies that make up the history of the European Cup; rather than follow a simple chronological order, the chapters follow eras and themes with the result that some less chronicled subjects are admirably covered. There is a complete chapter on Real Madrid and an extremely revealing chapter on the bribery and corruption scandals which Glanville has helped to expose – 'The years of the golden fix' reveals all and contains material of particular interest to historians of Derby County, whose defeat at the hands of Juventus in the 1973 semi-final was shrouded in controversy. Essential reading.

135 100 European Cups / Claude Girault, Guy Mislin and Mike Hammond; editor, Bruce Smith. Windsor: Burlington, 1992.
736p; illus   ISBN: 1-87305-710-5
                                 BL: YK.1993.a.14748

> When Red Star beat Olympique Marseille in a penalty shoot-out to win the 1991 European Champions Cup it was the 100th major European final. This book seizes on that landmark figure to present a full statistical survey of all one hundred competitions and their participants. Staggering research – one for the serious student.

136 Playing in Europe / edited by Mike Hammond. Warley: Sports Projects, 1992-
pbk

    Published annually   ISSN: 1357-0072
                                   BL: ZK.9.a.3682

> A who's who style publication to the teams and players in Europe's three major cup competitions – the

Champions Cup, UEFA Cup, and the Cup Winners' Cup. The first edition contained detailed information on more than 2,300 players from 130 European clubs. By the time the second edition was published, coverage had expanded to 2,600 players and 140 clubs.

137 Directory of finalists in European club competitions / Paul Marsh. Nuneaton: The author, 1993.
88p; pbk

Meticulously researched records of the European Cup, Cup Winners' Cup, Fairs Cup and UEFA Cup; lists every single player who has ever played in one of these four major European finals.

138 European cups review. Warley: Sports Projects, 1993-
illus; pbk

Published annually

ISSN: 1353-6958
BL: ZK.9.a.3145

The Domestic National Sides

✳ *England*

139 Young England: the story of the development of soccer talent / Kenneth Wolstenholme. London: Stanley Paul, 1959.
128p; illus

BL: 7925.b.17

A detailed account of the moves made by the FA to provide for England's future following disappointment in the 1950 World Cup, when England were beaten 1-0 by the USA; heavy defeats by Hungary then followed in 1953 and 1954. Effectively a 'blueprint for the future' presented by England's most famous commentator who witnessed, it might be agreed, the fruits of his labour in 1966 when England came good to win the World Cup final.

140 England v. Scotland / Brian James. London: Pelham, 1969.
xv, 271p; illus

SBN: 7207-0308 -5
BL: X.449/3731

Includes a report on each of the first 105 matches between two of the keenest international rivals, with full statistics and history.

☞ Also listed at: E157

141 A century of English international football, 1872-1972 / Morley Farror and Douglas Lamming. London: Hale, 1972.
240p; illus

ISBN 0-7091-3630-7
BL: X.629/4907

Excellent survey of the England team's progress presented in four main sections: Highlights of the Century 1872-1972; Full Results and Statistics; Analysis and Commentary on England's Players; Brief Biographies of Players.

142 Eng-land!: the story of the national soccer team / Anton Rippon. Ashbourne: Moorland Publishing, 1981.
144p; illus

ISBN: 0-86190-032-4
BL: X.622/11693

143 England's quest for the World Cup: a complete record / Clive Leatherdale; foreword by Sir Stanley Rous. London: Methuen, 1984.
xv, 334p

Bibliography: p333-334

ISBN: 0-413-546705 (cased) • ISBN: 0-413-55720-0 (pbk)
BL: X.629/2376-3 • BL: X.629/24482

Chronicles every England game in the World Cup finals and qualifying tournaments from 1950 to 1984 with a report on each accompanied by full statistics. This is a comprehensive and valuable research work.

☞ Subsequent ed. E150

144 The Woodcock Travel illustrated guide to England international footballers: detailed biographies of all 999 England players, 1872-1987 / compiled by J. M. Silk; sketches by M. D. James. Sheffield: Andromeda, 1987.
xx, 137p; illus; index; pbk

Bibliography: p xvi

ISBN: 0-9512634-0-4
BL: LB.31.a.2329

Published in a limited edition of 3,000 copies. Other publications offer the same information as this volume, usually with more detail, but the unique feature of this book is the 963 freehand portraits accompanying the text; just like the career records, some are rather better than others!

145 England: the football facts / Nick Gibbs; foreword by Bobby Robson; officially endorsed by the Football Association. Exeter: Facer, 1988.
256p; illus; pbk

Bibliography: p256

ISBN: 1-87054-100-6
BL: YK.1989.a.2099

An enormous compilation of all manner of facts and figures relating to English international football. Very informative.

146 An English football internationalists' who's who, 1872-1988 / Douglas Lamming. Beverley: Hutton, 1990.
300p; illus; pbk

ISBN: 0-907033-93-8
BL: YK.1991.b.7145

Biographical details of all the players honoured by their country during this period.

147 The England football fact book / Cris Freddi. Enfield:
Guinness, 1991.
264p; illus; index; pbk   ISBN: 0-85112-991-9
                                           BL: YK.1991.b.7403

In addition to biographical details of every England international player, this book gives many records and
trivia — hat trick heroes, sendings off, penalties, sub-
stitutes, attendances, death dates — in fact a
complete coverage of all elements of the national
side. Highly recommended.

148 England: the complete post-war record / Mike Payne.
Derby: Breedon Books, 1993.
336p; illus   ISBN: 1-87362-639-8
                                           BL: YK.1994.b.12687

An essential work for all those wishing to chart the
ups and downs of the England side; includes match
reports, both teams' line-ups, referees and attendances for every England full international game
since 1946. Includes several hundred photographs,
many published here for the first time.

149 The FA complete guide to England players since 1945.
London: Stanley Paul, 1993.
248p   ISBN: 0-09-177294-X
                                           BL: YK.1994.b.3598

An alphabetic reference book of all players who have
appeared for England since the Second World War,
with supporting statistics permitting an analysis of
how each player has fared and the relative impact his
performances have had on the success or failure of
the team. Invaluable research tool, especially for the
football journalist.

150 England: the quest for the World Cup: a complete
record 1950-1994 / Clive Leatherdale. 2nd ed. London:
Two Heads Publishing in association with Desert Island
Books, 1994.
352p; illus; pbk
(Desert Island football history series)
                                           ISBN: 1-897850-40-9

Essential reading for all students of the national
side. Starting with Wales in 1949 and finishing with
the memorable San Marino match in 1993, this book
provides a report of every single game, with accompanying statistics. A mine of information.

☞ Previous ed. E143

✳ *Northern Ireland*

151 European league and club histories: Northern Ireland
1890-1992 / Alexander Graham. Isle of Skye: The
author, 1992?

✳ *Republic of Ireland*

152 European league and club histories: Eire 1921-1991 /
Alexander Graham. Isle of Skye: The author, 1991?

153 Ireland on the ball: the international matches of the
Republic of Ireland soccer team — a complete record
March 1926 - June 1993 / Dónal Cullen. Dublin: Elo,
1993.
336p   ISBN: 0-9519593-5-2

This volume fills an important gap in the market, giving a complete record of all the matches played
during this period — not just the great games but
also the long-forgotten 0-0 draws! Certainly the definitive work on the Republic of Ireland team.

154 Ireland: the quest for the World Cup: a complete record
of every game from 1934-1994 / Clive Leatherdale;
foreword by Jack Charlton. London: Two Heads
Publishing in association with Desert Island Books, 1994.
256p; illus; pbk
(Desert Island football history)   ISBN: 1-897850-80-8

A record of every single game played by the Republic
of Ireland in the World Cup over this period.

155 The team that Jack built / Paul Rowan. Edinburgh:
Mainstream, 1994.
192p; illus; index   ISBN: 1-85158-670-9

The Republic of Ireland team grabbed many headlines
in 1994 — their creator, Jack Charlton, was never far
from the limelight himself and has become a national
hero in the Republic, much to his embarrassment on
occasions.

✳ *Scotland*

156 Association football: Scotland v England, 1872-1946 /
Chalmers Anderson. Edinburgh: C. J. Cousland, 1947.
36p; pbk   BL: 7919.cc.26

Early study of the contests between two of football's
fiercest rivals.

157 England v. Scotland / Brian James. London: Pelham,
1969.
xv, 271p; illus   SBN: 7207-0308-5
                                           BL: X.449/3731

One of the most keenly fought fixtures in the football
calendar, sadly no longer played on a regular basis.
This item includes a report on each of the first 105
matches between the two sides.

☞ Also listed at: E140

158 Welcome Inn's Scotland's history in the World Cup.
1982.

159 Who's who of Scottish internationalists, 1872-1982. Part
1: A-C / Douglas Lamming. Basildon: Association of
Football Statisticians, 1982?
iv, 51p; illus; unbound   BL: X.0629/617

The first part of a four volume series later amalgamated into a single publication giving biographical
details of all Scotland Internationals.

☞ See also: E166

160 Who's who of Scottish internationalists, 1872-1982. Part 2: D-K / Douglas Lamming. Basildon: Association of Football Statisticians, 1982?
65p; illus; unbound　　　　　　　BL: X.0629/617

☞　See also: E166

161 Who's who of Scottish internationalists, 1872-1982. Part 3: L-O / Douglas Lamming. Basildon: Association of Football Statisticians, 1982?
61p; illus; unbound　　　　　　　BL: X.0629/617

☞　See also: E166

162 Who's who of Scottish internationalists 1872-1982. Part 4: P-Z / Douglas Lamming. Basildon: Association of Football Statisticians, 1982.
63p; illus; unbound　　　　　　　BL: X.0629/617

☞　See also: E166

163 Scotland's quest for the World Cup: a complete record 1950-1986 / Clive Leatherdale; foreword by Alex Ferguson. Edinburgh: John Donald, 1986.
x, 247p; illus; pbk　　　　　ISBN: 0-85976-149-5
　　　　　　　　　　　　　　　BL: YK.1987.b.4385

This first edition of an excellent publication chronicles every game Scotland have played in the World Cup qualifying competitions and finals during this period. The second edition updated the story to 1994.

☞　Subsequent ed. E170

164 Scottish amateur internationals and internationalists 1927-1944 / George Campbell. 1986

Thoroughly researched work by one of Scotland's leading football historians.

165 Scotland: the team / Andrew Ward. Derby: Breedon Books Sport, 1987.
159p; illus　　　　　　　　ISBN: 0-907969-34-8
　　　　　　　　　　　　　　　BL: YK.1991.b.5702

A full history of the national team on a season-by-season basis.

166 A Scottish soccer internationalists' who's who, 1872-1986 / Douglas Lamming; foreword by Ernie Walker. Beverley: Hutton, 1987.
271p; illus; pbk　　　　　　ISBN: 0-907033-47-4
　　　　　　　　　　　　　　　BL: YK.1987.b.4224

A very comprehensive work containing biographies of all 947 players capped by Scotland up to and including the 1986 World Cup finals. Dozens of photos are included along with specialist sections on oldest and youngest débutants, birthplaces etc. Essential reading for all Scotland historians.

☞　See also: E159-162

167 The only game / Roddy Forsyth. Edinburgh: Mainstream, 1990.
223p; illus; index
　　ISBN: 1-85158-107-3 (cased) ● ISBN: 1-851581-08-1 (pbk)
　　　　　　　　　　　　　　　BL: YK.1991.b.2682

This is a celebrated study of Scottish football containing much of interest to the student of the national side.

168 Wembley wizards : the story of a legend / Paul Joannou. Edinburgh: Mainstream, 1990.
221p; illus

　　Bibliography: p220-221　　ISBN: 1-85158-320-3
　　　　　　　　　　　　　　　BL: YK.1991.b.1827

In 1928 England were beaten 5-1 at Wembley by the 'auld enemy', Scotland. Over 65 years later, it is still regarded as one of the great Scottish victories – the team which played that day became known simply as the 'Wembley wizards'. This is the story of the game and the side, with detailed individual coverage of all the personalities involved.

169 European league and club histories: Scotland 1890-1991 / Alexander Graham. Isle of Skye: The author, 1991?

170 Scotland: the quest for the World Cup: a complete record 1950-1994 / Clive Leatherdale; introduction by Alex Ferguson. 2nd ed. London: Two Heads Publishing in association with Desert Island Publishing, 1994.
256p; illus; pbk
(Desert Island football history series)
　　　　　　　　　　　　　　　ISBN: 1-897850-50-6

☞　Previous ed. E163

✳ *Wales*

171 Who's who of Welsh international soccer players / Gareth M. Davies & Ian Garland. Wrexham: Bridge Books, 1991.
240p; illus　　　　　　　　　ISBN: 1-87242-411-2
　　　　　　　　　　　　　　　BL: YK.1991.b.9473

Pity the poor Welsh football historian or statistician faced with a never ending list of Jones, Evans, Davies and the like! Considering the obvious pitfalls, this book is a magnificent achievement and certainly the definitive work covering those who have donned the Welsh shirt throughout history. Each player listed re

ceives a thorough treatment – height, weight, place and date of birth, date of death, positions played, international appearances, club record, honours and a pen portrait of his life and career. There are also head and shoulders pictures and some team photographs. An excellent example of what can be achieved through dedicated research. Essential reading for all students of the game from the Welsh perspective.

Overseas Football

✳ *General Studies*

172 Stanley Mortensen's international soccer book / Stanley Mortensen and others. London: Sampson Low, 1949.
156p; illus   BL: 7917.c.50

This is one of the earliest popular publications on this aspect of the game. The author achieved high status as a player with Blackpool and England, going on to score a staggering 24 goals in 25 games for his country.

173 Soccer revolution / Willy Meisl. London: Phoenix Sports Books, 1955.
192p; illus   BL: 7922.c.13

This important work was inspired by England's shock 6-3 defeat at Wembley in 1953 at the hands of Hungary, the 'Magnificent Magyars'. Six months later, England suffered a 7-1 reverse in Budapest. It was evident that England, having given football to the world, had lessons to learn from its former pupils. This is a study of the changing face of football at the time of an important transition from the old to the new. The author kept goal for Austria and is related to Hugo Meisl the famous manager of the highly successful Austrian 'Wunderteam' of the 1930s.

174 The international football book for boys / edited by Stratton Smith and others. London: Souvenir Press, 1959-

Published annually   BL: 7925.c.20
Published annually from 1959, this yields much of interest on the world scene, with many accompanying photographs.

175 Sport international / edited by Charles Harvey. London: Sampson Low, Marston, 1960.
415p; illus; index
Football section compiled by Bernard Joy   BL: 7923.w.6
☞ Also listed at: A78

176 World soccer: the international magazine. London: Websters, 1960-
Published monthly   ISSN: 0043-9037
                                    BL: P.P.8003.zs

177 Kenneth Wolstenholme's book of world soccer. London: Daily Mirror Newspapers, 1961.
120p; illus   BL: X.044/17

178 World soccer digest. London, 1961-
                                    BL: P.P.7618.fy

179 The world book of football champions. London, 1962-
                                    BL: 7925.h.26

180 European international football / Gordon Jeffery. London: Nicholas Kaye, 1963.
272p   BL: 7926.pp.14

Presented in four sections: A Brief Survey; The Story and Records of Full International Matches of 32 Countries; Specific Match Summaries; European Regional Competitions. This is one of the earliest attempts at a serious study of the game in the wider European context.

181 World football handbook / compiled by Brian Glanville. London: Hodder & Stoughton, 1964-

Published annually   BL: X.449/398
It was during the sixties that the British public really began to sit up and take notice of what was going on in the football world overseas. Glanville responded to this interest with the first world football handbook which gave information on many of the world's leading club and international sides.

182 The AB-Z of world football / Maurice Golesworthy and Roger Macdonald. London: Pelham, 1966.
278p; illus   BL: X.449/2270

Brief histories and records of clubs from around the world, numbering 180 in all. Excellent reference work.

183 Soccer: the international way / edited by Kenneth Wheeler, with 105 photographs. London: Kaye & Ward, 1967.
128p; illus   BL: X.441/930
☞ Also listed at: G234

184 Britain versus Europe / Roger MacDonald. London: Pelham, 1968.
312p; illus   BL: X.449/2961

Detailed chronicle of the performance of British sides against European opponents throughout the history of European competition.

185 Bobby Charlton's book of European football. London: Souvenir Press, 1969-1972?
128p; illus   BL: P.441/364

One of England's greatest ever exponents of the game here lends his name to a general work on European soccer – particularly strong on photographic content.

186 European football book no. 1. London: Stanley Paul, 1969.
106p; illus   ISBN: 0-09-098110-3

187 European football book no. 2. London: Stanley Paul, 1970.
128p; illus   ISBN: 0-09-103360-8

188 European soccer / edited by L. N. Bailey. London: Pelham, 1970.
234p; illus   SBN: 7207-0190-2
                               BL: X.629/3023

189 World football at your feet: what to watch and who to follow / Paul Trevillion. London: Stanley Paul, 1970.
124p; illus   SBN: 09-103180-X
                               BL: X.620/1508

Trevillion is best known for his action and sequence shots of players displaying their skills. His distinctive illustrations form the basis for this particular publication which introduces us to leading players from the worldwide football scene.

190 Scientific soccer in the seventies / Roger MacDonald and Eric Batty; illustrations designed by Rod MacLeod. London: Pelham, 1971.
160p; illus   SBN: 7207-0431-6
                               BL: X.629/3251

Studies the methods, tactics and strategies employed by the different footballing nations. Particular note is made of the nations competing in the 1970 World Cup competition.

☞ Also listed at: G236

191 Brian Glanville's book of world football. London: Dragon Books, 1972.
124p; illus   ISBN 0-583-30181-9
                               BL: X.619/6338

192 The Hamlyn book of world soccer / Peter Arnold and Christopher Davis. London: Hamlyn, 1973.
236p; illus   ISBN 0-600-33897-5
                               BL: X.625/100

Particularly strong on the history of the game in various parts of the world.

193 World soccer from A to Z / edited by Norman Barrett. London: Pan Books, 1973.
355p; illus   ISBN 0-330-23786-1
                               BL: X.611/3755

Very detailed coverage – 503 biographies of great players from all eras, histories of 113 famous clubs, 83 different competitions and a survey of 147 countries – excellent worldwide account.

194 Bass Charrington world football handbook / compiled by Brian Glanville. London: Queen Anne Press, 1974?-
255p; illus; pbk
(A Playfair publication)
    Spine title : World football handbook
                               ISBN: 0-362-00203-7

195 Football!: the story of all the world's football games / Nicholas Mason. London: Temple Smith, 1974.
xvi, 256p; illus   ISBN 0-85117-063-3
                               BL: X.620/7717

Useful book for students wishing to compare the nuances of association football with other codes of football played throughout the world. Rugby, Gaelic, American, Australian etc. are all given their place in this detailed and well researched publication.

196 The sportsman's world of soccer / edited by Martin Tyler. London: Marshall Cavendish, 1976.
152p; illus
(Golden hands books)
    'Some of this material has previously appeared in the part work "The Game"' – t.p. verso
                               ISBN: 0-85685-120-5
                               BL: X.0975/4(93)

☞ Also listed at: A119

197 The Hamlyn international book of soccer / contributors, Michael Archer and others. London: Hamlyn, 1977.
208p; illus; index   ISBN: 0-600-38247-8
                               BL: X.622/6117

An excellent reference source covering the history of soccer in Britain, Europe, North America, Australasia, Africa, Asia and South America with much additional material on famous players, great matches and tactical development. Well worth consulting.

198 World soccer skill / Dave Spurdens. Ipswich: Studio Publications, 1977.
3-61p; illus   ISBN: 0-904584-41-0
                               BL: X.622/6356

A description and explanation of the skills, tricks and ploys of famous players from the worldwide scene. The 54 famous names include Roberto Rivelino and Steve Heighway – evidently a wide-ranging survey!

199 Soccer: the world game / written and edited by Phil Soar and Martin Tyler. London: Marshall Cavendish, 1978.
185p; illus; index
    'Some of this material was first published in the part work "The game"' – t.p. verso
                               ISBN: 0-85685-490-5
                               BL: X.622/6752

☞ Subsequent ed. E213

200 The big matches / Brian Moore and Martin Tyler. London: Queen Anne Press, 1980.
189p; illus; index   ISBN: 0-362-00501-X
                               BL: X.622/9767

Well known television commentator and Gillingham follower Brian Moore here presents a selection of the most memorable matches from the world stage throughout history.

201 Soccer coaching: the European way / edited by Eric G.
Batty. London: Souvenir, 1980.
240p; illus   ISBN: 0-285-62354-0
                                BL: X.622/9097

An analysis of the differing methods employed
throughout Europe including contributions by leading
coaching figures. There are chapters by Greenwood,
Weisweiler, Sexton, Jezek, Baroti, Michels, Bluntstone, Shilton, Lea and Street.

☞ Also listed at: G163

202 Football and great footballers: star portraits, facts &
figures, training tips, games & quizzes, great match
reports. Harlow: Longman, 1981.
48p; illus, 1 plan; pbk   ISBN: 0-582-78522-7
                                BL: X.622/11823

Lightweight study included here as it is addressed directly at African students – may contain ephemeral
material of use to researchers studying the way
football is perceived by the African nations.

203 Kevin Keegan's international football book / compiled
by B. Apsley. Manchester: World International, 1981.
59p; illus   ISBN: 0-7235-6634-8
                                BL: X.622/13772

Lightweight study written during the author's playing
days with Southampton. He was well qualified to present this volume, however, having just returned from
three years in Germany with SV Hamburg where he
earned the nickname 'Mighty Mouse' and helped them
win the German Championship.

204 The Hamlyn world encyclopedia of football / written,
compiled and edited by Phil Soar, Martin Tyler and
Richard Widdows. London: Hamlyn, 1984.
184p; illus; 2 maps; index   ISBN: 0-600-34730-3
                                BL: X.622/22761

Good general world coverage but later eclipsed by
more comprehensive works.

205 Matches of the day 1958-83: a footballing history /
Derek Dougan & Patrick Murphy. London: Dent, 1984.
xiv, 178p; illus   ISBN: 0-460-04630-6
                                BL: X.622/21410

Descriptions of memorable matches seen on the
world stage, from Brazil v. Sweden in 1958 to England v. Denmark in 1983.

206 World club football directory. London: Queen Anne
Press, 1984-
    Published annually   BL: P.441/1105

207 World soccer skills / David Spurdens. London: Hamlyn,
1984.
128p; illus, plans   ISBN: 0-600-38552-3
                                BL: X.622/22330

208 World football / Steve Tongue. London: Treasure, 1986.
80p; maps; index   ISBN: 1-85051-157-8
                                BL: LB.31.b.2774

209 Europe 88. London: Associated Magazines, 1988.
1 folded sheet   ISBN: 0-85144-457-1
                                BL: YK.1988.b.5628

210 The European football yearbook. Exeter: Facer, 1988-
illus
    Published annually   BL: ZK.9.a.2059

This excellent annual publication is a largely statistical coverage of all the UEFA member countries and
their clubs – an extremely comprehensive reference
work.

211 The handbook of soccer: a complete guide to football,
the world game / Don Howe and Brian Scovell.
London: Pelham, 1988.
240p; illus; index   SBN: 0-7207-1792-2
                                BL: YK.1988.b.5889

212 Football in Europe / David Clayton. Cleethorpes:
Soccer Book Publishing, 1989-
illus; pbk
    Published annually   BL: ZK.9.a.2069

Very much one for the statistician; this gives all the
final league tables, results in the main cups and international line-ups – effectively a complete record of
the European scene for the season in question. Much
relatively obscure information is to be found here –
for example, the 1990/91 edition contains sixteen
sets of final tables and fifteen international line-ups
in the Romanian section alone and San Marino and
Faroe Islands receive full coverage on a par with
France, Spain, Italy and other high profile footballing
nations.

213 Soccer: the world game. Rev. ed. London: Hamlyn, 1989.
192p; illus; index
                                ISBN: 0-600-56350-2
                                BL: YK.1990.b.9281

Includes chapters on each of 25 European countries,
six South American countries plus Mexico, Algeria,
Cameroon, Morocco and Egypt. The introduction is by
Terry Venables, the current England manager.

☞ Previous ed. E199

214 The world's greatest football matches. London: Octopus
Books, 1989.
160p; pbk   ISBN: 0-7064-3890-6

General survey of great games throughout the history of world football.

215 Soccer research / Association of European Football
Statisticians. Norwich: The Association, 1990-
    Published monthly   ISSN: 0960-9695
                                BL: ZK.9.b.3301

The AEFS is dedicated to the promotion and study
of football statistics in the wider European sense
rather than simply on the domestic front.

216 Eurosoccer statistics / Mike Hammond. Birmingham:
Sports Projects, 1991.   ISBN: 0-946866-02-3

*One of the features amongst football followers in re-
cent years has been the significant upturn of
interest in the game over the Channel, a trend encouraged by the more comprehensive television
coverage now taken for granted. As writing on the
game in Europe has increased, the need for accurate
statistics and information has at the same time become paramount. This publication is something of a
landmark for football, being one of the first to offer
detailed statistical coverage for all 35 UEFA member
nations.*

217 European soccer who's who / Nich Hills. Enfield:
Guinness, 1992.
320p; pbk   ISBN: 0-85112-570-0
                                          BL: YK.1993.a.8401

*Over 2,500 players are listed alphabetically, detailing
their club, position and date of birth with a short pen
picture. Very much conceived in response to the growing interest in the overseas game prevalent at the
time of publication, an interest which has continued
to grow.*

218 The Guinness record of world soccer: the history of the
game in over 150 countries / Guy Oliver. Enfield:
Guinness, 1992.
x, 870p; illus

Bibliography: p865-866   ISBN: 0-85112-954-4
                                          BL: YK.1993.b.11640

*Promoted by the publishers as 'the most comprehen-
sive guide to the world's most popular game, covering
the history of all 169 members of FIFA'. Each country's entry is supported by masses of statistics and
text and there is a special coverage of results from
the Olympic Games and other less well known competitions. This book is specially recommended as a
possible starting point for any research project on
the world scene. Areas of interest can be identified
and then supported by consulting other more specialist works from the bibliographic listings in this
chapter.*

219 Shoot soccer: the world game. London: Hamlyn, 1992.
192p; illus; index   ISBN: 0-600-57691-4
                                          BL: YK.1992.b.8657

220 Nations of Europe / Ron Hockings and Keir Radnedge.
Emsworth: Articulate, 1993.
2 vols; 800p

Vol 1: Albania to Iceland; vol 2: Italy to Yugoslavia
                                          ISBN: 0-9517533-4-7

*A statistical history of international football from
1872-1992 – this massive survey covers every match
ever played by each European national team during
the period. In addition to the results, line-ups and
scorers from 8,000 matches, there is a review of the
history and achievements of each country.*

221 World football directory / Arthur Jones and Keir
Radnedge. IMS, 1993.

*Youth tournaments, World Club Cup, continental cups
and many lesser known competitions are all chronicled in this massive survey. Largely statistical, this
is a good research tool for those needing to unearth
the more obscure records from around the world.
Also includes an A to Z of all FIFA members with addresses of headquarters and over 2,000 club
addresses.*

222 Complete football international. 1994-
illus

Published monthly   ISSN: 1355-0543
                                          BL: ZK.9.a.3557

223 Rothmans European football yearbook / edited by
Bruce Smith. London: Headline, 1994-
400p; illus; pbk

224 Giving the game away: association football on different
continents / Stephen Wagg. Leicester: Leicester
University Press, 1995.
240p
(Sport, politics and culture)
     ISBN: 0-7185-1677-X (cased) • ISBN: 0-7185-1887-X (pbk)

*Extremely interesting account of the game as it is
perceived and practised against the background of
different cultural and political regimes. Rather different to the standard approach – well worth
consulting.*

✻ *Africa*

225 Football in Africa / Anver Versi. London: Collins, 1986.
vii, 172p; illus; pbk

                                          ISBN: 0-00-327808-5
                                          BL: YK.1987.b.617

*Substantially more text than statistics. One of Af-
rica's leading sports writers here presents the first
ever comprehensive coverage of the game which enjoys huge popularity throughout the continent. Since
the publication date our own interest in the game
there has been heightened by the exciting performances seen in World Cup games by Cameroon, Nigeria
and others. All the African nations are covered in
this excellent introduction to the subject.*

✻ NIGERIA

226 Football in Nigeria / Samuel Ekpe Akpabot. London:
Macmillan, 1985.
viii, 104p; illus; pbk

                                          ISBN: 0-333-37931-4
                                          BL: YK.1987.b.6030

*Having joined FIFA in 1959, Nigeria have always been
recognised as one of the more promising of the African nations. Yet, when this book was written, they*

had still to achieve the world exposure which came only recently with their appearance in the 1994 World Cup finals, where some of their football was a joy to watch. Essential reading for all researchers into the Nigerian and African game.

✻ SOUTH AFRICA

227 The world game comes to South Africa / Vivian Granger. London: Bailey & Swinfer, 1961.
xiv, 229p; illus

BL: X.449/862

When we think of African football we inevitably consider the North, the East and the West — the general football follower knows little of the game in South Africa although it has of course been played there for many years. Strangely this study was published in the very year in which South Africa was suspended from FIFA on political grounds. This is an interesting study particularly set against the time in which it was written.

✻ *Asia*

228 The little red book of Chinese football / Dave Twydell. Harefield: Yore, 1994.
70p; illus; pbk

ISBN: 1-874427-80-1

A concise history of football in China and Hong Kong.

✻ *Australia*

229 Introduction to Australian soccer / Tom Gough. Bognor Regis: New Horizon, 1983.
39p; illus, 1 map   ISBN: 0-86116-967-0
BL: X.629/23037

Australian soccer has not enjoyed a high international profile in general although the national side rose to fame as the 'Socceroos' when they qualifyed for the 1974 World Cup finals. Most English followers know little more of Australian soccer than the bizarre listing of club names encountered in the summer Football Pools coupons or, even more bizarrely, printed on a certain brand of sherbet sweets in the 1970s. Further enlightenment may be gained by consulting this short introductory study.

✻ *Europe*

✻ ALBANIA

230 Albania Football Club: a lighthearted but factual account of football in Albania / Dave Twydell. Uxbridge: The author, 1989.
48p; illus; pbk   ISBN: 0-951332-11-2

The title says it all — an unusual study from one of football's best known historians with an eye for delving into

the less accessible corners of the football world. Albania have never made it to the World Cup finals — this is their moment of glory in publishing terms containing much of interest alongside some curious anecdotal material.

✻ GERMANY

231 The Fussball book: German football since the Bundesliga / Dave Wangerin. Perton: The author, 1993.
228p; pbk   ISBN: 0-9522452-0-5
BL: YK.1994.a.2512

This spin-off publication from the fanzine 'Elfmeter' is the first ever English language book on German football. A detailed history of the Bundesliga from 1963 — essential reading for all students of the game as played by England's fiercest rivals.

✻ ITALY

232 Football Italia / Ray Della Pietra and Giancarlo Rinaldi. London: Virgin, 1993.
144p; illus; pbk

ISBN: 0-86369-702-X

The Italian passion for the game of football has always been well known and British football followers have come to share that passion, particularly since the 1990 World Cup held in Italy helped along by increased TV coverage of the continental game. Indeed, there is a distinct and ever-growing band of 'calcio' lovers and this book caters well for their needs. Essential reading for anyone researching the Italian game.

233 Forza Italia football / edited by R. Bonnet. London: Century 22, 1993.
80p; illus   ISBN: 0-907938-05-1

Rather more lightweight but also well worth consultation.

✻ SPAIN

234 The Real Madrid book of football / edited by Ramón Melcón & Stratton Smith. London: Souvenir, 1961.
143p; illus   BL: X.449/500

Only a magnificent European club could warrant treatment in a publication in this country. Real Madrid were just such a club in the fifties and sixties, winning the European Cup on the first five occasions, being undefeated at home from February 1957 to March 1965 and crowned as the first World Club champions in 1961 following victory over the South American club Penarol. This book presents a most interesting and informative survey of the club's history and achievements with many photographs and contributions from leading players.

235 The Real Madrid book of football / edited by Ramón
Melcón & Stratton Smith. London: World Distributors,
1962.
137p; illus
(Consul books; no. 772)   BL: X.449/521

❋ *North America*

236 The American encyclopedia of soccer / edited by
Zander Hollander. London: Everest, 1980.
544p

An extremely detailed guide to the history and development of the game in the USA.

237 NASL: a complete record of the North American Soccer
League / Colin Jose. Derby: Breedon Books, 1989.
352p; illus   ISBN: 0-907969-569
BL: YK.1993.b.5343

The definitive UK produced work on the NASL. The
League was established in 1968 in a determined effort to organise a nationwide football network in the
USA, but it had a troubled history. Many British
players had spells with US sides, often during the
twilight of their careers and these are all well covered
here. The League was dubbed 'elephants graveyard' by
Italian star Gianni Rivera and it floundered in its existing form in 1985. Excellent study.

238 The United States and World Cup soccer competition:
an encyclopedic history of the United States in
international competition / Colin Jose. London:
Scarecrow, 1994.
xiv, 350p; illus
(American sports history series; no. 2)
ISBN: 0-8108-2881-2
BL: YK.1994.b.7264

239 Dancing in the streets: tales from World Cup city / Don
Watson. London: Gollancz, 1994.
250p; pbk   ISBN: 0-575-05882-X
The author's personal view of the relationship between football, America, politics and culture in the
year in which they staged the World Cup finals.

❋ *South America*

240 Hockings' South American cups: a statistical history of
South American football since 1893 / Ron Hockings.
Emsworth: Articulate, 1991.
175p; illus   ISBN: 0-9517533-0-4
BL: YK.1992.a.11932

Football in South America is played and followed with
a passion that makes even the British game appear
lukewarm. This is a definitive study of the game and
its competitions throughout the continent.

241 International football in South America, 1901-1991 /
Miguel Angel Bestard; text translated by Helen Bonser;
edited by Michael Robinson & Mike Ross. Cleethorpes:
Soccer Book Publishing, 1992.
128p; illus   ISBN: 0-947808-21-3
BL: YK.1992.b.5170

A full country by country record of the international
game as played by South American countries with
many player profiles and photographs.

242 Football in Latin America / Tony Mason. London:
Verso, 1995.
192p
(Sport & Latin American studies)
ISBN: 0-86091-403-8 (cased) • ISBN: 0-86091-667-7 (pbk)

❋ BRAZIL

243 The Brazil book of football / edited by Stratton Smith
and others. London: Souvenir, 1963.
127p; illus
BL: 7926.h.2

The Brazilian team has always captured the imagination and interest of football followers far from South
America. Having won the World Cup both in 1958 and
1962, their popularity was at a sufficient high to warrant this English publication. It includes
contributions from some of their most illustrious figures – Pelé, Garrincha, Didi, Zagallo and Mauro.

❋ ECUADOR

244 Football in Ecuador: the grounds & history / Gustavo
Ramirez. Cleethorpes: Soccer Book Publishing, 1991.
57p; pbk   ISBN: 0-947808-18-3
BL: LB.31.a.3749

This history of the game in Ecuador includes 58 full
page ground photographs, a complete club listing as
well as comprehensive records of all the international
matches.

✳ *Statistics*

245 European league and club histories: [various countries] / Alexander Graham. Isle of Skye: The author, 1991-

> This series of publications have been produced on word processor by the author from his home on the Isle of Skye and are presented in spiral bound format. They comprise a statistical history of league tables, cup finals, club profiles and summary charts for each of the countries listed.

Albania 1930-1992	Luxembourg 1909-1992
Austria 1911-1991	Malta 1909-1991
Belgium 1895-1992	Norway 1902-1992
Bulgaria 1937-1991	Poland 1921-1991
Czechoslovakia 1925-1991	Portugal 1921-1991
East Germany 1948-1991	Romania 1921-1991
Finland 1930-1991	Spain 1928-1991
France 1932-1991	Sweden 1936-1991
Greece 1921-1991	Switzerland 1897-1991
Holland 1888-1954	Turkey 1922-1992
Holland 1954-1991	USSR 1936-1991
Hungary 1901-1991	West Germany 1945-1992
Iceland 1912-1991	Yugoslavia 1923-1992
Italy 1898-1992	

246 The international matches of [various countries] / David Clayton and Jan Buitenga. 1990?-

> Another example of a home-published work, this time detailing all international matches in chronological order with full supporting statistics. Countries covered are as listed below.

Czechoslovakia 1920-1990	Malta 1957-1990
DDR 1952-1990	Poland 1921-1990
Greece 1920-1990	Portugal 1921-1990
Holland 1905-1990	Romania 1922-1991
Iceland 1946-1990	Spain 1920-1991
Italy 1910-1990	Turkey 1923-1992
Latvia 1922-1990	USSR 1924-1989
Lithuania 1922-1940	Yugoslavia 1920-1990

Most Written About World Cup Tournaments

1st USA (1994) . . . . 18 books

2nd Spain (1982) . . . . 16 books

3rd Argentina (1978) . . . . . . 14 books

4th England (1966) . . . . 13 books

5th Italy (1990) . . . . 12 books

Grounds

PLAYERS AND SUPPORTERS ARE BOTH CRUCIAL to the game of football but there can be quite a gulf between them. The common bond uniting each with the other is the club and its ground. The ground is the club's physical and spiritual home and while the uninitiated might dismiss the playing venue as so much grass, bricks, concrete and steel, true supporters know otherwise and acknowledge the very real emotional attachment they have to the ground itself.

For many, there is a spiritual dimension to this emotion. Like great cathedrals, many football stadiums are monumental structures and observers of social behaviour are quick to pursue the analogy; pilgrimage, worship, devotion and faith are not uncommon words in football literature and there is no doubt that the football club plays a central role in the lives of many supporters. These strong emotional ties explain why a number of the books in this chapter have achieved cult status and have become best sellers.

Sceptics might argue that football grounds are too mundane a subject to be taken so seriously. They may make mocking comparison with *Great Supermarkets of the World* or even *NCP Car Parks Then and Now*, but truly, they miss the point. A kinder comparison would be with social histories of the public house (of which there are many) for both are 'homes' of a kind, where people meet and relax, enjoy themselves and take their ease. And it is the supporters, by and large, who display the strongest bond with their home town venues. Players, managers and coaches come and go – for them the ground is little more than a place of work.

But for supporters the association is much more enduring. Changes of school, job, house, even of partner may rock our lives, yet through them all the regular football follower will tread the same path to the same stadium, through the same turnstile to the same stand, year after year after year. On familiar 'ground' indeed. It brings to mind the sentiment expressed by Sherlock Holmes (a great traditionalist): 'Good old Watson! You are the one fixed point in a changing age'. It is with this comforting sense of constancy that I turn to summarise this chapter. It is certainly significant that no serious work charting the history and development of football grounds appeared until the 1980s, for it was only then that a threat to such constancy began to appear.

Modernisation, demolition, sharing arrangements and 'moving home' have become important issues in the last decade. It is thanks to Simon Inglis that some record of the true essence of the 'old style' football grounds was made on the very eve of their demise. His *Football Grounds of England and Wales* [F4] is a marvellous achievement, presenting detailed descriptions of all the Football League grounds along with a scholarly overview of the historical background to stadium design and development. The grounds depicted in his evocative photographs have now changed considerably as a result of new safety legislation. Subsequent publications by Inglis covered the grounds of Scotland [F6] and Europe [F7]. Both are authoritative and important works.

If Simon Inglis is the acknowledged authority on football architecture at first class level, then Tony Williams must surely take the honours when it comes to studying playing venues in the lower strata. His *Non-League Football Grounds of Great Britain* [F10] represents a phenomenal achievement in chronicling over 700 of the venues used at this level, many of which display a combination of reassuring charm and idiosyncrasy now lost forever from more famous homes.

To make up a trio of leading contributors to the literature of football grounds, it is fitting that Dave Twydell should complete the hat trick as the research involved in his publications is truly original. His speciality is the study of grounds long since vacated by their owners and his retrospective studies employ the techniques of local history and industrial archaeology to uncover the past in his own inimitable style. If Simon Inglis merits the title of 'stadiologist' then Dave Twydell is surely an 'ancient stadiologist' – his *Football League Grounds for a Change* [F31] charts the domestic movements of all the clubs who have played in the Football League whilst his ongoing *Gone But Not Forgotten* series [F32-36] records for posterity the homes of non-league clubs no longer in existence.

Completing the list of works charting the history and development of grounds is a section of titles specific to Wembley Stadium, home to the FA Cup Final, and many important fixtures since 1923. *The Story of the Building of the Greatest Stadium in the World* [F20], a scarce eight page book from 1923, is one of the earliest works about football stadiums, reflecting the magnitude of the achievement in the context of the times.

In the Safety and Design section are reminders of the serious crowd disasters which have occurred throughout the history of organised football and which have prompted both official reports and legislation. The 1985 fire disaster at Bradford, the Heysel Stadium tragedy of the same year, and the horrific consequences of Hillsborough in 1989 are only the most recent examples. This quick succession of disasters and the recommendations for ground safety procedures of Lord Justice Taylor [F50, F54] have set in motion a completely new era of football stadium design.

Simon Inglis is again at the forefront, acting as editor for a series of detailed reports published by the Football Stadia Advisory Design Council. These have assisted architects and football administrators to create magnificent new footballing homes which even die-hard traditionalists are growing to appreciate.

As we come full circle, from the nostalgia for the past to the technologically advanced aspirations for the future we remind ourselves that in time, 'Stadium 2000' will itself become the object of misty eyed reminiscence for future generations of football followers.

Researchers into this important aspect of association football will find much worthwhile and original material in this chapter, presented by a range of enthusiastic and talented experts.

Grounds ~ Contents

Grounds

1   I am a football ground / illustrations by Jose Ramon Sanchez; English text by Ruth Thomson. Oxford: Blackwell, 1977.
36p; chiefly illus
(Who am I? second series)

These illustrations originally published with Spanish text as: Soy un estadio. Madrid: Ediciones Altea, 1977
ISBN: 0-631-18520-8
BL: X.620/17547

I am only really happy
when there is a match,

because
I am a football ground.

2   Behind the scenes at the football match / Graham Hart; illustrated by Steve Smallman. Cambridge: Dinosaur for Cambridge University Press, 1983.
24p; illus
ISBN: 0-521-25849-9 (cased) • ISBN: 0-521-27530-X (pbk)
BL: X.629/23840

Includes material of interest to the Cambridge United follower.

3   Football club / Andrew Langley; photography by Chris Fairclough. London: Watts, 1983.
30p; illus; index
(Behind the scenes)
ISBN: 0-86313-039-9
BL: X.990/21977

4   The football grounds of England and Wales / Simon Inglis. London: Willow, 1983.
272p; illus

Published in association with the Football League and the National Dairy Council
Bibliography: p272
ISBN: 0-00-218024-3
BL: X.622/18485

Essential reading for all researchers of this subject; original and definitive, it includes much historical background and photographic material of value to historians and groundhoppers alike.

☞ Subsequent ed. F6

5   A chronological account of a journey: in search of York City / Malcolm Howe. York: Ebor Press, 1987.
44p; illus; pbk
ISBN: 0-9512338-0-7
BL: YK.1989.a.1386

Malcolm Howe was born in 1948 and has supported York City from boyhood. This is an account of his travels to 81 league grounds in pursuit of his team, giving his impressions of each one.

☞ Also listed at: B902

6   The football grounds of Great Britain / Simon Inglis. New ed. London: Willow, 1987.
368p; illus; pbk

Includes bibliography
ISBN: 0-00-218260-2 (cased) • ISBN: 0-00-218249-1 (pbk)
BL: YK.1987.b.5286

This volume includes additional material embracing 38 Scottish League clubs. It has become something of a cult book.

☞ Previous ed. F4; subsequent ed. F16

7   The football grounds of Europe / Simon Inglis. London: Collins, 1990.
228p; illus; index
ISBN: 0-00-218305-6
BL: YK.1990.b.1798

An authoritative and definitive work on European grounds with numerous photographs.

8   Full colour views of the Football League grounds / photography by Chris Ambler. Cleethorpes: Soccer Book Publishing, 1990.
104p; chiefly illus, plans; pbk
ISBN: 0-947808-14-0
BL: YK.1992.b.2995

Postcard-type views of all the League grounds – contains little text.

9   The non-league football grounds of Great Britain /
     edited by T. Williams. Taunton: The author in
     association with Atcost Buildings Ltd and the Football
     Association, 1990.
     576p; pbk   ISBN: 1-869833-10-4

     A massive survey – many non-league grounds still
     display features which have long disappeared from
     the major venues, affording a distinctive atmosphere
     peculiar to the non-league scene. Covers over 700
     grounds.

     ☞ Subsequent ed. F10

10   The non-league football grounds of Great Britain: a
     review of all senior club grounds from Conference to
     County level / Tony Williams; edited by James Wright.
     2nd ed. Taunton: The author, 1992.
     546p; illus; pbk   ISBN: 1-869833-25-2

     ☞ Previous ed. F9

11   Review of all-seated requirements for football grounds.
     Edinburgh: Scottish Office Education Department, 1992.
     4 stapled sheets

12   Fields of Fife / E. Thomson. Lytham St. Annes: The
     author, 1993.
     78p; pbk

     A most unusual study taking a look not at the major
     stadiums but at the non-league venues and various
     homely 'fields' known to the author in this part of
     Scotland. If you live in this region it is quite possible
     your back lawn may be listed!

13   Football grounds / edited by Dave Twydell. Addlestone:
     Dial, 1993.
     192p; chiefly illus; pbk
     (Aerofilms guide)   ISBN: 0-7110-2157-0
                                          BL: YK.1994.b.7732

     A largely photographic study with aerial views of all
     the major grounds – an important visual record at a
     time when many changes are occurring.

     ☞ Subsequent ed. F15

14   The Hampden story / Russell Galbraith. Edinburgh:
     Mainstream, 1993.
     221p; illus

     Includes bibliography   ISBN: 1-85158-445-5

     Hampden Park is considered Scotland's national sta-
     dium; it is also the home ground of Queen's Park. The
     ground's capacity, although much reduced in recent
     years, still outnumbers their home gate by a sub-
     stantial ratio on a regular basis.

15   Football grounds / edited by Dave Twydell. 2nd
     enlarged ed. Addlestone: Dial, 1994.
     224p; illus; pbk
     (Aerofilms guide)   ISBN: 0-7110-2301-8
                                          BL: YK.1995.b.4840

     This second edition of aerial views has been enlarged
     to include Scottish clubs and has fresh photographs
     of all the English stadia reflecting the many changes
     over the last year.

     ☞ Previous ed. F13

16   The football grounds of Great Britain / Simon Inglis.
     Rev. ed. London: CollinsWillow, 1994.
     416p; illus; pbk   ISBN: 0-00-218426-5

     ☞ Previous ed. F6

17   Football grounds then and now / Michael Heatley and
     Daniel Ford. Shepperton: Dial, 1994.
     160p; illus

         Also entitled: British football grounds then and now
                                          ISBN: 0-7110-2302-6
                                          BL: YK.1995.b.5487

     Includes some particularly early previously unpub-
     lished photographs of a number of grounds,
     illustrating the massive changes which have occurred
     in ground architecture throughout the century.

18   Guinness guide to League football grounds / Jon Ladd.
     London: Guinness, 1994.
     192p; illus; pbk   ISBN: 0-85112-779-7

19   Stadio mio: encyclopaedia of Italian football stadiums
     and clubs / Barrymore ÓhAilpéne. Lincoln: The author,
     1994.
     565p; illus
     (Professionisti serie A-B-C)   ISBN: 0-9521096-1-1

     Television coverage of the Italian League from the
     early nineties created a significant following amongst
     UK based football lovers. Some of the Italian grounds
     are the most technologically advanced in the football
     world – this is a comprehensive guide.

Wembley Stadium

The entries hereunder have all been included as they contain many references to Cup Finals and Internationals played at this world-famous venue.

20 The story of the building of the greatest stadium in the world. London: Sir Robert MacAlpine & Sons, 1923.
8p; pbk   BL: 7816.pp.27

This was published in the same year that the first FA Cup Final was held at Wembley Stadium.

THE STORY
OF THE BUILDING OF THE
GREATEST STADIUM
IN THE WORLD

21 Wembley presents 22 years of sport / Tom Morgan. Wembley: Wembley Empire Stadium, Pool & Sports Arena, 1945.
79p; illus; pbk   BL: 7918.aaa.2

☞ Subsequent ed. F22

22 Wembley presents 25 years of sport, 1923-1948 / Tom Morgan. 2nd ed. Wembley: Wembley Empire Stadium, Pool & Sports Arena, 1948.
103p   BL: 7919.c.18

☞ Previous ed. F21

23 Wonderful Wembley / Archibald Montgomery Low. London: Stanley Paul, 1953.
192p; illus   BL: 010349.u.24

24 Wembley Empire Stadium and Sports Arena / H. C. Hastings. London: Pitkins, 1956.
23p; pbk
(Pride of Britain)   BL: 7923.c.7

25 All roads lead to Wembley / Alastair Revie. London: Pelham, 1971.
176p; illus   ISBN: 0-7207-0443-X

26 Wembley: 50 glorious years in pictures / Colin Stuart. London: David Bruce & Watson, 1971.
109p; illus   ISBN: 0-85127-003-4
      BL: LB.31.a.5209

27 Wembley: fifty great years / Harry Gee. London: Pelham, 1972.
178p; illus   ISBN: 0-7207-0593-2
      BL: X.629/4666

28 Wembley 1923-1973: the official Wembley story. London: Wembley Stadium, 1973.
155p

Includes 48 pages by Brian Glanville entitled 'Football at Wembley'.

29 Summary of the salient sections of the Wembley Stadium report for the Football Association and the Sports Council / Rogers Chapman. West Drayton: Rogers Chapman, 1980.
13p; pbk

30 Glorious Wembley: the official history of Britain's foremost entertainment centre / Howard Bass. Enfield: Guinness Superlatives, 1982.
175p; illus; index; pbk   ISBN: 0-85112-237-X
      BL: X.622/18669

Former Grounds

31 Football League: grounds for a change / Dave Twydell. Harefield: The author, 1991.
423p; illus, maps   ISBN: 0-9513321-4-7
      BL: YK.1992.a.1873

Over the years most clubs have moved grounds; indeed the emotive issue of 'moving home' is taking a very high profile for many clubs at present. Dave Twydell studies all the Football League clubs and chronicles their domestic movements throughout history with a good balance of text, photography, diagrams and maps. The result is unique – I think

Twydell deserves the sobriquet 'Father of Football Archaeology' as he has surely created a new discipline; many of the techniques of industrial archaeology and local history are employed to fascinating effect.

32 Gone but not forgotten: part 1 / Dave Twydell.
Harefield: Yore, 1992.
52p; illus, maps
ISBN: 1-874427-25-9
BL: ZK.9.a.2832

Many non-league clubs fold, disappear or move over the years. This book recalls the former grounds of nine such clubs by text, maps and photographs. The five defunct clubs are Addlestone and Weybridge, St. Neots Town, Coventry Sporting, Post Office Engineers, and Catford Southend; the current clubs are Grantham, Ashford Town, Winchester City, and Tonbridge.

33 Gone but not forgotten: part 2 / Dave Twydell.
Harefield: Yore, 1993.
64p; illus, maps
ISBN: 1-874427-35-6

Includes the former grounds of Hillingdon Borough, Oswestry Town, Ilford, Shirley Town, Wycombe Wanderers, and Keighley.

34 Gone but not forgotten: part 3 / Dave Twydell.
Harefield: Yore, 1993.
64p; illus, maps
ISBN: 1-874427-60-7

Third in an ongoing series; looks at the grounds of Ellesmere Port, Kingstonian, Witton Albion, Walthamstow Avenue, and Cheshunt.

35 Gone but not forgotten: part 4 / Dave Twydell.
Harefield: Yore, 1994.
64p; illus, maps
ISBN: 1-874427-70-4

36 Gone but not forgotten: part 5 / Dave Twydell.
Harefield: Yore, 1995.
64p; illus, maps
ISBN: 1-874427-01-1

Safety & Design

37 Enquiry into the disaster at the Bolton Wanderers' football ground on the 9th March, 1946: report / R. Moelwyn Hughes. London: HMSO, 1946.
12p; pbk
(Cmd. 6846)
BL: B.S.18/40(78)

On 9 March 1946, 33 lives were lost before a quarter-final cup tie against Stoke City attended by 85,000 fans. In response to what was, at that time, the worst disaster in the history of football, the enquiry recommended limitations on crowd size and the licensing of grounds.

38 Hampden, Hampden, Hampden: report of the Working Party on the Future of Hampden Park. Edinburgh: Scottish Sports Council, 1975.
2, vi, 127p; illus, maps; pbk
ISBN: 0-9500813-3-7

39 Safety of Sports Grounds Act 1975. London: HMSO, 1975.
1, 13p; pbk
(1975 c. 52)
ISBN: 0-10-545275-0

40 Guide to safety at sports grounds (football) / Home Office and Scottish Home and Health Department. London: HMSO, 1976.
iv, 30p; 2 plans; pbk
ISBN: 0-11-340761-0
BL: BS.18/1086

The Ibrox Park disaster of 2 January 1971, in which 66 people were killed at the Rangers v Celtic derby, led ultimately to the Safety at Sports Grounds Act 1975. This guide highlights its major recommendations.

☞ Subsequent ed. F47

41 Report of the National Stadium Committee. Edinburgh: Scottish Sports Council, 1977.
82p

42 League football for the disabled spectator: an access guide to the Football League grounds of England and Wales. London: Royal Association for Disability and Rehabilitation, 1979.
96p; illus; pbk
BL: X.619/19443

Facilities for disabled spectators have long been in need of improvement but, despite studies such as this, conditions even today are in many cases inadequate. This early report promulgates ideas for the future as well as being a good statement of the state of play at that time.

☞ Subsequent ed. F48

43 Interim report / Committee of Inquiry into Crowd Safety and Control at Sports Grounds. London: HMSO, 1985.
92p; illus, plans; pbk
(Cmnd 9585)

Chairman: Mr Justice Popplewell
ISBN: 0-10-195850-1
BL: BS.18/1061

The Popplewell Inquiry looked into the Bradford City fire disaster and a football riot at Birmingham City on the same day. Many recommendations were made regarding evacuation procedures, regular inspections and the banning of smoking in wooden stands. An important report which did much to jolt football administrators into a more responsible attitude.

☞ See also: F45

44 Bradford disaster appeal: the administration of an appeal fund / Roger W. Suddards with contributions by Leolin Price and Hubert Picarda. London: Sweet & Maxwell on behalf of the Trustees of the Bradford Disaster Appeal, 1986.
169p; illus

> *Bibliography: p169* ISBN: 0-421-37990-1
> BL: YC.1988.b.370

> Donations for victims and their families poured in after the 1985 Bradford City fire disaster; this in itself raised important questions about the correct and lawful handling of an appeal fund. This detailed document provided many answers.

45 Final report / Committee of Enquiry into Crowd Safety and Control at Sports Grounds. London: HMSO, 1986.
85p; pbk
(Cmnd 9710)

> *Chairman: Mr Justice Popplewell* ISBN: 0-10-197100-1
> BL: BS18/1040

> The final version of the Popplewell Report following the interim findings of July 1985.

> ☞ See also: F43

46 Football: the club in the community: workshop report. London: Sports Council, 1986.
i, 165p; illus; pbk

> *Report of a workshop organised as part of Recreation Management 1986 – the 17th National Seminar and Exhibition at the Harrogate International Centre, 25-27th February 1986* BL: BS.387/185

47 Guide to safety at sports grounds / Home Office and Scottish Office. New ed. London: HMSO, 1986.
75p; illus; pbk

> ISBN: 0-11-340840-4
> BL: BS.18/853

> This revised version followed the Bradford City fire disaster of 1985.

> ☞ Previous ed. F40

48 Spectator's access guide for disabled people / compiled by Peter Lawton. 2nd ed. London: Royal Association for Disability & Rehabilitation, 1986.
368p; maps; index; pbk

> ISBN: 0-900270-01-2

> The 1979 guide had just 96 pages; some progress had evidently been made by 1986.

> ☞ Previous ed. F42

49 Football in its place: an environmental psychology of football grounds / David Canter, Miriam Comber and David L. Uzzell. London: Routledge, 1989.
192p; index; pbk

> *Includes bibliography* ISBN: 0-415-01240-6
> BL: YC.1989.a.6528

> Football grounds and their surroundings engender an atmosphere and environment which can waver alarmingly from unbounded joy to utterly threatening. This serious study raises many questions and offers thoughtful explanations for many of the problems of crowd behaviour whilst suggesting new ways of creating better conditions in and around the stadiums.

50 The Hillsborough Stadium disaster 15 April 1989: interim report / Rt. Hon. Lord Justice Taylor. London: HMSO, 1989.
71p; illus, plans; pbk
(Cm. 765) ISBN: 0-10-107652-5
BL: BS.91/240(765)

> The worst disaster in the history of British football occurred at the home of Sheffield Wednesday on 15 April 1989. At the FA Cup semifinal between Liverpool and Nottingham Forest 95 people were killed, 170 were injured and the relatives of one victim – Tony Bland – were given permission to disconnect his life-support machinery three years later. This interim report was the first detailed official response.

> ☞ See also: F54

51 Inquiry into the Hillsborough Stadium disaster: submission of the Chief and Assistant Chief Fire Officers' Association. Tamworth: Chief and Assistant Chief Fire Officers' Association, 1989.
16p; pbk

> Although fire itself did not play a part in the Hillsborough Disaster, the question of ingress and egress most certainly did. As a result the Fire Officers' Association were asked to tender their observations – this resulted in many clubs having to make important changes to their ground designs and procedures.

52 Guidance notes for the procurement of CCTV for public safety at football grounds / A. J. Ford. St Albans: Home Office, Police Scientific Development Branch, 1990.
32p; spiral
(Publication no. 4/90) BL: YK.1991.b.2513

> Control of violence and improvements in safety can certainly be aided by the use of closed circuit television equipment. This study offers guidelines to potential users.

53 Guide to safety at sports grounds / Home Office, Scottish Office. London: HMSO, 1990.
82p; illus; pbk ISBN: 0-11-341001-8
BL: BS.18/1078

54 The Hillsborough Stadium disaster 15 April 1989: final report / Rt. Hon. Lord Justice Taylor. London: HMSO, 1990.
vii, 109p; illus; pbk
(Cm. 962) ISBN: 0-10-109622-4
BL: BS.91/240(962)

> The final report, known universally as 'The Taylor Report', summarised many of the problems of the contemporary British game and put forward a variety of proposals, one of the most far-reaching being the introduction of all-seater stadiums for the major

clubs. This in itself changed the face of the game as many of the traditional standing terraces were to disappear forever.

☞ See also: F50

55 Sports stadia after Hillsborough: papers presented at the seminar held at the Royal Institute of British Architects, 66 Portland Place, London W1 on Thursday 29 March 1990 / edited by Owen Luder. London: Royal Institute of British Architects and the Sports Council in association with the Football Trust, 1990.
x, 102p; illus; pbk
　　　　　　　　　ISBN: 0-947877-72-x
　　　　　　　　　BL: YK.1992.b.3171

Changes in ground design, in particular the provision of new stands and the conversion of terracing to seating, had an inevitable knock-on effect for professions involved in design work. Architects are here given their first briefing.

56 Stadia handbook. London: Sports Council, 1990.

☞ Subsequent ed. F60

57 Euro-stadia '91. Lytham St Annes: Football League, 1991.

Published to accompany an exhibition on football stadiums held in Birmingham 11-12 September 1991.

58 Football stadia bibliography 1980-90 / compilers: Margaret R. Hastings, Denise Gamble; editor: Simon Inglis. London: Football Stadia Advisory Design Council, 1991.
172p; pbk
(Football Stadia Advisory Design Council information booklet; issue 2)　　ISBN: 1-873831-05-6
　　　　　　　　　BL: 2725.g.1566

Includes many references from trade and specialist periodicals. The serious student of this subject would do well to consult this item.

59 Seating: sightlines, conversion of terracing, seat types / editor, Simon Inglis; technical editor and illustrator, Maritz Vandenberg. London: Football Stadia Advisory Design Council, 1991.
24p; illus, plans; pbk
(Football Stadia Advisory Design Council information booklet; issue 1)

Contents: Sightlines / Roy Sheard; Conversion of terracing / Ernest Atherden; Seat types / Tony Sherratt
　　　　　　　　　ISBN: 1-873831-00-5
　　　　　　　　　BL: YK.1993.b.4868

The Football Stadia Advisory Design Council issued a series of information booklets on stadium design; this is the first of these with particular emphasis on the conversion of terracing to seating.

60 Stadia handbook. 2nd ed. London: Sports Council, 1991.

☞ Previous ed. F56; subsequent ed. F66

61 Stadium public address systems / Peter Barnett, J. Woodgate and S. Jones; edited by Simon Inglis. London: Football Stadia Advisory Design Council, 1991 .
24p; pbk
(Football Stadia Advisory Design Council information booklet; issue 3)　　ISBN: 1-873831-10-2
　　　　　　　　　BL: YK.1993.b.1592

No stone was left unturned by Simon Inglis and his team in seeking to improve spectator conditions and safety. Clear and speedy delivery of information can be an important factor . . . hitherto football clubs have been renowned for their inaudible PA systems!

62 Designing for spectators with disabilities: with guidance on the revised building regulations / contributors: John Geraint and others; edited by Simon Inglis and Callum Murray. London: Football Stadia Advisory Design Council, 1992 .
32p; illus; pbk
(Football Stadia Advisory Design Council information booklet; issue 7)　　ISBN: 1-873831-30-7

Yet a further effort to improve facilities for this important, but too often rejected, spectator group.

63 Digest of stadia criteria: featuring the requirements of FIFA, UEFA, FA, Football League, Scottish League, GM Vauxhall Conference, Beazer Homes League, Diadora League, and HFS Loans League / edited by Simon Inglis. London: Football Stadia Advisory Design Council, 1992.
92p; pbk
(Football Stadia Advisory Design Council information booklet; issue 4)　　ISBN: 1-873831-20-X

Clubs wishing to play at certain levels need to convince the football authorities that their facilities are up to scratch. Indeed, elevation from the lower leagues can be totally ruled by this factor, irrespective of playing ability. This publication states the requirements in detail.

64 Football stadia: facilities for people with disabilities. London: Centre for Accessible Environments, 1992.
44p; pbk

65 On the sidelines: football and disabled spectators / edited by C. Murray. London: Football Stadia Advisory Design Council, 1992.
32p; pbk
(Football Stadia Advisory Design Council information booklet; issue 6)　　BL: YK.1993.b.8744

66 Stadia handbook. 3rd ed. London: Sports Council and the Football Stadia Advisory Design Council, 1992.
20p; illus; pbk
　　Bibliography: p17-19　　BL: YK.1995.b.778

☞ Previous ed. F60; subsequent ed. F68

67   Stadium roofs / contributors: B. K. Bardhan-Roy and
      others; edited by Simon Inglis and C. Murray. London:
      Football Stadia Advisory Design Council, 1992.
      28p; illus; pbk
      (Football Stadia Advisory Design Council information
      booklet; issue 5)   ISBN: 1-873831-15-3
                                                  BL: YK.1993.b.7820

68   Stadia handbook. 4th ed. London: Sports Council, 1993.
      16p

          Includes bibliography

      ☞ Previous ed. F66

69   Terraces: designing for safe standing at football stadia /
      Simon Inglis. London: Football Stadia Advisory Design
      Council, 1993.
      52p; pbk
      (Football Stadia Advisory Design Council information
      booklet; issue 8)

70   Uncommon ground. Disablement Resource Unit, 1993.

          This guide for disabled spectators gives useful infor-
          mation on the special facilities offered at football
          grounds.

71   Design-build: a good practice guide where design-build
      is used for stadia construction / Football Stadia
      Development Committee. London: Sports Council, 1994.
      20p; pbk   ISBN: 1-872158-52-8

          Members of the civil engineering and construction in-
          dustries have responded quickly to a growing new
          market for purpose-built stadia — this guide lays
          down some basic ground rules.

72   Stadia. London: Sports Council Information Services,
      1994.
      19p; pbk
      (Select bibliography; no. 34)

73   Toilet facilities at stadia: planning, design and types of
      installation. London: Sports Council in association with
      the Football Trust, 1994.

The Playing Surface

74   The soccer club groundsman. London: Naldrett, 1951.
      108p

          The groundsman is one of the most important mem-
          bers of the football club staff. This early study is one
          of the few relating to this specialist craft. Members
          of the profession 'politely sacked' after turning their
          grounds into near swamps would learn the rudiments
          here for achieving a smooth and durable surface.

75   Association football club groundsman / Robert
      Hawthorn. London: Football Association, 1972.
      8, 97p; illus; pbk   BL: X.619/18273
          Similar but updated.

76   Thirty games a week: a study of the use of artificial grass
      pitches in Islington and Hackney / P. Birch for the
      Sports Council and the Greater London & South East
      Sports Council. London: Sports Council, 1975.
      33p; illus, 1 map; pbk   ISBN: 0-900979-26-7
                                                  BL: BS.387/79

          In the 1960s the technology for creating artificial
          playing surfaces took a great leap forward and their
          use became prevalent particularly in the USA. By
          1975 their use for British football was considered
          highly feasible. This study monitors their use and
          makes recommendations. In retrospect, although
          some professional clubs experimented, the idea was
          not to prove popular.

77   The case for better pitches: implications of a study of
      football in Lancashire. London: Sports Council North
      West Region with the Lancashire Football Association,
      1980.
      15p; pbk

78   Report of a workshop on sound constructions for sports
      pitches, held at West Ham Football Club, Upton Park,
      London, 18th January 1984 / edited for the National
      Turfgrass Council by Perry Crewdson; assisted by Janice
      King. Bingley: National Turfgrass Council, 1984.
      39p; illus; pbk
      (Workshop report; no.3)   BL: YK.1990.a.1601

79   Artificial grass surfaces for association football: report
      and appendices / an advisory group under the
      chairmanship of Sir Walter Winterbottom. London:
      Sports Council, 1985.
      127p; illus, plans; spiral
          At head of t.p.: Football Association, Sports Council
                                                  BL: BS.387/218

80   Artificial grass surfaces for association football: summary
      report and recommendations / an advisory group under
      the chairmanship of Sir Walter Winterbottom. London:
      Sports Council, 1985?
      67p; illus; spiral
          At head of t.p.: Football Association, Sports Council
                                                  BL: BS.387/218

Theory &
Practice

THIS CHAPTER COVERS THE PRACTICAL SIDE of the game – coaching and training, tactics and technique, fitness and injury, rules and refereeing. Whatever the level, from junior schoolboy to full international, some knowledge of all of these is required to make the game work. A large number of titles have been published devoted to these topics, especially in the last decade or so as the need to improve the British game has been increasingly recognised.

The first section covers Refereeing & Laws of the Game. The rules and discipline of association football are fundamental to its very existence and these are well documented from their earliest draft form, published in 1846, through to the laws we are familiar with today. The items in this section through to about 1938 chart the development of the laws from the 'primitive' to the 'modern' and throw light on the reasoning behind the gradual metamorphosis which took place.

Aspiring referees are well catered for and there are a number of key celebrity contributions from leading officials, notably Denis Howell [G27], Clive Thomas [G38] and Jack Taylor [G39]. Being a referee is still regarded by some as an unenviable job, but there are many who respond to its calling. Keeping abreast of rule changes is essential for anyone wishing to actively officiate at any level, so the golden rule is not to consult anything but the most up-to-date material. Even within the last few seasons, changes in back pass rules and offside interpretation must have caught many an amateur official unaware and there's always an 'expert' on the touchline looking for an excuse to give graphically explicit advice!

In the Coaching section the majority of items listed are variations on the simple theme of *how* to play. This begs the question, 'Does self-instruction really work'? Ask any footballer, past or present, how he learnt the game – amongst the older fraternity, there will be much talk of back street games played with tennis balls and more than a few misty eyed recollections of bundles of newspaper or rags tied with string; the thirty-somethings meanwhile, talk fondly of size five 'Fridos' banging relentlessly against garage doors (and the occasional party-pooping rosebush) whilst the younger stars of today will say that they learnt the game, naturally enough, by playing it! It is doubtful whether a single soul would attribute his success to the fact that he 'once read a book' which taught him all he knew.

In this respect there is something of a parallel between football instruction books and the vast market for slimming and fitness books. Millions aspire to that finely tuned body promised on the cover but all too often the desired result remains elusive. In the football world it is the wish of every youngster, often by parental proxy, to attain the skills and fitness of the professional, but usually to no avail. There are many titles from which to choose, from the early days of gentlemen players passing on their invaluable 'hints', through to the computer-graphic illustrated 'drills' now being promulgated by a myriad of coaches, many with suspiciously American-sounding names. This, then, is an area of football publishing largely employed in selling a dream – the 'how to play' books sell in large numbers, but do not produce great players.

What about coaches? They can exert an influence – average players can be turned into good players, and good players perhaps into great ones by the correct coaching. Yet there is a methodology in coaching itself which needs to be learnt; the greatest players are not necessarily able to go out onto the training ground and teach their craft to others less able. Teachers first need to be taught, and the abundance of coaching books available, especially from the 1960s onwards, satisfies this need. It is vitally important that such books exist – if only the right people would read them! Many are the men and women called upon to teach and supervise football in the junior schools with scarcely an idea where to start; a good book well digested and applied might be a suitable remedy.

Once an acceptable level of proficiency has been reached, the question of tactics inevitably arises – how to deploy the players on the field of battle to produce the best results. There have been a number of trends from the 'rushing game' to 'total football', 'push and run', the 'W' formation, '4-2-4' and now the 'diamond'. One fact remains indisputable; there are only eleven men from each side on the pitch at one time and only so many ways in which they can effectively combine. Despite the new terminology the cynic might suggest that revolutionary systems are nothing more than modern variations on an old theme. For students wishing to research this interesting element of football development this chapter covers the full range.

The demands of football are highly physical and the bodily damage that can so easily ensue is a constant hazard for those who play. There is a good selection of entries [G252-274] covering fitness and injury and these might profitably be consulted by club trainers and physiotherapists as well as medical or sports psychology students. There are some good early examples to set against the more technically advanced recent studies.

The final part of this chapter comprises a small number of entries under the heading The Science of Football. While playing the game is undoubtedly an art, there are many basic scientific principles at work in producing the fluidity of movement of both player and ball which combine to make football such an attractive and varied game. Students of sports science should find some useful material here.

The entries throughout this section of the bibliography are low on statistical content and allusions to individual clubs or players but in their own way can impart to the historian a feeling for the background to the practical side of the game's development which is a vital constituent to a full understanding. There are occasional surprises too for the photographic researcher – perhaps a view of a stadium interior or training ground, or an early shot of a player in action.

A little dry and serious most of the volumes may be – they are after all effectively soccer's text books – but there is still much of value to be gleaned from their pages.

Theory & Practice ~ Contents

Refereeing & Laws of the Game

1   The Cambridge rules of football. 1846.

The earliest attempt to draw up a common set of rules embracing the various and diverse elements of football as played at the major public schools – effectively represents the Football Association in embryonic form. No copies of this concise document are known to exist.

2   The Cambridge rules of football. 1848.

Committee chaired by H. C. Malden

3   Rules of football: the winter game / JCT. Uppingham: The Author, 1862.

Author is J. C. Thring   BL: D

This is an important historical document in the game's development. Thring's 'simplest rules' formed the basis from which the Football Association's own official rules were devised. Some of his rules are not consistent with the essence of football as we know it – Rule 2, for example, stated: 'Hands may be used only to stop the ball and place it on the ground before the foot'.

☞   Subsequent ed. G4

4   The winter game: rules of football / John Charles Thring. 2nd ed to which are added the Rules of the Cambridge University Committee and London Association. Uppingham: The author?, 1863.   BL: D

The author was a most important figure in the early framing of the laws of football which were formulated as an amalgam of the various codes prevailing at the public schools. He had been an Old Salopian in the 1840s, then moved up to Cambridge and on to Uppingham as a schoolmaster. It was from there in 1862 that he issued his rules entitled 'The Simplest Game' which, when amalgamated with the rules of Cambridge University in 1863, were published to act as the basis from which the Football Association rules were laid down and subsequently revised and developed over the years. This is an important early document in the history of the game, effectively responsible for all that the game now stands for.

☞   Previous ed. G3

5   The two codes of football. London: The Cricket Press, 1879.

41p   BL: D

The two codes herein referred to are the association and rugby versions of football.

☞   Subsequent ed. G8

6   The laws of association football. London: The Cricket Press, 1879.

14p

A duplicate of part of a work entitled: 'The Two Codes of Football', with a special titlepage and new pagination
BL: 7908.a.15

By this time a number of rule changes had occurred, not least of which was the agreement in 1877 that the conflicting London and Sheffield Associations would abide by the same set of rules.

☞   Subsequent ed. G7

7   The laws of association football. London: The Cricket Press, 1880.

13p; pbk   BL: 7908.a.28(2)

These laws, now further revised, included provision for the one-handed throw-in.

☞   Previous ed. G6; subsequent ed. G10

8   The two codes of football. London: The Cricket Press, 1880.

82p   BL: D

☞   Previous ed. G5; subsequent ed. G9

9   The two codes of football. London: The Cricket Press, 1881.

36p; pbk   BL: D

☞   Previous ed. G8

10 The laws of association football. London: The Cricket Press, 1882.

16p; pbk   BL: 7908.a.48(2)

A further revision in this year empowered the referee to allow a goal in the case of wilful handling of a goal-bound attempt.

☞   Previous ed. G7

11 The laws of the Football Association. London: Wright & Co, 1888-1894.   BL: 7912.a.84

By this time the laws were uniform for the four home countries – they had come to an agreement in 1883.

12 Laws of football (association). Revised to date. London: 'Pastime' Office, 1894.

27p; pbk   BL: D

In this year the referee was given effective control of the game – before this date players had to appeal to him before a decision could be made, rather akin to the umpiring system in cricket.

13 The laws of football as played at the New School, Abbotsholme, Derbyshire. Abbotsholme: Abbotsholme School, 1906.
1 sheet   BL: 7911.b.18

> *Scarce early item relating to schools' football.*

14 Laws of football: the correct decisions for all illegalities / Perseus. Preston: G. Toulmin & Sons, 1922.
24p

> *Pseud. of the Lancashire Daily Post*   BL: D
>
> *Almost fifty years after the formulation of the first association rules, many changes had occurred and some of the stranger early laws had been ousted. By this time the game more closely resembled what we know today although some important changes, notably to the offside rule, were still to come.*

15 Rules of summer football. Motherwell: H K Gollaher, 1922.
4p   BL: D

> *A curious small item seeks to explain a modified summer version of the winter game.*

16 Referees' handbook: question & answers with diagrams on the laws of the game / Robert Irving. Workington: R. Irving, 1923.
48p   BL: Mic.A.8116(1) (microfilm copy)

17 Referees' chart and players' guide to the laws of the game, 1938. London: Football Association, 1938.
48p   BL: 7908.eee.45

> *By this time the laws were substantially as we know them today. The offside rules had been redefined in 1925.*

☞ Subsequent ed. G21

18 Soccer fans: 'be your own referee' / Tom Smith. London: The author, 1947.
31p; pbk   BL: 7918.a.51

Soccer Fans
"BE YOUR OWN REFEREE"
by TOM SMITH

Ex Professional Football Player and Referee

PRICE 1/-

Most spectators need little invitation to offer their own, frequently incorrect, interpretations of the laws of football.

19 The laws of association football: the Football Association's illustrated handbook. London; Wakefield: Educational Publicity, 1948-
(Know the game!)   BL: W.P.3073/1

> *This is the first football edition of the extremely popular 'know the game' series. Despite many later editions, its format changed little over the years — many reluctant referees have turned to the series when pressed into action for schools or other minor games.*

20 How to become a referee. London: Naldrett Press, 1949.
53p; pbk
(Football Association pocket guides; no. 1)
BL: 7921.f.24/1

21 Referees' chart and players' guide to the laws of the game, June 1949. Rev. ed. London: Naldrett Press, 1949.
48p   BL: 7917.de.128

☞ Previous ed. G17; subsequent ed. G29

22 How to understand soccer control: referees' 'do's and don'ts' / compiled by V. Rae; contributors, H. Pearce and others. London: Victor Rae, 1950.
23p; illus   BL: 7921.aa.9

23 The Football Association coaching charts. No. 1-12. London: Football Association, 1951.
3 parts

> *Reissued 1952*   BL: Cup.1246.c.75
>   BL: 1856.g.13(30)

24 Universal guide for referees / Fédération Internationale de Football Association. London, 1953.
61p   BL: 7920.l.33

> *FIFA is the international organisation ruling on matters relating to the game worldwide. This was their definitive guide to the laws prevailing at that time.*

25 FA guide for referees and linesmen: an official FA publication. London: Heinemann, 1961.
71p; illus   BL: X.449/551

26 The 'middle' man: a booklet intended mainly for the younger referees / E. W. Lovick. Bury St. Edmunds: The author, 1962.
39p; pbk   BL: X.449/268

27 Soccer refereeing / Denis Herbert Howell. London: Pelham, 1968.
134p   BL: X.449/3227

> *The author was a well known refereeing figure who became Labour's Minister for Sport after retiring from the game.*

☞ Subsequent ed. G36

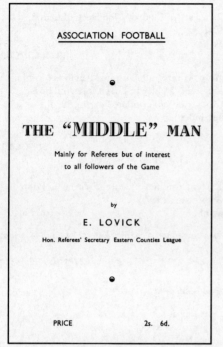

ASSOCIATION FOOTBALL

•

THE "MIDDLE" MAN

Mainly for Referees but of interest
to all followers of the Game

by

E. LOVICK

Hon. Referees' Secretary Eastern Counties League

•

PRICE   2s. 6d.

28   The FA guide to the laws of the game: a teaching
      programme / devised by Learning Systems Ltd. London:
      published on behalf of the Football Association by
      Heinemann, 1969.
      241p; illus; pbk   SBN: 434-25008-2
                                    BL: X.449/3993

29   Referees' chart and players' guide to the laws of the
      game, 1969-70. Rev. ed. London: Football Association,
      1969.
      52p   BL: X.619/10209
      ☞ Previous ed. G21; subsequent ed. G33

30   Association football: the Football Association's
      illustrated handbook. Wakefield: EP Publishing, 1970.
      48p; illus; pbk
      (Know the game)   ISBN: 0-7158-0101-5
      ☞ Subsequent ed. G32

31   Association football laws illustrated / Stanley Lover.
      London: Pelham, 1970.
      128p; illus   SBN: 7207-0434-0
                                    BL: X.620/1865

      Stanley Lover is one of the leading contributors to
      the literature relating to match control and the laws
      of the game.

      ☞ Subsequent ed. G34

32   Association football: the Football Association's
      illustrated handbook. New ed. Wakefield: EP Publishing,
      1973.
      48p; illus
      (Know the game)   ISBN: 0-7158-0513-4
      ☞ Previous ed. G30

33   Referees' chart and players' guide to the laws of
      association football / authorised by the International
      Football Association Board. London: Pan Books for the
      Football Association, 1973-
      63p; illus; pbk
          Published annually   BL: X.619/22170
      ☞ Previous ed. G29

34   Association football laws illustrated / Stanley Lover. 2nd
      ed. London: Pelham, 1976.
      128p; illus   ISBN: 0-7207-0879-6
                                    BL: X.629/10375

      ☞ Previous ed. G31; subsequent ed. G42

35   The referee's quiz book no. 1 / edited by Reg Paine.
      London: Pan Books, 1976.
      94p; illus; pbk
          'An official publication of the Football Association'
                                    ISBN: 0-330-24847-2
                                    BL: X.619/17117

      Self-testing is a useful method by which referees can
      check their knowledge of the laws although, like the
      Highway Code for drivers, a full knowledge on paper
      may not be enough when it comes to the real thing,
      where confidence and personality play such a part.

      ☞ See also: G40

36   Soccer refereeing / Denis Howell. Rev. ed. London:
      Pelham, 1977.
      159p; illus   ISBN: 0-7207-1003-0
                                    BL: X.629/11635

      ☞ Previous ed. G27

37   Association football match control: an illustrated
      handbook for the football referee / Stanley F. Lover;
      foreword by Sir Stanley Rous. London: Pelham, 1978.
      240p; illus; index
          Bibliography: p231-232; List of films: p231-232
                                    ISBN: 0-7207-1035-9
                                    BL: X.629/12005

      Sir Stanley Rous, writer of the foreword, was an out-
      standing referee himself, taking charge of the 1934
      FA Cup Final and devising the diagonal system of
      refereeing still in use today. As well as being FA Sec-
      retary and President of FIFA, he re-drafted the
      simplified set of 17 laws by which we play today. This
      is a very thorough study and includes a list of in-
      structional films as well as a full bibliography.

      ☞ Subsequent ed. G44

38   Soccer referee: a guide to fitness and technique / Clive
     Thomas and Tom Hudson. London: Duckworth, 1978.
     96p; illus, 1 plan

   Bibliography: p83
       ISBN: 0-7156-1278-6 (cased) • ISBN: 0-7156-1279-4 (pbk)
           BL: X.629/11870 • BL: X.619/18611

   Most publications for referees concentrate on the
   facts and interpretation of the laws – it is often forgotten that officials need to keep themselves fit in
   order to maintain effective control of an ever-quick-
   ening game. One of the leading officials here
   addresses this important subject.

39   Soccer refereeing: a personal view / Jack Taylor.
     London: Faber, 1978.
     96p; illus

       Contains questions with answers
       ISBN: 0-571-11298-6 (cased) • ISBN: 0-571-11299-4 (pbk)
           BL: X.629/12149

   Taylor was one of our highest profile referees, experienced at all levels right through to a World Cup Final,
   where he was called upon to make some difficult and
   controversial decisions.

   ☞ Also listed at: C479

40   The referees' quiz book / Reg Paine. London: Pan
     Books, 1979.
     93p; illus; pbk

       'An official publication of the Football Association'
                       ISBN: 0-330-25876-1
                       BL: X.0619/15107

   ☞ See also: G35

41   Soccer judge / Stan Lover. London: Mirror Books, 1980.
     128p; chiefly illus; pbk

       Questions with answers   ISBN: 0-85939-198-1
                       BL: X.629/13869

42   Soccer laws illustrated: officially approved and
     recommended by the Referees' Committee of FIFA with
     the laws of the game and decisions of the International
     Football Association Board / Stanley Lover. Rev. ed.
     London: Pelham, 1984.
     128p; illus; pbk
                       ISBN: 0-7207-1501-6
                       BL: X.629/23327

   ☞ Previous ed. G34; subsequent ed. G46

43   The golden rules of football / Ian Heath. London:
     Corgi, 1985.
     48p; illus; pbk
                       ISBN: 0-552-12598-9
                       BL: X.629/28126

44   Soccer match control: an illustrated handbook for the
     football referee / Stanley F. Lover; foreword by Sir
     Stanley Rous. Rev. ed. London: Pelham, 1986.
     256p; illus; index; pbk
       Includes bibliography   ISBN: 0-7207-1655-1
                       BL: YC.1986.a.2518

   ☞ Previous ed. G37

45   Football rules illustrated / George Sullivan. London:
     Simon & Schuster, 1987.
     96p; illus; pbk
                       ISBN: 0-671-61295-6

46   Soccer laws illustrated / Stanley Lover. Rev. ed. London:
     Pelham, 1988.
     128p; illus; pbk
                       ISBN: 0-7207-1852-X
                       BL: YK.1988.a.5037

   ☞ Previous ed. G42

47   Soccer. London: A & C Black, 1994.
     48p; illus, plans; index; pbk
     (Know the game)
       'Produced in collaboration with the Football Association'
                       ISBN: 0-7136-3681-5
                       BL: YK.1994.a.4774

48   The soccer referee's manual / David Ager. London:
     A & C Black, 1994.
     125p; illus; index; pbk
                       ISBN: 0-7136-3988-1
                       BL: YK.1994.a.13655

Coaching

49   Football and other out-door sports & games / edited by
     a Crack Hand. London: 1878.
     (The champion hand books)   BL: D
     A scarce example of a very early manual with signifi-
     cant football content.

50   How to play football: a booklet for juniors and seniors /
     Harry Earle and H. Bryett. Plaistow: Caines, 1898.
     15p; pbk   BL: D
     Scarce early ephemeral item.

51 Football, hockey and lacrosse / J. H. C. Fegan, T. Lindley, H. F. P. Battersby and J. C. Isard. 1900. xiv, 189p

(The sports library, 1899)　　　BL: 07912.ee.75(2)

In early manuals, football often shared its place with other sporting activities. There is an appreciable and informative football content in this volume.

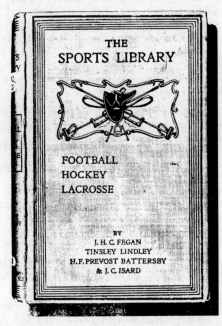

52 Football, and how to play it / Champions of the Game. London & Dundee: John Leng, 1905. 40p　　　BL: Mic.A.7125(9) (microfilm copy)

53 How to play association football / P. Walker. London: Blackie, 1905. 79p　　　BL: D

One of the more comprehensive early playing manuals.

54 Football guide, or, How to play soccer / S. Bloomer, J. T. Robertson, J. Kirwan, J. Ashcroft, W. Bull, A. Compton, A. McCombie, J. Cameron, and 'McW.'; edited by J. A. McWeeney. 1906.

(Spalding's athletic library; no. 14)　　　BL: 07908.i.14/14

Early instructional manuals are important sources for the football historian, containing as they do contributions from leading players and personalities of the day in an era when strictly autobiographical works were essentially unheard of. Amongst the contributors here are the legendary Derby, Middlesbrough and England forward, Steve Bloomer; Walter Bull, Spurs centre half; Ashcroft, the Arsenal goalkeeper; John Kirwan, Spurs and Chelsea outside left; Andrew McCombie, full back with Sunderland and Newcastle; John Cameron, secretary and manager of Spurs; and John Tait Robertson, Scotland, Rangers

and player-manager of Chelsea. An excellent source of reference for lesser known observations and anecdotes on the early years of this century.

55 Association football and how to play it / John Cameron. Health and Strength Ltd, 1908. 96p

A valuable early work which uses photographs of the author to illustrate how to play but it includes much more besides. Chapters include 'Football as a Profession', 'Football Reform', 'Present Day Football' and 'Famous Cup Ties'. Cameron played for Queen's Park and Everton before joining Spurs in 1898, going on to manage the club and later to become Secretary of the National Union of Association Players, forerunner to the PFA.

56 The complete association footballer / Bertram Saxellye Evers and Cyril Edward Hughes Davies. London: Methuen, 1912. x, 230p　　　BL: 2271.c.17

This is the earliest truly comprehensive study of how to play the game – a very weighty volume which may usefully be consulted by all historians of this era for an insight into all aspects of football in the early part of the century.

57 The science of soccer / F. Davison Currie. London: Routledge, 1919. 91p; illus　　　BL: Mic.A.10415(7) (microfilm copy)

Contains 25 diagrams and the laws of the game

58 Association football / Kenneth R. G. Hunt. London: Pearson, 1920. 91p　　　BL: Mic.A.7857(2) (microfilm copy)

The Reverend K. R. G. Hunt has been dubbed 'the muscular parson personified', playing for Wolves, Corinthians and as an England Amateur International. This instructional book presents a good evocation of the times from the playing perspective.

☞ Subsequent ed. G60

59 Association football / explained by Andrew Wilson, Andy Ducat, Jesse Pennington, J. Dawson. London: Athletic Publications, 1922. 57p; illus　　　BL: D

Most interesting for the contributions by four stars of the day: Andrew Wilson, Scotland and Dunfermline centre forward; Andy Ducat, Arsenal and Aston Villa player, famous as a cricketer-footballer double International, scoring over 23,000 runs for Sussex; Jesse Pennington, legendary England and West Bromwich Albion full-back; and, Jerry Dawson, 522 League appearances as Burnley goalkeeper from 1906-1929.

60 Association football / Kenneth R. G. Hunt. 2nd ed. London: Pearson, 1923. 114p　　　BL: 7911.cc.66

☞ Previous ed. G58

61   Football guide, or, How to play soccer / Philip Kelso.
London: Renwick, 1923.
77p
(Spalding's athletic library. Group 2; no. 14)
BL: Mic.A.8537(8) (microfilm copy)

Kelso was a famous Scot in the world of football,
manager of Hibernian and then Arsenal from 1904-
08. This guide was written towards the end of his
subsequent long management spell with Fulham. His
methods were strongly disciplinarian, his players being strictly discouraged from drinking and smoking.

62   First steps to association football / Kenneth R. G. Hunt.
London: Mills & Boon, 1924.
119p; illus
BL: Mic.A.7858(2) (microfilm copy)

A further contribution from one of a select band of
clergymen to play the game at the higher level.

63   How to play soccer: association football / four famous
players. London: Foulsham, 1927?
88p; illus; pbk

Cover title: Soccer
Contents: Forward play / Robert Kelly (Sunderland); Back
and half-back / Alf Baker (Arsenal); Wing play / Dicky
York (Aston Villa); Goal-keeping / Dick Pym (Bolton
Wanderers)

64   Stepping stones to cricket, football and hockey / Donald
MacCuaig. London: Longmans, 1927.
xv, 53p
BL: 07912.f.81

65   Association football / Leslie H. Bourke. London:
Warne, 1928.
64p; pbk
(Warne's recreation books)
BL: X.629/6699(15)

66   Football aids / Charles Murray Buchan. London: Daily
News, 1929.
125p; illus
BL: Mic.A.9930(9) (microfilm copy)

Buchan was a fine inside-forward, making a most effective contribution to the so-called 'Lucky Arsenal'
side created by Herbert Chapman in the late 1920s.
This manual was written during his Highbury days.

67   The boy's book of association football / John Tiarks
Ranke Graves. London: G. Bell, 1931.
xi, 164p; illus
BL: 7916.aa.27

One of the earliest works aimed entirely at the
younger element and something of a classic of its
genre. The author played for Casuals and Old Carthu-
sians and is the brother of poet Robert Graves, to
whom he dedicates the volume. The foreword is by A.
G. Bower, the Corinthian and England player. Many
photographic illustrations, largely of youngsters, are
used to portray the rudiments of play in this period
piece work."

68   Football: with hints from the secrets and tactics of
famous players. London: Conquest, 1931.
59p; pbk
BL: D

69   Football: how to succeed / Kenneth R. G. Hunt.
London: Published for the National Union of Teachers
by Evans, 1932.
32p; illus
BL: D

Still going strong after his first book in 1920 – this is
a much truncated version.

70   Games coaching for schools and colleges / Dorothy M.
Cooke; football and cricket contributed by Major H. J.
Selby and A. C. Douglas. London: Pitman, 1932.
xi, 332p
BL: 7916.cc.11

Schools and colleges sought to foster interest in the
game as it mounted in popularity – this is one of the
earliest comprehensive treatments explaining how it
might be taught effectively.

71   Soccer: experiences of the game with practical
instruction on training and on play in each position /
David R. Jack. London: Putnam, 1934.
viii, 336p; illus
BL: 7916.e.30

An extremely detailed study, well worth consultation.

72   Association football: an instructional book of the
Football Association / foreword by Sir Charles Clegg.
London: Evans Bros in conjunction with the Football
Association, 1935.
40p; pbk
BL: Mic.A.7129(7) (microfilm copy)

73   The Football Association coaching manual / edited by F.
N. S. Creek and others. London: Football Association,
1936.
180p
BL: 07908.e.19

The author played for Corinthians and England and
acted as official lecturer to the coaches of the Football Association as well as being a well known football
broadcaster. This is a comprehensive volume in itself
but was further expanded in the following entry.

74   Association football / F. N. S. Creek. London: J. M.
Dent, 1937.
xii, 239p; illus
(Modern sports)
BL: X.629/6646(5)

Introduced as the most complete modern analysis of
the game to date, combining the exceptionally wide
playing experience of the author with his analytical
and logical mind. The result is a definite gem of its
kind. As well as the instructional side, chapters include 'Soccer and its International Influence', 'The FA
Cup', 'Amateur Soccer' and 'University and Schools
Soccer'. It would be a mistake for football writers to
avoid instructional tomes of this kind – there is much
of interest here and some fine photographic illustrations.

75   Association football for boys / Cecil Thomas Rudd and
Edgar Murray Witham. London: James Nisbet, 1937.
64p
BL: 7908.eee.10

☞ Subsequent ed. G88

76 Football hints by famous Scottish players / Willie Waddell. 1945.

> The author played as a winger for Glasgow Rangers and was later to manage them as well as Kilmarnock. Here, during his playing years, he draws together guidance on playing matters from a number of leading Scottish players.

77 Games and sports by progressive practice: a handbook for training college students, teachers, and youth leaders / Jack Vinten Fenton. London: Allen & Unwin, 1945.
184p; illus   BL: 7918.aa.15

> The teaching of football to the younger element has always depended on equipping the teachers with the necessary tools to pass on knowledge to their students. Volumes of this kind are noble indeed in their intentions but there is an underlying sadness which seems to shroud this type of work, largely because we know in our hearts that they don't truly bring results of any significance. We have all seen the example of teachers or scout masters full of enthusiasm but totally ill-equipped for their 'football master' roles. Nevertheless, it contains some interesting football material.

78 Association football: an instructional book. London: Evans Bros, 1946.
40p   BL: 7918.b.43

79 Improve your football / John Harris. London: Lantern, 1947.
80p   BL: 7917.e.65

80 How to play association football / Denis Compton. London: Foulsham, 1948.
90p   BL: X.629/6605(24)

> Here one of the most famous of the footballer-cricketer breed allies himself firmly to the winter game. Most of his publications were of the cricketing variety so this is something of a curiosity in itself, written during his playing days with Arsenal.

81 How to play football: a practical guide with photographs and instructional diagrams / William Steel. London: C. & J. Temple, 1948.
206p; illus   BL: 7919.de.55

> Although an instructional book, it doubles as an account of Steel's career, with 19 pages of biography by Michael Piggott and many autobiographical elements in the body of the book. Steel was a Scottish International who had started his career with Dunipace Thistle before moving on to St. Mirren, Morton and later Dundee. Sandwiched between the latter two clubs, though, is his spell with Derby County from 1947 to 1950. Derby paid a British record fee of £15,500 so it was no surprise that this book should be published one year later. Photographs of the Derby squad and ground illustrate the text.

82 Stanley Matthews' soccer manual. London: Alan Fletcher Publications, 1948.
46p; illus   BL: 7920.aa.14

> Inevitably Matthews contributed to the instructional literature of his time. This was written during his Blackpool days.

83 Improve your soccer . . . with instructional pictures / Bernard Joy. London: Findon Publications, 1949.
80p; illus   BL: 7917.de.119

> The author played for Casuals and as an amateur for Fulham, Arsenal and England.

84 Playing football / J. B. Fair. London: Longmans, Green, 1949.
16p; pbk   BL: 7920.c.25

85 The professional footballer. London: Naldrett, 1949.
39p; illus; pbk
(Football Association pocket guides; no. 2)
                                               BL: 7921.f.42(2)

86 Teach yourself soccer / F. N. S. Creek. London: English Universities Press, 1949.
191p; illus
(Teach yourself books)   BL: W.P.706/90

> Creek had been contributing to instructional literature since 1936 – he was one of the most influential teachers over a long span of years, being particularly interested in the instruction of school age students. He was indeed a schoolmaster by profession.

☞ Subsequent ed. 135

87 Association football / Robert Taylor Hesford. London: Pitman, 1950.
ix, 153p; illus   BL: W.P.11671/36

88 Association football for boys / Cecil Thomas Rudd and Edgar Murray Witham. Rev. ed. London: James Nisbet, 1950.
63p   BL: 7921.aa.33

☞ Previous ed. G75

89 Constructive football / A. H. Fabian and Tom Whittaker. London: Edward Arnold, 1950.
vii, 150p; illus   BL: 7920.b.42

> This is one of the most common books of instruction, often cropping up on the lower shelves of secondhand bookshops. Fabian played for Derby County, Corinthians, Cambridge University and as an amateur for England, whilst Whittaker was secretary-manager of Arsenal. Derby manager Stuart McMillan provides a foreword to this interesting work which includes many action photographs of players of the time.

90 A manual of association football. London: Bond Publishing, 1950.
95p; illus   BL: 7919.d.17

91 Soccer / Peter Doherty. London: Foyle, 1950.
96p
BL: W.P.2940/5

This flame-haired Irishman was one of the finest players of his era, most famous during his time with Blackpool, Manchester City, Derby, Huddersfield and Doncaster Rovers; he was also a Northern Ireland International and National Team manager. This playing manual was published during his time as player-manager at Doncaster.

92 Play better football / Bernard Joy. London: The Star Publications Dept, 1951.
144p; illus
BL: 7921.de.40

Written following the author's amateur career with Corinthians and Arsenal.

93 Soccer for boys / F. N. S. Creek. London: English Universities Press, 1951.
88p
(Junior teach yourself books)
BL: W.P.5509/11

Yet another volume from Creek here targeting the juvenile market.

94 Soccer coaching / Walter Winterbottom. London: Naldrett, 1952.
247p; illus
BL: 7920.f.43

England manager Winterbottom, former player with Manchester United and Chelsea, here presents an official FA coaching manual regarded as a classic and translated worldwide into many languages.

95 Instructions to young footballers / Tom Finney. London: Museum Press, 1955.
112p; illus
BL: 7921.e.134

The Player of the Year for 1954 here passes on his vital experience to young students of the game. The winger's abilities were never truly rewarded in the silverware department – in 569 first class matches for Preston North End he never received a Championship or Cup Winners medal.

96 Soccer my way / Danny Blanchflower. London: Nicolas Vane, 1955.
48p
(My way sports coaching books; no. 1)
BL: W.P.593/1

Written shortly after his 1954 arrival at Spurs, the Tottenham legend and Northern Ireland manager had typically clear ideas of what 'his way' really was: 'The game is about glory. It's about doing things in style, with a flourish, about going out and beating the other lot, not waiting for them to die of boredom.'''

97 Success at soccer / edited by F. Butler. London: Phoenix Sports Books, 1956.
127p; illus
BL: W.P.7630/2

A selection of players give their tips on how to play the game. Contributors include John Charles, Johnny Haynes, Vic Groves, Bert Trautmann, Peter Doherty, Walley Barnes, Joe Mercer and Gordon Smith.

98 Modern soccer – the skills in play: an official coaching manual of the Football Association. London: Educational Productions, 1958.
v, 88p; illus
BL: 7924.aa.3

99 Tackle soccer this way / Duncan Edwards. London: Stanley Paul, 1958.
112p

This scarce title was published shortly after the death of Duncan Edwards in the Munich air crash. One of the greatest prospects the game has known here passes on the instructional tips he was never able to utilise fully himself. The book includes a brief biographical note on Edwards by William Luscombe.

100 Danny Blanchflower's soccer book. London: Muller, 1959.
127p; illus
BL: 7925.d.15

101 Football made easy: a plan for coaching / George Lewis Young as told to Bob MacNab. London: Stanley Paul, 1959.
124p; illus
BL: 7922.ee.40

The Glasgow Rangers and Scotland captain made his thoughts known shortly after his retirement; 53 Internationals certainly qualifies this defender to present his plan. The fact that he broke his nose 3 times and had a leg in plaster on 6 occasions says much about his brave and uncompromising style!

102 Association football: a coaching handbook for tropical areas / D. J. T. Millar and John Edward Cawley. London: Evans, 1960.
112p; illus
BL: 7925.l.6

You might think the methodology would be the same irrespective of climate and culture – indeed much of it is, but there are certain differences in the Tropics, not least the heat and the lack of good pitches, and facilities, which might challenge the usual coaching techniques. In 1962 Walter Winterbottom said: 'Watch Africa – that Continent will produce the World Champions before the end of the century.' And this at a time when 183 out of 200 clubs in Kenya employed a full time witch-doctor! This handbook is of certain interest to any researcher conducting a full study of the history and development of coaching.

103 Training for soccer: an official coaching manual of the Football Association / Walter Winterbottom. London: Heinemann, 1960.
ix, 200p; illus
BL: 7925.b.67
BL: 7926.cc.15

Comprehensive coverage from the England team manager of the time.

104 Soccer with the stars. London: Educational Productions, 1961.
62p; illus; index; pbk
(FA autograph book; no. 1)

'*A Football Association book*'
BL: 7923.ee.7

A collection of coaching hints from famous players.

105 How to play football / Cliff Jones. London: Associated
Newspapers, 1963.
35p; illus
(Weekend sports clinic)   BL: 7926.m.20

   Jones began his career with Swansea Town before a
   1958 move to Tottenham Hotspur, where he starred
   before joining Fulham in 1969. Here the Welsh International winger presents his tips in the year in which
   Spurs won the European Cup Winners Cup.

106 Skill in sport: the attainment of proficiency / Barbara
Naomi Knapp. London: Routledge & Kegan Paul, 1963.
xii, 203p; illus   BL: 7926.k.24

107 Soccer for schoolboys / John Norman Haynes. London:
Pelham, 1963.
110p; illus   BL: 7926.s.21

   In 1961 Fulham's Haynes became England's first
   £100 a week footballer – two years later he shares
   his passing and goal-scoring skills with aspiring
   youngsters.

108 How to play association football / David Bacuzzi.
London: W. Foulsham, 1964.
96p
(New sports library)   BL: 7923.nn.1/28

109 The strategy of soccer / Johnny Byrne. London: Pelham,
1965.
106p; illus   BL: X.449/1599

   Instructional and autobiographical work from the
   England centre-forward most closely associated with
   Crystal Palace and West Ham.

   ☞ Also listed at: C75

110 Tackle soccer this way / Denis Law. London: Stanley
Paul, 1965.
126p; illus   BL: X.449/1383

   European Footballer of the Year in 1964, Law here
   writes during his Manchester United days. His 'way'
   was often explosive, spectacular and highly individualistic, aptly summed up in a few lines of contemporary
   poetry by Gareth Owen –

            'And when he's hurtling for the goal,
              I know he's got to score,
            Defences may stop normal men,
              They can't stop Denis Law.'

   ☞ Subsequent ed. G117

111 Football coaching / John H. McKay. Chichester: Wiley,
1966.
242p   ISBN: 0-471-07147-1

112 Improve your soccer / Jimmy Hill. Harmondsworth:
Penguin, 1966.
144p; illus   BL: W.P.4003/122

   Prior to his high profile media career Hill had been a
   competent inside-forward with Brentford and Ful-

ham. He writes here though from his position as manager of Coventry City, a club he guided from the Third
to the First Division in just six years.

113 Soccer science / George Eastham with Ken Jones.
London: Pelham, 1966.
128p; illus   BL: X.441/634

   Eastham's approach was indeed almost scientific –
   ball control and precision passing were his trade-
   marks. The coincidental juxtaposition of this entry
   with the previous one by Jimmy Hill prompts a particular memory. Hill as Chairman of the Professional
   Footballers' Association had backed Eastham in
   1960 in a contract dispute with Newcastle United
   noted for its part in bringing an end to 'soccer slav-
   ery' and the removal of the wage ceiling for
   footballers.

114 Soccer techniques and tactics / Jimmy Greaves. London:
Pelham, 1966.
139p; illus   BL: X.449/1770

   'He was the Fagin of the penalty area; the arch-pick-
   pocket of goals.' This was Geoffrey Green's
   description of Greaves in his prime. He writes here as
   a Spurs player in the year of England's World Cup triumph, an occasion in which he played only a
   supporting role much to his personal disappointment.

115 The FA guide to training and coaching / Allen Wade.
London: Published on behalf of the Football Association
by Heinemann, 1967.
260p; illus

116 Soccer the modern way / Bobby Moore. London:
Stanley Paul, 1967.
110p; illus   BL: X.449/2785

   The title is an interesting one, perhaps indicative of
   the feeling that England's 1966 World Cup win might
   take domestic football into a new era. As captain of
   that legendary side Moore was renowned for his alert
   awareness and cool manner, qualities which, regret-
   tably, cannot be magically acquired via the written
   word.

117 Tackle soccer this way / Denis Law. New ed. London:
Stanley Paul, 1968.
127p; illus   ISBN: 0-09-075311-9
                                                           BL: X.449/3386

   ☞ Previous ed. G110; subsequent ed. G121

118 Football. London: Lutt, 1969.
44p; illus
(Magpie pocket books)
   A guide for children

119 How to play soccer / David Bacuzzi. London:
Foulsham, 1969.
96p; illus
(Pocket sports books)   SBN: 572-00648-9
                                                           BL: X.449/3737

120 Coach yourself association football / Allen Wade;
photography by Monte Fresco. London: Educational
Productions in association with the Football Association,
1970.
160p; illus; pbk
(Play the game)   ISBN: 0-7158-0164-3

The photographer went on to achieve leading status
in his profession, winning many awards for his football
images.

☞ Subsequent ed. G137

121 Tackle soccer this way / Denis Law. New ed. London:
Stanley Paul, 1971.
126p; illus   ISBN: 0-09-105740-X
BL: X.629/3283

☞ Previous ed. G117

122 Teaching soccer to boys / Alan Gibbon and John
Cartwright; with a foreword by Phil Woosnam. London:
Bell, 1972.
121p; illus   ISBN: 0-7135-1607-0

☞ Subsequent ed. G169

123 Beginner's guide to soccer training and coaching / Brian
Owen with Nigel Clarke. London: Pelham, 1973.
128p; illus
(Beginner's guide series)   ISBN: 0-7207-0683-1
BL: X.629/5743

124 Better soccer for boys / Thomas Henderson Docherty.
London: Pan Books, 1973.
94p; illus
(Piccolo books)   ISBN: 0-330-23438-2
BL: X.619/6654

Tommy Docherty writes here during his time as manager of Manchester United.

125 Book of football / John Goodbody and Allen Wade.
London: Macmillan, 1973.
112p; illus; pbk
(Topliners)
For adolescents   ISBN: 0-333-14372-8
BL: X.619/7432

☞ Also listed at: A103

126 Skill with a football / Douglas N. Hubbard; illustrated
by Kathleen Gell. Oxford: Blackwell, 1973.
52p; illus   ISBN: 0-631-14070-0

127 Soccer secrets of the stars / Ian Hutchinson and Paul
Trevillion. London: Pelham, 1973.
128p; illus   ISBN: 0-7207-0533-9
BL: X.629/5658

Methods and skills are analysed by Trevillion, one of
sport's foremost illustrators, and Hutchinson, a
Chelsea centre forward. He reveals one of his own secrets, the art of the long throw-in, in this interesting
approach in presenting the tricks of the trade.

128 Success in football / Mike Smith. London: J. Murray,
1973.
96p; illus
(Success sportsbooks)   ISBN: 0-7195-2822-4
BL: X.629/5854

☞ Subsequent ed. G151

129 Association football / R. Jones. London: Nelson, 1974.
56p; illus; index; pbk
(Sports for the Caribbean; book 1)   ISBN: 0-17-566152-9

One of a very few UK based publications aimed at an
ethnic market.

130 Football / Dennis Knight. London: Royal Sovereign,
1974.
16p; illus; pbk   ISBN: 0-900862-37-8

131 Football coaching: for play at all levels / Gordon Jago.
London: Stanley Paul, 1974.
128p; illus   ISBN: 0-09-121540-4
BL: X.620/7744

Jago was a player with Charlton Athletic before becoming player-manager at Eastbourne United in
1962. Managing and coaching positions with Fulham,
Queen's Park Rangers and Millwall were to follow, interspersed by spells abroad. He was renowned as a
coach with an analytical and innovative approach; he
was particularly successful in America with Tampa
Bay Rowdies.

132 Football's for schoolkids / Evan Owen. London: Evans,
1974.
80p; illus
(Checkers)
ISBN: 0-237-29041-3 (cased) • ISBN: 0-237-29007-3 (pbk)

133 Games for football training / Günter Lammich and
Heinz Kadow; illustrations by Klaus Zühl; translated
from the German by Robin and Hella Oliver; edited by
A. R. Mills. London: Nelson, 1974.
184p; illus

*Translation of 'Spiele für das Fußballtraining'. Berlin:
Sportverlag, 1966*   ISBN: 0-17-149060-6
BL: X.629/11847

Originally published in Germany in a year they would
rather forget – the German side lost to England in
the World Cup final at Wembley. A rather obsessive
interest amongst British coaches for the 'secrets' of
the Continental game led to a number of translations
of European manuals, of which this is one.

134 My learn to play football / Hugh Allenson; illustrated by
Michael Jackson. London: Hamlyn, 1974.
2-47p; chiefly illus
For children   ISBN: 0-600-36146-2

☞ Subsequent ed. G180

135 Soccer / F. N. S. Creek. Rev ed. London: Teach
Yourself Books, 1974.
ix, 165p; illus; pbk
(Teach yourself books)   ISBN: 0-340-18264-4
                                          BL: W.P.706/460

> Perhaps slightly worrying that Creek's ideas were still
> being promulgated, albeit in a revised edition, 38
> years after his first publication?

☞ Previous ed. G86; subsequent ed. G140

136 Teaching soccer skill / Eric Worthington. London:
Lepus Books, 1974.
184p; illus
(The physical recreation series)
   Bibliography: p176   ISBN: 0-86019-004-8

☞ Subsequent ed. G165

137 Coach yourself association football / Allen Wade;
photography by Monte Fresco. Wakefield: EP
Publishing in association with the Football Association,
1975.
160p; illus; pbk
   'An official publication of the Football Association' – cover
                                          ISBN: 0-7158-0177-5
                                          BL: X.619/18509

☞ Previous ed. G120

138 Football / Gerhard Bauer; translated from the German
by Wendy Gill. Wakefield: EP Publishing, 1975.
114p; illus
   Originally published: München: BLV, 1974
                                          ISBN: 0-7158-0594-0
                                          BL: X.629/10382

> On many occasions we have been told that the Brit-
> ish game lags well behind that on the Continent.
> Translations from an original German work, such as
> this one, serve as an interesting comparison to ideas
> prevalent in England. In truth, the differences are not
> readily apparent, however, despite the insistence by
> many coaches of the time that we must 'play the
> Continental way'.

139 Football / Danny Blanchflower; script by Iain Reid;
drawings by Horak. Paris: Chancerel; distributed by
WHS, 1975.
96p; chiefly illus; pbk
(Learn through strips)
   'From the Sunday Express' – cover
                                          ISBN 2-85429-010-0
                                          BL: X.611/8106

> This is an instructional book which demonstrates an
> original approach to teaching – Danny Blanchflower
> here passes on his experience through the medium of
> cartoon strips.

140 Football / F. N. S. Creek. New ed. Leicester: Knight
Books, 1975.
95p; illus; index; pbk
(Illustrated teach yourself)   ISBN: 0-340-19378-6
                                          BL: X.619/15196

☞ Previous ed. G135

141 Play football with Pelé / Pelé in collaboration with Julio
Mazzei; photographs by Domicio Pinheiro; translated
from the Portuguese by Jacquie Meredith. London:
Hodder and Stoughton, 1975.
97p; chiefly illus
   Originally published: Rio de Janeiro: Livraria Jos Olympio
   Editora, 1975   ISBN: 0-340-19329-8
                                          BL: X.622/5239

> This is a curious item; whilst most instructional
> books were presented by leading domestic stars, the
> worldwide popularity of the Brazilian rendered him a
> marketable commodity well beyond South America.

142 Playing football / Mike Graham-Cameron; illustrated by
Colin King. Cambridge: Dinosaur, 1975.
24p; illus; pbk
(Althea's dinosaur books)
   For children   ISBN: 0-85122-090-8
                                          BL: X.990/17476

143 Soccer / Bob Wilson. London: Pelham, 1975.
61p; illus   ISBN: 0-7207-0793-5
                                          BL: X.622/2217

144 Soccer / Phil Woosnam with Paul Gardner for 'Sports
Illustrated'. Authorised British ed. / revised by Allen
Wade. London: A. and C. Black, 1975.
96p; illus
   Originally published as '"Sports Illustrated" Soccer'.
   Philadelphia: Lippincott, 1972; Bibliography: p96
                                          ISBN: 0-7136-1586-9
                                          BL: X.629/10140

> The Welsh International, Woosnam, played for Man-
> chester City, Sutton United, Leyton Orient, West
> Ham and Aston Villa as an inside-forward in the fif-
> ties and sixties. The influencing factor in this
> publication though is his American connection – in
> the late sixties Woosnam played a leading role in the
> National Professional Soccer League as manager of
> Atlanta Chiefs, then as Executive Director of the
> North American Soccer League. This publication ema-
> nated in the States being published in Britain later in
> this revised format.

☞ Subsequent ed. G156

145 Junior soccer: a guide for teachers and young players /
John Jarman. London: Faber, 1976.
77p; illus; index
         ISBN: 0-571-10846-6 (cased) • ISBN: 0-571-10847-4 (pbk)
                                          BL: X.629/10935

Jarman is one of the unsung stalwarts of the coaching scene, unselfishly dedicating himself to the advancement of juniors and with a number of important senior posts to his credit. He wrote this informative guide whilst Director of Coaching for the Football Association of Ireland, and indeed it became a bestseller there. Jack Charlton, then entirely unconnected with the Irish football scene, prophetically wrote the foreword – it is quite possible that some of his Republic of Ireland players would have been taught in their schooldays by teachers using this very book, a point which the author himself has since picked up in the media with some pride and a pleasing sense of fulfilment.

146 Teach your child soccer / John Adams. London: Lepus Books, 1976.
95p; illus
(The teach your child series)
ISBN: 0-86019-025-0 (cased) • ISBN: 0-86019-021-8 (pbk)
BL: X.629/10420

147 Tackle soccer / Dave Sexton. London: Stanley Paul, 1977.
172p; illus
ISBN: 0-09-129900-4 (cased) • ISBN: 0-09-129901-2 (pbk)
BL: X.629/11550

Written in the year in which he left the management post at Queen's Park Rangers to take over at Manchester United. His four years there were followed by a spell at Coventry City before he became England assistant manager in 1983. He took a particular interest in new ideas in coaching and was later to play a leading role in developing the soccer 'school of excellence', which was set up to select and develop the best of our young talent. This book presents many of his ideas.

148 The FA guide to teaching football / Allen Wade. London: Heinemann for the Football Association, 1978.
xvi, 171p; illus
ISBN: 0-434-92210-2
BL: X.620/17933

149 Focus on soccer: a player's guide / written by Ken Jones in collaboration with Ray Marshall. London: Stanley Paul, 1978.
104p; illus
'Published in association with the Football League, based on the HTV series' – jacket
ISBN: 0-09-133860-3 (cased) • ISBN: 0-09-133861-1 (pbk)
BL: X.620/17975

One of a number of books published in association with instructional TV programmes.

150 Jack Charlton's book for young footballers / Jack Charlton. London: Stanley Paul, 1978.
63p; illus
'...based on the Tyne Tees Television series, "Play soccer Jack Charlton's way"' – t.p. verso
ISBN: 0-09-133850-6 (cased) • ISBN: 0-09-133851-4 (pbk)
BL: X.620/17805

Written during Charlton's early management years with Sheffield Wednesday after four years in charge at Middlesbrough. During the filming of the TV series Charlton revealed his distinctive way of handling his young pupils, often with amusing results as they struggled manfully to carry out his instructions.

☞ Subsequent ed. G190

151 Success in football / Mike Smith; with a foreword by Allen Wade. 2nd ed. London: J. Murray, 1978.
96p; illus
(Success sportsbooks)   BL: X.629/12072
☞ Previous ed. G128; subsequent ed. G175

152 The Beaver book of football / Tom Tully; illustrated by Mike Jackson; cartoons by David Mostyn. London: Beaver Books, 1979.
126p; illus; pbk
ISBN: 0-600-33699-9
BL: X.619/22523
☞ Also listed at: A127

153 Fair play: ethics in sport and education / Peter McIntosh; foreword by Sir Roger Bannister. London: Heinemann Educational, 1979.
213p; index
ISBN: 0-435-80579-7
BL: X.529/33042

The writer of the foreword – the first man to run a mile in under four minutes – achieved his feat in an era when fair play was taken for granted rather more readily than it is now. This scholarly work includes some original observations on football.

154 How to play soccer / Ken Jones; photography by Mark Moylan. London: Hamlyn, 1979.
4-61p; illus; index
ISBN: 0-600-38262-1
BL: X.620/8793
☞ Subsequent ed. G181

155 Let's play soccer / Stan Liversedge. London: Octopus Books, 1979.
96p; illus; index
ISBN: 0-7064-1004-1
BL: X.622/7049

156 Soccer / Phil Woosnam with Paul Gardner for 'Sports illustrated'. Authorised British ed. / revised by Allen Wade; reprinted with alterations. London: A. and C. Black 1979.
96p; illus
Bibliography: p96
ISBN 0-7136-1586-9
BL: X.629/12473
☞ Previous ed. G144; subsequent ed. G178

157 The young player's guide to soccer / Jim Bebbington. Newton Abbot: David and Charles, 1979.
96p; illus
Includes bibliographies
ISBN: 0-7153-7536-9
BL: X.629/12389

158 Coaching modern soccer: attack / Eric G. Batty.
London: Faber, 1980.
121p; illus
ISBN: 0-571-09840-1
BL: X.629/14866

159 Football. London: Sparrow Books, 1980.
24p; illus
(Discoverers)
For children   ISBN: 0-09-923650-8

160 Football: a complete guide to better soccer / Tom Tully;
illustrated by Mike Jackson; cartoons by David Mostyn.
London: Severn House, 1980.
126p; illus
ISBN: 0-7278-0685-8
BL: X.629/17286

161 The Football Association coaching book of soccer:
tactics and skills / Charles Hughes. London: British
Broadcasting Corporation, 1980.
236p; illus
ISBN: 0-563-17808-60
BL: X.622/9565

The author was later to become Director of Coaching
and Education to the Football Association and ultimately became embroiled in much controversy.

☞ Subsequent ed. G208

162 More skilful soccer / Robin Trimby. London: Gollancz,
1980.
128p; illus
ISBN: 0-575-02718-5
BL: X.629/13691

163 Soccer coaching: the European way / edited by Eric G.
Batty. London: Souvenir, 1980.
240p; illus
ISBN: 0-285-62354-0
BL: X.622/9097

A study of the varying methodologies prevalent in
Europe at the time. Includes chapters by Ron Greenwood, Dave Sexton, Frank Bluntstone and Fred
Street. Bluntstone was coaching in Greece at the
time whilst his fellow contributors all had close connections with the England coaching scene. Also
includes contributions from their European counterparts.

☞ Also listed at: E201

164 Successful soccer / Bobby Brown. London: Letts, 1980.
95p; illus; index; pbk
(World of sport)
ISBN: 0-85097-472-0
BL: X.629/19015

165 Teaching soccer skill / Eric Worthington. 2nd ed.
London: Lepus Books, 1980.
218p; illus
Bibliography: p218   ISBN: 0-86019-039-0
BL: X.629/14390

☞ Previous ed. G136

166 Coaching modern soccer: defence and other techniques
/ Eric G. Batty. London: Faber, 1981.
128p; illus
ISBN: 0-571-11772-4 (cased) • ISBN: 0-571-11773-2 (pbk)
BL: X.629/16527

167 Soccer: skills, tricks and tactics / Simon Inglis. London:
Usborne, 1981.
32p; illus; pbk   ISBN: 0-86020-545-2

☞ Subsequent ed. G184

168 Super soccer skills / Don Howe; planned and edited by
Norman Barrett; illustrated by Paul Buckle. London:
Granada, 1981.
64p; illus; pbk
(Dragon books)
ISBN: 0-583-30486-9
BL: X.629/16313

This former England, West Bromwich Albion and Arsenal player turned to coaching after suffering a broken
leg in 1966. He was the Arsenal coach and England
assistant manager when this short study was published.

169 Teaching soccer / Alan Gibbon and John Cartwright;
with a foreword by Ron Greenwood. 2nd ed. London:
Ben & Hyman, 1981.
158p; illus; pbk
ISBN: 0-7135-1257-1
BL: X.629/26457

☞ Previous ed. G122

170 How to succeed at soccer / Gerhard Bauer; translated
from the German by Beverly Worthington. London:
Orbis, 1982.
127p; illus, plans; pbk
ISBN: 0-85613-431-7
BL: X.629/21995

171 Pelé soccer training programme / text by Julio Mazzei
with William J. McGuire. London: Pelham, 1982.
24p; illus; pbk
ISBN: 0-7207-1439-7
BL: L.42/1885

Lightweight coverage only from the Brazilian legend.

172 Soccer / Mike Yaxley. London: Batsford Academic and
Educational, 1982.
63p; illus; index
(Competitive sports series)
ISBN: 0-7134-3980-7
BL: X.622/12607

173 Soccer: coaching and team management / Malcolm
Cook; foreword by Lawrie McMenemy. Wakefield: EP
Publishing, 1982.
140p; illus
ISBN: 0-7158-0833-8 (cased) • ISBN: 0-7158-0795-1 (pbk)
BL: X.629/20489

174 Soccer fundamentals / Ron Tindall. Newton Abbot:
David & Charles, 1982.
64p; illus; index
ISBN: 0-7153-8361-2
BL: X.622/13744

175 Success in football / Mike Smith; with a foreword by
Allen Wade. 3rd ed. London: J. Murray, 1982.
96p; illus
(Success sportsbooks) ISBN: 0-7195-3900-5
BL: X.629/18182

☞ Previous ed. G151

176 The way to play soccer / Tony Roche, Bob Trevor.
London: Collins, 1982.
61p; illus; index ISBN: 0-00-195378-8
BL: X.622/14527

180 My fun to play football / Hugh Allenson; illustrated by
Michael Jackson. Rev. ed. London: Hamlyn, 1984.
61p; illus ISBN: 0-600-38980-4
BL: L.45/2857

☞ Previous ed. G134

181 Soccer / Ken Jones. London: Hamlyn, 1984.
61p; illus; index; pbk
(Play the game) ISBN: 0-600-34765-6
BL: X.622/22396

☞ Previous ed. G154

*Reg Carter's impression of
the coach's lecture*

177 You can play football / Gordon Banks; illustrated by
Mike Miller. London: Carousel, 1982.
119p; illus; pbk

> *Subsequently reprinted as: You can play soccer. London:
> Severn House, 1982* ISBN: 0-552-54200-8
> BL: X.629/17488

Written after the England goalkeeper's retirement
from the game.

178 Soccer / Phil Woosnam with Paul Gardner. 2nd ed. /
revised by Allen Wade. London: Black, 1983.
96p; illus

> *Bibliography: p96* ISBN: 0-7136-2358-6
> BL: X.629/22232

☞ Previous ed. G156

179 Games, drills and fitness practices for soccer coaching /
Nick Whitehead & Malcolm Cook; foreword by Ron
Atkinson. London: Black, 1984.
128p; illus; index ISBN: 0-7136-2443-4
BL: X.622/19635

☞ Subsequent ed. G188

182 Soccer excellence: the revolutionary new training plan /
Wiel Coerver; new text for British edition by Mike
Langley; foreword by Bobby Robson. London: Sidgwick
& Jackson, 1985.
200p; illus

> *Translation of: Leerplan voor de ideale voetballer. 1983*
> ISBN: 0-283-99244-1 (cased) • ISBN: 0-283-99311-1 (pbk)
> BL: YC.1986.b.208

Coerver is the Dutch coach of great repute who takes
much of the credit for the fluid style of play for which
his national side has become known.

183 Football. London: Sangam, 1986.
192p; illus
(Wills book of excellence) ISBN: 0-86131-683-5

184 Usborne guide to soccer: skills, tricks and tactics /
Simon Inglis. 2nd ed. London: Usborne, 1986.
32p; illus; pbk ISBN: 0-7460-0120-7

☞ Previous ed. G167

185 Football / Ken Shellito. London: Carnival, 1988.
31p; pbk

> *For children* ISBN: 0-00-194705-2
> BL: YK.1989.a.658 • BL: Cup.937/455

The author was a player with Chelsea from 1957 to 1969 and thereafter turned to coaching and management; Queen's Park Rangers, Crystal Palace, Preston, Wolves, and Cambridge United all preceded this lightweight publication for children.

186 How to play soccer / Ronnie Glavin. London: Guinness, 1988.
128p; illus; pbk
ISBN: 0-85112-361-9
BL: YK.1989.a.2134

187 Soccer / Ken Goldman & Peter Dunk. London: Ward Lock, 1988.
80p; illus; index; pbk
(Play the game)
ISBN: 0-7063-6665-4
BL: YK.1989.a.2985

☞ Subsequent ed. G205

188 Soccer training: games, drills and fitness practices / Nick Whitehead & Malcolm Cook; foreword by Alex Ferguson. 2nd ed. London: A & C Black, 1988.
128p; illus; index; pbk
ISBN: 0-7136-5617-4
BL: YK.1988.a.5125

☞ Previous ed. G179; subsequent ed. G203

189 A consultancy approach for trainers / Keri Phillips and Patricia Shaw. London: Gower, 1989.
viii, 174p
ISBN: 0-566-02737-2
BL: YC.1989.a.11935

190 Learn football with Jack Charlton. Rev. ed. London: Stanley Paul, 1989.
63p; illus; pbk
ISBN: 0-09-174027-4
BL: YK.1989.b.1870

Written during Jack Charlton's tenure as manager of the Republic of Ireland.

☞ Previous ed. G150

191 Soccer: the skills of the game / Tony Book. Marlborough: Crowood, 1989.
135p; illus; index; pbk
ISBN: 1-85223-557-8
BL: YK.1992.b.6386

Bath City, Plymouth Argyle and Manchester City figured in Book's playing career; very much a latecomer to league football, he made his debut at the age of 29. A spell as Manchester City manager followed, but Book has spent much of his later years in coaching positions.

192 Soccer basics / Gary Mabbutt; edited by R. Bickersteth. London: Cockerel, 1989.
64p; illus; pbk
ISBN: 1-869914-12-0
BL: YK.1992.a.7940

Written whilst the author was playing for Spurs.

193 Successful soccer / David Brenner; illustrations by Paul Trevillion. Stradbroke: Sackville, 1989.
96p; illus
ISBN: 0-948615-31-1
BL: YK.1990.a.5281

194 Coaching youth soccer / Tony Waiters. London: A & C Black, 1990.
320p; illus; pbk
ISBN: 0-7136-3319-0
BL: YK.1990.a.6882

Waiters enjoyed a goalkeeping career with Blackpool, Burnley and England before a measure of management success with Plymouth Argyle. He later made a name for himself in Canada, leading the national team to the 1986 World Cup finals; a variety of coaching and scouting positions followed.

195 Knowabout soccer / Trevor Spindler and Andrew Ward. London: Automobile Association, 1990.
72p; illus; pbk
(Knowabout sport)
ISBN: 0-7495-0155-3
BL: YK.1991.b.938

196 The winning formula: soccer skills and tactics / Charles Hughes. London: Collins, 1990.
192p; illus; index
ISBN: 0-00-185354-6 (cased) • ISBN: 0-00-191160-0 (pbk)
BL: YK.1990.b.10253

If only the title were true – Football Association Director of Coaching, Charles Hughes, came in for much criticism from many factions within the game for his 'establishment' views on coaching and teaching. Insufficient use of ex-players in coaching positions was an accusation levelled at Hughes by the PFA and he carried much of the blame for the so-called 'decline' of British football. This volume presents some of his ideas.

197 The Guinness book of skilful soccer / Stephen Ford, Colin Woffinden. Enfield: Guinness, 1991.
159p; illus; pbk
ISBN: 0-85112-969-2
BL: YK.1991.b.6164

198 How to play soccer: a step-by-step guide / text by Liz French. Norwich: Jarrold, 1991.
47p; illus
ISBN: 0-7117-0513-5
BL: YK.1992.a.7494

One of a very small number of 'how to play' books presented by a female author.

199 Play football / Sheila Fraser; illustrated by Lisa Kopper. London: Watts, 1991.
20p; illus
For children
ISBN: 0-7496-0424-7
BL: YK.1991.a.2519

One of a small number of instructional works presented by female writers – this one for the very young.

200 Soccer skills with Gazza / Paul Gascoigne and Mel Stein; illustrations by Paul Trevillion. London: Stanley Paul, 1991.
112p; illus; pbk
ISBN: 0-09-174870-4
BL: YK.1991.b.2195

Gascoigne's undoubted skills inevitably had to be packaged in book form.

201 Football training can be fun / Graham Taylor. London: Stanley Paul, 1992.
79p; illus; pbk

  'An official FA publication'   ISBN: 0-09-177293-1
                                          BL: YK.1994.b.1242

  Taylor does not enlighten us as to the truth or otherwise of his title statement during his troubled tenure as England manager.

202 The soccer skills poster book / Paul Trevillion; edited by Tony Lynch. London: Stanley Paul, 1992.
32p; illus; pbk   ISBN: 0-09-177297-4
                                          BL: LB.31.c.6019

  Soccer skills presented in the author's own distinctive artistic style. Many illustrations used in the past few decades are recognisable as 'Trevillion'.

203 Soccer training: games, drills and fitness practices / Nick Whitehead & Malcolm Cook; foreword by Alex Ferguson. 3rd ed. London: A & C Black, 1992.
128p; illus; index; pbk   ISBN: 0-7136-3574-6
                                          BL: YK.1992.a.2549

  ☞ Previous ed. 188; subsequent ed. 210

204 Training to win: football / Rolf Wirhed. London: Wolfe, 1992.
96p; illus; pbk   ISBN: 0-7234-1778-4

205 Soccer / Ken Goldman & Peter Dunk. Rev. ed. London: Blandford, 1993.
80p; illus; index; pbk
(Play the game)   ISBN: 0-7137-2419-6
                                          BL: YK.1993.a.14877

  ☞ Previous ed. G187

206 Soccer techniques: a guide for teachers and coaches / Trevor Spindler. Aylesbury: T. Spindler, 1993.
112p; illus; pbk   ISBN: 0-9520030-0-7
                                          BL: YK.1993.a.12833

207 Team coach / Alan Brown. Braunton: Merlin, 1993.
48p; pbk   ISBN: 0-86303-626-0
                                          BL: YK.1994.b.14895

208 The FA coaching book of soccer tactics and skills / Charles Hughes. New ed. Harpenden: Queen Anne, 1994.
240p; illus   ISBN: 1-85291-545-5

  ☞ Previous ed. G161

209 Ryan Giggs' soccer skills / Ryan Giggs with Bobby Charlton. London: Boxtree, 1994.
128p; illus; pbk   ISBN: 1-85283-956-2

  Manchester United's young and old maestros here join forces. Welsh International Giggs is one of the most exciting players to have emerged in recent years.

210 Soccer training: games, drills and fitness practices / Nick Whitehead and Malcolm Cook; foreword by Alex Ferguson. 4th ed. London: A & C Black, 1994.
125p; illus; index; pbk   ISBN: 0-7136-3832-X
                                          BL: YK.1994.a.13974

  ☞ Previous ed. G203

211 The young soccer player / Gary Lineker. London: Dorling Kindersley, 1994.
32p; illus; index; pbk   ISBN: 0-7513-5165-2
                                          BL: YK.1995.b.3526

  A lightweight treatment for youngsters written under Lineker's name during his reign as a Japanese superstar.

Play in Specific Positions

212 Goalkeeping / Bob Wilson. London: Pelham, 1970.
112p; illus   SBN: 7207-0337-9
                                          BL: X.629/3005

  Written by the Scotland goalkeeper during his long career with Arsenal.

213 Association football: back defenders / Allen Wade. Wakefield: EP Publishing, 1972.
40p; illus; pbk
(Coach yourself)   ISBN: 0-7158-0167-8

214 Association football: goal-keepers / Allen Wade. Wakefield: EP Publishing, 1972.
40p; illus; pbk
(Coach yourself)   ISBN: 0-7158-0166-X

215 Association football: midfield players / Allen Wade. Wakefield: EP Publishing, 1972.
40p; illus; pbk
(Coach yourself)   ISBN: 0-7158-0168-6

216 Association football: strikers / Allen Wade. Wakefield: EP Publishing, 1972.
40p; illus; pbk
(Coach yourself)   ISBN: 0-7158-0169-4

217 Golden goals / Jimmy Hill and Brian Moore. Middlesbrough?: Cleveland Petroleum, 1972.
72p; illus

  An unusual book describing, with accompanying graphics, great goals and the way they arose. Includes spaces for stickers given away free at Cleveland petrol stations.

218 Shilton in goal: a player's guide / Peter Shilton; written in collaboration with Pete Barraclough. London: Stanley Paul, 1974.
80p; illus
ISBN: 0-09-121260-X (cased) • ISBN: 0-09-121261-8 (pbk)

Shilton transferred from Leicester to Stoke in this year with many games behind him but even more to come. This is the first of several volumes from the famous keeper.

219 Clemence on goalkeeping / Ray Clemence with John Keith; photographs by Harry Ormesher. Guildford: Lutterworth Press, 1977.
156p; illus; index
ISBN: 0-7188-7016-6
BL: X.620/17197

Doubles as an autobiography for the Scunthorpe United and Liverpool goalkeeper, written before his move to Spurs — valuable tips from an England International.

220 Goals!: a unique A to Z collection / Jimmy Greaves; edited by Norman Giller. London: Harrap, 1981.
161p; illus
ISBN: 0-245-53787-2 (cased) • ISBN: 0-245-53796-1 (pbk)
BL: X.622/11413

An unusual book which examines the end product which the game seeks to produce — no one would appear better qualified to present this study than Jimmy Greaves, one of the game's most prolific marksmen.

221 How to score goals / Malcolm Macdonald with Martin Samuel; photography by Bed Radford; graphics by Paul Buckle. Tadworth: Kingswood, 1985.
154p; illus
ISBN: 0-434-98064-1
BL: YK.1987.a.1140

The author scored 191 domestic league goals in his career with Fulham, Luton, Newcastle and Arsenal. Written whilst resting from his managerial career during a spell as a Worthing licensee.

222 Goalkeeping in action / Peter Shilton. London: Stanley Paul, 1988.
107p; illus; pbk
(Sport in action)
ISBN: 0-09-171261-0
BL: YK.1988.a.2599

Written during Shilton's Derby County days. A thorough study on his art from the England International, renowned as one of the world's best ever.

223 Goalkeeping / Alex Welsh. London: A & C Black, 1990.
127p; illus
ISBN: 0-7136-5789-8
BL: YK.1990.a.3786

224 Striker: skills and tactics / Gary Lineker with Tony Lynch; illustrations by Paul Trevillion. London: Stanley Paul, 1991.
96p; illus; pbk
ISBN: 0-09-173662-5
BL: YK.1991.b.6019

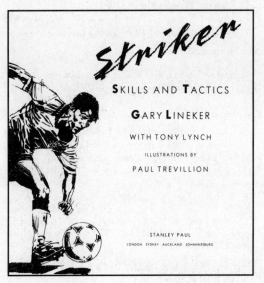

225 Shilton on goalkeeping / Peter Shilton. London: Headline, 1992.
160p; illus
ISBN: 0-7472-0718-6
BL: YK.1993.b.829

This update from Shilton appeared after his move to Plymouth Argyle as player and manager.

Tactics & Playing Systems

226 Football positional play no. 1: The kick-off / William MacPherson. Beith: The author, 1929.
1 sheet

No more published in this form   BL: 1879.cc.2(50)

This early example of niche marketing was evidently envisaged as one of a long-running series, but in the event, 'The Throw-in', 'The Back Pass', and 'The Retaken Free Kick' never saw the light of day. Instead the various component parts of the game were packaged together in the following entry by the same author.

227 Football positional play / William MacPherson. Beith: The author, 1930.
46p; pbk
BL: D

228 Soccer tactics . . . / Bernard Joy. London: Phoenix Sports Books, 1957.
127p; illus   BL: 7923.b.26

The author played for Casuals, Fulham and Arsenal as an amateur, and as an England amateur International. This is an important book studying tactical systems as they had developed to this date. Includes chapters on the Hungarians, Arsenal, Spurs 'push and run' and the classical Scottish style.

☞ Subsequent ed. G229

229 Soccer tactics: a new appraisal / Bernard Joy. Rev. and reset. London: Phoenix House, 1962.
127p; illus   BL: X.449/982

Effectively the same content as the previous entry.

☞ Previous ed. G228

230 Positional skills and play / Walter Winterbottom. London: Educational Productions, 1959-1962.
7 pt
(Coach yourself series)

Contents: Centre forward (1959), Full-back (1960), Goalkeeper (1960), Wing forward (1961), Wing half (1961), Centre half (1961), Inside forward (1962)
       BL: 7926.b.1
       BL: X.0449/52

England manager Winterbottom became the FA Director of Coaching and set up the first National Coaching System. His innovations in this field led to the award of a knighthood in 1978. This is one of his earliest publications.

231 Soccer: the British way / edited by Kenneth Wheeler. London: Kaye & Ward, 1963.
128p; illus

Contributors include John Sissons, Ron Springett, Bobby Tambling and Jimmy Armfield. As well as 'how to play' this also includes a section on 'how to watch'.

232 International coaching book: the master football coaches reveal their own methods / T. Stratton Smith; edited by Eric Batty. London: Souvenir, 1966.
110p; illus   ISBN: 0-285-50196-8

233 Understanding soccer tactics / Conrad M. J. L. Lodziak. London: Faber, 1966.
188p; illus   BL: X.449/2117

John Arlott reviewed this book in *The Observer*: 'Mr. Lodziak deals in words and clear diagrams with every possible formation. For everyone seriously interested in football this is required reading.'

234 Soccer: the international way / edited by Kenneth Wheeler, with 105 photographs. London: Kaye & Ward, 1967.
128p; illus   BL: X.441/930

☞ Also listed at: E183

235 Soccer for thinkers / M. Sinclair Allison. London: Pelham, 1967.
154p; illus   BL: X.449/2787

236 Scientific soccer in the seventies / Roger MacDonald and Eric Batty; illustrations designed by Rod MacLeod. London: Pelham, 1971.
160p; illus   SBN: 7207-0431-6
       BL: X.629/3251

Uses the 1970 World Cup finals to illustrate the methods, tactics and strategies employed worldwide.

☞ Also listed at: E190

237 Five-a-side football / R. W. Elliot. Speldhurst: Planned Action Ltd for the National Association of Youth Clubs, 1972.
44p; illus, plans; pbk
(Know the game)   ISBN: 0-901528-59-5

One of the earliest publications to concentrate on this particularly popular 'brand' of the game.

☞ Subsequent ed. G240

238 The professionals' book of skills & tactics / Ken Jones and Pat Welton; edited by Martin Tyler. London: Marshall Cavendish, 1973.
192p; illus
(Golden hands books)

This material was first published by Marshall Cavendish Limited in the part work: 'Book of Football'.' – t.p. verso
       ISBN: 0-85685-024-1

239 Tactics and teamwork / Charles F. C. Hughes. Wakefield: EP Publishing, 1973.
160p; illus; pbk

Cover title: Football tactics and teamwork
'Produced in collaboration with the Football Association' – Bookcover   ISBN: 0-7158-0174-0
       BL: X.619/15298

240 Five-a-side football / R. W. Elliot. 2nd ed. Wakefield: EP Publishing, 1977.
48p; illus; pbk
(Know the game)   ISBN: 0-7158-0543-6
       BL: WP.3073/116

☞ Previous ed. G237

241 Football: match winning skills and tactics / David Gregory; drawings by C. H. Juillard. London: Chancerel, Barrie and Jenkins, 1977.
3-93p; illus
(Action books)   ISBN: 0-905703-15-4
       BL: X.629/11919

242 Winning soccer tactics / Robin Trimby. London: Ward Lock, 1977.
95p; illus
(Hyperion books)   ISBN: 0-7063-5297-1
       BL: X.620/17243

243 The ABC of soccer sense: strategy & tactics today /
Tommy Docherty. London: Batsford, 1978.
144p; illus; index   ISBN: 0-7134-0539-2
                                      BL: X.620/18018

*Docherty has been a high profile and characterful
servant to the game and is able to draw on his very
varied experience to present his own particular ideas
on the way the game should be played.*

244 Basic soccer: strategies for successful player and program
development / George Ford. London: Allyn and Bacon,
1982.
xii, 259p; illus; index   ISBN: 0-205-07157-0
                                      BL: X.622/11952

*One of just a handful of soccer strategy and tactic
books written originally for the American market.*

245 The Hamlyn book of football techniques and tactics /
Richard Widdows; illustrated by Paul Buckle. Feltham:
Hamlyn, 1982.
192p; illus; index   ISBN: 0-600-34641-2
                                      BL: L.45/1666

☞ Subsequent ed. G247

246 Five a side football: a guide to mini football / Glenn
Hoddle with the assistance of Keir Radnedge. London:
Pelham, 1984.
95p; illus   ISBN: 0-7207-1510-5
                                      BL: X.629/25685

*One of very few publications on this very popular form
of the game played by all ages, largely at the amateur level, but particularly popular with the more
senior fraternity. When the boots are finally hung up,
the training shoes have been known to keep going for
much longer. Spurs favourite Hoddle was particularly
adept at this game which presents particular opportunities for those with vision and close control.*

247 The Hamlyn book of football techniques and tactics /
Richard Widdows; illustrated by Paul Buckle. London:
Treasure, 1988.
192p; illus; index   ISBN: 1-85051-292-2
                                      BL: LB.31.b.1595

☞ Previous ed. G245

248 Soccer strategies / Allen Wade; diagrams by Ken
Tranter. London: Heinemann Kingswood, 1988.
127p; illus; pbk   ISBN: 0-434-98156-7
                                      BL: YK.1989.b.2523

249 Soccer / Nic Paul; foreword by Glenn Hoddle. London:
Ward Lock, 1992.
80p; illus; index; pbk
(Tactics of success)   ISBN: 0-7063-7089-9
                                      BL: YK.1993.a.9402

250 Expressive soccer / Chris Swann. The author?, 1993.
37 leaves; spiral   ISBN: 0-9521272-0-2
                                      BL: YK.1995.b.979

251 Soccer techniques, tactics & teamwork / Gerhard Bauer;
introduction by Franz Beckenbauer. New York: Sterling;
London: Cassell, 1993.
159p; pbk   ISBN: 0-8069-8730-8
                                      BL: YK.1993.b.10566

*The introduction by Franz Beckenbauer is an all too
rare contribution in English language books by this
legendary German player and manager.*

Fitness & Injury

252 Football impetigo: an enquiry into a contagious affection
of the skin occurring amongst football players / Henry
George Armstrong. London: J. & A. Churchill,
1896.
12p; pbk

*A paper read before the Medical Officers of Schools
Association on 10th December 1895*
                                      BL: 07306.g.4(14)

This rare early item sought to explain the
prevalence of skin rashes amongst footballers
of the day. The findings of the report traced
the problem to the compound being used for
delineating the pitch markings.

253 Football injuries / R. H. Anglin Whitelocke.
London: J. & A. Churchill, 1904.
16p; pbk

*A paper read before the Medical Officers of Schools
Association in 1903*   BL: 07305.m.6(18)

Footballers have always sustained injuries, not least
in the early days of the game when unwieldy boots
and heavy footballs made life distinctly difficult. This is a most interesting early guide.

254 Training and diet for cricket, football and
athletics with diary for 1904 / C. B. Fry.
London?: Bedford Publishing Press, 1904.

*Corinthian footballer, cricketer and fine all-
rounder – Fry attributed much of his
prowess to his training and lifestyle. Today
we would call it a fitness programme.*

255 Recreative physical exercises and activities for
association football players and other games
players. London: Evans, 1937.
63p; pbk   BL: 07908.e.77

Medical Officers of Schools Association.

FOOTBALL IMPETIGO

AN ENQUIRY INTO A CONTAGIOUS AFFECTION OF THE SKIN
OCCURRING AMONGST FOOTBALL PLAYERS.

A PAPER READ BEFORE THE ASSOCIATION

On 10th December, 1895.

BY

H. G. ARMSTRONG, M.R.C.S.

MEDICAL OFFICER, WELLINGTON COLLEGE.

Published by order of the Association.

H. ALDERSMITH,
CHARLES SHELLY, } *Hon. Sees.*

January, 1896.

London:
J. & A. CHURCHILL, 11, NEW BURLINGTON STREET.
1896.

256 Recreative physical exercises and activities. London:
Evans, 1946.
34p; pbk
BL: 7918.bb.9

257 A medical handbook for athletic and football club trainers /
William David Jarvis. London: Faber & Faber, 1950.
144p
BL: 7384.b.44

More sophisticated methodology had been made
available by the time of this publication. Many of the
techniques appear quaint, however, against today's
advanced technology.

258 Strapping and bandaging for football injuries / John H.
C. Colson. London: Naldrett Press, 1953.
ix, 85p
BL: 7484.f.44

Sprains are one of the most common injuries in the
game – this guide concentrates on specific techniques to aid their speedy recovery.

259 Footballers and their injuries / William Hughes.
Wrexham: Football Association of Wales, 1955.
90p
BL: 7922.de.12

260 Football fitness / William George Watson. London:
Stanley Paul, 1973.
132p; illus
ISBN: 0-09-115780-3 (cased) • ISBN: 0-09-115781-1 (pbk)
BL: X.629/5579

With the odd exception, books before this date
tended to concentrate on the treatment of injury
rather than the development of fitness. This is a
comprehensive guide.

261 Football fitness and injuries / David S. Muckle and
Harold Shepherdson. London: Pelham, 1975.
142p; illus
ISBN: 0-7207-0801-X
BL: X.329/7866

Well informed advice indeed – Shepherdson was well
known as the blue-tracksuited England trainer for
many years, whilst Muckle acted as medical adviser
to FIFA.

262 The treatment of football injuries / Harry Harris & Mike
Varney. London: Macdonald and Jane's, 1977.
159p; illus; pbk
ISBN: 0-354-08510-7
BL: X.319/17578

Includes authentic case histories.

263 Football injuries / Muir Gray. Oxford: Offox Press,
1980.
xi, 114p; illus; index
ISBN: 0-9506989-0-3
BL: X.329/19290

☞ Subsequent ed. G265

264 Get fit for soccer: training, diet, travel, environment
factors / David Sutherland Muckle. London: Pelham,
1981.
151p; illus; index
Bibliography: p143-144
ISBN: 0-7207-1342-0
BL: X.322/10210

A comprehensive guide, including some of the fringe
elements in the quest for fitness, from the medical
adviser to FIFA.

265 Football injuries / Muir Gray. School ed. London:
Edward Arnold, 1982.
xi, 114p; illus; index; pbk
ISBN: 0-7131-0848-7
BL: X.329/16069

☞ Previous ed. G263

266 The FA guide to the treatment and rehabilitation of
injuries in sport / William J. Armour. London: Published
on behalf of the Football Association by Heinemann,
1983.
178p; illus; index
Bibliography: p173
ISBN: 0-434-02751-0
BL: X.322/13282

There is nothing worse for a footballer than being out
of the game through injury; getting back quickly becomes all-important – this guide covers the
rehabilitation period which must generally follow initial treatment.

267 Physical conditioning for winning football / William A.
Kroll. London: Allyn and Bacon, 1983.
xv, 300p; illus; index
Includes bibliographies
ISBN: 0-205-07940-7
BL: X.622/17490

268   Fit for soccer / Mike Yaxley; general editor Peter
Verney; medical adviser Alan Maryon-Davis. London:
Batsford, 1986.
96p; illus; index   ISBN: 0-7134-4729-X
     BL: YK.1987.a.40

*A thorough guide to the fitness side of the game –
Yaxley writes as physiotherapist and trainer of
Brighton and Hove Albion.*

269   Soccer injuries / Alan G. Smith. Malborough: Crowood,
1989.
96p; pbk   ISBN: 1-85223-186-6
     BL: YK.1990.b.6093

270   Get ready for soccer: a complete training programme /
Mervyn Beck and others. Marlborough: Crowood, 1990.
128p; illus; index; pbk   ISBN: 1-85223-267-6
     BL: YK.1991.b.3159

271   Soccer fit: training and health for soccer players /
Mervyn Beck. Swindon: Crowood, 1991.
95p; illus; index; pbk

     Bibliography: p94   ISBN: 1-85223-472-5
     BL: YK.1993.b.1232

272   Football against MS: souvenir brochure / Action and
Research for Multiple Sclerosis and Nationwide Building
Society. London: EMP, 1992.
133p; illus, 1 map; pbk

     With wallchart   BL: YK.1994.b.10749

*Football has on occasion been used as a vehicle to
support major health initiatives – this represents
one of the best known examples.*

273   Serum creatine phosphikinase – changes in running,
football and rugby: an intergroup comparison / Mary
Kelly. Dublin: Cospoir, 1993.
23p; illus

     Includes bibliography
     *At head of cover title: COSPOIR Sports Research
Committee; Department of Education*

*This unusual publication examines certain of the
physiological elements of football in comparison with
other sporting activities.*

274   The Italian football diet and fitness programme / Jane
Nottage and Claudio Bartolini. London: Thorsons, 1994.
x, 150p; pbk   ISBN: 0-7225-2950-3
     BL: YK.1994.a.7720

*Author Jane Nottage served as Paul Gascoigne's
personal assistant; this is an example of spin-off
marketing at its most blatant – quite who buys volumes such as this is a mystery. On his transfer to
Lazio, Gazza is rumoured to have forsaken his favourite Mars bars in favour of the odd pizza!*

The Science of Football

275   The principles of missile games: field athletic sports,
cricket, baseball, lawn tennis, football, bowls / Philip
Harwood Francis. Liverpool: T. Brakell, 1948.
70p   BL: 7919.aaa.37

*Amongst the vast number of 'how to play' books
there have always been a handful which seek to delve
slightly deeper in an effort to place sport firmly in the
same camp as science. This is an early effort at this
approach, including football as one of a number of
sports discussed.*

276   A study of targets in games: (tournaments, field athletic
sports, baseball, cricket, football, hockey, golf, lawn
tennis, bowls, etc.) / Rev. P. H. Francis. London: Mitre,
1951.
235p; illus; index   BL: 7920.a.46

A similar, but more detailed, treatment.

277   The mechanics of sport: an elementary instructional
handbook for all sportsmen, emphasizing the factors
governing ball control with particular reference to
football, cricket, and golf / Edwin Bade; illustrations by
H. J. Proctor. Kingswood: Andrew George Elliot, 1952.
107p; illus
(Right way books)   BL: W.P.1122/31

*Another pseudo-scientific approach. One cannot pro-
test that science has nothing to do with football;
every movement of the body, bounce and flight of the
ball is governed by scientific principles. This type of
analysis is particularly prevalent in the exacting confines of golf, for example, but less common in football.*

278   Science and football: proceedings of the first World
Congress of Science and Football, Liverpool 13-17th
April 1987 / edited by T. Reilly and others. London:
Spon, 1988.
xx, 651p; illus; index

     Includes bibliographies   ISBN: 0-419-14360-2

*A most unusual scholarly work which applies the laws
and disciplines of science and mathematical analysis
to many areas of the game, including ballistics, physi-*

ology and the treatment of injury; a fascinating and highly original publication of true technical quality.

279   Science and football II: proceedings of the second World Congress of Science and Football, Eindhoven, Netherlands, 22nd-25th May 1991 / edited by T. Reilly, J. Clarys and A. Stibbe. London: Spon, 1993.
xx, 480p; illus; index

> *Includes bibliographies*   ISBN: 0-419-17850-3
>   BL: YK.1993.b.6232

Three years after the first symposium, the second World Congress of Science and Football was held in Holland with the result that further papers and scholarly studies were brought together, all on the broad theme of science and its application to all facets of the game. The result is some very stimulating material – not for the faint-hearted though. This is one of very few soccer books which include algebraic equations. Viewed on a lighter note, it can be a comforting read; Roberto Baggio might be relieved to know that he missed the last and fatal penalty of the 1994 World Cup not due to lassitude and sheer terror but rather because of an unfortunate combination of the angle of incidence and co-efficient of friction!

280   Football / edited by Björn Ekblom. Oxford: Blackwell Scientific, 1994.
viii, 227p; illus; pbk
(Handbook of sports medicine and science)
                                                  ISBN: 0-632-03328-2

Football &
Society

LIKE MANY OTHER PASTIMES AND ACTIVITIES, there is far more to football than might conceivably be imagined by the uninitiated observer. Just as 'golf is a good walk spoiled' to the wags who have never played, so football is 'twenty-two grown men chasing a bag of wind' to those masters of the sweeping statement who choose to deride anything they fail to appreciate. Yet nothing could be further from the truth. Football, though indeed a simple game, has complex implications far beyond the confines of the field of play. In total, this can best be described as the 'culture' of football; something that embraces the role football plays in people's lives – the attitudes and behaviour of fans, the customs of the game; the collection of programmes and other ephemera; the badges, colours and strip of the participating teams – a whole host of intermeshing topics each deserving, and receiving, serious study.

Whilst many of the items listed in this chapter reflect the most lyrical and good humoured side of soccer it is regrettable that the first section, and one of the largest, is concerned with hooliganism and crowd control. Bad behaviour on the part of fans is something that has plagued football throughout its existence, but during the last two decades the problem has often forced itself dramatically on the attention of politicians and public alike.

Shameful though it may be that such problems have occurred at all, the significant amount of research undertaken into this topic, reflected in the number of reports and other works listed below, is surely an encouraging sign. This research has undoubtedly played a role in helping the football authorities curb the worst excesses of the 'English Disease' at a time when it looked to be taking an unshakeable hold. Permanent solutions though have not yet been forthcoming – even as I write, the date of 15 February 1995 has just been indelibly written into the 'Black Calendar' of football history as a mindless minority of English 'followers' rioted in Dublin at a friendly fixture between the Republic of Ireland and England.

Researchers into this darker side of football both at home and abroad will find much of interest in this section. It begins with one of the first ever official reports on crowd control, published by the Home Office in 1924 [H1] as a reaction to the overcrowding which occurred at the first Wembley Cup Final in 1923, between Bolton Wanderers and West Ham United. This however is a rather isolated example and it was not until 1966 that the first really substantial official report was commissioned. When it appeared, *The Chester Report* [H4] addressed the future of football in its broadest sense. While many of its recommendations were ignored, it effectively put football on the political agenda and, most importantly, its author Sir Norman Chester (1907-1986) went on to become football's foremost academic voice. By the time of his death he had established the Sir Norman Chester Centre for Football Research at Leicester University. The Centre has since formed close links with the Football Trust and has become the leading publisher of academic research in the field of crowd disorder and spectator psychology. Leading players in their team of sociologists and statisticians include Professor Eric Dunning, John Williams, Patrick Murphy, Rogan Taylor and Jackie Woodhouse. Their 1984 report, *Hooligans Abroad* [H30], stretching to 230 pages, was the first major publication from the Leicester University stable, firmly establishing football as a valid subject for academic research. Other works tackled the subjects of all-seater stadiums [H25], club membership schemes [H53], policing of matches [H57], children and football [H48], racism [H86], and women in soccer [H77]. These examples serve to give a flavour of the sort of material produced by the Sir Norman Chester Centre – there is much more besides.

I can already hear though, the dissenting voices of the sceptics, anguished cries of 'pretentious academic claptrap', and worse. Truth to tell, football academics do not claim to provide definitive answers. What they do, and do well, is address the problems, analyse carefully, raise awareness and present conclusions. This is a real and positive contribution to the development of the game. Academic research has an important role to play in safeguarding the game's future and helping to steer it in the right direction when it threatens to go off the rails altogether.

The social status of football is very different now from what it has been in the past. Students wishing to trace the growth of football in society, particularly during the early years, will find the definitive works of James Walvin [H13], Tony Mason [H20], and Nicholas Fishwick [H58] invaluable. At the other extreme, those in search of a statement of 'where it's at in the nineties' will find the modernist approach of Steve Redhead [H80] and Richard Giulianotti [H94-95] most enlightening.

All the titles referred to thus far deal with the sociological side of football spectatorship rather than the pure pleasure of supportership. In recognition of the sheer enjoyment which watching football can generate, titles covering the Art of Spectatorship are accorded a separate listing. Here one will find accounts explaining the appeal of soccer from a spectator's viewpoint; there is no more lyrical evocation of spectatorship as it is used to be than in the works presented by Percy Young [H98-100] whilst the later publications of Nick Hornby [H123] and Ian Ridley [H127] convey a similar passion updated in which the simple act of 'going to the match' has been superseded for many by the 'cult of fandom' more recently analysed by Steve Redhead [H133] and Kevin Baldwin [H142].

All the works in the Art of Spectatorship section help explain the whys and wherefores of supportership, and answer questions which many football followers must have asked themselves at one time or another. 'Why does it really matter that your team lost an FA Cup semifinal in the eighth minute of injury time to a disputed penalty? For goodness sake, there are people starving. . .'. It is difficult to justify, but the fact is that it *does* matter for millions of people worldwide. The volumes in this section will give as near to a rational explanation as you are ever likely to get.

In the next section are a number of works grouped under the banner Badges & Names, Club Colours & Strip. There is a very definite neo-heraldic element in football – playing attire (now more commonly referred to as 'strip'), club colours, nicknames and crests are all covered in this small section of curious and interesting works.

The following sections, Broadcasting, and Legal Cases present a limited number of specialist studies before the surprisingly lengthy list of titles which address Betting & the Pools. Betting on matches has been a feature of football since early times, but the birth of the Littlewoods Pools Organisation in 1923 extended football gambling to the public at large and it has been a part of life ever since. Of course, the majority of us never reap any financial rewards from our love of football – on the contrary it costs us a fortune. Not content with laying out huge sums for season tickets and travel to away games, we spend even more on items which serve to remind us of this annually perpetrated folly. I refer to the collecting of memorabilia and ephemera, an affliction suffered by many football followers. Entries in this section include items on football programmes, cigarette cards, postcards and football art.

Most football followers would admit to dreams of turning out for their favourite club, but these generally founder early in life. Not entirely content with this inevitable state of affairs, reputations may instead be won and lost through game simulations enacted through the medium of the table top, computer or fantasy league. A number of essentially ephemeral items have been published in this field but a definitive treatment is notable by its absence. The subject would suit a colourful 'coffee table' treatment – what about *Just Flick to Kick: a Century of Football Games*? I for one would certainly order a copy and I must confess to having more than a few items for inclusion lurking in the back bedroom just begging to be 'rediscovered'.

On a more serious note this chapter finishes with a selection of works which seek to apply the disciplines of economics and business analysis to the future of football. They recognise that no matter how much the game may be loved by the people, it simply cannot survive unless the financial books are balanced well enough to ensure continued viability and the consequent support of the bank manager. The skills of accountancy, marketing and business development are certainly becoming just as important as the fitness and ability of the on-field representatives of this global enterprise. These ideas are well summarised by the comprehensive *Out of Time* [H297] by Alex Fynn and Lynton Guest, very much a blueprint for the future.

Football will survive of course – it will suffer crises; players, managers and fans will commit inexcusable misdemeanours and many more words on the problems besetting the game will be written; but it will survive the immediate future because it is just too precious a commodity to be allowed to die. Whether it will be with us in five centuries time is more problematic although the prospect of Derby County being Inter-Galactic Champions for season 2495/96 is certainly something to ponder, as is the additional shelf space required to house a full set of *Rothmans*. Who knows where mankind will be then, or cricket and synchronised swimming for that matter . . . Whatever the future for football, though, the publications under the spotlight in this chapter will present historians with a snapshot view of the social importance of the game during the last one hundred years or so. The authors deserve to be applauded for their diligent efforts and, often, evident compassion in making such important and original contributions to the literature of association football.

Football & Society ~ Contents

Crowd Behaviour & Soccer Violence

1 Crowds / E. Shortt. London: Home Office Committee on Crowds, 1924.
28p; pbk
(Cmd 2088)

Examines safety aspects of the inaugural Cup Final at Wembley.

2 Digest of Scottish statistics nos. 1-37 (April 1953-April 1971). Edinburgh: HMSO, 1953-1971.

No. 1-8 issued by the Scottish Home Department; from no. 9 issued by the Scottish Statistical Office; continued by Scottish Abstract of Statistics;
Published annually   BL: BS155/21

Gives statistics on the numbers attending Scottish Football League and other football matches.

☞ See also: H8

3 Village on the border: a social study of religion, politics and football in a North Wales community / Ronald Frankenberg. London: Cohen & West, 1957.
xi, 163p   BL: 010370.b.83

Studies of this kind are now flavour of the month, but at the time of publication this was somewhat innovative in its approach and should certainly be of interest to the student of Welsh football.

4 Report of the Committee on Football. London: Department of Education and Science, 1968.
vii, 135p

Chairman: D. Norman Chester   BL: BS10/299

The Chester Report is not a report about hooliganism, but its recommendations on how the game should be run have had an impact for spectators. The name of Sir Norman Chester, who died in 1986, lives on in the Centre for Football Research at Leicester University from which many of the following publications emanated.

5 Soccer hooliganism: a preliminary report / J. A. Harrington. Bristol: John Wright, 1968.
iv, 57p; pbk   SBN: 7236-0199-2
          BL: X.100/26324

There has always been violence at football matches but it was in the swinging sixties that the problem became a serious one, spawning early academic studies like this.

6 Report of the Working Party on Crowd Behaviour at Football Matches. London: Ministry of Housing and Local Government, 1969.
17p; pbk

Chairman: Sir John Lang   SBN: 11-750219-7
          BL: BS128/223

7 Social trends / Central Statistical Office. London: HMSO, 1970-

Published annually   ISSN: 0306-7742
          BL: BS75/19

Includes information on attendances at football matches.

8 Scottish abstract of statistics. Edinburgh: HMSO, 1971-

Issued by the Scottish Office; continues Digest of Scottish statistics   BL: BS39/48

☞ See also: H2

9 Report of the inquiry into crowd safety at sports grounds / J. Wheatley. London: Home Office & Scottish Home and Health Department, 1972.
iv, 35p; pbk
(Cmnd 4952)   SBN: 10-149520-X
          BL: BS18/385

10 Football hooliganism and the skinheads / John Clarke. Birmingham: Centre for Contemporary Cultural Studies, University of Birmingham, 1973.
24p; pbk   ISBN: 0-7044-0489-3

Echoes of a time when all acts of football violence seemed to be committed by the tonsurally challenged.

11 Football mania – the players and the fans: the mass psychology of football / Gerhard Vinnai; translated by David Fernbach and Martin Gillard. London: Ocean Books, 1973.
121p

Translation of: Fußballsport als Ideologie
          BL: X.619/7057

One of the first books to recognise football supporters as a 'species' in their own right consuming the 'product' known as football, the two combining together to form a highly distinctive culture.

12 Football since the war: a study in social change and popular culture / Chas Critcher. Birmingham: Centre for Contemporary Cultural Studies, University of Birmingham, 1973.
33p; pbk   ISBN: 0-7044-0478-8

13 The people's game: a social history of British football / James Walvin. London: Allen Lane, 1975.
xi, 201p; illus

Bibliography: p187-193   ISBN: 0-7139-0768-1
          BL: X.629/7112

From public school ties to flat caps and beyond . . .

☞ Also listed at: A114

14   Football hooliganism and vandalism / Fred Milsom and
     Russell Swannell. Birmingham: Westhill College of
     Education, 1976.
     42p; pbk

     An inquiry into the experiences and attitudes of
     young football followers in the West Midlands.

15   Report of the Working Group on Football Crowd
     Behaviour. Edinburgh: HMSO, 1977.
     xviii, 41p; pbk

          Chairman: Frank McElhone   ISBN: 0-11-491514-8
                                                  BL: BS152/210

16   'Football hooliganism': the wider context / Roger
     Ingham and others. London: Inter-Action Inprint, 1978.
     149p; illus; pbk

          Bibliography: p145-147   ISBN: 0-904571-15-7
                                                 BL: X.519/27887

17   Public disorder and sporting events: a report / Joint
     Panel of the Sports Council and the Social Science
     Research Council. London: Sports Council, Social
     Science Research Council, 1978.
     3, iv, 60p; pbk   ISBN: 0-900296-71-2
                                  BL: BS387/117

18   The development of soccer as a participant and spectator
     sport: geographical aspects / John Bale. London: Sports
     Council, Social Science Research Council, 1979.
     3 leaves, 42p; illus, maps; pbk
     (Reviews / Joint Panel on Leisure and Recreation
     Research. ISSN: 0143-2931)

          Bibliography: p36-42   BL: BS387/135(4)

19   Soccer: the social origins of the sport and its
     development as a spectacle and profession / E.
     Dunning. London: Sports Council, Social Science
     Research Council, 1979.
     5, 38p; pbk
     (Reviews / Joint Panel on Leisure and Recreation
     Research. ISSN: 0143-2931)   ISBN: 0-900979-95-X
                                             BL: BS387/135(13)

20   Association football and English society, 1863-1915 /
     Tony Mason. Brighton: Harvester, 1980.
     x, 278p; illus, maps; index

          Bibliography: p259-267   ISBN: 0-85527-797-1
                                                BL: X.620/19159

     One of the best studies of the growth of football
     from the formation of the Association to the First
     World War. Essential for the student of Victorian and
     Edwardian soccer.

21   The soccer tribe / Desmond Morris. London: Cape,
     1981.
     320p; illus, coats of arms, music; index

          Bibliography: p318   ISBN: 0-224-01935-X
                                            BL: X.622/11350

A most unusual study using the disciplines of anthropology and behavioural psychology to explain the
popularity of football and the behaviour of its fans.
Some of the theories are outlandish, but this is a
fascinating and colourful volume. Oxford United were
the guinea pigs for much of the research as the
author was a director of the club and an Oxford Research Fellow.

22   Working class social bonding and the sociogenesis of
     football hooliganism: a report to the Social Science
     Research Council / Eric Dunning, Patrick Murphy and
     John Williams. Leicester: Sir Norman Chester Centre for
     Football Research, 1982.

23   Explorations in football culture / edited by Alan
     Tomlinson. Eastbourne: Leisure Studies Association,
     1983.
     202p; pbk
     (Conference papers / Leisure Studies Association; no. 21)

          Proceedings of a workshop of the British Sociological
          Association/Leisure Studies Association held in Sheffield on
          4 June 1982.   ISBN: 0-906337-24-0
                                       BL: YK.1992.b.8439

24   Football as a focus for disorder. London: Centre for
     Contemporary Studies, 1983.
     20p; pbk

          At head of cover title: Patterns of social violence

25   All seated football grounds and hooliganism: the
     Coventry City experience, 1981-84 / John Williams, Eric
     Dunning and Patrick Murphy. London: The Football
     Trust, 1984.
     44p

26   All sit down: a report on the Coventry City all-seated
     stadium 1982-83 / John Williams, Eric Dunning and
     Patrick Murphy. Leicester: Sir Norman Chester Centre
     for Football Research, 1984.
     2 vols

27   Crowd behaviour at football matches: a study in
     Scotland / Sue Walker and others. Edinburgh: Centre
     for Leisure Research, 1984.
     186p

          Sponsored by the Football Trust

28   Football spectator violence: report of an official working
     group / D. V. Teasdale. London: HMSO, 1984.
     61p; pbk

          Issued by the Department of the Environment
                                       ISBN: 0-11-751749-6
                                            BL: BS414/2197

29   The football world: a contemporary social history /
     Stephen Wagg. Brighton: Harvester, 1984.
     xv, 252p; index   ISBN: 0-7108-0258-7
                                  BL: X.629/23618

30   Hooligans abroad: the behaviour and control of English fans in continental Europe / John Williams, Eric Dunning and Patrick Murphy. London: Routledge & Kegan Paul, 1984.
xiv, 230p; illus, maps; index; pbk   ISBN: 0-7102-0143-5
                       BL: X.529/62290

    This is the first major study by the team from the Sir Norman Chester Centre for Football Research at Leicester University. Many other important works of research were to follow.

    ☞ Subsequent ed. H63

31   The Old Firm: sectarianism, sport and society in Scotland / Bill Murray. Edinburgh: John Donald, 1984.
ix, 294p; illus; index; pbk

    Bibliography: p282-285   ISBN: 0-85976-121-5
                             BL: X.800/40862

    Glasgow's Rangers and Celtic sides are collectively known as 'The Old Firm' – their traditional rivalry reflects the cultural, religious and historical differences between Scotland's Catholic and Protestant communities.

    ☞ Also listed at: B1067, B1200

32   A study of the behaviour of Aberdeen fans at the European Cup Winners Cup Final, 1983: a report prepared for the Football Trust. Edinburgh: Tourism and Recreation Research Unit, University of Edinburgh, 1984.
23p; pbk

33   We hate humans / David Robins. Harmondsworth: Penguin, 1984.
155p; pbk   ISBN: 0-14-007062-1
                       BL: X.529/67446

'Football violence from the inside – a disturbing and controversial account.'

34   European Convention on Spectator Violence and Misbehaviour at Sports Events and in particular at Football Matches: Strasbourg, 19 August 1985. London: HMSO, 1985.
10p; unbound
(Cmnd 9649); (Treaty series (1985); 57)

    The convention entered into force for the UK on Nov. 1, 1985
                        ISBN: 0-10-196490-0
                        BL: BS14/137(9649)

35   Feasibility study into the use of club membership cards to help combat football hooliganism / P. J. Skinner. London?: Central Computer Telecommunications Agency, 1985.
30p; pbk

36   Football and the community: programmes for implementation in Liverpool. Liverpool: Liverpool City Council, 1985.
51p

37   House of cards: the development of Leicester City members plan / Patrick Murphy, Eric Dunning and John Williams. Leicester: Zeel, 1985.
97p; illus, 1 plan; pbk   ISBN: 0-9510797-0-0
                         BL: YC.1986.b.1168

38   The anthropology of violence / edited by David Riches. Oxford: Basil Blackwell, 1986.
224p; index   ISBN: 0-631-14788-8
                         BL: YC.1987.b.1248

    Includes an essay by Dunning, Murphy and Williams on hooligan factions: 'Casuals, Terrace Crews and Fighting Firms: Towards a Sociological Explanation of Football Hooligan Behaviour'.

39   Football and the decline of Britain / James Walvin. Basingstoke: Macmillan, 1986.
viii, 139p; index
    ISBN: 0-333-42276-7 (cased) ● ISBN: 0-333-42277-5 (pbk)
       BL: YK.1988.a.3858 ● BL: YC.1986.a.2728

40   The Luton home only members plan: a preliminary report / John Williams, Eric Dunning and Patrick Murphy. London: The Football Trust, 1986.

41   Music, closed societies and football / Hans Keller; illustrated by M. Cosman. London: Toccata, 1986.
288p; illus

    Rev. ed. of: '1975 (1984 minus 9)'   ISBN: 0-907689-21-3

42   Off the ball: the football World Cup / edited by Alan Tomlinson and Garry Whannel. London: Pluto, 1986.
174p; pbk   ISBN: 0-7453-0122-3
                       BL: YK.1987.a.7195

    A selection of 12 essays written around the Mexico World Cup from the fans' viewpoint; includes 'White riots' by John Williams.

    ☞ Also listed at: E88

43   Spectator violence associated with football matches: a state of the art review / Eric Dunning, Patrick Murphy and John Williams. Leicester: Sir Norman Chester Centre for Football Research, 1986.

Prepared for the Sports Council on behalf of the Council of Europe

44   The crowd in contemporary Britain / edited by George Gaskell and Robert Benewick; foreword by Lord Scarman. London: Sage, 1987.
x, 273p; illus; index

Includes bibliographies   ISBN: 0-8039-8074-4
                            BL: YH.1987.a.709

45   Football and football hooliganism in Liverpool / John Williams, Eric Dunning and Patrick Murphy. Leicester: Sir Norman Chester Centre for Football Research, 1987.
51p

Prepared for The Football Trust and the Department of the Environment

46   Football and spectator behaviour at Watford: the 'friendly club' / John Williams, Eric Dunning and Patrick Murphy. Leicester: Sir Norman Chester Centre for Football Research, 1987.

Prepared for The Football Trust and the Department of the Environment

47   The Luton home only members plan: final report / John Williams, Eric Dunning and Patrick Murphy. London: The Football Trust, 1987.

Prepared for the Department of the Environment

48   Young people's images of attending football: a preliminary analysis of essays by Liverpool school children. Leicester: Sir Norman Chester Centre for Football Research, 1987.
58p

49   English football fans at the European Championships, 1988: a preliminary report / John Williams and others. Leicester: Sir Norman Chester Centre for Football Research, 1988.
45p; pbk

50   Football national membership scheme: report of the Minister for Sport's working party. London: Department of the Environment, 1988.
39p; pbk   BL: BS414/787

51   Hooliganism after Heysel: crowd behaviour in England and Europe, 1985-88 / John Williams, Eric Dunning and Patrick Murphy. Leicester: Sir Norman Chester Centre for Football Research, 1988.
38p

52   An investigation of the measures for improving spectator behaviour currently in use at seven English football clubs: summary of preliminary research findings and recommendations / John Williams, Eric Dunning and Patrick Murphy. Leicester: Sir Norman Chester Centre for Football Research, 1988.
19p

53   Membership schemes & professional football clubs / John Williams, Eric Dunning and Patrick Murphy. Leicester: Sir Norman Chester Centre for Football Research, 1988.
38p

54   Preston North End crowd survey: preliminary report / Patrick Murphy, Eric Dunning and John Williams. Leicester: Sir Norman Chester Centre for Football Research, 1988.

55   The roots of football hooliganism: an historical and sociological study / Eric Dunning, Patrick Murphy, John Williams. London: Routledge & Kegan Paul, 1988.
x, 273p; index;
    ISBN: 0-7102-1336-0 (cased) • ISBN: 0-7102-0146-X (pbk)
        BL: YC.1988.a.1057 • BL: YK.1988.a.1300

56   Bloody casuals: diary of a football hooligan / Jay Allan. Famedram, 1989.
142p; illus; pbk   ISBN: 0-905489-41-1
                       BL: YK.1992.a.5237

A look at the problem in Scotland from an insider's viewpoint.

57   Crowd control and membership at football: a survey of police officers with responsibility for policing football matches in England and Wales / John Williams, Eric Dunning and Patrick Murphy. Leicester: Sir Norman Chester Centre for Football Research, 1989.
29p; pbk

58   English football and society, 1910-1950 / Nicholas Fishwick. Manchester: Manchester University Press, 1989.
xii, 164p; index
(International studies in the history of sport)

Bibliography: p153-158   ISBN: 0-7190-2529-X
                          BL: YK.1989.a.5134

This was the period during which the game attained its greatest popularity when judged against attendances. An excellent study.

59   Football and football spectators after Hillsborough: a national survey of members of the Football Supporters' Association / John Williams, Eric Dunning and Patrick Murphy. Leicester: Sir Norman Chester Centre for Football Research, 1989.
55p; pbk

60   Football into the 1990s: proceedings of a conference
      held at the University of Leicester, 29/30 September
      1988. Leicester: Sir Norman Chester Centre for Football
      Research, 1989.
      131p

61   Football Spectators Act 1989. London: HMSO, 1989.
      28p
      (1989 c. 37)   ISBN: 0-10-543789-1

62   Football spectators: proposed membership scheme for
      England and Wales. London: Central Office of
      Information Reference Service, 1989.
      2p

63   Hooligans abroad: the behaviour and control of English
      fans in continental Europe / John Williams, Eric
      Dunning and Patrick Murphy. 2nd ed. London:
      Routledge, 1989.
      lix, 230p; illus; index; pbk   ISBN: 0-415-02550-8
                                        BL: YC.1989.a.6869

      ☞ Previous ed. H30

64   The Luton Town members scheme: final report (with
      new postscript) / John Williams, Eric Dunning &
      Patrick Murphy. Leicester: Sir Norman Chester Centre
      for Football Research, 1989.
      118p; pbk

65   Spectator behaviour, media coverage and crowd control
      at the 1988 European Football Championships: a review
      of data from Belgium, Denmark, the Federal Republic of
      Germany, Netherlands and the United Kingdom / John
      Williams and A. Goldberg. Leicester: Sir Norman
      Chester Centre for Football Research, 1989.
      58p; pbk

66   Steaming in: journal of a football fan / Colin Ward.
      London: Simon & Schuster, 1989.
      192p; pbk
      (Sports pages)   ISBN: 0-671-69710-2
                                       BL: YK.1990.a.5716

      Ward is the football hooligan who finally realised the
      error of his ways and decided to tell all. His firsthand
      account tells so much about the hooligan problem
      which even the most carefully researched academic
      studies are unable to pinpoint.

67   Football on trial: spectator violence and development in
      the football world / Patrick Murphy, John Williams and
      Eric Dunning. London: Routledge, 1990.
      xiii, 240p; illus; index; pbk
      Includes bibliographies   ISBN: 0-415-05024-3
                                        BL: YK.1990.a.5008

68   Hillsborough and after: the Liverpool experience / S.
      Coleman, A. Jemphrey and P. Scraton. Ormskirk: Edge
      Hill College, 1990.
      149p

69   Hooligans Deutschland – 'I say no hoolis': a personal
      view of the Millwall Community Scheme visit to
      Germany during April 1990 / prepared by Al Mills.
      London: Independent Millwall Supporters Association,
      1990.
      25p; illus; pbk   BL: YK.1993.b.592

      Millwall have a long history of supporter violence and
      as a response to this have promoted a variety of in-
      itiatives to counteract the problem. Four years after
      this publication, blessed with a superb new ground,
      Millwall fans invaded the pitch, attacked players and
      turned over cars in a play-off fixture against Derby
      County. Much genuine effort was destroyed at a
      stroke.

70   Policing football hooliganism: memoranda of evidence /
      Home Affairs Committee. London: HMSO, 1990.
      11, 107p
      (House of Commons papers 1990-91; 1)
                                        ISBN: 0-10-200191-X

71   Seven years on: Glasgow Rangers and Rangers
      supporters, 1983-1990 / John Williams with T. Bucke.
      Leicester: Sir Norman Chester Centre for Football
      Research, 1990.

      ☞ Also listed at: B1212

72   The soccer war / Ryszard Kapuscinski; translated from
      the Polish by William Brand. Cambridge: Granta, 1990.
      234p   ISBN: 0-14-014209-6
                                        BL: YK.1990.a.7325

      A study of football rivalry and friendship viewed in the
      wider European and world context against a back-
      ground of political affairs and hotspots visited by the
      author as a roving correspondent. An unusual study.

73   2nd report, session 1990-91: policing football
      hooliganism. Vol 1: Report together with the
      proceedings of the Committee / Home Affairs
      Committee. London: HMSO, 1991.
      46p
      (House of Commons papers 1990-91; 1-I)
      Chaired by Sir John Wheeler   ISBN: 0-10-272991-3

      ☞ See also: H81

74   2nd report, session 1990-91: policing football
      hooliganism. Vol 2: Memoranda of evidence, minutes of
      evidence and appendices / Home Affairs Committee.
      London: HMSO, 1991.
      vi, ii, 180p
      (House of Commons papers 1990-91; 1-II)
      Chaired by Sir John Wheeler   ISBN: 0-10-272291-9

75   Among the thugs / Bill Buford. London: Secker &
      Warburg, 1991.
      317p   ISBN: 0-436-07526-1
                                        BL: YK.1991.a.11761

      This American writer first encountered football hooliganism whilst travelling by train in Wales. The phenomenon mystified him completely so he decided to become one of them. His observations are perceptive but never truly convey an 'insider' status. Nevertheless this is a valuable study.

76   British football and social change: getting into Europe / edited by John Williams and Stephen Wagg. Leicester: Leicester University Press, 1991.
x, 258p; index

Includes bibliographies
ISBN: 0-7185-1371-1 (cased) • ISBN: 0-7185-1410-6 (pbk)
BL: YC.1991.a.4917

77   Can play, will play?: women and football in Britain / John Williams and Jackie Woodhouse. Leicester: Sir Norman Chester Centre for Football Research, 1991.
46p

Women either love or hate football; as spectators they are growing in number and there has been a resurgence in recent years in their desire to play the game in an organised manner. Here the research team from Leicester University lobby in favour of the women's game.

78   England and Italia '90: a report on the behaviour and control of English fans at the World Cup finals, 1990 / John Williams and Jackie Woodhouse. Leicester: Sir Norman Chester Centre for Football Research, 1991.

79   Football (Offences) Act 1991. London: HMSO, 1991.
2p
(1991 c. 19)   ISBN: 0-10-541991-5

80   Football with attitude / Steve Redhead. Wordsmith 1991.
120p; illus; pbk
ISBN: 1-873205-04-X
BL: YK.1992.a.7169

The author's compelling obsessions are football and music – here he combines these interests in a serious study of the crossover relationship between football, popular music and youth culture. A most unusual and extremely welcome addition to football literature. Includes many photographs by Richard Davis.

81   The government reply to the 2nd report from the Home Affairs Committee session 1990-91 HC 001: policing football hooliganism / Home Office. London: HMSO, 1991.
2, 14p
(Cm 1539)   ISBN: 0-10-115392-9

☞ See also: H73-74

82   A national survey of female football fans / Jackie Woodhouse. Leicester: Sir Norman Chester Centre for Football Research, 1991.

The football world has always been male dominated at managerial and at administrative levels with the result that the needs of women as supporters have been severely neglected. This survey seeks to identify

areas of need in an effort to persuade football clubs to wake up to their obligations.

83   A study of football crowd behaviour / C. Harper. Edinburgh: Lothian and Borders Police, 1991.
136p

84   Fans at the trackside: a national survey of disabled football spectators / John Williams. Leicester: Sir Norman Chester Centre for Football Research, 1992.

85   Football spectators and Italia '90: a report on the behaviour and control of European football fans at the World Cup finals, 1990 / John Williams. Leicester: Sir Norman Chester Centre for Football Research, 1992.

Prepared for the Council of Europe

86   Lick my boots: racism in English football / John Williams. Leicester: Sir Norman Chester Centre for Football Research, 1992.

87   Pre-match liaison between supporters in Europe: a report on the UEFA Cup ties Liverpool v Genoa 4th & 18th March 1992 / Rogan Taylor. Leicester: Sir Norman Chester Centre for Football Research, 1992.

88   Through the turnstiles / Brian Tabner. Harefield: Yore, 1992.
208p; illus
ISBN: 1-874427-05-4
BL: YK.1993.b.11841

This is a unique statistical study charting Football League attendances from the very first season with some supporting text and photographs. Useful information for the club historian.

89   What's the story?: true confessions of the Republic of Ireland soccer supporters / compiled and edited by Derek O'Kelly and Shay Blair. Dublin: Elo, 1992.
232p; illus
ISBN: 0-9519593-1-X

In 1990 the Republic of Ireland travelled to Italy for the World Cup and, predictably, took thousands of supporters with them. Inevitably there were some high jinks – when one particular group had regular encounters with the Italian police, "What's the story?" became their watchword – this is their story.

90   Football and football hooliganism. Leicester: Sir Norman Chester Centre for Football Research, 1993.
12p; pbk

91   Sport, space and the city / John Bale. London: Routledge, 1993.
xiv, 211p; illus, maps; index
Includes bibliographical references   ISBN: 0-415-08098-3
BL: YK.1993.a.5129

An overview of the place of sport, including football, in our society and in our cities, discussing both the beneficial and the problematic elements concerned.

92　Football against the enemy / Simon Kuper. London: Orion, 1994.

x, 223p; illus　　　　　　　　　ISBN: 1-85797-558-8

> Voted 1994 William Hill 'Sports Book of the Year' - explains in a sociological and political context what football really means to fans around the world.

93　Football hooliganism and crowd behaviour. London: Sports Council Information Services, 1994.

26p; pbk

(Select bibliography; no. 16)

94　Football, violence and social identity / edited by Richard Giulianotti, Norman Bonney and Mike Hepworth. London: Routledge, 1994.

vi, 268p; index

　　　ISBN: 0-415-09837-8 (cased) • ISBN: 0-415-09838-6 (pbk)

　　　　　　　　　　　　BL: YC.1994.a.2102

95　Game without frontiers: football, identity and modernity / edited by Richard Giulianotti and John Williams. Aldershot: Arena, 1994.

xiii, 381p

(Popular cultural studies; 5)

　　　ISBN: 1-857422-19-8 (cased) • ISBN: 1-857422-20-1 (pbk)

　　　　　　　　　　　　BL: YK.1995.a.1293

96　Understanding soccer hooliganism / John H. Kerr. Buckingham: Open University Press, 1994.

xi, 129p; illus; index

　　Includes bibliographies

　　　ISBN: 0-335-19250-5 (cased) • ISBN: 0-335-19249-1 (pbk)

The Art of Spectatorship

97　Characteristics of the crowd / William McGregor.

> *Published in: Football / B. O. Corbett, W. McGregor, etc. 1907.*　　　BL: Mic.A.7125(7) (microfilm copy)

> McGregor was known as the 'Father of the Football League' as he was the prime mover behind the foundation of the Football League in 1888 and became its first President. These observations on spectatorship came just four years before his death in 1911.

☞　See also: A32

98　Football: facts and fancies, or, The art of spectatorship / Percy Marshall Young. London: Dennis Dobson, 1950.

95p; illus　　　　　　　　　BL: 7921.aa.2

> 'On Wednesday afternoon 50,000 grandmothers lay dead. This curious coincidence allowed our football ground to be comfortably filled.' This is the opening line to a delightful lyrical study, with not a hooligan in sight.

99　The appreciation of football / Percy Marshall Young. London: Dennis Dobson, 1951.

93p; illus　　　　　　　　　BL: 7921.de.22

> Percy Young is highly recommended for all football romantics – this is a celebrated essay.

100　Football year / Percy Marshall Young; illustrated by Reginald Haggar. London: Phoenix Sports Books, 1956.

160p　　　　　　　　　　BL: 7922.ee.24

> You would expect any book 'dedicated to John Arlott' to be a worthwhile read. Each of the twelve chapters is a month – 'In August regrets are buried and hopes renewed; for then the year begins'. If the first words of this book strike a chord, then read on! Young is one of our very best football writers who signs off thus – 'It is a whacking good game'.

101　The spectator's handbook: an aid to the appreciation of athletics, boxing, cricket, association and rugby football and lawn tennis / John Barclay Pick. London: Phoenix Sports Books, 1956.

144p; illus　　　　　　　　BL: 7922.ee.23

102　The way there: a soccer encyclopaedia / compiled by Harold Richards. London: Stanley Paul, 1960.

126p; illus　　　　　　　　BL: 7925.g.8

> Includes much information aimed specifically at spectators.

103　I-spy football / 'Big Chief I-Spy' London: Polystyle, 1969.

48p; illus; pbk

> *Reissued 1974*　　　　　　ISBN: 0-85090-264-9

> This first edition of the popular spotting game for children is now something of a period piece itself. It may be of interest to compare the spotter's targets with those in the later edition as a measure of the changes which have occurred in the game.

☞　Subsequent ed. H119

104　Football for fans / Mark Osborne & John Rushton. London: Studio Vista, 1975.

64p; illus

　　　　　　　　　　ISBN: 0-289-70557-6

　　　　　　　　　　BL: X.629/10200

105 Let's go to the soccer match / Frank Peacock; editor
     Henry Pluckrose. London: Watts, 1977.
     32p; illus
     (Let's go series)   ISBN: 0-8516-6639-6
                                            BL: X.629/11446

     For children.

106 The love of soccer / David Brenner; foreword by
     Johann Cruyff. London: Octopus Books, 1980.
     96p; illus; index   ISBN: 0-7064-1202-8
                                            BL: L.45/534

     Noteworthy for the quality of its illustrations.

107 The travelling supporter's guide to Football League clubs
     / compiled by John M. Robinson and Glenys Robinson.
     Grimsby: Hobbypress, 1982.
     51p; illus, 1 map; pbk   BL: X.629/25416

     First in a regularly updated series giving important
     information on all the League clubs for travelling sup-
     porters. Out of date editions can provide researchers
     with interesting comparative details of ground ca-
     pacities, admission prices, etc.

     ☞ Subsequent ed. H109

108 Soccer madness / Janet Lever. London: University of
     Chicago Press, 1983.
     xv, 200p; illus, 1 map; index   ISBN: 0-226-47382-1
                                            BL: X.950/26179

JANET LEVER

     A look at supportership using the Brazilian
     scene to demonstrate the obsessive fervour
     which the game can engender.

109 The travelling supporter's guide to Football
     League clubs / John Robinson, editor. Grimsby:
     Hobbypress, 1984.
     72p; illus, 2 maps; pbk   ISBN: 0-947808-00-0
                                            BL: X.629/25609

     ☞ Previous ed. H107; subsequent ed. H111

110 City go nap as Quakers halt slump / Patrick Barclay;
     photographs by Michael Pearson. York: Jackson Wilson,
     1985.
     24p; pbk

     An evocation of lower division football in photographs
     published to coincide with an exhibition at the Im-
     pressions Gallery of Photography in York.

     ☞ Also listed at: B900

111 The travelling supporter's guide to Football League
     clubs. Grimsby: Hobbypress, 1985.
     80p; illus, 1 map; pbk   ISBN: 0-947808-02-7
                                            BL: X.629/27995

     ☞ Previous ed. H109; subsequent ed. H113

112 Home and away / George Rutherford. 1986
     The experiences of a fan who watches his football in
     Scotland.

113 The supporter's guide to Football League clubs / John
     Robinson, editor. 4th ed. Grimsby: Marksman, 1987.
     104p; illus, maps; pbk   ISBN: 0-947808-06-X
                                            BL: YK.1987.a.5635

     ☞ Previous ed. H111; subsequent ed. H114

114 The supporter's guide to Football League clubs / John
     Robinson, editor. 5th ed. Cleethorpes: Marksman, 1988.
     116p; illus, maps; index; pbk   ISBN: 0-947808-07-8
                                            BL: YK.1988.a.5296

     ☞ Previous ed. H113; subsequent ed. H117

115 In your blood: football culture in the late '80s and early
     '90s / Richard Turner. London: Working Press, 1990.
     90p; illus; pbk   ISBN: 1-870736-07-9
                                            BL: YK.1991.a.2739

     Informed observation on the prevailing trends
     amongst young soccer fans from a Stockport County
     follower. If you saw Stanley Matthews play at his
     prime, this book might make you feel just a trifle old.

116 Just to see a game / David A. Howgate. Southport: The
     author, 1990.
     64p; pbk

     Howgate is known in football circles as a 'groundhop-
     per' — someone who will travel around to experience
     the hospitality and facilities of other clubs 'just to
     see a game'. This is the first in a series of 3 books in
     which he chats about the game and supportership.

117 The supporter's guide to Football League clubs. 6th ed.
     Cleethorpes: Soccer Book Publishing, 1990.
     124p; illus; pbk   ISBN: 0-947808-11-6
                                            BL: YK.1994.a.11456

     This edition includes the Vauxhall Conference clubs.

     ☞ Previous ed. H114; subsequent ed. H121

118 From Accies to Ayr / Graeme Holmes. 1991.
     Groundhopping around Scotland.

119 I-spy football. Harrow: Michelin, 1991.
     48p; pbk   ISBN: 1-85671-061-0
                                            BL: YK.1992.a.2654

     For children — points are awarded for spotting elements
     associated with the game. Part of a popular series cov-
     ering different subjects — how many points, I wonder, for
     a man accepting a brown envelope at Watford Gap?

     ☞ Previous ed. H103

120 Just to see another game / David A. Howgate.
Southport: The author, 1991.
64p; pbk

> More general musings on the game in the second volume of this series as the author travels around the country.

121 The supporter's guide to Football League clubs. 7th ed.
Cleethorpes: Soccer Book Publishing, 1991.
132p; illus; pbk   ISBN: 0-947808-16-7

> ☞ Previous ed. H117; subsequent ed. H128

122 'Dicks out!': the definitive work on British football songs / Larry Bulmer and Rob Merrills. Tunbridge Wells: Chatsby Publishing, 1992.
200p; pbk   ISBN: 1-874546-00-2

> What a refreshing change! Club by club examples of terrace chants and songs from earliest times to the present. Includes most English League clubs, some from Wales and Scotland along with Cliftonville, Glentoran and Linfield from Northern Ireland. Alan Dicks, by the way, was in charge at Fulham during a tricky spell in 1991, hence the title.

123 Fever pitch: story of football and obsession / Nick Hornby. London: Gollancz, 1992.
256p   ISBN: 0-575-05315-1
                                   BL: YK.1993.a.4546

> Many of us wonder exactly why we follow football as we do. What does it really matter? This highly acclaimed book goes a long way towards a rational explanation, charting events in Hornby's life against his supportership of Arsenal. Researchers with little knowledge of the game will find this a revelation whilst aficionados will recognise themselves on every page.

124 Football and its fans: supporters and their relations with the game, 1885-1985 / Rogan Taylor. Leicester: Leicester University Press, 1992.
viii, 198p; index; pbk
(Sport, politics and culture)   ISBN: 0-7185-1463-7
                                   BL: YK.1993.a.3397

> The author, as founder of the Football Supporters' Association, presents a serious study of the role of the fan in relation to the game, particularly noting the financial contribution – 'It's the fans that pay the players' wages' is an oft quoted and essentially true phrase. An enlightening study from the earliest days onwards.

125 Just one more game: the trilogy / David A. Howgate.
Southport: The author, 1992.
68p; pbk

> David Howgate enjoys going anywhere just to see a game. This is the third little volume of his travels in which he offers interesting opinions on the sport he follows.

126 More than a job?: the player's and fan's perspectives / Roger Titford with Eamon Dunphy. Upavon, Pewsey: Further Thought Publishing, 1992.
128p; pbk   ISBN: 0-9518771-0-0
                                   BL: YK.1993.a.1088

> Supporters often declare that they feel success and failure more intensely than the players. Titford the supporter and Dunphy the player look back on a memorable season for Reading in the 1970s and compare notes in an entertaining and enlightening fashion.

> ☞ Also listed at: B690

127 Season in the cold: a journey through English football / Ian Ridley. London: Kingswood, 1992.
292p; illus; pbk   ISBN: 0-413-66250-0
                                   BL: YK.1993.a.12692

> Highly individual account of a fan's view of a year in the life of football. Ridley's quest was to explore every stitch of the rich tapestry of the game he loved – he did so with most interesting results.

128 The supporter's guide to Football League clubs. 8th ed.
Cleethorpes: Soccer Book Publishing, 1992.
120p; illus; pbk   ISBN: 0-947808-20-5

> ☞ Previous ed. H121; subsequent ed. H135

129 The supporter's guide to non-league football clubs / edited by John Robinson. Cleethorpes: Soccer Book Publishing, 1992.
112p; illus; pbk   ISBN: 0-947808-22-1
                                   BL: ZK.9.a.2989

> ☞ Subsequent ed. H134

130 Supporter's guide to Scottish football / edited by Angus Ross. Cleethorpes: Soccer Book Publishing, 1992.
96p; illus; pbk   ISBN: 0-947808-23-X
                                   BL: ZK.9.a.2445

> ☞ Subsequent ed. H136

131 The end: 80 years of life on Arsenal's North Bank / Tom Watt. Edinburgh: Mainstream, 1993.
347p; illus

> *Includes bibliographical references*   ISBN: 1-85158-567-2
                                   BL: YK.1994.b.4458

> The author, widely known as Lofty from the TV soap Eastenders, is also a keen Arsenal follower. As the traditional standing terraces begin to disappear, this element of spectatorship is being lost forever. This book will prove a valuable reference in years to come – it uses Arsenal as the subject, but includes much of general application.

> ☞ Also listed at: B42

132 The Kop: the end of an era / Stephen F. Kelly. London: Mandarin, 1993.
xxv, 258p; illus; pbk

                                   ISBN: 0-7493-1649-7
                                   BL: YK.1993.a.17431

A similar treatment to the Arsenal book above, this one studies the Liverpool Kop before the seating contractors move in. Includes reminiscences from inhabitants of football's most famous terrace.

33 Passion and the fashion: football fandom in the new Europe / edited by Steve Redhead. Aldershot: Avebury, 1993.
x, 205p
ISBN: 1-85628-462-X (cased) • ISBN: 1-85628-464-6 (pbk)
BL: YK.1993.a.12393

Steve Redhead has popularised the term 'fandom' as a description of the cult and culture of supportership and its crossover with other elements of modern society. He and his team here report on cultural changes in the European soccer scene drawing on specific studies of fans at Juventus, Napoli, Leeds United, Marseilles, and Manchester United.

34 The supporter's guide to non-league football clubs / edited by John Robinson. 1994 ed. Cleethorpes: Soccer Book Publishing, 1993.
112p; illus; pbk
ISBN: 0-947808-27-2

Details of the top 200 clubs.

☞ Previous ed. H129

35 The supporter's guide to Premier and Football League Clubs / edited by John Robinson. 10th [i.e. 9th] ed. Cleethorpes: Soccer Book Publishing, 1993.
120p; illus, 1 map; pbk
ISBN: 0-947808-25-6
BL: YK.1994.a.16732

☞ Previous ed. H128; Subsequent ed. H141

36 The supporter's guide to Scottish football / edited by John Robinson. 1994 ed. Cleethorpes: Soccer Book Publishing, 1993.
96p; illus; pbk
ISBN: 0-947808-26-4

Includes the Highland League clubs.

☞ Previous ed. H130

37 The supporter's guide to Welsh football / edited by John Robinson. Cleethorpes: Soccer Book Publishing, 1993-
illus; pbk

Published annually
BL: ZK.9.a.2941

Details the top 70 Welsh clubs including the Konica League of Wales and its two feeder leagues.

138 A view from the ground / Gwen McIlroy. Dundee: D. Winter, 1993.
243p; illus; pbk
ISBN: 0-902804-20-0

The author watches her football largely in Scotland and here presents her observations from the female fan's point of view in an interesting and unusual study with much coverage of Dundee football and specific concentration on Dundee United.

139 Red fever!: from Rochdale to Rio as 'United' supporters / Steve Donoghue. Wilmslow: Sigma Leisure, 1994.
v, 94p; illus; pbk
ISBN: 1-85058-415-X

A fan's account of his travels near and far following Manchester United.

140 'Shoot!': disabled supporters' guide to British football / edited by John Robinson. Cleethorpes: Soccer Book Publishing, 1994-
Published annually
BL: ZK.9.a.3649

141 The supporter's guide to Premier and Football League Clubs / edited by John Robinson. 11th [i.e.10th] ed. Cleethorpes: Soccer Book Publishing, 1994.
108p; illus, 1 map, plans; pbk
ISBN: 0-947808-36-1
BL: YK.1995.a.132

☞ Previous ed. H135

142 This supporting life: how to be a real football fan / Kevin Baldwin. London: Headline, 1994.
275p; illus; pbk
ISBN: 0-7472-4747-1
BL: YK.1995.a.1490

Increasing emphasis throughout the early nineties has been placed on the developing cult of 'fandom' and the paraphernalia which goes with it. This witty guide explains how to support your team – what to wear, what to eat and how to understand the mysteries of terrace behaviour and the language of the game.

Badges & Names, Club Colours, & Strip

43 English costume for sports and outdoor recreation from the sixteenth to the nineteenth centuries / Phillis Cunnington and Alan Mansfield. London: Black, 1969.
388p; illus
SBN: 7136-1017-4
BL: X.421/2855 • BL: 2020.g

Includes a good section on football with illustrations of the earliest attire.

144 Soccer crests / Frederick Compton Avis. London: The author, 1969.
64p; illus; index
BL: X.429/6114

There is a distinct heraldic element in many of the traditions of football. This colourful book illustrates about 180 club badges and shows a refreshing lack of bias towards the big clubs – Manchester United are not included but Ballymena United and Penzance are.

145   Football history map of England and Wales. Edinburgh: Bartholomew, 1976.
1 map (98 x 72cm)

Shows the colours and locations of all the clubs in the Football League, also their badges, dates of foundation, grounds and leading clubs not in the League. An unusual item, being a folding poster-map rather than a book – 160 clubs are represented.

146   Soccer club colours / Martin Tyler. London: Hamlyn, 1976.
60p; illus   ISBN: 0-600-38206-0
                          BL: X.629/10973

Two pages on 'The story of football strips' precede a largely pictorial record of 160 different colours in a club by club analysis for England, Scotland and the International sides. Many of the strips have long since changed and are now sold in reproduction form as nostalgia clothing.

147   The Scottish football map / pictures by George Ashton; text by Ken Gallacher. Edinburgh: Bartholomew, 1977.
1 map (102 x 78cm)   ISBN: 0-7028-0136-4
                          BL: Cup.600.e.1(34)

Colours, badges and locations of all the Scottish League clubs in folding poster-map format.

148   How they were formed: the biological evolution of football club names / Steve Spartak; illustrated by Samantha Thomson. The Glasshouse, 1993.
24p

A surreal little book, not to be consulted by those seeking serious explanations for the origins and names of leading clubs. The etymological answers range from the bizarre to the highly amusing and the downright confusing as the entry for Bristol Rovers may demonstrate: 'Bristol Rovers - Yet another Frenchman brought some cheese over, but no-one liked it much and so to entice customers he gave away some tools with it. Old people still remember to this day the sign outside his shop which read 'Brie's Tool Offers' and thus the name of the club was put into the larder'.

Broadcasting

149   Script for radio or television programme devised by Dave Shand entitled 'Soccer Hit Parade'. London: D. Shand, 1955.
1 sheet

Typewritten   BL: Cup.600.b.2(8)

150   Football on television / produced by The British Film Institute Educational Advisory Service; general editor, Edward Buscombe. London: British Film Institute, 1975.
v, 65p; illus; pbk
(Television monographs; 4. ISSN: 0306-2929)
                          ISBN: 0-851700-46-2
                          BL: X.0909/643(4)

Television has played a major part in the promotion of the game. This study offers an insight into its coverage. Since its publication, football has been incorporated into many TV dramas and sit-coms – Gary Lineker, Tommy Docherty, Bryan Robson and Graeme Souness are just some of the football personalities who have made acting appearances. A complete updated study of football on TV would surely be an interesting publication?

151   Guide to the pronunciation of some international association football teams. London: British Broadcasting Corporation, 1984.
40p; pbk   ISBN: 0-946358-07-9

An essential part of every commentator's armoury.

152   Match of the Day: the complete record since 1964 / compiled by John Motson; foreword by Graham Taylor. London: BBC Books, 1992.
224p; illus; index   ISBN: 0-563-36406-8
                          BL: YK.1993.b.9509

During its heyday of the late sixties and early seventies Match of the Day was truly a national institution. In those pre-video recorder days it regularly achieved the seemingly impossible – getting seasoned beer drinkers to vacate their local before closing on Saturday nights! This study charts every single game shown on the programme since its inception and is edited by one of the commentators most closely associated with it. In its own way it provides a good year by year overview of the football scene since 1964.

Legal Cases

153 Sport and the law / Edward Grayson. London: Sunday Telegraph, 1978.
78p; illus; index; pbk   BL: X.208/7099

> Includes many examples of legal cases involving football.

☞ See also: H155

154 Soccer in the dock: a history of British football scandals 1900-1965 / Simon Inglis. London: Willow, 1985.
213p; illus

> *Bibliography: p212-213*   ISBN: 0-00-218162-2
> BL: X.800/41919

> Soccer is no stranger to scandal – this covers both bizarre and tragic cases from this century.

155 Sport and the law / Edward Grayson; with forewords by Lord Havers, Denis Howell. London: Butterworths, 1988.
xviii, 376p; illus; index; pbk   ISBN: 0-406-25300-5
BL: YC.1988.a.8228

> An updated version with more football examples. Each passing year seems to bring more cases to the fore - 1995 has been a particularly interesting year.

☞ See also: H153

Betting & the Pools

156 Systematic method: how to win football competitions / A. Russell. Stockport: The author, 1907.
7p; pbk   BL: Mic.A.12621(10) (microfilm copy)

157 The Excelsior system. 1910.
1 sheet   BL: 1879.cc.2(8)

158 Report of the Commissioners of Her Majesty's Customs and Excise for the year ended 31 March . . . / HM Customs and Excise. London: HMSO, 1910-

> *Published annually*

> Gives receipts from duty for, amongst other things, pool betting. Taxed betting stakes are given for football and similar Pools.

159 The incomparable football forecasting system / W. J. Duckworth. Padiham, 1914.
pbk   BL: 1879.cc.2 (10)

> Although the Pools as we know them did not begin until 1923, bookmakers had been offering fixed odds betting for many years, hence such an early preoccupation with predicting results.

160 The logical football system. Birmingham: Logical Systems, 1920.   BL: D

161 Ready Money Football Betting Act, 1920. London: HMSO, 1920.
(1920 c. 52)

> An Act to prevent the writing, printing, publishing, or circulating in the United Kingdom of advertisements, circulars or coupons of any ready money football betting business.

162 Football: home and away 'certs.': profitable plans for a popular pastime. Manchester: 1923.
40p; pbk   BL: D

> Littlewoods Pools were set up in this year.

163 Football investment scientifically applied, or, Football backing as a science / Tremar. Plymouth: Plymouth Printers, 1924.
42p   BL: D

164 The Star pari-mutuel Racing and Football Pools / John William Jones. Liverpool: The author, 1930.
BL: D

165 Comber's new handbook of football combinations / Joseph Charlesworth Comber. Morecambe: The author, 1934.

> *Reproduced from typewriting*   BL: D

☞ Subsequent ed. H166

166 Comber's new handbook of football combinations: best methods for making football pay / Joseph Charlesworth Comber. 2nd ed. Morecambe: Visitor Printing Works, 1935.
47p   BL: D

☞ Previous ed. H165

167 Mathemagic: football points pool system / Alexander Morrison. Glasgow: Kirkwood, 1935.
21p; pbk   BL: D

168 Systematic football betting / The Mathematician, of the Racing and Football Outlook. London: Webster's Publications, 1935.
128p   BL: 7911.d.44

169 Making Pools pay / The Mathematician, of the Racing and Football Outlook. London: Webster's Publications, 1936.
128p   BL: 07908.de.89

> In this year the Football League tried to disrupt the distribution of Pools coupons by refusing to announce details of fixtures until a few days before games. This ridiculous subterfuge lasted only a few weeks.

170 Mathematician's Pool book: over one hundred new tables for systematically entering Football and Racing Pools / Mathematician of the Racing and Football Outlook. London: Webster's Publications, 1937-
Note: Published annually   BL: 08535.de.4

171 Profit from Football Pools / E. Johnstone. London: Routledge, 1937.
xviii, 203p   BL: 07908.h.9

174 How to win a fortune in Football Pools. London: Success Publishing, 1938.
63p   BL: Mic.A.7799(2) (microfilm copy)

175 The public and the Football Pools: results of Daily Telegraph and Morning Post inquiry. London: 1938.
19p
Reprinted from the Daily Telegraph and Morning Post
BL: Mic.A.11318(1) (microfilm copy)

176 Forecast to win / Clifford Regan. London: Hipwell Publications, 1946.
66p; pbk   BL: 7919.aa.5

177 Non-repeat football double- & treble: season card. Maghull: M. Owen, 1946.   BL: 7918.a.45

178 Scoop the Pools / Bernard Ward. London: Withy Grove Press, 1946.
112p; pbk
(Cherry tree specials)
Author is from the Sunday Empire News
BL: 12634.p.2/2

Reg Carter's depiction of the FA's ambivalent attitude to the Pools

A quote from George Orwell admirably illustrates the importance of the Pools at this time –
'During and between the war years the Football Pools did more than any one thing to make life bearable for the unemployed'.

172 £50,000 from the Penny Pools / Juniso. Berwick-on-Tweed: Martin's Printing Works, 1938.
29p
Author is J. W. Newham
BL: Mic.A.8545(4) (microfilm copy)

173 Football Pools: Sheppard's winning method. London: W. Foulsham, 1938.
48p
BL: Mic.A.13227(5) (microfilm copy)

179 Win at Football Pools / Raymond Bewsy. London: Citizen Press, 1946.
32p; pbk   BL: 7918.aa.56

180 Winning systems at horse racing, greyhound racing, Football Pools / Edward Manning. London: Pendulum Publications, 1946.
32p; pbk   BL: 7947.aa.24

181 The football log: Pools ready reckoner / T. J. Bradley. Manchester: The author, 1947.
1 sheet
Reproduced from typewriting   BL: Cup.1246.c.45

182 Football Pool annual. St. Ives, 1947-
     BL: P.P.2489.wka

183 Basic switch system, season 1948/49 / Anthony
     Grafton. Horsham: The author, 1948.
     1 sheet   BL: Cup.930/145 1884.b.15(133)

184 Football souvenir with Pools guide supplement / Rick
     Eldon and Leslie Bell. London: Linden Lewis, 1948.
     40p; illus   BL: 7917.e.80

185 Permutations for all / Bruce Morgan. London: Newgate
     Press, 1948.
     127p   BL: 7917.e.62

186 Precise forecasting / Anthony Grafton. Horsham: The
     author, 1948.
     6p

     Reproduced from typewriting   BL: 7919.b.38

187 Sporting Record Pools pointer / Harold King. London:
     Sporting Record, 1948-
     BL: W.P.9823

188 The Banker's guide to Football Pools / The Banker.
     London: Sporting Handbooks, 1949.
     x, 111p   BL: 7919.e.23

189 Daily Herald football handbook and Pools guide
     1949/50-1957/58 / compiled by C. A. Hughes. London:
     Daily Herald, 1949-1957.   BL: P.P.2489.wkk

190 Football forecasting / Jack Boulder. London: Axtell
     Publications, 1949.   BL: 7920.b.40

191 Pool statistics: first half / Bruce Morgan. London:
     Newgate Press, 1949-   BL: W.P.7336

192 Pools encyclopædia / Index. London: Pools Publishing,
     1949.
     135p   BL: 7917.de.113

193 Report of the Royal Commission on Betting, Lotteries
     and Gaming. London: HMSO, 1949-1951.
     (Cmd 8190)

     On football, the report comments in detail on the 're-
     markable growth in the popularity of Football
     Pools. . .'.

194 The weekly Football Dispatch Pools survey. London:
     Football Dispatch, 1949-   BL: P.P.2489.wkg

195 100 famous football systems / compiled and edited by
     W. N. Shaw. London: Postlib, 1951.
     80p

     W. N. Shaw is pseudonym for Walter Henry Swan
     BL: 7919.f.24

     ☞ Subsequent ed. H202

196 Sunday Dispatch Jack Boulder's book of fixed odds
     football. London: Associated Newspapers, 1951.
     64p   BL: 7921.de.35

197 Figurist Pools handbook. London: Figurist Press,
     1952-1955.

     Continued as: Flagstaff Pools guide and football facts
     BL: P.P.2489.wlg

     ☞ See also: H204

198 The all-in compucaster / compiled by G. E. Jones.
     Chorley: The author, 1953.
     1 sheet   BL: Cup.930/145 1884.b.15(170)

199 Pools pilot, or, Why not you? / Alan P. Herbert.
     London: Methuen, 1953.
     xii, 155p   BL: 7920.aaa.105

200 Pools Betting Act, 1954. London: HMSO, 1954.
     (1954 c. 33)

     An Act to regulate the disposal of moneys and to
     provide for the publication of certain accounts and
     information in connection with pool betting.

201 Drink and gambling in 1955: facts, figures and opinions
     to help preachers and speakers in preparation for
     Temperance Sunday, November 20th, 1955 / edited by
     Edward Rogers and Kenneth G. Greet. London:
     Temperance Council of the Christian Churches, 1955.
     15p; pbk   BL: 8436.d.37

202 100 famous football systems / compiled and edited by
     W. H. Swan. London: Postlib, 1955.
     80p   BL: 7922.bb.11

     ☞ Previous ed. H195

203 The private collection of synchro-sequence master
     formulas / Promath. London: Postlib Publications, 1955.
     2 vols (142p)   BL: 7921.e.116

204 Flagstaff Pools guide and football facts. London: 1956-
     Continues: Figurist Pools handbook   BL: P.P.2489.wlg

     ☞ See also: H197

205 Mantissa / Bernard Chancellor. Wingham: The author,
     1959.
     1 sheet   BL: Cup.600.d.1(25)

     In this year the Football League established copy-
     right over their fixtures and as a result won a
     substantial share in Pools profits – in many ways a
     turning point for the game.

206 Annual review of the Churches' Council on Gambling,
     including the annual report and financial statement for
     the year ending 31st December . . . . London: The
     Council, 1961-   BL: P.P.8002.dy

     Contains statistics (some from non-official sources)
     on all forms of betting and gaming.

207 The facts about the 'money factories': an independent
     view of betting and gaming in Britain now / Gordon E.
     Moody. London: The Churches' Council on Gambling,
     1972.
     76p; pbk   ISBN: 0-902891-03-0
                                        BL: X.519/42237

208 Understand your Pools & win / Francis Hart.
     Ilfracombe: Stockwell, 1973.
     74p   ISBN: 0-7223-0521-4
                                        BL: X.629/6070

     *Cyril Grimes did just that in 1972 – the wages clerk
     became the first half million pound winner for just a
     thirty pence stake.*

209 Interim report / Royal Commission on Gambling.
     London: HMSO, 1976.
     16p; pbk
     (Cmnd 6643)

          Chairman: Lord Rothschild   ISBN: 0-10-166430-3
                                            BL: BS77/83

210 X power / Ivor N. Bailey. London: The Winner, 1976.
     48p; pbk   ISBN: 0-901371-21-1
                                        BL: X.619/17175

211 Spend, spend, spend / Vivian Nicholson and Stephen
     Smith. London: Cape, 1977.
     215p; illus   ISBN: 0-224-01339-4
                                        BL: X.809/41667

     *This is the autobiography of the lady whose husband
     won £152,000 in 1961 – she and her husband Keith
     vowed to go on a spending spree and did exactly that.
     Keith was killed in a car crash and Viv remarried with
     disastrous results until not a penny remained. Back
     in a small house in Castleford she turned first to
     drugs and alcohol and then found solace in religion as
     a Jehovah's Witness. To all those who dream of a
     Pools win this is a sobering tale. Also made into a
     television play of the same title by Jack Rosenthal.*

212 Gambling statistics, Great Britain 1968-78 / Home
     Office. London: HMSO, 1980.
     43p; tables; pbk
     (Cmnd 7897)   ISBN: 0-10-178970-X
                                        BL: BS18/679

213 The Pools punters guide to a fortune / Dennis Jones.
     London: Foulsham, 1980.
     96p; pbk
          Author's name given incorrectly as Denis Jones
                                        ISBN: 0-572-01129-6
                                        BL: X.529/37334

     ☞ Subsequent ed. H214

214 The Pools punter's guide to a fortune / Dennis Jones.
     New ed. London: Foulsham, 1980.
     96p; pbk   ISBN: 0-572-01159-8
                                        BL: X.629/16783

     ☞ Previous ed. H213

215 How to win the Pools by really trying / G. B. Stone.
     London: Quilter Press, 1982.
     72p; illus; pbk   ISBN: 0-907621-11-2
                                        BL: X.629/19484

216 Football Pools with the Commodore 64 / Frank George.
     London: Collins, 1985.
     ix, 176p; illus; index; pbk   ISBN: 0-00-383069-1
                                        BL: X.622/25085

     *There was a time when hat pins, budgerigars and
     family birthdays were perfectly adequate – here the
     computer takes over the selection procedure!*

217 Jackpot / Philip Osborn. London: Futura, 1987.
     96p; illus; pbk   ISBN: 0-7088-3173-7
                                        BL: YK.1987.a.2231

     *Wins of a million pounds and more were commonplace
     by this time.*

Vivian Nicholson
and
Stephen Smith

JONATHAN CAPE
THIRTY BEDFORD SQUARE LONDON

218 Pools punters' guide to treble chance Pool permutations
     / written and compiled by M. Akers. Sheffield: MS
     Publications, 1988.
     vi, 127p; illus; spiral   BL: YC.1988.b.8860

219 Guide to winning the Pools / Dennis Jones. London:
     Rosters, 1989.
     126p; pbk   ISBN: 0-948032-49-9
                                        BL: YK.1991.a.9259

220 Bread and butter Pools / Dennis Jones. London:
     Rosters, 1990.
     90p; pbk   ISBN: 0-948032-49-9
                                        BL: YK.1991.a.9379

221   Pools buster: the Daily Express guide to winning a
fortune / Philip Osborn. London: Express Books, 1990.
96p   ISBN: 0-85079-218-5
                                                 BL: YK.1992.a.8566

222   Football Pools / Statistician. London: Foulsham, 1991.
127p; pbk
(Betting systems that win)
(Leisure know how)   ISBN: 0-572-01694-8
                                                 BL: YK.1992.a.3831

223   The Football Pools review / C. D. Lyth. Coventry:
Chazel Publishing, 1991.
23p; pbk   BL: YK.1993.a.6195

224   Perms that win the Pools / Gwilym Roberts. Newbury:
Raceform, 1991?
56p; illus; pbk   ISBN: 0-900611-81-2
                                                 BL: YK.1992.a.9713

With a foreword by Terry McDermott?

225   The 'secret' of winning / Compustat. Oban: Scotia
Business Information Services, 1992.
46p; pbk   ISBN: 1-897777-00-0

226   Win at fixed odds football betting / Malcolm Boyle.
Harpenden: Oldcastle Books, 1993-
256p; tables; pbk
        Published annually   ISBN: 1-874061-18-1
                                                 BL: ZK.9.a.3198

There has been a recent increase in popularity in pre-
dicting individual scores, scorers, etc.

Collecting Football Ephemera

227   A selection of programmes designed and produced in
the Leicester College of Arts and Crafts. Leicester:
Leicester City Football Club, 1934-1936.
8 parts   BL: 11914.d.22
An unusual early item relating to programme design.

228   Football programme collectors handbook, including
price guide, values of vintage items, how to spot rarities,
where to buy or sell, plus hundreds of facts on the hobby
/ Norman Lovett. Hull: British Programme Club, 1974.
94p; illus; pbk   ISBN: 0-9504273-0-6
                                                 BL: X.619/15013

The British Programme Club did much at this time to
develop the hobby of programme collecting and to
foster a spirit of togetherness amongst its members.

☞ Subsequent ed. H230

229   Collecting football programmes / Phil Shaw. London:
Granada, 1980.
128p; illus
        ISBN: 0-246-11399-5 (cased) • ISBN: 0-583-30424-9 (pbk)
                                                 BL: X.629/14494

Programme collecting is one of the most popular
football related hobbies. Includes many programme
cover illustrations.

230   Football programme collectors handbook (including
price guide) / Norman Lovett. Hull: British Programme
Collectors Club, 1980.
8, 98p; pbk   BL: X.529/37033

☞ Previous ed. H228

231   Good old soccer: the golden age of football picture
postcards / Eric Krieger. London: Longman, 1983.
120p; illus; pbk   ISBN: 0-582-40621-8
                                                 BL: X.629/23458

Footballers and teams were well represented on
postcards, particularly in the early years and humorous portrayals were very popular. This definitive guide
may provide club historians with a good source of illustrations.

232   Chris Stevens: artist in residence, Sunderland Association
Football Club / edited by Tony Knipe. Sunderland:
Ceolfrith, 1984.
20p; illus; pbk   ISBN: 0-904461-87-4

Contents not verified but thought to be a collection
of artistic representations of Sunderland Football
Club.

233   The sporting collector / Louis T. Stanley. London:
Pelham, 1984.
170p; illus; index   ISBN: 0-7207-1545-8
                                                 BL: X.622/22061

It is sad to report that football merits only a passing
mention in this book of sporting memorabilia whilst
cricket, racing, etc. are well covered. Football does
have a rich heritage and much in the way of historic
artefacts, yet this has seldom been publicised. There
is a superb volume entitled 'The Wisden Book of
Cricket Memorabilia' – if only someone would research
and publish the football equivalent, I'm sure it would
sell like hot pies on a November night at Stockport.

234 Cricket cigarette and trade cards / D. Deadman.
London: Murray Cards International, 1985.
272p; illus; pbk   ISBN: 0-946942-02-1

   *Researchers seeking unusual illustrations of football-
   ers 'in their whites' will find this a good source of
   identification.*

235 The Pinnace collection / Raymond John Spiller.
Basildon: Association of Football Statisticians, 1986.
114p; illus; pbk   ISBN: 0-946531-46-3

   *In 1923, Godfrey Phillips Ltd. launched their new
   brand of Pinnace cigarettes and gave away a massive
   series of real photo cards initially depicting football
   and rugby players. This book reproduces all 2,462
   photos. An excellent source of illustrations for
   authors, especially for lesser known sides of that era.*

236 Arsenal football programme collectors handbook: a
check list of football programmes from away matches,
1946-1987 / Leonard Evans. London: The author, 1987.
48p; pbk   ISBN: 0-9512697-0-4
                                    BL: YK.1988.a.2994

237 The definitive guide to football programmes: an
illustrated guide to the hobby of football programme
collecting / Julian Earwaker. Ipswich: Chapter 6
Publishing, 1987.
112p; illus; pbk   ISBN: 1-870707-00-1
                                    BL: YK.1989.a.420

   Includes many programme cover illustrations.

238 Half-time: (football and the cigarette card, 1890-1940) /
David Thompson. London: Murray Cards
(International), 1987.
104p; illus; pbk

   Bibliography: p2   ISBN: 0-946942-05-6
                                    BL: YV.1990.b.86

   *An invaluable research tool. Don't expect to find lots
   of pictures – it is a complete listing of all football
   subjects known to the publishers up to 1940. Collectors seeking to build up albums relating to a
   particular club can identify the cards required at a
   glance. Many lesser known players and clubs are included. Club historians and authors take note.*

239 Football under the skin: a historical glimpse of soccer in
Tyne and Wear 1879-1988 / edited by Alisdair R.
Wilson. Newcastle: Tyne and Wear Museums Service,
1988.
80p; illus; pbk   ISBN: 0-905974-37-9

   *In 1988 Tyne and Wear Museums staged an exhibi-
   tion entitled 'The Football Show'. It included many old
   photographs and items of memorabilia from the world
   famous collection of Harry Langton – this well illustrated catalogue accompanied the show.*

240 Sport and the artist. Vol 1: Ball games / Mary Ann
Wingfield. Woodbridge: Antique Collectors' Club, 1988.
359p; illus, plans; index

Bibliography: p350-352   ISBN: 1-85149-071-X
                                    BL: YV.1989.b.399

*Football art is a much neglected subject in general –
researchers will find much to build on in consulting
chapter 2 of this superb study. There are some delightful illustrated examples and a complete list of
artists and subjects exhibited at the 1953 exhibition
organised by the Football Association. Out of 1,700
submitted entries, 150 were selected to be shown at
Park Lane House in October/November 1953. If
enough examples could be traced I feel sure a complete volume on football art would be a great success.*

241 A collector's guide to Celtic in competitive matches
1946-47 to 1988-89 / Tom McGouran. Glasgow?:
Injectaprint, 1989.

   Complete programme listing for the period.

242 A collector's guide to Celtic in friendlies 1946-47 to
1988-89 / Tom McGouran. Glasgow?: Injectaprint, 1989.

   Delving ever deeper.

243 Glasgow Rangers collectors club guide to Rangers
programmes 1946-47 to 1988-89 / I. Manson. 1989.

244 The illustrated footballer / Tony Ambrosen. Derby:
Breedon Books, 1989.
62p; illus   ISBN: 0-907969-47-X
                                    BL: YA.1991.b.9112

   *A history of this popular genre including many illus-
   trations of the cards themselves. A valuable work on
   the ever growing hobby of football cartophily.*

245 Rangers home and away programme guide 1946-1989 /
Robert McElroy. 1989.

246 Arsenal football programme collectors handbook: a
comprehensive check list of all Arsenal football
programmes from home matches 1946-1990 including
all first team, reserve, youth and all other matches played
at Highbury / Leonard Evans. London: The author,
1990.
iv, 46p; pbk   ISBN: 0-9512697-1-2
                                    BL: YK.1991.a.7369

   ☞ Subsequent ed. H256

247 A collector's guide to Falkirk FC programmes 1946-47
     to 1989-90 / F. & A. Hullett. 1990.

248 A collector's guide to St Mirren FC programmes: home
     and away 1946-47 to 1990-91 / Derek Drennan. 1991.
     64p; pbk

249 Chelsea FC: the programme guide, 1905-1992 /
     compiled by Alan Delaprelle. Witham: Skript, 1992.
     145p; illus; pbk   ISBN: 1-874799-01-6
                                     BL: YK.1994.a.15639

     Full season-by-season first team programme listings
     – also includes cigarette and trade card listings of
     Chelsea subjects.

250 A dictionary of sporting artists, 1650-1990 / edited by
     Mary Ann Wingfield. Woodbridge: Antique Collectors'
     Club, 1992.
     354p   ISBN: 1-85149-140-6
                                     BL: YK.1993.b.415

     Best used in conjunction with Mary Wingfield's 'Sport
     and the Artist'. This gives biographical details of art-
     ists known to have depicted football subjects and
     most importantly, identifies the whereabouts of
     paintings where known to a particular gallery or col-
     lection. Likely to be of use to club historians seeking
     the less common illustrations.

251 Facsimile volumes of Chelsea Football Club
     programmes / Scott Cheshire. London: Chelsea Football
     Club, 1992.
     (The Chelsea chronicles)

     Vol. 1: 1905-06; Vol. 2: 1906-07; Vol. 3: 1907-08;
     Vol. 4: 1908-09; Vol. 5: 1909-10
     Limited ed. of 250 copies of each title

     This series of facsimiles of 'The Chelsea Chronicle',
     the early club programme, is a must for all Chelsea
     historians, reproducing all the programmes season by
     season. They tell us much about the way the game
     was run and perceived in those early years.

252 Hoole's guide to British collecting clubs / compiled by
     Les Hoole. Bradford: Adwalton, 1992.
     112p; illus; index; pbk   ISBN: 0-9520690-0-8
                                     BL: YK.1994.a.2230

     Includes listings of societies pertaining to the game
     of football.

253 In Soccer Wonderland / Julian Germain. London?: Why
     Not Publishing, 1992.
     24p; pbk

     Delightfully bizarre is probably the best description of
     this item, which is in effect the catalogue accompa-
     nying a football photographic exhibition entitled 'In
     Soccer Wonderland' held at the Photographers' Gal-
     lery, London and Impressions Gallery of Photography,
     York. The photographs are here presented as stick-
     ers in a pastiche of the sticker books so popular
     today. 24 subjects are included: number 10 is prob-
     ably the only example of full frontal nudity in this

     bibliography and number 20 is a rear view of a man
     with a Bobby Charlton haircut – he has a large blue-
     bottle on his head! A new and enlarged hardback
     edition was published in 1994 by Booth Clibborn Edi-
     tions.

254 Tottenham Hotspur: the programme & handbook guide,
     1946-1992 / compiled by Chris Ward and Steve Isaac.
     Witham: Skript, 1992.
     200p; illus; pbk   ISBN: 1-874799-00-8
                                     BL: YK.1994.a.15604

     ☞ Subsequent ed. H260

255 Arsenal FC: the 1st XI official programme guide,
     1946-1993 / compiled by Richard Lerman and Andrew
     Miller. Witham: Skript, 1993?
     226p   ISBN: 1-874799-02-4
                                     BL: YK.1994.a.136

256 Arsenal football programme collectors handbook: a
     comprehensive list of all Arsenal programmes from home
     matches, 1946-1993, including all first team, reserve, youth
     and all other matches played at Highbury / Leonard Evans.
     New, rev. ed. London: The author, 1993.
     64p; pbk   ISBN: 0-9512697-2-0
                                     BL: YK.1993.a.15004

     ☞ Previous ed. H246

257 Cricket cigarette and trade cards: a further listing / Alan
     Harris and Geoff Seymour. London: Murray Cards
     International, 1993.
     118p; illus; spiral   ISBN: 0-946942-13-7

     Best used in conjunction with the 1985 publication by
     Derek Deadman – a good source of identification of
     pictorial representations of cricketer-footballers in
     their summer garb.

258 Heart of Midlothian FC: the programme guide / J. Ure.
     Edinburgh: The author, 1993.
     192p; illus   ISBN: 0-9521660-0-3

259 The Scottish non-league programme collector's guide /
     edited by Andy Mitchell. The author, 1993.
     64p; illus

     Primarily a programme guide but also includes a
     check-list of all appearances in the Scottish Cup by
     non-league clubs and a general overview of items of
     interest to the Scottish non-league fan.

260 Tottenham Hotspur: the programme & handbook guide,
     1946-1993 / compiled by Chris Ward & Steve Isaac.
     Updated & rev. home ed. Witham: Skript, 1993.
     i, 204p; illus; pbk   ISBN: 1-874799-03-2
                                     BL: YK.1994.a.122

     ☞ Previous ed. H254

261 Aberdeen programme review / Kevin Sterling. 1994.

262 A collector's guide to Kilmarnock FC programmes /
     Richard Cairns.

Games

263 Rules for parlour football. London: Haslop, 1888.
1 sheet   BL: 1865.c.2(1)

Table top games based on football have been popular since the early days of the game. This scarce early rule sheet dates from the year in which the Football League was formed.

264 Bow Bells international football: rules. Bristol: H. R. Clarke, 1893.
2 parts   BL: D

265 The new game of football racing / invented by P. Pyne. 1905.
Typewritten   BL: 1865.c.2(40)

266 Spain's football billiards and football snooker / C. Spain. London: The author, 1924.   BL: D

☞ Subsequent ed. H267

267 Spain's football billiards and football snooker: rules / C. Spain. 2nd ed. London: The author, 1926.   BL: D

☞ Previous ed. H266

268 Rules of the game of table football / Arthur Smith. Cleethorpes: The author, 1930.
1 sheet   BL: 1879.cc.2(38)

Even before Peter Adolph from Tunbridge Wells invented the game Subbuteo in 1947 it was played in very similar format as Newfooty and Table Soccer. This is an ephemeral item from the early days of the game. Mr W. L. Keeling, founder of the Newfooty Company based in Liverpool, invented the game in 1929 and it has changed remarkably little since those days. Generations have tried to come up with something better but have been united in their failure. Table football, whatever its tradename, reigns supreme.

269 Foba. Southsea: Martin Shaw, 1933.   BL: D

270 Football commentary: a new 'soccer' game for one or more players / Rex Pogson. Birmingham: Cotterell, 1944.
12p   BL: 7917.de.31

This game was suggested by the method of dividing the field of play into squares, as a guide to listeners, in the early days of running commentaries on the wireless.

271 Pencil football: a game, with instructions / Philip Harrop. West Kirby: G. Harrop, 1947.
                                           BL: 1856.g.13(20)

272 Table association football / T. Waterman. 1963.
11p

Reproduced from typewriting with a typescript inserted
                                           BL: 7926.p.27

Table Football, Newfooty and then Subbuteo have delighted young and old alike for many years; indeed Subbuteo has become a cult game especially revered by those who played it during its sixties heyday. This small item is of interest but rather limited in its scope – collecting old football games is a growing hobby as the video game market appears to take over. Perhaps a well illustrated coffee table book on the subject would be a good idea.

273 Dream league football: a guide to success 1993-94 / Peter James Wroe. Egham: Dream League, 1993.
160p; pbk   ISBN: 1-8983480-1-4

The cult of fantasy football has achieved a very high profile in the early nineties. Contestants select a team of 'real' players whose performance in real life earns points for their manager. This is the game at its simplest, but computerised versions introduce many more variants. Personally, I still prefer Waddington's 'Table Soccer' and its 'endless hours of excitement. . . .'

274 Fantasy team / Jason Page and Richard Mead; illustrations by David Woodward. London: Bloomsbury, 1994.
128p; illus; pbk   ISBN: 0-7475-1908-0

275 The official Fantasy League manager's handbook / Andrew Wainstein; with illustrations by Dave Robinson and contributions by Fantasy League managers. London: Corgi, 1994.
257p; illus; pbk   ISBN: 0-552-14287-5

Economic & Business Studies

276   Conciliation Act, 1896 Association Football: report of a committee of investigation into a difference regarding the terms and conditions of association football players. London: Ministry of Labour and National Service, 1952.
19p; pbk   BL: BS23/26(93)

Financial security has never been easy for the majority of footballers due to their strictly limited career span, but it was particularly difficult in the era before the 'big money' contracts so prevalent today. This report is an important milestone in establishing better working conditions for the footballing fraternity.

277   Professional football / Commission on Industrial Relations. London: HMSO, 1974.
vi, 111p; pbk
(Report; no. 87)   ISBN: 0-11-700304-2

Another important document relating to the economic and working status of the professional player.

278   The financing and taxation of football clubs / Arthur Andersen & Co. London: The Football Association and The Football League, 1982.
122p

A firm of leading accountants advises clubs on the complexities of good housekeeping. Many financial irregularities have occurred in football from its earliest days – perhaps this should become compulsory reading.

279   The demand for Scottish football 1971-80 / John Cairns. Aberdeen: University of Aberdeen, Department of Political Economy, 1983.
73p; pbk
(Discussion paper / University of Aberdeen; 83-05)
    Bibliography: p72-73   BL: X.525/7899

A serious academic study charting trends in attendances and analysing reasons and remedies for some of the game's ills.

280   The economics of league structure: an analysis of the reorganisation of the Scottish Football League / John A. Cairns. Aberdeen: University of Aberdeen, Department of Political Economy, 1983.
43p; pbk
(Discussion paper / University of Aberdeen; no. 83-03)
    Bibliography: p43

281   Price-setting and revenue-sharing in the Scottish Football League / John Cairns. Aberdeen: Department of Political Economy, University of Aberdeen, 1983.
26 leaves; illus; unbound
(Discussion paper / University of Aberdeen; 83-09)

282   A survey of Football League clubs. London: Jordan & Sons, 1985.
iv, 105p; pbk   ISBN: 0-85938-197-8
                             BL: YC.1986.b.2528

    ☞ Subsequent ed. H288

283   Economics of Scottish professional football: a resource for teachers of economics / R. A. Crampsey. Glasgow: Education for the Industrial Society Project in co-operation with the Scottish Examination Board, 1986.
33p; spiral
    Bibliography: p31   ISBN: 0-946584-06-0
                            BL: YC.1987.b.5834

284   Financing and management in the football industry / A. J. Arnold; edited by G. Stewart. Hull: Barmarick, 1986.
29p; illus   ISBN: 0-906971-72-1

285   Report on association football clubs. London: ICC Business Ratios, 1986.
pbk

    ☞ Subsequent ed. H287

286   Football clubs: a report. Hampton: Key Note Publications, 1987.
pbk   ISBN: 1-85056-451-5

287   Report on association football clubs. 2nd ed. London: ICC Business Ratios, 1987.
pbk   ISBN: 1-85319-065-9
    ☞ Previous ed. H285; subsequent ed. H289

288   A survey of Football League clubs 1987. Bristol: Jordan & Sons, 1987.
12, 92p; illus; index; pbk   ISBN: 0-85938-243-5
                            BL: ZK.9.b.1197

    ☞ Previous ed. H282; subsequent ed. H293

289   Report on association football clubs. 3rd ed. London: ICC Business Ratios, 1988.
pbk   ISBN: 1-85319-266-X
    ☞ Previous ed. H287; subsequent ed. H291

290   Manager's simulation: football. Huntingdon: Elm, 1989.
1 loose-leaf vol; illus, forms
(PEG series. ISSN: 0954-030X)   ISBN: 0-946139-09-1
                            BL: Cup.937/249

291   Report on association football clubs. 4th ed. London: ICC Business Ratios, 1989.
pbk   ISBN: 1-85319-501-4
    ☞ Previous ed. H289

292 Soccer survey. Esher: Sports Marketing Surveys, 1990?-

Produced annually

A market survey with statistics of UK football products and participation. The data is based on personal interviews with sports participants. Football is such a big market in the widest business sense that companies are prepared to commission market research studies like this as an aid to business development.

293 A survey of Football League clubs: England and Scotland industry / commentary by Lynton Guest. Bristol: Jordan & Sons, 1990.
45, 77p; index; pbk   ISBN: 0-85938-332-6
                                             BL: YK.1992.b.1128

☞ Previous ed. H288

294 The Football Trust programmes in Scotland. Edinburgh?: Scottish Sports Council, 1991.
8p
(Information digest; FP10. ISSN: 0140-2803)

295 A game without vision: the crisis in English football / Dan Corry, Paul Williamson with Sarah Moore. London: Institute for Public Policy Research, 1993.
ii, 44p

Includes bibliographical references   ISBN: 1-872452-74-4

Football is, when stripped to its basics, a business like any other. If income fails to exceed expenditure then serious problems accrue. This analysis, taken from the economic viewpoint, sounds the alarm bells and suggests a more professional and visionary approach.

296 A guide to successfully marketing a football club / Christopher Owen Meredith. Bracknell: The author, 1994.
25 leaves; spiral   ISBN: 0-9523016-0-1

As many clubs struggle to make ends meet and others continue to run with huge losses, business expertise in the form of marketing skills is becoming an increasingly essential requirement. Football has certainly fallen behind other industries in general, although specific examples stand out in glorious contrast – Leicester City repackaged their sparsely attended reserve games as 'Family Fun Football' and attracted much larger crowds. There is much more to marketing than the ubiquitous 'Executive Suite', home to the 'Blue Blazered Florid' and his 80 minute match – clubs take note!

297 Out of time: why football isn't working / Alex Fynn and Lynton Guest. London: Simon & Schuster, 1994.
xi, 355p; illus; index; pbk   ISBN: 0-671-71220-9
                                             BL: YK.1994.b.11150

Many football clubs are losing money and a great number can boast of vast armies of 'used-to-go' spectators who now count themselves as armchair followers only. There is much about the game which is certainly as good as ever, if not better, but there is also an underlying malaise about its economic future. The authors here present a very serious study which effectively amounts to their blueprint for the future.

Football in Literature

THE GAME OF ASSOCIATION FOOTBALL is portrayed in fiction in widely differing ways – from the cosy childhood world of *Topsy and Tim at the Football Match* to the sinister violence and anarchy of *Albion! Albion!* Two questions occur to the interested reader: why is so little written about football? and, does what there is adequately describe and capture the essence of the game?

Football is such an all-pervasive thread in the fabric of modern life that it is reasonable to suppose that in many novels it would feature as a central theme and that many novelists would use it as a backdrop in much the same way as they might refer to eating, drinking or sleeping. But nothing could be further from the truth. Football and literature are not comfortable bedfellows nor even casual friends – distant relatives would be nearer the mark.

Several respected commentators, John Arlott and Brian Glanville foremost amongst them, have sought to explain why this should be so. They hypothesise that only a small proportion of football fans are keen readers of fiction, and that only a handful of novelists are keen enough on the game to have either the inclination or the ability to write about it with authority.

The number of good novelists who write about football is thus a small one. As if to fill this gap a number of relative novices, some from within the game itself, have boldly tried their hand. Reviews have been at best humorously tolerant, and at worst scathing – delivered with the manic ferocity of an over-the-top tackle leaving the hapless author in a deflated heap, utterly devoid of the confidence to try again.

All this apart, football fiction does exist and so does serious journalistic appreciation along with a smattering of poetry, a number of stage plays and some well observed football cameos in non-soccer works. Indeed the relative scarcity of material heightens the thrill of the chase and it has become something of a running game amongst football-loving 'literati' to uncover hitherto undiscovered sources. There are pitfalls though for unwary hunt participants looking for a good football read. Samuel Becket wrote *More Pricks than Kicks* long before Wimbledon ever went on tour and there is no mention of the Holte End in Somerset Maugham's *Up at the Villa*. Agatha Christie's *Endless Night* might well be the compelling drama of a European Cup Final decided on penalties but unfortunately it isn't. For those of us looking to reverse this almost conspiratorial exclusion of the world's greatest game from the pages of fiction, the advice 'seek and ye shall find' offers the most useful directive. This chapter of the bibliography should act as your guide.

The range of adult fiction is relatively limited. A good early example is Leonard Gribble's *They Kidnapped Stanley Matthews* [158]. Gribble also wrote *The Arsenal Stadium Mystery* [157] and a much later attempt on the same theme came from the pen of the great Pelé, although his *World Cup Murder* [184] is far less gentle than its predecessor.

This indeed is a feature of the more recent adult fiction which tends to spurn the innocent side of the game in favour of the sex, drugs, violence, alcohol and corruption which apparently inhabit the seedier depths of our national pastime. Jimmy Greaves, Terry Venables, Derek Dougan and Mel Stein are all men of the football world who have made efforts to transport their experiences to the printed page. The results are certainly of interest and present an insight into facets of the sport of which the average supporter may be unaware, but none of them has received significant critical acclaim. Many fans indeed prefer a more traditionalist approach and have not taken readily to such tacky portrayals. Rather better received and very professionally written was J. L. Carr's delightful *How Steeple Sinderby Wanderers won the FA Cup* [129] which in turn is in complete contrast to the realism and aggression of Dan Kavanagh's *Duffy* novels [172-74] and the *Skinhead* books of Richard Allen [195-100]. Although not totally football-related the latter two examples portray a violent side of football followers in the seventies which for a number of years became the scourge of the game.

No survey of football in fiction could be complete without reference to Brian Glanville, a fine novelist and a highly respected journalist and authority on soccer. Many of his short stories have a soccer theme and remind us of the human frailties and vulnerability associated with the footballing life. They are essentially tales about people who just happen to work in football and they are particularly sensitive efforts. His novel *Dying of the Light* [147] covers the particularly poignant subject of what happens to a professional footballer when he becomes an ex-pro' and finally an old ex-pro'. It makes sobering reading for those who might be seduced by the surface glamour of football. Sadly there are many who could have been the inspiration for this book.

Also worth mentioning are the two major series of books making up a considerable proportion of the listings. The Aldine football novels of the 1920s and 1930s generally presented the cheery face of football but with a touch of villainy thrown in for good measure. The stories usually centred on the triumph of good over evil, and honesty over deceit in which genuine endeavour would always prevail over shady skulduggery. The titles themselves are splendidly evocative of the era: *The Pit Boy Centre, The Filmland Forward, The Circus Saver, The Fighting Footballer* – what a team they might have made. It is debatable whether any of today's publishers would dare to present their readers with *Darkies on Tour* or even *The Gypsy Footballers* but such exotica was eagerly devoured by the youngsters of the day blissfully unhampered by the strictures of political correctness. We are reminded too that women's football, enjoying an increasingly high profile today, has already experienced one heyday. Researchers of this topic should consult *Captain Meg: Footballer* [I299/2] from the Aldine series or *Bess of Blacktown* [I299/27], in the *Football and Sports Library* series published in 1922 or, for a more contemporary view of the same subject, *Joanna's Goal* [I135] by the prolific Michael Hardcastle. His series of novels represents the second major library for juveniles and adolescents and such is the volume of his output that Hardcastle can justifiably lay claim to the title of most productive writer of football fiction.

This chapter also includes both fictional and biographical observation from authors not primarily known as writers on football and offers the researcher a less direct but nevertheless useful insight into the game. These items include the sport only incidentally – most well known amongst the full length novels are J. B. Priestley's *Good Companions* [I85] and Arnold Bennett's *The Card* [I27]. There are times when a distant observer can divine more about a subject or come closer to defining its true essence than the greatest expert. A good example comes from Paul Theroux in his *Kingdom by the Sea* [I232]. His short paragraph describing his shock, mystification and sheer disgust at a chance encounter with hooligans on a train says just as much about the alien nature of this unacceptable element as many a word written in a serious sociological study.

Rather less heavy and characterised by a strong vein of humour are the entries in the Poetry section. Cricket, with its pastoral overtones, has always been the poets' favourite and football has not generally been taken to heart by the rhymesters of our times. *The Poetry of Motion* anthology edited by Alan Bold [I191] includes a few worthwhile references to football while his *Scotland, Yes: World Cup Football Poems* [I180] have filled out a complete volume. Poetry is one area of football writing in which discoveries may still be made – many early periodicals, boys' annuals, programmes and fanzines include isolated examples penned in praise of a favourite player or team. Although some of these amateur efforts are gloriously naïve there seems to be sufficient material for a substantial anthology of soccer poetry to be compiled.

For those who prefer to tread the boards, the sections on Plays includes those few known examples of soccer on the stage. They include non-football productions with incidental cameos as well as those which have the game as a central running theme. One wonders whether *The Referee* [I197] and *The Football Club Supper* [I199] have been exposed to the glare of the footlights in recent years. Certainly Peter Terson's *Zigger Zagger* [I208] is a well known dramatic piece which took audiences and critics by storm when it was first performed at the National Youth Theatre in 1967. Contemporary reviews declared its impact as shocking – 'set on the chanting, jeering terraces of City Club, it inhabits the world of football hooligans, youths pitched out of school at fifteen, with or without dead end jobs, their present excitement and future faith all turning on the football . . . '. Much of the original dialogue appears archaic by today's standards but it still has much to say about the sociology and psychology of supportership.

A more light-hearted portrayal is the recent success story *An Evening with Gary Lineker* [I207]. It has a strong element of comedy albeit that the theme of the play marks one of the most darkly disappointing nights in the history of the English national side, England's defeat by West Germany in the 1990 World Cup semifinals. It is to be hoped that the box office success of this production encourages other writers to transport the game into the theatre – what price an Andrew Lloyd Webber musical?

Despite my opening remarks that non-factual coverage of football is not as widespread as might be expected, there is still a fair range of material to interest the student, writer or researcher wishing to explore this field. For an excellent overview of the subject the miscellaneous collections in the Anthologies section are certainly the best place to start. Glanville's *Footballer's Companion* [I240] contains many extracts from the works listed in this chapter and was one of the first books to explore the relationship between football and literature. The more recent *Joy of Football* [I242] was an updated version of Glanville's original and both *The Footballer's Fireside Book* [I241] and *The Kingswood Book of Football* [I243] contain similar material. John Arlott's *Concerning Soccer* [I235] includes some delightful essays from a master of his craft whose love of football has not been widely publicised; his piece explaining the emotions behind his love of Reading FC gives a shrewd insight into the reasons why a man of intelligence can feel such passion for his chosen club.

Certainly there will be something new for many football lovers in the pages of the books listed here. It is quite possible to know the history and statistics of the game intimately without ever having touched on the more lyrical elements of the sport. And for those who doubt that football and the written word could ever combine to produce pieces with the power to provoke profound recognition, laughter and even tears, there are entries here which might well be a revelation.

Football in Literature ~ Contents

Short Stories

✳ Single Author Collections

Bennett, Enoch Arnold

1 The matador of the five towns, and other stories.
London: Methuen, 1912.
vi, 325p   BL: NN.10

> The title story includes an extended football passage
> about a game between Knype and Manchester Rovers.

2 Ok noveloj . . . el, or, The matador of the five towns,
and other stories / tradukis Alfred E. Wackrill.
Londono: Brita Esperantista Asocio, 1919.
124p   BL: 012611.g.37

> Any researcher seeking, for whatever reason, a de-
> scriptive football related passage in Esperanto will
> find it here!

Cooke, Rupert Croft

3 A football for the Brigadier, and other stories. London:
Werner Laurie, 1950.
251p   BL: NNN.988

> Whilst football is included in the title of just one of
> the stories, the allusions are tenuous. One for the
> completist!

Fraser, George MacDonald

4 The General dances at dawn. London: Barrie & Jenkins,
1970.
205p   ISBN: 0-214-65269-6
                                          BL: Nov.16036

> Includes the football related tale 'Play Up, Play Up
> and Get Tore In' . . . 'from the moment when the
> drums beat "Johnnie Cope" at sunrise until it became
> too dark to see in the evening, the steady thump of a
> boot on a ball could be heard somewhere in the bar-
> racks'.

Glanville, Brian Lester

5 A bad lot. London: Severn House, 1977.
143p   ISBN: 0-7278-0309-3
                                          BL: Nov. 35278

> This author is one of very few novelists who have
> made serious efforts at writing short football sto-
> ries. It is a commonly held misconception in some
> circles that Glanville's stories are for children – some
> of his themes are in fact distinctly adult. He is an
> author well worth collecting. This particular collection
> contains ten football and boxing stories.

6 A bad streak, and other stories. London: Secker &
Warburg, 1961.
224p   BL: NNN.15912

7 The director's wife, and other stories. London: Secker &
Warburg, 1963.
252p   BL: Nov.437

8 Goalkeepers are crazy: a collection of football stories.
London: Secker & Warburg, 1964.
222p   BL: Nov.2189

> Almost certainly the most complete selection of
> football short stories – 23 in all – from the best
> known writer of this genre.

9 The King of Hackney Marshes, and other stories.
London: Secker & Warburg, 1965.
256p   BL: Nov.6717

> This unusual title relates to the keenly fought ama-
> teur games played on Hackney Marshes. A number of
> the stories are football related – the others relate to
> Jewish society in Britain. Glanville writes with author-
> ity and an insider's eye on both.

10 Love is not love, and other short stories. London:
Anthony Blond, 1985.
218p   ISBN: 0-8563-4189-4
                                          BL: X.950/40684

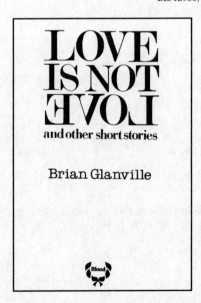

LOVE IS NOT LOVE

and other short stories

Brian Glanville

Blond

Naughton, Bill

11   The goalkeeper's revenge, and other stories / illustrated
     by Dick de Wilde. London: Harrap, 1961.
     119p
                                        BL: 012845.e.3

     ☞ See also: I203, I274

Sillitoe, Alan

12   The loneliness of the long-distance runner. London:
     W. H. Allen, 1959.
     176p
                                        BL: NNN.13909
     '. . . towards the end of the match, when Bristol
     scored their winning goal, the players could only just
     be seen, and the ball was a roll of mist being kicked
     about the field. Advertising boards above the stands,
     telling of pork pies, ales, whisky, cigarettes and other
     delights of Saturday night, faded with the afternoon
     visibility'.

Silver, R. Norman (pseud.)

13   Romance of the football field. London: Ward Lock,
     1906.
     229p

     Author's real name is George Knight
                                        BL: 012632.aaa.28

✻ *Anthologies*

14   Best sports stories / edited with an introduction by Paul
     Edwards. London: Faber, 1966.
     223p
                                        BL: X.909/7818
     Includes Brian Glanville's 'Goalkeepers are crazy' – 12
     pages.

15   British sporting stories / selected by John Arlott.
     London: News of the World, 1953.
     223p
     (News of the World readers circle series; no. B39)
                                        BL: 12299.de.29
     Includes 'Chapman's final' by Geoffrey Green and 'The
     Cup Final of 1934' by Frank Swift.

16   Sporting detective stories / edited by Ellery Queen.
     London: Faber & Faber, 1946.
     381p
                                        BL: 12729.aaa.16
     Of the twenty-two stories only one is about football:
     'The football photograph' by H. C. Bailey features De-
     tective Reggie Fortune 'investigating a burglary and
     finding a footballer' – 27 pages.

17   Twenty five football stories. London: Newnes, 1908.
     216p
                                        BL: 012629.k.80
     In the early part of the century 'Boy's Own' style
     football yarns were extremely popular. This is a good
     selection of early examples.

Children's Short Stories

✻ *Single Author Collections*

Adrian, Alec

18   Football thrills. Ilfracombe: A. H. Stockwell, 1945.
     63p; pbk
                                        BL: 7918.aa.19

Hardcastle, Michael

19   Dog bites goalie, and other stories. London: Methuen
     Children's, 1993.
     127p; illus
                                        ISBN: 0-416-18723-4
                                        BL: YK.1993.a.6872

Newman, Marjorie

20   Dan and the football; Dan and the special badge.
     Basingstoke: Pickering, 1984.
     63p; illus; pbk
     (Dan the parable man)
                                        ISBN: 0-7208-2345-5
                                        BL: X.990/23577

✻ *Anthologies*

21   The 'Boys' Realm' football (and sports) library no. 1-299.
     London: Boys' Realm, 1909-1915.
     No. 4 is missing from the Library set   BL: P.P.5993.ndo
     This series includes many football stories.

22   The Clipper book of favourite football stories /
     illustrations by Harry Winslade. London: Clipper Press,
     1970.
     42p; illus; pbk
                                        ISBN: 0-85108-009-X

23   Football stories / selected by Ian Woodward; illustrated
     by Francis Moseley. London: Transworld, 1984.
     143p; illus; pbk
     (Carousel books)
                                        ISBN: 0-552-52222-8
                                        BL: H.85/26

Novels

✱ *Adult Novels*

Bartlem, Neil

24 Soccer ace gunned down. Southport: Tabloid, 1993.
285p
ISBN: 1-874652-03-1
BL: H.94/253

Bateman, Robert Moyes Carruthers

25 Young footballer. London: Constable, 1958.
155p
(Sports fiction series)
BL: W.P.4522/3

Bell, Sam Hanna

26 The hollow ball. London: Cassell, 1961.
248p
BL: Nov. 2439

A young Belfast lad decides to exploit his skills as a footballer. But will he survive the tensions, the board-room intrigues and the inevitable disappointments?

Bennett, Enoch Arnold

27 The card: a story of adventure in the five towns.
London: Methuen, 1911.
vii, 305p
BL: 012618.aaa.34

Includes cameo football passages relating to potter-ies football. The leading clubs are Knype and Bursley.

Bruckner, Karl

28 The Terriers Football Club / translated by Stella Humphries; illustrated by Beryl Sanders. London: Burke, 1961.
183p; illus

Translation of: Die Spatzenelf
BL: 12847.d.9

Carr, James L.

29 How Steeple Sinderby Wanderers won the FA Cup.
London: London Magazine Editions, 1975.
ISBN: 0-904388-02-6
BL: Nov.23139

An unusual book deserving of a wide readership. Carr transports himself back to 1930 and the romance of the cup in a lyrical and witty tale of improbable glory. He dedicates it to '. . . those others of my generation who have shivered into their kit behind hedgerows and in ditches'. As well as being a good yarn, the book takes a swipe at some of the ills of the modern game. Benny Green commented in a review – 'He delivers with a kind of derisive gaiety some murderous blows at the fatheads who populate professional football'.

Cope, Kenneth

30 Striker. London: BBC, 1976.
96p

Based on the BBC television series of the same name
ISBN: 0-563-17192-8 (cased) • ISBN: 0-563-17203-7 (pbk)
BL: X.990/8340 • BL: X.981/20529

31 Striker, second leg. London: BBC, 1977.
96p; pbk
ISBN: 0-563-17288-6
BL: BS.129/38

Crampsey, Robert

32 The manager. London: Hodder and Stoughton, 1982.
190p
ISBN: 0-340-27569-3
BL: Nov.46042

Manager Bob Calderwood strives manfully to keep Barford Albion from relegation. Many allusions to the football scene in Scotland.

Curtin, Michael

33 The replay. London: Deutsch, 1981.
271p
ISBN: 0-233-97327-3
BL: Nov.44271

HOW STEEPLE SINDERBY WANDERERS WON THE F.A. CUP

J.L.CARR

LONDON MAGAZINE EDITIONS
1975

Davies, Hunter

34   Come on, Ossie! London: Bodley Head, 1985.
     132p; illus
               ISBN: 0-370-30895-6
               BL: YC.1987.a.5286

35   Ossie the millionaire. London: Bodley Head, 1987.
     144p; illus
               ISBN: 0-370-31111-6
               BL: YK.1987.a.7638

36   Striker. London: Bloomsbury, 1992.
     247p
               ISBN: 0-7475-1225-6
               BL: Nov.1993/757
     A satirical 'spoof' autobiography – the story of Joe Swift superstar takes him from Carlisle to Tottenham and on to Hamburg and AC Venice. Interesting approach.

Dougan, Derek

37   The footballer: a novel. London: Allison and Busby, 1974.
     240p
               ISBN: 0-85031-114-4
               BL: Nov.21761
     Poor boy from an underprivileged background finds success and problems in the world of football.

Douglas, George

38   Final score. London: Hale, 1975.
     192p
               ISBN: 0-7091-4953-0
               BL: Nov. 30370
     The manager of Benfield United is killed by a carbomb. Was he the intended victim and, if so, why?

Draper, Alfred

39   The death penalty. London: Macmillan, 1972.
     192p
               SBN: 333-13352-8
               BL: Nov. 17965
     A controversial decision on the field results in murder.

Durston, Jack

40   The great football mystery. London: Mellifont, 1934.
     64p; pbk
               BL: 12601.pp.15

Evans, Philip

41   The bodyguard man. London: Hodder & Stoughton, 1973.
     192p
               ISBN: 0-340-16566-9
               BL: Nov.1990/1568

42   Playing the wild card. Sevenoaks: Hodder and Stoughton, 1988.
     224p
               ISBN: 0-340-42369-2
               BL: Nov.1988/1438
     The story of young Welshman, Gary Byrne, and his exploits playing in Italy for Fiorentina. The publicity material describes the book as 'richly evocative of Italy, the glamour of stardom and the loneliness of exile'.

Fuller, Roy Broadbent

43   The second curtain. London: Derek Verschoyle, 1953.
     172p
               BL: NNN.5025
     This non-football novel includes one of the lesser known extended football passages.

Gill, Patrick

44   The battle for the cup. London: Mellifont, 1939.
     128p; pbk
               BL: 12637.p.1/8

45   The fighting footballers. London: Mellifont, 1937.
     64p; pbk
               BL: 12627.pp.28

46   The mystery of the centre-forward. London: Mellifont, 1939.
     128p; pbk
               BL: 12637.p.1/14
     Follows the fortunes of Hoxley United.

Giller, Norman See Greaves, Jimmy & Norman Giller

Glanville, Brian Lester

47   The dying of the light. London: Secker and Warburg, 1976.
     v, 184p
               ISBN: 0-436-18111-8
               BL: Nov.32454
     Len Rawlings was the greatest goalkeeper of his time but now he is a pathetic relic living in wretched obscurity – a poignant study of what can happen to a pro in retirement.

48   Goalkeepers are different. London: Hamilton, 1971.
     154p
               ISBN: 0-241-02121-9
               BL: X.990/3034
     This story about the rise of a talented young goalkeeper, Ronnie Blake, tells 'what it is really like to be a professional footballer'. Although strictly fiction, it does offer some valuable insights into the early seventies era.

49   The rise of Gerry Logan. London: Secker & Warburg, 1963.
     239p
               BL: Nov.1348
     From Jarrow City to Chiswick United, on to Rome and back again. A study of the worlds of British and Italian football in the early sixties.

Goodyear, Robert A. H.

50   The old golds: a romance of football. London: Lincoln Williams, 1934.
     272p
               BL: 20054.c.5

Greaves, Jimmy & Norman Giller

51   The ball game. London: Arthur Barker, 1980.
     156p   ISBN: 0-213-16744-1
                                             BL: Nov.41086

     The dust jacket blurb says it all: '. . . more action be-
     tween the goalposts and the bedposts as soccer
     superstar Jackie Groves scores in the States.'

52   The boss. London: Arthur Barker, 1981.
     154p   ISBN: 0-213-16784-0
                                             BL: Nov.42783

     Taken from the manager's point of view as he strug-
     gles to overcome a loss of form in the First Division.
     The boss in question is Steve Walker – hitting the
     bottle is one of the solutions he tries in overcoming
     the pressures of the game.

53   The final. London: Arthur Barker 1979.
     175p   ISBN: 0-213-16723-9
                                             BL: Nov.39530

     Described as an explosive novel about football and
     the people who play it at the highest level. The hero of
     the series is one Jackie Groves, a wayward US born
     striker with a taste for sexual adventurism. Reveals
     facets of the game we may not be familiar with but
     as a novel it did not receive critical acclaim.

54   The second half. London: Arthur Barker, 1981.
     182p   ISBN: 0-213-16798-0
                                             BL: Nov.44544

     A second chance in life for Groves closely parallels
     the troubles of co-author Jimmy Greaves, whose
     frank introductory note is all too clear – 'This book
     has, sadly, been well researched. The events and
     characters are imagined, but the drinking problems
     are real enough for millions of people. I have Alcoholics
     Anonymous to thank for helping me to beat the bot-
     tle and I hope this novel gives anybody with the
     problem the encouragement and motivation to con-
     quer it.'

Greenwood, Arthur

55   Soccer circus. London: P. R. Macmillan, 1961.
     271p   BL: 12845.m.14

Gribble, Leonard Reginald

56   The Arsenal stadium mystery. London: Harrap, 1939.
     280p   BL: NN.30902

     This Superintendent Slade mystery was made into a
     popular film; a footballer dies in front of 70,000 fans
     and Slade flushes out the culprit.

     ☞ Subsequent ed. I57; See also: M10

57   The Arsenal stadium mystery: a replay. Rev. ed. London:
     Herbert Jenkins, 1950.
     224p   BL: NNN.886

     ☞ Previous ed. I56

58   They kidnapped Stanley Matthews. London: Herbert
     Jenkins, 1950.
     222p   BL: NNN.821

     Another Slade mystery – popular with collectors but
     very elusive.

Gumley, F. W.

59   The football racketeers. London: Mellifont, 1944.
     96p; pbk   BL: 012641.n.114

60   The Hoodoo half-back: a soccer tale of thrills and
     mystery. London: Mellifont, 1942.
     96p; pbk   BL: 12637.p.1/44

61   The phantom footballer: a footer tale of mystery and
     adventure. London: Mellifont, 1939.
     128p; pbk   BL: 12637.p.1/12

Hatton, Charles

62   The White Hart Lane mystery. London: Longacre Press,
     1960.
     176p   BL: 12842.n.32

     Hungarian scientist Otto Kunniger develops a winning
     tactical formula, given to Spurs and subsequently
     stolen. PC George Dixon (of Dock Green), a Spurs
     stalwart, saves the day.

I

HISTORY IS MADE AT HIGHBURY

THERE WAS A SUDDEN,
expectant hush as Tom Whittaker walked into the
dressing-room of the Arsenal team at Highbury, that
same hush he has been greeted with for years, on every
Arsenal home-match day.

"The boss wants to see you all upstairs in a quarter
of an hour," he announced.

"O.K., Tom."

"Sure."

"Righto, Tom."

Life, suspended for a few moments for the almost
traditional announcement, flowed again. The eleven
first-team players idling in the dressing-room, waiting
for the time when they can start changing, picked up the
scraps of conversation they had let fall when the trainer
entered.

One of the trainer's assistants, standing by a table near
the door into the main corridor, continued with his task
of quartering a lemon. He let the knife he was using
rattle against the table's top. On to a cracked plate

9

Opening page of 'The Arsenal Stadium Mystery'

Hey, Stan See Lineker, Gary & Stan Hey

Hines, Barry

63   The blinder. London: Michael Joseph, 1966.
270p
BL: Nov. 7824

Great things are expected of young Lennie Hawk both
on and off the pitch.

Home, Stewart

64   Pure mania. Edinburgh: Polygon, 1989.
217p; pbk
ISBN: 0-7486-6035-6
BL: H.90/354

Football supportership and violence are the central
theme in this tale of the rise and fall of the 'Casuals'.

Hopkins, Tim

65   Jimmy Swift: a football novel. London: Macdonald and
Jane's, 1979.
iv, 91p
ISBN: 0-354-08048-2
BL: Nov.24326

Horler, Sydney

66   A legend of the league. London: Mellifont, 1940.
128p; pbk
BL: 12637.p.1/23

Jack Blair takes up professional football with struggling Deeppark Rangers in order to make enough
money to pay off his father's debts. Jack and his director friend, Thomas Hardy(!), overcome supporter
and boardroom oppposition to win the day. "'You
must stop to supper, Jack", said Thomas, "I want you
to meet my daughter." Vivid realism all round . . .

67   McPhee: a football story. London: Herbert Jenkins, 1923.
256p
BL: NN.8149

☞ Subsequent ed. I68

68   McPhee: prince of trainers. London: Newnes, 1930.
127p
BL: 12648.a.1/1

☞ Previous ed. I67

69   A pro's romance. London: Newnes, 1930.
128p
BL: 12648.a.1/2

Irwin, Michael

70   Striker. London: Deutsch, 1985.
231p
ISBN: 0-233-97792-9
BL: Nov.55327

Written in autobiographical form by 'Vincent Gilpin'
who progresses from park pitch to cup final and back
again. The book, whilst routine fare, has been critically
acclaimed for its descriptive passages concerning
on-the-field action — always a difficult part of the
game to portray realistically.

Jenkins, Robin

71   The thistle and the grail. London: Macdonald, 1954.
296p
BL: NNN.4857

This novel is unusual in its choice of subject, chronicling the ups and downs of Scottish Junior League
football, one of the lesser known areas of the game.

Kavanagh, Dan

72   Duffy. London: Cape, 1980.
181p
ISBN: 0-224-01822-1
BL: Nov.41225

Written under pseudonym by Julian Barnes. Duffy is a
bisexual ex-policeman who turns to private detection
and has a penchant for Sunday morning football. Along
the way he tackles football hooligans and associated
problems. Some interesting football allusions from this
accomplished author and Leicester City fan.

73   The Duffy omnibus. London: Penguin, 1991.
740p; pbk
ISBN: 0-14-015824-3
BL: H.91/4006

74   Putting the boot in. London: Cape, 1985.
150p
ISBN: 0-224-02332-2
BL: Nov.54360

The story involves Athletic, a London football club
languishing in the Third Division. Is someone trying to
ruin the club? Duffy provides the answers. The jacket
is one of soccer's most striking and potentially painful portrayals.

Lineker, Gary & Stan Hey

75   All in the game. Sevenoaks: Hodder & Stoughton, 1993.
Loosely based on Lineker's own career. Nice guy Darren
Matthews gets to grips with a move to Barcelona.

Maydwell, W. D.

76   Between the posts. London: Mellifont, 1940.
128p; pbk
BL 12637.p.1/22

77   Convict International. London: Mellifont, 1941.
96p; pbk
BL: 12637.p.1/38

Leading player of Burborough United, John Smith, is
arrested when he goes to Marble Arch Post Office to
collect a package. Can he ever prove his innocence?

78   The Football Pools mystery. London: Mellifont, 1940.
128p; pbk
BL: 12637.p.1/17

The Pools were used on a number of occasions as a
central theme for football novels, inevitably accompanied by much skulduggery.

79   The football racket. London: Mellifont Press, 1940.
128p; pbk
BL: 12637.p.1/16

An American millionaire sets out to buy a team of
best players that will achieve the 'impossible' by winning the League and the FA Cup in the same season.

Merrick, Phil

80   A game of two halves. Lewes: Book Guild, 1988.
173p   ISBN: 0-86332-279-4
BL: Nov.1990/111

'. . . describes the temptations which beset those at
the top of the soccer scene, when Bill Cunningham becomes an heroic figure.'

Montgomery, Douglas

81   On their way to Lisbon. Greenock: Seanachaidh, 1989.

Retrospective tale of Celtic's 1967 European Cup triumph in the Portuguese capital.

Morland, Dick

82   Albion! Albion! London: Faber, 1974.
213p   ISBN: 0-571-10597-1
BL: Nov.21899

A futuristic tale set in an England where anarchy
prevails and four football clubs are a controlling influence.

Parkes, Roger

83   Gamelord. London: Collins, 1990.
191p
(Crime club)   ISBN: 0-00-232311-7
BL: Nov. 1992/124

An investigation into a vicious assault leads to an
arrest made during an International in Munich.

Pelé

84   The World Cup murder / Pelé with Herb Resnicow.
Harpenden: No Exit, 1990.
318p; pbk   ISBN: 0-948353-74-0
BL: H.90/2091

The cover describes Pelé as 'the Dick Francis of the
football thriller'. This is a futuristic tale based on the
World Cup held in the United States, which of course
was reality in 1994. It is interesting that in the book
USA get to the final against East Germany! If the
novel had included Maradona's drugs episode, the
murder of poor Escobar and the red card antics of a
Syrian referee we would have said it was far-fetched. .
. truth is stranger than fiction?

Priestley, John Boynton

85   The good companions. London: Heinemann, 1929.
viii, 640p   BL: NN.15566

Although only a few pages relate directly to football,
this is one of the most oft-quoted non-football novels. Mr. Oakroyd walking down the Manchester Road
after watching Bruddersford United presents an
evocative, albeit idealised, portrait of supportership
in the early part of the century.

Pudney, John Sleigh

86   Shuffley Wanderers: an entertainment. London: Bodley
Head, 1948.
224p   BL: NN.39333

Saye, Charles

87   The footballer. London: New English Library, 1970.
128p   SBN: 450-006417
BL: W.715

Sheridan, Philip

88   Johnny on the spot. London: MacGibbon & Kee, 1965.
288p   BL: Nov.6911

Simons, Eric N.

89   The whistle blew: a football final. London?: Laurie, 1951.
255p

Stein, Mel

90   Danger zone. London: Fontana, 1980.
318p; pbk   ISBN: 0-00-615638-X
BL: H.81/57

Stretford Athletic and Thamesmead United meet in
a championship decider accompanied by murder, rape,
drugs and other staples of the football diet.

Venables, Terry   See   Williams, Gordon Maclean & Terry Venables

Verner, Gerald

91   The Football Pool murders. London: Wright & Brown,
1939.
284p   BL: NN.30667

One of a number of mystery novels taking the Pools
as its central theme.

Williams, Gordon Maclean & Terry Venables

92   They used to play on grass. London: Hodder and
Stoughton, 1971.
254p   ISBN: 0-340-15651-1
BL: Nov.17261

A futuristic tale of artificial pitches, players earning
£200 a week and managers under constant pressure
to deliver. . . . The book is more eagerly sought by collectors now that Venables is England manager – it is
regarded as something of a curiosity.

Yablonsky, Yabo

93   Escape to victory / based on a screenplay by Evan Jones
     and Yabo Yablonsky from a story by Yabo Yablonsky
     and Djordje Milicevic & Jeff Maguire. London: Severn
     House, 1981.
     164p
     ISBN: 0-7278-0742-0
     BL: Nov.44425

     The novelisation of one of the best known football
     films.

Young, Francis Brett

94   The black diamond. London: Collins, 1921.
     396p
     BL: NN.6863

     'The football season had opened with a flourish as far
     as Mawne United were concerned. In the North Brom-
     wich League they had beaten all their principal rivals:
     Wolverbury, Dulston and even the Albion Reserves. . .'
     – includes a number of well written football passages.

✽ *Teenage Novels*

Allen, Richard

95   Skinhead. London: New English Library, 1970.
     127p
     ISBN: 0-450-00556-9
     BL: W.597

     When this book was published the skinhead was a fa-
     miliar sight at football grounds throughout the
     country and trouble was never far away. Richard Al-
     len's novels are amongst the few which deal with this
     element of society.

96   Skinhead escapes. London: New English Library, 1972.
     125p
     ISBN: 0-450-01253-0
     BL: H.72/760

97   Skinhead farewell. London: New English Library, 1974.
     128p
     ISBN: 0-450-01975-6
     BL: H.74/737

98   Skinhead girls. London: New English Library, 1972.
     127p
     ISBN: 0-450-01295-6
     BL: H.72/1022

     Skinhead girls were not an unfamiliar sight at football
     matches at this time. These aggressively turned-out
     teenagers will now be pushing forty – how times
     change! Richard Allen presents an enlightening snap-
     shot.

99   Suedehead. London: New English Library, 1971.
     110p
     ISBN: 0-450-00954-8
     BL: H.71/641

100 Trouble for skinhead. London: New English Library,
     1973.
     125p
     ISBN: 0-450-01419-3
     BL: H.73/319

Black, Peter

101 The boy who bossed the town. London: Gerald G.
     Swan, 1947.
     35p
     (Football pocket library)
     BL: W.P.1624/2

Burrage, Edwin Harcourt

102 Football in Coketown; or, Who shall be captain?
     London: Best for Boys Publishing Co., 1893.
     178p
     (Best for boys library)
     BL: C.140.d.11(4)

Gall, Edward R. H.

103 The football commandos. London: New Arts Publishing
     Guild, 1946.
     80p
     BL: 012643.tt.45

104 The roving Rovers. London: Hennel Locke, 1952.
     189p
     (Boys' sporting fiction library)
     BL: W.P.B.21/1

     '. . . scratch your match with Hanford United or Eddie
     Bell will never play left-half for you again.' Tuffy Tufton
     gets to the bottom of this sinister threat!

Hardcastle, Michael

105 Top of the league. London: Heinemann, 1979.
     95p
     (Pyramid books)
     ISBN: 0-434-95833-6
     BL: X.990/15904

Woods, Whitley

106 The 'Cup of Fortune'. London: Gerald G. Swan, 1947.
     35p
     (Football pocket library)
     BL: W.P.1624/1

✽ *Children's Novels*

Adamson, Jean & Gareth Adamson

107 Topsy and Tim at the football match. London; Glasgow:
     Blackie, 1963.
     27p; illus
     BL: 12844.ee.18

     Rosy-cheeked wonderment from two of the best loved
     children's characters; includes some colourful illus-
     trations.

Adrian, Alec

108 The FA Cup comes west / illustrated by Geoffrey
     Whittam. Ilfracombe: Stockwell, 1971.
     31p; illus; pbk
     ISBN: 0-7223-0208-8

109　He wore a red jersey / illustrated by Geoffrey Whittam.
　　Ilfracombe: Stockwell, 1975.
　　40p; illus; pbk　　　　　　　ISBN: 0-7223-0809-4
　　　　　　　　　　　　　　　　　　BL: X.907/25054

Ahlberg, Allan

110　The great marathon football match / pictures by Janet
　　Ahlberg. Glasgow: Collins, 1976.
　　32p; illus
　　(Brick Street boys)　　　　　ISBN: 0-00-138058-3
　　　　　　　　　　　　　　　　　　BL: X.990/8394

Ahmed, Shasta

111　The elephant who wanted to play football / illustrated by
　　Mark Southgate. London: Blackie, 1989.
　　20p; illus　　　　　　　　　　ISBN: 0-216-92571-1
　　　　　　　　　　　　　　　　　　BL: YK.1989.a.3768

The Elephant who wanted to Play Football

Shahsta Ahmed
Illustrated by Mark Southgate

Blackie

Awdry, Christopher & Ken Stott

112　Edward plays football. London: Heinemann, 1991.
　　22p; illus
　　(Thomas the Tank Engine board books)
　　　　　　　　　　　　　　　　ISBN: 0-434-97621-0
　　　　　　　　　　　　　　　　　　BL: YK.1991.a.4544

Childs, Rob

113　The big day / illustrated by Tim Marwood. London:
　　Young Corgi, 1990.
　　96p; illus; pbk　　　　　　　ISBN: 0-552-52581-2

114　The big goal / illustrated by Tim Marwood. London:
　　Young Corgi, 1993.
　　79p; pbk　　　　　　　　　　ISBN: 0-552-52760-2
　　　　　　　　　　　　　　　　　　BL: YK.1994.a.10522

115　The big kick / illustrated by Tim Marwood. London:
　　Young Corgi, 1991.
　　79p; pbk　　　　　　　　　　ISBN: 0-552-52663-0
　　　　　　　　　　　　　　　　　　BL: YK.1991.a.10053

116　The big match / illustrated by Tim Marwood. London:
　　Young Corgi, 1987.
　　96p; pbk　　　　　　　　　　ISBN: 0-552-52451-4
　　　　　　　　　　　　　　　　　　BL: YK.1988.a.3378

117　Sandford on tour. London: Blackie, 1983.
　　112p　　　　　　　　　　　　ISBN: 0-216-91409-4
　　　　　　　　　　　　　　　　　　BL: X.990/20483

118　Soccer at Sandford. London: Blackie, 1980.
　　95p　　　　　　　　　　　　ISBN: 0-216-90890-6
　　　　　　　　　　　　　　　　　　BL: X.629/13008

Drake, Alan

119　Muddy the football / illustrated by Gordon Stowell.
　　London: University of London, 1963.
　　48p; illus; pbk
　　(Dolphin books; no. D7)　　　BL: W.P.4606/43

French, Vivian

120　Warren and the flying football / illustrated by Chris
　　Fisher. London: Young Lions, 1994.
　　63p; illus; pbk
　　(Staple Street pets)　　　　　ISBN: 0-00-674890-2
　　　　　　　　　　　　　　　　　　BL: YK.1994.a.17819

Gard, Elizabeth

121　Billy Boot's brainwave / illustrated by David Mostyn.
　　London: Beaver, 1982.
　　125p; illus; pbk　　　　　　　ISBN: 0-600-20490-1
　　　　　　　　　　　　　　　　　　BL: X.990/19133

Gora, Felix　See　Parma, Clemens & Felix Gora

Groves, Paul & Martin Pitts

122　The magic football. London: Edward Arnold, 1983.
　　32p; illus; pbk
　　(Winners)　　　　　　　　　ISBN: 0-7131-0876-2
　　　　　　　　　　　　　　　　　　BL: X.990/21473

Hardcastle, Michael

123 Attack!: a Mark Fox story. London: Fontana, 1982.
111p; pbk
(Mark Fox books; no.7)
    ISBN: 0-00-691758-5
    BL: X.990/18548

 Michael Hardcastle specialises in novels for children and is one of the most prolific writers of this genre. Mark Fox is his central character.

124 The away team. London: Methuen Children's, 1992.
121p
    ISBN: 0-416-15082-9
    BL: YK.1992.a.1779

125 Behind the goal. London: Pelham, 1980.
120p
    ISBN: 0-7207-1252-1
    BL: X.992/4020

126 Breakaway: a Mark Fox story. London: Armada, 1976.
125p; pbk
(Mark Fox books; no. 2)
    ISBN: 0-00-690955-8
    BL: H.79/1789

127 The first goal: a Mark Fox story. London: Armada, 1976.
127p; pbk
(Mark Fox books; no. 1)
    ISBN: 0-00-690954-X
    BL: H.79/1788

128 Free kick / illustrated by Trevor Stubley. London: Methuen Children's, 1974.
126p; illus; pbk
    ISBN: 0-416-79880-2
    BL: H.82/1009

129 Goal! / illustrated by James Hunt. London: Heinemann, 1969.
iv, 104p; illus
    ISBN: 0-434-94233-2

130 Goal in Europe: a Mark Fox story. London: Armada, 1978.
127p; pbk
(Mark Fox books; no. 5)
    ISBN: 0-00-691362-8
    BL: H.78/1040

131 Goalie / David Clark (pseud.); illustrated by Richard Kennedy. London: Benn, 1972.
31p; illus
(Inner ring sports)
    ISBN: 0-510-07835-4

132 Goals in the air. London: Heinemann, 1972.
96p
(Pyramid books)
    ISBN: 0-434-95794-1
    BL: X.998/3065

133 Half a team / illustrated by Trevor Stubley. London: Methuen Children's, 1980.
108p; illus
(Pied Piper books)
    ISBN: 0-416-87740-0
    BL: 12847.aa.3(62)

134 In the net / illustrated by Trevor Stubley. London: Methuen, 1971.
123p; illus; pbk
(Pied Piper books)
    ISBN: 0-416-66520-9
    BL: H.82/1005

135 Joanna's goal / illustrated by Elizabeth Haines. Glasgow: Blackie, 1990.
48p; illus
    ISBN: 0-216-92923-7
    BL: YK.1991.a.2341

136 Kick off: a Mark Fox story. London: Armada, 1981.
128p; pbk
(Mark Fox books; no. 6)
    ISBN: 0-00-691757-7
    BL: YK.1986.a.738

137 Mark England's cap / illustrated by Margaret de Souza. London: Heinemann, 1990.
62p
(A superchamp book)
    ISBN: 0-434-93065-2
    BL: YK.1992.a.1765

138 Mascot. London: Methuen Children's, 1987.
108p; illus
(Pied Piper books)
    ISBN: 0-416-00392-3
    BL: YK.1987.a.7450

139 Mascot. London: Mammoth, 1992.
345p; pbk
   Contents: Team that wouldn't give in; Soccer special
    ISBN: 0-7497-1317-8
    BL: YK.1993.a.1866

140 No defence. London: Deutsch, 1986.
160p; pbk
(Adlib paperbacks)
    ISBN: 0-233-97912-3
    BL: YC.1986.a.5549

141 On the ball: a Mark Fox story. London: Armada Books, 1977.
125p; pbk
(Mark Fox books; no. 3)
    ISBN: 0-00-691151-X
    BL: X.619/17862

142 One kick. London: Faber, 1986.
132p
    ISBN: 0-571-13775-X
    BL: YK.1986.a.20

143 Own goal / illustrated by Caroline Binch. London: Faber and Faber, 1992.
73p; illus
    ISBN: 0-571-16411-0
    BL: YK.1993.a.4740

144 Shoot on sight. London: Heinemann, 1967.
154p
    BL: Nov.9726

145 Shooting star: a Mark Fox story. London: Armada Books, 1977.
127p; pbk
(Mark Fox books; no. 4)
    ISBN: 0-00-691152-8
    BL: X.619/17863

146 Soccer captain. London: Orion Children's Books, 1994.
86p; illus
ISBN: 1-85881-060-4
BL: Nov. 1994/1334

147 Soccer is also a game. London: Heinemann, 1966.
153p

Subsequently reissued as: Soccer comes first. London: Dragon Books, 1971   BL: Nov.8120

148 Soccer special / illustrated by Paul Wright. London: Methuen, 1978.
128p; illus
(Pied Piper books)
ISBN: 0-416-56460-7
BL: 12847.aa.3/48

149 Soccer star / illustrated by Lis Toft. London: Heinemann, 1993.
42p; illus
(Banana books)
ISBN: 0-434-97688-1
BL: YK.1994.a.9586

150 The team that wouldn't give in. London: Methuen Children's, 1984.
110p; illus
(Pied Piper books)
ISBN: 0-416-23450-X
BL: X.990/21756

151 United! / illustrated by Trevor Stubley. London: Methuen Children's, 1973.
141p; illus; pbk
(Pied Piper books)
ISBN: 0-416-76390-1
BL: H.82/1008

Him, George *See Lewitt, Jan & George Him*

Lambert, Thelma

152 No football for Sam. London: Hamish Hamilton, 1991.
30p; pbk
ISBN: 0-241-12928-1
BL: YK.1991.a.592

Leslie, Stephen

153 Action football / illustrated by Robert Bond. London: Transworld, 1977.
88p; chiefly illus; pbk
(A tracker action book)
ISBN: 0-552-56008-1

Lewitt, Jan & George Him

154 The football's revolt / pictures and words by Lewitt-Him. London: Country Life, 1939.
26p; illus

Reissued London: Sylvan Press, Nicholson & Watson, 1944
BL: 012331.p.3 • BL: 12823.d.48

An unusual book. One of a few books with a football theme which is regarded as collectable by non-football enthusiasts. Sought after for its illustrations, it rarely appears on dealers' lists.

Lloyd, Andy

155 First team at football / illustrated by Mike Francis. London: Dragon, 1985.
91p; illus; pbk
ISBN: 0-583-30825-2
BL: X.990/25533

McCuaig, Ron

156 Tobolino and the amazing football boots / illustrated by Lee Whitmore. London: Angus and Robertson, 1974.
96p; illus
ISBN: 0-207-12886-3

McFall, Beth

157 Football / illustrations by Beth McFall. London: Collins Colour Cubs, 1987.
32p; illus; pbk
(Wil Cwac Cwac)
ISBN: 0-00-196151-9
BL: YK.1987.a.2428

Newell, Mary

158 Farmer Parsnip football trainer / illustrated by David Pearson. London: Hippo Books, 1982.
24p; illus; pbk
ISBN: 0-590-70100-2
BL: X.990/19696

Parkinson, Michael

159 The Woofits play football. London: Collins, 1980.
48p; illus; pbk
ISBN: 0-00-123528-1
BL: X.990/16259

Parma, Clemens & Felix Gora

160 Tom, the football hero / translated by Percy Marshall. London: Dobson, 1969.
30p; illus

Originally published: München: Parabel Verlag, 1968
ISBN: 0-234-77226-3

Pitts, Martin *See Groves, Paul & Martin Pitts*

Prior, Ted

161 Grug plays soccer. London: Hodder and Stoughton, 1985.
32p; illus; pbk
ISBN: 0-340-37607-4
BL: YK.1987.a.2115

Sibley, Kathleen

162 Adam and football / illustrated by F. D. Phillips. London: Dobson, 1972.
101p; illus
ISBN: 0-234-77621-8

163 Adam and the FA Cup / illustrated by Douglas Phillips. London: Dobson, 1975.
96p; illus
ISBN: 0-234-77365-0
BL: X.990/7886

164 Adam and the football mystery / illustrated by Douglas Phillips. London: Dobson, 1979.
109p; illus

ISBN: 0-234-72159-6
BL: X.990/15867

Smee, Nicola See Wilmer, Diane & Nicola Smee

Smith, Bryan

165 The day they stole the FA Cup. London: Blackie, 1982.
95p

ISBN: 0-216-91185-0
BL: X.990/19912

Based on a true incident: between the hours of 9.30p.m. on Wednesday 11th September and 7.30a.m. on Thursday 12th September 1895, the cup was stolen from the shop window of William Shillcock in Birmingham. It was never recovered.

£10 REWARD.

———

STOLEN!

From the Shop Window of W. Shillcock, Football Outfitter, Newtown Row, Birmingham, between the hour of 9-30 p.m. on Wednesday, the 11th September, and 7-30 a.m., on Thursday, the 12th inst., the

ENGLISH CUP,

the property of Aston Villa F.C. The premises were broken into between the hours named, and the Cup, together with cash in drawer, stolen.

The above Reward will be paid for the recovery of the Cup, or for information as may lead to the conviction of the thieves.

Information to be given to the Chief of Police, or to Mr. W. Shillcock, 73, Newtown Row.

Stops, Sue

166 Dulcie Dando / illustrated by Gliori Debi. London: Hippo, 1992.
28p; illus; pbk

ISBN: 0-590-55128-0
BL: YK.1993.b.1217

Stott, Ken See Awdry, Christopher & Ken Stott

Taylor, William

167 The worst soccer team ever. London: Puffin, 1989.
141p; pbk

ISBN: 0-14-034002-5
BL: H.90/1040

Waddell, Martin

168 Napper goes for goal / illustrated by Barrie Mitchell. Harmondsworth: Puffin, 1981.
103p; illus; pbk

ISBN: 0-14-031318-4
BL: X.990/24802

169 Napper strikes again / illustrated by Barrie Mitchell. Harmondsworth: Puffin, 1981.
112p; illus; pbk

ISBN: 0-14-031319-2
BL: X.990/18166

170 Napper super-sub / illustrated by Richard Berridge. London: Puffin, 1993.
175p; pbk

ISBN: 0-14-036040-9
BL: H.93/3116

171 Napper's big match. Harmondsworth: Puffin, 1993.
144p; illus; pbk

ISBN: 0-14-036039-5

172 Napper's golden goals / illustrated by Barrie Mitchell. Harmondsworth: Puffin, 1984.
150p; illus; pbk

ISBN: 0-14-031638-8
BL: X.990/24306

173 Napper's luck / illustrated by Michael Strand. London: Puffin, 1993.
175p; pbk

ISBN: 0-14-036041-7
BL: H.94/2485

Walt Disney Productions

174 Scrooge McDuck and the football field. Maidenhead: Purnell, 1979.
1 folded leaf; illus

> *Cover title: Walt Disney's Scrooge McDuck and the football field. — Leaf folded and cut to create three dimensional effect; six pictures in all*

ISBN: 0-361-04487-9

Wilmer, Diane & Nicola Smee

175 Benny and the football match. London: Collins Colour Cubs, 1986.
32p; illus; pbk

ISBN: 0-00-123823-X
BL: YK.1986.a.290

Wilson, Bob

176 Stanley Bagshaw and the short-sighted football trainer. London: Hamish Hamilton, 1986.
31p; illus

ISBN: 0-241-11783-6
BL: YK.1989.b.3556

Wright, Geoff

177   Charlie-Not-So-Good plays football. Bedford:
F. Coleman, 1984.
28p; illus; pbk   ISBN: 0-948103-00-0

❊ *Anonymous Works*

178   Moschops plays football. Bristol; Purnell, 1983.
24p; illus; pbk
(Moschops TV series)   ISBN: 0-361-05952-3
                                  BL: X.990/22268

Poetry

❊ *Single Author Collections*

Bateman, Fred

179   Captain Jack: a football story. Bilston: Orchard Press,
1904.   BL: 11603.aa.27(5)

*Many early examples of football verse exist in the
boy's papers of the time, but few were published in
their own right. This is a rare early example.*

Bold, Alan

180   Scotland, yes: World Cup football poems. Edinburgh: P.
Harris, 1978.
80p; illus
     ISBN: 0-904505-45-6 (cased) • ISBN: 0-904505-46-4 (pbk)
                                BL: X.619/18537

*The World Cup can be an inspirational force; this un-
usual poetry collection presents a celebration of the
experience from Scotland's viewpoint.*

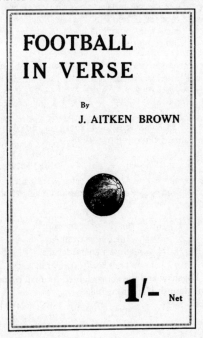

FOOTBALL
IN VERSE

By
J. AITKEN BROWN

1/- Net

Brown, J. Aitken

181   Football in verse. Edinburgh: Bishop, 1923.
44p   BL: 011645.e.59

Brown, W. J.

182   Football heroes: dedicated to the Queen's Park Rangers.
London: J. S. Carte, 1910.
1 sheet   BL: 1879.c.12(50)

     ☞   Also listed at: B669

Concanen, Matthew The Elder

183   A match at foot-ball: a poem, in three cantos. Dublin;
The Author, 1720.
42p

     The dedication signed: M. C., i.e. Matthew Concanen
     Reprinted as: A match at foot-ball, or, The Irish champions:
     a mock-heroic poem, in three cantos. London, 1721
                                BL: 1508/518
                               BL: 1078.h.12(1)

184   Poems upon several occasions. Dublin: E. Dobson, 1722.
xx, 99p   BL: 11632.bb.13

*Written well before the Football Association was
formed in 1863, this work contains poetry alluding to
football in its pre-organised days.*

Eachus, Samuel Henry

185   At the football match: a wreath of lyrical poems and
songs / Samuel Henry Eachus. Wolverhampton &
London: Steen, 1910.
ix, 42p; pbk   BL: 011650.eee.29(9)

Hall, Martin

186   Stan Cullis blues. Charisma Books, 1974.
96p; illus; pbk   ISBN: 0-85947-001-6

*Of interest to Wolverhampton Wanderers and Bir-
mingham City followers, if only for the title poem.
Cullis managed both clubs and played for Wolves from
1934. Included in this poetry tribute to soccer are*

the following lines on the man himself –

> 'The night Stan Cullis got the sack,
> Wolverhampton wandered round in circles,
> Like a disallowed goal,
> Looking for a friendly linesman'

Horovitz, Michael

187 The Wolverhampton wanderer: an epic of Britannia in
twelve books with a Resurrection & a Life / Michael
Horovitz; with illustrations by Peter Blake and others.
London: Latimer New Dimensions Ltd for Poetry
United, 1971.
v-xvii, 123p; illus   ISBN: 0-901539-15-5

An unusual item much sought after by non-football
book lovers for its poetry and accompanying illustrations, including some by David Hockney. Wolves are
included visually and in some of the poems which are
not exclusively football related.

Magee, Wes

188 The football replays. Higham Ferrers: Greylag, 1980.
8p   BL: X.909/45016

Toshack, John

189 Gosh it's Tosh / foreword by Kevin Keegan; preface by
John Keith; photography by Harry Ormesher. London:
Duckworth, 1976.
95p; illus
ISBN: 0-7156-1197-6 (cased) • ISBN: 0-7156-1198-4 (pbk)
                                        BL: Cup.1281/449

Unusual example of a member of the playing fraternity turning his hand to something more lyrical.

✳ Anthologies

190 Here we go: a poetry celebration of soccer. Blackburn:
BB Books, 1986?
42p; illus; pbk   BL: YC.1988.a.6176

A small anthology of poetry examples. This could lead
on to greater things – there are a sufficient number
of football poems to warrant a much heavier tome
than this.

191 The poetry of motion: an anthology of sporting verse /
edited by Alan Bold. Edinburgh: Mainstream, 1986?
201p; index   ISBN: 0-906391-70-9
                                        BL: YC.1987.a.2801

This Edinburgh born poet and journalist has done a
fine service here in bringing together numerous examples of sporting poetry – there are some delightful
and surprising football examples including those by
Ted Hughes and Michael Horovitz. Subjects include

Stanley Matthews, Hackney Marshes, England's
World Cup triumph of 1966, Kenny Dalglish, and the
'great wee Scotsman' Archie Gemmill. Much more besides.

192 The racing driver, the jockey, the footballer, the diver.
Knutsford: Stafford Pemberton, 1982.
8p; chiefly illus; unbound

193 Remember Hillsborough / Chris Searle and Steve Chew,
editors. Runcorn: Archive Publications in association
with Sheffield City Council Education Department; The
Sheffield Star, 1990.
93p; illus   ISBN: 0-948946-76-8
                                        BL: YA.1990.b.4634

The Hillsborough Disaster of 15 April 1989 inspired
many letters and tributes, many penned in verse.
Children, in particular, were encouraged by their
schools to express their emotions towards this most
tragic event. This is a poignant collection of the children's own poetry – it will ensure that the day is
indeed never forgotten.

194 The rising sons of ranting verse / Seething Wells ;
Cautionary tales for dead commuters / Attila the
Stockbroker. London: Unwin Paperbacks, 1985.
80, 48p; chiefly illus; pbk

Bound tête-bêche
Attila the Stockbroker's real name is John Charles Baine
                                      ISBN: 0-04-821057-9
                                        BL: X.958/32843

A most unusual treatment, reviewed by Steve Redhead in 'Football with attitude' as: '. . . anarchic fun;
seeks to create an underground and counter-culture
sense of soccer's "cerebral orgasm", evoking joyous
satires on Albanian football and the soccer predilec-
tions of Sun readers'.

195 Verses united: the poetry of football / edited by Ian
Horn; illustrated by Robert Nancollis. Durham: County
Durham Books, 1993.
77p; illus; pbk   ISBN: 1-897585-06-3

196 'Ere we go! / David Orme, Ian Blackman and Marc
Vyvyan-Jones. London: Piper, 1993.
63p; pbk   ISBN: 0-330-32986-3
                                        BL: YK.1994.a.5046

David Orme, Stoke City supporter and editor of the
Schools' Poetry Review, here chooses a varied and unusual selection –

> '"That's funny," said the worm,
>   As it went under Wembley,
>   "I wonder why the ground's
> So loud and trembly."' – Tony Mitton

Plays

❋ Published Playscripts

Andrews, W. H. & Geoffrey Dearmer

197 The referee: a football farce in one act. London: Deane, 1931.
23p; pbk
(YBP series of plays)   BL: W.P.2236/26

Surely this doesn't suggest that referees and farce are in any way related? This is the one act version – many epic counterparts remain unrecorded!

Ayckbourn, Alan

198 Time and time again: a comedy. London: French, 1973.
iii, 67p; 1 plan; pbk

Cast comprises 3 men & 2 women   ISBN: 0-573-01457-4

Clifton, Myles

199 The football club supper: a sketch in one act. London: French, 1929.
17p; pbk

Published in the same volume as: The 'ole in the road / 'Seamark', pseud.   BL: 11791.t.1/154

Courtenay, Sydney See Harvey, Lola & Sydney Courtenay

Dearmer, Geoffrey See Andrews, W. H. & Geoffrey Dearmer

England, Chris See Smith, Arthur & Chris England

Forsyth, Bill

200 Gregory's girl: an adaptation of Bill Forsyth's original film script / Andrew Bethell. Cambridge: Cambridge University Press, 1983.
72p; illus; pbk
(Act now)

Cast comprises 23 men & 16 women
                              ISBN: 0-521-27106-1
                              BL: X.950/21808

This is the acting version of the well-known film about a talented schoolgirl footballer and the boy who worships her from afar. Popular production for school drama classes.

☞ See also: I214

Harvey, Lola & Sydney Courtenay

201 Bill's football prize: a five minute sketch. London: Cavendish Music, 1929.
4p   BL: 11778.h.27

Little known early example on a football theme.

Holman, David

202 Football apprentices. Cambridge: Cambridge University Press, 1982.
87p; 2 plans; pbk
(Act now)

Cast comprises 1 woman & 15 men
                              ISBN: 0-521-28567-4

Nicholls, Derek & Ray Speakman

203 The play of The goalkeeper's revenge / Derek Nicholls and Ray Speakman from the writings of Bill Naughton. London: Heinemann, 1983.
90p; pbk   ISBN: 0-435-23724-1
                                      BL: X.958/19538

☞ See also: I11

Pinter, Harold

204 The dumb waiter: a play in one act. London: French, 1960.
33p; pbk

Cast comprises 2 men   BL: 11791.t.1/1459

'I saw the Villa get beat in a cup tie once . . .' A number of amusing football exchanges occur between Gus and Ben, most notably the short 'Playing Away' sequence.

205 A night out: a play. London: French, 1961.
52p; pbk

Cast comprises 2 men & 1 woman   BL: 11791.t.1/1480

Includes a number of football related vignettes.

Rosenthal, Jack

206 Another Sunday and sweet F A

Published as pages 241-299 in The television dramatist / Robert Muller. London: Payl Elek, 1973. ISBN: 0-236-15470-2   BL: X.989/22699

The play relates to Works League Sunday morning football in Manchester.

Smith, Arthur & Chris England

207 An evening with Gary Lineker. London: Warner
Chappell, 1992.
135p

> *Published in the same volume as: Trench kiss / Arthur Smith*
> ISBN: 0-85676-129-X
> BL: YK.1994.a.12796

Football's most widely known stage performance re-
writes the script on England's 1990 World Cup exit in
Italy when they lost out to the Germans in a semifinal penalty shoot-out. A humorous treatment of a
painful event throws considerable light on the essence of fandom from both the male and female
perspective.

*Speakman, Ray See Nicholls, Derek & Ray
Speakman*

Terson, Peter

208 Zigger Zagger. Harmondsworth: Penguin, 1970.
188p; music

> *Published in the same volume as: Mooney and his caravans*
> ISBN: 0-14-045009-2
> BL: X.908/19939 • BL: X.908/19940

Of the two plays in this publication, Zigger Zagger
deals with the football theme. First performed by the
National Youth Theatre in 1967, it relates to the
problems of football hooliganism and youth culture in
a performance described variously as 'funny' and
'alarming'. Zigger Zagger was a well-known football
chant at the time – I particularly recall 'Zigger Zagger, Zigger Zagger, Kevin Hector' ringing out at
Derby's Baseball Ground. Football supportership has
changed significantly since then, but Terson's play
still contains much of relevance.

Win, C.

209 Football fun: revue sketchlet. London: C. A.
Fitzmaurice, 1955.
7p

> *Reproduced from typewriting*
> BL: 11785.f.3

* *Unpublished Playscripts*

Hurt, Paul

210 Big time. 1990?

> Described as an explosive mixture of racism and foot-
> ball, hilarious and irreverent, bawdy and brutal.
> Effectively an observation of the non-league playing
> scene and its idiosyncrasies.

Mercier, Paul

211 Studs. 1993.

> Originally performed by the Passion Machine Theatre
> Company in Dublin, this play studies the plight of
> Dublin soccer team Emmet Rovers, whose fortunes
> are catapulted from obscurity to big time by the arri-
> val of an inspired stranger.

Williamson, David

212 Wearing colours. 1985.

> This is a one hour drama based on the 1985 Euro-
> pean Cup Final between Liverpool and Juventus, scene
> of the horrific Heysel Stadium tragedy. The author
> states that it was written 'specifically to counter
> the seemingly concerted efforts by government and
> media to pillory not only Liverpool supporters in par-
> ticular but football supporters generally'. The play
> toured fringe theatres and in 1993 was made avail-
> able on video.

213 The Celtic story 1888-1988. Wildcat Theatre, 1988.

> One of very few stage portrayals of the history of a
> specific club. Illustrates the potential, perhaps, for
> local writers and theatre groups to perform workshop
> style pieces on the folk history of football and their
> home town clubs.

Filmscripts

Forsyth, Bill

214 Gregory's girl: the filmscript / edited by Paul Kelley.
Cambridge: Cambridge University Press, 1991.
112p; pbk
ISBN: 0-521-38838-4
BL: YK.1991.a.4705

Highly acclaimed film classic about a footballing
schoolgirl and the lanky lad whose passions are
aroused by her winning ways.

☞ See also: I200

Ballet & Opera

Mason, Benedict & Howard Brenton

215 Playing away. 1994

Playwright Howard Brenton wrote the text for Benedict Mason's first opera, world premiered in Munich during 1994. This most unusual treatment of football on the stage centres on the European Cup Final, with 'United' playing in Munich and star player Terry Bond keeping pace with wife Lola and girlfriend Cynthia, both there to witness the final drama. Described as a vicious travesty of the Faust legend, it observes the general football scene, its stars, officials, hooligans and wheeler-dealers.

Oransky, V. & Igor Moiseyev

216 The footballer. 1930.

Most unusual treatment of football in the form of a humorous satirical ballet; the score is by Oransky and choreography by Moiseyev.

Shostakovich, Dmitri

217 Golden age. 1930.

Shostakovich composed this football ballet with choreography by Semyon Kaplan and Vasily Vainonen. The plot traces the conflict between Fascists and a Soviet football team on tour in the West. The climax is a dance by the footballers and the capitalist workers united in celebrating the joys of work. Surely one of the most unusual stage portrayals of the game.

Essays & Reminiscences

✳ *Single Author Works*

Croall, Jonathan

218 Don't shoot the goalkeeper. London: Oxford University Press, 1976.
2, 66p; illus; pbk
(Standpoints)
Bibliography: p65　　　　　　ISBN: 0-19-913232-1
　　　　　　　　　　　　　　　　BL: X.619/16747

Essays on various elements of football.

Glanville, Brian Lester

219 People in sport. London: Secker & Warburg, 1967.
255p　　　　　　　　　　　　　　BL: X.449/2621

Hattersley, Roy

220 Goodbye to Yorkshire. London: Gollancz, 1976.
163p; illus, 1 map (on lining papers); index
　　　　　　　　　　　　ISBN: 0-575-02201-9
　　　　　　　　　　　　　　　BL: X.800/25729

Roy Hattersley, politician and journalist, is well known for his allegiance to Sheffield Wednesday. Each of his publications listed here contains football material.

221 Politics apart: a selection of 'Listener' endpieces. London: BBC, 1982.
184p　　　　　　　　　　　ISBN: 0-563-20058-8
　　　　　　　　　　　　　　　BL: X.950/15621

222 A Yorkshire boyhood. London: Chatto & Windus, 1983.
215p; illus　　　　　　　　ISBN: 0-7011-2613-2
　　　　　　　　　　　　　　　BL: X.809/56384

Jones, Lawrence Evelyn

223 I forgot to tell you. London: Rupert Hart-Davis, 1959.
234p　　　　　　　　　　　　　BL: 010608.f.4

Includes some extended football passages.

Lawrence, T. E.

224 The mint: a day-book of the RAF depot between August and December 1922 / with later notes by 352087 A/c Ross. Unexpurgated text. London: Cape, 1955.
206p　　　　　　　　　　　　　BL: X.708/21326

It is rare for the great authors to include football observations in their works. Here Lawrence includes a delightful passage in which the progress of an amateur football game is lyrically described.

Legge, Gordon

225   In between talking about the football. Edinburgh:
      Polygon, 1991.
      144p; pbk
                                    ISBN: 0-7486-6112-3
                                         BL: H.91/3791

Macadam, John

226   The Macadam road. London: Jarrolds, 1955.
      192p; illus
                                         BL: 7921.e.125
      Reminiscences of this distinguished sports journalist
      include much on soccer.

McIlvanney, Hugh

227   McIlvanney on football. Edinburgh: Mainstream, 1994.
      283p; illus
                                    ISBN: 1-85158-661-X

Mallalieu, Joseph Percival William

228   Sporting days. London: Phoenix Sports Books, 1955.
      190p
                                         BL: 7919.bb.52
      Includes some excellent football references; the
      author was MP for Huddersfield and includes Hud-
      dersfield Town in his keenly observed pieces.

Miller, David

229   Sports writer's eye: an anthology. London: Queen Anne,
      1989.
      vii, 278p; pbk

          Title on spine: Sportswriter's eye   ISBN: 0-356-17652-5
                                         BL: YK.1990.a.800
      A collection of the author's own writings, mainly on
      football.

Nabokov, Vladimir Vladimirovich

230   Speak, memory: a memoir. London: Gollancz, 1951.
      237p
                                         BL: 10796.bb.16
      'Of the games I played at Cambridge soccer has re-
      mained a windswept clearing in the middle of a rather
      muddled period. I was crazy about goalkeeping.'

Shearwood, Kenneth Arthur

231   Whistle the wind / illustrated by A. I. Ingram. London:
      Rupert Hart-Davis, 1959.
      188p
                                         BL: 10864.g.86
      The author was centre half during the 1950s for
      Pegasus, the famous Oxford and Cambridge side. In-
      cludes observations on Oxford University football and
      a delightful piece on Mevagissey, for whom the author
      played in the Junior Football League of Cornwall.

Theroux, Paul

232   The kingdom by the sea: a journey around the coast of
      Great Britain. London: H. Hamilton, 1983.
      303p; maps
                                    ISBN: 0-241-11086-6
                                         BL: X.800/37113
      In this excellent book the American author travels
      around the coast of Britain on foot and by train. On
      page 9, on the 11.33 to Margate, he encounters 'The
      Skinheads'. The book is included here for the graphic
      description of their antics, which the author found
      both repugnant and utterly confusing. While he does
      not specify that they are of the football variety, soccer
      followers will certainly recognise the distinctive type.
      There is no specific football content beyond this.

233   The old Patagonian express: by train through the
      Americas. London: H. Hamilton, 1979.
      9, 340p; maps (on lining papers)   ISBN: 0-241-10285-5
                                         BL: X.981/21866
      This chronicles another of Theroux's odysseys by
      train, included here for his observations in San Salva-
      dor where he witnesses the clash of El Salvador and
      Mexico at the National Stadium. Pages 135-142
      chart his astonished and fearful reaction to the bi-
      zarre goings on during a 6-1 win for Mexico. A very
      refreshing piece of football writing – sometimes those
      who know nothing about the game can pinpoint its es-
      sence and expose its difficulties with incisive
      perception. This very graphic piece deserves inclusion
      in any future anthologies of football literature.

✳ *Anthologies*

234   At the end of the day: great writing about Scottish
      football / edited by Alan Taylor. Edinburgh:
      Mainstream, 1995.
      224p; pbk
                                    ISBN: 1-85158-676-8

235   Concerning soccer / John Arlott. London: Longmans,
      Green, 1952.
      ix, 186p; illus
                                         BL: 7921.e.53
      The 'voice of cricket' here observes the winter game. A
      variety of pieces including club studies on Arsenal,
      Bordeaux, Reading, Newcastle United, Blackpool, and
      Manchester United.

236   The Faber book of soccer / edited by Ian Hamilton.
      London: Faber, 1992.
      336p
                                    ISBN: 0-571-14402-0
                                         BL: YK.1992.a.1158
      An essential reference work. Very wide-ranging an-
      thology, including poetry examples.

237   Football classified: an anthology of soccer / edited by
      Willis Hall & Michael Parkinson. London: Luscombe, in
      association with Mitchell Beazley, 1975.
      190p; illus
                                         BL: X.629/7133
      A collection from the works of 30 writers.

238   Football final: selected writings on soccer / edited by Michael Parkinson and Willis Hall; foreword by the Duke of Edinburgh. London: Pelham, 1975.
144p; illus
ISBN: 0-7207-0874-5
BL: X.629/10264

   34 writers are included.

239   Football report: an anthology of soccer / edited by Willis Hall & Michael Parkinson. London: Pelham, 1973.
173p; illus
ISBN: 0-7207-0724-2
BL: X.629/5645

240   The footballer's companion / edited by Brian Glanville. London: Eyre & Spottiswoode, 1962.
543p
BL: 7926.cc.39

   This essential work of reference was the first comprehensive attempt to study the genre of football literature, serious journalistic prose and poetry. Most later anthologies were based very firmly on Glanville's format. Includes a chapter entirely on goalkeepers with a contribution by Albert Camus and a complete section of football poetry. The dust jacket features a painting entitled Chelsea v Spurs at Stamford Bridge by Lawrence Toynbee.

241   The footballer's fireside book / compiled by Terence Delaney. London: Heinemann, 1961.
xvi, 286p; illus
BL: X.449/967

   An excellent anthology which revealed hitherto little known football related literature when it was published. Includes some good poetry and a football report in Latin!

242   The joy of football / edited by Brian Glanville. London: Hodder & Stoughton, 1986.
283p; illus; index
ISBN: 0-340-39439-0
BL: YK.1986.b.681

   Effectively a comprehensive update of the author's earlier 'Footballer's Companion' as Glanville unearths many new pieces in his quest for examples of football literature.

243   The Kingswood book of football / edited by Stephen F. Kelly London: Kingswood, 1992.
xii, 466p; index

   Reissued as: A game of two halves. London: Mandarin, 1993. ISBN: 0-7493-1596-2

ISBN: 0-413-65770-1
BL: YK.1992.b.7373 • BL: YK.1993.a.16750

   Essential reference book for football literature students. A selection of quality writing in chapters entitled 'The Game', 'The Matches', 'The Teams', 'The Players', 'The Managers', 'The Fans', 'The Anguish', 'The Verse'. Particularly poignant pieces are those by Kelly himself on the Heysel Stadium and Hillsborough tragedies, and H. E. Bates on the Manchester United Munich air crash.

244   My favourite year: a collection of new football writing / edited by Nick Hornby. London: Witherby, 1993.
220p

   Published in association with 'When Saturday Comes'

ISBN: 0-85493-236-4
BL: YK.1994.a.81

   13 contributors give their impressions of a particularly memorable season for their preferred teams. Cambridge United and Raith Rovers jostle for space along with a piece on the Republic of Ireland by Roddy Doyle, 1993 Booker Prize Winner.

245   The Observer on soccer: an anthology of the best soccer writing / edited and compiled by Tony Pawson. London: Unwin Hyman, 1989.
256p; illus
ISBN: 0-04-440533-2
BL: YK.1990.b.2574

246   The Saturday men: a book of international football / edited by Leslie Frewin. London: MacDonald, 1967.
288p; illus
BL: X.441/813

   Wide-ranging and comprehensive anthology including over 50 writers.

247   Saturday's boys: the football experience / edited by Harry Lansdown and Alex Spillius London: Collins Willow, 1990.
224p; illus
ISBN: 0-00-218384-6
BL: YK.1991.b.351

   Accounts by writers more usually known for their interests unconnected with football.

248   Sporting literature: an anthology / chosen by Vernon Scannell. Oxford: Oxford University Press, 1987.
320p; index
ISBN: 0-19-212250-9
BL: YC.1987.a.3483

   Chapter 6 is entitled 'The Football War' and includes 23 extracts in 36 pages. Among them is a piece on early football in Wales from the Oswestry Observer of 1887. Includes poetry examples.

249   We'll support you evermore / edited by David Bull. London: Duckworth, 1992.
224p; pbk
ISBN: 0-7156-2447-4
BL: YK.1993.a.16665

   Twenty-four 'ordinary' fans recount their football experiences. John Arlott and Prime Minister John Major are amongst the contributors. The piece by Tessa Davies on 'Women and Football' has been singled out by reviewers as particularly perceptive and relevant.

Religious Tracts

Flower, Mrs Isabel

250   Jack and his master: a football match. Glasgow: Scottish
Temperance League, 1894.
32p; pbk   BL: 4412.g.18 (6)

*Drink and Scottish football were close partners at
the time and, indeed, on one or two occasions since.
But for every action there is inevitably a reaction and
Mrs Isabel Flower evidently held strong views.*

Goodwin, Gradwell Fleming

251   Christ on the football field: an address. London: SPCK,
1913.
16p; pbk   BL: D

*Football was an increasingly popular game at this
time and was inevitably used as a vehicle for the
propagation of Christian doctrine. This association
still persists – many football clubs have their origins
in Church teams and youth club football is a popular
recreation.*

Old Lancing Boy

252   Lessons from association football: being an address to
boys / an Old Lancing Boy. London: Christian
Knowledge Society, 1900.
24p; pbk   BL: Mic.A.9046(7) (microfilm copy)

*It has been said that football mirrors many facets of
society itself. Indeed Sir Walter Scott wrote that 'life
itself is but a game of football'. Here the 'Old Boy of
Lancing' seeks to impart the wisdom of football to his
young charges.*

JACK AND HIS MASTER:

A FOOTBALL MATCH.

BY

MRS. FLOWER, YORK,

AUTHOR OF

*"The Discipline of Alice Lee;" "Wynille Court;" "Tom Allardyce;
"Alick's Christmas Box;" etc., etc.*

GLASGOW:
SCOTTISH TEMPERANCE LEAGUE.
LONDON:
HOULSTON AND SONS, AND NATIONAL TEMPERANCE LEAGUE.
EDINBURGH: JOHN MENZIES AND CO.
1894.

Riddell, Mrs W. E.

253   A bright sunset, or, Recollections of the last days of a
young football player. Second ed. London: Hodder &
Stoughton, 1885.
vi, 142p

With a new titlepage and frontispiece; 1st ed. untraced
BL: 4955.de.28

*This religious tract tells of an accident which befell
sixteen year old William Easton Riddell, a Glasgow
youth.*

Educational Aids & Reading Books

254   Game of life: Uncle Tom's football team / T. J. S.
Rowland. Exeter: A. Wheaton, 1945.
31p; illus; pbk   BL: 7008.bb.6

*This fictional tale represents an unusual early appli-
cation of football as a medium for education. Players'
positions are used to illustrate to children the working of the human body. Researchers not having had
sight of this uncommon item might well speculate at
length what part is played by each member of the
team and whether the football commentator might
be pressed into action in the bodily functions department.*

255   The book of football / illustrated by Kingsley Sutton.
London: Evans, 1950.
64p; illus
(Evans Headway readers series)

256   Know about football / Brian Lester Glanville. London:
Blackie, 1963.
61p   BL: 7926.t.43

☞ Subsequent ed. I259

LIVING THINGS
HAVE
YOUNG ONES

**MR.
REPRODUCE**

**THE
LAST HOPE
OR SAVES
THE GAME**

MR. REPRODUCE, the goalkeeper, may be looked upon as the last hope of the side. When all else fails, it is up to him to save the game. He must be a very strong and reliable player. Living things do not live for ever. Old age and the end comes to all, sooner or later. If the race is to be kept up, young ones must be born to take the place of the parents.

The earliest living things are very tiny one-celled animals. When they reach a certain size they just divide into two, and so you have two creatures. These grow up and divide again. Other simple animals, like sponges, can be chopped up and each piece will grow into a new animal. But when animals become more complex this method is out of the question. You can't cut a kitten into two and make twins. Nature had to find a better method for getting young ones, so she invented the egg. Creatures like insects, spiders, worms, snails, frogs and fish lay hundreds of eggs, which they just leave to hatch out. Birds lay fewer eggs, but larger ones in nice hard shells with rich food inside. The parents keep them warm until the young are hatched. Then they feed them until they grow up. How proud the clucking hen is of her brood of chicks ! Animals that feed their young on milk have so few that they can't afford to lose any. So the mother develops the young ones in her own body until they are ready to be born. After birth she has to feed, protect and teach them how to look after themselves. Plants chiefly grow from seeds. Inside a fertile seed there is a tiny baby plant surrounded by a store of food. The young seedling feeds on this food until roots and leaves can carry on the work. Were you born under a gooseberry bush, or did the stork bring you ?

24

Sample page from 'The Game of Life: Uncle Tom's Football Team' by T. J. S. Rowland

257 Soccer / George Robb. London: Weidenfeld &
     Nicolson, 1964.
     78p; illus
     (Sports for schools)   BL: 7926.r.1/4

258 The story of football / Vera Southgate; with illustrations
     by Jack Matthew. Loughborough: Wills & Hepworth,
     1964.
     50p; illus
     (Ladybird easy reading books)
                    BL: W.P.9629/152 • BL: W.P.9629/155

     This is a particularly good book for young children
     wishing to grasp the essentially serious history of
     the game in an easily digested manner. Its make-up
     follows the format of adult books on the same sub-
     ject, charting the game from its ancient origins to
     modern times. Very cleverly conceived and nicely illus-
     trated.

259 Know about football / Brian Glanville. New ed.,
     reprinted with amendments. London: Blackie, 1970.
     63p; illus   ISBN: 0-216-88355-5

     ☞ Previous ed. I256

260 Reds and blues / Michael Hardcastle; illustrated by
     Richard Kennedy. London: Benn, 1970.
     32p; illus
     (Inner ring books. Second series)   ISBN: 0-510-07740-4

261 Football / text by R. M. Fisher and others; pictures by
     Gareth Floyd. Glasgow: Blackie, 1972.
     12p; chiefly illus; pbk
     (Sparks, stage three (green); 7)   ISBN: 0-216-89268-6

262 The football book / text by David Mackay; pictures by
     Simon Stern. Harlow: Longman for the Schools Council,
     1972.
     16p; illus; pbk
     (Breakthrough continuation readers. Blue set B)
     (Breakthrough to literacy)   ISBN: 0-14-062073-7

263 Les in Brazil / Richard Ward and Thomas Gregory.
     Cheltenham: Hulton Educational, 1973.
     170p; illus; pbk
     (Inswinger series)   ISBN: 0-7175-0619-3

     On occasions the popularity of football is used as a
     medium in education. The Les series of books was de-
     signed to develop reading skills in children. Les
     himself was very much a man of the seventies – some
     of his antics now appear amusingly dated.

264 Les in Europe / Richard Ward and Thomas Gregory.
     Cheltenham: Hulton Educational, 1973.
     138p; illus; pbk
     (Inswinger series)   ISBN: 0-7175-0618-5

265 Les joins United / Richard Ward and Thomas Gregory.
     Cheltenham: Hulton Educational, 1973.
     96p; illus; pbk
     (Inswinger series)   ISBN: 0-7175-0614-2

266 Les loves Betty / Richard Ward and Thomas Gregory.
     Cheltenham: Hulton Educational, 1973.
     124p; illus; pbk
     (Inswinger series)   ISBN: 0-7175-0616-9

267 Les signs on / Richard Ward and Thomas Gregory.
     Cheltenham: Hulton Educational, 1973.
     92p; illus; pbk
     (Inswinger series)   ISBN: 0-7175-0617-7

268 Les's first match / Richard Ward and Thomas Gregory.
     Cheltenham: Hulton Educational, 1973.
     84p; illus; pbk
     (Inswinger series)   ISBN: 0-7175-0615-0

269 Football / Duncan Scott-Forbes; editing and provision
     of additional material by Mike Esplen. London:
     Heinemann Educational, 1974.
     58p; illus, 1 plan; pbk
     (Heinemann guided readers. Intermediate level; 7)
                    ISBN: 0-435-27004-4
                    BL: X.908/29809

270 Investigation into football / Jennifer Curry. Glasgow:
     Blackie, 1974.
     40p; illus; pbk
     (Investigations)   ISBN: 0-216-89741-6

271 Football / Bob Wilson; illustrations by Oxford
     illustrators. Oxford: Blackwell, 1975.
     60p; illus; index
     (Blackwell's learning library; no. 81)
                    ISBN: 0-631-13210-4

272 Peter's football / Shirley D. Sutcliffe; illustrated by John
     Wood. Leeds: E. J. Arnold, 1975.
     24p; chiefly illus; pbk
     (Star family; 7)   ISBN: 0-560-00826-0
                    BL: X.990/7242

273 Football / Ken Wilson. London: Evans, 1976.
     43p; illus; pbk
     (Evans graded reading. Grade 5)   ISBN: 0-237-29122-3

     ☞ Subsequent ed. I276

274 The goalkeeper's revenge and other stories / Bill
     Naughton; retold by Peter Hodson; illustrated by Gareth
     Floyd. London: Heinemann Educational, 1976.
     vi, 42p; illus; pbk   ISBN: 0-435-27038-9
                    BL: X.990/7962

     ☞ See also: I11

275 Football. York: Published for the Nuffield-Chelsea
     Curriculum Trust by Longman Resources Unit, 1977.
     21p; illus; pbk
     (Nuffield working with science source materials for
     CPVE)   ISBN: 0-582-17395-7
                    BL: YK.1988.b.3987

276   Football / Ken Wilson. 2nd ed. London: Evans, 1978.
      43p; illus; pbk
      (Evans graded reading. Grade 5)   ISBN: 0-237-50361-1
      ☞ Previous ed. I273

277   Football flyers / M. Champion. London: Longman, 1978.
      ii, 38p; illus; pbk
      (Ready readers)   ISBN: 0-582-59482-0

278   Football workbook / Paul Farmer and Tony Attwood.
      London: Edward Arnold, 1978.
      80p; illus, maps; index; pbk   ISBN: 0-7131-0283-7
                                                 BL: X.611/8463

279   The football / N. T. Beniston. London: Longman, 1979.
      32p; illus; pbk
      (Living English readers for the Arab world; reader 1)
                                             ISBN: 0-582-76454-8
                                                 BL: X.808/37278

280   Football adventures in England and America / Alec
      Adrian; illustrated by Julian Moore. Ilfracombe:
      Stockwell, 1979.
      51p; illus; pbk   ISBN: 0-7223-1231-8
                                                 BL: X.619/19724

281   Top soccer / Michael Hardcastle. London: Harrap, 1979.
      48p; illus; pbk
      (The reporters series)   ISBN: 0-245-53394-X
                                                 BL: X.629/13009

282   Scottish football / prepared by Job Creation Project
      SCW 778-77 'Production of Geography Teaching
      Materials'; written by J. Murray Allan and others.
      Glasgow: Geography Department, Jordanhill College of
      Education, 1979.
      59 leaves; illus, maps; spiral
      (Resources for geography teachers)

         Cover title : The geography of Scottish football
                                             ISBN: 0-903915-34-0
                                                 BL: X.622/7465

283   Go for goal / Michael Hardcastle; illustrated by Ron
      Sandford. London: Benn, 1980.
      45p; illus; pbk
      (An inner ring hipster: red circle hipsters)
                                             ISBN: 0-510-07762-5
                                                 BL: X.629/13384

284   Johnny Black, footballer / Hendy Smith; illustrated by
      Ian Heard. Exeter: Wheaton, 1981.
      16p; illus; pbk
      (The Johnny Black stories; bk.1)   ISBN: 0-08-024372-X
                                                 BL: X.990/18089

285   Football / John P. Baker. Loughborough: Ladybird,
      1982.
      52p; illus
      (Learnabout)   ISBN: 0-7214-0697-1

286   Football / Simon Freeman; illustrated by George Fryer.
      London: Macdonald, 1982.
      64p; illus; index
      (Whizz kids; 23)
         ISBN: 0-356-06383-6 (cased) • ISBN: 0-356-06343-7 (pbk)
               BL: X.629/17811 • BL: X.629/17818

287   Spotlight on football / Michael Dean. London: Cassell,
      1982.
      58p; illus, 1 map; pbk   ISBN: 0-304-30595-2

288   Football / Graham Hart. Cambridge: Cambridge
      Educational, 1983.
      16p; illus; pbk
      (Openers)   ISBN: 0-521-28859-2
                                                 BL: X.629/19806

289   Froggy football / Richard & Nicky Hales and André
      Amstutz. London: Granada, 1984.
      24p; illus
      (Help your child to count)
         ISBN: 0-246-12467-9 (cased) • ISBN: 0-583-30728-0 (pbk)
                                                 BL: X.990/23783

290   Football / text by Didier Braun; artwork by
      Claude-Henri Julliard; scenario by André Marguin.
      London: Corgi, 1986.
      34p; illus; pbk
      (Action sports)
         Translated from French   ISBN: 0-552-54274-1
                                                 BL: YK.1987.b.4248

291   Football / text by Didier Braun; artwork by
      Claude-Henri Julliard; scenario by André Marguin.
      London: Hamilton Children's, 1986.
      34p; illus
      (Action sports)
         Translated from French   ISBN: 0-241-11865-4
                                                 BL: YC.1986.b.2896

292   Football club / John Colerne; illustrated by Chris
      Fairclough. London: Watts, 1987.
      29p; illus
      (People and places)   ISBN: 0-86313-608-7
                                                 BL: YK.1988.a.2056

293   Football / David Payne. Hove: Wayland, 1989.
      32p; illus   ISBN: 1-85210-707-3
                                                 BL: YK.1990.b.6309

294   Football and the National Curriculum / Kathy Bird,
      Malcolm McHenry, Kevin Collins. Cambridge: Daniels, 1993.
      74p; illus, maps; pbk   ISBN: 1-85467-163-4
                                                 BL: YK.1995.b.2068

295   Football / David Marshall. London: Heinemann Library,
      1994.
      32p; illus
      (Successful sports)   ISBN: 0-431-07434-8
                                                 BL: YK.1995.b.5099

Fiction Published in Serial Form

✳ *Aldine Football Novels*

BL: 12649.c.1

The following stories were published in magazine format by the Aldine Publishing Company. The numbers given alongside each title are the actual series numbers of the books as issued. The Library's holdings end with number 88.

296

1   Goal! / Sydney Horler. 1925.

2   The white moth: a romance of the football field / E. C. Buley. 1925.

3   The sportsman wins! / Roy Stephen. 1925.

4   A legend of the league / Sydney Horler. 1925.

5   Through to the final! / Charles Marviss. 1925.

6   The whirlwind centre / Charles Marviss. 1925.

7   Out for the cup / Travers Tree. 1925.

8   The wizard of the wing / Peter W. Batten. 1926.

9   The ball of fortune / Sydney Horler. 1925.

☞ See also: M6

10   The football detective / Edmund Yare. 1926.

11   A football impostor / T. Stanleyan King. 1926.

12   On the ball! / John Whistler. 1926.

13   The man who saved the club / Sydney Horler. 1926.

14   Benton's great year / Harold Graham. 1926.

15   In final and test match / Kay Gray. 1926.

16   A footballer's romance / Richard Worth. 1926.

17   Footsteps of fame / John Demaine. 1926.

18   Larsington's crack shot / Kay Gray. 1926.

19   The all-conquering game / T. Stanleyan King. 1926.

20   Straight for goal / Kay Gray. 1926.

21   A leader of the league / J. O. Standish. 1927.

22   The mystery centre / Richard Worth. 1927.

23   Two of a kind / Kay Gray. 1927.

24   Dan of the Rovers / Peter W. Batten. 1927.

25   Won from the wing / Richard Goyne. 1927.

26   The movie winger / Cross Dixon. 1927.

27   The great invincibles / Peter Woodruff. 1927.

28   The will to win / Kay Gray. 1927.

29   Expelled from football / Cross Dixon. 1927.

30   A last minute goal / Kay Gray. 1927.

31   The dandy goalkeeper / Peter Woodruff. 1927.

32   Foes in football / Tom Lloyd. 1927.

33   Dr Jim, full-back / Peter Woodruff. 1928.

34   The door of victory / Harold Graham. 1928.

35   The actor-footballer / Richard Worth. 1928.

36   The twin centre / Peter Woodruff. 1928.

37   The football fugitive / Howard Grant. 1928.

38   Fairmyle fights through / Old Cap.1928.

39   The worst team in the Army / Home Goal. 1928.

40   The football suspect / Howard Grant. 1928.

41   The goal of a lifetime / Kay Gray. 1928.

42   The midget winger / Richard Worth. 1928.

43   The club on the cliff / Home Goal. 1928.

44   The soccer men of 'Hunger Town' / Martin Mowbray. 1928.

45   The airman half-back / Peter W. Batten. 1928.

46   The busman centre-forward / Steve Sunderland. 1928.

47   The cup-tie murder / Cross Dixon. 1928.

48   'Play up, the waiters!' / Martin Mowbray. 1928.

49   The Star 'Spangles' team / Steve Sunderland. 1929.

50   The man who sold his side / Kay Gray. 1929.

51   The centre of the stage / Cross Dixon. 1929.

52   The phantom team / Roland Spencer. 1929.

53   The eleven who knew too much / Martin Mowbray. 1929.

54   A born footballer / Anonymous

Not held by BL – title advertised in preceding issue

55   A winner from Scotland Yard / Kay Gray. 1929.

56   The filmland forward / Cross Dixon. 1929.

57   A club under suspicion / Martin Mowbray. 1929.

58   The footslogger forwards / Roland Spencer. 1929.

59   [Not held by BL]

60   The black sheep of the club / Steve Sunderland. 1929.

61   The speed-king centre / Peter W. Batten. 1929.

62   The gipsy footballers / Home Goal. 1929.

63   The rebel goalkeeper / Martin Mowbray. 1929.

64   The footballers' secret / Steve Sunderland. 1930.

65   Dan of the Dockers' Team / Roland Spencer. 1930.

66   Won at Wembley / Kay Gray. 1930.

67   The poorest team in the league / Martin Mowbray. 1930.

68   The circus saver / Cross Dixon. 1930.

69   The man the Rangers wanted / Steve Sunderland. 1930.

70   The final test / Old Cap.1930.

71   A top-o'-the-world team / Martin Mowbray. 1930.

72   Champs of the Speed Iron League / Sid Melby. 1930.

73   The team from the Tropics / Home Goal. 1930.

74   Speedboat or football? / Cross Dixon. 1930.

75   Hissed off the field / Ernest Lionel Mackeag. 1930.

76   The football night club / Steve Sunderland. 1931.

77   Darkies on Tour / Home Goal. 1931.

78   The pit-boy centre / Peter W. Batten. 1931.

79   The stars who couldn't score / Stacey Ray. 1931.

80   Darkies on the Rhine / Home Goal. 1931.

81   The castaway champion / Fred Stowe. 1931.

82   By skill or bribery? / Martin Mowbray. 1931.

83   A crown at stake! / Old Cap.1931.

84   The white moth: a romance of the football field / E. C. Buley. 1931.

85   The football hikers / Steve Sunderland. 1931.

86   Through to the final! / Charles Marviss. 1931.

87   The whirlwind centre / Charles Marviss. 1931.

88   Sharland's soccer squad / Roland Spencer. 1931.

❊ *Aldine Football Novels New Series*

BL: 12649.c.2

297

1   The ball of fortune / Sydney Horler. 1933.

2   [Not held by BL]

3   The wizard of the wing / Peter W. Batten. 1933.

4   The football detective / Edmund Yare. 1933.

5   The twin centre / Peter Woodruff. 1933.

6   The door of victory / Harold Graham. 1933.

7   Out for the cup / Travers Tree. 1933.

❊ *Aldine Football Stories*

BL: 012803.dd.14

298

1   Born to win! / Jack Wylde. 1922.

2   Dick Daring and the mystery pro / T. Stanleyan King. 1922.

3   The football furies / Geoffrey Prout. 1922.

4   Play up ten men! / Hedley Scott. 1922.

5   Dick Daring scores again! / T. Stanleyan King. 1923.

6   The traitor of the team / Jack Wylde. 1923.

7   Barred from the game! / Anthony Thomas. 1923.

8   The idol of the crowd / Hedley Scott. 1923.

9   Dick Daring, International / T. Stanleyan King. 1923.

10   The masked forward / Hedley Scott. 1923.

11   The million pound goal / Roland Spencer. 1923.

12   The bogus referee / Hedley Scott. 1923.

❊ *Football & Sports Library*

BL: 12645.cc.1

The following three series were all published by Amalgamated Press. Only the titles known to be football stories have been listed with their original series number alongside.

299

1   From village team to pro! / C. Malcolm Hincks. 1921.

2   Captain Meg – footballer / Anonymous. 1921.

3   For league & love / Victor Nelson. 1921.

4   Captain Meg: further adventures / Anonymous. 1921.

5   From village club to fame / C. Malcolm Hincks. 1922.

6   Football Island / Anonymous. 1922.

7   What a team / C. Malcolm Hincks. 1922.

8   A marked man / Steve Nelson. 1922.

9   The fighting footballer / Geoffrey Gordon. 1922.

10   The football favourites / C. Malcolm Hincks. 1922.

11   The team with a bad name / Charles Pickford. 1922.

12   John Fleming – international / Paul Urquhart. 1922.

13   Nell o' Newcastle / Steve Nelson. 1922.

14   What's the matter with Millport? / J. S. Margerison. 1922.

15   The luck of Lorrimer / Paul Urquhart. 1922.

16   'Stick-it Ginger!' / Jock MacPherson. 1922.

17   Every inch a sport / C. Malcolm Hincks. 1922.

18   Fighting Frank / Paul Urquhart. 1922.

20   Jack Briton: footballer and fighter / Arthur S. Hardy. 1922.

21   Dashing Dick Steele / Geoffrey Gordon. 1922.

22   The Jonah of the team. 1922.

25   Ray of the Rovers / Malcolm C. Hincks. 1922.

26   Penalty Jack / Charles Pickford. 1922.

27   'Bess of Blacktown' / Don Gray. 1922.

30   Freddy the football fan / Henry T. Johnson. 1923.

31   Down on their luck / Malcolm Arnold. 1923.

32   Suspended for life / Jack Stephens. 1923.

40   Tom Pepper / Jock MacPherson. 1923.

❊ *Champion Library*

BL: 12644.aaa.2

300

21   The lad with the lightning left / Rupert Hall. 1933?

75   The Wizard of the Wanderers / Rupert Hall. 1933?

98   The football rebel! / Nelson Victor. 1933.

121   The masked footballer / Rupert Hall. 1934.

135   The football toreadors / Jack Maxwell. 1934.

Pseudonym for Ernest Lionel Mackeag

143   The millionaire footballer / Rupert Hall. 1935.

166   The hobo footballers / Rupert Hall. 1935.

❊ *Sexton Blake Library*

BL: 12814.e.3

301

163   The mystery of the shadowed footballer / Martin Frazer. 1948.

Reference Books

WHILE MANY OF THE ENTRIES in this bibliography portray the game in colourful and evocative prose, this chapter lists publications which are largely factual, containing little in the way of subjective observation. The who, what, why, when and where of association football have always been subjects eagerly addressed by supporters with a bent for statistical analysis and by writers and journalists who need accurate facts and figures.

The annual yearbook or directory has been a familiar sight in football publishing since the very early years, typically presenting details of clubs, playing staffs, previous season's results and current season's fixtures in a logically arranged and handily sized format. One of the earliest and most respected of such publications was the *Athletic News Football Annual* [J5] which fulfilled for the winter game the sort of function so admirably performed for cricket by Wisden. These early annuals are now extremely scarce and eagerly sought by collectors and researchers alike.

Titles of this kind were profuse. Often they were published by newspaper groups on a regional basis and their coverage is usually plain from their title. Researchers of particular clubs and areas will find such publications well worth consulting, always likely to offer up that elusive name or date and evoking the immediacy of the era under study. Certainly one of the best ways to travel back to a particular season is to procure a directory for that year, even if the same information might be available in updated format. Uniformity was a feature of the annuals over successive years and even now the pocket sized publications such as *Playfair* differ little in appearance from their earlier counterparts.

A major innovation occurred in 1970. In that year Rothmans launched their *Football Yearbook* [J103], which has since become a standard work of reference. In over 900 pages it presented a full retrospective of the 1969/70 season along with fixtures for the year ahead, coverage of the European scene, and much on world football. The first edition promised 'more than half a million facts and figures and tremendous value for money at only 18 shillings'. Twenty-five years later Rothmans is still going strong and it is difficult to fault this claim. Rothmans was important for a number of reasons. The publication of such a high-quality reference work by a major international company raised the profile of its subject matter and introduced many soccer followers to a side of the game they may not have been aware of. It made football facts and figures much more accessible – indeed the blue and yellow covers of Rothmans became an annual 'must have' Christmas gift for many a football buff. It also set the standard for a new kind of reference book, different from the lightweight pocket compilations which had been the norm. This set a distinct trend which has since been followed by many imitators. By linking a respectable company with the association game the *Rothmans Football Yearbook* was also important in its implications for sponsorship. The foreword, by 'Rothmans of Pall Mall' makes their own stance absolutely clear: 'It seems fitting that Rothmans, makers of cigarettes throughout the world, should now be associated with the world's most widespread and popular sport'. How fitting this might still be to a more health conscious society is a moot point, but the real importance of this event is that it strengthened the links between football and major company sponsors whose own fields of activity were not directly sports related. The recent major involvement of Carling, Coca Cola, Guinness and Barclays Bank in football and football publishing has been a logical extension of the Rothmans concept, helping the game in its broadest sense and extending the scope and range of Rothmans-style publications to its current healthy status. Major directories are now available which chronicle the game in England, Scotland, Wales, Northern Ireland and the Irish Republic whilst the non-league scene is superbly covered in its own right.

Whilst directories and annuals such as these serve up a mind-boggling array of factual material, much of what they present is specific to the particular year of publication so researchers seeking an all-time overview, or requiring deeper detail, must look elsewhere. Their specialised needs are invariably answered by the impressive range of purely statistical material which has been generated largely in the last fifteen years.

Like most sports, association football readily lends itself to statistical analysis – scores, scorers, career records, dates, transfers, attendances – this sort of data is the backbone of the game. Personalities and their heroic deeds may be the true flesh and blood of football but the statistics behind the great stories tell a larger tale. A solid and reliable databank of statistical information is vital for the writers, publishers and journalists who need to lace their prose with hard facts and figures. At this point it is appropriate to mention the Association of Football Statisticians, the organisation responsible for so many key statistical publications in the field of association football.

Founded in 1978, the AFS now embraces over 1,400 members in thirty-eight countries and enjoys the official backing of the Football League and Football

Association in both England and Scotland. The projects undertaken by their members require an almost frightening level of thoroughness in their research, but this is a challenge to which they have risen in indomitable fashion. By producing a steady flow of publications specifically conceived to fill gaps in existing knowledge, the Association has built up a range of work covering the game at all levels through all eras. The results of their research are usually published as economically as possible – no glossy covers or illustrations – and are usually issued in strictly limited editions. While not all the items listed under the Statistics and Records section emanate from the AFS stable, their influence, and particularly that of Ray Spiller their founder, cannot be overstated. It is worth noting too that the traditional vision of statistics as simply column upon column of painstakingly written figures is fast becoming outdated, as advanced technology has begun to make important inroads into the discipline – a number of the most recent statistical works have been generated by computer, enabling all manner of cross-statistical analyses and series to be generated in a fraction of the time which a manual exercise would take.

In addition to these directories and statistical works, there have been a number of encyclopaedias published over the years which form a most useful adjunct to the football historian's library. While generally low on detail, they present a wide-ranging overview which can serve as an excellent quick reference source. Foremost amongst the early examples is that by Frank Johnston [J178], the first comprehensive publication of its ilk, whilst the later work of Maurice Golesworthy [J179] ran to many revised editions and was the standard encyclopaedic work from 1956 to 1976 before being superseded by the work of Phil Soar and Martin Tyler [J192]. More recently the *Guinness Football Encyclopaedia* [J202] and the 'ultimate' work of Keir Radnedge [J205] have kept well abreast of the times. A smattering of football dictionaries and a number of works relating to football fixtures and league tables complete the comprehensive range of reference works covering association football. From the items listed in this chapter, it should be possible to produce an answer to any football query one may care to ask – a fine testimony to the all-encompassing work undertaken by the dedicated compilers and editors whose specialist skills and knowledge have filled such an important niche in football literature.

Reference Books ~ Contents

Directories, Yearbooks & Guides

1   The football annual / Charles William Alcock. London: 1872-1908.

Library set lacks the issues for 1878, 1890, 1894, 1901/2
BL: P.P.2489.wf

2   The Sporting Chronicle annual. London: Sporting Chronicle, 1876-

Library holdings begin at 1896   BL: P.P.2489.dd

The *Sporting Chronicle* was one of the leading journals of the day for sports coverage and, like many daily or weekly publications which followed it, produced annuals which were effectively summaries of the year just gone and previews of the year to come. Early examples of these are very scarce but they can be of real value to researchers of the game in its infancy.

3   The all England cricket and football journal and athletic review. Sheffield: 1877-1879.   BL: P.P.1852.d

Early journal containing some football material.

4   Scottish Football Association annual / edited by John MacDowall. Glasgow: Scottish Football Association, 1885-1900?   BL: P.P.2489.wah

Scarce early coverage of the game in Scotland.

5   The Athletic News football annual. London: 1887-1946.

Subsequently incorporated into the Sunday Chronicle football annual   BL: P.P.2489.wfc

The *Athletic News* was published on a Monday morning following the weekend fixtures and gave a thorough account of every league game; it was avidly read by its many regular followers. Not surprising then, that the annual received equal acclaim and came to be regarded as the Wisden of football. In 1946 it was incorporated into the *Sunday Chronicle Football Annual* which in turn metamorphosed into the *News of the World Football Annual*, still published today. Early editions of Athletic News Annual are scarce and eagerly sought by collectors. The AFS did a great service in reprinting early issues in facsimile.

☞ See also: J74; J96

6   Association football, cricket, and lawn tennis guide for Sheffield, Rotherham, and north-east Derbyshire. Football edition. Rotherham: H. Garnett, 1888.
96p   BL: Mic.A.9569 (6) (microfilm copy)

Scarce guide of interest to historians of the game in Derbyshire and Yorkshire.

7   Johnson's football guide / compiled by 'Wab'. Nottingham: 1890-

Library holdings begin at 1904   BL: P.P.2489.wgn

8   The Scottish League handbook / edited by 'Pertinax'. Glasgow: Nisbet, 1890-   BL: 7908.de

The Scottish League was formed in 1890. This scarce early handbook covers the first ever season of the League.

9   The Welsh Association football annual. Wrexham: Football Association of Wales, 1891-1893.

Just three issues were published.

10   Boot's football guide / James Anderson Peddie. London: Alfred Boot and Son, 1892.
45p; pbk   BL: D

11   Bristol & District Football League, established 1892: rules, with fixtures and list of clubs. Bristol: Bristol and District Football League, 1892.
32p; pbk   Mic.A.9916(5) (microfilm copy)

12   Floyd's football guide: the official handbook of the Devon County Football Association / edited by A. E. Floyd. Plymouth: J. Smith, 1893.   BL: D

13   The Sussex Association football annual / compiled by E. W. Everest. Brighton: W. E. Nash, 1893-
BL: P.P.2489.wgg

14   The association football handbook / edited by N. L. Jackson. London: 1894-1895.

Only two issues published   BL: P.P.2489.wfa

15   Moffatt's handbook and guide to football and cricket / William Moffatt. London: Moffatt & Paige, 1894.
48p; pbk   BL: D

16   Mortimer's 'Handy' football guide for South Wales and Monmouthshire. Cardiff: G. & J. Lennox, 1895.

Only one issue published   BL: P.P.2489.wgf

Scarce early guide of significant interest to historians of Welsh football.

17   Old Un's football handbook. Pontypridd: Glamorgan Times Newspaper Co., 1896.
BL: 7912.a.69(6)

More early material offering information likely to assist researchers of the early days of the game in Wales.

18   The Birmingham Daily Gazette football guide. Birmingham: Birmingham Daily Gazette, 1897-1903.

Continued as: The Birmingham Gazette & Express football guide   BL: P.P.2489.wgr

☞ See also: J27

19 Hampstead football news. London: 1897-1899.
BL: P.P.1832.mai

20 Smirk's handbook: association football season / E. H.
Smirk. Preston: 1897-
BL: P.P.2489.wgh

21 The South-Bucks district football handbook. Chesham:
1899-
BL: P.P.2489.wgo

22 The football handbook. Dundee: 1900-1904.
Continued as: Leng's football handbook   BL: P.P.2511.pb
☞ See also: J33

23 Manchester Evening News football handbook /
compiled by F. Silson. Manchester: 1900-
BL: P.P.2489.wgv

24 The Northern Athlete football guide 1901-2 / John
Henry Morrison. Newcastle: Northern Publishing, 1901.
128p   BL: Mic.A.10957(1) (microfilm copy)

25 The Golden Penny football album. London: 1902-1904.
Continued as: The Daily Graphic football album
BL: P.P.1859.bc
☞ See also: J31

26 Wirral District association football handbook.
Birkenhead: J. Maddocks, 1903-   BL: D

27 The Birmingham Gazette & Express football guide.
Birmingham: Birmingham Gazette & Express, 1904-
Continues: The Birmingham Daily Gazette football guide
BL: P.P.2489.wgr
☞ See also: J18

28 Leicestershire football annual. Hinckley, 1904-
BL: P.P.2489.wgp

29 Manchester Evening Chronicle football guide.
Manchester: 1904-   BL: P.P.2489.wgu

30 The Norfolk football annual / edited by S. E. Baker.
Norwich: 1904-1907.   BL: P.P.2489.wgq

31 The Daily Graphic football album. London: 1905-
Continues: The Golden Penny football album
BL: P.P.1859.bc
☞ See also: J25

32 Frank Sugg's football annual / edited by Frank and
Walter Sugg. Liverpool: 1905-   BL: P.P.2489.wgm
Frank Sugg played for Derby County, Everton and
Burnley in the 1880s. He also played cricket for York-
shire, Derbyshire and Lancashire and in two Tests
against Australia.

33 Leng's football handbook. London: 1905-1915.
Continues: The football handbook   BL: P.P.2511.pb
☞ See also: J22

34 Post football guide. Nottingham: The Post, 1905-
*1905 edition subsequently reprinted in facsimile by the
Association of Football Statisticians*
BL: P.P.2489.wgi
The Nottingham Post has a particularly good reputation for football coverage and their annual football
guide is both informative and collectable.

35 Spalding's association football annual / edited by 'McW'.
Spalding's Athletic Library, 1906-
Author is J. A. McWeeney   BL: D

36 The Warrington football annual and sports record /
compiled by 'Ovalist'. Warrington: 1906- BL: P.P.2489.wgw
Predominantly rugby, as the 'Ovalist' epithet indi-
cates, but may include material of interest to soccer
followers.

37 The Southend and south-east Essex football annual.
Southend: 1908-   BL: P.P.2489.wgk(2)

38 The Daily Chronicle football guide / compiled by
'Corinthian'. London: 1909-   BL: P.P.2489.wfh

39 The football directory: giving the names and addresses
of secretaries of the principal clubs, leagues, and
associations for the season / compiled by Archibald
Sinclair. London: Cricket Press, 1909-
BL: P.P.2489.wkt

40 Gamage's association football annual / edited by Alfred
Davis and H. R. McDonald. London: Caxton, 1909-1929.
Library set incomplete; not published during war years.
BL: P.P.2489.wfi
Generally regarded as one of the best of the football
annuals for the period. Many hundreds of pages and
masses of information in each volume.

41 The Sports Gazette national association football guide.
Middlesbrough: Sports Gazette, 1909-
Compiled by 'Old Bird'   BL: P.P.2489.wgx

42 The Morning Leader annual 1910/11. London: 1910.
98p
*Subsequently reprinted in facsimile by the Association of
Football Statisticians*

43 The Racing and Football Outlook football annual.
London: 1912-   BL: P.P.2489.wfk

44 The Umpire football annual. Manchester: 1913-1918.
Continued as: The Empire News football annual
BL: P.P.2489.wgt
☞ See also: J48; J75

45 Yorkshire News football guide. York: Yorkshire News,
1913-   BL: P.P.2489.wgs(2)

46 The Carlisle Journal football annual. Carlisle: Carlisle Journal, 1919- BL: P.P.2489.wgl

47 Daily News football annual. London: Daily News, 1919-1929.

> *Continued as: News-Chronicle football annual*
> BL: P.P.2489.wfn

☞ See also: J66

48 The Empire News football annual. Manchester: Empire News, 1919-1945?

> *Continues: The Umpire football annual;*
> *Continued as: Sunday Empire News football annual*
> BL: P.P.2489.wgt

☞ See also: J44; J75

49 The Sheffield Telegraph football guide and annual. Sheffield: Sheffield Telegraph, 1919- BL: P.P.2489.wfy

☞ Also listed at: B704

50 All sports football annual. London: 1921-1928.

> *Continued as: Answers football annual* BL: P.P.2489.wfp

☞ See also: J65

51 Football special Northern Union annual. London: 1921- BL: P.P.2489.wfr

52 The 'Handy' football guide. Darlington: Echo Printing Works, 1921-

> *Published annually* BL: P.P.2489.whf

53 Northern Echo football guide. Darlington: 1921- BL: P.P.2489.wgz

54 The Nottingham Journal football guide. Nottingham: Nottingham Journal, 1921- BL: P.P.2489.whe

55 Success football annual and form guide. London: 1921- BL: P.P.2489.wfo

56 Tit-Bits football annual: complete records & fixtures. London: Newnes, 1922-1923.

> *Two issues published* BL: P.P.2489.wfs

57 The Lincolnshire football guide / edited by 'Critique' of the Lincolnshire Chronicle. Lincoln: Lincolnshire Chronicle, 1924- BL: P.P.2489.whd

58 London and Provincial Wireless Programme, football, racing and amusement guide. London: 1924- BL: P.P.2496.tf

59 The Northern Athlete football guide. Newcastle-on-Tyne: 1924- BL: P.P.2489.whg

60 Westminster Gazette football guide. London: 1925- BL: P.P.2489.whh

61 The Bucks. football annual. Aylesbury: 1926- BL: P.P.2489.whi

62 Sheffield Independent football guide. Sheffield: Sheffield Independent, 1926- BL: P.P.2489.wfx

☞ Also listed at: B705

63 Topical Times football annual. London: Topical Times, 1927-1939. BL: P.P.2489.wfu

This is not the annual well known as a Christmas present to generations of young boys from 1959 – rather this is the adult soft-back pocket edition with summary and preview information for the season in question. It is one of the most popular annuals of this period; interesting advertisements provide a nice period feel.

64 Daily Express football annual. London: Daily Express, 1928-1930. BL: P.P.2489.whl

65 Answers football annual. London: 1929-

> *Continues: All sports football annual*

☞ See also: J50

66 News Chronicle football annual. London: News Chronicle, 1930-1960.

> *Published in two editions – Northern and Southern;*
> *Also entitled: News Chronicle & Daily Dispatch football annual.*
> *The volumes for 1930/31-1932/33 were issued in a combined edition; not published 1940-1945.*
> *Continues: Daily News football annual;*
> *Continued as: The football annual*
> BL: P.P.2489.wfn

This entry well illustrates one of the particular features relating to the chronology of these pocket size football annuals, namely the various name changes which occurred over time as the newspaper sponsors themselves were amalgamated or absorbed. The market for such items was particularly competitive, each publisher seeking the loyalty of its own readers.

☞ See also: J47; J95

NEWS CHRONICLE

FOOTBALL

ANNUAL
1950–51

by

CHARLES BUCHAN

•

LONDON
"News Chronicle" Publications Department
12/22, Bouverie Street, E.C.4

67   Sports Telegraph football annual. Blackburn: Sports
      Telegraph, 1932-1933.   BL: P.P.2489.whm

68   The Answers book of football. London: 1934.
      96p; illus   BL: P.P.2489.who

69   Handbook for season . . . containing lists of officials,
      committees, rules, league fixtures. Tunbridge Wells:
      Tunbridge Wells and District Football League and
      Charity Cups Competition, 1935-   BL: P.P.2489.wfz

70   The Leader football annual. London: 1935-
                                               BL: P.P.2489.whp

71   Answers football handbook. London: 1936-
                                               BL: P.P.2489.whr

72   Football. London: 1946-   BL: P.P.1832.maa

73   Football up-to-date annual. London: 1946-1948.
                                               BL: P.P.2489.whu

74   Sunday Chronicle football annual: incorporating the
      Athletic News football annual. London: Sunday
      Chronicle, 1946-55.

      *Subsequently merged with Empire News football annual to
      become The Empire News and Sunday Chronicle football
      annual*   BL: P.P.2489.wlb

      ☞ See also: J5; J92

75   Sunday Empire News football annual. Manchester:
      Sunday Empire News, 1946-1950.

      Continues: Empire News football annual
      Continued as: Empire News football annual
                                               BL: P.P.2489.wht

      ☞ See also: J48; J88

76   Daily Worker football annual. London: Daily Worker,
      1947-1952.

      Library holdings incomplete   BL: P.P.2489.wku

77   The Newservice amateur football year book. London:
      Newservice, 1947-   BL: P.P.2489.whw

      One of the first annual publications covering the
      game at amateur level.

78   Silver football handbook. London: Promise Press, 1947.

      Continued as: Sport football handbook
                                               BL: P.P.2489.wkq

      ☞ See also: J82

79   The Football Association book for boys. London:
      Naldrett, 1948-   BL: P.P.6753.ala

      Although boys' annuals are specifically excluded from
      the bibliography, I make no excuses for making this an
      exception as a good period example of the genre. The
      contents will give the researcher a fine evocation of
      the times, excellent anecdotal material, good illustra-
      tions and some pretty appalling riddles.

80   The Football Association year book. London: Football
      Association, 1948-   BL: P.P.2489.whz

      This is the first of the official publications of the
      Football Association, published every year since.

81   Playfair Books football annual. London: 1948.

      Continued by: Playfair football annual
                                               BL: P.P.2489.wkw

      This began a run of one of the best known pocket
      sized annuals – well-thumbed copies still turn up at
      programme and book fairs; excellent information
      source, good period advertisements and a nostalgic
      evocation of the post-war years.

      ☞ See also: J85

82   Sport football handbook. London: Topical Publications,
      1948.

      Continues: Silver football handbook;
      Continued as: Sport football annual
                                               BL: P.P.2489.wkr

      ☞ See also: J78; J86

83   Sporting Record football annual. London: Sporting
      Record, 1948-   BL: P.P.2489.wke

84   The Football Association pocket guides. London:
      Naldrett Press, 1949.
      2 parts   BL: 7921.f.24

85   Playfair football annual. London: Queen Anne Press,
      1949-

      Continues: Playfair Books football annual;
      From 1962/63 edition includes: The football annual
                                               ISSN: 0079-2322
                                               BL: P.P.2489.wkw

      ☞ See also: J81; J95

86   Sport football annual. London: Topical Publications,
      1949-

      Continues: Sport football handbook

      ☞ See also: J82

87   Daily Mail football guide. London: Daily Mail, 1950-
                                               BL: P.P.2489.wks

88   The Empire News football annual. Manchester: Empire
      News, 1951-1955.

      Continues: Sunday Empire News football annual;
      *Continued as: Empire News and Sunday Chronicle football
      annual*

      ☞ See also: J75; J92

89   North of Scotland football clubs handbook. Dundee:
      Simmath, 1951.

90   The Scottish League football yearbook. Dundee:
      Simmath, 1953.

91   The Scottish football book. London: Stanley Paul, 1955-

> *Published annually*   BL: P.P.2489.wlf

> ☞   Also listed at: A184

92   Empire News and Sunday Chronicle football annual. Manchester: Empire News and Sunday Chronicle, 1956-1960.

> *Merger of Empire News football annual and Sunday Chronicle football annual*
> *Continued as: News of the World and Empire News football annual*

> ☞   See also: J74; J88; J96

93   The Topical Times football book. London: Topical Times, 1959-   BL: P.P.1860.aar

> Many a boy has woken up on Christmas morning to pick out, in the still dark recesses of his bedroom, the blurred outline of a pillow case and the glorious combination of flat expanse and sharp corners straining at the linen that could only be the *Topical Times Football Book*. Although boys' annuals are specifically excluded from the bibliography, this one has been retained as a fine example of its genre. Editions from the sixties and seventies present the true flavour of the times – no matter what the serious studies may say, the lighter side of the game is best revealed through an item like this, though there is also much of serious interest. Notwithstanding that, where else could you find out the name of Jimmy Gabriel's dog and create your own league table of players' wives?

94   Eagle football annual. London: 1961-   BL: P.P.6758.fi

> Comments as above, but I was always a TT boy at heart.

95   The football annual. London: News Chronicle, 1961.

> *Continues: News-Chronicle football annual*
> *From 1962/63 incorporated into Playfair football annual*
>   BL: P.P.2489.fkc

> ☞   See also: J66; J85

96   News of the World and Empire News football annual. London: News of the World, 1961-1964.

> *Continues: Empire News and Sunday Chronicle football annual*
> *Continued as: News of the World football annual*
>   BL: P.441/129

> ☞   See also: J92; J98

97   The Caxton football annual / edited by A. H. Fabian and G. Green. London: 1962-   BL: P.P.2489.fkj

> Issued to complement the renowned four volume *Association Football* by Fabian and Green.

> ☞   See also: A77

98   News of the World football annual. London: News of the World, 1965-

> *Continues: News of the World and Empire News football annual*

Continuation of a very old established and respected pocket size annual, finally taking on its more familiar name. Still running today, it is now in its 109th edition.

> ☞   See also: J96

99   The Scotsport football annual. London: 1965-
>   BL: P.441/2

100   Northern Ireland soccer yearbook / edited by Malcolm Brodie. Belfast: Howard Publications, 1966-
illus; pbk

> *Later editions entitled: Northern Ireland football yearbook*

> Prior to this date, coverage of Northern Irish soccer appears to have been rather neglected. This relatively early yearbook remedied that; Malcolm Brodie has become an acknowledged authority on his subject.

101   Daily Mirror book of football / edited by Kenneth Wheeler. London: Hamlyn, 1970.
95p; illus   ISBN: 0-600-39624-X
>   BL: P.443/85

102   The Football League book no.1 / edited by Harry Brown; assisted by Bob Baldwin and Walter Pilkington; photographs by Peter Robinson. London: Arthur Barker, 1970.
144p; illus   ISBN: 0-213-00169-1

> Not a directory or guide as such, more akin to an adult version of a boy's annual – included here as a landmark example of its kind, containing much of interest presented largely in narrative and photographs.

103   Rothmans football year book / compiled by Tony Williams and Roy Peskett. London: Queen Anne Press, 1970-   ISSN: 0080-4088

> Very much a key publication in soccer publishing history. Prior to this, most information directories had been slim pocket size editions understandably limited in what they could fit in to the space available. Rothmans changed all that, presenting a larger and much weightier format which has continued in reassuringly uniform appearance to this day. In the foreword to the first edition FIFA President Sir Stanley Rous expressed the hope that it would become to football what Wisden was to cricket. This hope has surely been met – almost 1,000 pages cover the full range of the English and Scottish game, coverage becoming more comprehensive as the publication has found its feet. Complete sets are now very much in demand. Tony Williams deserves full credit for creating Rothmans, the first of his valued contributions to the world of football publications.

104   Rothmans Football League club guide. London: Queen Anne Press, 1975-   ISSN: 0306-9621

> A guide to all the clubs, consistent with the usual Rothmans high standards.

105   League of Ireland yearbook / edited by Tony Reid.
      Dublin: Tara, 1977?-

      The first comprehensive coverage of the Republic of
      Ireland soccer scene.

106   The FA non-league football annual / edited by Tony
      Williams. London: Macdonald and Jane's, 1978-1980.

      Continued as: Rothmans FA non-league football yearbook
                                              ISSN: 0142-6257
                                              BL: P.441/865

      Tony Williams's commitment in starting this publica-
      tion has been thoroughly justified over the years, as
      it has grown into a veritable 'Bible' for non-league fol-
      lowers. Essential work of reference.

      ☞   Also listed at: A234; See also: J108

107   Clydesdale Bank Scottish Football League review.
      Glasgow: Clive Allan Stuart for the Scottish Football
      League, 1980-

      Published annually   ISSN: 0260-8804
                                              BL: P.2000/877

      Definitive coverage of football north of the border,
      very much in the vein of Rothmans.

108   Rothmans FA non-league football yearbook. Aylesbury:
      Rothmans Publications, 1981-1983.

      Continues: The FA non-league football annual;
      Continued as: FA non-league directory
                                              ISSN: 0262-4850
                                              BL: P.441/865

      Continuation of the essential non-league reference
      work being embraced by the Rothmans empire and
      gaining in stature year by year.

      ☞   See also: J106; J110

109   Sunday Telegraph Canon football year book. London:
      Sunday Telegraph, 1983-1985.

      Spine title: Canon football year book
      Continued as: Telegraph football yearbook
                                              ISSN: 0266-0296
                                              BL: P.441/1051

      It was inevitable that Rothmans could not have it all
      its own way – weighty competitors such as the Sun-
      day Telegraph yearbook add spice to the market and
      keep everyone on their toes.

      ☞   See also: J114

110   FA non-league directory / edited by Tony Williams.
      Feltham: Newnes Books, 1984.

      Only one issue published
      Continues: Rothmans FA non-league football yearbook
      Continued as: Non-league directory   ISSN: 0267-8772
                                              BL: P.441/865

      Further continuation of this essential reference work
      under a slightly different guise.

      ☞   See also: J108; J113

111   Football League club directory. Feltham: Newnes Books,
      1984-1988.

      Published annually;
      Continued as: Daily Mail Barclays League football club
      directory   BL: ZC.9.a.289

      Further competition to Rothmans. Informative, useful
      and well presented – not surprising, as it is edited by
      the prolific Tony Williams who had introduced the
      'desk directory' concept thirteen years previously.

      ☞   See also: J117

112   Northumbrian football yearbook / edited by Bob
      Barton. Newcastle upon Tyne: R. Barton, 1984-
                                              ISSN: 0267-6060
                                              BL: P.441/1079

113   Non-league directory / edited by Tony Williams.
      Feltham: Newnes Books, 1985-

      Published annually;
      Also entitled: Official Football Association non-league
      directory
      Continues: FA non-league directory   BL: ZC.9.a.290

      Tony Williams's essential work of reference is ac-
      corded official status at last. Recent editions have
      stretched to over 1000 pages, making this a truly re-
      markable feat of organisation which looks set to run
      and run.

      ☞   See also: J110

114   Telegraph football yearbook. London: Telegraph, 1986.

      Only one issue published;
      Continues: Sunday Telegraph Canon football year book;
      Continued as: The Daily Telegraph football year book
                                              BL: P.441/1051

      ☞   See also: J109; J116

115   The BBC Radio Wales sportstime yearbook / edited by
      Terence O'Donohue. 1987-   ISBN: 0-9507168-1-2

116   The Daily Telegraph football year book / edited by Jack
      Rollin and Norman Barrett. London: Daily Telegraph,
      1987-

      Continues: Telegraph football yearbook   BL: P.441/1051

      The first issue included a full review of the 1986/87
      season with results, appearances, scorers, tables
      etc. As a 1987/88 yearbook though, it has one rather
      bizarre omission, namely the fixtures for the season
      ahead. Apparently the publishers were so anxious to be
      the first yearbook on the shelf for that season that
      they had to go ahead and print prior to the permis-
      sion of the Football League to publish the fixtures!

      ☞   See also: J114

117   Daily Mail Barclays League football club directory.
      London: Harmsworth, 1988-

      Continues: Football League club directory

      ☞   See also: J111

118 Football League year 1989 / edited by Barry J. Hugman. London: Arena, 1988.
240p; illus   ISBN: 1-85443-015-7
                                            BL: YK.1989.b.4765

Barry Hugman has been a most influential figure in the world of football publishing — this is one of his many publications.

119 Panini's football yearbook. London: Panini, 1988-
                                            BL: ZK.9.a.1353

More famous for their football stickers series for juveniles (plus a few Peter Pan-ish adults) Panini here enter the directories arena, but in truth add little to the material offered by the larger established operators in this specialised market.

120 B and Q Scottish Football League review. Glasgow: Scottish Football League, 1990-1991.
Note: Two issues published

Definitive Rothmans style coverage of the Scottish football scene — a valuable work of reference.

121 The Irish football yearbook. Fareham: Marshall Gillespie, 1990-

Later editions published in conjunction with Ulster Television
                                            ISSN: 0965-5565

This annual publication presents a comprehensive coverage of the game in Northern Ireland. An essential work of reference.

122 Irish football handbook / edited by Gerry Desmond and David Galvin. Cork: Red Card Publications, 1991-

This Rothmans style handbook covers Republic of Ireland football in extremely comprehensive form — details of all the clubs, line-ups, players, records and much more. Essential work of reference.

123 Playfair non-league football annual / edited by Bruce Smith. London: Macdonald, 1991-1992.

Continued as: Non-league football pocket annual
                                            BL: ZK.9.a.2279

Pocket size quick reference edition on the non-league game giving a good overview, though not as comprehensive as the much weightier non-league directory published by Tony Williams. Handy for taking along to matches or on that dream European trip, as Williams's hefty tome would undoubtedly be regarded as an offensive weapon or excess baggage.

☞ See also: J129

124 Welsh football almanac / edited by Mel ap Ior Thomas. Blaenau Ffestiniog: Thomas, Collins & Dumphy, 1991-

Published annually   BL: ZK.9.a.2031

Includes full details of the season just gone, along with histories of the various competitions, clubs etc. A valuable addition to the available literature on the Welsh game. Essential reference work.

125 The Welsh football yearbook / edited by Mark Jones. Norfolk: Soccer International, 1991-

Promoted as the first Welsh football yearbook, although there was one which ran for three years from 1891! In truth though, this is the first comprehensive modern coverage of the game in Wales, with full page details of thirty clubs and coverage of virtually every League in the Principality. Much on the non-league game too, along with full records of the Welsh Cup and Amateur Challenge Cup. An excellent publication produced annually and an essential tool for all serious followers of the game in Wales.

126 Official Premier League yearbook. London: Stanley Paul, 1992.

Continued as: The official FA Carling Premiership yearbook
                                            BL: ZC.9.a.3405

The foundation of the Premier League in 1992 presented both problems and opportunities for publishers of football directories. The main problems related to statistics and records since the change in league structure effectively altered the terms of reference which had applied hitherto. The First Division became the Premier League, the Second Division became the First Division. Confusion reigned but created new publishing opportunities; the Premier League now has its own yearbook — this was the first of what is sure to become an annual publication.

☞ See also: J130

127 The Scottish Football League review. Scottish Football League & Sports Projects, 1992.   ISBN: 0-946866-08-2
Comprehensive coverage of the game in Scotland.

128 FA Premier League pocket annual / edited by Bruce Smith. St Albans: Words on Sport, 1993-

This pocket size book is a useful quick reference work with a full club and player directory covering the Premiership. Ideal for journalists or broadcasters requiring information quickly.

129 Non-league football pocket annual / edited by Bruce Smith. St Albans: Words on Sport, 1993-
illus; pbk

Continues: Playfair non-league football annual
                                            BL: ZK.9.a.2279

☞ Also listed at: A248; See also: J123

130 The official FA Carling Premiership yearbook. London: Stanley Paul, 1993-

Continues: Official Premier League yearbook
                                            BL: ZC.9.a.3405

Consistent with the name changes which have always been a feature of the annual directories market, sponsors inevitably take centre stage on such occasions. So long as Carling remain sponsors of the Premiership this publication will run relatively unchanged. What is a dead certainty, though, is that a new sponsor will inevitably take over at some point. It is anybody's guess what the next Premiership year-book title might be – meanwhile this presents a comprehensive and informative coverage.

☞ See also: J126

131 Premier football review. Warley: Sports Projects, 1993-
Note: Published annually   ISSN: 1353-6966
                            BL: ZK.9.a.3148

132 The Endsleigh football directory. London: Harmsworth, 1994.
illus; pbk

Extremely detailed coverage of the Endsleigh League which comprises the First, Second and Third Divisions of the Football League. The Premiership is also chronicled here in detail.

133 Non-league club directory / edited by James Wright. Taunton: Tony Williams Publications, 1994-
1200p; illus; pbk   ISBN: 1-869833-22-8

Monumental piece of research and presentation. An invaluable reference work.

134 Tartan special. Renfrew: Scottish Football League Review, 1994.
128p; pbk   ISBN: 0-86108934-0

Generally described as the premier reference book for Scottish football followers seeking an up-to-date overview. Comprehensive coverage indeed.

Statistics & Records

135 Football book of records, 1888-89 to 1922-23 / G. D. Henderson. London: Athletic Publications, 1923.
95p   BL: Mic.A.7679(7) (microfilm copy)

Statistics and records were not a strong point of early football literature but this relatively scarce example is an exception which covers the years from the foundation of the League until the date of publication.

136 The Football League: the competitions of season . . . / W. M. Johnston. The author, 1932-1940.

Published annually

For eight seasons during the thirties Billy Johnston, editor of the Arsenal FC programme for many years, kept his own hand-written records on a season-by-season basis. He privately published his painstaking efforts in eight volumes, limiting each to no more than forty copies – results, scorers, transfers and much else of interest is presented in these unique and extremely scarce records, later published in facsimile by the AFS.

☞ See also: J165

137 Flagstaff book of football facts. London: Flagstaff, 1958-
                            BL: 7923.n.41

138 Report / Association of Football Statisticians. Basildon: AFS, 1978-
illus

   Six issues a year   ISSN: 0263-1342
                            BL: P.441/962

When the Association of Football Statisticians was founded in 1978, the organisers inevitably had a vision of what they might achieve, but surely this has been surpassed by the reality of what has actually been accomplished. They now have over 1,400 members in 38 countries and enjoy the official backing of the Football League and Football Association of both England and Scotland. Their work is pioneering and painstaking and the research tasks they undertake are almost frightening in their magnitude. The results of their labour are indeed a massive contribution to the game of football and an invaluable source of research information for journalists and scholars alike. Since 1978 they have published regular AFS reports, currently at number 88 and well on the way to a century. The reports contain far more than statistics – many articles and interviews of an historical nature are included. Subscription to the AFS guarantees postal delivery of reports, an excellent way for football scholars to keep in touch with what is happening in the world of football and associated research.

139 Rothmans book of football league records, 1888-89 to 1978-79 / Ian Laschke. London: Macdonald & Jane's, 1980.
352p   ISBN: 0-354-08552-2

Extremely comprehensive research from the foundation of the League presented to the expected high standard of a Rothmans publication.

140 Annual / Association of Football Statisticians. Basildon: AFS, 1981-
illus

   Three issues yearly   ISSN: 0263-0354
                            BL: P.441/956

Each annual covers one season commencing with the 1888/89 season; 37 annuals have been published to date. Each issue gives all the line-ups and scorers for every League game for every team for the season covered. Extremely thorough and originally presented statistical work.

141 Best over 82 seasons: an examination of long term performances in the Football League / David Lee. 1981. 20p; pbk

> A novel piece of individual research creating a picture of relative club performances over the whole life of the Football League. By the way, this was not the fourteen year old version of the David Lee we now see skating past defenders in Bolton Wanderers' quest for honours.

142 The draw experts: with special Pools guide including details of the top 2,100 matches which the home clubs failed to win from 1888-1981 / Norman Lovett. Hull: British Programme Collectors Club, 1981-1982. 4 vols; pbk (Facts and figures on the Football League clubs; nos.33-36) BL: X.0629/552

> If there is a pattern in the incidence of draws, then Norman Lovett has surely uncovered it. I always believed it was pot-luck but evidently Mr Lovett felt otherwise – whether or not he ever won a Pools jackpot remains unrecorded.

143 The ex-league clubs (1888-1981) / Norman Lovett. Hull: British Programme Collectors Club, 1981. 24 vols; pbk (Facts and figures on the Football League clubs; nos. 4-27) BL: X.0629/552

144 The Hamlyn A-Z of British football records / compiled by Phil Soar. London: Hamlyn, 1981. 192p; illus; index

> *Bibliography: p192* ISBN: 0-600-34662-5
> BL: X.622/11458

> A substantial volume containing many interesting items which have made the headlines throughout football history.

> ☞ Subsequent ed. J157

145 The record breakers (1888-1980) / by Norman Lovett. Hull: British Programme Collectors Club, 1981. 4 vols (Facts and figures on the Football League clubs; nos. 28-31) BL: X.0629/552

> Norman Lovett produced a series of reports each chronicling various elements of records and statistics; a little idiosyncratic in their presentation but nonetheless of value at the time. Doubtful whether there is anything here, though, which cannot be found in more recent and substantial publications.

146 Report / Bureau of Non-League Football Statistics. Romford: The Bureau, 1981-1982. 9 vols

> *Published monthly;*
> *Continued as: League tables, cup draws, results, news*
> ISSN: 0263-1342
> BL: P.441/1090

> Following in the steps of the AFS, the Bureau of Non-League Football Statistics recognised the need for a comprehensive statistical coverage of the lower leagues, which enjoy an avid following. This publication set the ball rolling and it has gathered pace ever since. The non-league scene is now exhaustively documented.

> ☞ Also listed at: L1334; See also: J147

147 League tables, cup draws, results, news / Bureau of Non-League Football. London: The Bureau 1982-

> *Published monthly;*
> *Continues: Report / Bureau of Non-League Football Statistics* BL: P.441/1089
> Also listed at: L1335; See also: J146

148 War report no. 1: season 1915-16 / Association of Football Statisticians. Basildon: AFS, 1982? 46p; illus; pbk

> *Written by Phil Hollow and others* BL: X.0629/601(1)
> Detailed statistical coverage of the footballing activity which survived the disruption of the Great War. This innovative AFS series filled important gaps in formally recorded football data.

149 War report no. 2: season 1916-17 / Association of Football Statisticians. Basildon: AFS, 1982? 47p; pbk BL: X.0629/601(2)

150 War report no. 3: season 1917-18 / Association of Football Statisticians. Basildon: AFS, 1982? 42p; illus; pbk BL: X.0629/601(3)

151 War report no. 4: season 1918-19 / Association of Football Statisticians. Basildon: AFS, 1982? 48p; illus; pbk BL: X.0629/601(4)

152 War report no. 5: summary / Association of Football Statisticians. Basildon: AFS, 1982. 28p; illus; pbk BL: X.629/19653

> The four previous parts of this series were amalgamated in this summary report to present an overall statistical picture of the Great War years.

153 War time report / Association of Football Statisticians. Basildon: AFS, 1982? 8 parts; pbk

> This eight booklet series covers football during the Second World War, again filling an important void for one of the lesser documented eras of the game's history.

154 The early years. Basildon: AFS, 1983-1984. 4 vols; illus; pbk ISBN: 0-946531-19-6

> A most interesting and valuable four part series covering the years between the formation of the Football Association in 1863 and the foundation of the Football League in 1888. Typical of the quest for completeness pursued by the AFS, this series presents important observations on the game during its formative years.

155 The Football League appearances and goalscorers 1888-1984. Basildon: AFS, 1983-
illus; pbk   BL: X.629/21474

A progressive series charting appearances and scorers during the lifetime of the Football League.

156 A record of Scottish League football: dates, results and final tables / Gordon Smailes. Basildon: AFS, 1983.
4 vols; illus; pbk   BL: X.629/21472

A four part series which gives a complete statistical record of the game in Scotland from the 1890 foundation of the League right up to 1983. An extremely valuable and thorough piece of research.

157 The Hamlyn A-Z of British football records / compiled by Phil Soar. Completely rev. 2nd ed. London: Hamlyn, 1984.
204p; illus; index

Bibliography: p204   ISBN: 0-600-34728-1
                                    BL: X.622/22331

☞ Previous ed. J144

158 The AFS book of inter league matches: a complete record / Ray Spiller. Basildon: AFS, 1985.
100p

At one time matches between the Football League and the Scottish League were a regular and popular feature of the season, used as a sort of International trial and played largely at the provincial grounds. Nowadays, although such matches are played at more junior levels, the full inter league games have effectively ceased. Ray Spiller here presents all the line-ups, results and scorers for every game in this original piece of research.

159 Digest of football statistics. London: Football Trust, 1985-

Published annually   BL: ZK.9.b.5814

In 1979 the Football Trust was founded by the combined efforts of the Pools companies to provide financial support for worthy projects connected with the game at all levels. Part of the Trust's remit was to sponsor the provision of statistics giving leading indicators on trends in the game. Attendances, regional variations, demographic make-up of spectatorship, arrests, finances, indeed all elements of the non-playing side of the game are covered. Potentially very useful to those working within the football industry and dependent trades.

160 Non-league annual / Paul Marsh. Basildon: AFS, 1985?-

A thorough statistical presentation of the non-league football world. Much of value to historians of the game at this level.

161 Record of League of Ireland football, 1921-22 to 1984-85 / N. MacSweeney. Basildon: AFS, 1985.
184p; pbk   ISBN: 0-946531-24-2

Comprehensive coverage of football in the Republic of Ireland from the statistical and records viewpoint.

162 Scottish League appearances and goalscorers / Jim McAllister, 1985.

Fills an important gap in statistical coverage of the Scottish game.

163 Scottish League clubs: the records / Mike Watson. 1985.

Valuable research work for Scottish statisticians.

164 Guinness soccer firsts / John Robinson. Enfield: Guinness Superlatives, 1986.
128p; illus; index; pbk   ISBN: 0-85112-800-9
                                    BL: YK.1986.b.1069

Contains over 1,000 records on the firsts in football – the first player to score a hat-trick, the first to score for England etc. Includes many photographs.

☞ Also listed at: K58; Subsequent ed. J169

165 The W. M. Johnston facsimile. Basildon: AFS, 1986.
8 vols; 1512p

Facsimile of one man's personal hand-written records covering the eight seasons from 1931/32 to 1938/39. Gives full staff lists for each club, results, goalscorers, transfers, diary and lots more. A remarkable journal giving much valuable detail.

☞ See also: J136

166 Goalscorers 1919-1931 / Brian Mellowship and Alex Wilson. Basildon: AFS, 1987.
3 vols

Every single goalscorer for these twelve seasons is listed on a match-by-match basis for all the Football League and FA Cup games – great for resolving arguments. Issued in a limited edition of 200 sets.

167 Soccer starfacts / Peter Oakes and Francis Wolstencroft. Manchester: The Star, 1987-
illus

Published annually

Studies all the First Division clubs giving game-by-game coverage of league line-ups, goalscorers, attendances, referees and league positions – not content with just that, they also present the number of fouls, corners and goal attempts for every single game in the First Division!

168 Classifieds / Ray Spiller. Basildon: AFS, 1987?-

These innovative little books reproduce, in facsimile, the familiar result pages of a national newspaper with League tables, scorers, half-time scores and attendances. Excellent source of information for the statistician and the historian presented in an 'as it happened' format; this is an ongoing series.

169 Soccer firsts / John Robinson. 2nd ed. Enfield: Guinness, 1989.
128p; illus; index; pbk   ISBN: 0851123678
                                    BL: YK.1990.b.2089

☞ Also listed at: K62; Previous ed. J164

170   The Breedon book of Football League records /
      Gordon Smailes. Derby: Breedon Books, 1991.
      256p; illus   ISBN: 0-907969-98-4
                                             BL: YK.1993.b.8275

      Similar in content to Tony Brown's 'ultimate' statis-
      tics book, this gives every Football League result
      since 1888, every end of season table, all the leading
      scorers and plenty of additional statistical informa-
      tion. Nicely presented and well illustrated, maybe
      more user friendly than Brown's book, but any re-
      searcher interested in this field should ideally use
      them both for the fullest picture possible.

      ☞ Subsequent ed. J173

171   The Guinness non-league football fact book / Tony
      Williams. Enfield: Guinness, 1991.
      256p; illus; index   ISBN: 0-85112-970-6
                                             BL: YK.1991.b.8390

      Packed with information, this is the essential work of
      reference for non-league followers and all to the high
      standard which has become a hallmark of Guinness
      publishing.

172   The ultimate Football League statistics book / Tony
      Brown. Basildon: AFS, 1991.
      451p; pbk   ISBN: 0-946531-38-2

      Computer generated work of awe inspiring detail giv-
      ing every Football League result from 1888 to 1991,
      which equates to over 141,000 in all. This is the ulti-
      mate argument solver, as indeed the name suggests.
      Full League tables are also included along with all
      manner of other statistical wizardry and trivia. This
      is a remarkable achievement by any standards and
      will become the standard work of reference for League
      results.

      ☞ Subsequent ed. J177

173   The Breedon book of Football League records /
      Gordon Smailes. 2nd ed. Derby: Breedon Books, 1992.
      256p; illus   ISBN: 1-873626-33-9
                                             BL: YK.1993.b.251

      An updated version of the earlier edition.

      ☞ Previous ed. J170

174   The Football League 1888-1992 / Tony Brown.
      Basildon: AFS, 1992.

      Presents every Football League team's total results
      tally against every other Football League opponent.
      Always useful if your team gets badly beaten by your
      work colleague's club – as a desperate measure it
      might be possible to prove that your club is well
      ahead on an all-time results basis!

175   Three English leagues / Tony Brown. Basildon: AFS,
      1992.
      200p

      Covers the Premier League, Football League and GM
      Vauxhall Conference, giving each club's all-time re-
      sults against each of their opponents along with
      all-time League tables showing who really is the best
      since time began! Invaluable for the statistician and
      journalist needing to dig out those elusive facts and
      to prove whatever he fancies proving to suit his case
      on the day. Astonishing research.

176   The ultimate Scottish Football League statistics book /
      Tony Brown. 1993.
      225p

      Contains the results of every Scottish League match
      since the League began in 1890 to the end of
      1992/93. Also gives full home and away tables, scor-
      ing records, all-time tables and the overall
      performance of each club against each of its rivals.
      Over 54,000 results are presented in this limited
      edition publication – the most comprehensive statis-
      tical results coverage ever produced for the Scottish
      League.

177   The ultimate Football League statistics book / Tony
      Brown. Rev. ed. Soccer Data, 1994.
      470p   ISBN: 0-946531-76-5

      This new edition is complete to the end of 1993/4. It
      contains all Premier and Football League results in a
      club versus club format, showing at a glance how all
      the previous meetings have finished. Very useful for
      assessing comparative performances between two
      specific clubs (say Liverpool v Everton) for all periods
      in their history.

      ☞ Previous ed. J172

Encyclopaedias

178   The football encyclopaedia: a historical and statistical
      review of the game / edited by Frank Johnston. London:
      Associated Sporting Press, 1934.
      320p   BL: 7916.ee.26

      Arsenal manager George Allison writes in the preface
      to this collectable volume that it fills an important
      gap in literature relating to the great national game.
      Although far more comprehensive books have been
      published since, this was indeed innovative at the
      time. Well worth consultation, includes all manner of
      information and a range of brief club histories cover-
      ing English, Scottish, and Irish clubs. The Irish
      section chronicles lesser profiled clubs such as Bray
      Unknowns, Dolphin and St James's Gate. A gem of a
      volume likely to yield an unknown snippet or two even
      to the more knowledgeable historians.

      ☞ See also: C535

179 The encyclopaedia of association football / compiled by Maurice Golesworthy. London: Hale, 1956.
179p; illus

> One of the most comprehensive encyclopaedic works which ran to many editions, still well worthy of consultation today.

☞ Subsequent ed. J180

180 The encyclopaedia of association football / compiled by Maurice Golesworthy. New and rev. ed. London: Hale, 1958.
188p; illus

☞ Previous ed. J179; Subsequent ed. J181

181 The encyclopaedia of association football / compiled by Maurice Golesworthy. New and rev. ed. London: Hale, 1959.
190p; illus

☞ Previous ed. J180; Subsequent ed. J183

182 Encyclopaedia of sport / edited by Charles Harvey. London: Sampson Low, Marston, 1959.
327p; illus   BL: 7925.d.17

183 The encyclopaedia of association football / compiled by Maurice Golesworthy. New and rev. ed. London: Hale, 1961.
190p; illus

☞ Previous ed. J181; Subsequent ed. J184

184 The encyclopaedia of association football / compiled by Maurice Golesworthy. 6th ed. London: Hale, 1963.
224p; illus

> *There appears to have been no 5th ed.*

☞ Previous ed. J183; Subsequent ed. J185

185 The encyclopaedia of association football / compiled by Maurice Golesworthy; foreword by Sir Stanley Rous. 7th ed. London: Hale, 1965.
224p; illus

☞ Previous ed. J184; Subsequent ed. J187

186 Encyclopaedia of sport and sportsmen / edited by Charles Harvey. London: Sampson, Low, 1966.
624p; illus   BL: X.449/2361

187 The encyclopaedia of association football / compiled by Maurice Golesworthy; foreword by Sir Stanley Rous. 8th ed. London: Hale, 1967.
224p   ISBN: 0-7091-0079-5

☞ Previous ed. J185; Subsequent ed. J188

188 The encyclopaedia of association football / compiled by Maurice Golesworthy; foreword by Sir Stanley Rous. 9th ed. London: Hale, 1969.
224p; illus   ISBN: 0-7091-1066-9

☞ Previous ed. J187; Subsequent ed. J189

189 The encyclopaedia of association football / compiled by Maurice Golesworthy; foreword by Sir Stanley Rous. 10th ed. London: Hale, 1970.
222p; illus   ISBN: 0-7091-1874-0

☞ Previous ed. J188; Subsequent ed. J191

190 Purnell's encyclopaedia of association football / edited by Norman S. Barrett. London: Purnell, 1972.
254p; illus   ISBN 0-361-02111-9
     BL: X.625/82

☞ Subsequent ed. J195

191 The encyclopaedia of association football / compiled by Maurice Golesworthy; foreword by Sir Stanley Rous. 11th ed. London: Hale, 1973.
222p; illus   ISBN: 0-7091-4047-9

☞ Previous ed. J189; Subsequent ed. J193

192 Encyclopaedia of British football / edited by Martin Tyler and Phil Soar. Glasgow: Collins, 1974.
254p; illus

> *The greater part of the material published in this book was first published by Marshall Cavendish in the partwork 'Book of football'*   ISBN: 0-00-106181-X
>   BL: X.625/125

☞ Subsequent ed. J194

193 The encyclopaedia of association football / compiled by Maurice Golesworthy; foreword by Sir Stanley Rous. 12th ed. London: Hale, 1976.
239p; illus; index
     ISBN: 0-7091-6040-2 (cased) • ISBN: 0-7091-5840-8 (pbk)
     BL: X.620/16409 • BL: X.611/7449

☞ Previous ed. J191

194 Encyclopaedia of British football / Phil Soar and Martin Tyler. 2nd ed. London: Marshall Cavendish, 1977.
232p; illus, 1 map

> *The great part of this material was first published in the partwork "Book of football"' – title page verso*
>   ISBN: 0-85685-309-7
>   BL: X.625/563

☞ Previous ed. J192; subsequent ed. J196

195 Purnell's new encyclopaedia of association football / edited by Norman S. Barrett; contributors Brian Glanville and others. Rev. ed. Maidenhead: Purnell, 1978.
190p; illus; index   ISBN: 0-361-04200-0
     BL: X.622/7003

☞ Previous ed. J190

196 Encyclopaedia of British football / Martin Tyler and Phil Soar. 3rd ed. London: Marshall Cavendish, 1979.
232p; illus   ISBN: 0-85685-594-4

☞ Previous ed. J194; subsequent ed. J197

197 Encyclopaedia of British football / Phil Soar and Martin Tyler. 3rd updated and revised ed. London: Willow, 1983.
246p; illus
ISBN: 0-00-218049-9
BL: X.622/18222

☞ Previous ed. J196; subsequent ed. J198

198 Encyclopaedia of British football / Phil Soar, Martin Tyler. 4th ed. London: Willow, 1984.
248p; illus; index
ISBN: 0-00-218135-5
BL: X.625/950

☞ Previous ed. J197; subsequent ed. J199

199 Encyclopaedia of British football / Phil Soar. New ed. London: Willow, 1987.
261p; illus
ISBN: 0-00-218290-4
BL: LB.31.b.3015

☞ Previous ed. J198

200 The Hamlyn encyclopaedia of soccer / Ian Morrison. London: Hamlyn, 1989.
176p; illus
ISBN: 0-600-56370-7

201 The football almanac / Peter Stewart. Moffat: Lochar, 1991.
158p; illus; index
ISBN: 0-948403-77-2
BL: YK.1991.a.10276

☞ Subsequent ed. J203

202 The Guinness football encyclopaedia / edited by Graham Hart. London: Guinness, 1991.
216p; illus; index
ISBN: 0-85112-998-6
BL: YK.1991.b.9248

Effectively an A-Z of the English and Scottish game, with some European and world soccer thrown in for good measure. Clubs, players, managers, grounds, cups etc. are all covered. This and subsequent editions would prove a good general reference work to have to hand for those engaged in football research projects.

☞ Subsequent ed. J204

203 The football almanac / Peter Stewart. New ed. Glasgow: N. Wilson, 1993.
288p; illus; index; pbk
ISBN: 1-897784-08-2

☞ Previous ed. J201

204 The Guinness football encyclopaedia / edited by Graham Hart. 2nd ed. Enfield: Guinness, 1993.
218p; illus; index
ISBN: 0-85112-730-4
BL: YK.1994.b.2168

By this time, Guinness has established a respected reputation for their sterling work in football publishing. As with their other more familiar product, the quality is high and the contents no less eagerly consumed. Particularly suitable for those just beginning to learn about the history of the game.

☞ Previous ed J202

205 The ultimate encyclopaedia of soccer / Keir Radnedge. London: Hodder, 1994.
256p; illus
ISBN: 0-340-62319-5

A definitive illustrated guide to world soccer with many photographs and biographies of 225 all-time greats. The index is particularly detailed, making this an ideal reference work to keep by one's side.

206 The world encyclopaedia of soccer / Michael L. LaBlanc and Richard Henshaw. London: Gale Research, 1994.
xvi, 430p
ISBN: 0-81038-995-9
BL: YK.1994.b.14921

A very substantial work, well worthy of consultation as a comprehensive reference source giving a broad overview of the game on a world basis.

Dictionaries

207 Soccer reference dictionary / compiled by F. C. Avis. London: The author, 1954.
135p
BL: 7921.a.82.

Another early attempt at a quick reference work, worth consultation as a curiosity but containing little which is not chronicled in later more comprehensive works.

☞ Subsequent ed. J208

208 Soccer dictionary / compiled by F. C. Avis. 2nd ed. London: The author, 1966.
96p
BL: X.449/2150

☞ Previous ed. J207; subsequent ed. J209

209 Soccer dictionary. 3rd ed. London: F. C. Avis, 1970.
104p; illus
ISBN: 0-14-489034-8
BL: X.629/3078

☞ Previous ed. J208

210 Elsevier's football dictionary: English-German, German-English / compiled by Horst Sirges. Amsterdam, Oxford: Elsevier, 1980.
x, 286p
ISBN: 0-444-41890-3
BL: X.629/14392

Occasionally someone publishes a book for which the apparent market is particularly narrow. This substantial work seems to be just such an example, although perhaps it is more appropriate today than it was in 1980.

Bibliographies

211 Sport in Britain: a bibliography of historical publications, 1800-1987 / Richard William Cox. Manchester: Manchester University Press, 1991.
xxxiii, 285p   ISBN: 0-7190-2592-3
                                                              BL: 2020.f

> Includes a full range of sports with some examples relevant to football.

212 A football compendium: a comprehensive guide to the literature of association football / compiled by Peter J. Seddon; edited by C. McKinley and A. E. Cunningham. Boston Spa: The British Library, 1995.
xx, 522p; illus; index   ISBN: 0-7123-1075-4

In 1977 E. W. Padwick published a bibliography of cricket – I have thumbed through this on many occasions over the years, finding myself regretting that no football equivalent exists and wondering what form a soccer volume might take. The resulting *Football Compendium* does not intend to imitate Padwick, indeed it differs in a number of ways – what it does intend to do is fill a frustrating gap in football literature, stimulating interest and further research and opening up the door of football's rich library of material to a wider audience, young and old, expert and novice alike.

League Tables & Fixtures

213 The football calendar, containing laws of both sections of the game, list of clubs, playing grounds and fixtures for season / compiled by G. H. West. London: 1875-1879.
> *Library set missing the issue for 1878/79*
                                                       BL: P.P.2489.wag

214 The Scottish football calendar / compiled by Robert Black. Edinburgh: 1878-   BL: P.P.2489.waf

215 The national football calendar for 1881 / edited by C. W. Alcock and N. L. Jackson. London: 1881.
142p   BL: P.P.2489.wgc.

> Very scarce early item presented by two of the game's leading figures – worth consultation for all researchers of football during the years leading up to the formation of the League.

216 The football calendar. London: 1886-1894.
> *No more published*   BL: P.P.2489.wgb

217 Football scoring card for the Lancashire League. Lancashire League, 1892-
1 sheet   BL: 1865.c.2(14)

218 Scottish League fixtures. Leith: MacKenzie & Storrie, 1892.   BL: Mic.A.12664(9) (microfilm copy)

219 Football chart: showing position on League Table. Liverpool: G. F. Stirling, 1912.
1 sheet   BL: 1865.c.2(100)

> Curious early item of ephemeral interest only.

```
          THE
      NATIONAL

  FOOTBALL CALENDAR
          FOR
        1881

         ◆

       EDITED BY
C. W. ALCOCK and N. L. JACKSON.
By authority of the Committee of the Football
          Association.

    PRICE SIXPENCE.

  CRICKET PRESS,
17, PATERNOSTER SQUARE, LONDON. E.C.
```

220 Football competitions simplified / T. C. P. Birmingham: TCP, 1920.
12p; pbk
> *Author is T. C. Parsons*   BL: D

221 Cox's league diary and football yarns containing league fixtures. Liverpool: 1922.   BL: P.P.2489.wha

222 The football diary for season .... London: T. de la Rue, 1924.   BL: P.P.2489.wfi

223 Competitors' football fixture card: League, First (Second, Third) Division, all clubs' fixtures for season 1930/31. 1930.

4 pt   BL: Cup.1251.e.1

224 Fixtures ready made: football, cricket, hockey, etc. / W. R. Blezard. London: Garrick, 1934.

48p; pbk   BL: Mic.A.9827(11) (microfilm copy)

Creating a fixture list can be a nightmare for club secretaries, no matter at what level of the game. This was an early attempt at providing useful guidance.

225 The arrangement of league fixtures and knock-out competitions. London: Published officially for the Football Association and the Football League by Naldrett Press, 1950.

12p; pbk   BL: 7920.ee.16

Official FA guidance from the days before we relied on computers.

226 Football Association diary. London: Football Association, 1951-   BL: P.P.2489.wlc

227 Football League tables: 1889 to the present / editor Jim Mallory; assistant editor Jeanette Tannock. Glasgow: Collins, 1977.

153p; pbk   ISBN: 0-00-435009-X
                                        BL: X.619/17852

Rather innovative at the time of publication but not containing anything which is not available in more up-to-date format in recent works.

☞ Subsequent ed. J228

228 Football League tables: 1889 to the present / editor Jim Mallory; assistant editor Jeanette Tannock. Rev. ed. Glasgow: Collins, 1978.

154p; pbk   ISBN: 0-00-411634-8
                                        BL: X.619/18876

☞ Previous ed. J227

229 Tables of the Midland and Athenian League / Ray Spiller. Basildon: AFS, 1985.

58p; pbk   ISBN: 0-946531-26-9

Includes every single final League table from the date of formation.

230 Tables of the Northern League and the Isthmian League / Ray Spiller. Basildon: AFS, 1985.

54p; pbk   ISBN: 0-946531-27-7

Includes every single final League table from the date of formation.

231 Tables of Cheshire County, North West Counties League, Northern Counties (East), Southern League, Northern Premier Alliance / Ray Spiller. Basildon: AFS, 1986.

100p; pbk   ISBN: 0-946531-36-6

All the final League tables from the date of formation.

232 Tables of the Central League and Football Combination / Ray Spiller. Basildon: AFS, 1986.

All the reserve team final League tables from the date of formation.

233 Tables of the Western League, Delphian League, Lancashire League, Birmingham and District League, Hellenic League / Ray Spiller. Basildon: AFS, 1986.

100p; pbk   ISBN: 0-946531-41-2

All the final League tables from the date of formation.

CHAPTER
K

The Lighter Side
of the Game

WE ARE REGULARLY REMINDED that 'football is a funny old game'. Does this mean that the sound of laughter rings out loud and clear during a match, from players and spectators alike? Not a bit of it! Watching football is diverting, absorbing, thrilling, disappointing, infuriating and uplifting in turn, but occasions for laughter in the midst of serious battle are few and far between; a referee falls over, the linesman drops his flag, the ball strikes firmly home in that area known decorously as the lower abdomen or an announcement is relayed over the tannoy – 'Will Mr John Smith please return home immediately, your wife has just given birth'. These are the predictable hardy perennials guaranteed to relieve the tension and provoke a wave of ironic mirth. Add a smattering of goalkeeping errors, some fine own goals and the occasional streaker or unscheduled canine pitch invasion and there, in a nutshell, is the humour of football.

One might conclude therefore that the game itself does not generate many genuinely funny moments. What football does provide though is a shared experience for its followers, a common backdrop against which like-minded people can throw their darts of wit. And what of the hapless Aunt Sallys who make up the targets? Teams, players, managers, commentators, officials and fellow supporters – all are cruelly exposed to be mercilessly pilloried in the fashion which characterises so much football humour. Our national game is a great vehicle for humour and banter and there is no shortage of those wanting to go along for the ride.

Because of this incidental nature of football humour, there is relatively little published on the subject. Many serious football studies contain amusing elements and anecdotes as a matter of course but researchers will find in this chapter only those publications which deliberately address the humorous or comic side of the game.

Jokes, strange incidents, quotations and quiz trivia abound. Particularly good examples for the trivia buff are the Jack Rollin *Soccer Shorts* books [K61, K65], whilst tales of the unexpected are well covered by Andrew Ward [K63] and David Prole [K57]. There are several good sources of quotations including the fabled *Colemanballs* series [K29]. Quiz fans are well catered for [K90-144] and Roy Ullyett [K76] provides an amusing visual commentary on contemporary incidents.

It should be noted that there is one major and deliberate omission from this section. The last decade has spawned the growth of a new style 'observational' or 'alternative' humour in the football world, as in the world of comedy itself. It seems that now, more than ever before, the printed word is able to generate genuine belly laughs and fits of uncontrolled giggling among football followers. The particular outlet for humorist writers of this type has been the fanzine. Call it satire, pure wit, surreal observation or just an astute knack for tuning into the more amusing nuances of the game, but it cannot be denied that much of this new material is genuinely funny. It is distinct enough to constitute a genre in its own right and has therefore been treated in a separate chapter within this bibliography.

A serious game football may be, but some of the best and most enjoyable reading is to be found amongst the lighthearted entries which follow and it should not be spurned by the serious historian.

The Lighter Side of the Game ~ Contents

Humour

1   Football yarns / compiled and edited by 'Phil'.
Liverpool: T. Kilburn, 1921.
128p   BL: D

2   Laughs in short pants: fun on the football field /
compiled by S. E. Thomas. London: Brightsome
Publications, 1947-   BL: 12332.f.16

3   Shack's guide to soccer / Len Shackleton in
collaboration with David R. Jack; photographs and
cartoons by Mickey Durling. London: Nicholas Kaye,
1956.
123p; illus   BL: 012306.de.6

   One of football's more waggish characters subtitled
   this book 'The bookball handfoot'.

4   Soccer for suckers / Dennis Barry Jackson. Kingswood:
Right Way Books, 1960.
55p   BL: 7925.bb.85

5   Football daft / Michael Parkinson; cartoons by
'Graham'. London: Stanley Paul, 1968.
127p   BL: X.449/3243

6   How to play football: being a comprehensive guide to
the playing of the game / Sir Norbert Pratt-Fall; edited
and collected by Mr William Rushton; posed and enacted
by Mr Roy Hudd and Mr Richard Ingrams; with tasteful
plates by Mr Lewis Morley. Walton-on-Thames:
Margaret & Jack Hobbs, 1968.
45p; illus   BL: X.619/10170

   An Edwardian style coaching manual definitely not
   for the serious minded — many long-shorted and
   moustachioed photos complement this amusing
   piece. Chapter 1 is opened by one of the game's lesser
   known mottoes — 'Ho football ho! For thou art a noble
   sport. So much for all those pooftahs who leap about
   on the tennis court'.

7   Not all a ball / John Moynihan. London: MacGibbon &
Kee, 1970.
220p   SBN: 261-63173-X
                                 BL: X.809/7442

8   Park football / John Moynihan; illustrated by John
Jensen. London: Pelham, 1970.
142p   SBN: 7207-0396-4
                                 BL: X.629/2829

   There have always been thousands more playing their
   football in the parks than on the professional field of
   play — even the 'greats' had to start somewhere.
   That atmosphere, folklore and humour are all nicely
   captured here.

9   The wit of soccer / compiled by Kenneth
Wolstenholme. London: Frewin, 1971.
120p; illus   ISBN 0-09-101590-1
                               BL: X.629/4427

   The 'quips, anecdotes and pungent witticisms' re-
   counted here now appear sadly dated. Nevertheless,
   some good material and a nice evocation of the pre-
   fanzine age when gentle humour still prevailed.

10 The little red book: the thoughts of Bill Shankly / Bill
Shankly. Liverpool: Scouse Press, 1973.
56p; pbk   ISBN: 0-901367-09-5

   Includes a number of classics from the legendary Liverpool manager.

11 Away wi' the goalie! / John Fairgrieve; illustrated by
Rod. London: Stanley Paul, 1977.
126p; illus   ISBN: 0-09-129910-1
                               BL: X.989/52117

   A humorous look at Scottish football.

   ☞ Subsequent ed. K14

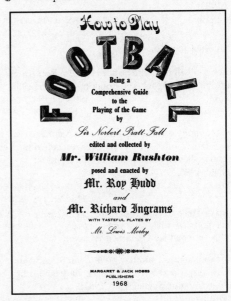

How to Play
FOOTBALL
Being a
Comprehensive Guide
to the
Playing of the Game
by
Sir Norbert Pratt-Fall
edited and collected by
Mr. William Rushton
posed and enacted by
Mr. Roy Hudd
and
Mr. Richard Ingrams
WITH TASTEFUL PLATES BY
Mr. Lewis Morley

MARGARET & JACK HOBBS
PUBLISHERS
1968

12 Football makes me laugh / compiled by Malcolm
Macdonald. London: Pelham; Walton-on-Thames: M. &
J. Hobbs, 1979.
96p; illus   ISBN: 0-7207-1107-X
                               BL: X.629/12727

   ☞ Also listed at: C329

13 Football crazy / Colin McNaughton. London: Heinemann, 1980.
32p; illus

ISBN: 0-434-94991-4
BL: X.992/1984

14 Scottish football laugh-in / John Fairgrieve. Rev. ed. Dalkeith: Lang Syne, 1982.
120p; illus; pbk

ISBN: 0-946264-03-1

☞ Previous ed. K11; subsequent ed. K15

15 Scottish football laugh-in / John Fairgrieve. 2nd rev. ed. Dalkeith: Lang Syne, 1982.
136p; illus; pbk

ISBN: 0-946264-743-0

☞ Previous ed. K14

16 The Sunday footballer / Tony Stephens. Roks, 1982.
179p

Another evocation of football as played by mere mortals.

17 Let's have a ball / Roy Bartlett. Bognor Regis: New Horizon, 1983.
184p

ISBN: 0-86116-812-7
BL: X.629/22607

18 Stop the game: I want to get on! / Jimmy Greaves with Norman Giller; illustrations by Roy Ullyett. London: Harrap, 1983.
96p; illus; pbk

ISBN: 0-245-54010-5
BL: X.622/18535

☞ Also listed at: C225

19 Subsoccer: football from the bottom down / Rob King; with cartoons by Rod McLeod. London: Souvenir, 1985.
165p; illus

ISBN: 0-285-62706-6
BL: YC.1986.a.879

20 Football is a funny game: according to the Saint and Greavsie / Ian St. John and Jimmy Greaves; edited by Bob Patience; illustrations by Jake Tebbit. London: Stanley Paul, 1986.
104p; illus

ISBN: 0-09-166120-X
BL: YK.1987.b.288

The two strikers formed a surprise partnership as TV football pundits with the comic touch. This is the first of a series of light-hearted volumes.

21 The Saint and Greavsie football book / Ian St. John and Jimmy Greaves; edited by Bob Patience; illustrations by Jake Tebbit. London: Stanley Paul, 1987.
128p; illus

ISBN: 0-09-173456-8
BL: YK.1987.b.6727

22 Football is still a funny game / Ian St. John and Jimmy Greaves; edited by Bob Patience; illustrations by Robin Bouttell. London: Stanley Paul, 1988.
127p; illus; pbk

ISBN: 0-09-173737-0
BL: YK.1989.b.811

23 Extra time and it's still a funny old game / Ian St. John and Jimmy Greaves; edited by Bob Patience; illustrations by Robin Bouttell. London: Stanley Paul, 1989.
122p; illus; pbk

ISBN: 0-09-174251-X
BL: YK.1990.b.5232

24 Where's the bar?: an alternative guide to non-league football / edited by Martin Lacey. Sheffield: Juma, 1990-
illus; pbk

Title varies   BL: ZK.9.b.5668

Humorous articles and skits on the upper end of the lower echelons of the game.

25 Life at the tip: Les Bence on the game / Merv Grist. London: Virgin, 1993.
201p; illus; pbk

ISBN: 0-86369-613-9
BL: YK.1994.a.8279

A season's diary in the inglorious life of Les Bence, manager of Athletico Whaddon, playing in the Multivite Vegeburger / Singleton's Valve Replacement League. Thought to be ever so loosely based on Trowbridge Town.

26 The far corner: a mazy dribble through north-east football / Harry Pearson. London: Little, Brown, 1994.
256p; illus

ISBN: 0-316-91189-5

The north-east has always been described as a hotbed of soccer. This amusing account perpetuates that truism. I only need to quote from the publicity blurb to present a flavour of the contents — 'tales of heroism, human frailty and the difficulty of eating an egg mayonnaise stottie without staining your trousers . . .'.

27 The official Baddiel & Skinner fantasy football diary / David Baddiel and Frank Skinner. London: Little, Brown, 1994.
33p; illus

Bibliography: p33   ISBN: 0-316-91316-2

Based on the surreal cult TV series 'Fantasy Football'.

Quotations

28 Sports quotes / Jonathon Green and Don Atyeo.
London: Omnibus, 1979.
216p; illus; pbk   ISBN: 0-86001-606-4

29 Private Eye's Colemanballs / illustrated by Larry;
compiled and edited by Barry Fantoni. London: Private
Eye, 1982.
93p; illus; pbk   ISBN: 0-233-97490-3
                                    BL: X.958/13207

Commentators are renowned for their heat-of-the-moment gaffes; David Coleman was particularly adept, so much so that he lent his name to the genre which the satirical magazine Private Eye made their own. This includes 24 pages on football – 'And there'll be more football in a moment but first we've got the highlights of the Scottish League Cup Final'.

30 The book of football quotations / compiled by Peter
Ball and Phil Shaw; illustrated by Simon Ellinas. London:
Stanley Paul, 1984.
258p; illus; index; pbk
   Bibliography: p243-244   ISBN: 0-09-158461-2
                                    BL: X.809/63654

A comprehensive selection of real gems, both serious and humorous.

☞ Subsequent ed. K32

31 Private Eye's Colemanballs 2 / compiled and edited by
Barry Fantoni; illustrated by Larry. London: Private Eye,
1984.
96p; illus; pbk   ISBN: 0-233-97700-7
                                    BL: X.958/26193

32 The book of football quotations / compiled by Peter
Ball and Phil Shaw. Rev. ed. London: Stanley Paul, 1986.
260p; illus; index; pbk
   Includes bibliography   ISBN: 0-09-166161-7
                                    BL: YK.1987.a.4270

☞ Previous ed. K30; subsequent ed. K35

33 Private Eye's Colemanballs 3 / compiled and edited by
Barry Fantoni; illustrated by Larry. London: Private Eye,
1986.
96p; illus; pbk   ISBN: 0-233-97985-9
                                    BL: YC.1987.a.12422

34 Private Eye's Colemanballs 4 / compiled and edited by
Barry Fantoni; illustrated by Larry. London: Private Eye,
1988.
93p; illus; pbk   ISBN: 0-233-98337-6
                                    BL: YC.1989.a.1110

35 The book of football quotations / compiled by Peter
Ball and Phil Shaw. 2nd rev. ed. London: Stanley Paul,
1989.
256p; illus; index; pbk   ISBN: 0-09-174057-6
                                    BL: YK.1990.a.697

☞ Previous ed. K32; subsequent ed. K40

36 The Guinness dictionary of sports quotations /
compiled by Colin Jarman. Enfield: Guinness, 1990.
298p; index; pbk   ISBN: 0-85112-922-6
                                    BL: YK.1991.a.551

One of the best, includes many football examples.

37 Private Eye Colemanballs 5 / compiled and edited by
Barry Fantoni; illustrated by Larry. London: Private Eye,
1990.
92p; illus; pbk   ISBN: 0-552-13751-0
                                    BL: YK.1991.a.9571

38 Sports quotes of the eighties / compiled by Peter Ball,
Phil Shaw. London: Mandarin, 1990.
231p; illus; pbk   ISBN: 0-7493-0366-2
                                    BL: YK.1990.a.4423

39 Private Eye Colemanballs 6 / compiled and edited by
Barry Fantoni; illustrated by Larry. London: Private Eye,
1992.
96p; illus; pbk   ISBN: 0-552-13996-3
                                    BL: YK.1993.a.3877

40 The Umbro book of football quotations / compiled by
Peter Ball and Phil Shaw. 4th ed. Stanley Paul, 1993.
192p; illus; index; pbk   ISBN: 0-09-177626-0
                                    BL: YK.1994.b.5757

The most comprehensive recent source for football alone contains the serious, the amusing and the obscure – ideal material for football writers.

☞ Previous ed. K35

41 Private Eye Colemanballs 7 / compiled and edited by
Barry Fantoni; illustrated by Larry. London: Private Eye,
1994.
illus; pbk   ISBN: 0-552-14279-4

42 Scottish football quotations / compiled by Kenny
MacDonald. Edinburgh: Mainstream, 1994.
224p; index; pbk   ISBN: 1-85158-643-1

Comprehensive selection of gems from north of the border.

43 The sporting word: prize quotes from the world of sport
/ compiled by Desmond Lynam and David Teasdale.
London: BBC, 1994.
256p; pbk   ISBN: 0-563-36971-X

Records & Trivia

44 The Clipper annual of football facts. London: Clipper Press, 1969-
illus, maps

Title and publisher varies

45 The football handbook to end all football handbooks / Chris Lightbown; with cartoons by Paul Rigby. London: Wolfe, 1974.
144p; illus
SBN: 7234-0532-8
BL: X.629/6571

☞ Also listed at: L1

46 The Guinness book of soccer facts and feats / Jack Rollin. Enfield: Guinness Superlatives, 1978.
255p; illus; index
ISBN: 0-900424-45-1
BL: X.0622/907

☞ Subsequent ed. K47

47 The Guinness book of soccer facts & feats / Jack Rollin. 2nd ed. Enfield: Guinness Superlatives, 1979.
251p; illus; index
ISBN: 0-85112-203-5
BL: X.620/18929

☞ Previous ed. K46; subsequent ed. K49

48 A record book of Scottish football / edited by Forrest Robertson. Paisley: Wilfion Books, 1979.
70p; pbk
ISBN: 0-905075-06-4

49 The Guinness book of soccer facts & feats / Jack Rollin. 3rd ed. Enfield: Guinness Superlatives, 1980.
255p; illus; index
ISBN: 0-85112-213-2
BL: X.622/22836

☞ Previous ed. K47; subsequent ed. K50

50 The Guinness book of soccer facts and feats / Jack Rollin. 4th ed. Enfield: Guinness Superlatives, 1981.
256p; illus; index
ISBN: 0-85112-227-2

☞ Previous ed. K49; subsequent ed. K53

51 The book of football lists / Jimmy Greaves with Norman Giller. London: Sidgwick & Jackson, 1983.
192p; illus; pbk
ISBN: 0-283-99034-1

☞ Subsequent ed. K54

52 The book of football lists / Robert Hutton Moss. London: W. H. Allen, 1983.
234p; pbk
ISBN: 0-352-31427-3
BL: X.629/22574

53 The Guinness book of soccer facts & feats / Jack Rollin. 5th ed. London: Guinness Superlatives, 1983.
256p; illus; index
ISBN: 0-85112-240-X

☞ Previous ed. K50

54 The book of football lists / Jimmy Greaves with Norman Giller. London: Panther, 1984.
236p; illus; pbk
ISBN: 0-586-06250-5
BL: X.629/25495

☞ Previous ed. K51

55 Football crazy! / compiled by Jimmy Hill. London: Robson, 1985.
240p; illus
ISBN: 0-86051-356-4
BL: X.629/2755-7 • BL: YK.1986.a.1496

56 Soccer: the records / Jack Rollin. Enfield: Guinness, 1985.
136p; illus; index
ISBN: 0-85112-436-4 (cased) • ISBN: 0-85112-449-6 (pbk)
BL: X.622/24979

☞ Subsequent ed. K60

57 Funny game, football: curiosities, coincidences, statistics and other soccer trivia / collected by David Prole; illustrated by Ken Jackson. Derby: Breedon Books, 1986.
106p; illus; pbk
ISBN: 0-907969-21-6
BL: YK.1990.a.4607

One of the best sources for researchers seeking the more bizarre elements of the game.

58 Guinness soccer firsts / John Robinson. Enfield: Guinness Superlatives, 1986.
128p; illus; index; pbk
ISBN: 0-85112-800-9
BL: YK.1986.b.1069

☞ Subsequent ed. K62; Also listed at: J164

59 Football: startling stories behind the records / Jim Benagh. New York: Sterling Pole; Distributed by Blandford, 1987.
128p; illus; index
ISBN: 0-8069-6618-1 (cased) • ISBN: 0-8069-6619-X (library ed.)
ISBN: 0-8069-6858-3 (pbk)
BL: YK.1989.a.132

60 Soccer: records, facts and champions / Jack Rollin. 2nd ed. Enfield: Guinness, 1988.
144p; illus; index; pbk
ISBN: 0-85112-360-0
BL: YK.1989.b.106

☞ Previous ed. K56

61 Soccer shorts / Jack Rollin. Enfield: Guinness, 1988.
128p; illus   ISBN: 0-85112-321-X
                                     BL: YK.1989.a.54

First in a fascinating series by one of football's best
known writers. Researchers and authors will find it an
excellent source of trivia and anecdotal material.

62 Soccer firsts / John Robinson. 2nd ed. Enfield:
Guinness, 1989.
128p; illus; index; pbk   ISBN: 0-85112-367-8
                                     BL: YK.1990.b.2089

☞ Also listed at: J170; Previous ed. K58

63 Soccer's strangest matches / Andrew Ward. London:
Robson, 1989.
x, 206p; illus   ISBN: 0-86051-600-8
                                     BL: YK.1990.a.3354

The best source for coverage of bizarre games in the
history of football: elephants, stilts, prisoners, blind-
folded players, fancy dress – all this and much more.

64 The football fact book / Jack Rollin. Enfield: Guinness,
1990.
256p; illus; index   ISBN: 0-85112-901-3
                                     BL: YK.1990.b.9823

☞ Subsequent ed. K69

65 More soccer shorts / Jack Rollin. Enfield: Guinness,
1991.
128p   ISBN: 0-85112-992-7
                                     BL: YK.1991.a.11141

66 Ian St John's book of soccer lists / Ian St. John with
Geoff Tibballs. London: CollinsWillow, 1992.
192p; pbk   ISBN: 0-00-218435-4
                                     BL: YK.1993.a.8821

☞ Subsequent ed. K73

67 The book of football records. Derby: Breedon Books,
1993.
256p; illus   ISBN: 1-873626-30-4

68 The Breedon book of Scottish football records /
Gordon Smailes. Derby: Breedon Books, 1993.
170p; illus   ISBN: 1-873626-42-8

69 The Guinness football fact book / Jack Rollin. 2nd ed.
Enfield: Guinness, 1993.
255p; illus; index   ISBN: 0-85112-716-9
                                     BL: YK.1993.b.14642

☞ Previous ed. K64

70 Shoot A-Z of football records / Ian Morrison. 1993.

71 The Cassell soccer companion: history, facts, anecdotes
/ David Pickering. London: Cassell, 1994.
359p   ISBN: 0-304-34231-9
                                     BL: YK.1995.b.1036

Described as a glorious treasure trove of soccer
facts, this publication is arranged in A-Z format,
starting with 'A's, the nickname of Banstead Athletic Football Club, and ending with 'Zulus', the
extraordinary spoof football team that toured England in the wake of the Zulu War of 1879 – an
excellent quick reference book with some unusual entries.

72 The crazy world of soccer / cartoons by Bill Stott.
Watford: Exley, 1994.
74p; illus; pbk   ISBN: 1-850154-95-3

73 Ian St. John's book of soccer lists / Ian St. John with
Geoff Tibballs. Rev. ed. London: CollinsWillow, 1994.
192p; pbk   ISBN: 0-00-218486-9

☞ Previous ed. K66

Cartoons

74   Football mad / Peter Moloney. Manchester?: Gallery Press.

75   Tom Webster of the Daily Mail among the sportsmen. London: Associated Newspapers, 1920-1939.
96p; chiefly illus

> *Published annually*   BL: 12316.s.26
>
> Webster was one of the best known cartoonists of his age; his annuals include many football examples – excellent source of illustrations for club historians.

76   Roy Ullyett's sports cartoon annual: cartoons from the Daily Express. London: Daily Express, 1956-

> *Also entitled: Daily Express sports cartoon annual*
>
>   BL: P.P.6661
>
> Ullyett performs a similar service to Tom Webster from the 1950s onwards. As well as being a good source of illustrations the cartoons are effectively a season-by-season commentary and tell much of the flavour and politics of the game as each year passes.

77   Roy of the Rovers football annual. London: Amalgamated Press, 1957-

> *Further editions published as: Tiger: book of Roy of the Rovers; Roy of the Rovers*   ISSN: 0262-3498
>
>   BL: P.P.6753.alu • BL: P.P.6758.fa
>
> Although this bibliography excludes boys' annuals, 'Roy of the Rovers' has been included as an exception. Roy Race of Melchester Rovers is surely football's most famous cartoon creation, appearing here in his famous red and yellow strip. Features include a history of the origins and early years of Melchester Rovers along with a behind the scenes tour of Melchester Stadium and everyday stories of footballing folk – '...de-

> termined to break himself of his bad shooting habit, Len clutched a miner's lamp in each hand as he weaved and swerved among his pals, the ball at his toes'.

78   Mordillo football / Guillermo Mordillo. London: Hutchinson, 1981.
69p; all illus   ISBN: 0-09-146460-9

>   BL: L.45/1333
>
> A collection of football cartoons by this famous cartoonist.

79   The best of *Fitba' Daft*: a selection of football cartoons / E. W. Wright. Edinburgh?: Portain Press, 1986.
64p; illus; pbk   ISBN: 0-948341-03-3

> The game in Scotland provides ample material of the humorous variety.

80   Duffer's guide to football / 'Gren'. Bromley: Columbus, 1986.
80p; illus; pbk   ISBN: 0-86287-290-1

81   At the end of the day: a collection of vaguely amusing cartoons culled from the pages of the alternative football press / Liam Sluyter. Edinburgh: Mainstream, 1990.
134p; illus; pbk   ISBN: 1-873216-00-9

82   The Viz Billy the Fish football yearbook. London: John Brown, 1990.
48p

> Second only to *Roy of the Rovers* this cartoon strip enjoyed a widespread cult following in the late 1980s, appearing in the adult comic *Viz*. Billy 'The Fish' Thomson was born half-man half-fish and his heroic exploits for Fulchester United parody the popular footballing stories of children's comics. This book includes all the story strips from 1983 to date.

83   The armchair guide to football / Tim Bradford. Harrogate: Take That Books, 1994.
32p; illus; pbk   ISBN: 1-873668-07-4

84   Roy of the Rovers: the playing years / Colin M. Jarman and Peter Acton. Harpenden: Queen Anne, 1994.
224p; chiefly illus   ISBN: 1-85291-548-X

> From his first appearance in the *Tiger* comic in 1954 to his tragic helicopter accident in 1993, Roy Race won most of the game's major honours and was credited with having scored around 5,000 first-class goals. There is something of the Sherlock Holmes persona in Race – we sometimes confuse reality with fiction, perhaps because we would sooner believe he really did exist. This substantial volume perpetuates the myth in most admirable fashion.

Joke Books

Although football is a game which can generate tremendous humour, it is not generally renowned as a subject for straightforward jokes. The following is a selection of those that do exist. Further entries can be found in the club histories section as some of the major clubs have published their own joke books.

85   Football howlers / Victor Rae. London: The author, 1951.
23p; illus; pbk   BL: 012331.m.212
'What flies high, lights low, wears shoes and has none?' 'A football' is the howl-inducing answer to this eighteenth century riddle!

86   Best football jokes / compiled by Edward Phillips. London: Wolfe, 1970.
63p
(Mini ha-ha books)   SBN: 7234-0163-2
                                                   BL: X.989/17750

87   More best football jokes / compiled by Edward Phillips. London: Wolfe, 1976.
63p; pbk
(Mini ha-ha books)   ISBN: 0-7234-0699-5
                                                   BL: X.907/14389

88   The world's best football jokes / compiled by Edward Phillips; illustrated by Graham Morris. London: Angus & Robertson, 1991.
96p; illus; pbk   ISBN: 0-207-16957-8
                                                   BL: YK.1991.a.9184

89   The official Green Army joke book / John Byrne. Dublin: O'Brien, 1994.
80p; illus; pbk   ISBN: 0-86278-393-3
                                                   BL: YK.1994.a.18026
Liberal servings of Southern Irish humour.

Quiz Books

Football followers love to test their knowledge of the game. Many repeat questions crop up time and again in the entries in this section and as the years pass questions become obsolete as new records are broken. Good fun but unlikely to be of real value to the serious researcher.

90   Soccer enquire within / John A. Graydon. London: Findon, 1946.
64p; pbk
An early example illustrating the soccer fan's fascination for facts and trivia – 'over 300 questions and answers on every conceivable soccer subject'.

91   S. Evelyn Thomas' football fanfare / with drawings by Jack Ketton. London: The author, 1948.
63p; pbk   BL: 7919.cc.53
Quizzes, photographs and cartoons in this early example of 'fun for the football fan'.

92   Soccer quiz: 200 questions and answers / Victor Rae. London: 1950-
15p; illus
Published annually   BL: 7921.aa.19
An early example of a popular genre.

93   Football quiz / Jack Cardwell. Birkenhead: Gannet Press, 1959.
79p   BL: 7923.g.59

94   Shoot soccer quiz book. London: IPC Magazines, 1970-
illus
Published annually; for children   BL: P.441/285

95   Football fan: star and quiz book. London: H. Darton, 1971.
52p; illus
For children   ISBN: 0-85593-000-4

96   Football quiz book no. 1 / compiled by Gordon Jeffery. London: Collins, 1972.
128p; pbk   ISBN: 0-00-690557-9

97   Football quiz book no. 2 / compiled by Gordon Jeffery. London: Collins, 1973.
128p; pbk   ISBN: 0-00-690724-5

98   The question and answer book of football. London:
     Hamlyn, 1973.
     63p; illus   ISBN: 0-600-37408-4

     ☞ Subsequent ed. K100

99   Football quiz book no. 3 / compiled by Gordon Jeffery.
     London: Collins, 1974.
     128p; pbk   ISBN: 0-00-690949-3

100 The question and answer book of football. Rev. ed.
     London: Hamlyn, 1974.
     63p; illus   ISBN: 0-600-37412-2

     ☞ Previous ed. K98

101 The Armada football quiz book / Gordon Jeffery.
     London: Armada, 1975.
     126p; illus, 2 maps; pbk   ISBN: 0-00-691038-6

102 Football: how much do you really know? / John
     Tagholm; illustrated by Robin Anderson. London:
     Independent Television Books, 1975.
     128p; illus; index; pbk
     (Look-in books)

          Bibliography: p126   ISBN: 0-900727-42-X
                                        BL: X.619/15315

     ☞ Subsequent ed. K105

103 The football quiz book / Graham Spiers; introduction
     by Mike Channon. London: Croom Helm, 1975.
     138p; illus; pbk
               ISBN: 0-85664-203-7 • ISBN: 0-85664-233-9
                                        BL: X.629/10212

104 The Puffin soccer quiz book / David Prole; illustrations
     by Illustra Design. Harmondsworth: Puffin, 1975.
     95p; illus, 1 map; pbk   ISBN: 0-14-030792-3
                                        BL: X.619/15245

105 Football: how much do you really know? / John
     Tagholm; illustrated by Robin Anderson. London:
     Severn House, 1976.
     128p; illus; index
     (Look-in books)

          Bibliography: p126   ISBN: 0-7278-0182-1
                                        BL: X.629/10953

     ☞ Previous ed. K102

106 Football quiz / Gordon Jeffery. London: Armada, 1976.
     96p; illus; pbk   ISBN: 0-00-690951-5
                                        BL: X.619/17525

107 Purnell's questions and answers book of football /
     designed and edited by David Roberts. Maidenhead:
     Purnell, 1976.
     63p; illus; index

          Spine title: Questions and answers book of world football
                                   ISBN: 0-361-03260-9
                                        BL: X.622/5349

108 Brian Moore's football quiz book / illustrated by Gary
     Rees. London: Independent Television Books; Arrow
     Books, 1977.
     95p; illus, 1 map; pbk
     (Look-in books)
                                   ISBN: 0-09-915540-0
                                        BL: X.619/18356

109 Football quiz / Gordon Jeffery. London: Armada, 1977.
     96p; illus; pbk   ISBN: 0-00-691290-7
                                        BL: X.619/18052

110 Football quiz / Gordon Jeffery. London: Armada, 1978.
     96p; illus, 1 map; pbk   ISBN: 0-00-691385-7
                                        BL: X.619/18916

111 'Roy of the Rovers' football quiz book / edited by Barrie
     J. Tomlinson. London: Mirror Books, 1978.
     128p; illus; pbk   ISBN: 0-85939-141-8
                                        BL: X.619/18887

112 'Roy of the Rovers' football quiz book 1979-1980 /
     edited by Barrie J. Tomlinson; introduction by Trevor
     Francis. London: Mirror Books, 1979.
     128p; illus; pbk   ISBN: 0-85939-164-7

113 The Scottish football quizbook / compiled by John
     Gibson and others. Ayr: Kyle, 1979.
     71p; 1 map; pbk   ISBN: 0-906955-00-9
                                        BL: X.629/15044

114 The 2nd Scottish football quizbook / compiled by John
     Gibson and others. Ayr: Kyle, 1980.
     75p; 1 map; pbk   ISBN: 0-906955-15-7
                                        BL: X.629/15061

115 Beaver football quiz / Tom Tully; illustrated by Bob
     Harvey and David Mostyn. London: Beaver, 1980.
     110p; illus; pbk   ISBN: 0-600-20177-5
                                        BL: X.629/14674

116 Football quiz / Gordon Jeffery. London: Armada, 1980.
     62, 40p; illus, maps; pbk   ISBN: 0-00-691740-2
                                        BL: X.629/14040

117 The Terry Venables soccer quiz book. London:
     Scholastic Publications, 1980.
     111p; illus; pbk
     (Hippo book)   ISBN: 0-590-70037-5
                                        BL: X.629/14010

118 Test your soccer knowledge / Philip Evans; illustrated
     by Bob Harvey. Sevenoaks: Knight, 1980.
     127p; illus; pbk   ISBN: 0-340-25823-3
                                        BL: X.629/26955

119 Football quiz 1981/82 / Gordon Jeffery. London:
     Fontana, 1981.
     128p; illus; pbk   ISBN: 0-00-691945-6

120 Football quiz / Gordon Jeffery. London: Fontana, 1982.
     127p; illus, 1 map; pbk   ISBN: 0-00-692066-7
                                        BL: X.629/18812

121 The soccer quiz book / Chris Coley; assisted by Bob Nocton; introduced by Bryan Robson. East Ardsley: EP Publishing, 1983.
64p; illus; pbk
ISBN: 0-7158-0882-6 • ISBN: 0-7158-0852-4
BL: X.629/2230

122 The league football history facts & quiz book. Grimsby: Hobbypress, 1984.
56p; illus; pbk
BL: X.629/27067

123 Quiz book for football experts. London: Cockerel, 1986.
240p; pbk
ISBN: 1-86991-402-3

124 The Scottish quizbook / Jim Bruxton and Brian Pendreigh. Edinburgh: Lennox, 1986.
128p; pbk
ISBN: 0-9511520-0-9
BL: YC.1988.a.10639

125 A question of football / Emlyn Hughes. London: Arthur Barker, 1987.
109p
ISBN: 0-213-16944-4
BL: YK.1992.a.1916

126 Football quiz book / Ian Thomson and Mansel Davies. London: Sphere, 1988.
139p; pbk
ISBN: 0-7474-0111-X
BL: YK.1989.a.1912

127 A question of football / Emlyn Hughes. London: Arthur Barker, 1988.
110p
ISBN: 0-213-16958-4
BL: YK.1991.a.9619

128 Bob Wilson's soccer quiz book / Bob Wilson with William Walker. London: Willow, 1989.
208p; pbk
ISBN: 0-00-218356-0
BL: YK.1990.a.78

129 The Guinness soccer quiz book / Julian Farino. Enfield: Guinness, 1989.
127p; illus, maps; pbk
ISBN: 0-85112-368-6
BL: YK.1990.b.1234

130 The official FA soccer quiz book: more than 1,000 questions to test your football know-how. London: Rosters, 1990.
157p; illus; pbk
ISBN: 1-85631-008-6
BL: YK.1994.a.5358

131 Trevor Brooking football quiz book / Trevor Brooking with William Walker. London: Ward Lock, 1990.
128p; illus; pbk
ISBN: 0-7063-6968-8
BL: YK.1990.a.7580

132 Jack Charlton's soccer quiz book / Jack Charlton with William Walker. London: Collins Willow, 1991.
vii, 168p; illus; pbk
ISBN: 0-00-218423-0
BL: YK.1991.a.9271

133 Junior Football Association quiz book. London: Rosters, 1991.
200p; pbk
ISBN: 1-85631-044-2

134 Gary Lineker's soccer quiz book. London: CollinsWillow, 1992.
176p; pbk
ISBN: 0-00-218436-2
BL: YK.1994.a.1013

135 The great Scots soccer quiz book / Colin McCullough. Scotland?: The author?, 1992.
80p; pbk
ISBN: 1-872769-60-8
BL: YK.1994.a.4640

136 Scottish football quizbook / quizmaster Alan Campbell. Argyll: Argyll Publishing, 1992.
70p; pbk
ISBN: 1-874640-05-X
BL: YK.1995.a.494

137 The Shoot! soccer quiz game book / compiled by William Walker. Enfield: Guinness, 1992.
160p; illus; pbk
ISBN: 0-85112-586-7
BL: YK.1992.b.8728

138 Alan Hansen's soccer quiz book / Alan Hansen with William Walker. London: CollinsWillow, 1993.
172p; illus; pbk
ISBN: 0-00-218528-8
BL: YK.1994.a.2234

139 The FA quiz book / David Barber. London: Stanley Paul, 1993.
96p; pbk
ISBN: 0-09-177623-6
BL: YK.1994.a.3521

140 Jack Charlton's World Cup quizbook / Jack Charlton with William Walker. London: CollinsWillow, 1994.
190p; illus, 1 map; pbk
ISBN: 0-00-218475-3
BL: YK.1994.a.11564

141 The official FAI soccer quiz book / compiled by Michael Hayes; introduced by Jimmy Magee. Dublin: Sportsworld, 1994.
94p; illus
Cover title: Official FAI World Cup quiz book

142 Football / Neil Cook and Paul Harrison. London: Puffin, 1995.
32p; illus; pbk
(100 questions & answers)
For children
ISBN: 0-14-037409-4

143 Soccer crossword puzzles / Joel Rothman.
16p; pbk

144 He shoots, he scores: 30 fact filled football crosswords / compiled by Roy & Sue Preston. London: Macmillan Children's, 1995.
64p; pbk
ISBN: 0-330-34106-5

Fanzines

THE DECISION TO INCLUDE FANZINES in this bibliography was not a difficult one. Not only their contents, but the very fact of their existence says much about the past, present and future of association football and it would have been a grave omission to have excluded them.

That said, the fanzine holdings of the British Library are far from complete. This is not because the Library is averse to holding them, quite the contrary, but rather that the fanzine publishers are often unaware of their obligation to send copies to the Library. Those publishers who do send in copies of their fanzines have the satisfaction of knowing that their titles will appear in the weekly list of new British publications which the Library publishes. This may have no small impact on sales, but most publishers have not in the past taken advantage of this opportunity.

Until recently, fanzines have had very much an 'underground' existence but the market continues to grow by the day and there is now more awareness and sophistication on the part of both publishers and readers than there was in the formative years of fanzine culture. If this listing can help in gaining a broader readership for fanzine material and a wider recognition of its value then it will have been more than worthwhile.

Very few of the titles listed carry an International Standard Serial Number (the unique identifying number used by libraries and the book trade to facilitate ordering), or even clearly state the name or address of the publisher or distributor. For this reason most of the entries below are brief. Where titles are held by the British Library, it has sometimes been possible to supply some of this information. On the whole though, these titles are most easily obtained through the specialist dealers who stock them. With some exceptions, the vast majority of these publications date from the mid 1980s onwards and, typically, comprise between twenty and fifty pages in soft back format. Many are published at irregular intervals.

It is only in publishing terms however that fanzines are ephemeral or 'fugitive'. They are now firmly established as a very important part of football literature. They are the 'young pups' snapping at the heels of authority, occasionally overstepping the mark and receiving a sharp rebuke, but always letting the footballing powers that be know that they are around, whilst displaying an unnerving unpredictability which has made them largely unpopular with players, managers and administrators alike.

The term 'fanzine', a contraction of 'fan magazine', was first coined in the United States in 1949 where it referred to magazines published for science fiction fans. The same concept was applied on home soil in the mid 1970s as followers of punk and 'new wave' music sought to express their individuality and rallied against the established and increasingly commercial face of the music industry, expressing their views in fanzines such as *Sniffin' Glue*, *Ripped and Torn*, and *48 Thrills*. It was a logical progression for this new wave of self-expressionist printed matter to be applied to other areas of popular culture and association football was ready and waiting.

Early club-oriented fanzines were *Terrace Talk* [L620] from York City and *City Gent* [L73] from Bradford City, first published in 1984, but the greatest titles which covered football in its wider sense – *Off the Ball* [L1131], *When Saturday Comes* [L1145] and *The Absolute Game* [L1204] were all landmark publications which established a style of writing and menu of material eagerly devoured and quickly imitated by football followers everywhere. Many more club-oriented titles were spawned and by the late 1980s the number of available titles was approaching 200. Contemporary reviewers of this refreshing new genre were sufficiently impressed to label the trend a 'phenomenon'. Now, just a few years later that sounds an understatement, as the list of titles currently available extends to around a thousand whilst the all-time title list exceeds two thousand. New titles seem to appear every week and definitive lists are out of date as soon as they are published. The proverbial multiplication abilities of the rabbit seem almost ordinary when compared to the exponential growth prevalent in the 'zine scene!

It is not the intention of this introductory overview to present a full history of fanzine publishing as this has been well covered by publications like *El Tel was a Space Alien* [L4] and *Whose Game is it Anyway?* [L5] both of which offer an historical overview and rationale whilst also presenting a selection of typical material from some of the better known titles. Both these anthologies are ideal for any researcher seeking an introduction to fanzine culture, as indeed are the *When Saturday Comes Specials* [L6-7, L9]. Particular mention should be made of *The 'Foul' Book of Football* [L2] presenting the best of a publication straight from the 'Private Eye' stable. *Foul* appeared in 1972, well ahead of its time – it was to be another fourteen years before *When Saturday Comes* was to be published. The two titles are much closer in terms of style and content than the chronology would suggest.

Many of the strands referred to briefly thus far are brought together in Richard

Haynes' book *The Football Imagination* [L11], the first in-depth analysis of fanzine culture and an essential reference work.

Researchers content just to consult the various anthologies on offer need to be cautious. These titles are glossy repackagings of fanzine material in a book format – they are no substitute for the real thing. It is the club-based and general titles which show the true fanzine in all its glory and it might be appropriate at this stage to offer the completely uninitiated a pointer as to the essential nature of the beast.

Fanzines are written by the fans for the fans – they are not published by the football club and , apart from one or two enlightened exceptions, are not officially endorsed by the club authorities. The method of publication is essentially amateur – many fanzines are photocopies of typewritten sheets stapled together, with 'letraset' headings, a cartoon or two and a few handwritten annotations. They look amateurish because that is precisely what they are; even the best examples, compiled on word processors and put together by professional printers, betray their evidently amateur origins but therein lies some of the appeal. The fanzines are a refreshing antidote to the glossy uniformity and 'safe' content of official club programmes which often do little more than fulfil a public relations role. Inviting contributions from all comers, and generally printing most of what they receive, the typical content of any fanzine is truly democratic. Some of the most humorous, well written and erudite material to be found in a fanzine is quite likely to find itself juxtaposed with badly written, appallingly mis-spelt and insensitively expressed material. For most readers this is an attraction rather than a criticism, since most of the weekly or monthly football magazines to be found on the newsagents' shelves offer up predictable fare which too often skirts around the real issues.

Fanzines do debate serious issues and generally address the problems with a candour and perception far beyond that displayed by influential figures within the game. Football hooliganism, identity card schemes, all-seater stadiums, TV coverage – these are just a few of the issues which have galvanised the fanzine writers. Notwithstanding this real concern, one of the most immediately recognisable characteristics of these publications is their propensity to include the more bizarre, humorous and utterly inane sides of the game which 'sensible' publications would never admit: which ground serves the best meat pies; did Thomas Hardy ever watch Dorchester Town; is there a scientific correlation between my team's home results and the time it takes the bloke in seat B108 to consume his pea mix; and why do married men with children of their own still play Subbuteo against their best friend and end up arguing about a disputed goal scored by centre forward Henri Matisse at the china cabinet end? These are some of the most sensible questions which the fanzine writers are likely to pose – some are a little more bizarre.

Surreal though much of the fanzine material may be, it does create a sense of fellowship, linking fan to fan to create a sort of brotherhood which can transcend team allegiance altogether. Some of the material falls on completely stony ground but by and large the cryptic language of fanzine culture is a uniting factor amongst supporters of differing persuasions.

This short digression gives just a hint of what it's all about. Basically, anything goes! If there is a recurrent theme to be discerned though, it is generally praise and amused affection for the past, criticism and amused regard for the present, concern and amused conjecture for the future . . .

Readers who have got this far will either have decided by now that fanzines are not for them, or will be eager to get hold of the real thing. Because most fanzines are not available in public libraries or through newsagents, clues as to the best hunting grounds might be useful for those whose curiosity is aroused. *When Saturday Comes*, which is more readily available, includes regular lists of available titles and sales outlets; 'Sportspages', the specialist book shop with branches in London and Manchester, stocks a full range of current titles; and Steve James of AFN Distribution issues regular catalogues of past and present titles for sale. Steve James has become one of the leading authorities in the culture of the 'alternative football network'. At the time of writing, he is working in conjunction with Chris Harte of the Association of Sports Historians on the compilation of an up-to-date and comprehensive list of titles which will surely add significantly to the list given here. Meanwhile, the Manchester Institute for Popular Culture continues to build up an archive of fanzine material, laying claim to the most complete collection in existence.

It is evident that the ongoing work of specialist researchers, dealers and selected sales outlets in promoting fanzine literature is instrumental in exposing the genre to a wider audience. More importantly, it serves to show that fanzine writing is something more than the crazed ramblings of frustrated supporters desperately trying to be heard. By giving academic recognition and blessing to publications regarded with some suspicion and distaste by football's decision makers, perhaps the tide may turn. If the authorities can learn to absorb the best messages served up by the fanzines, whilst developing a thick skinned tolerance of the leftovers, then football's 'alternative' publishers and contributors, the fans themselves in fact, may yet have an important influence on the future of the game. It is an influence they thoroughly deserve because it has been created from nothing – there are some very talented and forward thinking people amongst the ranks of the 'ordinary fans'. If their voices can be heard, and readers can be entertained at the same time, fanzines will deserve a place in football history which may yet be recognised by future generations as being influential above and beyond our current perception.

Fanzines ~ Contents

Fanzine Anthologies & Alternative Studies

1   The football handbook to end all football handbooks / Chris Lightbown; jacket illustration by Derek Alder; other illustrations by Paul Rigby. London: Wolfe, 1974.
144p; illus   ISBN: 0-7234-0532-8

   ☞ Also listed at: K45

2   The 'Foul' book of football no. 1 / Andrew Nickolds and Stan Hey. Cambridge: 'Foul' Publications, 1976.
128p; illus; pbk

    Cover title: The best of 'Foul', 1972-75
          ISBN: 0-9504655-0-X
          BL: X.0615/508(1)

   Foul first appeared in October 1972 and ran to 34 issues over four years. Its title was a deliberate parody of contemporary magazines such as Shoot and Goal; it was very much the Private Eye of the football world and indeed put out by the same distributors and typesetters. Regarded as the precursor to When Saturday Comes, it holds a vital place in fanzine culture. This compilation presents the best of Foul from 1972-1975 – essential reading.

3   Sing when you're winning: the last football book / Steve Redhead. London: Pluto, 1987.
144p; illus; pbk

    Bibliography: p144
          ISBN: 0-7453-0144-4
          BL: YK.1987.a.7338

   Whilst not a book about football fanzines, this is very much a work which relates to football as alternative culture. Steve Redhead's ideas and observations are essential reading for all those studying football as popular culture.

4   El Tel was a space alien / edited by Martin Lacey. Sheffield: Juma, 1989.
illus; pbk
(The best of the alternative football press; vol. 1)
          ISBN: 1-872204-00-7
          BL: ZK.9.b.3873

   Compilation of material from 14 leading fanzines, including a six page introduction on fanzine history; essential reading.

5   Whose game is it anyway?: the book of the football fanzines / compiled by Phil Shaw. Hemel Hempstead: Argus, 1989.
96p; illus; pbk
          ISBN: 0-85242-997-5
          BL: YK.1991.b.7298

   An anthology of fanzine material with an excellent introductory overview of the history and development of fanzines – essential reading for all research students in this field. Includes a foreword by John Peel.

6   Offside. London: Queen Anne Press?, 1990?
(When Saturday Comes special; no. 1)

   The first WSC special was well received and makes essential reading for all fanzine students.

7   Bookable offence. London: Queen Anne Press, 1990.
96p; illus, maps; pbk
(When Saturday Comes special; no. 2)
          ISBN: 0-356-19522-8
          BL: YK.1990.b.9767

   This second special includes a range of material which is distinctly recognisable as coming from the WSC stable.

8   Get your writs out!: another dose of the alternative football press / edited by Martin Lacey. Sheffield: Juma, 1991.
illus; pbk   ISBN: 1-872204-02-3

   A follow-up compilation to El Tel – another essential work in the still rather limited range of fanzine compilation volumes.

9   Late tackle / editor, Andy Lyons. London: Queen Anne Press, 1991.
95p; illus; pbk
(When Saturday Comes special; no. 3)
          ISBN: 0-356-20317-4
          BL: YK.1992.b.2686

   Maintaining the usual WSC high standards – this is their third special.

10   The 1st eleven: the half decent retrospective. Harpenden: Queen Anne Press, 1992.
240p; illus, maps; pbk
          ISBN: 1-85291-522-6
          BL: YK.1994.b.2587

   Presents issues 1 to 11 of 'When Saturday Comes', the pioneering fanzine which now enjoys a cult following and has developed into a real voice in the world of football.

11   The football imagination: a study of football fanzine culture / Richard Haynes. London: Avebury, 1995.
178p
    ISBN: 1-85742-212-0 (cased) • ISBN: 1-85742-213-9 (pbk)
   This is the first in-depth study of football fanzine culture, documenting the genealogy of football fanzines and studying the ethnography of those who read and write in the fanzine market – an essential reference work for all students of fanzine literature.

FA Premiership & Football League

VOL. 2   MAY
NO.   20   1951

The OFFICIAL MAGAZINE of the
ARSENAL FOOTBALL SUPPORTERS' CLUB
POLICY : TO HELP, NOT HINDER

NOT THE 8502

Bristol City

92 The bountyhunter
93 The bumpkin report
94 One team in Bristol.
       BL: ZK.9.a.3260
   There are two fanzines of this title
95 Over the gate
96 Take your seats
97 Ultra!

Bristol Rovers

98 9 months
99 The gashead
100 The second of May
101 Trumpton Times

Burnley

102 The 29th
103 Claret & blue review
104 Marlon's gloves.   BL: ZK.9.a.2928
   Continues Who ate all the pies?
105 No nay never
106 Supporters' club review
107 Who ate all the pies?: a biased
   look at Burnley FC. (1992-)
       BL: ZC.9.a.3688
   There are two fanzines of this title

Bury

108 Where were you at The Shay?
       BL: ZK.9.a.3054

Cambridge United

109 The Abbey rabbit.   BL: ZK.9.a.3064
110 The globe
111 Rah rah rah!
112 Why is custard yellow?

Cardiff City

113 Blue news 'n' views
114 Bluebird Jones
115 The bluebird magazine
116 Bobbing along
117 Cover the grange
118 Do the ayatollah
119 Intifada
120 My love is blue
121 O bluebird of happiness
122 Supporters' club newsletter
123 The thin blue line
124 Watch the bluebirds fly!

Carlisle United

125 The Brunton roar
126 The Cumberland sausage: north
   of Watford, south of heaven – a
   Carlisle United alternative.
   *Absorbed: North of Watford, south
   of heaven*
       BL:ZK.9.a.3017
127 CUSC news
128 For fox sake
129 The foxy ferret. (1993-)
       BL: ZK.9.a.3044
130 North of Watford, south of
   heaven
131 So, Jack Ashurst, where's my shirt?
132 Watching from the Warwick.
   (1994?-)   BL: ZK.9.a.3224

Charlton Athletic

133 Addickted
134 Andyana Jones and the Valley
   crusade
135 The drop
136 Goodbye horse
137 Lennie Lawrence
138 Memories are made of this
139 Remember, remember, the 5th of
   December. (May 1993-)
       BL: ZK.9.a.3035
140 Robins report
141 Valiants viewpoint
142 Voice of The Valley

Chelsea

143 The blues brothers
   Covers Chelsea, Linfield and
   Rangers
   ☞ Also listed at: L1002, L1078
144 Carefree . . . (Aug. 1992-)
145 Chelsea blue
146 Chelsea calling
147 Chelsea chat
148 Chelsea collector
149 Chelsea independent.
       BL: ZK.9.a.3281
150 The Chelsea reports
151 Cockney rebel.   BL: ZC.9.b.5686
152 Combinations reserved
153 The red card
154 SW6
155 True blue
156 West standers

Chester City

157 Hello Albert. (Mar. 1990-)
       BL: ZK.9.a.3175
158 The onion bag.   BL: ZK.9.a.3266
   Covers Chester City and Dee
   Rangers
   ☞ Also listed at: L717
159 Southern branch supporters' club
   newsletter

Chesterfield

160 The crooked spireite

Colchester United

161 Always see him in 'The Lamb' on
   a Saturday night
162 The blue eagle: a Colchester
   United fanzine written by
   supporters for supporters. (1993-)
       BL: ZC.9.a.3770
163 Floodlight
164 Official magazine of the
   Colchester United football
   supporters' club. (Nov/Dec.
   1966-)
       BL: P.441/62
165 Out of the blue
166 Supporters' club magazine
167 U's news

Coventry City

168 Sky blue army
169 Sky blue special
170 The westender

Crewe Alexandra

171 Gradi rag
172 He's not Danny Grady
173 Super Dario land. (1993-)
       BL: ZK.9.a.3051
174 The railwaymen of Gresty Road
175 To work upon the railway

Crystal Palace

176 Eagle eye
177 The eastern eagles fanzine.
       BL: ZK.9.b.6714
178 One more point. (1993-)
       BL: ZK.9.b.7524
179 Orne blikket
180 So glad you're mine
181 Suffer little children
182 Supporters' club magazine

Darlington

183 Feetham's fanfare
184 Mission impossible.
BL: ZK.9.a.3366
185 Supporters' club news & views

Derby County

186 Bloomer shoots, Shilton saves
187 C-stander. (1990-) BL: ZK.9.a.3185
188 Hey big spender. (1992-)
BL: ZK.9.a.3063
189 Interesting very interesting
190 Ivor Ram
191 The mutton mutineer
192 Programme collector review
193 Ramlines
194 The sheep
195 We'll be back in '91

Doncaster Rovers

196 Raise the roof

Everton

197 Blue wail
198 The Evertonian
199 The Goodison roar
200 Gwladys sings the blues. (1994-)
BL: ZK.9.a.3686
201 London area newsletter
202 Speke from the Harbour
203 When skies are grey. (1988-)
BL: ZK.9.a.3087

Exeter City

204 The Exe directory. BL: ZK.9.a.3265
205 In exile. (1993?-) BL: ZK.9.a.3240
206 We'll score again

Fulham

207 Cottage pie
208 The cottager
209 There's only one F in Fulham.
(Mar/Apr. 1988-) BL: ZK.9.a.3132
210 Where's ARA? (Dec. 1993-)
BL: ZK.9.a.3090

Gillingham

211 Brian Moore's head looks
uncannily like London Planetarium
212 Capital gills
213 The donkey's tale
214 Go away
215 Priestfield press

Grimsby Town

216 The mariners magazine
217 Sing when we're fishing.
BL: ZK.9.a.3056

Hartlepool United

218 Monkey business
219 Scandinavia newsletter

Hereford United

220 Bullseye
221 Hereford bull
222 Talking bull. BL: ZK.9.a.3102

Huddersfield Town

223 Hanging on the telephone.
BL: ZK.9.a.3101

Hull City

224 Fearful symmetry
225 From Hull to eternity
226 Hull, hell & happiness
227 Look back in amber
228 On cloud seven
229 Southern supporters' newsletter
230 Tigers eye

Ipswich Town

231 The blue arrow
232 Blue: for the love of Ipswich.
(1994?-) BL: ZK.9.a.3164
233 Dribble! BL: ZK.9.a.3078
234 A load of cobbolds: an alternative
look at Ipswich Town.
BL: ZK.9.a.3103
235 News of the blues
236 Suffolk punchline
237 Those were the days. (1990-)
BL: ZK.9.a.3385
238 Townsfolk
239 Without a care in the world

Leeds United

240 Crossbar
241 The hanging sheep
242 Just a quick word lads please
243 Marching altogether
244 The peacock news
245 The square ball
246 Taking the peacock
247 Till the world stops.
BL: ZK.9.a.3067
248 We are Leeds

Leicester City

249 Filbo fever
250 For fox sake
251 The fox. BL: ZK.9.a.2956
252 London branch newsletter
253 The moon
254 Where's the money gone?

Leyton Orient

255 The donut
256 Frankly speaking. BL: ZK.9.a.3261
Covers Leyton Orient and
Dagenham & Redbridge
☞ Also listed at: L714
257 Leyton Orientear. BL: ZK.9.a.2942
258 Pandamonium. (1991-)
BL: ZK.9.a.3323

Lincoln City

259 The banker
260 The bonker
261 Deranged ferret!
262 The imps: supporters' club official
magazine. (1967-) BL: P.441/106
☞ Also listed at: B379

Liverpool

263 All day and all of the night
264 Another wasted corner. (1993?-)
BL: ZK.9.b.6717(1)
Continues: One minute to go
265 The Kopite
266 One minute to go. (Dec.
1990-1993)
Continued by: Another wasted corner
BL:ZK.9.b.6717(1)
267 Our days are numbered
268 Through the wind & rain. (1989?-)
BL: ZK.9.b.6823
269 When Sunday comes.
BL: ZK.9.b.6873
270 You'll never walk alone

Luton Town

271 Depleated
272 The hatter
273 Mad as a hatter! BL: ZK.9.a.3352
274 Town

Manchester City

275 Blue print. (1987-)
BL: ZK.9.b.6245
276 The city set
277 Cityzen

278 Electric blue. BL: ZK.9.b.6878
279 Junior blues news
280 King of the kippax. (1988-)
      BL: ZK.9.b.7689
281 The kippax: a celebration
282 Main stand view
283 Out of the blues
284 Purple reign
285 Singing the blues
286 Supporters' mag
287 This charming fan
288 True blue

Manchester United
289 Blackburn reds
290 By the swords United
291 Celtic United news
      Covers Manchester United and Celtic
      ☞ Also listed at: L886
292 Cula review
      Covers Manchester United and Celtic
      ☞ Also listed at: L887
293 Echoes from Old Trafford
294 Hell fire club
295 In league with the devils
296 Independent view: the alternative fanzine for Manchester United supporters. (Aug. 1993-)
      BL:ZK.9.b.6120
297 The K stand
298 London & district supporters' magazine
299 London & district newsletter
300 London fan club newsletter
301 Man-U-magic
302 Northern exposure
303 Our day will come
      Covers Manchester United and Celtic
      ☞ Also listed at: L896
304 Red attitude
305 The red devil
306 Red issue
307 Red news: the champions fanzine. (1989-) BL: ZK.9.b.6794
308 The Shankill skinhead
309 There's only one United
310 Tiocfaidh ar la
      Covers Manchester United and Celtic
      ☞ Also listed at: L899
311 Title reports 92/93
312 United supporteren

313 United we stand
314 Voices from the devil
315 WDWR: Walking down the Warwick Road. BL: ZK.9.a.3344

Mansfield Town
316 Alternative Mansfield matters
317 Follow the Yellow Brick Road
318 The mill on the maun
319 Size 10 boots

Middlesbrough
320 Ayresome angel
321 Bread 'n' Boro. (1992-)
      BL: ZK.9.a.3223
322 Fly me to the moon
323 Never mind the boy's end

Millwall
324 Bossa nova baby
325 The dengerous
326 The lion roars. BL: ZK.9.a.3232
327 No one likes us. BL: ZK.9.a.3142
328 Someone likes us

Newcastle United
329 Alas Smith & Smith
      Covers Newcastle United and Sunderland
      ☞ Also listed at: L492
330 Black and white
331 Boardbuster
332 The famous number nine
333 The giant awakes. (Feb/Mar. 1993-) BL: ZK.9.a.3222
334 Half mag half biscuit.
      BL: ZK.9.a.3086
335 Half magpie, half biscuit. (Aug/Sept. 1992-Jan. 1994)
      Continued by: Half mag half biscuit
      BL:ZK.9.a.3086
336 Jim's bald heed
337 London magpie
338 The mag. BL: ZK.9.b.6661
339 Mighty Quinn
340 The Norwegian mag
341 The number nine
342 Once upon a Tyne
343 The supporter (1978-)
      ISSN: 0142-6788
      BL: P.2000/657
      ☞ Also listed at: B570
344 Talk of the toon. (1991-)
      BL: ZK.9.b.6672

345 Talk of the Tyne
346 Who wants to be in Division One anyway?

Northampton Town
347 WALOC: what a load of Cobblers!

Norwich City
348 Attack
349 The beautiful Barclay
350 The canary
351 Capital canaries
352 The citizen
353 The cityzen
354 Ferry 'cross the Wensum
355 A fine city
356 Fleck again
357 I can drive a tractor
358 Liverpool are on the tele' again! (1990-) BL: ZK.9.b.7305
359 Never mind the danger
360 On the ball
361 Sing when we're ploughing
362 Spud international
363 A tint of yellow

Nottingham Forest
364 400 yards
      Covers Nottingham Forest and Notts County
      ☞ Also listed at: L374
365 (The almighty) Brian
366 Forest forever. BL: ZK.9.a.3123
367 The forest tree
368 The forester
369 Garibaldi
370 Saturday afternoon/Sunday morning
      Covers Nottingham Forest and Notts County
      ☞ Also listed at: L379
371 The Trent Times
372 The tricky tree. BL: ZK.9.a.3402
373 Woodcutter's

Notts County
374 400 yards
      Covers Nottingham Forest and Notts County
      ☞ Also listed at: L364
375 The better half
376 Flickin & kickin'
      Covers Notts County and subbuteo
      ☞ Also listed at: L1309

377 No more pie in the sky
    Covers Notts County and Stockport County
    ☞ Also listed at: L482

378 The pie.   BL: ZK.9.a.3537

379 Saturday afternoon/Sunday morning
    Covers Notts County and Nottingham Forest
    ☞ Also listed at: L370

380 The thin yellow stripe

381 The wheelbarrow

Oldham Athletic

382 Beyond the boundary.
    BL: ZK.9.a.3068

383 Boundary bulletin

384 The exploding latics inevitable

Oxford United

385 Raging bull. (1988?-)
    BL: ZK.9.a.3648

386 The supporter

387 Supporters' club magazine

Peterborough United

388 The Peterborough effect.
    BL: ZK.9.a.3186

Plymouth Argyle

389 Central heating

390 The evergreen

391 The green piece

392 Pasty news

393 Rub of the greens. (1990?-)
    BL: ZK.9.a.2943

394 Way out west. (Aug/Sept. 1993-)
    BL: ZK.9.a.3239

Port Vale

395 The memoirs of Seth Bottomley

396 Valiants

397 The Wright's pie

Portsmouth

398 Blue & Wight

399 The blue & Wight. (1992-)
    BL: ZK.9.b.6793
    Isle of Wight Pompey Supporters' Club magazine.

400 The chimes

401 Down the park

402 Frattonise

403 The greatest city

404 More dead wood than the Mary Rose

405 More money than sense

406 Northern blues news

407 The Pompey chimes

Preston North End

408 53 miles west of Venus

409 Deepdale digested

410 Deepdale rudge. (Spring 1993-)
    BL: ZC.9.a.3827

411 Gonzo

412 Hyde! Hyde! What's the score?

413 The North End melon

414 The PNE view

415 Preston other paper

416 Preston pie muncher.
    BL: ZK.9.a.3155

417 Preston's pride and joy

418 Sleeping giant

419 Tales from the River End

420 Tommy who?

421 Win on the plastic

Queen's Park Rangers

422 All quiet on the Western Avenue

423 Beat about the bush

424 In the loft. (1984-)   BL: ZK.9.a.3187

425 A kick up the R's

426 Loyal supporters' association newsletter

427 Ooh, I think it's my groin!

428 QPR crudentials

429 Rangers roar

430 The superhoop

431 Superhoops

432 Superhoops – Ah!

433 The whingeing donkey

Reading

434 Elm Park disease

435 Elm Park news

436 Taking the biscuit

437 There ain't no red in Reading or Tottenham
    Covers Reading and Tottenham Hotspur
    ☞ Also listed at: L551

Rochdale

438 The 92nd club

439 The dark blues

440 Exceedingly good pies. (1993-)
    BL: ZK.9.a.3062

Rotherham United

441 Dreaming of an Eric Twigg pukka pie

442 Mi whippet's dead

443 Moulin rouge. (1994-)
    Continues The scrap book
    BL:ZK.9.a.3322

444 The scrap book. (Spring 1994)
    Only 2 issues published;
    Continued by: Moulin rouge
    BL:ZK.9.a.3322

445 Two up two down

446 We've won the kop choir loo

447 Windy & dusty

Scarborough

448 Beyond the 843

449 The Scarborough warning

450 Who's Neil Warnock?

Scunthorpe United

451 Any old iron?

452 Get a grip, ref!

453 Iron filings

Sheffield United

454 The blades: official magazine of the Sheffield United district supporters' club. (Aug/Sept. 1967)
    Only one issue published
    BL:P.441/97

455 Flashing blade. (Mar. 1986-)
    BL: ZK.9.a.3034

456 The greasy chip buttie (1993-)
    BL: ZK.9.b.7018

Sheffield Wednesday

457 The blue & white wizard. (Feb. 1993-)   BL: ZK.9.b.6953

458 Boddle, taking the Wednesday into insanity.   BL: ZK.9.a.3263

459 Cheat!!

460 The eyes of the kop

461 Just another Wednesday

462 The London owl

463 Medalian Atkinson

464 A view from the East Bank: an unusual look at Sheffield Wednesday Football Club. (Sept. 1992-)   BL: ZK.9.b.5287

465 War of the monster trucks. (Feb. 1993-)   BL: ZK.9.a.3446

Shrewsbury Town

466 A large scotch.   BL: ZK.9.a.3341
467 Up the blues

Southampton

468 De-valued
469 Junk mail
470 London Saints' newsletter
471 On the march
472 Red stripe
473 The ugly inside

Southend United

474 Blues news.   BL: ZK.9.d.696
475 Roots Hall ramblings
476 The Roots Hall roar
477 The seasider
478 Supporters' club outlook
479 True blues magazine

Stockport County

480 1-0 County
481 County calling!
482 No more pie in the sky

    Covers Stockport County and
    Notts County
    ☞ Also listed at: L377

483 The tea party

Stoke City

484 All stoked up
485 Come back Bill Asprey
486 The jolly potter
487 The oatcake
488 Potters monthly
489 She stood there laughing
490 The Victoria voice. (1993-)
    BL: ZK.9.b.6984

Sunderland

491 5573
492 Alas Smith & Smith

    Covers Sunderland and New-
    castle United
    ☞ Also listed at: L329

493 ALS: the independent Sunderland
supporters' magazine.
    BL: ZK.9.a.2980
494 CAT
495 It's an easy one for Norman: an
alternative look at Sunderland
AFC. (June/July 1993-)
    BL: ZK.9.a.3225

496 London branch newsletter
497 A love supreme: the independent
Sunderland supporters' magazine.
    BL: ZK.9.a.2980
498 The number 9.   BL: ZK.9.a.3365
499 The red & white Rokerite
500 Roker raw
501 Roker roar
502 The Roker roar
503 SAFCSA newsletter
504 The Sunderland newsletter
505 Wear all going to Wembley: a
Sunderland supporters' magazine.
    BL: ZK.9.a.3238
506 Wise men say
507 You wot!

Swansea City

508 3,526: the score again Swansea
City
509 Better than sex
510 The dud
511 The Geordie swan
512 The Jack. (Nov. 1993-)
    BL: ZC.9.a.3771
    Continues: Love peace and Swansea
    City incorporating Jackmail
513 Jackmail
514 The London swan
515 London swans newsletter
516 A lot to answer for
517 Love, peace and Swansea City
518 The Manchester swan
519 Nobody will ever know
520 South of Morfa
521 The swan.   BL: W.225(45)
522 Swanning around London
523 Swimming in Swansea Bay
524 Voice of the vetch

Swindon Town

525 The 69er
526 Bring the noise
527 Randy Robin. (Mar. 1994-)
    BL: ZK.9.a.3343
528 Swindon Town Telegraph

Torquay United

529 Bamber's right foot: the unofficial
Torquay United fanzine. (1994-)
    BL: ZK.9.a.3264
530 The gullible gull-post. (1994-)
    BL: ZK.9.a.3442
531 The gull's cry
532 Mission impossible

533 TILT
534 You wot!: the anti-racist
alternative Torquay United mag.
    BL: ZK.9.b.7781

Tottenham Hotspur

535 Cock-a-doodle-doo: lilywhite &
blue (Aug. 1994-)
536 Goalden cockerel
537 The lilywhite: the official organ of
the Spurs supporters' club (1st
volume). (Aug. 1950-Feb. 1964)
    BL:P.P.1832.mad
538 The lilywhite (2nd volume)
539 Mabbs ahoy
540 My eyes have seen the glory
541 The new lilywhite
542 Off the shelf
543 Spur. (1988-)   BL: ZK.9.b.6669
544 Spur of the moment.
    BL: ZK.9.a.3088
545 The spur (supporters' club
magazine)
546 The Spurs historiette. (1983-1985)
    BL: P.441/1037
    ☞ Also listed at: B802
547 The Spurs reports
548 Spurs review
549 The Spurs screws
550 Team. (Mar. 1964-)
    BL: P.P.1832.mad/2
551 There ain't no red in Reading or
Tottenham
    Covers Tottenham Hotspur and
    Reading
    ☞ Also listed at: L437
552 Tottenham supporteren
553 A view from the shelf
554 (We will) follow the Tottenham

Tranmere Rovers

555 Come on you Rovers
556 Friday night fever
557 Give us an R
558 The Prentonian
559 Three men in a boat
560 White magic

Walsall

561 Blazing saddlers. (Dec. 1993-)
    BL: ZK.9.a.3107
562 Moving swiftly on
563 Saddle sore

Watford

564 Bra!: the collected works of
    Gladys Protheroe 1985-1992
565 Clap your hands, stamp your feet
566 The horn
567 The hornet express
568 The hornet news
569 More tea vicar
570 Mud, sweat and beers
571 The supporter
572 The Watford book of soccer
573 The yellow experience. (1991-)
    BL: ZK.9.a.3386

West Bromwich Albion

574 The Albion chronicle. (Oct. 1992-)
    BL: ZK.9.a.3262
575 Almost a chance
576 Fingerpost.   BL: ZK.9.a.1334
577 Grorty Dick.   BL: ZK.9.a.3342
578 Last train to Rolfe Street.
    BL: ZK.9.a.3404
579 The throstle

West Ham United

580 The Boleyn scorcher
581 The east end connection
582 Fortunes always hiding
583 Home alone
584 Never mind the Boleyn
585 On a mission from god

586 On the terraces. (1994-)
    BL: ZK.9.a.3584
587 Over land and sea. (1988?-)
    BL: ZK.9.a.3125
588 Scandinavian bubbles
589 Supporter mag
590 UTD United
    Covers West Ham United and
    Dundee United.
    ☞ Also listed at: L927

Wigan Athletic

591 The cockney latic
592 The latic fanatic. (1993?-)
    BL: ZK.9.a.3243

Wimbledon

593 Big one Hans!
594 Carlton, Carlton
595 Don's outlook
596 Go, Jo, go!! (May 1991-)
    BL: ZK.9.a.3287
597 Grapevine
598 Hoof the ball up?
599 Roger Connell's beard
600 Sour grapes
601 Tenant's extra
602 There's only one Mark Dziadulewicz
603 Vidaho
604 Wandering Hans
605 What about Dante?

Wolverhampton Wanderers

606 Bully's boots, beers & burgers
607 A load of bull
608 Manchester Wolves
609 The wolf

Wrexham

610 The furious Harry
611 The reliant robin
612 The sheeping giant: a totally
    biased view of Wrexham AFC
    from the Tanat Valley. (1990-).
    BL: ZK.9.a.3091

Wycombe Wanderers

613 The Adams family
614 Chairboys gas
615 Roobarb roobarb

York City

616 In the city
617 New frontiers. (1993-)
    BL: ZC.9.a.3786
618 The shippo shout
619 Supporters' club review
620 Terrace talk
621 Terrace toughs
622 To be a yokel
623 Win, lose or draw

Former Members of the Football League

Accrington Stanley

624 The barber's pole
625 Crown jewels
626 The Norwegian they

Aldershot

627 Enigma
628 Hotshots
629 Shots in the dark
630 Talk of the town

Barrow

631 Give 'em beans!
632 National supporters' club
    newsletter
633 Zigger. (Sept. 1967-) BL: P.441/105

Bradford Park Avenue

634 Aye aye rhubarb pie!
635 Fightback!
636 The wings of a sparrow

Halifax Town

637 The sound of The Shay

Maidstone United

638 Fools gold
639 The foundation stone
640 Golden days
641 Hailstones
642 SAM
643 Show me the way to go home
644 The spirit of London Road
645 Yellow fever

Non-League & Amateur

Crawley
705 One team in Sussex
706 Scorcher

Cray Wanderers
707 Cray chatter

Croydon
708 Blues news

Dagenham
709 Come on Dagenham, use yer forwards!
710 The dagger
711 The dagger magazine
712 Farewell to . . .
713 They looked good in the bar

Dagenham & Redbridge
714 Frankly speaking.   BL: ZK.9.a.3261
     Covers Dagenham & Redbridge
     and Leyton Orient
     ☞ Also listed at: L256
715 Raise your game

Dartford
716 Light at the end of the tunnel

Dee Rangers
717 The onion bag.   BL: ZK.9.a.3266
     Chester City/Dee Rangers
     ☞ Also listed at: L158

Dorking
718 Weekend affair

Dover Athletic
719 Dover soul
720 Rhodes Boyson, oo's ee play for?
721 Tales from the River End

Dudley Town
722 Lacey's ledger

Dulwich Hamlet
723 Champion Hill Street blues

Easington United
724 Mouth of the Humber

East Grinstead
725 Wasps whispers

Enfield
726 Attack
727 In defence
728 Talk of the town end

Fareham Town
729 Bailey is back – again
730 A miller's tale

Farnborough Town
731 Simon's haircut

Farsley Celtic
732 Monthly review

Ferryhill Athletic
733 The hill

Fleetwood Town
734 The codhead

Frickley Athletic
735 Bluesman

Gateshead
736 A different corner. (1993-)
                    BL: ZK.9.a.3403

Gloucester City
737 The T-ender
738 The tiger roar

Grantham Town
739 2052
740 Winston Churchill picked an army

Gravesend and Northfleet
741 No idea

742
743 *[Numbers not used]*
744

Halesowen Town
745 Follow your instinct
746 Yeltz news

Halfway FC
747 Don't get sucked in

Harwich & Parkeston
748 Shrimpers review

Hastings Town
749 The ghost of United

Hayling United
750 Play fair

Hednesford Town
751 The just after Christmas cracker
752 The pits

Hendon
753 Lambs to the slaughter
754 The sleeping giant

Herne Bay
755 Field of dreams

Hitchin Town
756 Chirp!
757 Club chat

Holywell Lions
758 You lion gets!

Huntsman Inn FC
759 Jibberer

Kettering Town
760 Poppies at the gates of dawn
761 White ball in the net

Kidderminster Harriers
762 The soup

Kingstonian
763 NHS
764 The searcher

Lancaster City
765 The Lancaster town & City historian
766 The mad axeman

Leyton Wingate
767 Kick bollock & bite
768 The supporter

Tunbridge Wells
831 Beachy's head
832 Trout rising

Uxbridge
833 Alternative Uxbridge

Warrington Town
834 Come on you yellows!

Waterlooville
835 Flippin' heck ref that was a foul surely!
836 Foul
837 The Looville rag

Wealdstone
838 The Elmslie ender
839 Long ball down the middle

Welling United
840 On a wing and a prayer
841 Wings review
842 Winning isn't everything

West Bromwich Albion Strollers
843 The floppy dick

Westgate Harriers
844 Sod off Iraq

Weston Super Mare
845 A gull's view
846 Who are these people?

Weymouth
847 Floodlight
848 Terrarising
849 Travelling club magazine

Whitley Bay
850 Sitting in the lounge of the Bay

Willenhall Town
851 A load of locks

Windsor & Eton
852 Jesus was a Windsor fan

Witney Town
853 The 'real shed' review

Witton Albion
854 Bishop, 3-1
855 Not the Albion review

Wivenhoe Town
856 Look for floodlights

Woking
857 The cardinal sin
858 Wubble yoo

Wokingham Town
859 The amber and black

Woodbridge Town
860 Whoosh!

Worcester City
861 Down the pan

Worksop
862 The toothless tiger

Worthing
863 Dynamo's news

Yate Town
864 Nightmare on Lodge Road
865 The posse review

Yeovil Town
866 Drink up ye cider
867 Huish roar
868 She fell over
869 To be a yokel

Scotland ~ The Football League

Aberdeen
870 The granite kipper.
   Continued as: The red final
   See also L876
871 If things were perfect
872 London supporters' Club news
873 The northern light
874 Paper tiger
875 Pittodrie profile. (Aug. 1992-)
   BL: ZK.9.d.994
876 The red final. (1994-)
   Continues: The granite kipper
   See also: L870

Airdrieonians
877 Only the lonely

Albion Rovers
878 Over the wall

Arbroath
879 Tomato soup & lentil

Ayr United
880 4-1
881 The honest truth

Berwick Rangers
882 From the Grove to the Harrow

Celtic
883 The cage to the jungle
   Covers Celtic and Cliftonville
   ☞ Also listed at: L1060
884 The celt
885 Celtic supporters' association monthly
886 Celtic United news
   Covers Celtic and Manchester United
   ☞ Also listed at: L291
887 Cula review
   Covers Celtic and Manchester United
   ☞ Also listed at: L292
888 Faithful through and through

889 From the nursery
890 Hail hail
891 The Irish roar
Covers Celtic and Ireland
892 Jungle drums
893 News from paradise
894 Not the view
895 Once a Tim
896 Our day will come
Covers Celtic and Manchester United
☞ Also listed at: L303
897 Over & over
898 The shamrock
899 Tiocfaidh ar la
Covers Celtic and Manchester United
☞ Also listed at: L310
900 Tiocfaidh ar la!
Covers Celtic, Ireland and politics

Clyde
901 The Clyde underground
902 Clyde-o-scope

Clydebank
903 Alternative kilbowie komment
904 Le chic
905 Clydebank historian
906 Clydebank monthly

Cowdenbeath
907 The blue Brazilian

Dumbarton
908 The gibbering clairvoyant
909 View from the rock

Dundee
910 The beloved
911 Dens-scene
912 The Derry rumba
913 Eh mind o' gillie
914 It's half past four & we're 2-0 down
915 The morning after
916 Past the post
917 The sleeping giant

Dundee United
918 Can I bring my dog?
919 Falkirk & district newsletter

920 The final hurdle
921 Freakscene
922 Glasgow arabs news rag
923 One team in Dundee
924 Psycho arab
925 Tangerine dream
926 The United review
927 UTD United
Covers Dundee United and West Ham United
☞ Also listed at: L590
928 When the hoodoo comes

Dunfermline Athletic
929 East end bounce
930 Par trek
931 Parallel lines
932 Walking down the Halbeath Road

East Fife
933 Away from the numbers
934 The Bayview bulletin
935 Where's the tunnel?

East Stirling
936 Who is Dougie Henry?

Falkirk
937 The Falkirk unofficial fanzine
938 Rupert's roar

Forfar Athletic
939 The loonatic

Hamilton Academical
940 Crying time again
941 HASH

Heart of Midlothian
942 Always the bridesmaid
943 The boys done well
944 Dead ball
945 Doon by Gorgie
946 Five jam parts
947 The good, the bad & the ugly
948 Gorgie granite news
949 The Gorgie view
950 Gorgie wave
951 The gravedigger
952 Heartbeat
953 Hearts review
954 Hearts (stat) attack
955 The hearts supporter

956 The jam piece
957 Jambo
958 The jambo
959 Manor news
960 No idle talk
961 Still musn't grumble
962 Trophy please?

Hibernian
963 The attacker
964 Aye monotonous
965 Down the slope
966 Hibby hippies greatest hits
967 Hibees Glasgow gossip
968 Hibees here, hibees there
969 The Hibernian
970 Hibs kids
971 Hibs monthly
972 Hibs OK?
973 The north east Hibernian
974 The proclaimer
975 TANEHSH

Kilmarnock
976 Killie Ken
977 Paper roses

Meadowbank Thistle
978 AWOL
979 Cheers
980 London branch bulletin
981 Mr Bismarck's electric pickelhaube
982 Roll on 4.40
983 The thistle

Montrose
984 Mo Mo super Mo

Motherwell
985 Waiting for the great leap forward
986 Wherever you may be

Partick Thistle
987 Dear John
988 The Harry rag
989 The jagazine
990 The Johnny Flood experience
991 One team in Glasgow
992 Sick in the basin
993 What a sensation!
994 Worse than East Fife

Queen of the South
995 The alternative Queen's speech
996 Nightmare on Terregles Street

Queen's Park
997 Off the ball
998 The web

Raith Rovers
999 Stark's bark
1000 The wild rover

Rangers
1001 Aye ready

1002 The blues brothers
      Covers Rangers, Chelsea and Linfield
      ☞ Also listed at: L143, L1078
1003 Follow follow.   BL: ZK.9.a.2320
1004 Number one
1005 The Rangers historian
1006 Strangers on Rangers
1007 The teddy bear
1008 Third division
1009 True blue
1010 World shut your mouth

St Johnstone
1011 Old McDiarmid had a farm
1012 The Sassenach saintee

1013 True faith
1014 Wendy who?

St Mirren
1015 Love street syndrome
1016 There's a store where the creatures meet

Stenhousemuir
1017 The duffle

Stirling Albion
1018 The beanos
1019 Rave on!

Scotland ~ Former League & Non-League

Arthurlie
1020 The home of football

Auchinleck Talbot
1021 Three in a row

Dalry Thistle
1022 China's

East Kilbride Thistle
1023 The jag mag

Elgin City
1024 The champions
1025 The last line of defence

1026 Oot the windae
1027 Over the turnstile
1028 The playboy

Fraserburgh
1029 The happy haddock

Huntly
1030 Up Sandy!

Inverness Caledonians
1031 Another kind of blues
1032 (On a) life support machine

Inverness Thistle
1033 18 hours from Rotterdam
1034 Black and red all over

Irvine Meadow
1035 Up the work rate

Kilwinning Rangers
1036 The buffie

Nairn County
1037 75/76

Pollock Juniors
1038 Fulton, one-nil

Wales

Bangor City
1039 Now with wings
1040 On top form
1041 Spirit of '62

Barry Town
1042 Supporters' club news

Caernarfon Town
1043 The oval ball

Colwyn Bay
1044 Claret and booze

Merthyr Tydfil
1045 The Brecon Road beat
1046 Dial M for Merthyr
1047 The junior martyr
1048 Tiny Taff's adventures

Newport AFC
1049 Homeward bound
1050 Never say Dai
1051 Pyramuddle
1052 Welcome to Gateshead

Pontlottyn Blast Furnace
1053 And then there was one . . .

Rhyl
1054 We are Rhyl

Northern Ireland

Ards
1055 The butcher's apron
1056 We're all going down to Davy Lee's

Ballyclare Comrades
1057 Calling all comrades!

Bangor
1058 The brown bottle
1059 A close shave

Cliftonville
1060 The Cage to the Jungle
Covers Cliftonville and Celtic
☞ Also listed at: L883
1061 The casbah
1062 The little red

1063 Seeing red
1064 The wee red

Coleraine
1065 For it's a grand old team

Crusaders
1066 Where cornerboys collect

Glenavon
1067 The silence of the bann-shees
1068 Walking down the Tandragee Road

Glentoran
1069 For ever and ever
1070 The Glentoran gazette
1071 Never mind the bluemen
1072 A nightmare on Dee Street

Larne
1073 The harbour rat
1074 No sheep at Inver
1075 Under the moon

Linfield
1076 Blue for you
1077 Blue print
1078 The blues brothers
Covers Linfield, Rangers and Chelsea
☞ Also listed at: L143, L1002
1079 F stands for Linfield
1080 One team in Ulster
1081 TBS
1082 The Windsor roar

Portadown
1083 Better red than dead

Republic of Ireland

Bohemian AFC
1084 The Dalymount road
1085 The gypsy
1086 Only fools and horses

Bray Wanderers
1087 No way referee

Cork City
1088 No more plastic pitches

Derry City
1089 Brandyballs

Drogheda United
1090 Kick off

Galway United
1091 Standing room only

Kilkenny City
1092 Every man a football artist

Limerick United
1093 Limerick you're a lady

Shamrock Rovers
1094 Glenmalure gazette
1095 Hoops supporters' club newsletter
1096 Hoops upside your head
1097 Some ecstasy

Shelbourne
1098 Dully misses again
1099 From home to home

St Patricks FC
1100 Green and white

Isle of Wight

Cowes Sports
1101 99% of gargoyles look like Pete Groves

General

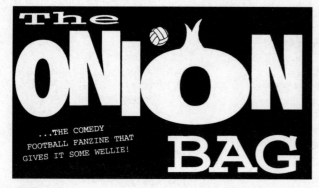

Special Interest Groups

1148 Against the tide
   Women and football.

1149 All ears
   Fanzine for radio fans, especially followers of Radio 5 sport.

1150 Andy the Aardvark's pub guide to Norwich

1151 Born kicking: the fanzine for women who love football.
   Sunderland: 1990.   BL:ZA.9.a.2981

1152 Foot and mouth
   Catering facilities at League grounds.

1153 Football magazine
   The history of football.

1154 The football pink
   Fanzine for gay football supporters.

1155 Game for a LAFF: the fanzine for librarians as football fans.
   London: LAFF, 1991-
   BL:ZK.9.a.2134

1156 Ivor Thirst good pub guide to the Football League. Vol. 1: The Midlands.
   Where to drink on your footballing travels.

1157 Ivor Thirst good pub guide to the Football League. Vol. 2: The North West.
   More places to drink . . .

1158 Kick off 91-. Portsmouth: Sporting Editions, 1990-
   Published annually
   ISSN: 0956-7240
   Women and football.

1159 North East programme club magazine

1160 Planet football
   Football and art.

1161 Programme monthly. Kirkcaldy: Programme Monthly, 1981-
   BL:W.225(69)

1162 The rusty staple
   Programme collectors' fanzine.

1163 Scottish football historian

1164 The sports historian. London: British Society of Sports History, May 1993-
   Published annually
   Continues: Bulletin (British Society of Sports History). ISSN: 0966-1042   ISSN: 1351-5462
   BL: ZK.9.a.2237
   Dedicated to serious historical research.

1165 Under the wires
   The world's first football and trainspotting crossover fanzine.

Music Crossover Titles

1166 Boys own
   General football and music.

1167 The end
   Football and music in Liverpool.

1168 The expression she pulled
   General football and music.

1169 Further too
   General football and music.

1170 The globe
   Football and music in Cambridge.

1171 Manchester, north of England
   Football and music in Manchester.

1172 Scour
   Football and music in Paisley.

1173 Walter Zenga's right buttock
   General football and music.

1174 Zico was a punk rocker
   General football and music.

1175 Zoot skazine
   General football and music.

Fanzine Collecting and Listings

1176 AFN distribution fanzine catalogue
   A periodically published catalogue of fanzines for sale via the Alternative Football Network championed by Steve James. This catalogue is one of the best sources of identification and acquisition for fanzine collectors.

1177 The best of the football fanzines / editor, John Robinson.
   Cleethorpes: Fanzine, 1990.
   48p; illus   ISBN: 0-9515167-0-1
   BL: ZK.9.b.3388

1178 By far the greatest team
   Concentrates on fanzine reviews.

1179 Fanzine classics

1180 Fanzine collector

1181 Fanzine monthly. Edinburgh: Fanzine Monthly, 1989?-
   BL:ZA.9.a.2984

1182 The football fanzine & independent supporters' magazine directory. Mountain Ash, 1992-
   BL:ZK.9.a.2868
   Two issues have been published to date, each giving a compre-

hensive listing of all known fanzines up to the date of publication. Original and valuable research by Steve James, one of the country's leading authorities on fanzine culture.

1183 Scottish 'zine scene
1184 Tom, Dick and Harry

    A comprehensive listing of past and present fanzines.

Supporters' Organisations

1185 Avon calling

    Football Supporters' Association – Avon area.

1186 Don't just stand there

    Football Supporters' Association – East Midlands.

1187 End to end. National Federation of Football Supporters' Clubs.

1188 Football supporter. Football Supporters' Association.

1189 FSA newsletter. Football Supporters' Association.

1190 Get a grip. Football Supporters' Association – Teeside.

1191 Guide to non-members areas. Football Supporters' Association.

1192 In touch. Football Supporters' Association – North Wales and Cheshire.

1193 London FSA newsletter. Football Supporters' Association – London.

1194 Loyal supporter. Football Supporters' Association – Greater Manchester.

1195 Maybe it's because: the magazine of the London Branch of the FSA. Liverpool: Football Supporters' Association London Branch, 1990-   BL:ZA.9.b.535

    Scandinavian supporters of London teams.

1196 Membership or registration? Football Supporters' Association

1197 Reclaim the game. Football Supporters' Association

1198 Scana news. Football Supporters' Association – Cheshire and North Staffordshire.

1199 The sharp end. Football Supporters' Association.

1200 Supporters United newsletter. Supporters United.

1201 Tales from the river bank. Football Supporters' Association – Merseyside.

1202 Up for grabs now. The Football Supporters' Association of Birmingham University.

1203 The voice. Football Supporters' Association – South Wales.

National & International

1204 The absolute game: a Scottish football fanzine. Edinburgh, May/June, 1988?-

    6 issues per year

        BL:ZK.9.b.3084

    The leading fanzine covering Scottish football in general. North of the border equivalent of When Saturday Comes.

1205 Alive and kicking

    Soccer in the United States.

1206 Alk echo

    Covers German football.

1207 Allez allez

    Coverage of the French soccer scene.

1208 The alternative Ulster

    Coverage of Northern Ireland.

1209 Archie! Archie! what's the score?

1210 Arconada . . . Armstrong!

    Covers the Northern Ireland national side.

The Absolute Game

A Scottish Football Fanzine

1211 Blaue Stunde

    General coverage of the Greek soccer scene.

1212 Diable rouge

    A quarterly fanzine covering Belgian football.

1213 The dribble

    Covers Scottish football.

1214 Dwy droed chwith

    Coverage of Welsh football.

1215 Elfmeter

    Leading fanzine covering the German League.

1216 Erin go Bragh

    Covers the Republic of Ireland national side.

1217 European football
General coverage of the European scene.

1218 Fan Treff
German football.

1219 Flair's back in fashion
Covers the England national side.

1220 The football liar
Scarce publication covering Scottish football in the early 1950s.

1221 Forza!
Coverage of Italian football.

1222 From Berwick to Dumfries
Covers Scottish football.

1223 FSA fans guide to Sardinia
Guide for England fans travelling to the 1990 World Cup.

1224 Furz
German football.

1225 Goal
Scarce 1960s coverage of Scottish football.

1226 Halb Zeit
General coverage of German soccer.

1227 The hand of god
Continues: The Italian job
Covers the England national team.

1228 Hard lines
1980s coverage of the Scottish game.

1229 Head the ball
General coverage of Irish football.

1230 The Italian job: the England & International football fanzine. Aylesbury: D. Bissmire, 1989-1990.
Only 6 issues published; Continued as: The hand of god
BL:ZA.9.b.485
Coverage of the England team.

1231 It's not unusual
Coverage of football in Wales.

1232 Japan soccer
Coverage of the Japanese J League.

1233 Kleeblatt spezial
General coverage of the game in Germany.

1234 Libero
The game in Italy.

1235 The long ball
Irish soccer.

1236 A lotta balls
Scottish football.

1237 Magic news
Another in the ever-growing list of issues covering the game in Germany.

1238 Munchen rulps
Specific coverage of the Munich area.

1239 Olé, olé, olé
Republic of Ireland national side.

1240 On the one road
Irish football.

1241 The pirate news
Coverage of Swedish football.

1242 Power echo
Coverage of the German Second Division.

1243 Pride and passion
Irish soccer.

1244 Proper shaped balls
Welsh soccer.

1245 Punt
Scottish football.

1246 The punter. Glasgow: Scotrun Publications, 1989-
BL:ZK.9.b.2491
The game in Scotland.

1247 Put the boot in
Irish football.

1248 Que sera, sera
Covers Scotland and the 1990 World Cup.

1249 Rigore
Soccer in Italy.

1250 Rojo, blanco y azul
Red, white and blue . . . covers the Spanish football scene.

1251 Schwaben echo
General German football.

1252 SFS bolletinen
Minority interest item covering Swedish statistics.

1253 Sick as a parrot
Spanned just eight issues in the early 1980s – covers Scottish football.

1254 Soccer hene
Coverage of African football.

1255 Soccer info
General European football.

1256 The sound of the crowd
Scottish football.

1257 Stimme der Reichshauptstadt
General coverage for Germany.

1258 Supporterunionens handbok
Scandinavian soccer.

1259 Swedish football for English readers
Concentrates solely on the Swedish scene.

1260 Tartan Esercito 1990
Scotland and the 1990 World Cup.

1261 Terrace talk
German soccer scene.

1262 This way up
Scottish football.

1263 Too sexy by far
Welsh football.

1264 A traveller's guide to football in Luxembourg
Specific coverage of the lesser known scene in Luxembourg.

1265 A traveller's guide to Greek football
Aimed at supporters wishing to follow the Greek soccer scene.

1266 Twlltin pob
The game in Wales.

1267 Two left feet
Welsh football.

1268 Ultra voice
General coverage for Germany.

1269 Voll Daneben
General German coverage.

1270 We hate Jimmy Hill
Covers Scottish football.

1271 Welsh football: the independent national soccer magazine for Wales. Prestatyn: Welsh Football, 1992-
BL:ZK.9.a.2353
Less imaginatively titled than it might have been.

1272 The Welsh footballer
General coverage of the football scene in Wales.

1273 When Domenica comes
Leading fanzine covering Italian soccer.

1274 Das World Cup zine
Covers the 1990 World Cup.

Domestic Leagues & Regional

1275 Always look on the bright side
   London area football.

1276 Are you sitting comfortably?
   Soccer in the south-east.

1277 Avon soccerworld
   Football in the County of Avon.

1278 Bring back the green
   South Tyneside football.

1279 Bristol soccerworld
   Covers Bristol and Avon.

1280 BUM
   Birmingham area football.

1281 Capital soccer review
   London area.

1282 Don't panic
   South London football.

1283 Football north. Blackburn: Topal,
   1988-   BL:ZK.9.a.732
   Covers northern England.

1284 Football utopia
   South-east England.

1285 Going it alone
   Covers the Football League.

1286 Groin strain
   London soccer coverage.

1287 Is it red
   Soccer in north-west England.

1288 One man and his dog
   Coverage of Scottish junior football.

1289 Onside
   Football in the Newbury area.

1290 Pride of the south
   General coverage for southern England.

1291 A river runs through it
   Special issue covering Nottingham football.

1292 Sheep shaggers
   Soccer in western England.

1293 Six tame sides
   General coverage of Tameside football.

1294 The snotty pest
   Liverpool football with some politics thrown in.

1295 Soccer Essex
   General coverage of the Essex soccer scene.

1296 The soccer scene
   Banbury area football.

1297 Soccer talk magazine
   Coverage of central Wales.

1298 The South-East Enders
   Coverage of south-east London football.

1299 Start!
   Covers Lancashire football.

1300 Storming with menace
   Football in south-west England.

1301 Tales from the riverbank
   General coverage of London football.

1302 Tayside football review
   General coverage of Tayside soccer.

1303 Three D Mark II
   English and Scottish Second and Third Divisions.

1304 West Country football
   Concentrates solely on the soccer scene in western England.

1305 What's the score?
   Coverage of Merseyside football.

Simulated Football & Games

1306 A 30 point weekend
   Fanzine for the Fantasy League supporter.

1307 The back page
   Another item for fantasy football followers.

1308 Bob's finger
   One of a number of fanzines dedicated to the Subbuteo aficionado.

1309 Flickin' and kickin'
   Subbuteo shares the coverage here with Notts County.
   ☞ *Also listed at: L376*

1310 It's a thinking man's game
   Publication for the football quiz buff.

Humour

1311 Football krazy
1312 Les Bence's manager's notes
1313 The magic sponge

1314 Sick over a parrot
1315 Sweet FA

Personalities

1316 And now you're gonna believe us
> Pays homage to Maurice Johnston.

1317 Ooh Gary Gary
> The one and only Gary Lineker.

Non-League Football

1318 6-leagues under
> Coverage of Kent.

1319 Club soccer

1320 End 2 end
> Covers Conference League and main feeder leagues.

1321 Grassroots
> Covers the lower levels of non-league football.

1322 Groundhopper
> Around the grounds of non-league football.

1323 The groundhopper's journal

1324 Hopper tunities

1325 Let's get talking

1326 Netstretcher

1327 The non-league digest

1328 Non-league football fanfare

1329 Non-league football focus

1330 Non-league north-west

1331 Non-league traveller

1332 One step from heaven
> Aptly titled fanzine which covers the Vauxhall Conference League which affords direct access to the Football League.

1333 Pyramid football: the magazine for non-league fans by non-league fans. London: Pyramid Football Magazine, 1984-   BL:ZA.9.a.2982
> Leading magazine covering the non-league scene.

1334 Report / Bureau of Non-League Football Statistics. Romford: The Bureau, 1981-1982.
9 vols
> *Published monthly;*
> *Continued as: League tables, cup draws, results, news*
> ISSN: 0263-1342
> BL: P.441/1090
☞ Also listed: J146; See also: L1335

1335 League tables, cup draws, results, news / Bureau of Non-League Football. London: The Bureau 1982-
> *Published monthly;*
> *Continues: Report / Bureau of Non-League Football Statistics*
> BL:P.441/1089
> Leading magazine covering the English non-league scene.
> Also listed: J147; See also: L1334

1336 Scottish non-league review
> Leading organ covering the non-league scene north of the border.

1337 West Middlesex review
> Specific coverage of non-league in this area.

Films

FOOTBALL IS A GAME OF EXCITEMENT, glamour, athleticism, emotion and beauty. It is unpredictable, has a cast of thousands, no formal script and a host of superstars to play the roles of both heroes and villains. Despite all this it has received little attention from film producers. This is probably because watching football, whether live or on the TV screen, satisfies the spectators' appetite for all these things without the need for fictional enhancement. What more could possibly be offered by the fictionalisation of the game for transfer to the large screen?

Such efforts as have been made are often embarrassingly hackneyed; choreographed on-field sequences look exactly what they are, whilst the appearance of serried ranks of supporters bedecked in sparkling new scarves, rosettes and the ubiquitous 'bobble hat' merely reinforces the artificiality of the drama. Paradoxically, it is the very dearth of examples, and the relative inadequacy of its treatment, that spurs enthusiasts to seek out instances of football in the movies. Nor is the subject entirely devoid of serious academic or historic significance – something may be learned of styles of play, the accoutrements of dress and the place of football in society by a careful examination of its treatment on film.

Knowledge in this field has been greatly increased recently by Phil Crossley of the British Film Institute. His painstaking research worldwide has unearthed many hundreds of titles with a footballing theme or cameo content and has made him the leading authority on the subject. It is to be hoped that his research may find publication in the near future. The following filmography is selective rather than comprehensive, designed as a way-marker for students interested in a further pursuit of the subject.

Films

1   Harry the footballer / directed by Lewin Fitzhamon.
Hepworth, 1911.
650 ft – ca. 11 mins at 16 fps; b&w.

Possibly the first reference to football in a British fiction film. Made by Cecil Hepworth's company, one of the most important wholly British film companies in existence at the time, and starring Hay Plumb and Gladys Sylvani. This is a fairly typical melodrama of the Edwardian era: Harry the star footballer is kidnapped by members of the opposition club but rescued by his doughty girlfriend in time to get to the match and score the winning goal. This is a silent film (sound was introduced in 1928/29) and one of relatively few early British films to have been preserved.

2   The cats' cup final / directed by Arthur Melbourne Cooper. Empire Films, 1912.
360 ft – ca. 6 mins at 16 fps; b&w animation.

This is the first British animated film to have had a soccer theme. Described in the contemporary trade press as 'an ingenious trick film', it consisted of toy cats playing a game of football.

3   The cup final mystery / directed by Maurice Elvey. Motograph, 1914.
2600 ft – ca. 43 mins at 16 fps; b&w.

Another football melodrama, this time including several sequences shot in and around the Crystal Palace ground.

4   A footballer's honour / directed by Lewin Fitzhamon. Britannia Films, 1914.
2600 ft – ca. 43 mins at 16 fps; b&w.

With a plot that sounds uncannily like that of *Harry the Footballer*, this film represents a considered attempt by the movie business to cash in on the increasing popularisation of football.

5   The rival captains / directed by Ethyle Batley. British Oak, 1916.
970 ft – ca. 16 mins at 16 fps; b&w.

Swifts versus Rangers, and the rival captains are also rivals for the hand of the heroine. This film is most notable in film history terms as being made by Britain's first female director.

6   The ball of fortune / directed by Hugh Croise. Mercury, 1926.
6500 ft – ca. 87 mins at 20 fps; b&w.

Notable for the inclusion of the legendary Billy Meredith, appearing as himself. Based on the novel by Sydney Horler.

☞ See also: I296/9

7   The great game / directed by Jack Raymond.
Gaumont-British Picture Corporation, 1930.
79 mins; b&w.

This was possibly the first British football film to use the technique of incorporating actual match footage, namely the 1930 FA Cup Final between Arsenal and Huddersfield Town. A match played between two specially recruited teams of professionals was also shot for inclusion in the film. A remake of this film appeared in 1952.

8   Up for the cup / directed by Jack Raymond. British and Dominion Film Corporation, 1931.
76 mins; b&w.

A comedy based around the misadventures of an unsophisticated Yorkshireman (Sydney Howard) in London to watch the Cup Final.

9   Oh, Mr Porter! / directed by Marcel Varnel.
Gainsborough Pictures, 1937.
85 mins; b&w.

Will Hay, Moore Marriott and Graham Moffatt in perhaps their finest hour. Not a football film, but a good example of a football related sub-plots. Hay is the totally incompetent station master of the isolated and sleepy Irish village of Buggleskelly, when a gang of gunrunners claim they are Buggleskelly Wednesday FC wanting to hire an excursion special for an away match. Hay is slightly puzzled by their claim that they are taking their own goalposts with them in sealed wooden crates and his suspicions are further aroused when Jeremiah Harbottle (Marriott) informs him that there is no such team. Buggleskelly's only club are The Swifts and Harbottle is their centre forward!

10   The Arsenal stadium mystery / directed by Thorold Dickinson. G&S Films, 1939.
87 mins; b&w.

Probably Britain's most enjoyable football film which has Slade of the Yard (Leslie Banks) pacing the marble halls in an effort to find the killer of a footballer, nobbled during a charity match, on the Highbury pitch, between Arsenal and The Trojans. The 1938 Arsenal Championship team were heavily featured in the film and manager George Allison played a central role. A genuine game (Arsenal v Brentford) was used as the basis for the match sequences and then intercut with footage of a game between Arsenal players and a side made up of Oxford and Cambridge footballers. The end result is a pleasing comedy-thriller, based on the book by Leonard Gribble, with interesting sidelights on the Arsenal stadium itself, newly redeveloped in the 1930s.

☞ See also: I56

11 Spotlight on the Pools / produced by Anthony
Gilkinson. Rayant Pictures, 1949.
18 mins; b&w.

> Not a feature film, more of a documentary, short, but
> worthy of inclusion in this filmography as a reminder
> of how great a phenomenon the Football Pools were
> at that time. Very informative on the subject but also
> notable for some excellent footage in and around The
> Valley for the Charlton v Burnley game with splendid
> shots of the East Terrace crammed to bursting point.

12 The love match / directed by David Paltenghi. Group 3,
1954.
85 mins; b&w.

> Not to be confused with Claude Chabrol's 1974 film of
> the same name (*Partie de Plaisir*)! This is much more
> easily understood though and is thoroughly typical of
> the 1950s popular British film-making. Football forms
> the backdrop to a broad farce starring Arthur Askey
> following the progress of his son who is starting a ca-
> reer with the local team. Notable for the action
> sequences at Bolton Wanderers' Burnden Park; in-
> deed there is almost a role in itself for the Railway
> End, now the much maligned Normid End blessed by
> the presence of a supermarket. Here it is that Askey
> the engine driver pulls his train to a halt to watch a
> stirring match played in front of a packed crowd; flat
> caps and Woodbines much in evidence.

13 The Saturday men / directed by John Fletcher. Graphic
Films, for the Ford Motor Company, 1962.
28 mins; b&w.

> An evocative documentary shot as the cameras
> spend a week following the West Bromwich Albion
> team in an era just prior to the swinging sixties and
> the onset of superstardom. There is little glamour
> here, but certainly shades of *Saturday Night and
> Sunday Morning* as the Albion men go about their
> business. It features many connected with the club
> at that time, including supporters, club members and
> directors, but most well-known are the young Don
> Howe and Bobby Robson. A slice of life impression of
> 60s' soccer which shows just how far conditions for
> players have advanced in the last thirty years.

14 Cup fever / directed by David Bracknell. Century Film
Productions, 1965.
63 mins; b&w.

> Made for the Children's Film Foundation, a prolific
> producer of kids' movie fare in the UK. Barton United,
> a children's team in Manchester, have to overcome
> sundry obstacles as their unscrupulous rivals try to
> prevent them winning the Junior Football League Cup.
> They are treated to a training session at Old Traf-
> ford where they are greeted by Matt Busby and
> coached by the United team.

15 Goal!: World Cup 1966 / directed by Ross Devenish and
Abidine Dino. Frigo Productions, 1966.
108 mins; col.

> They might easily not have bothered to fix up the 117

cameras reputedly used to shoot this record of the
1966 World Cup Finals held in England, but thank
goodness they did. Not only does it record in intimate detail the greatest footballing moment in
England International history, it probably rates as
the best of the full length documentary records of a
World Cup. Notable also as being the first opportunity for millions of football followers to see the game
portrayed in colour on film and at very close quar-
ters. In this respect a precursor for the sort of TV
coverage which we now accept as a daily diet. Other
British World Cup documentaries include *The World at
their Feet* (1970), *Heading for Glory* (1975), and *G'ole*
(1983).

16 Bloomfield / directed by Richard Harris. World Film
Services; Limbridge Productions, 1969.
95 mins; col.

> Also known as *The Hero* this has nothing whatsoever
> to do with *Jimmy* of the same name but instead has
> Richard Harris directing himself as an ageing Israeli
> soccer star, a symbolic clock ticking away in the
> background, Romy Schneider as his girlfriend implor-
> ing him to 'Give eet up!' and Harris being offered a car
> to throw the game. Not highly acclaimed but never-
> theless an interesting insight into the terrors of the
> twilight zone of a professional's career.

17 The Italian job / directed by Peter Collinson. Oakhurst
Productions; Paramount Pictures, 1969.
100 mins; col.

> Another non-football film but one with a running foot-
> ball theme as Michael Caine and his cronies home in
> on Turin for a meticulously planned bullion job. Their
> cover is that they are a party of England football
> supporters in the city for an International — many
> scarves and favours in evidence. Today's travelling
> fans have a reputation for trouble but did they ever
> cause chaos on such a grand scale?

18 Kes / directed by Ken Loach. Woodfall Film
Productions, 1969.
112 mins; col

> A landmark film in British cinema, bringing a new
> naturalism to the screen. This story of a young boy's
> attachment to his pet kestrel poignantly illustrates
> the narrow options open to those without money,
> family stability and adequate education. Filmed on lo-
> cation around Barnsley it is not a football film but
> includes an amusing football cameo as actor Brian
> Glover referees a school match rather less than
> even-handedly.

19 The goalkeeper's fear of the penalty / directed by Wim
Wenders. Produktion 1 Im Filmverlag der Autoren;
Österreichischen Telefilm, 1971.
101 mins; col.

> *Original title: Die Angst des Tormanns beim Elfmeter*
> Very much a serious film despite its rather jocular ti-
> tle. Goalkeeper Bloch walks out of a game in Vienna,
> commits a murder and flees to the Austrian border

to look up an old flame. It is the journey of a man getting too old for his job and living off his nerves — contemporary reviews insisted that 'every frame haunts you for weeks'. It is probably not a film to be watched by those gallant custodians pushing forty.

20 The lovers / directed by Herbert Wise. Gildor Films, 1972.
    89 mins; col.

This spin-off from the TV series starred Richard Beckinsale and Paula Wilcox, fuelled with the straining ardour of the permissive society but finding the reality just a little different, living at home with middle-class parents in Manchester. Not a football film, but this comedy offering does see football mad Beckinsale taking his girlfriend on a romantic date to the Stretford End at Old Trafford. A good element of football backdrop then; when the terraces finally disappear for ever such snippets of nostalgia might take on an historic significance which could never have been appreciated at the time.

21 Stubby (Fimpen) / directed by Bo Widerberg. Bo Widerberg Films, 1974.
    89 mins; col.

A Swedish offering in which a six year old child gets to play for the local league team, moves on to the Swedish side one game later and scores a string of 'Roy of the Rovers' goals in the World Cup qualifying games culminating in the defeat of the USSR at Dynamo Stadium. But Stubby gives it all up to learn how to read and write in this fantasy tale which also doubles as a satire on fame and exploitation in the world of soccer.

22 Yesterday's hero / directed by Neil Leifer. Cinema Seven Productions, 1979.
    95 mins; col.

Another from the ageing footballer school, this one scripted by Jackie Collins and starring Ian McShane long before his 'Lovejoy' days. The film's football adviser, Frank McLintock, has McShane make a cup final comeback with two goals against Leicester Forest whilst John Motson commentates over footage of the Southampton versus Nottingham Forest League Cup Final. All the ingredients are there — boozing striker, hard line managers and rock star chairman. McShane's father, incidentally, was a professional footballer. One of the football films with the greatest number of tenuous connections to the game, it is truly one for the trivia buffs and its billing by a contemporary reviewer as 'irresistibly bad' surely makes it compulsory viewing for all students of football and film.

23 Gregory's girl / directed by Bill Forsyth. Lake Film Productions, 1980.
    91 mins; col.

Forsyth's second feature was this highly entertaining comedy about a Scottish schoolgirl who becomes a wizard in the school football team whilst spurning the amorous advances of the shambolic Gregory who, for good measure, she replaces as centre forward. Regarded as a classic of its type and likely to be enjoyed by all those who love their football.

  ☞ See also: I200; I214

24 Victory / directed by John Huston. Lorimar Productions; Victory Company; Tom Stern, 1981.
    117 mins; col.

An offering from the United States, more generally known as *Escape to Victory* and probably unsatisfactory both for fans of prison escape dramas and for followers of football — Sylvester Stallone and Michael Caine team up with Pelé, Bobby Moore, Oesvaldo Ardiles and a sundry collection of Ipswich Town players as a squad of PoW soccer stars escaping from a Paris stadium. Certainly a curiosity and one of the better known and most widely distributed films with a football theme. If you have seen only one of the offerings in the filmography, this is probably it.

25 Those glory, glory days / directed by Philip Saville. Enigma; Goldcrest, 1983.
    90 mins; col.

The shape of things to come, in that this film was one of the first to be made for Channel 4 Television. Scripted by sports journalist Julie Welch, it tells of her adulation of the great Tottenham Hotspur side of the early 1960s; it includes a cameo appearance by Danny Blanchflower. This is one of the better known football related films which makes some telling observations on the art of teenage fandom.

26 Young giants / directed by Terrell Tannen. Entertainment Enterprises, 1983.
    97 mins; col.

This American feature sees Pelé coming to the aid of his childhood mentor, a dying priest (John Huston) whose orphanage is under threat from corporate baddies who want to kick the kids' football team out on to the street. Under Pelé's coaching guidance they win a fund-raising 'feud match' against the local rich kids' school and all is well. This is a good example of how football may be used to mirror moral issues and emotions.

27 Hero / directed by Tony Maylam. Worldmark Productions; Soccer International Productions, 1986. 86 mins; col.

Surprising how often Michael Caine crops up in these entries, this time as a narrator in another official documentary of the World Cup. The film concentrates on the progress of ten key players, including Diego Maradona, to the exclusion of some of the better moments of the 1986 tournament.

28 Virile games (Muzny Hry) / directed by Jan Svankmajer. Krátky Film; Jiri Trnka Studio, 1988.
    17 mins; col.

A Czech film from the master of bizarre animation, ruminating on the lot of the armchair fan. Soccer violence takes on a new meaning as our viewer finds himself drawn into the action from the squalid confines of his flat. Much use of plasticine and a spirited rendition of 'Blue is the Colour' in Czech – animation has come a long way since *The Cats' Cup Final*. Not one for the football traditionalist, it probably says something of importance about the way the game is perceived but it might take some working out.

29 Arrivederci Millwall / directed by Charles McDougall. National Film & Television School, 1989.
50 mins; col.

Originally shown in cut form on TV, this is one of the few scripted films to examine the ever topical problem of hooliganism. It follows a party of Millwall supporters as they prepare for England's World Cup match in Bilbao in 1982. Loutish behaviour on the ferry to Spain, imprisonment and ultimately the death by misadventure of one of the party render this a depressing film for true fans of football but at least it forces us to face the type of problems depicted and to ponder on how such difficulties might be eradicated.

30 Ultra / directed by Ricky Tognazzi. Numero Uno International; RAI-2; Sacis Productions, 1990.
86 mins; col.

An Italian film depicting their own hooligan problem, much of the footage follows a group of fans on the train from Rome to Turin travelling to the game. The essence of the film is the struggle of one fan to break away from the hooligan clan, get married, go straight, and get a job, but his ambitions are tragically thwarted when he decides to take the rap for a murder accidentally committed by his best friend. The emphasis on mindless violence and vulgarity is convincing, even if it is what we don't wish to see. Like the previous entry, this is one for the football sociologist rather than the season ticket holder.

31 Cup final (Gemar Gavia) / directed by Eran Riklis. S. R. Local Production, 1991.
107 mins; col.

Those who say that football is only a game might reflect on the fact that it has been used as a political, diplomatic and propagandist tool. Whilst it can be divisive it can also draw warring factions together in the pursuit of a common interest. Such is the theme of this Israeli film set in 1982 as Israel invades Lebanon. A shared passion for football proves to be a bond between captors and captives in what is generally regarded as a competent and gripping piece of film-making showing football as the powerful force it undoubtedly is.

Music

MAKING A FOOTBALL RECORD is rather like having eight pints of 'Old Thumper', followed by a fiery curry, the night before a big day at work – at the time it seems like a great idea but in the cold light of day it's a clear case of 'never again'. Banal lyrics, suspect musicians and singing voices of doubtful quality epitomise 'footy records', a venture embarked upon with depressing regularity by many a star-struck player or team rolling along on a wave of success or notoriety.

The few serious observers who have given this phenomenon even a cursory review generally have no hesitation in dismissing the genre. Steve Redhead, for example, in *Football with Attitude* writes, 'The tracks are almost universally awful and, with the exception of the Anfield Rap, I cannot recommend, on aesthetic grounds, a single one!'. This response is fairly typical, but perhaps the time has come for a reappraisal. Certainly, I cannot be the only fan prepared to admit that not only do I have a sneaking regard for football records, I even have a burgeoning collection and know other aficionados whose own collections make mine a mere bagatelle. 'Coming out' is something I would urge all football discophiles to seriously consider – the tide may be about to turn.

So, where is the charm? I believe the appeal lies in the patently idiosyncratic and essentially ephemeral nature of the material on offer. Why should men who can't sing make records? Furthermore, why should people buy them? Probably for the same reasons that kids collect plastic models from cereal packets, or bric-a-brac freaks turn to bakelite egg cups and fifties tableware. Certainly much of what is on offer is truly kitsch and the nature of the beast is 'of the moment' – the first time acquisition is invariably on impulse and the later disposal can follow equally swiftly. This is the only explanation why so many football records end up in attics, spare rooms, charity shops or, more usually, car boot sales. For this reason items which originally were readily available (remaindered more often than not), have become so scarce and thus, in some instances, valuable. On the whole, though, this scarcity is reflected largely in a difficulty of acquisition rather than in high value – most football records sell from fifty pence to just a few pounds, even for the gems. Although supply is strictly limited, demand for the moment is correspondingly low. The result is that no formal market for second hand football recordings has developed so that the few tortured souls seeking to enhance their holdings are frustrated in their search for those elusive titles. Perhaps record dealers should take note – attending a mammoth fair at Birmingham's National Exhibition Centre recently I noticed all the dealers had most efficiently segmented their stock into a myriad of categories yet I didn't encounter a single trader who had a section for football records. Whilst most of the dealers had some in stock they were generally categorised as 'miscellaneous', which entails a search akin to hunting for a needle in a haystack. Time, perhaps, to suitably label up a cardboard divider and watch the sales roll in to the benefit of collector and dealer alike.

Now to the listing. Although I believe this is the most comprehensive presentation published to date, I am well aware that it is far from complete. Rumour has it that every first class English and Irish club, excepting Crewe Alexandra, has at one time cut a record – inevitably this leaves yawning gaps in the lists, but indeed one of the reasons for addressing this subject in the bibliography is to 'raise awareness' with a view to establishing a more comprehensive coverage. It only needs one collector from each club to provide their definitive discography for the effective logging of all known football records to be complete.

So, where is the value in that, one might query. Apart from the obvious quest for completeness which characterizes many collecting fields, there is a serious quasi-academic side to football discophily. Certainly the tone and content of the varied material on offer mirrors the contemporary atmosphere and issues within the game. The dignified gentility of Victor Silvester's 1966 *World Cup Waltz* seems appropriate to the Bobby Moore era while the rather more aggressive renditions of terrace chants provided by Teamwork on their *Terrace Talk* single seems right for 1982. The assertiveness of recent singles by, for example, Ian Wright and Vinny Jones is in sharp contrast to the wistful crooning of John Charles in the early 1960s. Perhaps, too, a listing of this sort might be of use to radio and TV researchers seeking lesser known material to use in profile and documentary programmes – indeed a number of the scarcer titles have begun to surface in just such a manner in the last year or so.

Perhaps all this may convince the reader that it is time for football records to be regarded less derisively and more as a valid part of football culture. Those whose appetite is now whetted may experience fruitful rummaging in the antique fairs and village fêtes where abandoned discs might be rescued from undeserved obscurity; team records, player records, commentaries, charity recordings and novelty items are all likely to surface and the listings herein mirror those categories. Whilst it has been said that the Manchester United calypso, paying homage to the Busby Babes in the 1950s was the first commercially available football 'pop' song, there is in fact a much longer tradition. Right from the earliest days of the organised game in the late nineteenth century, music hall artists soon learned that songs with football allusions were likely to please an audience and this trend continued throughout the present century – Gracie Fields's rendition of *Pass, Shoot, Goal* in 1931 is a typical example. But it was largely the advent of commercial radio and the 'popification' of football in the late 1960s and early 1970s which led to the golden age of football vinyl. Certainly this was a medium for commercially aware clubs and players which had hitherto not been so accessible and many committed themselves to vocal contributions hastily put together on the back of a championship win or cup final appearance. Nowadays the stars of football are more inclined to video productions, and in the same way the availability of video souvenirs of major games has reduced the need for the splendid range of commentary LPs which were an annual fixture well into the 1980s.

Certain enthusiasts within the music industry have recently sought to bring about a resurrection of the football recording artists of yesteryear with the result that a number of compilation albums and tapes have emerged in recent years. The *4-2-4* and *Flair* albums of the late 1980s, followed by the *Bend It* cassettes and CDs of the 1990s offer an excellent introduction for those seeking to widen their knowledge of the subject. Certainly Mike Alway and the London based Exotica company have, in these compilations, provided a forum for further development – indeed the *Bend It* series is well on the way to achieving cult status, its annual offerings being eagerly awaited and a source of much mirth.

Finally, a qualification regarding the following list. All the examples cited have been commercially available and should in no way be confused with examples of sound archive material, which is a different and altogether more extensive matter. Nor do the lists include examples of popular music which simply contain references to the association game. Researchers interested in this extension to the field of study should refer to *Football with Attitude* (p113), by Steve Redhead, to find a short listing of football/music crossover titles.

Meanwhile, peruse the following lists, fill in the gaps and rummage around in that spare room for the record you know you have, even though your subconscious might not like to admit it. 'Ta-ra-ra-boom, let the crusade begin, yeah yeah yeah'. Happy listening!

Music ~ Contents

FA Premiership & Football League

Arsenal

1 Good old Arsenal ; The boys from Highbury / Arsenal 1st Team Squad. 1971.   Pye Records: 7N45067.

'Good old Arsenal, we're proud to say that name, while we sing this song, we'll win the game.' Almost 25 years after the first recording Arsenal supporters are still singing this verse at games.

2 Arsenal we're on your side ; Half time / North Bank. 1972.   Polydor: 2058225

3 The official Arsenal march ; Arsenal boogie / The Highbury Marchers. 1972.   Columbia: DB8899

4 Roll out the red carpet ; Kings of London / Arsenal 1st Team Squad. 1978.   Lightning Records: LIG 544

5 Super Arsenal FC / Arsenal 1st Team Squad. 1979.

6 We're back where we belong ; Spot the ball / Arsenal 1st Team Squad. 1989.   Dover Records: DE1N 1-2

Sung by the 1988/89 League Champions – the sleeve front shows the victorious team group and the rear shows the squad accepting public acclaim at Islington Town Hall. Also includes facsimile autographs.

7 Nessun Dorma 2 ; The victory song. 1993.

8 Shouting for The Gunners ; Shouting for The Gunners (instrumental) / FA Cup Final Squad. 1993.   London Records: LON342

9 Arsenal we're right behind you ; London pride / North Bank.

Aston Villa

10 A S T O N V I L L A / Dave Ismay and the Holte End.
Also on: Flair

Blackpool

11 Blackpool, Blackpool / The Nolan Sisters.
Also on: Flair

'We gave them Stanley Matthews and we gave them Mortensen. We won the cup in '53 and we'll do the same again. So come on down to Blackpool, you can see the lights as well, and join in with the Blackpool Kop as they begin to yell, Blackpool, Blackpool . . .'

AFC Bournemouth

12 Here come The Cherries / Bournemouth Squad and Foursite Saga.
Also on: Flair

Bradford City

13 You know we're going to win / Bradford City Squad. 1987.
Also on: Flair

Brentford

14 Come on you Brentford / The Bees Band.
Also on: Flair

Brighton and Hove Albion

15 The boys in the old Brighton blue / Brighton FC. 1983.   Energy: NRG 2

Also on: Flair; also available on 12" single

Bristol City

16 One for the Bristol City / The Wurzels.

Charlton Athletic

17 The red red robin / Charlton Athletic FC and Billy Cotton.
Also on: Flair

Chelsea

18 Chirpy chirpy cheep cheep / Chelsea Squad and Peter Osgood. 1970.

☞ Also listed at: N205

19 Peter Osgood ; Chelsea / Stamford Bridge. 1970.   Penny Farthing: PEN 715

☞ Also listed at: N206

20 Blue is the colour ; All sing together / Chelsea Squad. 1972.   Penny Farthing: PEN 782.

Generally regarded as the best known football squad recording made by a league side.

21 Back on the ball ; Back on the ball (Club mix) / Chelsea 1st Team Squad. 1984.   W & A Records: YZ23.
Blue vinyl

The sleeve is in the form of a fold out poster with photographs of the 1955, 1970 and 1984 squads.

22 Play the game ; Come on ref. / Team Spirit with John Hollins. 1985.

☞ Also listed at: N187

23 Blue is the colour ; Chelsea we love you / Chelsea Squad. 1987.

Blue vinyl, 12" single

24 Blue is the colour / Chelsea FC and various artists. 1994.
    CD   Monde CD: 19
    CONTENTS: *Blue is the colour / Chelsea FC ; We'll keep
    the blue flag flying high / The Boys from The Shed ; Flying
    high '94 / True Blue Crew ; Chelsea heaven Chelsea hell /
    True Blue Crew ; The liquidator / Billy Blue Beat ; Ten
    men went to mow / Billy Blue Beat ; Chirpy chirpy cheep
    cheep / Chelsea FC ; Football is / Chelsea FC ; Give me
    back my soccer boots / Chelsea FC ; Let's all sing together /
    Chelsea FC ; Song sung blue / Chelsea FC ; Stop and take
    a look / Chelsea FC ; Son of my father / Chelsea FC ;
    Alouette / Chelsea FC ; Liquidator (1970 mix) / Billy
    Blue Beat ; We'll keep the blue flag flying high / The Boys
    from the Shed ; Grand old team / Billy Blue Beat.*

25 No one can stop us now / Chelsea Squad. 1994.

26 Chel-sea of blue / Ron Harris with players and fans.
    Also on: Flair

    ☞ Also listed at: N182

27 Why I love Chelsea / Mr Martini.   Exotica Pélé: 5C
    On: Bend it '93, CD and cassette

Coventry City

28 The Coventry City song ; Football football / Alan
    Randall and Sheps Banjo Boys. 1970.
                                      Domino Records: 110
    Randall is best known as a foremost George Formby
    soundalike – he delivers these songs in the distinctive
    style of the loveable Lancastrian.

29 Go for it ; Sky Blue / Coventry City Squad. 1987.
                                            Skyblue: SKB1

30 Count me in ; Sky Blues song / Coventry City Squad

31 Jimmy Hill's Sky Blues / Coventry City FC
    Also on: Flair

Crystal Palace

32 Glad all over ; When Eagles fly / Crystal Palace Squad.
    1990.   Parkfield: PMS 5019

33 Power to the Palace ; Flying high / Crystal Palace FC
    Also on: Flair

Derby County

34 The Rams song ; The supporter's lament / The Carl
    Wynton Sound. 1975.   Zella Records: JHSPM 176

35 The Derby County story / BBC Radio Derby. 1985
    Limited edition double cassette
    An unusual but valuable offering. Interviews, commen-
    tary and historical dramatisation are nicely
    combined to produce a most effective club history in
    audio form.

36 Uwarya ; Grass miracle / Uwarya. 1994
    Cassette
    Described as a 'screaming' new dance track. This in-
    cludes actual recordings of the Derby fans in full voice
    at the Crystal Palace game on 22 October 1993.

37 We will follow you ; Sure beats going to work on Sunday
    / Syndrome.   White Line Records: WL1

Everton

38 Spirit of the Blues ; Forever Everton / Everton Squad.
    1972.

39 The boys in blue ; The boys in blue (instrumental) /
    Everton Cup Squad. 1984.   Precision Records: EFC1

40 Here we go / Everton Squad. 1985.   Columbia: DB 9106

41 Everybody's cheering the Blues / Everton Squad. 1986.

Fulham

42 Fulham stomp / Fulham FC.

43 Viva el Fulham / Tony Rees and The Cottagers.

Hartlepool United

44 Never say die / Hartlepool Squad.
    Also on: Flair

Ipswich Town

45 Come on The Town ; Ipswich football calypso / Edward
    Ebeneezer and Ipswich supporters.
    Also on: Flair

46 Ipswich, Ipswich / Ipswich FC.

Leeds United

47 Leeds United calypso / Ronnie Hilton and Leeds United
    players. 1964.

48 Leeds, Leeds, Leeds / Leeds United FC. 1972.

49 Here we go again / Leeds United and the Hot Shots.
    1991.

50 Leeds, Leeds, Leeds / Leeds United FC. 1992.
    12" single and cassette

Leicester City

51 This is the season for us ; The tank / Leicester City FC.
    1974.   Decca: F13508
    Also on: Flair
    'The tank' is a tribute to the substantial Leicester
    defender, Graham Cross.

Leyton Orient

52 Fantastico / Orient Squad. and The OK Band. 1978
Also on: Flair
'Away we go to Wembley-O, it's fantastico.'

Liverpool

53 The Kop Choir ; The Kop Choir / The Kop Choir. 1972.
LP   Hallmark Records: SHM794
The album is called 'The Kop Choir' and both sides
feature the Kop Choir so there can be no doubt as to
the contents of this scarce record of live 'atmos-
pheric' recordings of the Liverpool faithful in full
throat recorded during the Chelsea and Bayern Munich
games. The sleeve carries a message from Bill Shankly
and a photograph of the squad. This is a unique me-
mento of an institution which has now vanished for ever.

54 We can do it ; Liverpool Lou ; We shall not be moved ;
You'll never walk alone / Liverpool FC. 1977.
EP   State Records: STAT50

55 Hail to the Kop / Liverpool FC. 1978.

56 Liverpool we're never gonna stop ; Liverpool anthem /
Liverpool FC. 1983.   Mean Records: MEAN102
Red vinyl

57 Sitting on top of the world / Liverpool FC. 1986.
Picture disc   Columbia: DB9116

58 Anfield rap (red machine in full effect) / Liverpool FC.
1988.   Virgin: LFC1
7" and 12"

59 Kenny D the pride of Liverpool ; The team / Liverpool
FC and Peter Howitt. 1989.
12" single   Sublime Records: LIMET 115

60 Liverpool we love you ; Liverpool we love you (version)
/ The Kopites.   Bradleys: BRAD317

61 Paisley crazy / Liverpool FC and the fans.

62 The pride of Merseyside ; Don't care much any more /
Joe Fagin.   GFM Records: GFMX 110
Picture disc and 12" single
Lyrics are by Liverpool player and entrepreneur Craig
Johnston. One side of the disc is completely pictorial
– Bill Shankly, The Kop, Alan Hansen and Kenny Dalglish.

Luton Town

63 D-Pleated ; Terrace mix / The Surgeon.

64 We're Luton Town / Luton Town FC.

Manchester City

65 City and United 1956: the Manchester football double /
The Lord Kitchener Fitzroy Coleman Band. 1956
1956 was the season United won the League and City
lifted the FA Cup.

66 The boys in blue ; Funky City / Manchester City Squad.
1972.

Manchester United

67 United Manchester United / Manchester United 1972
Squad.
LP

68 Manchester United / Manchester United FC. 1976.
Decca: F13633

69 Onward Sexton's soldiers ; Come on you Reds / The
First Team Squad. 1979.   RCA: MAN1
Red vinyl
'Onward Sexton's soldiers we know how to win,
Buchan makes the passes, Macari slots them in.'

70 Glory glory Man United / Manchester United FC. 1983.
EMI: 5390
Also available on picture disc

71 We all follow Man United / Manchester United FC. 1985.
     Also available on picture disc   Columbia: DB9107

72 We will stand together / Manchester United. 1990.

73 United we love you (radio version) ; United we love you
     (karaoke version) / Manchester United and the
     Champions. 1993   Living Beat: LBES 026

     The sleeve is a fold-around poster of Steve Bruce and
     Bryan Robson holding aloft the 1992/93 Premiership
     Trophy.

74 Come on you Reds / Manchester United. 1994.

75 Football classics: Manchester United / Various artists.
     1994.   Cherry Red Records: Monde 16
        CD
        CONTENTS: *Manchester United calypso / Edric Connor*
        with Ken Jones and his music ; Red Devils / The Georgie
        Boys ; Ryan Giggs we love you / The Rainbow Choir ; Ryan
        Giggs / George Best ; George Best Belfast boy / Don
        Fardon ; I love George Best / The Devoted ; Popstar /
        George Best ; Echoes of the cheers / Don Fardon ; The
        Manchester football double / Lord Kitchener Fitzroy
        Coleman Band ; United Manchester United / MUFC *1972*
        Squad ; Look around / MUFC *1972 Squad ; Yellow*
        submarine / MUFC *1972 Squad ; Oh what a lovely morning*
        / MUFC *1972 Squad ; Storm in a tea cup /* MUFC *1972*
        Squad ; Precious memories / MUFC *1972 Squad ;*
        Congratulations / MUFC *1972 Squad ; Never be alone /*
        MUFC *1972 Squad ; Chirpy chirpy cheep cheep /* MUFC
        1972 Squad ; Love again live again / MUFC *1972 Squad ;*
        Saturday afternoon / MUFC *1972 Squad ; Raindrops keep*
        falling on my head / MUFC *1972 Squad ; The Munich air*
        disaster / Harry Gregg ; Flowers of Manchester / Ian
        Campbell and his group

76 Just one of those teams ; Na na hey hey (instrumental) /
     Manchester United Supporters Club.

77 Rah rah rah for Manchester United / The Dollies.
        On: Bend it '93, CD and cassette   Exotica Pélé: 5C

78 Stretford enders / Burke and Jerk.

Mansfield Town

79 Mansfield magic / Mansfield Town FC.
        Also on: Flair

Millwall

80 The ballad of Harry Cripps / Millwall FC

     Cripps was tremendously popular at Millwall in the
     1960s and 1970s – his crunching tackles were a leg-
     end in themselves and, regrettably, a 'leg-end' for
     some of the recipients who left the Den with shat-
     tered limbs.

81 Let 'em come ; Come on you Lions / Millwall FC.

Newcastle United

82 United Newcastle United / Newcastle United players
     and Bobby Webber.
        Also on: Flair

Newport County

83 Come on the County / The Supporters and the Colin
     Woodman Sextette. 1973.
        Also on: Flair

Northampton Town

84 Rising to the top / Sacred Hearts.
        Also on: Flair

Norwich City

85 Something to shout about / Norwich FC and Accent.
        Also on: Flair
     'Mark and Dave and Peter Mendham, other teams
     just can't defend 'em!'

86 On board the yellow submarine / Norwich City FC.
                                      Exotica Pélé: 1C
        On: Bend it '91, CD and cassette

Nottingham Forest

87 We've got the whole world in our hands ; The Forest
     march / Nottingham Forest and Paper Lace. 1978.
                                      Warner Bros: K17710

88 Come on the Forest ; Forest theme / The Fans. 1979.
                                      Soccer Records

89 Brian / Fat and Frantic. 1991.

Notts County

90 County's the team for me / Jimmy Willan, Pete Quilty
     and the Notts County Choir.

Oldham

91 The boys in blue / Oldham Athletic. 1990.

92 The Roger rap / Oldham FC and Beyond the Boundary.

Oxford United

93 My oh my / Oxford United and Prism. 1986.

Peterborough United

94 Posh we are / Peterborough United and the Graham
     Walker Show Band.
        Also on: Flair

Plymouth Argyle

95 Farewell Third Division / Plymouth Argyle Squad and Mount Charles Band.
Also on: Flair

Portsmouth

96 Pompey, city with a heart / Portsmouth players and Southampton All Stars Orchestra accompanied by the Milton Glee Club.
Also on: Flair

Queen's Park Rangers

97 The Loftus Road runners / QPR Squad.
Also on: Flair

98 QPR the greatest / QPR Squad. and Mark Lazarus.

Scarborough

99 We play for Scarborough / Scarborough Squad. 1987.

Scunthorpe United

100 Scunthorpe United / The Del Viking Show Group.
Also on: Flair

Sheffield United

101 I'm following Sheffield United / Alan Martin & Bobby Knutt.
Also on: Flair

One of those 'comedy' recordings which it is just impossible to describe!

Sheffield Wednesday

102 Steel city ; Move on up / Hillsboro' Crew. 1986.
Virgin Records: VS908

The sleeve is a period photograph of a terrace scene in which every spectator appears to be wearing a flat cap. The record was made in support of 'Artists Against Apartheid'.

Southampton

103 The Saints / Southampton FC.

Stoke City

104 We'll be together ; We need you / Stoke City FC with Gordon Banks and friends. 1972.   Trent Records: JT 101

105 We'll be with you / The Potters and Stoke City supporters.
Also on: Flair

Sunderland

106 Sunderland all the way ; I'm feeling happy / Sunderland Squad and Bobby Knoxall. 1973.   RCA: 2362
Also on: Flair

107 Roker rave ; Ain't no stopping us now / Sunderland Squad. 1992.

108 Sunderland are back in the First Division / Fine Art.

Swansea City

109 Bringing back the glory days / Swansea Players Squad.

Tottenham Hotspurs

110 Singalong Spurs / Tottenham Hotspur FC. 1967.
EP.
CONTENTS: *Glory, glory hallelujah ; Hello Dolly ; You made me love you ; Bye bye blackbird / Terry Venables ; I belong to Glasgow / Mackay & Gilzean ; For me and my gal ; Keep right on to the end of the road ; Carolina in the morning ; Maybe its because I'm a Londoner / Mullery & Knowles ; Strollin' / Greaves ; I was Kaiser Bill's batman ; When Irish eyes are smiling / Jennings & Kinnear ; It's a grand old team ; Glory, glory, hallelujah*

111 Nice one Cyril / Cockerel Chorus. 1973.
Youngblood: YB107

☞ Also listed at: N195

112 Ossie's dream ; Spurs are on their way to Wembley / Tottenham Hotspur FC. 1981.   Rockney: Shelf 2

113 Tottenham Tottenham / Tottenham Hotspur FC. 1982.

114 Hot shot Tottenham ; Ossie's dream '87 / Tottenham Squad with Chas 'n' Dave. 1987.   Rainbow: RBR16

115 And David Seaman will be very disappointed about that / The Lillies. 1991.
Flexidisc

116 The victory song ; Glory, glory Tottenham Hotspur / Chas 'n' Dave. 1991.   Glory Records

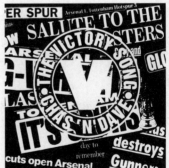

117 When the year ends in 1 / Tottenham Hotspur FC and Chas 'n' Dave. 1991.   AIA1324

118 The hot Spurs boogie / Glitterbest.   Exotica Pélé: 5C
On: Bend it '93, CD and cassette

119 Tip top Tottenham Hotspur.   Exotica Pélé: 1C
On: Bend it '91, CD and cassette

Tranmere Rovers

120 Wembley way / Tranmere Rovers Squad. 1990.

West Bromwich Albion

121 Albion day / West Bromwich Albion Players Squad.
     Also on: Flair

     Celebrates the FA Cup Final of 18 May 1968 when Albion beat Everton 1-0. The winning goal was scored by Jeff Astle, himself a recording artist of some note . . . which note, Jeff has not quite decided yet.

West Ham United

122 I'm forever blowing bubbles ; West Ham United / West Ham United Cup Squad. 1975.   Pye: 7N45470

Wimbledon

123 The Dons song / Wimbledon FC. 1988.

124 We are Wimbledon ; Wimbledon FA Cup theme / Wimbledon FC. 1988.

Wolverhampton Wanderers

125 We're back / Wolves Squad. 1988.

Wrexham

126 I mewn I'r Gol ; We're gonna score / Brymbo Male Voice Choir. 1978.   Tryfan Records: TRF116S

     This is some of the most harmonious singing you are likely to encounter on a football record, delivered in tune by a real Welsh male voice choir.

127 This is Arfon Griffiths / Wrexham supporters and Arfon Griffiths.
     Also on: Flair

     Welsh International Griffiths was both player and manager for his home town club and was awarded the MBE for his services to football. The record begins with a stirring speech from the man himself.

Wycombe Wanderers

128 The Wanderer / Dion. 1962.   HMV: POP 971

129 The Wanderer / Dion. 1976 (re-issue).   Philips: 6146700

York City

130 Here we go / York City Squad. 1984.
     Also on: Flair

Former Members of the Football League

Maidstone United

131 The MUFC Club song / Maidstone United FC players.
     Also on: Flair

Non-League & Amateur

Burton Albion

132 Here we go / Burton Supporters and Ind Coope Burton Brass Band.
     Also on: Flair

133 Hit the road to Wembley / Bernard Bagan and Take Five.

Fisher Athletic

134 Come on the Fish / Fisher Athletic FC.
     Also on: Flair

Gravesend and Northfleet

135 Here comes the Fleet / The Swanscombe End.
     Also on: Flair

Kingstonian

136 These nearly, nearly glory glory days / The Norbitones.
     Also on: Flair

Leatherhead

137 Nut rocker / Bee Bumble and The Stingers.

Wealdstone

138 We are the Stones / The Defenders.
     Also on: Flair

     'We go to places as far away as Barrow, but one place we always like to win is Harrow!'

Scotland

Aberdeen

139 The northern light of old Aberdeen ; The European
song / Aberdeen FC Squad.   AFC1
     White vinyl

Celtic

140 Celtic your favourites in green ; Saturday / Celtic Squad.
1973.   Polydor: 2058332

141 The Celtic rap ; Boot mix / Celtic Squad. 1988.
     12" single   Skratch Music: CFC12

142 The Celtic song / Glen Daly.

143 Over and over / Celtic 1st Team Squad.

Clyde

144 Song of the Clyde / Clyde FC and Fraser Bruce
     Also on: Flair

Kilmarnock

145 Flags of glory / David Shaw.
     Also on: Flair

Partick Thistle

146 Firhill for thrills / Partick Thistle FC.
     Also on: Flair

Raith Rovers

147 The Raith Rovers songs / Crooked Jack at the Kiwi
Tavern, Auchertool.
     Also on: Flair; LP

Rangers

148 The Glasgow Rangers boys (vocal) ; The Glasgow
Rangers boys (instrumental) / The Boys in Blue Players
Squad. 1987.   Spartan Records: GRB1
     12" single

149 Follow, follow / Buddy Logan.
     Also on: Flair

Republic of Ireland

Finn Harps

150 The Finn Harps song / Hugh McLean and the Blue Glows.
     Also on: Flair

     'Once there was a football team in dear old Donegal.
People thought that in the League they had no
chance at all . . .'

Personalities

Banks, Gordon

151 Banksie (a tribute to Gordon Banks) ; National (Health)
Anthem / Chris Renshaw and The Keepers. 1973.
Pye: 7N45285

'Pelé and Eusébio found he was the best, Uncle Alf
knew he would stand the test.' The career of one of
the world's greatest goalkeepers is heralded in similar verse throughout this tribute recording.

Barrett, Les

152 Julie Brown loves Captain Cook / Les Barrett.
Exotica Pélé: 5C

On: Bend it '93, CD and cassette

Curious offering from the Fulham winger whose career
in the sixties and seventies coincided with an era
when footballers and pop were more closely associated than ever before or since.

153 Love me / Les and Paul Barrett.   Exotica Pélé: 1C
On: Bend it '91, CD and cassette

Best, George

154 George Best, Belfast boy / Don Fardon. 1970.
Youngblood: YB1010

155 An open letter to George Best ; Bovver boys / The
Group. 1972.   The Famous Charisma Label: CB197

156 George Best advertises grooming aids.   Exotica Pélé: 2C
On: Bend it '92, CD and cassette

157 George Best – promotional interview with Kenneth
Wolstenholme.   Exotica Pélé: 1C
On: Bend it '91, CD and cassette

You would have to hear it to believe it – blatant yet
utterly naive endorsement of a 'new kind of leisure
coat' from football's best known boutique owner in
casual conversation with a commentating superstar.

158 George, you've broken my heart / Her.   Exotica Pélé: 5C
On: Bend it '93, CD and cassette

159 I love George Best / The Devoted.   Exotica Pélé: 1C
On: Bend it '91, CD and cassette

One of a number of gems devoted to the number one
heart throb of his era.

Bonds, Billy

160 Billy Bonds MBE / Barmy Army.   CI Sound
*On: Pay it all back Vol. 2, LP; also available on flexi disc
issued with West Ham fanzine 'On the terraces'*

Buchan, Martin

161 Old Trafford blues / Martin Buchan.

Cantona, Eric

162 Cantona superstar / Her.   Exotica Pélé: 5C
On: Bend it '93, CD and cassette

163 Ooh ah Cantona / Oo la la.

Inspired by one of the enigmatic Frenchman's own
speeches . . . 'I want to say I love you, I don't know why
but I do.'

Charles, John

164 La fine / John Charles. 1960.   Exotica Pélé: 1C
On: Bend it '91, CD and cassette

165 Love in Portofino / John Charles and the William
Gallassini Orchestra.   Exotica Pélé: 2C
On: Bend it '92, CD and cassette

If you send a Welshman to Italy, then maybe a song is
the natural result. This and the following entry are
two of the earliest examples of a footballer commit-
ting himself as a solo recording artist – the result is
not at all bad.

Charlton, Bobby

166 Bobby Charlton ; City summer / Tribute. 1973.
Jam Records: JAM48

Finger in the ear time for brother Bobby in this folksie
rendition – 'His name is Bobby Charlton and this is
Bobby's song, All the people love him 'cos he's never
done no wrong.' And today's players talk about pressure?

Charlton, Jack

167 Jack Charlton's Geordie Sunday / Jack Charlton.
Exotica Pélé: 1C

On: Bend it '91, CD and cassette

Time to reach for the Hovis as Big Jack consults the
dialect dictionary in this overly sentimental tale of a
Geordie childhood.

Clemence, Ray

168 Side by side / Ray Clemence with Peter Shilton.

No hard feelings as two of England's rival keepers
prove what great mates they are – what does it matter who goes between the sticks as long as England
win. Trouble is, we didn't!

☞ Also listed at: N208

Clough, Brian

169   You can't win 'em all ; It's only a game / Brian Clough with J. J. Barrie, Peter Taylor and Stuart Webb. 1980.

MCA: 658

What an unlikely foursome – a management duo, a real musician and a club director. The result is predictable; let's just say the title of the 'A' side is an apt one.

☞   Also listed at: N209

Dalglish, Kenny

170   Just like Kenny / Mad Jocks and Englishmen.

Fashanu, Justin

171   Do it 'cos you like it / Justin Fashanu.   Monde: 15CD
On: 4-2-4 football classics, LP and CD

Gascoigne, Paul

172   Fog on the Tyne (revisited) / Lindisfarne with Paul Gascoigne. 1990.   Best: ZB44083

It was inevitable that someone with Gazza's marketing profile would get in on the recording scene. This is one of a number of offerings.

173   Geordie boys ; Gazza rap / Paul Gascoigne. 1990.

Best: ZB44229

174   Cry, Gazza, cry / Spitting Image.

It could only happen to him – a celebration of his world famous lachrymal outburst from the masters of latex lampoonery.

175   Gascoigne please / Mr Martini.   Exotica Pélé: 1C
On: Bend it '91, CD and cassette

176   Let's have a party / Paul Gascoigne and friends.   Best

177   Nice one Gazza / New Cockerel Chorus.

George, Charlie

178   I wish I could play like Charlie George.   Exotica Pélé: 1C
On: Bend it '91, CD and cassette

This endearing song features a group of children longing to be blessed with the visionary skills of this Arsenal and Derby icon.

Giggs, Ryan

179   Ryan Giggs we love you / The Rainbow Choir.
On: Bend it '92, CD and cassette   Exotica Pélé: 2C

The Rainbow Choir echo the sentiments of the entire Brownie movement as they serenade their wonderful Welsh winger.

Gilzean, Alan

180   I belong to Glasgow / Alan Gilzean with Dave Mackay. 1967.
On: Singalong Spurs, EP

☞   Also listed at: N199

Greaves, Jimmy

181   Strolling / Jimmy Greaves. 1967.

Harris, Ron

182   Chel-sea of blue / Ron Harris with Chelsea players and fans.

☞   Also listed at: N26

Hateley, Tony

183   Where have you been lately Tony Hateley? / The Disco Zombies.

Hoddle, Glenn

184   Diamond lights ; Diamond lights (instrumental) / Glenn and Chris (Hoddle and Waddle). 1987.
EP and picture disc   Record Shack: Kick 1

Not many footballers were actually good enough singing artists to appear on 'Top of the Pops' – Glenn and Chris were no exception but they had a good agent!

☞   Also listed at: N213

185   It's good-bye ; It's good-bye (instrumental) / Glenn and Chris (Hoddle and Waddle). 1987.   Record Shack: Kick 2
Includes free flexi disc interview

Enough good byes to last a lifetime – hopefully.

☞   Also listed at: N214

Hollins, John

186   Peace ; A peace of reggae / Peace Band with John Hollins. 1979.

187   Play the game ; Come on ref. / Team Spirit with John Hollins. 1985.

☞   Also listed at: N22

Hughes, Emlyn

188   Christmas time / Emlyn Hughes with Suzanne Dando & kids.

Liverpool's famous captain had entered the world of TV by the time this seasonal offering came hurtling down the chimney.

Jennings, Pat

189   When Irish eyes are smiling / Pat Jennings with Joe Kinnear. 1967.
On: Singalong Spurs, EP

☞   Also listed at: N193

Jones, Vinnie

190 Wooly Bully / Vinnie Jones. Monde: 15CD
    On: 4-2-4 football classics, LP and CD
    No comment required!

Keegan, Kevin

191 Head over heels in love / Kevin Keegan. 1979.
                           EMI: 2965
    One of the few footballers brave enough to go solo in
    an attempt at a seriously sentimental song.

192 England ; Somebody needs / Kevin Keegan.

Kinnear, Joe

193 When Irish eyes are smiling / Joe Kinnear and Pat
    Jennings. 1967.
    On: Singalong Spurs, EP
    ☞ Also listed at: N189

Knowles, Cyril

194 Maybe it's because I'm a Londoner / Cyril Knowles and
    Alan Mullery. 1967.
    On: Singalong Spurs, EP
    ☞ Also listed at: N204

195 Nice one Cyril / Cockerel Chorus. 1973.
                       Youngblood: YB1017
    'Nice one Cyril, Nice one son, Nice one Cyril, Let's have
    another one.' This is still heard in various guises to-
    day around UK football grounds.
    ☞ Also listed at: N111

Lee, Francis

196 Sugar sugar / Francis Lee with Bobby Moore and the
    1970 England World Cup Squad. Exotica Pélé: 1C
    On: Bend it '91, CD and cassette
    ☞ Also listed at: N202

Lineker, Gary

197 Europe united / Gary Lineker with Roy of the Rovers. 1990.
    The Queen Mother of football here joins forces with
    soccer's most famous fictional creation to boost the
    spirit of togetherness required at a time when the
    game's image needed bolstering.

198 Ooh Gary Gary / Her. Exotica Pélé: 2C
    On: Bend it '92, CD and cassette
    Despite the sometimes unflattering anatomically in-
    clined nicknames given to England's superstar striker
    by his fellow professionals (or maybe even because
    of!), there can be no doubt that Gary is popular with
    the ladies. This fact is here celebrated in a catchy
    musical number.

Mackay, Dave

199 I belong to Glasgow / Dave Mackay with Alan Gilzean.
    1967.
    On: Singalong Spurs, EP
    Mackay was born in Edinburgh, but it's the sentiment
    that counts.
    ☞ Also listed at: N180

McFarland, Roy

200 Roy McFarland / Rockin Johnny Austin.
                   Confection Records: LC7871
    On: Flair
    Celebrates the talent of one of the best centre
    halves ever to have played for England – pity the lyr-
    ics weren't of equal quality. 'Wave your scarves and
    start to cheer, the superstar of the Rams is here . . .'

Matthews, Stanley

201 Sir Stanley Matthews. Exotica Pélé: 1C
    On: Bend it '91, CD and cassette
    Thoughts on the game rather than a musical offering.

Moore, Bobby

202 Sugar, sugar / Francis Lee with Bobby Moore and the
    1970 England World Cup Squad. Exotica Pélé: 1C
    On: Bend it '91, CD and cassette
    ☞ Also listed at: N196

Morgan, Willie

203 Willie Morgan on the wing. Exotica Pélé: 1C
    On: Bend it '91, CD and cassette
    This title and tune spawned terrace chants through-
    out the nation – simply substitute the name of your
    favourite winger and there you have it . . . that's if
    your team plays wingers of course; it doesn't scan if
    you say 'in a deep-lying left sided midfield role.'

Mullery, Alan

204 Maybe it's because I'm a Londoner / Alan Mullery and
    Cyril Knowles. 1967.
    On: Singalong Spurs, EP
    ☞ Also listed at: N194

Osgood, Peter

205 Chirpy chirpy cheep cheep / Peter Osgood and Chelsea
    FC. 1970.
    ☞ Also listed at: N18

206 Peter Osgood ; Chelsea / Stamford Bridge. 1970.
                   Penny Farthing: PEN 715
    ☞ Also listed at: N19

Rosenior, Leroy

207 Leroy's boots / Barmy Army.

    On: The English Disease, U sound; also available on flexi disc issued with West Ham fanzine, 'On the terraces'

Shilton, Peter

208 Side by side / Peter Shilton with Ray Clemence.

    ☞ Also listed at: N168

Taylor, Peter

209 You can't win 'em all ; It's only a game / Peter Taylor with Brian Clough, J. J. Barrie and Stuart Webb. 1980.
                                      MCA: 658

    ☞ Also listed at: N169

Venables, Terry

210 Bye bye blackbird / Terry Venables. 1967.

    On: Singalong Spurs, EP

When Venables picked up the mike for a range of karaoke style singalongs long before that term was invented, he might not have guessed that he would be the future holder of that supremely dignified position known as the England Manager. Anyway it's all good fun and he'd probably do the same again given a chance.

211 Lucy what do you want to make those eyes at me for / Terry Venables. 1974.

212 I've got you under my skin / Terry Venables.
                                        Exotica Pélé: 2C

    On: Bend it '92, CD and cassette

Waddle, Chris

213 Diamond lights ; Diamond lights (instrumental) / Glenn and Chris (Hoddle and Waddle). 1987.
                                Record Shack: Kick 1

    EP and picture disc

    ☞ Also listed at: N184

214 It's good-bye ; It's good-bye (instrumental) / Glen and Chris (Hoddle and Waddle). 1987.
                                Record Shack: Kick 2

    Includes free flexi disc interview

    ☞ Also listed at: N185

Wright, Ian

215 Do the right thing / Ian Wright. 1993.
                             M&G Records: MAGS 45

    Also available on CD and 12" single

This record probably boasts the most unpleasant pictorial sleeve in the entire discography – a graphic close up of Wright's wide open mouth. Definitely one for his dentist.

World Cup & International Squads

✱ *England*

216 The day we won the cup ; Ramsey's men / Roy Hudd. 1966.   Polydor: 56136

One of the most collectable and extremely scarce recordings celebrates England's victory in good old music hall fashion.

217 England 1966: the World Cup waltz / Victor Silvester Orchestra.   Exotica Pélé: 2C

    On: Bend it '92, CD and cassette

Undoubtedly the most genteel offering in the entire listings – perfect with a large pink gin.

218 World Cup Willie / Lonnie Donegan. 1966.

England's leonine mascot is celebrated in this well known but surprisingly scarce little ditty. 'There's a football fella you all know his name, And the papers tell us he's in the hall of fame. Wherever he goes, he'll be all the rage, Cos he's the new sensation of the age . . . Dressed in red, white and blue he's World Cup Willie.'

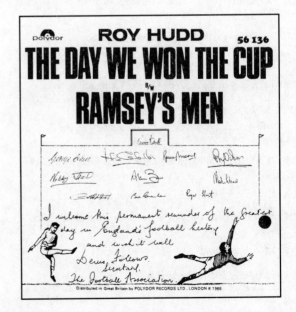

219 Back home ; Cinnamon stick / 1970 England World
Cup Squad.   Pye: 7N17920

> Generally regarded as the best known World Cup
> squad recording.

220 The world beaters sing the world beaters / 1970
England World Cup Squad.   Pye: NSPL 18337
LP

221 Here we are ; Here we are (instrumental) / England
Squad and Magnum Brass. 1975.   Inline Records: ENS 1
LP

> The most endearing and rather sad feature of this
> record is the photograph and sleeve message; 'Dear
> Supporter, I sincerely hope this record will be a big
> success and that all the England supporters will
> learn the words so they can sing it well together. I
> feel this will help the England team wherever we play.
> Best wishes, Yours sincerely, Don Revie England Team
> Manager.' I really don't know whether to laugh or cry.

222 This time we'll get it right / 1982 England World Cup
Squad.   K Tel Records: NE 1169
LP

223 This time we'll get it right ; England we'll fly the flag /
1982 England World Cup Squad.   England Records
Also available on 7" picture disc & 7" red, white and blue disc

> The picture disc is particularly collectable – squad
> portraits on one side, team autographs on the other.

224 Oh sweet England / England Supporters. 1986.

225 We've got the whole world at our feet ; When we are far
from home / 1986 England Squad.   Columbia: DB9128

226 World Cup party / 1986 England Squad.
LP

227 All the way / 1988 England Squad with Stock, Aitken
and Waterman.   MCA: Goal 1
Also available on 12" single

228 Back home ; Barrelhouse Cam in Vietnam / Crackous
Rock an Roll. 1989.   HTB Records: BAR6
Flexidisc free with 'Hit the bar' fanzine

> This is an extremely raucous rendition of the England
> squad's rousing 1970 version.

229 World in motion / 1990 England Squad and New Order.
12" single and cassette   Factory/MCA: FAC2937

230 England my England / The Lads of the Village.

231 Viva England ; The young footballer / Ian Sludge Lees.

✱ *Scotland*

232 Easy, easy / 1974 Scotland World Cup Squad.
LP   Polydor: 2383282

233 Easy, easy ; Scotland Scotland / 1974 Scotland World
Cup Squad.   Polydor: 2058452

> Of the home international sides Scotland need less
> encouragement than the others to enter the record-
> ing studio. The lyrics are always loosely based around
> conquering the world although a number have pre-
> empted the mounting sense of failure on the world
> football stage by opting for the humorous approach.

234 Ally's tartan army / Andy Cameron. 1978.
                                       Klub: KLUB 03

235 Don't cry for us Argentina ; We'll be there over there /
Andy Cameron. 1978.   Klub: KLUB 06

236 Easy, easy ; We'll be there over there / Scottish football
supporters. 1978.   Polydor: 2059020

237 Hey Argentina / Scotland Sons. 1978.

238 Hoat pies for us Argentina / Bill Barclay. 1978.

239 Olé ola (Mulher Brasileira) / 1978 Scotland World Cup
Squad and Rod Stewart.   Riva: 15

240 Marching to Argentina / Tartan Lads. 1978.

241 Scotland bonnie Scotland ; Into the dead of night /
Hampden's Heroes. 1978.   State Records: STAT 73

242   World Cup fanfare / Band of the Scots Guards. 1978.

243   We have a dream / 1982 Scotland World Cup Squad.
                             Wea: K 19145

244   Big trip to Mexico ; Carry the hopes of Scotland / 1986 Scotland World Cup Squad.   Columbia: DB9130

      'We're the squad, you know us all by name, We got here the hard way, no easy game, We're not afraid of anyone's fame, We'll give all we've got to bring the trophy hame!'

245   Say it with pride / 1990 Scotland World Cup Squad.
      Also available on 12" single   RCA: PB 43791

246   Scotland Scotland / Andy Stewart and Rabble FC. 1990.

247   The Black Douglas.

✳ *Republic of Ireland*

The Republic's success during the last decade has caused their supporters and their squad to make a number of recordings. I believe there are many more examples than those listed here, but I have not had sight of them. More information required please.

248   The boys in green / 1988 Eire Football Squad.

249   Jack's heroes ; Whiskey in the jar / The Pogues and The Dubliners. 1990.   Pogue Mahone: YZ 500

250   Put 'em under pressure / 1990 Eire Football Squad.
      12" single

✳ *Northern Ireland*

251   Yerman / 1982 Northern Ireland Squad and Dana.
      This is the only instance I can recall when a Eurovision Song Contest heroine has cut a footy record.

252   Come on Northern Ireland / 1986 Northern Ireland Squad.

World Cup Theme Tunes

253   World Cup Cha Cha Santiago '62.   Exotica Pélé: 1C
      On: Bend it '91, CD and cassette

254   The England World Cup march / Joe Loss and his orchestra 1966.   Exotica Pélé: 1C
      On: Bend it '91, CD and cassette

255   Mexico Grandstand: BBC 1970 World Cup Grandstand theme.

256   The world at their feet: 1970 World Cup theme.

257   Lap of honour: 1974 World Cup theme / London Stadium Orchestra.

258   Action Argentina ; Nanaskin / South Bank team. 1978.
      Weekend Records: DJS 10867

259   Argentine melody (Cancion de Argentina) / San José and Rodriguez Argentina.   MCA: 369
      Rodriguez Argentina is also known as Rod Argent
      The 1978 BBC World Cup Grandstand theme tune.

260   World Cup Argentina '78 / Ennio Morricone & his orchestra.

261   El Mundial: theme for Spain 1982 / Placido Domingo.

262   Matador: 1982 ITV World Cup theme / Jeff Wayne. 1982.   CBS: A2493

263   Aztec gold: ITV World Cup '86 theme.

264   Aztec lightning: 1986 World Cup Grandstand theme / Heads.   BBC: RESL 184

265   Viva la Mexico: 1986 World Cup theme / Black Lace.

266   Nessun dorma: BBC World Cup Grandstand theme ; 'O sole mio / Luciano Pavarotti. 1990.   Decca: PAVO3
      Of all the World Cup themes this deserves a special mention. It may sound far-fetched, but this had a massive influence in 'popularising' opera. Much of what has happened to Pavarotti since has been as a direct result of Italia '90. Such is the power of football!

267   To be number one: 1990 official FIFA World Cup song.

268   Tutti al mondo: 1990 ITV World Cup theme.

269   Un' estate Italiana: official FIFA World Cup theme ; Un' estate Italiana (karaoke version) / Eduardo Bennato and Gianna Nannini. 1990.   Virgin: 112913

270   Can't get a ticket for the World Cup / Peter Dean.

271   Official World Cup theme / Colourbox.

OFFICIAL SONG OF FIFA WORLD CUP ITALY 1990

EDOARDO BENNATO - GIANNA NANNINI

UN'ESTATE ITALIANA

Supporters' Anthems & Terrace Chants

272   Que sera sera, whatever will be will be / Doris Day. 1956.
Philips: PB 586

Doris Day's well known rendition is just one of a number of versions of this song, now firmly established as one of soccer's best known anthems, invariably sung when it looks as if the game is moving towards inexorable defeat.

273   You'll never walk alone / Gerry and the Pacemakers. 1963.   Columbia: DB7126

Rodgers and Hammerstein's tearjerker from 'Carousel' still has the power to move even in the completely different context of football. It has been adopted as one of football's most famous anthems, particularly favoured by Liverpool, who regard it as their own.

274   Terrace talk ; Sucker for the game / Teamwork with Marshall Doctors and Nicky Parker. 1982.
Kingdom: KV8023

Side 'A' is a compilation of some of the best known terrace chants. Side B is quite a poignant lament by an imaginary also-ran from the professional ranks.

275   Abide with me / Inspirational Choir. 1984.   Epic: A4997
1985 reissue – Portrait: A4997

This anthem is seldom heard on football grounds nowadays, but time was when it was sung with true feeling by 100,000 fans prior to kick off at every FA Cup Final. It is one of the most moving sounds from the football archives. This version is one of a number recorded.

276   The last football song ; Here we go / Hoagy and the Terrace Choir. 1984.   Silvertown: ST58

277   Abide with me / Vic Reeves. 1991.   Sense: SIGH713

278   Your swaying arms / Deacon Blue. 1991.
Columbia: 6568937

279   Football hustle / Kop Unlimited Orchestra.

280   Olé olé olé: the name of the game / The Fans.

281   Play the game / The Supporters.

282   Que sera, sera / Anne Breen.

283   Que sera, sera / Shakin' Stevens.

284   Red white and blue / Gerry Marsden and England Supporters Club.

285   Viva Espana (football version) / UK supporters.

286   We are the champions / Combined Supporters Clubs.

Charity & Disaster Appeals

287   Love can be cruel. 1985.
In aid of Bradford City Fire Disaster Fund

288   You'll never walk alone ; Messages / The Crowd. 1985.   Spartan Records: BRAD1
In aid of the Bradford City Fire Disaster Fund

The Crowd included over fifty names from the world of sport and entertainment, amongst them Rick Wakeman, Paul McCartney and Peter Cook.

289   It's on our doorstep / Chelsea, Fulham and QPR. 1987.
For Children in Need

290   The worst song ever ; Worst song ever (sick as a parrot mix) / The Boss Squad. 1988.   Polydor: FOOTY1
In aid of Sports Aid

The Boss Squad comprised many top managers – Brian Clough, Alex Ferguson, George Graham, Bobby Robson, Jack Charlton and Terry Venables all make the team, supported by Jimmy Greaves, Ian St. John and John 'Shnozz' Sillett from the media.

291   Ferry 'cross the Mersey ; Abide with me / Gerry Marsden, Paul McCartney, The Christians and others. 1989.   PWL: 41
In aid of the Hillsborough Disaster Fund

Abide with me is a live recording taken from the six o' clock evening mass at Liverpool's Catholic Cathedral on Sunday 16 April 1989.

Humour & Novelty

292 Football results ; The astronauts / Michael Bentine. 1962.

Parlophone: 4927

Highly entertaining reading of the day's results as a dignified Bentine lapses into manic excitement when he realises that his eight draws could be up.

293 Bovver boys ; Piraeus Football Club / The Group. 1972.

The Famous Charisma Label: CB 197

A bizarre offering written by Neil Innes – the Piraeus Football Club squad have great difficulty in reaching the end of their club song as it involves calling out the team's names – Papadopolous is the shortest!

294 Bickenhill Rovers skin'ead supporters / Jasper Carrot.

Well known comedian and Birmingham City man Jasper Carrot presents an amusing spoof football club record in his own inimitable style.

295 Earl's a winger / Richard Digance.

296 Football / Mickey and the Soul Generation.

297 Football crazy / Robin Hall and Jimmy McGregor.

'He's football crazy, he's football mad . . .'; several versions of this 1960s refrain were produced, this one being the best known of them.

298 Football crazy / Rolf Harris.

Bearded antipodean star resorts to broad Scots accent in this version of a well known football ditty – not a didgeridoo or wobble board in sight, not many buyers either.

299 Goalie's ball / James.

300 Here we go, here we go / The Essential Wally Party Medley.

Here we go is undoubtedly one of the chants of the nineties – this invariably irritating and earsplitting chorus is here recorded for posterity.

301 Oh no not football / Goal to Goal featuring Jazzie J.

A group of Liverpool girls bemoan the fact that they can't escape the 1990 Italy World Cup – 'Oh no not football on my TV', all sung to the classical strains of 'Just one Cornetto'!

302 Only a 1000 a day ; Do do be do / Cockerel Chorus.

303 Pump up the ball / Shoot and DJ Bear.

304 We want a goal / The 80's Band.

305 We're on the ball / Glen Daly.

Compilations

306 4-2-4 football classics. 1988.   EL Records

LP and later on CD

This compilation should be at the core of any collection, being the first of its kind. The original record is extremely difficult to acquire.

307 Flair: the other world of British football. 1989.

Double album   Confection records: LC7871

Again, an essential acquisition – the sleeve blurb states that it presents 'the most panoramic and largest collection of soccer recordings ever assembled' – 47 tracks in all. The album included a free 24 page Flair Magazine featuring George Best, Stan Bowles and Duncan McKenzie along with Norman Wisdom and Graham Kerr the 'Galloping Gourmet'!

308 Bend it '91.   Exotica Pélé: 1C

CD and cassette

This first Bend It compilation extended the *Flair* concept to include many examples from overseas along with delightful recording oddities from domestic shores – Frankie Howard, Alec Guinness, Bruce Forsyth and Sophia Loren all make the credits.

309 Bend it '92.   Exotica Pélé: 2C

CD and cassette

More exotic fare as Harold Wilson, Arthur Askey, Donald Duck and Her Majesty the Queen of England deliver their football homilies.

310 Bend it '93.   Exotica Pélé: 5C

CD and cassette

Ever-increasing resourcefulness as Diana Dors, Hilda Ogden, Bamber Gascoigne and Sid James muscle in amongst more conventional musical fare.

311 Bend it '94.

CD

The first Bend It compilation not to appear in tape format – one senses that new examples from the archives may be dwindling as this latest offering includes many overseas excerpts.

312 101 songs about sport / Sportschestra.   Agit Prop

Double album

Includes some football examples.

Commentaries & Commentators

❋ General

313 Matthews to Moore 1948-1966: the golden age of
football, commentary and interviews from the BBC
Sound Archives. 1992.   BBC Enterprises Ltd
Double cassette (ISBN: 0-563-40983-5)

Serves as a complete history of post-war broadcast
football up to England's 1966 World Cup victory. Includes some marvellous material – well worth seeking
out.

314 BBC Sports Report: 40 years of the best. 1987.
Cassette

Includes an introduction by Eamonn Andrews as a
foretaste to many famous radio voices and, of
course, the legendary theme tune.

315 Quite extraordinary ; At the end of the day / I Ludicrous.
Kaleidoscope Records: KS 707

The sleeve shows a team group style photograph of a
number of commentators including Frank Bough,
David Coleman, Alan Weeks, Arthur Ellis and Kenneth
Wolstenholme. *Quite Extraordinary* is an amusing
tribute to David Coleman

316 Luton Town v Bristol City 1975: commentary excerpt by
Eric Morecambe.
Exotica Pélé: 2C
On: Bend it '92, CD and cassette

'0-0 at the moment, for Luton, and Luton have got a
free kick coming up now which Bobby Thomson's just
going to take. Yes. Anderson . . . it's there, wa-hey
how about that . . . knockout, that's fabulous that!'
Morecambe delivers a real live commentary as only he
could.

❋ World Cup

317 World Cup '66: recordings of final and extra time,
semi-finals, quarter finals and interviews. 1966.
Double album   Centaur Productions: CPC 1234

This should certainly be a candidate for any football
fans desert island portfolio. Commentator 'Geevers'
Wynne-Jones, a Welshman of course, sums up better
than any Englishman might. 'Good ol' England! England who couldn't play football! They've got it in the
bag! . . . It's a magnificent victory the result of years
of planning, this enormous crowd standing cheering
madly, and the sun shines brightly on this treasured
isle. England's such a happy place, Wembley such a
wonderful spot, on this World Cup afternoon . . .'

318 World Cup 1966 and 1970.
LP   Quality Recordings Ltd: QP 5/70

Includes England 4 West Germany 2 from 1966 along
with the memorable Brazil 4 Italy 1 from 1970.

319 Flashback '66 / Match and DJ Bear with Kenneth
Wolstenholme. 1992.   High Cue Music: SUMM 2

Includes a reconstruction of the great man's 1966
World Cup Final commentary along with a cartoon
strip depiction of Geoff Hurst's third goal on the rear
of the sleeve.

❋ European Competitions

320 Chelsea kings of Europe: 1971 European Cup Winners
Cup Final – Chelsea v Real Madrid.
LP   Quality Recordings Ltd: QP 8/71

Chelsea won this replayed final 2-1. The sleeve states
that the record is dedicated to manager Dave Sexton and his players, preserving for the football fan
the drama and thrills of that magical replay night in
Athens. A footnote apologises for the omission of
Dempsey's opening goal which is instead described at
half time by Peter Lorenzo.

321 European Cup: the match 1968 – Manchester United v
Benfica. 1973.   Quality Recordings Ltd: QP 12/73
LP

This emotive recording celebrates United's historic
performance at Wembley, emerging 4-1 victors over
the Portuguese champions.

322 We've kopped the cup: 1976 UEFA Cup Final –
Liverpool v Bruges.   Quality Recordings Ltd
LP

Liverpool were victorious 4-3 over two legs.

323 Liverpool conquer Europe: European Cup Final 1977 –
Liverpool v Borussia Mönchengladbach.
LP   Quality Recordings Ltd: QP 24/77
*3-1 to the Reds – Peter Jones and Alan Parry com-
mentate.*

324 Liverpool, the legend of Europe: 1978 European Cup
Final – Liverpool v Bruges.
LP   Quality Recordings Ltd: QP 27/78
*Liverpool's 1-0 win at Wembley is superbly covered by
the Radio Merseyside team.*

325 Forest's Euro double: 1979 European Cup Final v
Malmö, 1980 European Cup Final v Hamburg.
LP   Quality Recordings Ltd: QP 83/80
*Celebrates Forest's remarkable double feat – both
games were won 1-0.*

✱ *FA Cup*

326 Chelsea's Cup: 1970 FA Cup Final – Chelsea v Leeds.
LP   Quality Recordings Ltd: QP 4/70
*Chelsea beat Leeds 2-1 in the replay after a 2-2 draw
at Wembley.*

327 1971 FA Cup Final: Arsenal v Liverpool.
LP   Quality Recordings Ltd: QP 7/71
*Arsenal's 2-1 victory is captured by Bryon Butler,
Maurice Edelston and Peter Jones.*

328 1972 FA Cup Final: Leeds v Arsenal.
LP   Quality Recordings Ltd: QP 9/72
Leeds won this centenary final 1-0

329 Sunderland's Cup: 1973 FA Cup Final – Sunderland v
Leeds.   Quality Recordings Ltd: QP 11/73
LP
*One of the most dramatic Cup Finals of all time as
Sunderland beat the mighty Leeds United 1-0. I knew
a chap at university who played this album nearly
every night, much to the irritation of his rather studi-
ous, poetry-loving room mate.*

330 Liverpool's Cup: 1974 FA Cup Final – Liverpool v
Newcastle.   Quality Recordings Ltd: QP 15/74
LP
*Includes material from Radio Merseyside on the
homecoming of the victorious Liverpool team, who
romped to an easy 3-0 win.*

331 Hail to the Hammers: 1975 FA Cup Final – West Ham v
Fulham.   Quality Recordings Ltd: QP 16/75
LP
*Hammers won 2-0 in one of the duller finals on re-
cord.*

332 Super Saints: 1976 FA Cup Final – Southampton v
Manchester United.   Quality Recordings Ltd: QP 19/76
LP

*Includes How the Cup was Won; Saints Receive the
Cup; Welcome Home and When the Saints Come
Marching In. An excellent souvenir of this memorable
1-0 win for Southampton.*

333 Battle of the giants: 1977 FA Cup Final – Manchester
United v Liverpool.   Quality Recordings Ltd
LP
*United came out on top 2-1 – Peter Jones and Alan
Parry relay the drama.*

334 Bobby's dazzlers: 1978 FA Cup Final – Ipswich v
Arsenal.   Quality Recordings Ltd: QP 26/78
LP
*Roger Osborne scored the surprise winner in this 1-0
triumph for the Suffolk club.*

335 Match of the century: 1979 FA Cup Final – Arsenal v
Manchester United.   Quality Recordings Ltd: QP 29/79
LP
*Near apoplexy for Peter Jones and Alan Parry as a
last gasp goal from Alan Sunderland wins the game
for Arsenal 3-2.*

336 Liverpool's FA Cup Finals: radio excerpts from their
Cup exploits. 1980.
Gold flexidisc

✱ *League Cup*

337 1971 League Cup Final: Spurs v Aston Villa.
LP   Quality Recordings Ltd: QP 6/71
Celebrates a 2-0 win for Spurs.

338 League Cup Final 1972: Chelsea v Stoke City.
LP   Quality Recordings Ltd
Stoke were victorious 2-1.

339 1973 League Cup Final: Tottenham Hotspur v Norwich.
LP   Quality Recordings Ltd: QP 10/73
Celebrates a 1-0 victory for Spurs.

340 Wonderful Wolves: 1974 League Cup Final –
Wolverhampton Wanderers v Manchester City.
LP
Wolves were triumphant 2-1.

341 League Cup Final 1976: Manchester City v Newcastle
United.   Quality Recordings Ltd: QP 18/76
LP
*Commentary by Simon Smith with no ursine assis-
tance whatsoever, as City beat Newcastle 2-1.*

342 Villa's hat trick: Aston Villa v Everton 1977 League Cup
Final replay.   Quality Recordings Ltd
LP
*Villa won this marathon 3-2 only after a second re-
play at Old Trafford.*

343   Fabulous Forest: 1978 League Cup Final – Forest v Liverpool, Wembley and Old Trafford replay.
LP   Quality Recordings Ltd

Forest won the replay 1-0 at Old Trafford.

344   Forest are magic: 1979 League Cup Final – Forest v Southampton.   Quality Recordings Ltd: QP 28/79
LP

Forest take the Cup two years in succession by winning 3-2.

✳ *Scottish Cup*

345   Scottish Cup Finals 1965-70: famous Celtic victories. 1970.   Quality Recordings Ltd: QP 3/70
LP

Includes 3 wins and 2 runner-up spots for the Glasgow club.

346   Rangers kings of Scotland: 1976 Scottish Cup Final – Rangers v Heart of Midlothian.   Quality Recordings Ltd
LP

Souvenir of a 3-1 victory for Rangers.

✳ *Home Internationals*

347   1969 Home International Tournament: England v Scotland.   Quality Recordings Ltd: QP 2/69
LP

After England's superb 4-1 victory the Scottish manager, Bobby Brown, tipped them for the 1970 World Cup. The commentator here is David Francey.

Name Index

This is an index of all names – both of individuals and organisations – which appear in the entries in A Football Compendium. Entries are given for all authors, editors, compilers, illustrators etc, as well as corporate bodies such as the Football Association or the Association of Football Statisticians. Entries may refer to books or other items about that person or organisation, as well as those written, or issued, by them. There are no entries under club names – these may be found in the separate Club Index. Names beginning with Mc or Mac have been interfiled as if spelt Mac. A number of qualifying terms, such as group (for musical/recording groups) and fictional (for fictional characters) have been used where it is thought this might be helpful.

A

Abbotsholme School G13
Aberystwyth & District League B1301
Accent (group) N85
Ackland, Norman A230
Action and Research for Multiple
  Sclerosis G272
Acton, Peter K84
Adams, Jack A186, B1061, B1195
Adams, John G146
Adams, P C B993
Adamson, Gareth I107
Adamson, Jean I107
Adamson, Steve B698-700
Adrian, Alec I18, I108-109, I280
Advisory Design Council F66
Aflalo, F G A14, A23
Ager, David G48
Agnew, Paul B667, C180
Ahlberg, Allan I110
Ahlberg, Janet (illustrator) I110
Ahmed, Shasta I111
Aitken, Andrew A32
Aitken, Charlie B59
Aitken, Mike A191, B1135, B1138,
  C275, C370
Aitken, Roy C1, C63
Akers, M H218
Akpabot, Samuel Ekpe E226
Alan, Jay H56
Alaway, Robert B B988
Alcock, Charles William A4, A8,
  A11, A31-32, J1, J215
Alcock, Kevin B40
Alder, Derek (illustrator) L1
Aldridge, John B409, C2
Alister, Ian B75
Allan, David A B1249, B1270-1271,
  B1284, B1298, B1300
Allan, J Murray I282
Allan, Jay H56

Allan, John B1183-1184, B1186
Allard, Dave B347
Allen, Clive C3
Allen, John C117
Allen, Richard I95-100
Allen, Robert C39
Allen, Roland D4
Allen, Ronnie C4
Allen, Samuel Henry B765
Allenson, Hugh G134, G180
Allgood, Johnny
  See Goodall, John
Allison, George A43, C5-6, J178, M10
Allison, M Sinclair G235
Allison, Malcolm C7
Allison, William B1193
Allman, Geoffrey B664, B824
Ally McCoist Testimonial Committee
  C327
Almond, Bobby E80
Alternative Football Network L1176
Alway, Mike A162
Amateur Football Alliance A231, A236
Amateur Football Association A227
Amateur Football Defence Federation
  See Amateur Football Alliance
Ambler, Chris (illustrator) F8
Ambrosen, Tony B935-936, H244
Ames, L E G C8
Amstutz, André I289
Anderson, Chalmers D42, E156
Anderson, Ian B1241
Anderson, Keith D45
Anderson, Robin (illustrator) K102,
  K105
Anderson, Viv C9
Andrews, Eamonn N314
Andrews, Gordon B A207, C585, C589
Andrews, W H I197
Antique Collectors' Club H240, H250
Ap Dafydd, Myrddin
  See Myrddin ap Dafydd
Appleton, Arthur B746, B1018

Apsley, B E203
Archer, Ian A190, B1074, B1167
Archer, Michael E5, E197
Ardiles, Ossie C10, M24
Argentina, Rodriguez N259
'Argus' B252
Arlett, Reg C11
Arlott, John C220, C264-265, C545,
  C563, E33, G233, H100, I15, I235,
  I249
Armfield, Jimmy A84, C12, G231
Armour, William J G266
Armstrong, Henry George G252
Arnold, A J B124, B922, H284
Arnold, Malcolm I299/31
Arnold, Peter E122, E192
  For other works by this author see
  Graham, Matthew
Arnott, Robert B333
Arsenal Football Supporters' Club B5
Arthur, Max B498
Arthur Andersen & Co H278
Ashcroft, J G54
Ashton, George H147
Askey, Arthur M12, N309
Association of European Football
  Statisticians E215
Association of Football Statisticians
  A25, A138, B802, B908, C526,
  C529-530, C532-534, C536-537,
  C616-617, D33-38, D40-41, D46,
  D53-63, D65, E9, E159-162, H235,
  J138, J140, J148-156, J158, J160-
  161, J165-166, J168, J172, J174-175,
  J230-234
Astle, Jeff C13
Atcost Buildings Ltd F9
Athenian League A249, J229
Atherden, Ernest F59
Atkinson, Ron C14, G179
Attaway, Pete B614
Attila the Stockbroker I194
Attwood, Tony I278

G

H

M

S

X

Y

Z

Club Index

This index guides the user to books and other items about individual clubs and national sides. It also includes some fictional clubs. Note that many of the items under 'Key Personalities' refer to autobiographical or semi-autobiographical material included here because of the incidental information which may be derived from these sources relating to the club itself. Early volumes of reminiscences or early coaching guides in particular may be rich sources for such information.

A

Eastbourne United
Key Personalities G131

Edinburgh City
Club Histories B1255, B1285, B1289

Edinburgh St Bernards
Club Histories B1256, B1285, B1291

El Salvador
Supporters I233

Elgin City
Club Histories B1257-1258
Fanzines L1024-1028

Ellesmere Port
Grounds F34

Ely City
Club Histories B973

Emmet Rovers (fictional)
Literary Appearances I211

Enfield
Fanzines L726-728

England
Fanzines L1219, L1227, L1230
Film Appearances M29
History E139-142, E144-145, E147-149
Key Personalities E148, G54, G58-60, G62, G69, G73-74, G83, G86, G93, G97, G109, G114, G116, G135, G140, G168, G177, G194, G219, G222, G225
Managers C228, C369, C415-416, C421-422, C424-426, C477, C488-490, C508, G94, G103, G201, G230
Sound Recordings N216-231, N315, N317, N347
World Cup B945, E31-33, E38-40, E73-74, E90, E143, E150, N317

ES Clydebank
Club Histories B1289

Everton
Club Histories A16, A30, B278-300
Fanzines L197-203
Key Personalities C16-17, C38-39, C135-136, C140-141, C209, C219, C295-296, C301, C306-309, C314-316, C340, C346, C369, C386, C417, C419-420, C433, C501, C506, C520, C55, G97, J32
Sound Recordings N38-41, N342

Exeter City
Club Histories B301-302
Fanzines L204-206
Key Personalities C22, C498

F

Falkirk
Club Histories B1117-1121
Fanzines L937-938
Programmes H247

Fareham Town
Fanzines L729-730

Farnborough Town
Fanzines L731

Farsley Celtic
Fanzines L732

Ferryhill Athletic
Fanzines L733

5th Kirkcudbrightshire Rifle Volunteers
Club Histories B1300

Finchley
Club Histories B974

Finn Harps
Sound Recordings N150

Fiorentina
Literary Appearances I42

Fisher Athletic
Sound Recordings N134

Fleetwood Town
Club Histories B975
Fanzines L734

Fordingbridge Turks
Club Histories B976

Forfar Athletic
Club Histories B1122-1123
Fanzines L939

Forres Mechanics
Club Histories B1259

France
Key Personalities C78-79

Fraserburgh
Fanzines L1029

Frickley Athletic
Fanzines L735

Fulchester United (fictional)
Key Personalities K82

Fulham
Club Histories A30, B303-309
Fanzines L207-210
Key Personalities A81, C36-37, C99-100, C228, C253-254, C261, C328-331, C353, C382-385, C388-390, C424-426, C472, G61, G83, G97, G107, G112, G131, G221, G228-229
Sound Recordings N42-43, N289, N331

G

Gainsborough Trinity
Club Histories B948

Galston
Club Histories B1289

Galway United
Fanzines L1091

Gateshead
Club Histories B923-924, B946, B1018
Fanzines L736
Key Personalities C197, C376-377

Genoa
Supporters H87

Gillingham
Club Histories B310-314
Fanzines L211-215
Key Personalities C8, C59, C406

Glasgow Celtic
See Celtic

Glasgow Rangers
See Rangers

Glenavon
Club Histories B1321
Fanzines L1067-1068

Glenbuck
Club Histories B1260-1261
Key Personalities C442-444

Glentoran
Club Histories B1322
Fanzines L1069-1072
Key Personalities C38-40, C150, C337, G97

Glossop
Club Histories B946
Key Personalities C445

Spa
Club Histories B1314

Spain
History E246
Key Personalities A84

Sporting Lisbon
Key Personalities C167

St Albans City
Fanzines L809

St Austell
Fanzines L810

St Helens
Fanzines L811
Key Personalities C483-484

St Johnstone
Club Histories B1222-1224
Fanzines L1011-1014
Key Personalities C325-327

St Mary's
Club Histories B1339

St Mirren
Club Histories B1225-1229
Fanzines L1015-1016
Key Personalities G81
Programmes A173, H248

St Neots Town
Grounds F32

St Patricks FC
Fanzines L1100

Stafford Rangers
Fanzines L812

Stalybridge
Club Histories B946

Steeple Sinderby Wanderers (fictional)
Literary Appearances I29

Stenhousemuir
Club Histories B1230
Fanzines L1017

Stevenage Borough
Fanzines L813-814

Stirling Albion
Club Histories B1231-1232
Fanzines L1018-1019

Stockport County
Club Histories B731-733
Fanzines L480-483
Key Personalities C36-37
Supporters H115

Stoke City
Burnden Park Disaster F37
Club Histories A16, A30, B734-743
Fanzines L484-490
Key Personalities C18, C86, C188, C296, C298, C355-360, C402, C447, G113
Sound Recordings N104-105, N338

Stourbridge
Fanzines L815-816

Stranraer
Club Histories B1233
Stretford Athletic *(fictional)*
Literary Appearances I90

Stroud
Fanzines L817

Sudbury Town
Club Histories B1002

Sunderland
Club Histories A16, A30, B744-756, B1018
Fanzines L491-507
Key Personalities A31, C24, C38-39, C60, C81, C108-112, C183, C196, C325-327, C422, C440-441, C499-500, G54, G63
Memorabilia H239
Programmes H232
Sound Recordings N106-108, N329

Supermarine
Fanzines L818

Sutton United
Club Histories B1003-1004
Fanzines L819-821

Swansea City
Club Histories B757-764
Fanzines L508-524
Key Personalities C135-136, C183, C284, C297, C405, C454, C482
Sound Recordings N109

Swansea Town
Key Personalities G105

Sweden
Key Personalities C330-331, C418

Swifts (fictional)
Film Appearances M5

Swindon Town
Club Histories B765-773

Fanzines L525-528
Key Personalities C40, C402

Symingtons
Club Histories B1016

T

Tampa Bay Rowdies
Key Personalities G131

Tandragee Rovers
Club Histories B1325

Telford United
Fanzines L822-823

Terriers (fictional)
Literary Appearances I28

Thames Association
Club Histories B948

Thames Ironworks
Club Histories B861, B864
See also West Ham United

Thamesmead United (fictional)
Literary Appearances I90

Thetford Town
Fanzines L824

Third Lanark
Club Histories A173, B1276-1278, B1287, B1291

Thistle
Club Histories B1287, B1291

Thornton Dale Reserves
Fanzines L826

Tintagel
Key Personalities C298

Ton Pentre
Key Personalities C405

Tonbridge
Fanzines L827
Grounds F32

Tooting and Mitcham
Fanzines L828-829
Key Personalities C466-467

Torino
Key Personalities C302-304

Torquay United
Club Histories B774-775
Fanzines L529-534
Key Personalities C298, C486

U

V

W

Title Index

This is a list of all the book and film titles, recordings and other items which appear in A Football Compendium. All titles are arranged alphabetically. Articles (A, An, and The) at the beginning of a title are ignored for the purpose of filing as is punctuation such as colons (:) and apostrophes ('). When more than one book or other item with the same title appears, these are listed alphabetically by the name of the author or, if there is no author, the name of the club to which they refer, or the date of publication. Titles beginning with dates file at the beginning of the index. Titles beginning with a number file as if the number was spelt out, i.e. 100 years of Welsh soccer, files immediately before The hundred years story of the Nottingham Forest FC 1865-1965.

1879-1979 West Bromwich Albion Football Club centenary brochure B837

1921-1981, 60 years in the Scottish League: Alloa Athletic Football Club B1044

1969 Home international tournament: England v Scotland (sound recording) N347

1971 FA Cup Final: Arsenal v Liverpool (sound recording) N318

1971 League Cup Final: Spurs v Aston Villa (sound recording) N337

1972 FA Cup Final: Leeds v Arsenal (sound recording) N328

1973 League Cup Final: Tottenham Hotspur v Norwich (sound recording) N339

1975 (1984 minus 9) H41

1984-85: the double year / Wealdstone FC B1009

The 1992 European championship E125

A

The A-Z of Manchester football: 100 years of rivalry 1878-1978 B443

An A to Z of Reading Football Club B687

The A to Z of soccer A94

The A-Z of Tranmere Rovers B820

The AB-Z of world football E182

The abbey rabbit L109

The ABC of soccer sense: strategy & tactics today G243

Abercorn: a history B1234

Aberdeen: a complete record 1903-1987 B1035

Aberdeen FC handbook and history 1949-50 B1029

Aberdeen: final edition B1038

Aberdeen Football Club: a pictorial history B1036

The Aberdeen football companion: a factual history, 1946-86 B1032

Aberdeen greats B1037

Aberdeen programme review H261

Abide with me (sound recording) N275, N277, N291

The absolute game: a Scottish football fanzine L1204

Accrington Stanley: a complete record, 1894-1962 B906

Accrington Stanley to Wembley B905

Across the great divide: a history of professional football in Dundee B1103

Act now (series) I200, I202

Action Argentina (sound recording) N258

Action books (series) G241

Action football I153

Action replays C352

Action sports (series) I290-291

The actor-footballer I296/35

Adam and football I162

Adam and the FA Cup I163

Adam and the football mystery I164

The Adams family L613

Addickted L133

Adlib paperbacks (series) I140

Aerofilms guide (series) F13, F15

AFC Bournemouth official club history and championship souvenir B118

AFN distribution fanzine catalogue L1176

The AFS book of Cup Final players D38

The AFS book of inter league matches: a complete record J158

Against all odds C322

Against the odds: an autobiography C426

Against the tide L1148

Against the world: playing for England C288

Ain't no stopping us now (sound recording) N107

Airdrieonians FC: 100 years and more B1040

The airman half-back I296/45

Alan Breck's book of Scottish football A180

Alan Hansen's soccer quiz book K138

Alan Mullery C389

Alan Mullery: an autobiography C390

Alas Smith & Smith L329

Albania Football Club: a lighthearted but factual account of football in Albania E230

Albania to Iceland E220

Albion!: a complete record of West Bromwich Albion 1879-1987 B842

Albion! Albion! I82

B

C

D

E

Everton player by player B297
The Everton quiz book B291
The Everton story B286
Everton: the official centenary history B285
Everton winter, Mexican summer: a football diary C419
The Evertonian L198
Every inch a sport I299/17
Every man a football artist L1092
Every picture tells a story: the pictorial history of the
  Midland Counties Football League A250
Everybody's cheering the Blues *(sound recording)* N41
The ex-league clubs (1888-1981) J143
Exceedingly good pies L440
The Excelsior system H157
The Exe directory L204
Exeter City: a complete record 1904-1990 B301
Exeter City: a file of fascinating football facts B302
Exiled! L69
Expelled from football I296/29
The exploding latics inevitable L384
Explorations in football culture H23
The expression she pulled L1168
Expressive soccer G250
Extra time and it's still a funny old game K23
The eyes of the kop L460

F

F stands for Linfield L1079
FA autograph book G104
FA Carling Premiership pocket annual J129
FA Carling Premiership: the players: a complete guide to
  every player C607
The FA coaching book of soccer tactics and skills G208
The FA complete guide to England players since 1945
  E149
FA Cup D18
The FA Cup 1871-81 D33
The FA Cup 1881-91 D34
The FA Cup 1891-1901 D35
The FA Cup 1901-11 D36
The FA Cup 1911-25 D37
The FA Cup: a post-war history D29
FA Cup centenary gift book for boys 1872-1972 D15
The FA Cup: club by club records D39
The FA Cup comes west I108
The FA Cup Final 1970: Chelsea v Leeds Utd. D14
FA Cup Final victory: commemorating the 25th
  anniversary of West Bromwich Albion's Cup Final
  victory B845
FA Cup giant killers D32
FA guide for referees and linesmen G25
The FA guide to teaching football G148

The FA guide to the laws of the game: a teaching
  programme G28
The FA guide to the treatment and rehabilitation of
  injuries in sport G266
The FA guide to training and coaching G115
FA news: official journal of the Football Association A244
FA non-league directory J110
The FA non-league football annual A234, J106
FA Premier League pocket annual J128
The FA quiz book K139
The FA Trophy D67
The FA Vase D68
The Faber book of soccer I236
The fabulous 'Dixie' C141
Fabulous Forest: 1978 League Cup Final – Forest v
  Liverpool, Wembley and Old Trafford replay *(sound
  recording)* N343
Facsimile volumes of Chelsea Football Club programmes
  H251
Fact book *(series)* B675
The facts about a football club, featuring Queens Park
  Rangers B675
The facts about the 'money factories' H207
Facts and figures on the Football League clubs,
  (1888-1978) *(series)* B356, B396, B445, B495, J142-143,
  J145
FAI World Cup '94 handbook E110
Fair play: ethics in sport and education G153
Fairmyle fights through I296/38
Faithful through and through L888
Faithful through and through: a survey of Celtic's most
  committed supporters B1084
Falkirk & district newsletter L919
Falkirk through the years B1117
The Falkirk unofficial fanzine L937
The fall and rise of Derby County FC throughout the
  1980's B266
Family of four C15
Famous football clubs *(series)* B7, B49, B102, B184, B194,
  B436, B458-459, B663, B671, B707, B724, B735 B782,
  B831, B850
Famous names in soccer C580
The famous number nine L332
Fan Treff L1218
Fans at the trackside: a national survey of disabled football
  spectators H84
Fanseye L1108
Fantastico *(sound recording)* N52
Fantasy team H274
Fanzine classics L1179
Fanzine collector L1180
Fanzine monthly L1181
The far corner: a mazy dribble through north-east football
  K26
Far from a madding crowd L802
Farewell souvenir to Tommy Walker C494
Farewell Third Division *(sound recording)* N95

G

H

I

J

K

L

Limerick you're a lady L1093
Lincoln City bygones B382
Lincoln City centenary souvenir 1883-1983 B381
The Lincolnshire football guide J57
Lineker: golden boot C314
Linfield: 100 years of Linfield Football and Athletic Club
   B1324
Linlithgow Rose: 100 years 1889-1989 B1269
The Linnets: an illustrated, narrative history of Barry
   Town AFC 1888-1993 B1303
The Lion of Vienna: Nat Lofthouse, 50 years a legend
   C319
The lion roars L326
Lions through the lens B551
The liquidator *(sound recording)* N24
The little red L1062
The little red book of Chinese football E228
The little red book: the thoughts of Bill Shankly K10
A little thing called pride: an autobiography C472
Liverpool / *Day* B410
Liverpool / *Graham* B398, B400-401
Liverpool 1893-1978: results, league tables, would you
   believe it items B396
Liverpool: a complete record 1892-1986 B402
Liverpool: a complete record 1892-1988 B411
Liverpool: a complete record 1892-1990 B418
Liverpool: a pictorial history B424
Liverpool anthem *(sound recording)* N56
Liverpool are on the tele' again! L358
Liverpool: champions of champions B419
Liverpool, champions of Europe: the players' official story
   B391
Liverpool – club of the century B412
Liverpool conquer Europe: European Cup Final 1977 –
   Liverpool v Borussia Mönchengladbach *(sound recording)*
   N323
Liverpool FC official annual B392
Liverpool FC: season 1959-60 B403
Liverpool Football Club B389
Liverpool greats B415
Liverpool in Europe B425
Liverpool in Europe: the complete record from 1964
   B426
Liverpool Lou *(sound recording)* N54
Liverpool, my team C256
Liverpool: player by player B420
The Liverpool quiz book B406
The Liverpool story B393, B395
Liverpool supreme B404
Liverpool: 10 seasons at Anfield 1984/85 to 1993/94
   B431
Liverpool, the legend of Europe: 1978 European Cup
   Final – Liverpool v Bruges *(sound recording)* N324
Liverpool: the official centenary history, 1892-1992 B422
Liverpool we love you *(sound recording)* N60
Liverpool we're never gonna stop *(sound recording)* N56
The Liverpool year B413

Liverpool's Cup: 1974 FA Cup Final – Liverpool v
   Newcastle *(sound recording)* N330
Liverpool's FA Cup Finals: radio excerpts from their Cup
   exploits *(sound recording)* N336
Liverpool's sporting pages C402
Living English readers for the Arab world *(series)* I279
Living for kicks C302
Living with a legend C51
A load of bull L607
A load of cobbolds: an alternative look at Ipswich Town
   L234
A load of locks L851
Loadsamoney L54
The Loftus Road runners *(sound recording)* N97
The logical football system H160
London & District newsletter L299
London & District supporters' magazine L298
London and Provincial Wireless Programme, football,
   racing and amusement guide J58
London area newsletter L201
London Branch bulletin L980
London Branch newsletter / *Leicester City* L252
London Branch newsletter / *Sunderland* L496
London Fan Club newsletter L300
London football clubs series *(series)* B793
London FSA newsletter L1193
London Lions L27
London magpie L337
The London owl L462
London pride *(sound recording)* N9
London Saints' newsletter L470
London Supporters Club news L872
The London Swan L514
London Swans newsletter L515
London's Cup Final, 1967: how Chelsea and Spurs
   reached Wembley B197, D12
The loneliness of the long-distance runner I12
The long ball L1235
Long ball down the middle L839
The long Good Friday: the story of Charlton Athletic
   1905-1990 B188
Look around *(sound recording)* N75
Look back in amber L227
Look for floodlights L856
Look-in books *(series)* K102, K105, K108
The loonatic L939
The Looville rag L837
A lot to answer for L516
A lotta balls L1236
Loud L1126
Love affair: some saints B1228
Love again live again *(sound recording)* N75
Love can be cruel. 1985. *(sound recording)* N287
Love in Portofino *(sound recording)* N165
Love is not love, and other short stories I10
The love match *(film)* M12
Love me *(sound recording)* N153

M

N

O

P

Q

S

T

U

United: the story of Manchester United in the FA Cup B539

United to win C14

United we love you (karaoke version) *(sound recording)* N73

United we love you (radio version) *(sound recording)* N73

United we shall not be moved C323

United we stand / *Cantwell* C80

United we stand / *Manchester United* L313

United we stand / *Moncur* C379

United we stood: the unofficial history of the Ferguson years B540

United's fight for the Cup B555

Universal guide for referees G24

The unknown Maxwell C368

The unofficial World Cup book E81

Up for grabs now L1202

Up for t'cup: the story of Scarborough FC in the FA Cup 1887-1985 B698

Up for the cup D26

Up for the cup *(film)* M8

Up front L685

Up Sandy! L1030

Up the arse L22

Up the Blues L467

Up the Blues: into the 2nd Division B718

Up the 'Boro!: the diary of Middlesbrough Football Club's promotion season 1991-1992 B548

Up the cherries: the complete story of Bournemouth and Boscombe FC 1899-1959 B117

Up the city: the story of Chelmsford City FC B222

'Up the Clarets': the story of Burnley Football Club B156

Up the town: an illustrated history of Ipswich Town Football Club B344

Up the work rate L1035

Up, up and away: Brighton & Hove Albion's rise to the 1st Division B133

Up wi' the bonnets!: the centenary history of Dundee Football Club B1105

Upon St Andrew's Day 1841-1901: a list of football teams A254

Ure's truly C487

U's news L167

Usborne guide to soccer: skills, tricks and tactics G184

UTD United L590

Uwarya *(sound recording)* N36

V

Vale of Leithen FC 1891-1991 B1279

Vale of Leven FC cup-tie history B1280

The valiant 500: biographies of Charlton Athletic players past and present B190

Valiants L396

Valiants viewpoint L141

The Valiants' years: the story of Port Vale B653

Venables: the autobiography C489

Venables: the inside story C490

Verses united: the poetry of football I195

The Victoria voice L490

Victory *(film)* M24

The victory song *(sound recording)* N7, N116

Victory was the goal: soccer's contribution in the war of 1939-45 A47

Vidaho L603

A view from the East Bank: an unusual look at Sheffield Wednesday Football Club L464

A view from the ground / *McIlroy* H138

The view from the ground / *Gellhorn* B1109

A view from the Piggeries L691

View from the Rock L909

A view from the shelf L553

A view from the terraces: one hundred years of the Western Football League, 1892-1992 A247

View from the Tower L57

Villa bugle L31

Villa meets Beaunanza! L50

Village on the border: a social study of religion, politics and football in a North Wales community H3

The Villan L32

Villan meets Beaunanza! L33

Villa's hat trick: Aston Villa v Everton 1977 League Cup Final replay *(sound recording)* N342

Villazine L34

Vinnie: a kick in the grass C286

Vintage claret: a pictorial history of Burnley Football Club B157

Vintage 'Port B938

Virile games *(film)* M28

Viv Anderson C9

Viva el Fulham *(sound recording)* N43

Viva England *(sound recording)* N231

Viva Espana (football version) *(sound recording)* N285

Viva la Mexico: 1986 World Cup theme *(sound recording)* N265

The Viz Billy the Fish football yearbook K82

The voice L1203

The voice of soccer A55

Voice of the beehive L83

Voice of the Valley L142

Voice of the Vetch L524

Voices from the devil L314

Voll Daneben L1269

W

The W. M. Johnston facsimile J165

Waddle: the authorised biography of Chris Waddle C491

Waiting for the great leap forward L985

X

Y

The yellow peril L652
Yellow submarine *(sound recording)* N75
Yeltz news L746
Yerman *(sound recording)* N251
Yesterday's hero *(film)* M22
York City B901
York City: a complete record 1922-1990 B904
The York City Shipton Street quiz book B903
A Yorkshire boyhood I222
Yorkshire News football guide J45
Yorkshire soccer heroes C625
You can play football G177
You can play soccer G177
You can't win 'em all *(sound recording)* N169
You cheating bastard! L777
You get nowt for being second C57
You know we're going to win *(sound recording)* N13
You lion gets! / *Holywell Lions* L758
You lion gets! / *Red Lions FC* L795
You made me love you *(sound recording)* N110
You wot! L507
You wot!: the anti-racist alternative Torquay United mag
  L534
You'll never walk alone L270
You'll never walk alone *(sound recording)* N54, N273, N288

You'll never walk alone: the official illustrated history of
  Liverpool FC B407, B414, B423
Young England: the story of the development of soccer
  talent E139
Young footballer I25
The young footballer *(sound recording)* N231
Young giants *(film)* M26
Young people's images of attending football H48
The young player's guide to soccer G157
The young soccer player G211
The young sportsman A22
Younger's World Cup review, 1978 E69
Your book of soccer A75
Yours sincerely C228
Your swaying arms *(sound recording)* N278
You've got to be crazy C602

Z

Zico was a punk rocker L1174
Zigger L633
Zigger Zagger I208
Zoot skazine L1175

Subject Index

Please note books about specific clubs and national sides are listed in the separate Club Index.

A

African Football E225-227, G102, L1254

Albanian Football E230, E245, I194

Alcoholism A205, A208, C37, C224, I52-54

All-seater Stadiums
See Stadiums

Amateur Football A227-251, B952-1027, B1024, D64, G74

American Football (Soccer) E106, E113, E236-239, G144, G156, G178, L1205

Anthems N272-286
See also Music

Army Football A30

Art & Artists H240, H250

Artificial Pitches
See Playing Surfaces

Attendances H7, H88
See also Scottish Football. Attendances

Australian Football (Soccer) E229

Austrian Football A71, E245

B

Badges H144-147

Ballet I216

Baseball C402

Belgian Football E245, L1212

Betting H156-226

Bibliographies J211-212

Black Footballers C9, C19, C582, C584

Bogota Incident E45

Bradford City Fire Disaster C129, F43-45, N287-288

Brazilian Football E243, H108

Broadcasting C55, H149-152
See also Match of the Day; Media Coverage

Bulgarian Football E245

Burnden Park Disaster F37

C

Cartoons K74-84

CCTV
See Surveillance Equipment

Chairmen C592
See also Clubs. Management

Champions' Cup
See European Cup

Chants
See Anthems

Chinese Football E228

Cigarette Cards B63, B157, H234-235, H238, H244, H249, H257
See also Ephemera; Trade Cards

Clergymen C450
See also Religion

Clubs
Administration B623, B675, B816, B890, C293, C495, H290
Financial aspects H278, H284
See also Economics Studies
Management B743, C298, C320, C347, C370, C386, C570-571, C592, C599, C610-611, I52
Marketing H296
Membership schemes H35, H37, H40, H47, H50, H53, H57, H61, H64
Names H148, H151
See also Badges; Colours; Grounds; Strip

Coaching A15, A17, B890, E189-190, E198, E201, E207, G23, G49-211, G232, G236
See also Trainers

Coca-Cola Cup
See Football League Cup (England)

Collecting H227-262, L1176-1184

Colours A102, A110, A118, A125, A128, A202, H145-147

Commentaries N313-347

Commentators A96, A122, C6, C55, C60, C185, C352, C509

Crests
See Badges

Cricketer-Footballers A17, C8, C43-54, C80-81, C102-104, C114-123, C151-152, C160-163, C189-195, C220, C224-235, C238-241, C258-259, C264-265, C270, C332, C395, C500, C585, C589, G59, G254, H234, H257, J32

Crosswords K143

Crowd Behaviour F37, F49, H1, H6, H9, H15, H27, H44, H46, H54, H65, H71, H83
See also Soccer Violence

Crowd Safety
See Crowd Behaviour

Czechoslovakian Football E245

D

Defenders B95-96, B740, B742, B886-888, G213

Dictionaries J207-210

Diet G254, G264, G274

Disabled Spectators F42, F48, F62, F64-65, F70, H84, H140,

Disasters A129, N287-291
See also Bradford City Fire Disaster; Burnden Park Disaster; Heysel Stadium Disaster; Hillsborough Stadium Disaster; Munich Air Crash

Drama I197-213

Dream Football
See Games

Drybrough Cup B1150

Dutch Football E245, G182

E

Economics Studies A104, A109, A143, B124, B922, H276-297
See also Clubs. Financial aspects

Ecuadorian Football E244

Ephemera D20, H227-262, L1162
See also Cigarette Cards; Postcards; Trade Cards

Estonian Football E133

Ethics G153

European Championship E124-126, H49, H65

European Competitions
British Club Histories B280, B391, B425-426, B470, B510, B566, B606, B788, B805, B1060, B1088, B1153, B1190, B1196, B1216
European Cup D21, E127-138, I81, I215
Finals B1079, N321, N323-325
See also Heysel Stadium Disaster

Address List

✉ All-Party Football Committee
House of Commons
London SW1A 0AA

☎ 0171 219 3000

✉ Association of Football Statisticians (AFS)
22 Bretons
Basildon
Essex SS15 5BY

☎ 01268 416020
01268 543559 (Fax)

✉ Association of Sports Historians
4 Hollington Court
Chislehurst
Kent BR7 5AJ

✉ Centre for Sports, Science and History
Main Library
Birmingham University
Edgbaston
Birmingham B15 2TT

☎ 0121 414 5806

✉ Féderation Internationale de Football Association
(FIFA)
FIFA House, Hitzjweg 11
CH-8030
Zurich
Switzerland

☎ 00411 3849595
00411 384 9696 (Fax)

✉ Football Association (FA)
16 Lancaster Gate
London W2 3LW

☎ 0171 262 4542
0171 402 0486 (Fax)

✉ Football League
319 Clifton Drive South
Lytham St Annes
Lancashire FY8 1JG

☎ 01253 729421

✉ Football League Executive Staffs Association
4 London Circus
Leamington Spa
Warwickshire CU32 4SU

✉ Football League of Ireland
80 Merrion Square South
Dublin 2
Eire

✉ Football Licensing Authority
27 Harcourt House
19 Cavendish Square
London W1M 9AD

☎ 0171 491 7191
0171 491 7882 (Fax)

✉ Football Supporters' Association
PO Box 11
Liverpool L26 1XP

☎ 0151 709 2594

✉ The Football Trust
Walkden House
10 Melton Street
London NW1 2EB

☎ 0171 388 4504
0171 388 6688 (Fax)

✉ GM Vauxhall Conference
24 Barnehurst Road
Bexleyheath
Kent DA7 6EZ

☎ 01322 521116
01322 526793 (Fax)

✉ Institute of Groundsmanship
19-23 Church Street
The Agora
Wolverton
Milton Keynes MK12 5LG

☎ 01908 312511

✉ National Federation of Football Supporters' Clubs
87 Brookfield Avenue
Loughborough
Leicestershire LE11 3LN

☎ 01509 267643

✉ National Football Intelligence Unit
PO Box 8000
Swing Gardens
London SE11 5EN

☎ 0171 238 8000
0171 238 8040 (Fax)

✉ Northern Ireland Football Association
20 Windsor Avenue
Belfast BT9 6EE

☎ 01232 667290

✉ Northern Ireland Football League
96 University Street
Belfast BT7 1HP

☎ 01232 242888

✉ The Premier League
16 Lancaster Gate
London W2 3LW

✉ Professional Footballers' Association (PFA)
2 Oxford Court
Bishopgate
Manchester M2 3WQ

☎ 0161 236 0575
0161 228 7229 (Fax)

✉ Referees' Association
Cross Offices
Kingswinford
West Midlands DY6 9JE

☎ 01384 288386

✉ Republic of Ireland Football Association
80 Merrion Square South
Dublin 2
Eire

✉ Scottish Amateur Football Association
Beechwood
Gateside Road
Barrhead
Glasgow G78 1EP

☎ 0141 881 4025

✉ The Scottish Football Association
6 Park Gardens
Glasgow G3 7YF

☎ 0141 332 6372
0141 332 7559 (Fax)

✉ Scottish Football Commercial Managers Association
60 Union Street
Keith
Banffshire

✉ Scottish Football League
188 West Regent Street
Glasgow G2 4RY

☎ 0141 248 3844
0141 221 7450 (Fax)

✉ Scottish Professional Footballers' Association
Fountain House
1/3 Woodside Crescent
Glasgow G3 7UJ

☎ 0141 332 8641
0141 332 4491 (Fax)

✉ The Scottish Sports Council
Caledonia House
South Gyle
Edinburgh EH12 9DQ

☎ 0131 317 7200
0131 317 7202 (Fax)

✉ Sir Norman Chester Centre for Football Research
Department of Sociology
University of Leicester
University Road
Leicester LE1 7RH

☎ 0116 2522741
0116 2522746 (Fax)

✉ The Sports Council
16 Upper Woburn Place
London WC1H 0QP

☎ 0171 388 1277
0171 388 5740 (Fax)

✉ The Sports Council for Northern Ireland
House of Sport
Upper Malone Road
Belfast BT9 5LA

☎ 01232 661222

✉ The Sports Council for Wales
Welsh Institute of Sport
Sophia Gardens
Cardiff CF1 9SW

☎ 01222 397571
01222 222431 (Fax)

✉ Union of European Football Associations (UEFA)
Jupiter Strasse 33
PO Box 16
3000 Berne
Switzerland

☎ 0041 31 321735

✉ Welsh Football Association
Plymouth Chambers
3 Westgate Street
Cardiff CF1 1DD

☎ 01222 372325

✉ The Welsh League
16 The Parade
Merthyr Tydfil
Mid Glamorgan CF47 0ET

✉ Women's Football Alliance
9 Wyllyotts Place
Potters Bar
Herts EN6 2JB

☎ 01707 651840

✉ World Association of Friends of English Football
PO Box 2221
D-30022 Hanover
Germany

Specialist Bookdealers in New and Secondhand Sports Literature

✉ AFN Distribution (Fanzines)
25 Thomas Street
Miskin
Mountain Ash
Mid-Glamorgan CF45 3BU

✉ Archways Promotions
50 Lochrin Buildings
Tollcross
Edinburgh EH3 9ND

☎ 0131 228 8182

✉ Extra Cover
101 Boundary Road
St. Johns Wood
London NW8 0RG

☎ 0171 625 1191

✉ John M W Whittaker
51 Western Hill
Durham DH1 4RJ

☎ 0191 384 3202

✉ Sport in Print
3 Radcliffe Road
West Bridgford
Nottingham NG2 5FF

☎ 0115 945 5407

✉ Sportspages
Caxton Walk
94/96 Charing Cross Road
London WC2H 0JG

☎ 0171 240 9604

✉ Sportspages
Barton Square
St Ann's Square
Manchester M2 7HA

☎ 0161 832 8530